Hitler and the Middle Sea

Inscribed to General Franz Halder
He might disagree with some of
my findings, but no matter
what, he will agree that
we remain "stets"
fast friends

Walter Ansel

HITLER AND THE MIDDLE SEA

Duke University Press
Durham, N.C.   1972

L.C.C. Card No. 77–132026
I.S.B.N. 0–8223–0224–1

Printed in the United States of America
by Seeman Printery, Inc.

Contents

Illustrations

Maps and Charts

Hitler and the Middle Sea

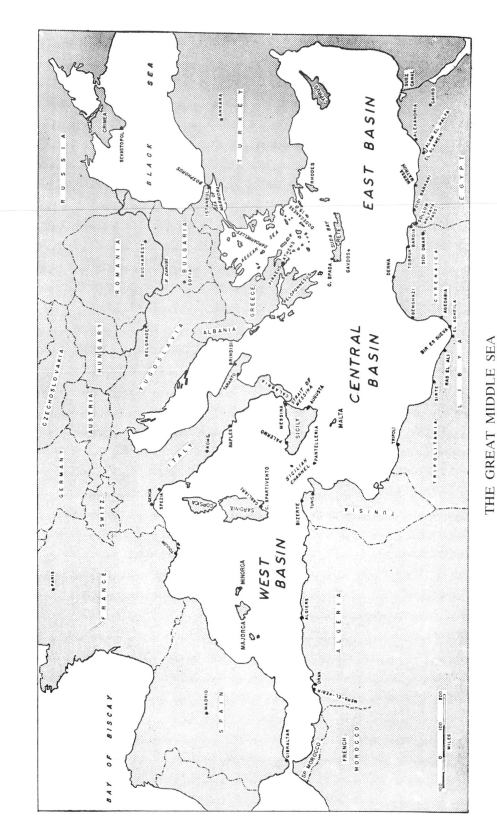

THE GREAT MIDDLE SEA

After Potter and Nimitz, *The Great Sea War*. By permission of Prentice-Hall, Inc.

1. Search for a New Strategy

From the English Channel to the Mediterranean: Summer of 1940

If Adolf Hitler ever looked out over the sea and marveled, no one remembers it. If ever while young he thought of going to sea and finding out what lay beyond, he never said so. No; if the thought had occurred to him he would by nature have tried to outwit the water barrier by flying over it in one of the newfangled flying machines. To him the sea remained alien and awesome, to the point that these feelings affected his thinking about power on the sea—*Seegeltung*, as he called such power. In his post–World War I talk and writing he derided the old German slogan, "Our future lies on the water," as preposterous and denounced the corresponding endeavors to develop sea power as criminally mistaken. He had no use for the sea in the north above the English Channel or in the south between Europe and Africa, that great Middle Sea of ancient times. His failure on the Channel we shall briefly review before heading south, where time would bring fresh opportunities. These prospects were remote and politically complex, yet they were destined to favor German arms, whose action in the Mediterranean at the right time and place could have changed the course of the war.[1]

1. Hitler MK, pp. 298–301, 706; Hitler SB, pp. 152–55. Hitler did not publish this second book, written in 1928; it was found during the war. In it he talked glibly about naval matters—ship armament, propulsion, and technical problems gleaned from books and papers—but showed little understanding of naval strategy. His interest in airplanes began early with model construction. See J. Greiner, *Das Ende*, pp.101–5. (A list of references with full titles will be found just preceding the index.)

This fine body of water had many natural attributes, to which its long history gave added significance. Here man made his earliest important advances as he migrated from east to west through three natural sea basins—East, Central, and West. He started where he emerged from the Nile Valley on the shore of the East Basin, which lay south and east of the island of Crete. Soon he was voyaging by oar and sail from the Nile Delta north along the Palestinian coast to the region of Lebanon and thence west via Cyprus, the Turkish coast, and the island of Rhodes to the north coast of Crete. From there it was an easy sail home under a prevailing westerly breeze to Africa and the Nile. Within this rough triangle, Crete grew renowned as a maritime focal point. The island provided the south boundary of an ideal seafaring laboratory—the Aegean Sea. Its many islands made island hopping easy and rewarding. It also made sailors, whose routes in time touched all points of the East Basin. They probed beyond into the Central Basin between Crete and Sicily/Italy, and finally into the West Basin between Italy and Spain, where an outlet to the Atlantic beckoned. The sea had become a bridge instead of a barrier. The year was about 2000 B.C.[2]

By this time a race of seamen had established Crete as the Britain of the pre-ancient world, a Britain of the East Basin whose equally splendid isolation and sea lore produced the glories of the Minoan culture. The great Sea Kings of Crete controlled the water round about their island base and kept it safe to flourish as Europe's first civilized society.

Minoan influences ran strong for centuries—until after 1400 B.C., when the world's first thalassocracy succumbed to a series of natural disasters made worse by invaders from the north. The invaders took over. This first Fall of Crete closed an era of 600 years from 2000 to 1400 B.C. during which the island base ranked high in Mediterranean strategy; it still does today, and did so even in Hitler's peculiar private strategy, which is the special interest of this study.

Crete fell prey to repeated conquests and thus lost her homeland identity; she never again was the exclusive home of a great people. Homer sang of the Minoans and their fair land, begirt by the sea and supported by ninety cities. A thousand years later Saint Paul found

---

2. In the bottom of the Mediterranean there are really only two main drainage deeps or basins—the west deep and the east deep, separated at the Strait of Sicily. Midway of the east deep the sea narrows to 155 miles between Crete and Derna in Africa. East of that line to the Palestinian coast lies the topside water of the East Basin of this study.

refuge in one of the few sheltered coves on her rugged south coast. She then belonged to Rome. From 1204 to 1669 Venice's sea power leaned heavily on Crete's central location; walled ports were built on the north coast to serve Venetian ships. Unsteady Turkish rule followed and turned the natives away from the sea to the hills and insurrection. Cretan men adopted some Turkish habits of dress—high boots and baggy trousers—yet they remain apart, self-reliant in personal strength and weaponry. Greece's war of liberation swept them along. After 1898 a commission, formed by the Great Powers and headed by Greece's Prince George, governed Crete until 1913, when she formally joined the kingdom of Greece. She remained distant and individual like her illustrious son, Eleutherios Venizelos, who had engineered union with Greece. While Crete had achieved freedom, she never regained her ancient glory on the sea.

But ours is another day and another story; one of a drive by Teuton Air Kings nearly 4000 years later to go the ancients one better and take the island through air assault in the year A.D. 1941; from Crete they hoped to rule the whole East Basin and its access to the Aegean Sea, which led to Russia. Crete and her near neighbor islands form a sort of southern protective boom athwart the Aegean; no passage through the boom is over 35 miles wide. Rhodes, 50 miles long, forms the eastern link next to the Turkish coast; to the west lie smaller Scarpanto and tiny Caso, which link up to Crete, stretching 140 sea miles farther westward. There two stepping-stones, the islands Antikithira and Kithira, complete the chain to the mainland. At the start of World War II the eastern three islands in the boom—Rhodes, Scarpanto, and Caso—were Italian outposts, while Crete and company to the west belonged to Greece, soon to become an ally of Britain. Of course both sides wanted Crete, in the middle. The resulting contention brought on the German paratroop assault of May 1941 that made Crete the first island to be taken through the air.

On the chart Crete has the look of a long slinky sea dragon, head to west, belly snugging the thirty-fifth parallel of latitude, and the scalloped tail trailing eastward. Two dangerous horns jut north from the forehead, which is set off at the back by a tasseled cap. It is Akrotiri headland, and under its lee lies Crete's prized strategic possession for war or peace, Suda Bay. From horns to tail tip the beast measures a good 140 sea miles, 6 miles through at the throat, just east of Suda, and 35 at the belly. So Crete is a substantial piece of land, at the gateway to three continents. Space factors are advantageous: from Suda, Greece lies 50 or so miles northwest, Turkey 120 northeast, the Libyan promontory of Africa 150 miles south and a bit west. Cyprus is 275 miles east, Syria another 50. But Suda Bay was the why of it all, a grand expanse of sheltered water, open to the east, that could anchor upwards of thirty deep-draft ships—a whole fleet.

These were my chart impressions on takeoff from Phaleron Airport (Athens), one of the eight mainland airfields used twenty years earlier by German attack forces. The islands fly past below, and Melos, about halfway, has scarcely been identified when a great lofty land appears ahead. It far surpasses the tidy chart image; mountains climb southward ever higher into snow, almost to the south coast, where it all plunges back to the sea with no visible ledges for anchorage; even boat landings look dubious. A mountainous spine seems to run the whole length. The plane dips toward the more inviting north coast and lands alongside Suda Bay. This is no tiny island lost at sea, but a big land with a shape and character of its own.

Akrotiri headland shelters Suda well on the north, but less on the west where the land recedes to a low three-mile-wide neck that separates the head of Suda Bay from the sea to the northwest. There, on the open Gulf of Canea, is the capital city, Canea (Khania), with about 40,000 inhabitants clustered around its small man-made Venetian port. At the middle of the dragon back 70 miles to the east is the larger port, the tourist and commercial center, Heraklion (Iraklion, or Candia), which offers entry to the ancient Minoan seat of Knossos a few miles inland. About halfway between these two main settlements on the coast is the small way-port of Retimo (Rethymnon); it too lies on the single coastal road that runs the length of the north shore. Spurs from this artery climb inland into the hills and stop, short of the south coast. In 1941 some 450,000 Cretans depended on this thin and primitive road net for all their wants, including movement of troops and equipment for defense. Levantine caïques offshore complemented the land route.

This whole region, among the best for seafaring, is even better for flying. By distances, wind, weather, and visibility it was ideally suited to the air power of 1941. Here, with boundless visibility and gentle breezes, the German flyers were not to be denied their chance at victory as they had been in the fogs and gales of the English Channel during the summer and fall of 1940.

The Channel ——! What delusions it fostered that summer! A

whole chain of them. The most fateful was Hitler's abiding faith that arrival on the Channel would bring peace with Britain. He believed that, with his "race to the sea" won, the war was over and that the British would soon be ready to talk settlement. War with Britain he had never wanted and when it came he wanted only enough to produce bargaining—a limited war. An obsession of settlement in sight took over the early summer days in Germany in a veritable peace rage that coined its own queer quips, such as "When will peace break out?" As time passed one aberration spawned another. On 19 July at a self-congratulatory Reichstag rally and against a total lack of encouragement from London, an uncertain Führer made his thin gesture for peace: "I see no ground that should force the continuation of this struggle." He had already grown wary enough of England's defiance to order practical preparations for invading her along the Channel coast. Luftwaffe planes began to soften the target. But England stood firm. Instead of softening, the British stiffened from one crisis to another until the routine grew monotonous. They wished Hitler would come.

Invasion? The craft and forces were assembled, yet the season for it was running out. Should, or indeed could, Invasion go? Should landing assault fly in the face of Air failure? In this puzzlement the immense momentum of the German victories on land oozed away. Professional opinion paltered while a perplexed Führer procrastinated. . . . Air power tried harder, nothing changed. At length, on 17 September, Hitler had his supreme command announce indefinite postponement of Operation *Sea Lion*, the code name for Invasion, and thereupon turned elsewhere to fulfill his private destiny. Stalemate by air and by sea sounded a faint note of defeat, the first of the war, which apparently went unheard, unheeded.

Neither the fact of stalemate nor the strategy at stake was fully apprehended; not in Germany, Britain, or America. Who, during those wild tumbled days, would have dared declare Invasion dead? Or who discerned failure in Hitler's abandonment of the military initiative over his most dangerous foe? Failure it was, but not necessarily absolute or fatal. Time would bring other chances to get at Britain, chances to retrieve. A natural setting for these opportunities lay in the Mediterranean. Toward its milder climate drifted the professional thought of British and Germans alike.

Even before the onset of dilemma England, the Mediterranean and its strategic islands had received some notice in German high counsels. Not that inaction on the Channel dismayed these high-riding men of victory. On the contrary, for them Greater Germania was on top, holding a wide choice and a deep reserve of psychological initiative; time was on her side, they reasoned, and about final victory there was no question at all. Yet where or how? It took the postponement of *Sea Lion* to spark interest in a new strategy and to fix it for a time in the south. Something had to be done to nudge victory along. History would never forgive him, remarked Hitler, if he failed to use this interlude.

Interlude till when or what? The professionals meant the approaching winter lull when Channel operations would drop to zero. Where else could they still punch at Britain, their primary and end target? Their Führer had in mind a totally different end target. His pause was a slack period until attack eastward on Russia could begin in the spring—a strictly limited period whose end pointed toward his grand private design. He could afford no embroilment that might jeopardize his East Plan; indeed, any pause had to contribute to that plan.

Action Russia! That was heart's desire, running deep and strong. If possible, Hitler wanted Britain associated with him; but with or without her, he had to have Russia. It was life's fulfillment! This ultimate goal of Hitlerian mythology envisioned a Germania astride the European heartland, with Adolf at her side. Britain would administer the sea; he the Continent. All thinking, deciding, and scheming remained tributary to this grandiose concept; and no plan or action could be fairly judged unless projected on that broad canvas. The undercurrent of this thinking is strongly apparent in the groping toward a new strategy.

One man on whom the strategic selection weighed heavily all through the summer of 1940 was General Alfred Jodl, principal military adviser to the Führer at Supreme Command Armed Forces, OKW.[3] Even during the peak of the peace publicity (June 1940)

3. OKW (Oberkommando der Wehrmacht—Supreme Command of the Armed Forces) was a complex staff mechanism that had been evolved for the conduct of Hitler's type of warfare. Its agencies covered all phases of war making by policy or strategy—i.e., by persuasion or coercion; but rather than generating plans and directing their execution, the various branches of OKW did the paperwork that implemented Hitler's personally devised plans and decisions. Thus Field Marshal Wilhelm Keitel, as Chief OKW, was more of an administrative chief over the functioning of the OKW agencies than a superchief of staff who might originate plans and advise the Führer on them. Keitel was usually in on all military decisions, but General Jodl acted as Hitler's top military adviser, and Jodl's relatively small

Jodl could not ignore the reality of England over there: the strongest foe, dangerous and still free to choose and fight. He strove to submerge his misgivings in the Führer's extravagant hopes, but it was no go. What if peace failed? The question dug deeper with thoughts of a prolonged war and prods from young assistants in Warlimont's L Section. By 30 June General Jodl had recorded his soul searching (conditioned by previous exposure to Hitler) in a brief, highly significant summary, "The Continuation of the War Against England." This document deserves forward notice for its record of Hitler's strategic policy toward Britain, both as to direct attack on her homeland and indirect peripheral action against her power in the Mediterranean. Events proved it to be a remarkably stable and prophetic guide to German plans and operations. Virtually all of the ideas can readily be identified as coming straight from Hitler, though relieved here and there by a Jodl touch. During this time Jodl must have raised critical points, only to receive, in reply, pat Hitler rejoinders which later were repeated endlessly. Faithful reflector that he was, Jodl strove to write his Führer's ideas into a frame of practical professional strategy that might harmonize with the times.

His efforts led to (1) the establishment of the Air Battle of Britain in first priority, (2) the initiation of Invasion planning (but only for the "death blow" after air success), and (3) a dim recognition of the Mediterranean as an alternative theater. Air war predominated as General Jodl evaluated two general courses of action:

(*a*) War against the British home island;

(*b*) War expanded to the periphery of the British Empire [in the Mediterranean].

An understanding of course *a* reveals how much or little enthusiasm may have been left for course *b*. Under *a* were listed three possibilities:

1. Siege by sea and by air against all ship traffic to and from England, and by air attack against the RAF and British war industries;
2. Terror attacks on population centers;
3. Landing attack to occupy England.

---

staff, called the Defense Section or L Section (L for *Landesverteidigung,* "national defense") under General Walter Warlimont, did his paperwork. The operational direction from OKW was mostly done or inspired—and always approved—by Hitler. Warlimont IH is an authoritative work on OKW and its relationship to the services and war waging. See especially at this point pp. 19–81.

Jodl elaborated and justified the sequence of action in typical cock-sure Hitler words: the air battle won, siege, propaganda, and terror attacks could follow to "*increasingly weaken the base of sustenance, cripple, and finally break the will of resistance of the people, who will thereupon force the government to capitulate.* A landing should then be undertaken, not to overthrow Britain militarily, . . . but to give England, crippled in war economy and scarcely capable of air action, the death blow, if one should still be required." It scarcely seemed necessary to consider the periphery, but he went on. Just as he had insisted that preparation for a landing should begin, he now included a thought or two on preparing an alternative strategy in the Mediterranean. It is the first such record about war in that sea.

For *b*, Jodl suggested:

The fight against the British World Empire can be conducted only through or over countries which are interested in the breakdown of the British Empire and hope for a lucrative inheritance. These are in the first place Italy, Spain, Russia, and Japan. The activation of these countries is a political matter. German military support to Italy and Spain in limited measure is possible (for example, for mining the Suez Canal [by air] or for seizing Gibraltar). Aside from this, through counterintelligence methods, help can be brought to the Arab countries. The most efficacious is an Italian attack operation against the Suez Canal, which in connection with the seizure of Gibraltar closes off the Mediterranean.

The power words were Hitler's, every one.[4]

Jodl may have struck them up at this point merely to raise the issue of the Mediterranean, for in Hitler's book Britain was to endure as his seagoing partner. He had said as much on 18 June to Mussolini in Munich, while the two discussed armistice terms for France and those for Britain, should she too see the light. "The British Empire is, after all, a force for order in the world," he told his amazed Axis partner, and went on to wonder aloud whether it would be a good thing to destroy the Empire. While these doubts endured, it nevertheless became Axis policy, often voiced, that the Middle Sea was Italy's sphere. Any operations the Duce initiated there were to receive immediate official German approval.

4. IMT, Doc. 1776. Jodl's summary documents an unhealthy mixing of policy and strategy and hopes to do things by political measures when the time for such measures was long past. It also documents the German mood of the time with telling phrases: "Ultimate German victory is only a matter of time—Germany can choose a warfare that spares her strength and avoids risks. . . . Enemy attack on a large scale is no longer possible. . . . With the knockout of the RAF, Britain is at the end of action capability against Germany." The confidence of the whole paper lessened interest in alternative strategy; still, it was entered on the books.

This did not deter the Führer from devising his own landsman's Mediterranean strategy. It was simple and direct: lock up the two end gates at Gibraltar and Suez, and thus deny Britain access. The definitive German word was *abschliessen*—lock it up, seal it off. The concept was defensive. It aimed to keep the Continent safe against British incursion from the south, but contemplated no strategic own use of the sea toward a decisive objective. Hitler regarded the whole area as suspect and degenerate. "Let us stay Nordic," he used to quip, to check speculation about the Mediterranean. On principle he preferred to leave it to Italy.[5]

Not so with the professionals generally, nor with General Jodl, who for a time became the Mediterranean's chief exponent at OKW. These men held offensive rather than defensive ideas. They wanted the sea to expand German power toward victory over Britain, and herein their concept diverged from the Führer's. General Jodl could scarcely have been aware of the divergence when he closed his remarkable summary on the political note of peace: "Since Britain no longer fights or can fight for ultimate victory, but only to retain her possessions and her world position, she will, in all expectation, incline toward peace if she learns she can still achieve her objective relatively cheaply. Her complete overthrow she will resist to the bitter end." He thus returned to his Führer's unhealthy confusion of policy and strategy, reiterating confidence in a political settlement, although such a choice was no longer open. The killing had long since become too earnest for an easy shift to dealing. It was 30 June 1940.

One day later, as though arranged to follow up, the Führer confirmed to Ambassador Alfieri of Italy the spirit and substance of the Jodl summary as his Mediterranean strategy. His shallow knowledge of the subject leaned heavily on case problems which events—or Mussolini—from time to time presented. The German leader's reactions seemed to be welcomed by the Italian, who took pains to keep his partner informed. The exchanges fell out of balance: Hitler did not hesitate to comment and suggest, while Mussolini generally had to be content with praise and agreement. The meeting with Alfieri came during the happy days at Tannenberg, the Führer headquarters in the beautiful Black Forest country. Secure in victory, he contentedly picnicked with his guests while expounding his planned "generous offer of peace" to Britain.

5. Hitler SC, pp. 58, 388. The true feelings of Hitler often showed through his casual table talk at Führer Field Headquarters mess.

Against such expansive thoughts Jodl's provision for a prolonged war had given Hitler pause. While Alfieri reported that Hitler exuded confidence, he also noted signs of perplexity over Britain: Germany could confront her with a solid, united Europe—Spain and Gibraltar included. Of course "the end of hostilities in France permitted Italy . . . to concentrate all her force against Britain in the Mediterranean." He went on about action against the Suez Canal, for which Germany could furnish long-range aircraft to work out of the Italian island of Rhodes. As for Greece, a word of warning: she had permitted the Allies to establish a beachhead at Salonika in World War I. Obviously, such a base, far up in the Aegean, could make trouble in many places. The Balkans should be kept quiet, said Hitler, as though his mind was already in Russia. If it was, his confusion in targetry was being compounded with that deeper confusion of policy and strategy. Of this Alfieri took no special notice when he departed as pleased and reassured as his host.[6]

What had happened was that after the fall of France Hitler tried to wage a cool war. He waged peace under the misapprehension that the peace initiative was all his. What nonsense this made became manifest on 3 July 1940 when British ships off the French African port of Oran acted out the truth.

In the afternoon of that day the British Naval Task Force H, based on Gibraltar, cruised off Mers-el-Kebir (two miles west of Oran), where strong French naval forces were moored. The British commander had been ordered to obtain assurances that none of the French ships would fall into Axis hands. After prolonged fruitless exchanges and in the face of French refusal, the British ships opened fire. They disabled most of the French ships.

The news broke into Tannenberg like a thunderclap; the whole place quivered and then exploded in tumult. What was up? What were the British after? Had they gone mad? Even then Britain's full meaning failed to get through, and to Hitler it probably never did. His private convictions had taken a knockout blow; his entire scheme of things, thought through and through so carefully, shook to the roots. What about peace? He refused to abandon it; yet surely this was no time to proffer a generous settlement. Actually, the British had robbed him of the peace initiative and sunk it. They wanted no peace with him! Moreover they had defied Hitler's solid European concept.

6. Warlimont KFA, pp. 177, 192, 201; also Warlimont IM; and Weichold DF. Admiral Weichold was chief of German Naval liaison in Rome in 1941–42.

Two influences grew out of the incident: a forced but defensive interest in sea power and a stronger but uneasy interest in the Mediterranean.

Hitler's triumphal reentry into Berlin for delivery of the peace speech at once fell into question. He did return on 6 July, as scheduled; but Reichstag assembly and peace speech dropped out. Instead, Germany's Führer stood on a balcony and let the crowds cheer. Eventually the shouting subsided and he turned on his military staff in anger. The Foreign Office had just delivered fresh unfavorable reports; Churchill had raised the Commons to its feet with defiant oratory. Hitler abandoned Berlin for his beloved mountains; he had to "think himself clear."

Count Ciano, Italy's foreign minister, had come to Berlin to listen. Before departure Hitler received him on 7 July for a review of the changed situation. Ciano's diary noted that his perplexed host seemed inclined to continue the fight "with a storm of wrath and steel upon England," that he "wanted to weigh every word of his speech." Six days later Hitler, in conference with his Army leaders, confessed his inability to turn Italian interest (Ciano) away from seizure of the Ionian islands toward Cyprus and Crete. Action against the west coast of Greece and the off-lying islands was a pet scheme of Ciano's, and Hitler's effort to substitute Cyprus and Crete documented his earliest known interest in Crete. General Halder recorded the remark at the conference on 13 July. The Führer had been map-traveling, and his thoughts seem to have centered on closure of the Aegean by Axis possession of Crete. Cyprus may have been added simply because it was British. For Rhodes, Hitler promised Ciano the same planes he mentioned to Alfieri for operations against the Suez Canal during the Italian offensive into Egypt. Mussolini soon replied by letter with a list of immense operational troubles in an attack on Egypt. Mediterranean projects thus burgeoned in both Axis camps. The Hitler/Ciano exchanges of 7 July expanded the Hitler/Jodl Mediterranean thought by the significant addition of Cyprus and Crete.

Meanwhile, Invasion England labored to the fore under Army sponsorship. Indeed, it was the main topic at the 13 July conference when General von Brauchitsch, commander in chief of the Army, and General Halder, his chief of staff, presented their grand cross-channel plan for overwhelming England from Thames mouth to Lyme Bay with a mighty tide of men and machines. To the soldiers' surprise Hitler gave approval out of hand with scarcely a question, as though he were ready for it. That done, he went into a general survey of the situation, beginning with the Italians, their island predilections in the Mediterranean and his own, their African claims and his (only the coast plus French and Belgian Congo), and ending in quandary over England. General Halder recorded:

The Führer is greatly puzzled by Britain's persisting unwillingness to make peace. He sees the answer, as we do, in Britain's hopes in Russia and therefore counts on having to compel her by main force to agree to peace. Actually, that is much against his grain . . . . a military defeat of Britain will bring about disintegration of the British Empire. This would not be of any benefit to Germany. German blood would be shed to accomplish something that could benefit only the United States and others.[7]

The picture grows broader, but no clearer. *Sea Lion* is to be prepared; the solid European front has been launched; Russia appears faintly in the eastern background, with the Balkans close alongside. Crete and Mediterranean islands take a place. Italy shows more interest in safeguarding her own African empire than in driving into Britain's. The Axis goals diverge.

Little or no consideration was granted to Axis strategy. In fact, a combined war effort appealed to neither of the Axis leaders. Talk about loans of extra units or materials cropped up occasionally; but there was no unified planning or execution against agreed targets, and certainly no thought of unified command. Differing national mores and temperament would naturally make problems; yet the most serious obstacle was the divergence of the leaders' aims. In place of "unified war," in Axis vernacular it became "parallel war," waged exclusively at targets of self-interest. These targets could overlap, sometimes almost coincide, but not their purpose. Here lay the nub of Axis troubles.

By the time Hitler came down from the Mountain in mid-July 1940 he was already deeply immersed in a search for an alternative strategy to implement (or get around) his policy of settlement with England. When he finally delivered his radically altered peace speech in Berlin on 19 July, the peace dove had gasped her last, and her misguided backer had plunged into the absorbing and more practical study of crushing Russia. Even as he had convinced himself that Britain would settle after France, he now argued, perhaps more for out-

7. Halder, 2:20, 21; Warlimont KFA, pp. 184, 192, 203, 204. General Halder as chief of the Army General Staff led the Army High Command (OKH, Oberkommando Heer).

side consumption, that Russia's fall meant striking the "last Continental dagger" from Britain's hand. That was the true solution! This beguiling slogan swiftly transformed Russian campaigning into a "detour on the way to England."

At OKW, Generals Keitel and Jodl experienced extreme difficulty in dissuading their Führer from ordering an immediate shift to Russia. They were concerned over the lack of eastern road nets, bridges, and rail beds. Finally Hitler agreed these would have to be strengthened and adapted. Thereupon he resolved loudly and "unalterably" to smash Russia in the spring of 1941. Thenceforth each day's work could lend shape and background to this grand design of finality. Anything that looked appropriate and helpful to the East Plan, the Führer could now place in proper sequence. For instance, closure of the Mediterranean, or at least the Aegean, could secure the prospective south flank of the drive into Russia. Meanwhile, pressure on England by air and invasion threat might still bring settlement, which would at once secure the rear and the south flank. Invasion therefore took momentary precedence. Craft began to assemble, the Luftwaffe deployed to Channel bases, and planes began to stab at England and her Channel traffic. A happy Führer rested in his mountain fastness, armed with high resolve.

He held a noteworthy strategy conference there with the service and OKW chieftains on the last day of July. The main theme, Invasion England, ended deep in Russia! Since Navy landing-craft problems and adjustments to Army tactical requirements in England had grown crucial, Grand Admiral Erich Raeder, commander in chief of the Navy, led off. Progress, although encouraging, he reported, did not warrant counting on a readiness date for the landing earlier than 15 September. He wanted the Army's expansive landing plans narrowed to a secure front of about 60 miles (instead of some 240); but the best course might be to postpone *Sea Lion* until the spring of 1941. Naturally, he had no knowledge that postponement would interfere with attack on Russia; and Hitler gave no sign. Instead, he took the unusual step of opening an exploratory discussion on the question: How can we bridge the gap until May [and Russia]? By air war, submarine warfare, Gibraltar?

Brauchitsch, the Army commander in chief, well aware of Hitler's designs on Russia, and wanting none of them, jumped in to suggest support of two German armored divisions to the hoped-for Italian drive on Suez. Recent reports from General von Rintelen, chief of

Army liaison in Rome, had indicated that Italy would require German aid. The Army now sought to exploit this through establishment of a bona-fide Mediterranean front. A shift south would gain time for *Sea Lion* to prove himself (or die), and time for the Russia plan to fade. The Brauchitsch proposal offered the first opportunity, and possibly a decisive one, for Army and Navy to combine on the conquest of the Mediterranean; Raeder failed to join Brauchitsch, and Hitler considered the Army sally good only for diversion. He brushed it off.

Then he went back to the main problem—England; and there, on the Channel, Raeder joined him, but only for 1941. Such postponement was the answer that Hitler seemed to want, for he immediately questioned its acceptability and began to reel off his predetermined decisions about England, which pointed toward *no invasion at all*:

Air war starts now. . . . If results are unsatisfactory, then Invasion preparation will be checked.

If the impression comes that the British are being beaten down, and that in due time results are forthcoming, then attack [that is, landing].

Diplomatic action—Spain, North Africa—discussed.

Order: Preparations shall continue; decision in 8–10 days about actual attack.

Army arrange for readiness 15 September, broad front.

Thus the unsure Invasion policy set forth by Jodl in late June had held through, while Mediterranean strategy was downgraded to a diversionary move. The growing eastern obsession remained secret. But not long.[8]

At this point Admiral Raeder having departed, Hitler leaped joyfully into the thick of the East Plan for the first time of general record. First he disparaged invasion chances and likewise any chance of bringing England down within reasonable time by siege. That left only the question: On what could England be pinning her rising hopes? It seemed to him they were pinned primarily on Russia. *"But if Russia is destroyed, then Britain's last hope is extinguished,"* he exulted. "The master of Europe and the Balkans is then Germany!" His galloping thoughts transported him from one power phrase to an-

8. Halder, 2:46-50; FC 1940, vol. 2; Skl War Diary, pt. A, July-Aug. 1940. Grand Admiral Raeder was chief of Naval Operations as well as commander in chief of the Navy. His command post in Berlin was known as OKM (for *Oberkommando Kriegsmarine*); its Naval Operations Office was Skl (for *Seekriegsleitung*). There remains one more high command to record: OKL (for *Oberkommando Luftwaffe*, "High Command Air Force"), over which Reichsmarschall Hermann Göring reigned. The three service high commands were thus OKH (Army), OKM (Navy), and OKL (Air).

other—*smash, beat to pieces*—the sooner the better! He quickly sketched the whole eastern campaign; five months and 120 divisions would do it. The Mediterranean had already taken on south-flank significance. General Halder could record a second Führer decision for the day—the unofficial, private one: *"In the course of this conflict Russia must be eliminated*—Spring 1941."

It was no news to the Army High Command (Brauchitsch and Halder). Only the night before the two top soldiers had thought the problem through and reached conclusions and plans of their own. Late the same evening General Halder recorded the Open Options:

1. Attack Gibraltar.
2. Support Italians in North Africa.
3. Attack British through Haifa.
4. Attack Suez Canal.
5. Incite Russians to drive on Persian Gulf.

Then he summarized the conclusions upon which he and von Brauchitsch had agreed:

The question whether, if a decision cannot be forced against Britain, we should, in the face of a threatening British-Russian alliance and the resulting two-front war, turn first against Russia must be answered thus: We had better keep on friendly terms with Russia. . . . Visit to Stalin would be desirable. Russian aspirations in the Straits and Persian Gulf need not bother us. In the Balkans, which fall within our economic sphere, we could keep out of each other's way. Italy and Russia will not hurt each other in the Mediterranean. In these circumstances we could deliver the British a decisive blow in the Mediterranean, shoulder them away from Asia, help the Italians build their Mediterranean empire, and with the aid of Russia, consolidate the Reich we have created in western and northern Europe. Then we could confidently face war with Britain for years.

Here was the first record of significant, and in itself remarkable, expansion of German politicostrategic thought toward the south— evolved, moreover, by the soldiers. From this source had issued the Brauchitsch proposal of the following day: to support the Italians in North Africa. The summary gave a profound evaluation of German opportunities, propounded a logical policy, and backed it with a feasible strategy. It never received its due.[9]

9. In these days of late July the Navy also explored the strategic possibilities of the Mediterranean, and at the same time an interior Skl study weighed the chances of eliminating Russia during 1940 while the Luftwaffe kept England neutralized. *Sea Lion* could then be unleashed in 1941, if still necessary. Admiral Raeder personally favored a decision over Britain before all else.

So by 1 August 1940, three key sources had drawn the Mediterranean into strategic reckoning: OKW in the person of Jodl, who saw advantages in peripheral war there; OKH in the persons of Brauchitsch and Halder, who saw a chance to deal Britain a decisive blow; and Hitler, who wanted merely to secure the south (Mediterranean) flank of his East Plan. A navy study of the new theater began belatedly. Anxiety over what Britain might do there, and reminders from the German Naval liaison officer at Rome, Rear Admiral Weichold, finally shifted attention south. The Luftwaffe stayed apart in Göring's inner track, alongside the Führer, and concentrated on "Grand Air Offensive" against England. Göring called it *Eagle Onslaught!*[10]

Eagle joined *Sea Lion* to conquer England by fright; the actual Führer and Luftwaffe directives prescribed a certain target sequence against the RAF until total air supremacy should be achieved. Once that was done, anything could happen, even England's collapse. Weather, however, proved intractable, and unanticipated operational snags impeded the massive plane onslaughts—the first in history. It took until mid-August, through stumbling starts to work up to full power, and then the effort fell far short of the vaunted blitz from the blue. Hitler seized on 15 August to declare England under total blockade by air and sea. The RAF swiftly responded in redoubled bomb drops into Germany. What of air supremacy over Germany, to say nothing of over England? Toward the end of August, when cumulative Luftwaffe effect began to tell on the RAF installations, the impatient Führer and his Air chief shifted target to London. This gave the RAF Fighter Command a much-needed respite. *Eagle* had turned buzzard.

His supposed teammate, *Sea Lion*, grew day by day, but continued to show conceptual deficiencies. Army envisioned a fantastic landing front of 240 miles, which Navy rejected. On 26 August Hitler decided for Navy's narrower 60-mile front; the quarrel inspired General Jodl at OKW to reestimate the problem of England in extension of his summary of 30 June. He found the Navy's narrow landing so des-

10. By 9 August, after the British had begun to reinforce their RAF units on Malta, Admiral Weichold from Rome expounded the significance of the island to his home office in Berlin. He called for elimination of the island base in order to insure freedom of action to the Italian Navy and to assure overseas connections with Libya. He drove hard on these ideas, designated Malta a "thorn in the flesh of Italian sea warfare," and was among the early ones to urge united German-Italian action in the Mediterranean "before it should become too late."—Weichold WM, pp. 164, 165, and as detailed to me by him in Germany in 1960.

perate and risky from the Army's point of view that a turn to "other means of forcing Britain to her knees" would be justified, and therewith he reverted to the Mediterranean—Egypt and Gibraltar. To these ideas his concluding words added a new ring of Axis Union: "Through discussion with the Duce, this end fight now beginning against Britain will be waged not alongside each other [in parallelism] but *together*." Hitler had given an offhand go-ahead for the new togetherness, but when it came to approving plans for Army and Navy to undertake specific studies of moving German armor into Libya, he hedged. Only sharply limited planning received authorization. By this time of late August, *Eagle* had lost much of his élan; thereby the freshened Mediterranean strategy gained credibility.[11]

In a little while Gibraltar planning got code name *Felix*; it had already taken the lead on paper and in OKW talk, for Gibraltar seemed closer and more tangible than Suez. And although General Franco ostensibly would command in chief, the actual operational command would be German. L Section developed a three-phase frame for strategic planning: (1) surprise Luftwaffe bombing of British naval forces in Gibraltar; (2) systematic bombing and shelling of the harbor defenses and any remaining ships; (3) ground assault from the land side of the Rock. Thus, by the beginning of September, *Felix* lacked only equipped forces under a vigorous commander to give him life. Before all else, however, came the political agreement with the Caudillo and blessings from the Duce.[12]

During this late August of 1940 a political storm blew up around a border dispute between Hungary and Rumania. Unrest there could imperil the stream of Rumanian oil that fueled the German engines of war; action had to be taken to keep the Ploesti petroleum fields secure. Diplomats from Germany, Italy, Rumania, and Hungary met in Vienna to compose the boundary differences while German strategists met in Berlin to plan the necessary military support to keep the oil coming. On 29 August the Axis foreign ministers, Ribbentrop and Ciano, wrung a "no contest" rejoinder from the Rumanians for a settlement favorable to Hungary. The conference adjourned.

The strategy conference under General Jodl held on because the Führer had decided "to send a strong military mission to Rumania after the new frontiers . . . had been fixed." Jodl reviewed the boun-

11. H. Greiner, p. 125; Warlimont KFA, pp. 193–96. Helmuth Greiner served as diarist of L Section OKW.
12. OKW Ops War Diary, pp. 57–88; H. Greiner, pp. 152–72.

dary troubles for the service representatives and followed with the strategic objective: "to occupy and secure the Rumanian petroleum district." Plans were discussed, and L Section was charged with collating the data and preparing operational instructions for the occupation. A draft directive was ready by 2 September, approved by Jodl, then sequestered in reserve for the time when events should justify issuance. Security of oil was the inception—beachhead in Rumania became the result, a beachhead that could give access in several directions. This decision, made on 30 August 1940, marked the genesis of the German Balkan drive that climaxed in June 1941 on Crete.

General Jodl had roused his proceedings with interesting word from on high about Libya: "The Führer is of a mind to send strong forces, perhaps two armored divisions," to assist the Italians there. Operations would be timed to coincide with attack on Gibraltar. Together, these actions could "destroy Britain's power position in the Mediterranean and create a favorable pre-condition for joint German-Italian sea warfare against the British Navy." Hear, hear! It is hard to distinguish if this is Jodlian missionary work or joint dreaming with his Führer. They have moved a long way in identifying the significance of this body of water, but when comes the morning, will they let the dream stick? At least they seemed capable of sound dreaming. One additional blessing a switch south might bring: it might obviate Invasion England.

One could have expected the German Navy to be the first to plump for such a scheme; there had in fact been sailor talk on the subject, which now, maybe aided by Jodl's welcome news, came on with a rush. Admiral Weichold in Rome furnished abundant ammunition. On 1 September he wired his Berlin superiors:

A weighty problem in the eastern Mediterranean is the possibility of *occupying Crete*. This would represent for the Italian side an important push forward with advantages to a strategic defensive . . . at the same time solving the problem of the Aegean. Even more important for the British does possession of Crete (along with elimination of Rhodes) appear. . . . [From] Crete they could cut the Italy-Libya line that supplies the offensive against Egypt and make it impossible.

The whole Mediterranean and especially the East Basin seemed suddenly to grow in strategic value.

Background accents, meanwhile, churned up tensions that burdened sound evaluation. Rumania's King Carol abdicated on 6 September in favor of his son Prince Michael, who turned governing over to General Antonescu and armed him with dictatorial powers. Close alignment with Germany seemed likely. Air assault against London had mounted steadily. A new Atlantic subject came into prominent notice: seizure of Atlantic islands. Swiss sources discussed Britain's need to occupy some islands as substitutes for Gibraltar, should it be attacked. Skl (Seekriegsleitung) in Berlin wondered about surprise occupation of the Canaries or the Cape Verdes or even the Azores. This speculating reached the Führer and took root with him in a new island madness. The Navy came to abhor it.

At the very outbreak of war in 1939 Admiral Raeder had arranged for direct access to the Führer. He instituted a system of monthly Führer conferences that became an institution from which flowed the Navy's war and its influence on German strategy in general. The talks served to inform Hitler about Navy plans and operations and to obtain his approval and support for them. At the same time Raeder received information on Führer views and plans so that the Navy could get in its licks on general strategy and above all maintain its independence. Independent and apart—the Navy remained almost too much so. Raeder was frequently left isolated in a corner. Conferring with this untrammeled younger operator was not the admiral's forte. He felt uncomfortable, and so did Hitler, except for brief periods when the two seemed to be in consonance, soaring together over the future. They endeavored to mollify each other, which to Hitler often meant duping the older man. The record discloses constants and variables on each side which shed light on the intents and aspirations of both men.

At Führer conference, then, of 6 September 1940, Admiral Raeder used *Sea Lion*'s dubious readiness as an entree to propose the alternative of fixing firmly on the Mediterranean. He expounded "the decisive strategic significance of waging German-Italian [united] war in that sea and for a combined drive from Gibraltar to Suez." Control over this was vital, he explained, to Axis interests in the whole of the southeast European–African area to guarantee unlimited raw materials and strategic bases against the British Empire. Seizure of Gibraltar should be readied at once, "*before the U.S.A. steps in.*" Action there should be contemplated "*as one of the main blows against Britain.*"

Skl's high-powered fancies had pulled Admiral Raeder along toward quick and effective supersession of the age-old British Navy and Empire; Hitler let the admiral believe that he happily joined in. For he directed Keitel then and there to get operational preparations against Gibraltar under way at once—something he knew had already been under way in OKW for two weeks. He had approved *Felix*'s preparatory measures on 24 August and given them high priority. If he granted the Navy chief the honor of originating the idea, it would make a happy start, at any rate, and from this pleasant point of departure the conferees sailed on to explore the question of American interest in the British Empire; her interest in entering the war, possibly by occupying the Atlantic islands or seizing a beachhead in West Africa. The happy exchanges held over to a key discussion on 26 September.[13]

As August was the time of Grand Air Offense for *Eagle*, so September was the time of invasion peak for *Sea Lion*, who got restive early in the month as the Channel hop-off ports filled with invasion craft and troops all along the coast challenged with one common battle password. *Eagle*, still working on London, strained to rise in crescendo to the approaching climax. But the final word to go never came. On 17 September *Sea Lion*, at the Führer's direction, gave up to *Indefinite Postponement*. Gradually, the Luftwaffe slipped farther and farther into the shadows of its failing offensive. Stalemate had arrived on the Channel.

Two important actions took place in the south: (1) The Italians in Libya advanced into Egypt, and (2) General de Gaulle, off Dakar in a British naval force, called on the French command ashore to surrender.

The Italian thrust had a long history of order upon order, threat upon threat, from Mussolini, to get Marshal Graziani to move. At last he moved, on 13 September. By evening that day, advance forces of General Berti's army reached the outskirts of Sidi Barrani, 54 miles inside Egypt. Resistance offered by the withdrawing British was light. By 16 September General Berti completed the occupation of the place and sat down to enjoy his questionable laurels. They were scattered to the winds on the next night, 17 September, from seaward by shells from the British Mediterranean Fleet. In Berlin Skl noted that additional interference could come from Crete, which New Zealand and Australian troops, newly arrived in Egypt, might occupy and make into a British air base.

General de Gaulle's peculiar gesture off Dakar brought political

13. FC 1940, 2:-17–36; Skl War Diary, 26 Sept. 1940.

rather than strategic repercussions. He signaled an ultimatum on 23 September to Governor Boisson ashore. When the challenge was defied, the British ships took the port, and the ships lying there, under fire. French guns ashore and afloat, including those of the battleship *Richelieu*, replied. For two days fighting with guns, bombs, and even torpedoes rose and fell. A French unit put to sea to do battle. Hits were made, casualties were suffered, but nothing changed in the status of Dakar or of its ships. The British withdrew, having rekindled French resentment over 3 July at Mers-el-Kebir. The French seethed with desire to get at *les Anglais!* Their home-based bombers, with German approval, attacked British installations and ships at Gibraltar. General Huntziger, Vichy minister of war, called on Field Marshal von Brauchitsch with proposals for alignment with Germany. This became the end product—the possibility of political realignment. The incident prepared a way for Admiral Raeder's conference with Hitler on the day after de Gaulle and the British abandoned their misguided bluff.

The project Admiral Raeder then took up in dead earnest was that of clearing up Hitler's target confusion. The Navy chief never wavered in his conviction that Britain was the one to beat. Though he personally had no liking for *Sea Lion*, he held firm to the position of strategic decision over Britain before all else. His staff had made a precautionary estimate of Russia, but authoritative word of the approved East Plan filtered through to Raeder last of all. He refused to believe it. But incontrovertible evidence closed in finally to drive him toward a personal power thrust against his dangerous folly. A special Führer conference in private was arranged "to present views on the progress of the war." The admiral's prime leverage rested in *Sea Lion's* demise, which made room for a new strategy. He would prove that the East Plan violated sound strategy and would propose something better.[14]

It was five in the afternoon of 26 September when Admiral Raeder entered the Führer's study and settled himself to sink the East Plan. He did not rush the target, but led up cannily through the Hitler mood he had found most amiable and responsive—the one induced through pictures of continued grandiose conquest. The imagery never failed to arouse the architect, builder, and above all, the politician in Hitler,

14. IMT, Doc. 066. In it, Admiral Raeder in January 1944 set forth his recollection of and objectives in that private meeting with the Führer. See also FC 1940, 2:17–36 for Sept. 1940; Raeder, 2:246–49.

who would then obligingly "take over the conn," and together the two would sail on and on.

This time Raeder began with Britannia. He expounded the importance of the Mediterranean to her empire, dropping hints as he progressed about what a great figure Germania would be if *she* took over the sea. "It [the Mediterranean] is the pivot of Britain's world empire," he declared, "and in it Italy is becoming the main target. Germany must wage war against Britain with all means at her disposal . . . before the United States can intervene effectively." Therefore, "the Mediterranean question must be cleared up *during the coming winter months.*" Somehow, Raeder's design fitted the Führer's mood and the admiral pursued his plan. "Gibraltar must be taken—the Canary Islands made secure beforehand by the Luftwaffe— the *Suez Canal* must be taken." An advance could be made through Palestine and Syria, to bring Turkey under. And then, having worked his way close to Russia, Raeder took the big leap. In such circumstances, said he, "*the Russian problem will appear in a different light. . . . It is doubtful whether advance against Russia on the north will be necessary.*"

The direct mention of attack on Russia—a ticklish subject never before discussed between them—drew no reaction whatever, as though the subject had been settled. Hitler never batted an eye. That he did not was a giveaway, for it could mean only one thing: attack on Russia had already hardened (as Jodl had explained to his incredulous staff) into one of those "unalterable Führer resolves" against which it would be foolish to contend.

Undaunted, Raeder sailed on, through the Red Sea to East Africa, then to India, and finally back for a last crack at the Mediterranean and Northwest Africa's shore. In a prophetic vein he declared that area to be of decisive importance. "All indications are," he pointed out, "that Britain, with the help of de Gaulle . . . *and possibly also the U.S.A.*, wants to make this region a center of resistance and to set up air bases for attack on Italy. . . . In this way Italy could be defeated." Steps should be taken at Dakar, he declared. "The possibility of French action against the British is . . . very promising. . . . Support to the French is desirable, possibly by permitting the use of the battleship *Strasbourg*." As Admiral Raeder closed his drive, he extracted tacit consent to relax *Sea Lion*'s instant readiness. (Postponement of *Sea Lion* until spring was made official on 12 October.)

That Hitler agreed was a positive sign of the chance for an alternative strategy. But what of policy? Would its aim remain on Russia?

There was the rub; a change in private policy was at stake, and had been all along. What mattered most to Hitler was the political future of any plan. It had to be a future that included him. Raeder's South Plan, founded on a solid continental base with France, Spain, and Italy, promised world empire in Africa and supremacy at sea, in the admired British manner. The thought, fresh and timely, came as air assault and Invasion were fading; and Hitler's knowledge of British dependence on the Mediterranean deepened. It was no brand new idea; he had heard it before, but was unready for it. He did not want England destroyed in any case; yet he felt guilty at backing off. Here came Raeder with a proposal to substitute a South Plan for an East Plan. At this very moment Hitler was ripe for it. An expanded South Plan could possibly solve the problem of England and that of Russia too.

If the silent admission of an East Plan depressed the admiral, Hitler's now knowledgeable and genuine interest in the Mediterranean gratified him. After the conference the Führer got hold of Captain von Puttkamer, his naval adjutant, to confirm his lively interest. Even during the conference he showed general accord by a promise to "confer with the Duce" after Japan's entry into the alliance, and to explore cooperation with France, Italy, and Spain. "Agreement can be reached," he held, "about African colonies; Britain and the U.S.A. must be excluded from Northwest Africa. If Spain cooperates [on Gibraltar], the Canary Islands—and possibly also the Azores and Cape Verde Islands—will have to be seized beforehand by the Air Force." Moreover, Hitler thought that Russia could be encouraged to advance south against Persia and India, to gain an outlet on the Indian Ocean.

Admiral Raeder departed the conference, well satisfied. "The Führer agrees," he wrote in his report. Together they had steamed around in new waters and dealt in new dimensions; seeking surcease from *Sea Lion* on the Channel, they found salvation in a South Plan in the Mediterranean. Solved were both problems England and Russia, but above all, the way to empire for Germania's Führer.[15] This instance was not the first counseling success for the long-headed chief of the Navy; his counsel had triumphed before—that is, for a time.

15. Puttkamer, pp. 41, 42, and consultation with the author; FC 1940, 2:32–36; Skl War Diary, 26–27 Sept. 1940; and IMT, Doc. 066.

The occupation of Norway originated with him; and although Norway later became a burden, at the time the North Concept was rated a bold stroke of genius. Now the South Plan drew respect and attention.

Like most politicians, Hitler favored straddled solutions, which, through an expanded target, could include private objectives and still look strategically sound. Detour through Russia on the way to England attempted to meet all strategic demands from the outside. Here was Raeder, offering world conquest by staying on the target of Britain. He had revised the old slogan to read: "Detour through Mediterranean and Africa on the way to World Empire," with Britain and Russia thrown in. For a project with a promise of such magnitude, there could be little doubt about genuine interest on the part of Hitler.

Confirmatory evidence came to notice immediately. The first signs appeared the next day, 27 September 1940, casting a new light on policy. It was the signing of the Tripartite Pact by Germany, Italy, and Japan. This pact, Hitler saw at once, could serve as the foundation for a new policy.

But which should come first? Policy or strategy? Here a new-found confidence in a shifted strategy forced a switch in policy.

2. Policy for a New Strategy

European Union: October 1940

On Friday 27 September 1940 news lines out of Berlin warmed with high expectation of a political blitz for this day. Everyone expected that the great historical event Dr. Goebbels had been trumpeting would be the formal entry of Spain into the Axis. Her foreign minister, Serrano Suñer, had dallied in Berlin long enough; it was time he paid up by joining. As late as yesterday, news headlines said so flatly. Yet this changed dramatically just before high noon when all eyes in the reception hall of the Reichskanzlei fixed on Berlin's Japanese ambassador, Saburo Kurusu, as he strode in, accompanied by resplendent attachés. His country has force and believes in it. He took a chair at the long table beside Italy's Ciano, whose visage beamed from an air colonel's uniform. Next to Ciano sat the Führer, toward the center where Foreign Minister von Ribbentrop stood ready to speak. As the rustle subsided, Ribbentrop began to intone the high purposes of the meeting. In short, universal peace was the goal today, which would be furthered by the signing of the Tripartite Pact. He finished. Each envoy rose, paid tribute to peace, and signed for his country. Kurusu, briefest and last, brushed his hieroglyphs one under the other on the white paper. There was the blitz! Any doubt about the global span of the war was surely dispelled. It made the big news of the day. It may have been the first omen of Pearl Harbor.[1]

1. OKW Ops SitConf reported (p. 63), "Today a German-Japanese pact has

In six short articles the three powers pledged mutual assistance to any signer attacked from without; they recognized a new German-Italian order in Europe, and a new Japanese order in Greater East Asia. The aim was Union of Policy. Outside comment for the most part found the target to be the United States. For our study, the really significant item appeared in the preamble on Axis policy. It provided for the enlistment of other signers: in Europe like-thinking governments could join this new political bulwark against Britain, and in the Far East, one against America. Japan added global dimension to a European arrangement. Let America beware, and perhaps Russia too, just a little, though she could join. The pact reaffirmed existing arrangements with her. Hitler had taken pains to apprise Stalin in advance of the whole business, a favor which the Russians appreciated. It was widely held that they would soon join. In the afterglow of the ceremony, Hitler took Ciano aside briefly to lay on a meeting with Mussolini at the Brenner Pass a week away, 4 October. Further political blitz was already in the making. It concerned France.

De Gaulle off Dakar and discussion with Raeder had catalyzed Hitler's brooding over England. He went exploring by chart in the Mediterranean and discovered many things new; Jodl's prods may have stirred ideas that Raeder's talk developed and endorsed. France, for example, emerged in clearer light as a strong power at both ends of the Mediterranean: in the west her continental position balanced Morocco and Algeria in Northwest Africa, and in the east her Syrian shore looked out on the East Basin. A "going together" with her found sudden fresh merit in the minds of these men and their staffs. Why should not France declare for the Tripartite Pact? A favorable answer, in General Jodl's thinking and that of the L Section, is discernible in the record. Even the day before, when Raeder clinched the argument, Jodl confided to Warlimont that he had "used every opportunity to convince the Führer of the extensive opportunities in joint German-French interests . . . against England," and "it seemed a change was going to take place." But sober Jodl knew what was at stake when he added, "One ought always to recognize [it would mean] a complete change in fundamental principles of carrying on the war and in the

been concluded, as well as a German-Spanish agreement." OKW Ops War Diary differed when it reported that conversations with Suñer were "unsatisfactory, since he demanded as a reward for Spain's entrance into the war . . . all of French Morocco and extension of economic and military aid." The signing of the Tripartite Pact is described by Schmidt, pp. 191-92; and by Guido Enderis, the *New York Times* man on the spot.

war aims." Quieting Italian and Spanish annexation fever would present difficulties. Nevertheless he would hold to the "importance of influencing the Führer further in this direction." By 1 October Warlimont had submitted a plan for "the inclusion of France in the fight against England, *which is now intended.* . . ." A tide of high hopes crowded hard realities out in conversion to an incredible cause: union with France.[2]

A like trend took strong hold in OKH after General Huntziger's visit to Field Marshal von Brauchitsch on 26 September. The two soldiers got on well. Huntziger as French representative on the Armistice Commission in Wiesbaden had worked hard for cooperation between the two countries, but to little avail. Now promoted to minister of war, he came fired by the spirit of Mers-el-Kebir and Dakar to assure Brauchitsch of "utmost loyalty." Dakar had proved that France "sincerely wished to fight side by side with Germany." He imparted new information about French forces and their distribution, told of troubles at Vichy and in the French colonies, and described Marshal Pétain's efforts to form a "community of European nations." The term cobelligerent gained currency. When one has hoped long it is easy to believe. Has union with France really been sanctified by Führer decision? It seems doubtful, though Jodl dares brace Hitler on what form cobelligerency shall take. Staff thinking in various power posts may have run headlong far beyond the master's. General Halder added an echo from the Raeder Mediterranean tour de force of 26 September when he credited the admiral with stressing the dangers to Northwest Africa. Ribbentrop in the Foreign Office, he noted, was alone opposed. No one could tell exactly where the line of truth ran.[3]

The spirit of the time was surely on the side of accommodation. But was the Führer's? To prize out the truth, Army Commander in Chief von Brauchitsch bearded Hitler in Berlin. He returned on 30 September loaded with Headquarters policy bits that confirmed an expanding image of western empire for which Hitler himself seemed to speak. General Halder entered his commander in chief's words:

2. OKW Ops War Diary, pp. 123–32. Warlimont's plan contemplated no inclusion of French land forces in combatting the British homeland, but occupied France would furnish its share of other support to the fight against Britain; armament industry would be set in motion. Command would be exercised through the Armistice Commission. In OKW generally, the purpose went: Harness France to our cart. She had allayed the Führer's suspicions at Dakar.—OKW Ops SitConf, p. 58.

3. OKW Ops SitConf, p. 66; Halder, 2:113–18.

Political developments are still in suspense. Tripartite Pact presses naturally for political decision . . . advisable to come at last to some decision about . . . France, but the game is still moving . . . outcome not foreseeable. . . . A letter has been written to [Stalin] to interest him in dividing up the estate of Britain and to induce him to join up with us. If the plan succeeds . . . we can go all out against Britain. The question whether Germany can pay herself out of British booty or has to look to France for compensation is decisive for our relations with France, so that right now the trend seems to be toward better relations . . . hinges on Italy's attitude. Therefore conference with the Duce . . . following agenda:

(1) Prosecution of the war in the Mediterranean;
(2) Italian demands on France;
(3) Settlement of war costs.

Not even so heavy a schedule sufficed for this German powerhouse on the make. Further OKW talk took off into Germania's boundaries-to-be: on the Continent and overseas on islands and in African colonies. At home, Alsace-Lorraine, parts of Burgundy, and lands to the northeast toward the Channel would be lopped from France (Belgium and Holland must already have been swallowed).

Then over the blue water: "In addition Germany puts forward a claim to the Azores, the Canary Islands [belonging to prospective ally Spain], and Dakar, if necessary in an exchange, and then that familiar strip of Africa from the west to the east coast." Perhaps the sailor hankering for colonies and overseas bases had driven up this island madness; it may have presented a gauge of expansion westward that could sate Hitler, as master of Germania, in place of his favored expansion eastward into Russia.

While the two army leaders evinced no concern over the proposed robberies, Stalin's elevation to membership made surprising and pleasing news. Maybe Hitler could still be turned off from the east. Certainly demonstrated was the width and depth of his scheming and dreaming, what it would take to satisfy him, how Italian ambitions cumbered a turn toward France, and above all, how intent Hitler was on exacting payment from the supposed losers for a war provoked by Germany. On the side, the Mediterranean had achieved new meaning. As General Jodl so well knew, and said, a shift from the east to south and west ran counter to the deeply rooted private principles (or mythology) of Hitler on which the war was based. He yearned for seas of land in the east, not seas of water in the west. The two goals would be hard to interchange. Actually, Hitler feared the water; he had no place for it. We may be caught in one of those peculiar false Hitlerian Fronts that marked torment over a move, logical and attractive in itself, and so admitted by him, yet far removed from his own urges. Norway was one such that he carried through, but in agony and as a side issue. To turn the grand total of the Main Effort around, would this not mean making Adolf Hitler over?

In these ideas for the west, Brauchitsch and Halder must have recognized their own thoughts of two months ago. Then they spoke of a visit to Stalin; now a letter is en route to him. Then the outline read: with the aid of Russia, consolidate the Reich in western Europe and face war with Britain for years; now it reads, get Russia to join up and go all out against Britain. The Mediterranean figured in both, but the Atlantic islands and Africa were new. Their mention may mark the addition of an empire element.

A deep undercurrent of the East Plan persisted, though not necessarily in direct conflict, for some preparatory measures could serve either plan. A case in point was the dispatch of a military mission to Rumania which achieved Führer decision on 30 August. We have already remarked the decision as the genesis of the Crete operation: it could count for the south and at the same time be a hedge toward the east. The mission to Rumania got under way.

All innocent of the changing trends, old calvaryman Erik Hansen relaxed happily with his command of the 4th Infantry Division in the lovely countryside around Orléans on the Loire. The war was over, chores were few—some training drills, and for the rest, a pleasant carefree life. Then things began to happen. The division was ordered to Dresden for conversion to armor, and General Hansen received personal orders to report to OKH at Fontainebleau. On arrival, an old friend on the staff, Generalleutnant Paulus, took him in hand to explain a change of duty to chief of Military Mission Rumania. The diverse troop and material strength presented something of a force: the 13th Motorized Division, minus two battalions, plus an armored regiment, an air section, engineers with a strong bridging column, other outsized attachments, and of course, training personnel and gear. Obviously more than training Rumanians and protecting oil preserves was in mind. Many fingers were in the pie, General Hansen said, and many objectives almost in sight. But none of them disturbed him much. He prepared to report for a personal, definitive briefing by the Führer on 1 October.

Field Marshal Keitel received him, told him to talk up to the

Führer—it was what he liked—and ushered him in at 1300.[4] General Hansen tried to speak out, to offer comment, to liven things up. It was no use. He could barely get a word or two out before an inspired Führer cut in with a fresh launch into a half-hour's speech on the "political situation, etc., the grounds and objectives of the mission, and what it must work toward." It plainly was a pet cause that concerned the security of the Aegean (like the Hitler talk with the Italians early in the summer). He said nothing about oil-field security. Instead, he turned back the clock to World War I and the British beachhead at Salonika. That must not happen in this war. Mission tasks, Hansen found, "culminated in the again and again stressed need of having in the Balkans a friendly, reliable, and battleworthy partner [Rumania] in case of Invasion into Europe by the British as in World War I at Salonika." Hitler reckoned, said Hansen, "on a [British] landing in Greece . . . in foreseeable time; they had preparations under way in the Middle East. General Hansen concluded, "a look to the south into Greece was my chief task." No word had been uttered about Russia, neither here nor in Fontainebleau at OKH. The General departed from Germany in a special train for Bucharest on 12 October, in total ignorance of the East Plan: his task was to counter Britain.

Fears of this sort were deep-rooted in the past and well-established in Hitler. They formed a central complex of Fortress (*Festung*) security for self and Germania. When they pressed, he took pains to work up pacifying counters within himself. This sequence appeared again and again. In this instance the repetition confirmed Hitler's private plan to forestall Britain by seizing Greece. Its refrain harmonized well at a distance with the budding South Plan. The designs on Greece were wholly independent of Italian plotting against Greece. Thus there was ground for some exchange on the subject with Musso-

4. Told to me by General Hansen in Germany, 1960, and documented by his own writing. The many fingers in the pie included the Foreign Office, which dealt with new-in-the-saddle General Antonescu of Rumania; he wanted his army modernized, equipped, and trained. The Luftwaffe was another, which refused to place an Air section under Army command. OKH and OKW were in it, and varied on mission deployment and objectives. Finally came the Führer with private instruction. Both policy and strategy were hatching. An OKW directive of 20 September 1940, signed by Keitel, set forth the tasks of the Army (Hansen) and the Air Force (Wilhelm Speidel) missions. The tasks expanded from these basic ones: to protect the oil fields from attacks by a third power; to train Rumanian armed forces to carry out certain assignments according to a definite plan drawn up in the interests of Germany; to prepare for operations by German and Rumanian forces in case of war with Soviet Russia.

lini at the forthcoming Brenner meeting. All was in order. The German contingent set out on 3 October aboard the plush Führer train.

Right from the start the conference at the Brenner on the next day struck a happy tone that held through three solid hours, as Ciano recorded. This was the partners' first reunion since 18 June at Munich, when, in a flush of victory, they discussed terms for France and peace with Britain. The subjects were still alive in a cooled situation that had changed strategically more than either leader apprehended. They still felt themselves very much on top as Hitler's resurvey began: "The war is won! The rest is only a question of time," and then in effect apologized for *Sea Lion*'s reluctance and *Eagle*'s failure. "England is under terrific strain. Why does she keep on?" The answer was twofold: hope of American and of Russian intervention. The Tripartite Pact checkmated America and forty German divisions on the eastern frontier stopped Russia. Hitler diverged into political means of getting at Britain, say by added alignment of France and Spain in a solid Europe. In spite of his small faith in friendship with France, he hammered again and again at a need for *European coalition*, including France, against Britain. This prime proposition, up to now a purely political one, swept his hearers along with moving words. Now for the implementing strategy he proposed:

(*a*) Gibraltar must be taken (presumably by Germany) . . . and
(*b*) Suez (by Italy), for which Germany can furnish armor and air help.

Not a word about a united Axis strategy. But in Ciano's words, partner Hitler had "put at least some of his cards on the table and talked . . . about his plans for the future."[5]

Now came Mussolini's turn; he responded in total, affable agreement. It was a love feast. The Duce parroted all that had gone before about England. Spain should be put off in Morocco and be promised economic aid at home. For his part he wanted only Nice, Corsica, and Djibuti. Once these were handed over by France, peace could be signed with her—reserving of course to Germany the use of French bases against England. Hitler could freely agree to the Italian claims; but a separate peace with France, that was something else. He wanted to sound out the French. Mussolini thereupon took wing into Egypt.

5. Ciano DP, pp. 395, 396; Halder, 2:135–40, for 15 Oct. 1940. The latter entries originated with the German Foreign Office liaison officer with OKH, von Etzdorf. See also Schmidt, p. 192.

The second phase of his campaign would begin a drive for strategic Matruh. Positive orders had gone out, and when Matruh fell, the final third phase "will lead to the Nile Delta and the occupation of Alexandria." Glorious thought! No help was needed for the second phase; for the third he might request some armor, a few heavy tanks and Stuka bombers. That was all.

In this cheerful camaraderie the two leaders settled down to talk together alone. All was rosy; the mood favored confidences. As later events indicate, Hitler omitted report about Rumania and the mission, but there are signs that Mussolini bragged about plans against Greece. Ciano had pressed for such an attack, and the Duce sorely needed a strictly Italian victory. Until now German restraint had kept him out of Yugoslavia and Greece. At this feast of friendship Hitler may have relented. What harm could it do, since he himself would shortly be committed in the Balkans? Let the Italians go ahead into Greece—but later. Howsoever the thing went, he would be ready to profit through Rumania. The surmise fits the scene, the Hitlerian method, and the later straws of evidence. General Jodl had a fixed impression that something of the sort had gone on.

Assent by Hitler meant another step toward Crete.[6]

"The Führer retired to the Berghof for a few days in order to think over quietly the new political scheme," recorded OKW's L Section conference log for 5 October. Out of the Brenner meeting had come an abundance of political kernels to mull over and sift out. Hitler's drill toward decision required a pacing up and down in self-debate. Endless monologues weighed one solution after another. Gradually the essentials of the problem, heavily charged with personal drive, emerged, and he could let the inner voice speak. Problems of violence (strategy) went well for him, but problems of diplomacy (policy) that offered nothing to overwhelm, nothing to smash and drive upon, went harder. During his sojourn of 5 to 9 October at the Berghof he determined to sound out the French personally, the Spanish, and significantly, also the Russians. He could see Laval and Marshal Pétain of France while proceeding to Spain's border for

6. Shortly before 23 October when rumors about the coming Italian attack on Greece circulated, General Jodl remarked to General Warlimont that he thought "it possible that at the Brenner Pass conference the Führer gave his consent to the Duce for an attack on Greece, without informing his military entourage."—OKW Ops SitConf, pp. 84, 85. Jodl was a member of the entourage. No other person was so well qualified or placed for making such an observation. He made it several days before the Italian attack.

exchanges with General Franco. Upon his return would come talk with Molotov, Russian foreign minister, in Berlin. The deep old urge to crush Russia seemed to be waning. Through Molotov he would test the Russians' temper; perhaps they were ready to join the Tripartite Pact. Hungary, Rumania, and Bulgaria had lined up; even the Scandinavian states planned to join. That France might swing into line had become a strong hope. So much for policy; in the realm of strategy a new campaign found currency: The "Battle of the Mediterranean."[7]

In Italy a strong champion for such a united strategy emerged in the person of Marshal Badoglio, chief of the Italian armed forces. Soon after the Brenner Conference he spoke for an early meeting with Field Marshal Keitel of OKW, "to arrange the operation plans for the winter when the main effort should be shifted to the Mediterranean, to expel the British from Egypt and Gibraltar." Keitel replied affirmatively, but that the meeting should wait until the planned political parleys had laid the requisite foundation.

It was odd how press and speech reports in England paralleled Axis gropings. British newspaper guesses, quoted widely in German war diaries, often seemed to anticipate Axis policy and strategy. This trend showed all through the Invasion crisis and swelled again when Britain sensed a German search for a new departure. That *Sea Lion* had gone to sleep for the season was easy to see. (On 12 October a brief OKW paper directed "that preparations for the landing in England . . . until spring are to be maintained merely as measures of political and military pressure. . . .") After the Brenner meeting the British prophesied Axis blows in the Near East and Italian agitation against Greece. "A valuable goal in this regard," the Skl diary quoted from a British newspaper, "would be Crete," and on 5 October 1940 added comment from its liaison officer in Rome: "Elimination of Malta and the occupation of Crete must be pursued in order to anticipate possession by the British." So far Hitler seemed to be the only other German leader the least interested in Crete, and his interest held.

All at once on 10 October the British raised a terrific hullaballoo over a German push into the Balkans. Troops and material, said press notices, jammed the routes through Hungary toward Rumania; move-

7. Field Marshal von Brauchitsch brought this news from Berlin for record by his chief of staff on 11 October. Halder, 2:133. See also OKW Ops SitConf for 11–12 October.

ments were also reported in the far north into Finland. Russia too showed concern. What could be going on now?

But of all people, Mussolini, so recently embraced at the Brenner, could rightly ask the question too, and in pain. He seemed in the dark, like any common Balkan roadside peasant watching the German troops roll by. Or so he acted in the presence of Ciano and his military staff—not a word at the Pass, not a word later, about "this German occupation of Rumania." He raged on to Ciano (12 October) that he would pay Hitler back in his own coin. "He will find out I have occupied Greece from the newspapers." On 14 October Mussolini fixed a date for hop-off into Greece. The day selected was 26 October.

Presumably the Duce's anger fed on the old complaint of being constantly faced by German *fait accompli*. The truth is Mussolini must have known about the mission (but maybe not early enough, nor by polite word from the Führer) before 8 October. General Hansen learned later that on that day the Italian envoy at Bucharest was still trying to wedge Italian participation into the German mission complement. The effort succeeded with an air contingent that arrived in Bucharest on the same day as Hansen, 14 October. To prepare for such participation took time. There was a note of play-acting about the Duce's explosion. A finding of collusion between the two dictators on Rumania and Greece can be put off until Hitler in turn explodes in verbal fireworks over Italian entry into Greece.

Hansen's movement took off in full sight through Germany and Austria on 10 October—no secret, no mystery; instead, fanfare and celebration all along the route in circus fashion. Crowds gathered at rail stations, decked with flags and slogans, and waved the procession through Hungary to Rumania, where at Bucharest on 14 October a red-carpet welcome greeted General Hansen. He deployed the swollen mission elements as they arrived, ostensibly to stiffen Rumanian defenses around Ploesti petroleum plants in the north, yet with primary readiness to drive south over the Danube. Nothing specific on the East Plan reached him until mid-November, and then Hansen redeployed without orders. Headline press notice of the mission's completed arrival and disposition, which the Italians called the "German occupation of Rumania," suited German policy to a tee, especially the British notices, for they unwittingly gave themselves warning to stay out of the Balkans, in particular out of Greece.[8]

8. General Hansen's written and verbal remarks (Germany, 1960). From Italian

In Berlin the German Führer awaited further British repercussions to his push southeast. Beyond the agreeable news stories, nothing of substantive consequence came out and even the press stories soon wore thin. Italian indignation raised only languid interest in Hitler, while arrangements proceeded for the policy pilgrimage into the west to sound out France and Spain. Connected to the latter was the Atlantic islands question. During a conference on 14 October Hitler queried Admiral Raeder about Navy overseas support to the islands: could the Navy transport troops and material to the Canaries, the Azores, and perhaps the Cape Verdes? To any sailor's amazement, Raeder replied in the affirmative, "provided the transport operation could get under way before the occupation by air. . . ." Raeder may have been thinking of Norway; maybe he had been infected by the wide-swinging Skl empire dreams. At any rate Hitler accepted the affirmative answer and carried it with him aboard the special Führer Headquarters train as it sped west through Belgium and into France. It halted in the evening of 22 October at little Montoire, above Tours, where Deputy Premier Laval of Vichy France came on board. The conversation, according to the Führer's interpreter, Dr. Paul Schmidt, was brief; it dealt mainly with arrangements for meeting Marshal Pétain two days hence. Laval impressed the Germans favorably; he got out a few suggestions in a friendly spirit and seemed anxious to cooperate. These were things Hitler had come to hear; he rolled on confidently through the night toward the Spanish border to collar Franco.

French Hendaye on the sea, a little below Biarritz, was the appointed rendezvous. At the edge of town were the adjoined rail platforms for the French narrow-gauge and the Spanish wide-gauge rails, which there crossed the Bidassoa River from the west over the international bridge. The Caudillo's train appeared on the bridge about three in the afternoon, a good hour behind time, but on this fine day of 23 October, who cared? Certainly not Hitler who chatted with Foreign Minister von Ribbentrop on the French platform. It could have been a last-minute briefing for himself and Ribbentrop that the Führer carried on, and that Dr. Schmidt, his interpreter, overheard. Hitler seemed to be backing off on the question of compensating Spain for her expected entry into the war. Suñer at one time

---

colleagues he never heard a word of the Duce's indignation, and he found such a reason for the later Italian march into Greece to be ridiculous. Hansen thought the Duce's uproar a fake.

had demanded Oran and all Morocco, plus wholesale economic aid. In this latest summing up, Hitler held that Spain should be compensated out of colonial booty from France, but only to the extent that France, when she joined, could be compensated out of booty from Britain. "I want," Hitler said, "in talk with Pétain to induce the French to start active hostilities against England, so I cannot now suggest to them cession of territory. . . . [If] an agreement with the Spaniards became known, the French colonial empire would go over bodily to de Gaulle." These few sentences went to the heart of Spain's enlistment, thought Schmidt. The Hendaye conference thus began hedged round by political handicaps.[9]

If policy was cluttered, its strategical companion, seizure of Gibraltar, enjoyed the advantage of specific Führer enthusiasm. Such support or lack of it could prove crucial to any project: Suez, for example, never really generated much Hitlerian drive; *Sea Lion* lacked it altogether. Both lay over the incomprehensible, mysterious sea. But as for the Rock, that remnant British bastion on the Continent—cracking it offered a grandstand play Hitler could go for: sudden, startling, short-term, efficacious, like the Fort Eben Emael drop on the Belgian-Dutch border in May 1940. Moreover, his direct interest in the project was likely to add extra political accommodation to meet Spain's demands. Hendaye was to have its chance at both policy and strategy, though no one on the scene could realize the length of its reach.

The arrival ceremony over, and the squat Spanish guest comfortably settled in the Führer conference car, Hitler began his familiar German success story. Schmidt could reel it off by heart: Britain is beaten, fails to realize it, she is under heavy air and sea attack, German victory is inevitable. Then suddenly, a radical shift to Gibraltar. British loss of it would exclude the English from the Mediterranean! Now he came out with it: a proposal for "the immediate closing of an alliance," to include Spain's entry into the war in early 1941. Gibraltar would be taken in January and turned over to Spain, along with additions in Africa. The elated Führer had worked to the point with a rush; he offered the prize all neatly gift-wrapped.[10]

Imperturbable, the Caudillo sat in silence. He was no glowing,

9. Schmidt, pp. 193–97. Paul Schmidt is the sole direct witness on record for many of the Hitlerian foreign affairs conferences. His familiarity with the method and with the personalities and his keen observation, which events proved, make him a valuable source.

10. H. Greiner, pp. 156–57; Schmidt, pp. 194–95.

responsive Duce who beamed approval as the Führer drove to his climax. He just sat until the fever abated. At length he began with tentative questioning words about Spain's dire economic straits—the urgent need for wheat, tons of it, and armament to guard the coasts against British counterattacks and about big guns to reduce the Rock. The Canary Islands—could their loss be prevented? He doubted the speedy conquest of Britain; after England fell she would fight from Canada. Hitler's assurance had failed to convince, and Schmidt noted his growing discomfort; at one point it brought him to his feet, as though to break off, but "he immediately sat down again." The Spaniard was giving the German an unusually bad time. Of the incident he later admitted to Mussolini that "rather than go through it again he would prefer to have three or four teeth pulled!" It was an apt expression for the involved and closely hedged terms that Franco at length conceded he *might* sign. He entered ands, ifs, and buts about colonial extensions, foodstuff and armament deliveries, and a final tricky one about a date for the Spanish participation coming into force. Hitler agreed to most of the nonmilitary items, but insisted that action against Gibraltar start by 10 January. The Spaniards—Suñer was there too—now took refuge in the lateness of the hour, for a feast in the Führer's de luxe dining car—very likely to celebrate a pact—had been promised. Reconciliation of the differences, they suggested, could be pursued by the two foreign ministers, Suñer and Ribbentrop. On this indecisive note the meeting broke up. The two leaders conversed in the afterdinner glow—to no firm result; nor did the foreign ministers the next day reach agreement. Franco succeeded in avoiding commitment.

Two hours behind schedule, the Führer train chugged off toward Montoire, north of Tours, to meet Marshal Pétain. Success with the French was made all the more important by disappointment and unconcealed Hitlerian disgust over Franco's evasion. Laval attended with the Marshal at Montoire station in the late forenoon of 24 October 1940.

Aged Pétain, Marshal of France, sat straight in his appointed place. His uniformed figure was not lost on Lance Corporal Hitler, who had his private ideas of heroes and perhaps even a place among them for a French one of World War I. Later the staff said the old soldier's bearing and dignity deeply moved the Führer; he showed it as he began a gentle recital of French sins, to lead into his theme of collaboration with the slogan, *Britain is beaten.* Someone must assume the war's costs—either England or France. If it is England, "then France can take the place in Europe which is her due in a *European community* against Britain, and can retain fully her position as a colonial power." Hitler suggested that France defend her colonies and win back those lost to de Gaulle. Next he dug into French reaction to the second Mers-el-Kebir. The Marshal knew what was meant; he countered that France could make no new war and asked in turn about a final peace and the return of prisoners of war. The exchanges continued along such lines and in an agreeable spirit. Laval chimed in to place on record France's help in nonwarmaking fields. "The conversations," recorded Greiner in the Operations War Diary of OKW, "took an absolutely satisfactory course, though there were no immediate results." A far-reaching willingness to cooperate in "the spirit of Montoire" became apparent. Führer and staff had reason to feel encouraged.[11]

A face-to-face meeting with the high personage of World War I did something to Hitler. Opposite him sat Le Maréchal de France; there was not one other. His rank and uniform alone meant Empire to the sensitive Austrian as he drank in the drama and its imagery; he could superimpose himself on it. Was he not a German Bonaparte dealing as an equal with the last vestige of Continental Empire? Before him sat the proof.

More than that, the encounter with Pétain decided Hitler for union in the west. The strong effects appear in an extensive briefing he gave immediately afterwards to his Army commander in chief, who promptly passed the remarkable mixture of strategy, policy, and postwar dreams on to General Halder for record, point by point:

(*a*) In basics the Spanish Operation [Gibraltar] is not yet clear. Question of prior occupation of Canary Islands through air landing can crop up. Spain itself is willing to go along, but wants to let cooperation with us become known only after military action begins. Accession to the Axis promised verbally, but not yet signed. In face of Britain, apparently still highly apprehensive.

(*b*) Greece: Italy now has nine divisions in Albania. Apparently Ciano

11. OKW Ops War Diary, pp. 169, 178, 179; Documents GFP, vol. 11, Doc. 227; Halder, 2:128–39, 147–49, 154. Deputy Premier Laval, about to become as well Vichy France's foreign minister, took to the "ideas of the Führer warmly," recorded the OKW Ops War Diary, and he also offered specific thoughts about any announcement of France's entry against Britain. Hitler tendered Pétain a confidential but padded summary of German military strength—186 first-line divisions, 20 armored, 12 motorized. Beginning in 1941 the Navy would add 25 new submarines a month. In reply the Marshal assured the Führer that the RAF had not to this point used United States planes in combat.

is again promoting occupation of Corfu and Greek coast to the south. Führer thinks this is nonsense and wants to write to Mussolini. Over and over Führer draws attention that warfare in the easterly Mediterranean will lead to quick success if *Crete* is occupied. Air landing.

(*c*) England is to be attacked further by Luftwaffe in full force. Possibility of her yielding not excluded. To be checked is, if Luftwaffe can carry out occupation of Canaries, cooperation at Gibraltar and Libya, furthermore at Crete.

(*d*) Tripartite Pact: Joined—Hungary, Bulgaria, Slovakia, and Spain; Yugoslavia about to, Greece possibly. Announcement only after European circle is closed. Countermeasures if Roosevelt is elected.

(*e*) Russia: Molotov 10 November, Berlin. Answer from Stalin to Führer letter: He concurs with Führer ideas. Molotov will come to Berlin. Then Russia expected to join Tripartite Pact.

(*f*) France: A clear declaration of position has been asked of Pétain. She will have to give up land in the region of Nice (not the town itself); Corsica, Tunis to Lake Chad, Djibuti will be demanded.

(*g*) No definite assent on Morocco given. If France can be compensated elsewhere, Spanish wishes can be considered. Gibraltar, after taken by German troops, will be turned over to the Spaniards.

(*h*) Peace Works Program: Autobahns (11 meters wide!)—four great east-west routes, three great north-south routes.

(*i*) Poland:No self-sufficient Poland. Germany will supply the material, Poland the manpower.

The final two points offered giveaway clues to the Führer's Montoire mood, at the peak of its European Union and South Plan commitment.[12]

As noted so often before, Peace Works Programs always signified a Führer in the surge of postwar imagery on the point of reaching a crest; this showed at the meeting with Admiral Raeder on 26 September too. Hitler the builder fancied a postwar millennium in which autobahns systems crisscrossed his continental domain. Buoyant effusions offered unfailing evidence of confident decision and release; for the moment he had his final definitive answer. Private policy could now gaze out in quiet satisfaction toward empire in the West and South, instead of the East. The moving encounter with Marshal Pétain had provided the last indispensable lift.

Yet voids remained. Frontal activity, so evident in past decision making, was unimpressive here. A genuine front for driving overseas—where the new plan had to lead—had not materialized. For that matter, how could action on the alien sea replace the cherished dream of crushing Bolshevism in grand Feldherrian maneuvers on the land

12. Halder, 2:148–49.

seas of Russia? The new concept was born outside of Hitler; it had never been a part of his mythology. He unwittingly disclosed the personal pinch in the last item when he conciliated the urge to go east by substituting Poland, as a German slave state, for Russia. And the Russians—to be sure, they could now earn absolution by signing the Tripartite Pact. Molotov's visit would consummate the deal.

To recapitulate: the two senior armed services and the professionals of OKW drove for a sound relationship between policy and strategy, and Hitler responded favorably. Logic was on the professional side, which Hitler readily recognized, in spite of diverging inner feelings. From stalemate on the Channel, strategy has thus progressed past Jodl's late-June peripheral Mediterranean suggestions, through the OKH estimate and expanded proposal of 30–31 July, to the late-September production by Admiral Raeder and Hitler of a complete South Plan based on a policy of Western European union and peace with Russia. For operational clarity these thoughts could be fitted into three main concurrent strategic undertakings:

(1) Keep England under intensified siege by sea and air.
(2) Reduce British dominion over the Atlantic by air descents on principal islands, initially on the Canaries.
(3) Exclude Britain from the Mediterranean and the Balkans through seizure of Gibraltar, Crete, and Suez by airborne and ground assaults.

Given political accommodation and firm, free, strategic command, such a sequence stood a fair chance of success. It minimized the peril of enchainment in a two-front war and fixed on the most dangerous foe by a method that retained flexibility for intensification or relaxation. The far-fetched Atlantic island scheme might have been settled for reinforcement of the Canaries alone. Gibraltar presented a comparatively easy target of profit in prestige and strategy. Suez would be the hardest; yet it might wither into irrelevance if the other goals, especially Crete, were achieved. Exploitation of the strategic and political initiative in the west for European union—that was the call!

Into these confident reflections there broke a sudden clangor of alarm out of Italy. As the homeward-bound Führer train hesitated at Yvoir on the Belgian border early on 25 October 1941, a message arrived from Rome. It gave notice that Italian troops in Albania were about to march into northwestern Greece. For days rumors of such a move had circulated, yet this had happened over and over in the past without consummation. "German occupation of Rumania" of 12 October may have tipped the balance. Invasion of Greece was about to begin. Hitler headed his train south while dickering over where and when he and Mussolini could meet. They fixed on Florence for 28 October. With the usual delays in deployments there was still hope the thing could be called off. However, if it succeeded, both Italy and Germany might profit. Wait and see, seemed to be the attitude; perhaps the Duce had merely advanced the Führer schedule.[13]

Florence did its utmost, or rather, the Fascist party did. "A greeting such as the Romans gave their Caesars," Hitler exulted to his man Linge after a triumphal entry. From a balcony of the Palazzo Pitti, Führer and Duce responded to the cheering multitude below. Mussolini laid it on thick, and Hitler showed that it worked. Word had reached him at Bologna of Italian entry to Greece at 0600 this day, 28 October 1940. There was no longer any reason to hold back.[14]

By and by, when Führer and Duce had had enough, the two sat down with their foreign ministers. Hitler at once expressed "full support for the operation begun by Italy against Greece," recorded Ciano. In the next breath German parachute troops were put at the Duce's disposal "for the occupation of Crete." No one took hold of the glib bluff. No more was heard about Crete.

Hitler bemused his partner with a sketch of the trip to the west. The French would guard North Africa. Their support would be a psychological help when the British realized they faced "a compact continental bloc." The Axis view of the war as won was now clear to Laval and Pétain. Franco had proved difficult throughout a nine-hour conference. Hitler growled out his tooth-pulling preference and then lapsed into his favorite theme, Russia. Molotov was due in Berlin soon; Russian energies would be steered toward India. Such Russian rapprochement "will create an Axis front that stretches from Japan to

13. H. Greiner, pp. 182–85; Warlimont KFA, pp. 202–7; OKW Ops War Diary, pp. 164–82, 234; and OKW Ops SitConf, pp. 84–87. The sources indicate a confusion of the dates and means Mussolini employed to inform Hitler. First he sent a warning letter about 19 October. It fixed no hop-off date, but a message of 23 October fixed on 26 October. This last may have been the Yvoir message received on the 25th. Later Hitler claimed he wanted to delay the invasion until Crete could be occupied by German airborne troops. A further, more obscure reason was to wait until after the United States presidential election. By that time in November bad weather would have insured postponement until his own favored time of spring 1941.

14. H. Greiner, p. 185; Ciano DP, p. 18; Warlimont KFA, pp. 201–11. At 0300 on 28 October the Italian representative in Athens presented an ultimatum to the Greek government. It demanded occupation of strategic points in northwest Greece and declared that troops would enter Greece at 0600 to effect the occupation.

Spain." Britain, still staggering under intensified air and shipping losses, "will suffer collapse as rapid and complete as France." Threadbare as these words were growing, they still testify to Hitler's personal attempt to switch back from the east to Britain and the west. Mussolini responded in lusty agreement.

He got over his miff about favoritism to France when the Führer twice solemnly pledged no peace until Italy's territorial demands should be satisfied. "The meeting ended," Ciano wrote, "in expressions of perfect harmony . . . on all points." In fact, nothing at all of consequence had been said about the main issue, Greece—why the Italians had attacked or what they hoped to accomplish. Such information as the German military pried out of Italian opposites left a totally negative impression of a clumsy attack plan over poor terrain with insufficient force and in the worst season. An outline of objectives offered nothing new: seizure of the opposite Greek coast to enhance control over the Adriatic, and the capture of Salonika to insure control over the Aegean. The former was Ciano's objective; the latter, possibly a sop to Hitler. The status of the Libyan campaign remained obscure. Mussolini had closed with the banality, "We will have improved our Mediterranean position in the struggle against Britain." But the Germans wanted no mere improvement in Italy's backyard; they wanted decision in Africa. As Hitler came away, his partner's left-handed venture galled him more and more.

While this was going on, a veritable Crete craze seized the German staffs. The Führer's idea had grown on his helpers until everyone wanted to be in—except the Luftwaffe, the most concerned. Navy discussion and a study dated 21 October contributed interest, but the main pulse came from OKW and the Army. General Jodl reduced his own thoughts to paper, and in OKH General Halder made repeated reference to Crete planning. The Luftwaffe recorded only a disbelief in British capability of bombing Rumanian oil preserves from Crete, a capability which was among Hitler's reasons for taking the island.

In its study "A Critical Examination of Britain's Situation" Navy postulated that a British offensive in the Mediterranean impended:

The Britons have undergone an inner change of policy which prompted action in the African and Mediterranean theater. . . . *A strengthening of the Suez position of decisive importance for the outcome of the war will be the main objective.* . . . Occupation of Greece is unlikely, but that of Crete could be of great importance for naval supremacy in the eastern

Mediterranean and for countering the Italian offensive in Egypt. . . . It is necessary to combat these dangers without delay through political and military counterstrokes.

The Navy drive for action in the south had begun with conversion of the Führer, but because of total lack of naval means in the theater had acquired a defensive cast. Its chief interest lay in the general stimulus offered to the South Plan, and in particular the emphasis given to Crete. All at once German strategy turned to keeping Britain out of Crete. The initiating impulse had come from Hitler.[15]

Thus when on 26 October General Jodl considered the Navy study, he wove into it his own and his master's ideas. The impracticality of an airborne effort was plain: the Italian Dodecanese bases were inadequate for a large-scale takeoff. Not only that: the British would take Crete to menace Greece and North African operations. However, preventive action might still be feasible, "though it would demand commitment of the entire Italian fleet." If Britain's Alexandria Squadron were first whittled down to second place—O happy thought—seizure of Crete from Rhodes might indeed become practicable. It made pure Hitlerian logic, all tidily balanced, as on the Channel: once the RAF Fighter Command was out, England would be at Germany's mercy. Here the concluding tasks became these:

1. Resume promptly the Italian offensive into Egypt for the seizure of Matruh as an air base.
2. From Matruh, attack British squadron at Alexandria with all means.
3. After sufficient reduction of the [Naval] squadron, begin operations against Greece; occupy Crete at the same time.

This production of Jodl's constituted the earliest quasi-official solution for control of the East Basin, with Crete as a key objective. Chief of OKW Keitel authorized use of the plan in the forthcoming talks with the Italian attaché, General Marras, as an acceptable South Plan.[16]

Army plans for the South had likewise progressed. General Kübler, commanding the 39th Corps in the projected Gibraltar operation reported at OKH and went on to Besançon in France, where his troops drilled in terrain like that of the Rock. Generous armored

15. FC 1940, 2:44, 45.
16. The evolution of these ideas between Hitler and Jodl may explain the latter's remark to Warlimont of 22 October about the Führer's accession to the Italian invasion of Greece.

support to the Italian thrust into Egypt was still recommended. "But," wrote General Halder on 26 October, "if a real job is to be done, Crete and Egypt must be carried out simultaneously. . . . We must enlist Bulgaria and Turkey . . . for access to Syria. In this context, perhaps, Italian military pressure on Greece might fit." The reference to Bulgaria and Turkey provides the first record of an overland march to get at Suez by the back door. Evidently, it had been in talk for a while. On the following day the general added, "German air control over Suez and Haifa could deprive the British of means of life in the eastern Mediterranean. Desired would be an attack on Crete." So the soldier's strategy for the East Basin outdid the sailor's. Strategy sought to drag policy along in a wide sweep from the Azores far out in the Atlantic through the Mediterranean to the Persian Gulf. Focal points were Gibraltar, Crete, and Suez. What a grand expanse it made! And for the moment, Russia had dropped out.

Then came the chill of the ill-timed Italian march into Greece. Hopeful anticipation of speedy success turned to anxious foreboding of a British arrival in Crete. Once lodged there, how could the British be got out?[17] Early German notice of Crete as a key position ends here in October 1940. The island has been identified with airborne conquest for control over the East Basin and eventually the whole Mediterranean. Greece gradually blotted Crete out; for a time the island was all but forgotten.

To judge by later remarks, thoughts about the island and the march into Greece bothered Hitler soon after he turned north from Florence. To him it must have been clear the Italians would bog down, Crete would fall to Britain, and Germany would find herself committed to a hopeless botch in the Mediterranean, where he, her leader, had never wanted to be in the first place. What probably cut deepest was the peril to the dormant East Plan—his very own private option. He adjourned to the Berghof to "think himself clear." Time and again he protested his innocence of foreknowledge about the Italian move; the vehemence of the protests alone made them suspect. Yet he kept on, to whip up his ire the more. His neat blueprint of the Balkans, safe and sound, had been childishly fouled, and woe betide the fouler. "Greece? A *Schweinerei*"—a swine's mess! "The Führer is so wrought up," Jodl told Warlimont on 2 November, "he has lost

17. OKW Ops War Diary, pp. 192–94; H. Greiner, pp. 183–85; Halder, 2:151–61. For lack of sea power, Halder stressed action through Syria by land power here for the first time. He wanted the German main effort shifted to the Mediterranean.

all desire to cooperate with Italy." For him it was the bitter morning after. The remark and its mood presaged a change, a reversion to his own twisted obsessions.[18]

To attempt further proof of collusion between the two partners on Greece turns out to be pointless. Evidence of Hitler's complicity in the Italian plans against Greece is substantial, and also of his intent to occupy Greece himself when it suited him. Contrary to established public opinion, the sack of Greece was never alone a case of Italian failure and German rescue. The Germans would have come anyhow. In loose talk at the Brenner, Hitler may have agreed in principle to his partner's proposal to invade, as Jodl intimated, yet hardly for the year's worst season and in such feeble strength. Mussolini's ignorant timing, his shifty execution, raised only suspicion and disgust. All prospect of unified strategy, let alone common policy, dropped out. Dictators cannot endure coequal union. Lack of confidence and mutual trust remained the fundamental failure. The trial period had held about one month—the month of October 1940.

From here on, German policy is dealt out in measured doses by Hitler so that his warriors and people may become inured to it and by degrees come to accede to it, even cheer it. First his strategy must win the east for policy to act upon. He began another halting turn away from Britain toward the refuge of his savage past in a fix on that fat, easy shot—Russia. While he had always admired Britain and shrunk from attacking her overseas, he had always despised Russia and could never refrain from belaboring her overland. After Russia was done, Britain could deal with the master of the Continent or take the unlimited consequences.

Yet in the eyes of the men around Hitler, his quitting one target did not irrevocably commit him to another in the opposite direction; May or June 1941 was still far off; changes would still be possible during the detailed planning as the picture clarified. They underrated the depth and strength of his resolve, his powers of persuasion and deceit, and moreover, the power of the East Plan itself as it expanded to monstrous, compulsive proportions.[19]

18. OKW Ops SitConf, p. 102. Hitler could pump up a show of anger. He may have done so here to permit enlargement of Italian shortcomings and to ease his reversion to the east. He certainly wanted to blacklist the Mediterranean.

19. Halder, 2:164, n. 5, and 165, n. 9.

3. Problem Russia

A suspicion of Hitler's relapse plagued Chief of L Section General Warlimont and moved him to protest to his superior, General Jodl, about an apparent split in strategy between the two ends of the Mediterranean. Thereupon Jodl unveiled the new scheme as fair salvage from the original concept of a combined Axis drive from Gibraltar through Suez. But he disclosed a radical switch in prospect when he added, "The Führer is so dissatisfied with Italy's action in Greece . . . that he has lost all inclination for close military cooperation with Italy. . . . It is doubtful whether the intended commitment of German troops in Libya will come about." As a sop Jodl offered a possible advance by the German army from bases in Rumania and Bulgaria into Greece (just as Hitler had forecast to General Hansen). Meanwhile at the western end of the sea the strike against the Rock would be under way in concert with Spain, but not Italy. Warlimont found this revision of the winter's work wholly unsatisfactory, adding that the Italian fleet would be chained to standing by at home to fend off a British sortie from Alexandria and that this would exclude any junction of heavy German and Italian ships in the Atlantic against the British heavy units. Such blue-water action had been talked of, even reduced to paper in August, by the Naval representative in L Section, Lt. Commander Junge, and passed to General Jodl. On 2 September Jodl noted Führer agreement with the added thought that such a combination would be facilitated by the prior seizure of Gibraltar and Egypt, as planned. The junction had never been recorded as a serious objective; now it came too late. Things had changed. Jodl rested his case on the availability of the Luftwaffe to bomb Alexandria and mine the Suez Canal; besides, the Rock's fall would cause repercussions in East Basin strategy. He digressed lamely to collaboration with France, which he knew Warlimont strongly supported. Other measures for saving union in the West were turned over. But what could be the use if not a single combined task of strategy could be effectuated? Warlimont registered a final dig by suggesting that pressure might be renewed on the Italians to occupy Crete, whose strategic significance was all the more compelling now. It was no use; Crete had faded too.[1]

Not so for Britain's Admiral Cunningham and his Mediterranean Fleet as it cruised westward of Crete and looked in on old Navarino, the spacious bay on the southwest corner of Peloponnesus. It was as well known and useful as Suda, and in some ways more convenient. The way things were going over the Italian march into Greece, both bays might come into greater use. German air reconnaissance gave proof on 2 November with reports of three battleships, two carriers, five cruisers, fourteen destroyers off Navarino and fighter planes over Crete and the Ionian Sea. London broke the news on 4 November— "British troops have landed in Crete." The fleet had given cover for this landing. Hitler could quip, "I told you so," to Jodl at their forenoon review of the same day.

. But rather than depressed, the Master seemed buoyed up; the news bore him out precisely on British occupation of Crete. A further older and deepening concern was Italy's plight in Libya and Egypt. Two days before, General von Thoma's unfavorable survey of the Italian effort had reinforced his negative impression. The commander in chief of the Army, who presented von Thoma, also got across the urgency of sticking on target Britain. The straddled plan that Jodl imparted to Warlimont disclosed Hitler's quandary and self-debate, and now on 4 November news of British action, as usual, forced decision. In retaliation for Crete, Hitler decided to speed the seizure of Gibraltar. The last hope of a sensibly unified South Plan evaporated. Jodl summoned Army representatives and alerted his

---

1. OKW Ops SitConf, pp. 102, 103; OKW Ops War Diary, 2 Nov. 1940. Germany's superbattleships *Bismarck* and *Tirpitz* were nearing sea readiness. Combined German and Italian big-ship action in the Atlantic receives only these fleeting references.

directive producers. An exciting buzz of fresh Führer decision stirred the air. It was high time.[2]

The first entry of General Halder's at the afternoon session with the Führer on 4 November presented Hitler's rationalization and downgrading of the North African dilemma:

Nothing to be done there before fall 1941 [which meant after Russia]; he enlarged on his disappointment in the Italian leaders: "They wanted only to save their own bloodshed." A dubious operation to send German troops over seas we do not command and with an ally who will not go all out to keep them open. Now Spain, Franco has promised to join us. . . . Press Spain's entry into the war. The British might land on West Africa or on Spanish or Portuguese islands. Spain will have to be helped in defense of islands. Which ones OKW is checking.

By this time he had worked up to a panorama of familiar visions; the series began at the newest addition, Gibraltar, skipped to Greece and through Turkey, to climax in the broad spaces of Russia. "She remains the whole problem of Europe," Hitler declared. "Everything must be done to be ready for the great showdown." In passing through Greece and Turkey he executed an odd juggle that implied the use · of a neutral Russia to keep Turkey down. Perhaps he meant to use Stalin and then turn on him. Perhaps it was mere timing; that Russia had to be crushed was certain, but just when, might still have been open. *Sea Lion* was hung on at the end, but "not to go before spring."[3]

This review sounded like a throwback to midsummer. If one got down to cases, the air of bogus excitement still hovered over the same stale, unresolved dilemma of England and Russia. Had nothing at all been decided since 31 July? Not a solitary thing? The off-again-on-again routine was old hat. Bewilderment showed when the Army leaders conferred to ascertain what came next. Out came a swinging shotgun answer: Be ready to fire in all directions. Certainly east at Russia, maybe north at England, but as soon as possible south and

2. Halder, 2:159–61, gives the revealing points set down for the commander in chief of the Army to present when von Thoma reported to the Führer. Decision was due. The Halder queries demonstrated how far adrift the German war plans really were: What should the Army prepare for? The need to stay on Britain with siege was the controlling factor. In addition there was Gibraltar, which could be done; the eastern Mediterranean would be far harder. Crete could be useful, and also a drive through Syria. But the long time needed there might have sufficed to bring decision over England by sea and air. Therefore to be decided was how far preparations for shifting the war's main effort to the eastern Mediterranean should go. These penetrating questions ignored the East Plan, joined Navy against Britain, and witnessed the unity in theory of the services for the direction of the war.

3. OKW Ops War Diary, 4 Nov. 1940; Halder, 3:151–67.

west at Gibraltar. On this last one, General Halder had already told his chief, "The Rock alone won't do it." He meant, won't resolve Problem England. It is the earliest hint of using assault on Gibraltar, Operation *Felix*, as ersatz for *Eagle* and *Sea Lion* together. On strategic grounds Halder afterwards favored taking Malta over Gibraltar. That the Army General Staff and its chief rated the tiny island south of Sicily high, so early, has pertinence to a later competition in targetry between Crete and Malta.

General Jodl struck a balance in OKW too; he accented "Führer decision" as he passed the main points to Warlimont for reduction to a catchall Führer Directive No. 18, "Guiding Principles for the Conduct of the War in the Near Future." It would bring the Gibraltar attack out as a full-blown operation under its name *Felix*. As background material Jodl included authority to continue North Africa plans on paper, orders for Luftwaffe attack on British air bases that threatened Rumanian oil (Lemnos, Salonika, Crete), and orders for "*immediate reinforcement*" of forces in Rumania. He then turned to that curious obsession, the Atlantic islands. Jodl's language could only mean "the Führer has spoken": "Simultaneously with attack on Gibraltar, the Canary and Cape Verde islands are to be occupied." He seemed anxious to pump up a fiction of fateful and far-reaching Führer decisions.

So toward evening of the notable Monday 4 November 1940, Jodl felt strong enough to tackle the shellback rebels at Navy. Word went out to Admiral Fricke, head of operations at SkI. By then the Führer's rambling tour had jelled operationally around Gibraltar, to which Jodl added a few leftovers from his 26–28 October plan against Alexandria, its fleet, and Suez. These actions appeared as merely postponed. With his accompanying words down pat in that peculiar German logicality that ignores or glosses over reality, Jodl unrolled his canvas.

Navy's head of operations, Fricke, was easily his equal, used to testing the strength and direction of the wind high up. His past performance at sifting out true Führer intent and softening its impact on the Navy had proved unfailing. Italy's march into Greece, Jodl said, had become "a most regrettable blunder. On no occasion had the Führer authorized such independent action. Britain's strategic position was improved by her occupation of Crete and Lemnos. . . . Support of the Italian offensive against Greece with one German corps is being considered. . . . An advance through Rumania and Bulgaria toward Salonika/Larisa will be attempted." These prophetic revelations come close to admission of complicity in the Italian push into Greece. Jodl continued: "The Führer does not plan to attack Suez through Turkey and Syria as proposed by some Army crusaders. It is anticipated that Russia will remain neutral." Here again emerges that peculiar quirk of using a neutral Russia as a stay on Turkey.

With the East Basin thus settled, Jodl turned west toward Gibraltar and the Atlantic for rousing action closer to the Navy's true interest. His language gathered the power of the offense.

The Führer is determined to occupy Gibraltar as soon as possible. Spain is ready to enter the war. . . . Our Army is ready to send troops; when they cross the border the following sequence obtains:
    (*a*) Air Force attack on British fleet in Gibraltar;
    (*b*) Occupation of Canary Islands; . . .
    (*c*) Occupation of Cape Verde Islands.

The last extravagance was too much for Fricke. He called a halt. Some of the early Navy exuberance over island bases had rubbed off on the Führer and stayed with him (for other than Navy reasons), while further study by the sailors revealed its absurdity. Fricke therefore protested the Cape Verde Island landing—out there 400 miles west of Dakar on the bulge of Africa. It might raise unfavorable world opinion and encourage British-American counter action. He pursued the same reasoning against Jodl's proposal to deploy German troops on Spain's border "to keep Portugal's little fellows in line." The plan was reaching too far.

One after the other Fricke's objections were listed for review by the Führer and the commander in chief of the Navy. As it stood, the list presented Jodl's processing of Hitler's plans with the Navy at this final, fateful point of turn away from European union and the South Plan. It included only strategical problems:

    (*a*) Provide facilities for defense of the Strait of Gibraltar.
    (*b*) Occupy the Canary Islands. . . .
    (*c*) Protect the coastal road along the southwestern French coast, from the seaward side, for the transfer of German troops to Spain.
    (*d*) Occupy the Cape Verde Islands.
    (*e*) Review the importance of Portugal to naval strategy.
    (*f*) Release the French fleet to take over its tasks within the overall plan [favored by the Navy].

At the very end Jodl added these warnings: "The Führer has decided that preparations for an eastern campaign, as well as for the execution of Operation *Sea Lion* in the spring, shall continue." These words weakened newcomer *Felix* and set him against the failure on the Channel in a sort of get-even scheme of great psychological effect. What a blow to Britain's prestige the world over when the Rock falls! It would bring along strategic returns by the challenge to British sea supremacy in the whole Mediterranean. The German Navy could warm to these pleasant prospects.[4]

Führer Directive No. 18—a number originally reserved for Invasion England—issued on 12 November 1940 to propound "guiding principles for the [changed] conduct of the war" now reaching from France through Spain (Gibraltar) to Egypt, the Balkans, and Russia, with a final apology for England. A certain stress still favored the west through fake proselytizing of France and quite specific directions as to the order of business in taking Gibraltar. Four familiar phases were prescribed:

(1) Reconnaissance in Spain by special units and assembly of troops in France;
(2) Air assault on British naval forces in Gibraltar, followed by entry of German troops into Spain from France;
(3) Ground assault on the Rock from the land side and deployment of troops against any British threat of entry into Portugal;
(4) Support to Spanish closure of the Strait of Gibraltar.

Fricke seemed to have scored, for descents on the Atlantic islands were left for further investigation. In Egypt, support to the Italians was to await their capture of Matruh (from which Alexandria could be attacked by air). For the Balkans the Army would prepare "to occupy *Continental Greece* north of the Aegean out of Bulgarian bases, as necessary." Although Russia was to be sounded in talks with Molotov—he had arrived in Berlin on the very day the directive was released—Hitler ordered that "regardless of the results of these discussions, all preparations for the east, which have been ordered ver-

4. FC 1940, 1:54–82 and 2:31–36; Warlimont KFA, pp. 224–29. British naval thought labored under its own delusive island foolishness and transmitted it to the United States. Captain S. W. Roskill, R.N., wrote in his *White Ensign* (Annapolis, 1960), p. 94, "As the only possible alternative to Gibraltar lay in gaining possession of the Spanish and Portuguese Atlantic islands, preparations were made to occupy some or all of them." But islands in mid-ocean without offensive power nowadays become burdens.

bally, are to continue." Then came the lame admonishment about England: the services were to strive to improve their plans for invasion landings "since changes in the situation might make it possible or necessary to return once more to Operation *Sea Lion* in the spring of 1941."[5] October's trial of a substitute policy and strategy had failed. That a shift away from the east was tried at all lends this period meaning in history.

Concern about Russia was naturally no new pain to German thought. Russia had been a part of life forever as the bigger half of a two-front horror in which Germany would be crushed between east and west. But when Hitler checkmated England, as the chief foe in the west, and Russia in the east, by the Nonaggression Pact with her on 23 August 1939, the bogey vanished. He said he wanted to make sure of this once and for all, though his main private cause was to subjugate and exploit Russia. To get on her border he struck east into Poland, and then west to clear his rear for further action east. France fell in the west, but England surprised him by defiant refusal to deal. Gradually, Hitler got used to a specious substitute solution of England merely neutralized, while he went about crushing Russia.

During the first year of war, relations with Moscow prospered— until the blitz speed of German western success rocked the continental balance. Russia's uneasiness became manifest in her seizure of the small Baltic buffer states on the north flank and her separation of Bessarabia from Rumania in the south. In August 1940 Russia stiffened her border forces opposite Finland, and in October after General Hansen's arrival in the Rumanian capital the number of Russian snoopers redoubled. When Italy marched into Greece, Russia occupied three islands in the Rumanian Danube delta. Political advances toward Bulgaria followed. So now in the second week of November 1940, as Molotov packed his bag to move on Berlin, feeling between the two governments was not all sweetness and light.

Supposedly, Hitler had reserved an important role for Russia in his New Order of European Union. Signing the Tripartite Pact could give her a free hand in the southeast toward the Persian Gulf. Eventually Britain would have to give in, and Russia could share in the spoils—so Ribbentrop had apprised Stalin when he invited Foreign Minister Molotov to Berlin for an exchange of views. By the time he

5. OKW Ops War Diary, 6 Nov. 1941; Jacobsen, pp. 153–56. General Jodl by stretching a little could console himself that Hitler had almost adopted his proposals of 26–28 October to get after Britain's Mediterranean Fleet at Alexandria by air attack.

arrived on 12 November, Russia, instead of being drawn toward the southeast, had been sucked into the Balkan vortex by the Italian attack on Greece. Everything about the carefully planned scenario had changed.

But at the first meeting, this deterred Ribbentrop not one bit from propping up the old scene and plot: he hammered at the tired theme of a beaten Britain, whose holdings in the south were ready for picking. He advocated close relations with Japan in the east and German/Russian movement south together, Russia toward the Persian Gulf; the Dardanelles Convention could be liberalized for her, and she could join the Tripartite Pact. In reply Molotov set a fretful tone by avoiding substance and concentrating on the semantics of the new terminology: Greater East Asia, what precisely did it mean? Or New European Order and spheres of influence, how could these terms be defined? The Russian raised other trivialities. When Hitler joined the talks he attempted to conciliate by explaining the war's course, the reasons for Germany's moves and her aims; he went on at length, stood firm for Russo-German harmony and for opposition to the United States. Molotov stuck to his pinpricks and hunger for knowledge on ticklish points. What was Finland up to? What did the New Order imply? What about Bulgaria? Who indeed was looking out for Russia? Interpreter Paul Schmidt heard the amazing barrage hail down on Hitler and waited for the explosion. It did not come. The Führer carefully eschewed all show of annoyance, politely repeated the purpose of the pact and Germany's role. Russia would be cut in on all settlements, he promised. It was growing late. He invoked a curious cause to break off: evening RAF attacks were expected; the meeting had better adjourn. If he wanted to expose Molotov to the rigors of combat, the peril of beaten Britain's planes was hardly the way to inspire respect and confidence. The exchanges had made no headway whatever.[6]

Late news of the day indicated that Britain was very much alive, and it echoed Molotov's skepticism. The news also fitted Hitler's alert about an RAF attack. What had happened was that a British air strike had crippled Italy's fleet—another major Italian disaster. Britain's Mediterranean Fleet had followed up the landing on Crete with a foray into the Ionian Sea toward Italy's fleet base at Taranto inside the heel. At about 1800 on 11 November 1940 Admiral Cunningham released the carrier *Illustrious* with supporting cruisers and destroyers

6. NSR, pp. 217–59; H. Grenier, pp. 315–18; Jacobsen, pp. 157–61; Puttkamer, and Puttkamer to Ansel, 1959.

to carry out Operation *Judgment*—a double strike by torpedo planes at the Italian heavy ships behind their netted mooring in Taranto port and roadstead. Twenty planes armed with bombs, flares, and twelve torpedoes flew 170 miles from their carrier to score the first big coup for the aircraft torpedo arm with hits on three battleships; two had to be beached and the third sank. The impact reached Pearl Harbor proportions—half of Italy's battleships out of action and serious damage on other ships.[7]

Back in Berlin the German hosts must have squirmed as the trickle of news boosted British stock higher and higher. That Cunningham had sewed up control over the vital East Basin seemed clear; he had thereby improved the possibility of overseas help to Greece and Crete. None of the conferees made any recorded mention about the Taranto debacle; none was needed. Molotov sharpened his tart remarks on troublesome German involvement with Finland in the north and with Rumania in the south. He danced from one scene to the other. Hitler strove to divert and convert him through contemplation of Britain's dismemberment, piece by piece. It must have been bait, for he had steadily discouraged such thoughts in his advisers and in Mussolini. But along these suspect lines the repartee continued. Dr. Paul

7. Cunningham, pp. 283–88; Hampshire and comment. *Illustrious* launched two strikes of 12 and 8 planes at 2035 and 2128. The 170-mile flight was flown at 90 knots at 7500 feet. Flare droppers and dive bombers broke off to silhouette the six battleships in the outer harbor, then went on for a diversionary bomb attack on cruisers in the inner port. Down from the west and in through barrage balloons and antiaircraft fire, the torpedo craft planned to drop their fish at 1000-yard range. Old battleships *Cavour* and *Dulio* took hits and the new spick-and-span *Littorio*. She and *Dulio* beached, *Cavour* sank. Two British planes failed to regain *Illustrious*. The night's work impressed Hitler, the innovator; he talked about a torpedo arm for getting after the British fleet in Alexandria and ordered Göring to pursue it. A quarrel between Göring and Raeder over who would control the torpedo planes killed the project (we shall get deeper into this story presently), but not for the Japanese Navy, whose representatives in Berlin photographed and studied the results of the British attack. In the United States, Admiral Stark, chief of Naval Operations, worried about the possibility of Japanese attack on ships in Pearl Harbor. He pressed for strengthening the defenses and their joint readiness by Army and Navy to repel attack. His concern led to a letter of 24 January 1941 from Secretary of the Navy Knox to Secretary of War Stimson; it set forth the practicability of Japanese attack and recommended specific countermeasures. (As a member of the War Plans Division of the CNO, this reporter had been designated to restudy the situation and to prepare the letter.) Except for Admiral Stark no one on high believed a Japanese attack to be feasible. During this same time of early 1941, Admiral Isoroku Yamamoto, fleet commander, devised the plan of Pearl Harbor attack and sold it to the Japanese Navy in March, and in the next month tentatively to the Imperial General Headquarters. How much did Taranto contribute? In answer to the question, General Genda of Japan, while a visitor at the U.S. Naval Institute on 3 March 1969, answered that Taranto had "no" effect. As a commander in the Japanese Navy he was a leading Pearl Harbor attack planner. The question was elaborated and repeated; the answer remained negative.

Schmidt, who recorded for Germany, characterized the exchanges as the sharpest of his career.

The unproductive skirmish centered on Finland, then on Rumania, and back again. Hitler carried the Finland question to the point of intimating that Germany would fight beside Finland; Molotov backed off, whereupon his host returned to the inviting British pie. He let himself go like a circus fakir or a slick barker on the streets of Vienna; his harangue was in total disagreement with what he had said before on the subject. He uttered scarcely a single honest word, but trumpeted death to the chief foe. Never before had he so brutally chopped up the Britain of his mythology, and now he was doing it for a rank, suspect outsider. What was up? It is certain that Hitler had gone all-out for something, but that something was not the making of a firm ally out of Russia. Was he trying to prove how impossible, even dangerous, dealing with her could be?

All of the proof was not yet in. Having used up Finland, Molotov beat a tactical retreat by reverting to the more or less accepted Russian plaint over Turkey and the imprisoned Black Sea. From there, quiet mention of the Danube Commission, sitting in Bucharest, gave easy access back to Rumania and her German guarantees. There the Russian pushed and snarled without ceasing; it was his true target. Get the guarantees lifted or downgraded! "What would Germany say if Russia gave the same guarantee to Bulgaria? . . . What exactly was the German position on the Bosporus?" Waxing uglier at each jab, Hitler countered and recountered by asking whether the Bulgars had asked for guarantees. The Russian's third reiteration was too raw for him. Said he bristling, "If Germany sought areas of friction with Russia she would not need the Bosporus for that." Abruptly the talk turned back to Hitler's sale of Britain, but now with reservations; "there is no *absolute certainty* the plan can be carried through." His probe of the Russians was finished; he had his measure of them, had had it all along. Perhaps his armed services needed proof. He had produced it.

In the security of a bomb shelter for the second time, Ribbentrop resumed the fruitless arguments. Molotov took pains to register a fresh interest: the freer use of the western entrance of the Baltic between Denmark and Sweden. This alarming suggestion could imply the very tie-up of Russia and Britain that Hitler had diligently been preaching against. If Molotov's remark in itself proved nothing, it could be twisted into verbal ammunition for the latest Führer slogan,

"Preventive war in the east." An outline plan for it got under way in L Section under Lt. Colonel von Lossberg.[8]

Suppose the Russian had snapped up the pie. Surely Hitler had considered such a long shot and prepared for it. On reflection, it could only have done him good. A Russia freshly committed to a pact that pursued the general line of 1939's friendship would clear the air and tell him where he stood for the immediate future. Beyond that, a Russia making southeast would be open to slaughter on its west flank. Britain might, in the meantime, have seen the light.

No; Hitler anticipated, even wanted, rejection and went all out to get it. After the bitter disenchantment with the South Plan he needed to test and reassure himself and to secure some leverage against his professionals. He deliberately adopted their prime target, Britain, held her up to Molotov's view while offering to tear her to shreds for Russia. He goaded the sour Russian into revealing how dangerous to Germany the Russian cause could become on the north and the south. Fatherland in peril became obvious to everyone! Long ago, on 31 July, Hitler had unveiled to his Army chiefs an expedition of murder and robbery on a national scale into the east; it had now by 13 November been sanctified into salvation of the homeland. And he was believed. In some quarters he still is, as the believers point knowingly at Problem Russia of today. Out of the Molotov visit grew the trumped-up picture of a Red Army in Finland that could cut off nickel and Swedish iron from Germany, and another army in Rumania that could cut off her oil and thus lay Germany's war flat. "From here," wrote his Naval aide, "a stone started rolling, and to bring it to rest again would be hard. For Hitler had firmed his decision and no one and nothing could dissuade him, unless a completely unforeseen situation worked up." For anyone free to see (perhaps it required hindsight) events did work up just such a situation with Crete and the East Basin. From 13 November 1940 forward Hitler's fatal target confusion took over, under the slogan of Preventive War—a convenient cover for fulfillment of his very own Evangel.[9]

8. Schmidt, pp. 209–20; Lossberg, pp. 104–7; Warlimont IH, pp. 150, 151.

9. Puttkamer, pp. 42–46 and in correspondence to this reporter. Molotov's mission to Berlin of November 1940 failed as badly as Chamberlain's to Munich in September 1938. There were similarities and differences. Both meetings were intent on halting German aggression and succeeded only in insuring it. Hitler came out of both meetings angry and more determined than ever to go ahead. A belief that appeasement at Munich encouraged him to push on is wholly mistaken. Instead he was furious at his own weakness for having met at all with the British on a matter of purely continental concern. He came away determined to show them.

Problem Russia was no longer a problem, nor was England, except among the doubters. Admiral Raeder was the most steadfast and open in opposition; he acted as South Plan's chief proponent and East Plan's chief opponent. Just prior to Hitler's return to the mountains in the afternoon of 14 November Raeder appeared for conference. Molotov had hardly got out of town; Raeder realized that if ever, now was the time to strike against going east. He brought several late studies that urged action in the East Basin and Crete: Seizure of Suez (via Crete) could decide the war; Gibraltar was not enough. "The British fleet must be deprived of its bases and, if possible, destroyed." Hold fast to Britain, he urged, and warned of overextension in Russia.

Amiable and relaxed, the Führer avoided taking issue; the admiral confidently steamed out into the Atlantic islands. Only the Spanish Canaries could be considered, he said; then he went on to squelch the Azores. Hitler at once took off: "Britain would take the Azores the moment any Germans entered Spain and would cede them to the United States; the Azores," he continued, "afforded him the only opportunity for attacking America [by air] . . . thereby forcing her to build up her antiaircraft defenses . . . instead of helping England." The next day L Section recorded that the Führer also had designs on the Azores for use when peace should break out. These wild words are a matter of record. Equally mad and arresting was Raeder's response. Though risky, he ventured, with luck a drop on the Azores could succeed. It might have been the only way to divert Hitler until the spell passed. He ordered "immediate further investigation." He had his East Plan; why worry about these lead-ins?[10]

On return to his own headquarters, the admiral made happy entry into Skl's War Diary: "Altogether the discussion offered opportunity for a very searching talkout about the great strategical . . . questions for the further conduct of the war and led to basic far-reaching accord

He accelerated his pace against Czechoslovakia and Poland and the war. Munich is no demonstration of the evils of appeasement. Hitler was unappeasable to Chamberlain and Molotov.

10. FC 1940, 2:37–58. Skl War Diary, 15 Nov. 1940; Halder 2:180–85; H. Greiner, pp. 309–20. Messerschmitt had under development a new fighter-bomber, touted to have a range of over 4000 miles. This was the new plane that Hitler proposed to use against the United States. Figures of this sort unfailingly inspired Führer speculation and trick solutions to tough strategic problems. (Our exploding technology of today shows similar effects.) To complete the island story: on 6 December 1940 the OKW Ops War Diary recorded that General Jodl thought the Canaries were adequately defended by Spain, that occupation of Madeira and the Cape Verdes no longer was considered, and ideas of preparations for occupation of the Azores would very likely *go to sleep* . . . for lack of time before *Felix*.

with the Führer as commander in chief." The old gentleman had succumbed to the relaxed and disarming Führer mood. The conference reflected a Hitler with mind made up, floating happily in unbounded release. He took off for the mountain fastness, not to fret in dilemma, but to contemplate at ease his "unalterable resolve" and its glorious execution. Russia herself had never been the problem; only the timing of her demise had.

Not one of the service chiefs agreed with their Führer at heart. Navy was the most forthright in opposition; Army, though opposed, hoped to maneuver around or out of the East Plan. At this time Army leaders felt no irrevocable commitment (Halder KT, 2:164–66). Göring, while personally opposed, took no stand. He busied himself to make Gibraltar an exclusive air show—to rub out the Channel failure. In the middle of the Molotov debate he proposed to Hitler that von Richthofen of the 8th Air Corps, should command in chief over *Felix*. Hitler made him no answer, but passed along the anti-Russian conclusion that was being confirmed in the Molotov talks. Göring would have to wait, to get his exclusive Luftwaffe show until May 1941 on Crete. The very forces and commanders recommended for *Felix* would eventually take over at Crete.

4. Felix—Marita—Barbarossa

Plans and Orders: December 1940

The old gospel of the East thus reaffirmed, the time was right for an interlude of play mixed with light skirmishing toward the showdown. Planners on high busied themselves, but not too hard, over the lead-in performances by *Felix* of Spain and *Marita* of Greece, to be climaxed by Crusader *Barbarossa* in Russia. First a midwinter blitz southwest would blast open a fresh season of war at Gibraltar, followed close by a confounding thrust through Bulgaria into Greece. Then in May 1941, when the agitated world knew not where to turn, the great javelin of men and machines would plunge east into the vitals of Russia, the promised land. We still gasp at the width of the sweep: from the Atlantic to the Black Sea deep into Russia. At OKW, papers about it collected under an innocuous code name, *Fritz*; and at OKH under *Otto* a rail and road improvement projected eastward. Fritz and Otto, what an innocent pair! But could such banalities raise anyone up out of himself? Who could these silly names inspire? Before the papers got very heavy, the Master took a hand; he rechristened his life's fulfillment *Barbarossa* after the old German hero of knighthood against the infidel. Swashbuckling old Redbeard would bear out his saga and return to crusade in the spirit of German fighting men.

But first a break, after the prolonged dilemma. People on high took leave. At the Berghof a procession of important policy figures passed by.[1] The first was Serrano Suñer, Spain's foreign minister, with Ciano, on 17 November. Ribbentrop tried in advance to move the Spaniard to outright commitment to war. He failed, and Hitler fared no better, though the record said the meeting had gone off pleasantly. Planners in OKW already complained of time growing short for the Gibraltar operation during January. On 18 November, another Berghof guest had been less than enthusiastic about joining the war. This was King Boris of Bulgaria. His reserve induced Hitler to add two divisions to *Marita*'s planned push through Bulgaria, which brought the total to twelve divisions. On 20 November Hungary joined the Tripartite Pact in a ceremony at Schloss Belvedere in Vienna.

In an aside afterwards Hitler handed Ciano a long letter of reconciliation and reassessment for the Duce. Three weeks had passed in silence between the two partners. Mussolini had suffered repulse in Greece and disaster in Taranto, while Hitler had achieved decision in Berlin. In pity, mingled with Axis fence mending, his letter opened with an avowal of devotion to the Duce and promise of all possible aid for this time of crisis. He reminded Mussolini of his neglected suggestion for the seizure of Crete and analyzed the consequences. He fitted pieces of the abandoned South Plan together with bits from General Jodl's scheme of 26 October to encourage and guide action in the Mediterranean. It was evident that European coalition had lost primacy. Uncommitted countries had reacted to events along lines of "wait and see," Hitler thought, because they felt "that the last word in this war has possibly not yet been spoken after all." From Crete Britain could now threaten not only Rumania's oil but all of southern Italy and Albania. This circumstance ruled out a "successful ground offensive from Albania before March." The I-told-you-so strain about Crete he repeated once again. The military "situation [was] threatening and . . . downright unnerving." What to do about it?[2]

Recommended actions appear in the two categories of policy and strategy. Under policy came pressure on Spain to enter the war and enlistment of Yugoslavia. As for Spain, Hitler hoped that Franco could be persuaded by the first of 1941. By then all units would be letter-perfect, poised to take the Rock and close the strait. Two divisions would cross into Northwest Africa to keep it secure. The sense

1. OKW Ops War Diary, 19 Nov. 1940; OKW Ops SitConf, pp. 113–19, "Operation Felix." L Section prepared a timetable that meshed every operation toward 1 May as the start of *Barbarossa*. Weather and Luftwaffe lacks blocked *Marita* until March.

2. Jacobsen, pp. 183–87.

of Hitler's note followed Admiral Raeder's prophetic argument of September that the defection or fall of Northwest Africa to the British could lead to Italy's downfall. But Gibraltar in German hands would cancel this threat, "force Britain's transport south around Africa," diminish her power in the East Basin, and thus contribute to the Balkan campaign.

Yugoslavia, the other political highlight, lay on the west flank of the projected Balkan thrust, and without "assurance from her about security the campaign cannot be risked . . . , means other than force must win her over." The true aim Hitler had already on 1 October explained to General Hansen and now revealed it to Mussolini in almost identical words. "I am determined, Duce, if the English attempt to build up an important position in Thrace, to engage them with decisive forces. And against all risks." Of all his phobias the thought of another British beachhead on Europe disturbed him most. Indeed, one of the Gibraltar campaign's strong attractions was the chance of driving Britain from her last European outpost. Thus political uncertainties menaced both Gibraltar and the Balkan plan.

Further strategic action against Britain, however, offered help. As though launching a brand-new inspiration, Hitler declared, "The most important objective in the Mediterranean is smoking out the British fleet, through combined German-Italian air action." But this required first of all North African takeoff bases within range of Alexandria, and here Mussolini came in: a renewed Italian land drive to seize Matruh, only 88 miles from Graziani's Sidi Barrani base. It was in fact the key of the letter. "This winter has to see the Mediterranean cleaned up, for at the beginning of May I have to have my forces back." The sound of combined operating was deceptive, for Hitler next defined two overlapping but separated operational theaters. One, which included Albania and Egypt, belonged to Italy, and the other, which took in all of the East Basin, including of course Alexandria and Suez, belonged to Germany. "Three or four months would make it a graveyard for the British fleet and a decisive prerequisite for the operations in Greece." Conquest of the Nile Delta could then be put off until the fall of 1941. "These measures should relieve tension and regain for the Axis a positive spirit of the initiative. . . . These are the thoughts," Hitler assured Mussolini, "that the warm heart of a friend conveys to help overcome the crisis and turn apparent failure into defeat of the foe."

Nonsense! They were second thoughts about a problem abandoned in a huff and since sharply intensified by events, which included a frightening demonstration of Britain ruling the sea and Italy helpless on land and sea. Hitler's paper drive for a Matruh air base was the first serious German effort to get after Britain's Mediterranean sea power. Just as the instructions for a mission to Rumania forecast the campaigns of the Balkans and Crete, this letter marked the beginning of Luftwaffe planning to contest the air over the East Basin. Operation *Judgment* at Taranto with its air-launched torpedoes was responsible.[3]

The failure of the Germans to develop an effective aircraft torpedo arm offers a sharp demonstration of the wrong kind of command relations. Emotional strains ran so high between the Luftwaffe, secure in Göring's inside track with Hitler, and the Navy, fighting for its very life, that the prime object of sinking ships got lost. Moreover, the Luftwaffe never could understand the paramount importance of making holes in hulls below the waterline. This is what sinks ships, not bravely blasting their armored topsides with bombs and machine-gun fire. The German attitude makes a strange tale that goes back some years to the Spanish Civil War of the thirties.

Hitler reacted typically to the vision that Taranto inspired; he saw a new air magic for wresting control of the Mediterranean from Britain—he would simply arm his planes with torpedoes instead of bombs. But a long air-torpedo story had gone before. During the Spanish Civil War a German Luftwaffe officer, formerly in the Navy, by the name of Harlinghausen made the first air-launched torpedo kill on a ship as it entered Valencia harbor. Later when World War II came on, Harlinghausen urged Göring to develop the air-launched torpedo as a weapon against British naval forces in Scapa Flow. Göring acceded, but staff underlings opposed the idea. Why bother to throw a torpedo in the water to have it strike a ship when you could hit her direct with bombs? It looked like another of those worthless Navy schemes for getting in on the Luftwaffe. The Navy, which had the torpedoes, did some limited experimenting and developing with the few planes under naval operational control and put them to work against British coastal sea traffic. By late 1940 they were making kills, and Navy wanted to keep them at it. When Air Inspector General Field Marshal Milch and the Chief of the Air General Staff General

---

3. Puttkamer, p. 46. Mussolini replied on 22 November. He agreed with the indispensability of an air offensive against the British fleet and of Luftwaffe entry into the Italian preserve. Hitler had elaborated his wishes to Ciano at the meeting on 18 November.

Jeschonnek, at Hitler's express wish for a Torpedo Group South, ordered the torpedo planes via Luftwaffe channels to cease using torpedos in the north, the Navy got up to do battle. "Intolerable interference in Naval Command," and about the use of "a Navy weapon that can only be fired by specially trained naval personnel." Reports and retorts shot back and forth. People at OKW took sides. What good were the few torpedoes anyhow to the south and especially in the shallows of Alexandria and Gibraltar?" Only infallible Führer decision could deal with the impasse.

He heard Admiral Raeder on 3 December and three days later directed the Luftwaffe "to suspend for the present commitment of torpedo aircraft in the Mediterranean." So for the nonce Navy kept its torpedoes and pride at an incalculable cost to operations in the very sea its own chief had again and again stressed. Often such quarrels that range out of control are fueled and pumped higher by staff agitation. This episode fired enough new ill-feeling to doom the air-launched torpedo for Germany. Her Führer cogently summed up his thought about just such a possibility to General Jodl:

> If there were no superior office which could decide, the danger would exist that, for example, in the present case the launch of torpedoes from aircraft would not be further developed at all or would even be discontinued because two branches of the armed forces could not agree on whom this task should devolve. . . . One must draw from such controversies the lesson that OKW must hold a tight rein in order to attain the best possible commitment of the strength of all three armed services. To guarantee this is the task of the OKW. This applies even today, when his, the Führer's, authority in the end always makes it possible to arrive at decision. . . . Into his position might some day step a man who would indeed be an excellent politician, but perhaps might not have so much military knowledge and audacity as he. Such a man would require a very strong OKW; otherwise the danger could exist that the forces of the three branches might fall apart rather than be combined for unified effect. . . .

Well and good. Yet Hitler himself temporized rather than decided; he failed to decide and direct how the Navy and Air Force should combine on an air torpedo arm under one command. The thing remained split between two warring camps.[4]

4. FC (German original), 3 Dec. 1940, annex 2; OKW Ops War Diary, 6 Dec. 1940, pp. 35–37; developments in the early days were told to me by General Martin Harlinghausen in Germany in 1960. In 1940-41 he served as chief of staff of the 10th Air Corps, which in January 1941 redeployed from Norway to the Battle of the Mediterranean. Admiral Cunningham (Cunningham, p. 289) testifies to excellent air torpedo work by the Italian Air Force. On 3 December 1940 two struck H.M.S. *Glasgow* in Suda Bay.

The fresh approach to an air offensive against British sea targets lost much of its steam. Hitler pressed for attack by bombs, even without Matruh; flights from the Dodecanese Islands, from Sicily and Italy, were planned. On 5 December Field Marshal Milch left for Rome to arrange southern air basing; on 10 December a Führer directive added force to the project, named the effort Special Operation Mediterranean, ordered attack on the British fleet in Alexandria, and on traffic in the Suez Canal and in the Strait of Sicily. The waters around Greece were named for possible action. Far away in Norway the 10th Air Corps packed up to move to sunny Sicily.

But in the southern objective area Britannia steamed where she willed: a supply convoy was to run the length of the sea from Gibraltar to Alexandria; fleet units made free with Cretan and Grecian inlets in exploitation of the Taranto triumph. Greece's soldiery chased the Italian aggressors back over the Albanian border. Distress calls went up, first for German motor transport, then for air transport. Soon Marshal Badoglio fell casualty to the uproar, which only roared higher. From Rome, von Rintelen telegraphed Berlin, "The time has come to help." German high commands fished around idly for the most convenient means; nor was the Führer much interested.

He was happily engrossed in the policy requirements of *Felix* and *Marita*. At Air and Navy bidding the final objective of the latter had been extended to the south tip of Peloponnesus, which meant all mainland Greece. Hitler moved forward on all paper and ceremonial fronts. Old *Sea Lion* got a couple of well-publicized kicks to remind the British, but strangest of all was a flurry over a rumored request from Ireland for help against occupation by the British. "The Führer is deeply engrossed in the possibilities of occupying Ireland; he is of the opinion that Ireland in German hands would mean the end of England," recorded L Section in its situation evaluation in late November. He spoke to Raeder in the same vein on 3 December. "Possession of Ireland can work the end of the war." He might as well have made it "Possession of England," which is about what the admiral thought of this folly. Had the war really got so far? The rumor may have started from intercepted British messages about the transfer of an important headquarters to Ireland. German plans for placing observers in Ireland were completed; L Section compiled data on the availability of captured British weapons for dropping into Ireland and drafted points for a treaty with her. But recall the air attack on

America from the Azores; Ireland was not much wilder. It was pure Hitleriana; moreover, it held on.[5]

England really was suffering. Each darkness was a nightmare of tense waiting. London was not spared; the Midlands, Liverpool, Birmingham, and satellite towns hurt the worst. It was the time of the senseless blast at Coventry with no follow-up except shudders. In the southwest the Luftwaffe seemed intent on blasting a wasteland barrier from the English Channel to Bristol Channel. Was it to make an invasion beachhead of Cornwall? The whole south coast from Plymouth, to Portsmouth, and on, took its share of horror. Food stocks dwindled; evacuation of children was talked about. What good were the Mediterranean victories if bombs and hunger and terror at home all but blotted them out?

To counter, the RAF raised the power and reach of bombing into Germany from Stettin in the north to Lake Constance in the far south. A program of mutual destruction could thus proceed without let up, neither side winning for lack of strategic objectives. It was senseless.

However, to Hitler, his own objective was clear and simple; total hegemony over the Continent and elimination of British capability to interfere. Plans beyond this last had matured sufficiently for his review, in particular those for the curtain raiser, Gibraltar; he wanted to see the blitz commanders—General Kübler for the Army task force and General von Richthofen of the 8th Air Corps for the Luftwaffe—"to discuss their tasks in detail." There was still one fatal lack: Spanish consent. Yet on 2 December General Jodl announced the good news to head planner Warlimont: the Caudillo had assented to early February for attack on the Rock. To nail it down Hitler re-dispatched his counterintelligence chief Admiral Canaris to Franco with a personal letter.Details could proceed and directives issue. In a regular Führer conference of 3 December Admiral Raeder reported the Navy ready. The Army followed two days later. The center of the stage belonged to *Felix*.

The early days of each succeeding month had evolved a repetitive scenario of high excitement and crisis leading to a show of Führer decision and restatement of plans at plenary session; 4 September ushered in the air switch to London, 4 October the Brenner meeting and the decision to explore a South Plan and western union; 4 No-

5. OKW Ops SitConf, pp. 113, 129, 130, 133; Halder, 2:192. The Ireland alarm was doubly suspect because of Göring's hand in it. The scheming held on for some time.

vember saw the confused aftermath of Italian failures and decision to shed them and turn irrevocably toward the east. Now 5 December did more than all the others: it validated the mighty sweep from Gibraltar to the Caspian in three successive campaigns—*Felix* (Gibraltar), *Marita* (Greece), *Barbarossa* (Russia) (though the Army still called him *Otto*). It was the first time of record the three were discussed in proper order.

But the record is clouded on Caudillo consent. Hitler thinks it is clear. He has convinced himself Franco means Yes, when in his Spanish way he means Yes and again, No. Coupled with anxiety over the general Mediterranean situation, the wishful conviction of Yes supplied an emotional charge that produced on 5 December a recital that settled everything.

The land warriors assembled for a long session in the somber study of the Chancellery: the Führer, backed by Keitel and Jodl and adjutants; for the Army, von Brauchitsch and Halder, supported by artillerist Brand. Brauchitsch led in with report of *Felix* readiness, his timing, duration, and that command would be by Field Marshal von Reichenau (a Hitler favorite). Then came *Marita*, which would have to wait until snow and ice cleared in March. He finished with rail construction eastward for *Barbarossa*. Toward this great day in May the preliminaries would have to closely mesh their timing. As he finished, the Army chief requested a Führer review of the entire situation. It opened the monologic floodgates to an exhaustive discourse covering the whole sequence, not alone the strategy but the political purposes behind it. General Jodl had a protocol record prepared of this veritable blueprint of Hitler's intent for 1941. It was entered in the war diary and from it Germany never got free.[6]

He deplored Italian ineptitude in deep pessimism and thence worked up to grand Teutonic triumph in Russia. Italy was stalled in Libya and was about to lose Albania—this was why Yugoslavia bided her time over joining the Axis. Yet there in the Balkans the true problem was Russia, pressing in Bulgaria and wherever else weakness might show. "Should it even be possible to force England," recorded General Halder, "to ask for an armistice, she would still try to make Russia her Continental dagger." The Führer had got at his private

6. Halder, 2:210–17; OKW Ops War Diary 2, 5 Dec. 1940, pp. 12–29, containing the Jodl protocol; H. Greiner, pp. 162–67, 242–43, 323–28; "Operation Felix," pp. 12–16. The sources agree in general, but not in sequence, with the on-the-spot record of General Halder.

devil quickly, and with the same hungry zest. Not even British submission could stop the eastern crusade.

Nothing could be done in Libya; the only possible help could be the planned air offensive from Sicily and southern Italy against the British fleet; then of course, there were the side effects of Gibraltar's seizure—they would ease the sting of Italian setbacks, the shift of German troops to Northwest Africa would bend Vichy France toward Germany, and loss of the Rock would deal Britain a heavy psychological blow. He moved eastward to size up Greece.

German forces in Rumania had kept the oil fields safe; but *Marita* was necessary to "clarify the situation once and for all," unless Greece settled with Italy and compelled the British to leave. Diplomatic relations with Greece were still intact for just such use. "In such case German intervention would be superfluous, since hegemony over Europe would no longer be at stake" (General Halder recorded). "Decision over European hegemony will come in the struggle against Russia." Here was the key! Deployment for attack into Greece is therefore absolutely indispensable, and useful in any case because the troops would become immediately available for the east. Rumania would join, and on the north flank, Finland. So far the operational sequence in the War Diary of OKW Operations was:

1. Air attack on the British Mediterranean fleet . . . begin 15 December.
2. Ground force attack on Gibraltar start February, complete in four weeks.
3. Greece, early March . . . end in March but maybe not until end of April. Draw Yugoslavia to Axis side.

Hitler made allowance in timing for trouble with Yugoslavia and for an extended Balkan campaign. For final action in Russia he feared two British beachheads: one strategical in Greece, the other political in Moscow, which might prematurely turn Russia against him. The first he would counter by occupying Greece; the second by occupying Russia. He would then be supreme. Britain would come around or go under. Many recent acts and signs bore out this simple scheme. It embodied the latest expression of Hitler's very soul.

When Brauchitsch thereupon questioned Luftwaffe power to keep Britain down and support the East Campaign at the same time, Hitler had ready statistical proof of the Luftwaffe's growth over the RAF. "Moreover, night raids into England can continue during the short campaign into Russia." But how short is a short campaign? Some boasts, skimmed from talk at Führer Headquarters, had whittled the time down to three weeks, or half the time for France—and yet over space factors more than thrice as big. "The Russian armed forces are inferior to the German; if Russia's army is once hit hard she will go into a greater collapse than France in 1940," said Hitler. "The campaign will end at the Volga." The general line ran from Archangel in the north to Astrakhan on the Caspian in the south.

General Halder presented the full OKH East Plan. The theater was divided into north and south subtheaters because of the Pripet Marshes in the center. Advantages of road and rail nets in the northern subtheater gave it a main effort headed for Leningrad by its left army group, while its companion group next to the south carried the true main effort toward Moscow over Smolensk. In the southern subtheater a third army group was aimed to take Kiev. The initial commitment of 137 divisions, backed by a powerful second wave, bespoke the grandiose proportion of the campaign. The eager Führer moved to reexpound his field doctrine: encircle and destroy "to render every Russian formation encountered incapable of regeneration." Moscow as a target can wait! The remark left the impression that the capital was secondary. Russian fighting formations came first! This ambiguity about targets gave the soldiers the first tremors of uneasiness which eventually became crucial. Should the field targets consist only of human bodies? Positions or land areas? (Economy and industry, drawn forward later, received only passing mention.) Was Hitler already transferring to the operational field his familiar target confusion? His knack for gimmickry and technical scheming was always astounding, yet in the vital problem of targetry he exhibited a politician's distractability and penchant for straddle and cheap victory. A similar wish for many options showed in target dates, but to a lesser degree. Weather patterns pointed at no hop-off into Russia before 15 May 1941. This date then provided the linchpin on which all else would have to turn.

A countback—padded for weather, deployment delays, and operational vagaries—fitted *Marita* into the first week of April 1941, rather than March. General Halder now took the word again to present the OKH plan: five infantry divisions would drive through friendly Bulgaria, and when ordered, into Greece. The Rhodope Mountains on the northern boundary of Greece squeezed the maneuver room, but mobile forces could probably work down the narrow

Struma valley to get at and breach the Metaxas Line. This should leave two armored and one and a half motorized divisions available for advance on Athens. The east flank would be guarded by other formations against Turkey. This heavy commitment could roll over anything in its path, and just this invincibility was what Hitler had preached. He gave hearty approval, adding only that at some point Italian forces would have to be drawn in. He further suggested glider descents on Aegean islands, especially on Lemnos off the Dardanelles. So, on paper, the drive into Greece was ready as a German enterprise and not just as a rescue of bogged-down Italians.

Felix against the Rock as the opening blow for 1941 naturally drew earnest professional interest. On 5 December 1940, it attained an emotional peak. An age-old symbol of British power and security was to be scaled and taken by Germans in a special trick performance.

Gibraltar's 260 years under Britain came about only because Admiral Sir George Rooke in 1704 had the gall and foresight to hoist the Union Jack and lay claim for Queen Anne. In fine summer sailing during July 1704 Sir George cruised west through the Strait of Gibraltar with some forty British and Dutch sail of the line after fruitless operations in the West Basin for the Archduke Charles's claim to the Spanish crown. Rooke's pass at Barcelona and at the French fleet farther up had only disgusted him and Prince George of Hesse-Darmstadt, who commanded the embarked Dutch troops. Now off Lagos twenty-two ships under Admiral Shovell joined, to swell the total to sixty-three under five British and two Dutch admirals. The overpowering concourse turned back through the strait and anchored off Rio Martín (Tetuán) on the Barbary Coast to take counsel.

"It was resolved to make a sudden attack on Spain's Gibraltar," well known to be weak. Four days of scheming and preparing at anchor brought the fleet to a high fighting pitch. It sailed on 31 July and at noon on 1 August anchored in the roomy Bay of Gibraltar. By 1500 Prince George and his heterogeneous force of British marines and Dutch infantry, all told 2400 men, had landed at and occupied the connecting neck to mainland Spain. The Rock was cut off, but defiant. General Diego de Salinas, backed by 80 regular soldiers and 470 militiamen, answered "No!" to the demand for surrender. Ship bombardment began, the town burned, seamen landing parties took the south mole and worked across the Rock. When the north mole fell silent, Prince George advanced from the neck. On the evening of the third day Salinas gave up. Hesse-Darmstadt hoisted

Charles's standard. Rooke promptly objected. He claimed the Rock for Queen Anne and had the Union Jack hoisted; it stayed. Britain had acquired its most useful outpost in the Mediterranean. Years of negotiating and skirmishing, one serious Spanish attack in 1727, and actions during the European edition of the American Revolution failed to shake British possession. The Rock became a symbol of British integrity.

In concluding his monologic review of the situation Hitler approved the matured project, and as he did, he came out with an astonishing blow-by-blow account of fixed events for the Rock's fall. They attest to his personal participation in the planning step by step and at each turn. It was his kind of job, his kind of personal answer to Britain, the only kind he was capable of: tricky, small commitment but full of surprises, and all based on air-land power. In such context, the *Felix* minutiae take on extra significance.

Horizontal bombing was to hold through for five days; then dive bombers would pinpoint targets, drive British ships to sea, and silence land batteries facing north so that his own artillery, emplaced by this time in Spain, could plow up the land neck in advancing barrages to explode mines and blast the Rock's casemates. Infantry would then move forward, supported by the heaviest tanks, while mountain troops scaled the steep seaward side. German artillery was to outweigh the British 1½ to 1, and the total expenditure was to come to 8500 tons, to be transported by sea from Italy to Malaga. By this time Hitler had the Rock fast in hand and was ready for a shift to the sea strait between Europe and Africa. On either shore, batteries would be set up to stop all sea traffic. The Führer's unbounded faith in artillery to do this was the same curious tendency that had surfaced earlier on the Strait of Dover. It was idle to object. That landlubber *Felix* possessed the capabilities imputed, no one present disputed. No voice rose in protest as in *Sea Lion*, whom the Führer at this very time declared dead. In his mind, *Felix* had moved in as a worthy substitute.

General Jodl, who was to unfold the plan to the Caudillo, set his departure for Madrid on 11 December, six days off, so promising seemed the prospect. Admiral Canaris was already on the spot to confirm consent for 10 January as F-Day. Yet Franco, who commanded in chief, could hardly grant entry without passing on the German plans. Twice he had requested details and had been given no satisfaction, for the Germans first wanted his unlimited commitment. The arrogance of it occurred to no one in OKW. During the afternoon of 7 December the final tactical polish, with a fascinating review of devices and precise moves by General Kübler's ground forces, was talked through step by step. Arrival of mountain troops, scaling the tough seaward (eastern) side, at its commanding northern tip would win the day. The Führer plodded along through each danger-fraught heave toward the peak. He gave air support its share of comment as he went and then repeated his insistent cry that, on arrival at the peak, the strait had to be closed. No other undertaking had been honed so fine, drilled to such perfection: it had to work. He was content and said so as he departed while discussion continued. General Warlimont submitted Führer Directive No. 19, Operation *Felix*, for signature. Affirmative word from Canaris at Madrid was all that was needed to start the wheels turning.

They stuck where they were. On Sunday 8 December a message arrived from Canaris: Franco had refused consent, point-blank. Instead of bursting out in temper, Hitler accepted this turn in stride, almost as though he had expected it. Franco's reasons of food shortages, loss of the Canaries, and so on, did not vary. In a helpful spirit he concluded that Spain could only prove a liability to the Axis and requested that camouflaged preparations continue. On that weak straw Hitler hung a weak hope. He instructed Canaris to squeeze out any date whatever. What would Franco settle for? This hope died too; Canaris had already tried for a substitute, and the Generalissimo then made himself clear: "Spain will enter the war only when England is on the point of collapse." They were almost the identical words Hitler had used to define his conditions for the invasion of England. Surrogate *Felix* foundered on the same shoal as *Sea Lion*.

Staff commotion over the upset reached General Halder. Acting for his absent commander in chief, he sought out Keitel at home to hear the news and lend a hand. He heard that the Führer occupied himself with "the extreme reaction of the dangerous spreading disaffection in French Morocco." He concluded, "if anything happens in North Africa, the remainder of France must be occupied." All confidence in union with France evaporated. General Halder outlined a plan for occupying the rest of her. For Hitler, despite his talk that being shed of Spain freed him for deals with France, the incident clearly encouraged a reversion to his original suspicions about her. This became the direct effect of *Felix*'s failure, although Hitler kept hoping Spain would come through. Führer Directive for total occupation of France even took *Felix*'s number—No. 19—but under the name Operation *Attila*. It defined a change of heart (but waited until the Allied landings in Northwest Africa in November 1942 for execution). "Hitler rejected the thought put forth from one quarter to go ahead with Operation *Felix* without Spain's consent."[7]

Thus Franco's stubborn stand became decisive in the west. That he did stand fast proved to be a major German reverse directly chargeable to Hitler. It made the third major failure in a series which ran:

(1) Dunkirk: failure to eliminate the BEF, 23–27 May 1940;
(2) England: failure to close with her cross-channel, summer 1940;
(3) Gibraltar: failure to close the Mediterranean at the Rock, January 1941.

Germany's resort to war had generated strategic demands that Hitler's psychopolitical approach could not meet; its continued perverse application to problems of pure strategy caused all three failures. Either the strategy (for which he was unprepared) had to prevail or policy had to change. Politician Hitler could no more discern this than he could hold steady aim on a selected decisive strategic target. He was not alone, nor ever will be.

On top of the bad news from Spain, came worse news from both Italian fronts. A surprise British counteroffensive struck at Sidi Barrani and caught the Italians flatfooted. From 9 December on they were swept up in disaster lots, each day more frightful than the one before. General Wavell's re-formed, tank-reinforced 8th Army had Italy's 10th army on the run: four forward divisions were cut to bits, and the remaining four were threatened with encirclement back at Bardia. Fantastic figures soon emanated from British sources—600 guns, 100,000 soldiers taken, and the like. Alarms of more to come ran the length of the coast to Tobruk, to Bengasi, and even to Tripoli. The final danger of eventual British link-up with dissident French in Tunisia loomed ominously.

Albania caved in too. Greek fighters threw the Italian soldiers back in defeat. Deep in despair Mussolini cried out to his son-in-law, Ciano, "It is grotesque and absurd, but a fact. We have to ask for a truce through Hitler." It never came to that, though Alfieri skirted near it in his approach to Hitler on 7 December, and Badoglio's abrupt dismissal as chief of the armed services showed high tension.

7. Warlimont KFA, pp. 285–89; Halder, 2:218, 219; OKW Ops War Diary 2, 8–10 Dec. 1940, pp. 43–51.

Slowly the Albanian crisis eased under a curious tactic of evading combat. But the Libyan trouble would not go away. British forces sealed up fragments of Italy's 10th Army in Bardia and drove on Tobruk. Mussolini avoided the outright request for direct combat help, but did not scruple over presenting outsized demands for replacement materials. At the top level the German professionals considered broadening the 10th Air Corps's targets to include, besides British sea forces, the most dangerous British ground thrusts. Hitler remained stuck with his timidity about committing German troops overseas. He sharply reminded General von Rintelen at Rome that there was still plenty of room for defense.[8]

If the end of 1940 revealed Axis strategy in deep calamity, it did the same for Axis policy. Western union languished near death, although as late as 12 December the chief of L Section, Warlimont, could record in the War Diary, "French readiness to collaborate has received a decisive impetus since the first discussions and there can be no doubt of the sincerity of the Pétain government." The entry recapitulated his opinion on return from meetings with the French. A detailed report was painstakingly drafted and rushed to the Führer on the hill. General Jodl added his personal boost: "We should strike while the iron is hot! Further reverses to our ally [Italy] could result in a stiffened French attitude." But meanwhile that evil Hun, Operation *Attila*, for the occupation of Vichy France, had invaded the sanctum to spread doubt. Hitler's reviving mistrust of French reliability was fortified just at this time when Pétain fired Laval, the strongest French exponent of collaboration. At this news Hitler turned his back on France and reverted to his erstwhile mood of conqueror.[9]

This same day of 13 December, as though sealing the turn away from the west, saw the issue of Führer Directive No. 20 for *Marita*—the hoped-for true Norway of the East Campaign. It opened with a specious purpose: "a dangerous situation in Albania makes it important to keep the British from establishing an air base under the protection of a Balkan front." Blame for invading Greece was thus hung on Italian failure, a story told so often it achieved credibility. The plan unfolded in repetition of the Führer's instructions to General Hansen of long ago on 1 October:

8. Warlimont KFA, pp. 271–80; OKW Ops War Diary 2, 10 Dec. 1940; OKW Ops SitConf, 8–12 Dec. 1940, pp. 142–45.
9. A detailed account of efforts to reach agreement with France is given in Warlimont IH, pp. 136–41.

(*a*) Set up a gradually increasing force in southern Rumania;

(*b*) In March, after good weather begins, send this force to occupy the northern Aegean coast via Bulgaria, and if necessary occupy the entire Greek mainland.

Power to overwhelm the stalwart Hellenes reached the absurd figure of twenty-four divisions, reinforced with armor, bridging, and other materials, which looked like plain padding for *Barbarossa*. There might have been a thought about reluctant Yugoslavia. Field Marshal List would command in the field over the 12th Army, supported by the 8th Air Corps (late of *Felix*). The Luftwaffe had also to occupy British bases on Aegean islands by airborne landings. "Immediately after *Marita* all forces are to withdraw to new assignments." *Barbarossa*, of course.

By now *Barbarossa*'s growing demands had need of that lift offered only by a Führer directive. Drafting these guides that married intuitive Hitlerian "musts" to sound professional practice and tradition was an art that took keen insight, capacity for juggling, screening, and tacking on inconspicuous bits for use in extremis or for the record. This last item has proved invaluable for history. In the present case, roughing out a first draft in L Section fell to the Army representative, Lt. Colonel Bernhard von Lossberg. He and his Navy colleague Lt. Commander Junge had, after the fall of France, promoted Invasion England. In the middle of that they were rocked by the news of the Führer's resolve to turn instead on Russia. Neither liked it, nor did their head, General Warlimont. They drove on *Sea Lion*, and lost. Then when *Felix*, a remaining chance, fell out too, Lossberg had to submit his first painful draft of Directive No. 21 for *Fritz* (soon to be *Barbarossa*). It was based on a previously submitted OKH plan.

On the same day, Junge submitted "a survey, as requested, of the situation, which might obtain for the Navy in case of a two-front war against England and Russia." He concluded soundly and simply that so long as defeat of Britain alone demanded all of her powers, Germany ought to avoid the extra burden of war against Russia. It was bound to affect naval operations against Britain unfavorably. Warlimont studied the draft and the two-front warning and redrafted, corrected, and submitted both to General Jodl on 16 December, having added to Junge's warning a comment on the critical fuel problem that a two-front effort would create. Jodl was unreceptive. He played back the latest Hitler argument: "The German army will never be so strong again; Russia continues to demonstrate that she will block Germany at every turn." Helmuth Greiner, L Section's historian-recorder, concluded that Jodl probably regarded the L Section objections as old stuff, already sufficiently heard from Admiral Raeder. None of the efforts affected the plotted course eastward.[10]

While undergoing changes Directive No. 21's draft floated about OKW from L Section to Jodl to Führer and back again. Suddenly on 18 December it received swift approval plus an order for immediate distribution, and made news on two counts. First, and of great consequence, Hitler had altered the basic mission of the main effort in the center; and second, he had struck out the old code name *Fritz* in favor of his own choice, *Barbarossa*. The central main effort was now to peel off force from its main thrust at Moscow (as wanted by the Army) to help the northern effort first destroy Russian forces in White Russia and the Baltic states: "Only after the successful completion of this decisive mission are the operations aimed at Moscow . . . to be continued." Was his absorption with bodies really fear of Moscow, the nerve center? His tampering with purely professional operational business boded ill for the eastern strategy. The shift in name, however, made the operation all his own with an emotional tone of holy crusade which under the banner of *Barbarossa* would kill infidel Russians. This theme he pursued in briefings from here onward.[11]

Admiral Raeder arrived for Führer conference in the afternoon of 27 December. He skipped the usual prefatory summary of own operations and sailed at once into concern about the Middle Sea. One gauge of Britain's total command, he said, is that she has dared to withdraw ships from there to the Atlantic. How about Italy? Can she survive these reverses? Can Germany do anything to prop her up? The Führer thinks that eventually supporting operations can be undertaken around Tripoli; best, though, would be control over North Africa from Spanish Morocco. "Therefore seizure of Gibraltar is necessary." He took the words right out of Raeder's mouth; but before agreeing, the admiral loosed a salvo about the Mediterranean in gen-

10. OKW Ops War Diary 2, 12–17 Dec. 1940, pp. 56–65; H. Greiner pp. 329–30; Lossberg, pp. 42–48; Halder, 2:209–39. At this time, 16 December 1940, Warlimont also submitted the proposed organization of the Luftwaffe's first airborne corps, the 11th Air Corps, to consist of the 7th Parachute Division, a Sturmregiment, and the 22d Air Landing Division (from the Army), plus appropriate aircraft. It was to be commanded by General der Flieger Kurt Student. The 11th Air Corps will figure prominently in the story of Crete.

11. Philippi and Heim, pp. 42–45; Hubatsch, pp. 84-88. Führer Directive No. 21 *Barbarossa* is a five-page document rendered complete in Hubatsch.

eral: (1) Italy's survival is doubtful; (2) expulsion of Britain's fleet is no longer feasible; (3) the hoped-for *decisive results are no longer realizable in the Mediterranean.* He shifted back to Gibraltar, elaborated all the expected gains, and called anew for Operation *Felix.* Hitler promised to try again through policy channels.

Raeder next took up the siege of England and its incompatibility with attack into Russia. "Britain's import problem is war decisive," while nothing about Russia was or ever could be. "Commandment of the hour is a clear unequivocal . . . main effort against Britain, which means reallocation of combat materials with utmost energy and dispatch and deliberate deferment of demands unconnected with England's reduction." One senses in Hitler's total silence an apologetic *nolo contendere.* "Grave doubts" said Raeder, "assail me about *Barbarossa* before settlement with England. The fight against her is carried by Air and Navy . . . far-reaching combat needs arise, all the more because Britain has transferred her armament, aircraft, and shipbuilding industries to America. Thus her dependence on imports achieves absolute war decisiveness." Hitler's mollifying tenders disclose his discomfort; he offered the admiral 160 Luftwaffe 88-mm guns for the Danzig area. Raeder said he would look into it. The long, earnest Navy drive closed on this switch east. Yet for the Mediterranean, Raeder had offered no Navy help. Surely there must have been something it could have done there.

Raeder's presentation was nevertheless a forcible year-end estimate. It probably contributed to a letter Hitler was composing for Mussolini. He again tried to inspire action against Britain at sea with a used punch line, "By skillful commitment of our air forces, in three or four months the Mediterranean could become the graveyard of the British fleet." But as for staying on target England, Raeder's effect was nil. The balance he had struck for the year at war brought the failures into sharper focus and disclosed their expanding meaning. For all its war tumult, all its great victories and upheavals, crowded, uproarious 1940, had in sum arrived at finality only over Britain's unaltered security at home as well as in the Mediterranean and Hitler's unalterable resolve to crusade in Russia. The year's toil and carnage had failed to unite Europe, failed to bring the Middle Sea under, failed to subdue Britain—who still ruled the waves and thereby held Europe captive, rather than through her supposed political influence on Russia. The sum made a thinly masked general failure. Yet not so for the German leadership, whose faultless, closely joined scheme of action via *Marita* and *Barbarossa* had by now been checked and confirmed: 1941 would surely bring fulfillment in victory.[12]

12. In his letter to Mussolini on 31 December 1940 Hitler's balance sheet contrasts sharply with his letter of 20 November. Its Mediterranean plans have been superseded by growing British victories. He offered little solace, urged action against British sea power as noted, and said nothing could be done on land until the fall of 1941, and in Albania no fresh decision could be reached until March. He was letting the Partner stew. Raeder's conference notes are given in FC 1940, 2:68–80, and elaborated in Raeder, 2:249, 250.

5. Practical Beginning—
The Battle of Crete

British Occupation: November 1940 and Early 1941

To ships of the Royal Navy, Crete, rising loftily out of the sea, was a familiar sight and a welcome one. The island's heights and promontories made good landmarks, and Suda Bay offered convenient anchorage for fueling and refreshment. The bay was more central than Alexandria; it gave light forces bound for Italian waters a gain of 350 miles. There were other strategic advantages, particularly as to air, and all of them led naturally toward growing British interest in securing the bay after Italy invaded Greece.

The interest went back to high councils in London and Paris early in 1940 while France was still in the war. Orders to the commanders in chief of the Middle East and Mediterranean directed that "if Greek territory is attacked by Italy, expeditions . . . to Crete are to start immediately." On 21 May 1940 Greece gave Britain and France authority to land troops on Crete. Ten days later, Admiral Cunningham reported that "the British forces could be landed within 24 to 30 hours of the orders being given." He was "wholeheartedly in favor of this project." In July after the fall of France, Britain canceled the plans; she did not want to be the first to violate Greece's neutrality. Nevertheless, Crete remained a forward item in the Royal Navy's war plans.[1]

1. Cunningham, pp. 230-33. For the prime minister in London, Admiral Cun-

In June 1940 Italy brought the war to the Mediterranean; tension grew between her and Greece, an ally of Britain. By October the signs were unmistakable. On the 21st the chiefs of staff in London considered a plan "to earmark . . . a small force and move it to reinforce Crete." It was decided at this time by these professional heads that any assistance to Greece should be limited to the proposed Crete reinforcement. This early limit should be well noted, for policy makers soon urged a ground-force expedition to Greece. The British commanders in chief in the Mediterranean (Army, Air, and Navy) were alerted by London's questions of practicability and timing of such a limited move. A week later, on 28 October, Italy's thrust into Greece from Albania precipitated action.

At 0130 on 29 October, Admiral Cunningham sailed with the fleet to the westward of Crete to block Italian interference, and on 31 October landed (from other ships) guns, their crews, and a battalion of troops at Suda. Soon a brigade headquarters, another battalion, naval base elements, and a few antiaircraft guns followed, in all about 2500 men. It was the first troop commitment to the Battle of Crete and was made more than six months ahead of the Germans who landed by air on 20 May 1941.

Perhaps because the project had received such enthusiastic Navy backing and because the prime minister had on 3 November spoken of Suda-to-be as a second Scapa, a feeling of Navy responsibility took hold. From the start German air action was expected, yet a dearth of RAF planes for defense in the air discouraged the thought of air counter action. With the powerful fleet on hand, it grew natural to think of ships as the main bulwark. In Cairo the joint planning staff recognized the air threat and the need of strong ground forces. A study of 30 October determined that if the Germans overran Greece, Crete's defense would require "a brigade group and Suda could not be used by the Navy during daylight." On 3 November the chiefs of staff in London expressed the same view after approving a general policy of "holding Crete, whatever happens on the mainland."[2]

Reference to the mainland has special pertinence because Churchill had already begun a powerful bid for commitment of troops to

---

ningham's plans for the eastern Mediterranean savored too much of the defensive, and he said so in official dispatches. "It was in the sort of 'prodding' message," wrote Cunningham, "that Mr. Churchill was often so ungracious and hasty. . . . Such messages . . . were not an encouragement, merely an annoyance. Moreover, as they implied something . . . lacking in . . . leadership, they did positive harm."
2. Cunningham, pp. 282–90; Davin, pp. 3–7, 12–19.

Greece on political grounds. His reaction to Crete had to come a day later than Hitler's in Florence, but it came promptly and of a like general tenor: Get hold of the island! To Anthony Eden, his secretary of state for war, who was on tour in Africa, Churchill cabled the day after Italy's attack: "An effort should be made to establish ourselves in Crete." It would be a great prize, he said, worth the risk and "almost equal to a successful offensive in Libya." The comparison should be noted: Churchill's first thought was for Crete, to which he added a confusing policy note on 3 November about Greece, "Collapse of Greece without an effort by us will have a deadly effect on Turkey and on the future of the war." World War I was still with him. He must have urged these ideas on the chiefs of staff, for they immediately began expressing thoughts in rebuttal. Sir John Dill, chief of the Imperial General Staff, opposed expeditionary aid to Greece and advocated instead holding Crete alone, as a naval and air base. It was the first stand about air basing. A fresh estimate of 4 November agreed, and the service chiefs joined in approval. Thus professional sentiment, including that on the scene, supported Crete without Greece; the prime minister wanted to work both in. These are the first signs of cleavage. Churchill wielded great powers of persuasion. He had always enjoyed sloganeering and naming things.

His designation of Suda as a "second Scapa" missed the mark completely. The extensive ground approaches of Suda, the climate and its visibility, the location far from home support—all presented a defense problem far different. From Scapa's misty home waters ships can sail in comparative freedom; shore-based antiaircraft batteries can make the air approaches to the anchorages highly dangerous. Hostile planes must approach over 250 miles without fighter cover and can bomb only if at the end visibility permits. In Suda's unlimited visibility, antiaircraft batteries could only attract dive bombers that had less than 100 miles from Greece to target, free of fighter interference. Only air power on the island could make Crete secure. Fortress Suda alone was not the problem, but the whole island—which meant a three-services combined operation under a single command. It would have been the first one of the war on either side. Of course "Scapa Suda" was intended to convey strength and security. It was a bluff.

When the island as a whole came into view, natural hazards added themselves to human mistakes. Deep transverse gorges cut the horny dragon-back into tight land compartments. Lateral communication the ancients had solved by sea; now the moderns would try by air and sea. Roads were few and primitive, and for lack of priority and energy in British arrangements they remained so. One narrow macadam road that threaded a tortuous way along the north coast linked the four principal natural centers of life that would be fought over: in the far west was Maleme Sector, running west from Signal Hill (Mount Monodhendhri) through Maleme village and airfield to the west end of the island; adjoining on the east was Canea-Suda Sector, from Signal Hill east through Galatas village, Canea town, Suda and beyond, to Georgeoupolis on Almiro Bay; then came Retimo Sector east from Georgeoupolis through Retimo village and airfield to Stavromenos; and finally still farther east was Heraklion Sector, composed of the largest port town, its airfield, and the immediate environs. These were the natural sectors. They differed from the later strategic sectors of defense only at Maleme Sector, whose fighting boundary on the east ran beyond Signal Hill to the outskirts of Canea. The question became, which of the sectors would prove decisive for all Crete?

The fact of an airfield in three sectors at once drew attention for the opening phases of combat. England had learned all about air prelude to invasion, but here those lessons did not apply, for lack of British air power. As Crete stood, she presented a naked England. There still was plenty of time for covering her. Heraklion in the east had the only all-purpose airfield. Retimo, 40 miles westward, had only a grass landing strip alongside the coastal road. Maleme Field, 11 miles west of the capital Canea, lay on the sea-delta of the almost dry Tavronitis River. It had been intended as a fighter base for Britain's Fleet Air arm; from it the planes were to defend the main base of Canea/Suda, and also carry out fleet tasks. That this air contingent would help defend Suda must have strengthened a belief in naval responsibility for Crete's security. The RAF showed reluctance to make any plane commitment; moreover, it made no move to coordinate airfield defense or supply with the Fleet Air Arm or with the ground force. Before the day of battle neither the RAF nor the Fleet Air Arm contributed a thing to local ground defense of the airfields. Maleme Field, which took on preeminence because of its proximity to the Suda base, was poorly sited for defense by British means. Both the field and Suda lay on the shortest approach for hostile planes out of Greece and at the end of the longest own supply lines out of Egypt. Could the island only have been turned around to face south, thought many defenders, the job would have been so much easier.

As it was, these two vital points were sited advantageously for attackers from Greece. Heavy Axis air attack fell on Suda and Canea on 1 November 1940. Here were the opening shots in the battle for Crete.

Whatever the handicaps, combat success depends first on sustained command leadership, which was something Crete's defense forces never got until battle was imminent. In the six months before invasion command of these forces changed seven times. Brigadier Tidbury, the first appointee, had the longest tenure, of two months during November and December. He was ordered "to defend the naval fueling base at Suda Bay and, in cooperation with Greek forces . . . prevent and defeat any attempt by hostile forces to get a footing" (Davin, p. 12). When London agreed that the local Greek Army division could be sent to Albania, the British forces were charged with the defense of the whole island. Another infantry battalion and two commando units arrived, but these were small change for Tidbury's staggering job. He believed in "night and day digging on defensive positions" around Suda, but this could not be enough. The outlying airfields were left to the remaining Greek Army recruit units. It is noteworthy that Brigadier Tidbury was clear on Maleme's need of a "separate and independent force." He seemed to apprehend that terrain features kept Maleme isolated. He also saw that the German main effort would come by air against Suda as the prime objective. Landings were thought probable at the other two fields as well. The ideas seem sound; they rose from familiarity with the problem. In time they could have evolved a sound operational plan. But they never had a chance, for lack of continuity in command. After Brigadier Tidbury departed in January, the command changed every three or four weeks. Crete had no papa to fight for her needs.

General Wavell paid a visit on 13 November. A few days before, the London chiefs had considered the assignment of a Mobile Naval Base Defense Organization (MNBDO) of marines, intended for just such an island task (though a bit out of date for this island) to take over on Crete. Perhaps its adequacy was on Wavell's list during his visit. Surely, no serious enemy threat was on hand in the sleepy island; Tidbury's efforts must have been plainly visible. General Wavell decided that the problem was not critical and departed under the misapprehension that "a small force would be quite sufficient for the naval fueling base." Apparently Admiral Cunningham agreed. Interest in Crete subsided.

There were compelling reasons for lack of Army interest. For some weeks, in the tightest secrecy, even toward London, the Middle East Command had been preparing an offensive against the Italians in the Western Desert, and the Navy was getting set for the Taranto strike. The Army operation was to secure the west flank. If the drive got rolling it could even hope to take Tripoli, far in the west, and thereby drive the Italians out of North Africa. London received only vague hints, but on 8 November Anthony Eden returned from Cairo with the great good news of the actual plans. As secretary of war, he must have approved them. Churchill, while anxious for action, could hardly have been happy that the plans had been kept from him.

On second or third thought he wondered if a drive of such length was really necessary. Was not the thinking behind it basically defensive? More gripping still, what would it do to the prime minister's ever stronger private urge for building a Balkan front in Greece, with Crete in reserve? The cleavage over Crete had already begun between the political and strategic leaderships. Here personal differences between Churchill and Wavell may have pushed it deeper.

Crete faded, as a sort of a stepchild that got only a lick and a promise from the Middle East Command. That MNBDO might take over could have been one excuse; let the marines have it. By and large, however, the neglect can be charged to competition with the drive toward Tripoli, or even to discord between Churchill and Wavell, which affected both projects adversely. Greece was mainly political, with strategic Crete thrown in; but Tripoli was mainly strategic. Events crowded Crete still farther into the background.

The fleet's night action of 11–12 November against the Italian ships in Taranto led off; then on 8 December the Army, with the blessings of a belatedly informed prime minister, struck in the Western Desert. Sidi Barrani fell at once, and on 16 December Sollum and Fort Capuzzo, which cleared Egypt of Italians. Offshore the Navy chimed in with light-craft shore bombardments. On 17 December the main fleet put into Suda Bay for fuel, having completed a sweep against the Dodecanese Islands. Three days later Admiral Cunningham entered Grand Harbor, Malta, on his flagship the *Warspite*; the guard was paraded, the band played, and from shore points, crowded with Maltese, came wild cheers of welcome. For seven months no big ship had entered. On touring the yard, the admiral was greeted on all sides by workmen singing "God Save the King" and "Rule Britannia." It was a happy time.

As the drive in Africa held on toward Bardia in Libya, Britain could rejoice over her own first real victories, and without advice from London. Wavell had scored something of a coup. On 26 December he met with his Navy and Air colleagues to firm the decision to give precedence to the capture of Tobruk. Crete and Greece received no mention, though Churchill still pressed for plans about Crete.

Meetings such as this one, which occurred about weekly to settle interservice business, exemplified the British committee system of command. For the British it may have been the most workable arrangement, yet it lacked a directly responsible head man. General Wavell usually chaired the conference, or at times a minister of state, like Eden. Admiral Cunningham wrote of these command relations at this time:

The Libyan offensive brought the three Commanders in Chief . . . closer together and made them realize that success could only be obtained by continual coordination and cooperation; that each service depended on the others; that the campaign by Sea, Land and Air was really one. Before, . . . we had been inclined each to pursue a vague shadowy object, . . . each using his own arm without much consultation. . . . After Libya closer consultation became a sine qua non (Cunningham, p. 295).

It was not enough; the crying need was a theater commander. Since no one was so designated, Churchill tried from afar to act as one for each theater of war in turn by firing off rockets of critique and acclaim. His dispatches, in the British tradition, attempted to season plaint with praise and always humorous quips. They often hit home; they often misfired in annoyance. The danger came in the commander's response. If it made a boomerang hit that hurt, the thing was no longer funny. This happened to General Wavell. It was a nonsensical system of warmaking.[3]

An early December call by Churchill on the London chiefs for a reckoning brought only an insignificant increase in Crete's authorized armament. Yet on 8 January they maintained that an expedition into Greece, which seemed to be working up, would run the "risk of

3. Grenfell, pp. 85–90. Bernard Fergusson, General Wavell's aide, in Fergusson, pp. 51–53, recounts a talk between Dill and Wavell about the latter's difficult relations with Churchill. Said Dill, "I don't think he will ever forgive you for that last sentence in your signal about Somaliland." Wavell had replied to the prime minister's angry message, in which he accused Wavell of having given up Italian Somaliland in the summer of 1940 without a fight, as proved by the light British casualties. Wavell's reply listed the heavy Italian casualties and ended with the quip: Heavy butcher's bill not necessarily indication of good tactics. "It was this unlucky phrase," writes Fergusson, "which had annoyed the prime minister and started the rot in his relations with Wavell."

a second Dunkirk." About the same time Wavell added his weight by counseling that even if Greece gave way, Crete should be given priority. By 10 January, nevertheless, Churchill had won approval of the contrary. He cabled to Cairo: "Nothing must hamper capture of Tobruk, but thereafter all operations in Libya are subordinated to aiding Greece. . . . We expect and require prompt and active compliance with our decisions, for which we bear full responsibility." This was severe language to a trusted commander in the field. The decision was a fateful one; 10 January 1941 was to become notable otherwise.

Obediently Wavell proceeded to Athens on 13 January to discuss military aid. He offered General Metaxas, head of the government, one artillery regiment and sixty armored vehicles. The offer was declined because the support offered was too small to be effective, but large enough for a pretext that could bring a German invasion. Wavell returned to Cairo via Crete. Nothing came out of the visit. The change of command routine had just begun on Crete and the garrison drifted along with its shortages and lack of direction. Now was the time to leave Greece out: conscience had been satisfied with the proffer of help that could not be accepted. Perhaps General Wavell thought Crete was now in the clear. The irretrievable moment to save the island was at hand.

But would enough have been done, anyhow? A reconnaissance party reported a dearth of labor, but surely 450,000 Cretans could have helped some; moreover, 14,000 Italian prisoners of war from Albania were on hand for roadmaking and other work. Later, thousands of imported Cypriot and Palestinian laborers clogged the works. The wretched roads and wire communications systems remained wretched. Motor transport was short; but what good could have come from more trucks without better roads? Suda's administrative arrangements for a complete infantry division progressed slowly; troop accommodation lagged. Out of convenience rather than combat requirement, Canea-Suda swelled far beyond its true battle importance. Above all, if the battle was to include hostile air bombardment and landings, weapons to counter them should have been singled out. This meant, besides fighters, armor and medium artillery, neither of which the attacker could bring by air. There is no evidence of established priorities, nor did an approved defense plan govern. This may have been when Crete was lost—in the lazy six months before battle. They were relatively pleasant carefree months.

6. Marking Time

Early 1941 on the German Side

Nothing much was going on—only some talk justifying this and blaming that; the new year came in quietly. A feeling of stalemate pervaded the German air. Where did things stand, anyhow? The Führer rested content in his mountains; only one excursion during the holidays had carried him to the Channel front—to be with his men, of course. He did not care for the Channel; since Dunkirk this had been his sole appearance in that area of sea and air combat. Orders for land combat in the opposite direction were now on the planning books; indeed, final troop movements against Greece (*Marita*) could begin any time, though the actual shooting would still be far off. Briefings for the new year and month were under way—mere repetitive routines for matters already settled. Then came a ripple of excitement from Libya with news of fresh fighting.[1]

On 5 January British troops overran the Italians in Bardia and lunged on against Tobruk. The fall of Tobruk would deprive Italy of her key forward strongpoint in Libya and at the same time provide

1. During this trip to the Channel, Hitler on Christmas Day read off the sins of France to Admiral Darlan, who acted as Marshal Pétain's deputy in the French government. Laval, who wanted to collaborate with Germany, had been ousted on 13 December 1941, and this enraged Hitler. He thought Weygand in Morocco had forced Laval's departure. Admiral Darlan sought to explain the ousting and to deliver a letter from the Marshal. Documents GFP, vol. 11, p. 955. According to Paul Schmidt, Hitler's rough language "rolled off the old sea dog like spray from an oilskin," but it nevertheless became clear that "a going together" with France stood at a low point.

Britain with a small but useful air and sea way-port and land fortress due south of Crete. The East Basin would become more British than ever, and Egypt more secure by land. Hitler seemed not in the least dismayed; he simply turned the clock back. Were not things still far more favorable than before the war? "A turnabout unfavorable to Germany is out of the question. For even the loss of North Africa would militarily only restore the situation to what it was before 25 June when war against France ceased. The entire German situation is consequently incomparably more favorable than on 1 September 1939 [when war began]." Small solace for a year and more of war and the West still at loose ends.

The odd excuse, in which Hitler really expressed his negative feeling for the Mediterranean, came out at a Berghof briefing for the new year on 9 January. This mountain retreat had become Führer headquarters and Germany's capital. At the bottom of the hill sat Keitel and Jodl in a miniature chancellery. Mussolini would soon come to the mountain to talk out the newest Libyan crisis; but first we hear the 9 January warm-up sessions.

Field Marshal von Brauchitsch attended for the Army; the other service representatives were underlings. This made the occasion special. The Führer used it to get his gospels for the South, West, and East over direct to the men on the staffs who executed orders. It was their indoctrination on high into the new mysteries: Fricke for Naval operations, Jeschonnek for Air; and to back up von Brauchitsch for Army, there were his quartermaster general and his operations chief. Keitel and Jodl represented OKW. Around noon on 9 January 1941 they filed into the Führer Berghof conference room of the wide window and wonderful views. The magnificent peaks and gorges were in winter array. No wonder the Führer preferred these surroundings of rugged power! He said they inspired him. But if he sought to inspire and proselyte these men by power words, we know he was also reconverting, reassuring Adolf Hitler. He launched immediately into Italian troubles in Libya and Albania, then on to France and her effect on Northwest Africa. All of the topics bore on policy and strategy in the Middle Sea.

Undoubtedly Italy's problems controlled, but she was weak. Hitler highlighted some of her incurable frailties: division in her leadership—Ciano with his own ideas of expansion, the Duce with his own, though he stood firm for the Axis; then the familiar Latin mentality. In trying to influence them, great care had to be exercised not to reveal one's own intent, "for there is danger that the royal house transmits information to England!" To Fricke's suggestion of a "strict Italian organization of armed forces under German guidance," Hitler named inferiority feelings as the main obstruction; a feeling of overwhelming British superiority left them "in no way up to the tasks to be met." To which Fricke added in his record, "They will not commit their fleet."

Still, Italy must not lose all Libya, Hitler continued. Militarily it is not so significant, but psychologically such loss will work in deeply. "Therefore," he declared, "I have determined to activate at once an armored blocking force and seal off the British advance" toward Tripoli. (His intent was only to block defensively.) Since transport has to wait until 20 February, "final decision need not be met until then." He is hedging. The Narvik nightmare in Norway still plagues him. Ever since, he has hedged on overseas commitment; specifically since August on North Africa. This cautious beginning affords the first portent of Rommel and his Afrikakorps. Right off, von Brauchitsch chimes in with a proposal of initial strength: 8000 men and 1400 vehicles, not including tanks, in twenty shiplifts would do it.

The equivocal note about final commitment carried over to Albania. If German troops were to be sent at all, the Führer held, "they must be strong enough to force any Greek switch position west of Salonika from the rear." He wanted all of Greece; moreover, the German force for Albania had best get on station before *Marita* began knocking on Greece's northern doors. In sum, a drive through Albania must facilitate Hitler's independent drive from the north, rather than merely rescue Italians. A comparatively new breed of cats, mountain troops, would be used in Albania. That front had already received substantial German aid by air-transport flights of the three-engined Ju-52 planes; hundreds of them had poured 17,000 Italian men and tons of gear into the gaps. (Both mountain troops and Ju's will come to notice on Crete.)

As for *Attila*, whose threat to occupy all France is to keep her compliant and mindful of making Algeria and Morocco toe the mark, recent thought about its execution raised the question of the heavy ships in Toulon. "Possession of Toulon," Hitler surmised, "and the French fleet [by air drops] will pin down British naval strength and thus free the Italian fleet to fix on the eastern Mediterannean." About three weeks before, OKW had thrashed out these fancies and found them impracticable. It came down to keeping the French ships from escaping to sea. Union with France is moribund. Airborne forces as a landing weapon wax more and more versatile in the Führer's mind. He throws paratroops around in great abandon. They fit his abiding confidence in surprise.

The afternoon session brought out what the visitors were there for—a progress report of the war's past and an indoctrinating prognosis of its future, ending in world-stunning victory. The audition was graduating into a regular act that would be repeated with variations and additions at monthly intervals through March to a final climax of Armageddon in June. L Section's War Diary reports how the Führer began sagely at the root with a review of the strategic superiority of Germany over France and England together, of Germany's sound and massive industrial-economic and labor-force base, all of which still counted advantageously on this day as at the beginning of war.

These fundamentals established, Hitler skirted the European littoral from Norway through France to the Balkans. Norway he regarded as safe, and the occupied lands to the west subject only to threats of British air raids (no invasion danger). Relations with France were clouded by a shifting mood of hopes for change; Weygand in North Africa was dangerous. Preparations for *Attila* were not being hidden. Spain continued to vacillate. Then a wide hop eastward: only Rumania was a true friend; Bulgaria, while loyal, feared Russian pressure; Yugoslavia still stood aloof. Taking Europe as a whole, the Führer concluded with the assurances already quoted: "A turnabout unfavorable to Germany is out of the question. For even the loss of North Africa would militarily only restore the situation to what it was before 25 June 1940." The entire German situation was consequently incomparably more favorable than on 1 September 1939. Hitler's next remarks revealed the fatal weakness of this excuse.

Two ill-defined clouds—England and Russia—still blurred the horizon. Hitler fixed on England, which was of course Admiral Fricke's prime concern. He recorded the Führer words:

Landing in England not possible unless heavy paralysis has set in and unquestionable command of air is held by Germany. Absolute success of Invasion must be certain; otherwise it would, according to the Führer, be a crime. Britain's aim must remain to strike us down on the Continent and bring about the war's decision. Resources to do this she does not have. . . . The weight of attack must be directed at her imports and armament industry; terror attacks of the air force make no sense; imports and their carriers [ships] are what must be destroyed. Possibly combined Air and Naval attacks against imports can produce results by July or August. The Führer is even today basically prepared for a negotiated peace with Britain. Present leading personalities in England however reject this. . . . The U.S.A. and Russia hold Britain erect; diplomatic signs point that way. Minister Eden is pro-Russian. Britain's sole hope rests in holding through until a Continental bloc is formed against Germany.

But that Stalin, he's a shrewd head; "possessed by a *Drang nach Westen*," he wants to fall heir to an impoverished Europe. Wherever possible he will make trouble. Hitler offered a remarkably prophetic hypothesis. If the British could hold on, with forty or fifty divisions, get help from the United States and Russia, "then a very difficult situation would arise for Germany. That must not occur." He explained how on principle he always attacked "the most important" target first, to get ahead a bit; which to him obviously and perversely meant Russia. So having proved the point to himself and his captive listeners he went on to propound a basically mistaken continental and global strategy:

Therefore, Russia must now be smashed. Either the British will then yield or Germany will continue the war . . . under the most favorable conditions. A beaten Russia will permit Japan to turn all energies against the United States and thereby prevent the latter from entering the war.

Time was of great consequence, he held. Since Russia must in any case be crushed, now is the time. He had arrived at the exalting moment of fulfillment and rededication to his mission: he warmed to it as he spelled out the primary moves of one master-stroke after the other. The extraordinary performance moved on to a vision of grand final triumph, whose awesome heights would mount with each repetition as the season advanced!

Germany will be unassailable [and he himself too]. The gigantic space of Russia hides immeasurable riches. Germany must dominate this space economically and politically, but not annex it. Therewith she will control all possibilities for fighting in the future against continents; when this operation is carried out, Europe will hold its breath.

There was his true purpose—to make the biggest bang ever, for surprise, recognition, and acceptance, even by Britain. The urge was personal in the extreme.[2]

2. The attending young fighters, rather than justification for war, needed promises of untold riches and great conquests. Hitler again stressed Russian troops as the main target and north flank reinforcement too at the expense of the seizure of Moscow. He speculated that forty to fifty divisions would be sufficient to keep the

Stunning effect was one thing that enthralled this man. At the 5 December meeting with the Army chiefs he had contented himself with collapse—a total breakdown—in Russia greater than that of France in the spring of 1940. Now a month later, on 9 January 1941, he sees "Europe holding its breath" when *Barbarossa* leaps into action. Month by month the magnitude of the effect rises in a calculated missionary campaign of oratory. His Volk he already has for whatever he undertakes, and that is the tragedy—he has been able to identify the longings and yearnings of a great people with his own demonic visions and to harness their energies to making them come true.

The very next day operations at sea in the Mediterranean struck an arresting note. Pursuant to a month-old Führer directive, the Luftwaffe had got busy from bases in Sicily. With the battleship *Warspite*, the *Valiant*, the carrier *Illustrious*, and destroyers in company, Admiral Cunningham was steaming southeast through the Strait of Sicily in Operation *Excess*. The object was to pass a valuable convoy from Gibraltar to Malta and the East. During the forenoon of 10 January a skirmish occurred with Italian destroyers. One of them sank. Shortly a British destroyer exploded a mine with her bow, and then came an Italian torpedo plane attack on the battle line. Just when that flurry had subsided, about 1230, three German Stuka formations came over the fleet from the north and at once concentrated upon their chief rival, the carrier *Illustrious*. Her planes were flying low to work against the departing Italian torpedo planes, so the Stukas had the edge on high. Cunningham watched from *Warspite*'s bridge and wrote later:

At times *Illustrious* became almost completely hidden in a forest of great bomb splashes. . . . We were watching complete experts. Formed in a large circle over the fleet they peeled off one by one on reaching the attack position, . . . attacks pressed home to point-blank range, and as they pulled out of their dives some were seen to fly along the deck of the *Illustrious*. . . . In something like ten minutes she was hit by six 1000-pound bombs . . . badly on fire, steering gear crippled, her lifts out of action and with heavy casualties. Yet she survived. Another twenty-five dive bombers came over. My heart sank . . . wondering how, with all her heavy damage, she could stand up to it. . . . I saw every gun in the *Illustrious* flash into action. . . . Eventually she arrived off Malta at 0945 P.M. and was taken safely into harbor.

East under after conquest. Once again he employed his familiar power words— *smash, beat to pieces, break up*—to rouse himself.

The day was over and with it Britain's freedom on the Mediterranean Sea. No one felt it more deeply than her Naval commander in chief on the spot:

We had plenty to think about. In a few minutes the whole situation had changed. At one blow the Fleet had been deprived of its fighter aircraft and its command of the Mediterranean was threatened by a weapon far more efficient and dangerous than any against which we had fought before.

The 10th Air Corps had arrived to sever the sea at the Strait of Sicily and to neutralize Malta. Thus air made the initial German bid to retrieve Axis fortunes in the south. It foreshadowed air versus sea in the Battle for Crete and occurred on the day Britain halted her drive on Tripoli. A bad day for her—10 January 1941.[3]

Conversion of this sea into a "graveyard of the British fleet," as Hitler boasted to Mussolini at the year's end, seemed on the way. Spirits picked up, especially in Italy. Further help for her would be taken up at the forthcoming Axis summit meeting. Meanwhile on 11 January Führer Directive No. 22 issued from the Mountain for the long delayed "German Participation in the Mediterranean Operations." It ordered the Army to set up the composite blocking unit with antitank weapons and land mines to stem the British armored tide in North Africa before it overran Tripoli. The code name *Sonnenblume* (sunflower) came along later. The 10th Air Corps would intensify its assault on British naval forces, communications, and bases. Help to the Albanian front with the code name *Alpenveilchen* (mountain violet) followed in corps strength, but events soon overhauled these directions. The *Violet* withered and died. *Sunflower*, on the other hand, blossomed into a great strategic project.

Order writing and implementation was growing carefree and confused because the experienced writers and checkers of L Section sat out of touch in the distant north at an old cavalry school near Krampnitz, while General Jodl and his typists on the Hill got out papers of

---

3. Cunningham, pp. 301–5; see also Warlimont KFA, pp. 144–45. On 11 January 1941 cruisers *Gloucester* and *Southampton* were bombed and hit. *Gloucester* survived; *Southampton* had to be sunk by a British torpedo after fires got out of control. General Martin Harlinghausen, who at the time was chief of staff of the 10th Air Corps, tells of the action and his later effort to pry help out of the Italian Navy on the sea in support of 10th Air Corps work in the air. His scheme was to have Italian destroyers patrol and deny the strait during dark. If contact occurred, the 10th Air Corps would close on it at break of day. (The corps was handicapped by lack of reconnaissance planes.) It was a sound scheme, as the head of Italy's navy, Admiral Riccardi, agreed, but for it he could find no destroyers, although there were some eighty on the books. Harlinghausen to Ansel.

accomplished fact on Führer decisions. It was the odd unprofessional way of Führer headquarters that often seemed to rely solely on the oft repeated magic: "The Führer has ordered," which supposedly made everything happen.

After receiving the jumbled Directive No. 22, Warlimont, Chief of L Section, took off for the Mountain to improve contact and iron out troubles. He arrived just ahead of the Italian conference delegation. While left to its own devices in the north his section had, as its records reveal, generated a strategy of its own. These ideas Warlimont now tried to sell piecemeal to his superiors as they discussed various problems. General Jodl soon let him know the proposals were way off target. They patently aimed at concentration on the Mediterranean at *Barbarossa*'s expense through conciliation with France, enlistment of the Arab world in the Middle East against the British there, and seizure of the Rock even without Franco's consent. Jodl knew that the last went directly counter to Hitler's expressed intent and said so. He had already replied affirmatively to Warlimont's direct query, "Does the Führer still hold fast to carrying out *Barbarossa*?" by recounting the exhaustive discussions of 9 January and Hitler's renewed resolve to go east, adding in Hitler's words, "Colossus Russia will prove to be a pig's bladder that a pinprick collapses." Danger of Russian interference in *Marita*, which his assistant raised, Jodl said was not expected; rather she might work up trouble by egging the Turks on against Germany and by secret help to the British in Greece. As for the Aegean islands, the Luftwaffe had directed the newly constituted airborne corps under General Kurt Student to test the airborne capture of Lemnos for control of the Dardanelles. It was clear, there was little room for the "decisive solutions" from L Section. Warlimont had to content himself with leaving a few action-pending papers. He must have departed disconsolate; no improved liaison had been achieved, and his sole sale had been the code names *Mountain Violet* and *Sunflower*.

Mussolini and company arrived on 18 January at the little railroad station near the Berghof. Ciano remarked to his diary that the spontaneous cordiality of their reception reversed the chill of the weather and immediately lifted the Duce's black mood. It was wellgrounded, this high unhappiness, for the Greek Army pressed at two crucial points in Albania, and the British pounded on the gates of Tobruk. If the Duce had feared condolences, their total omission and the Führer's confident voice swept his sorrows away. The relaxed exchanges that followed on this Saturday and then the easy Sunday clarified a number of issues: the Germans showed a specific wish for one more fling at Franco and a strong concern over Russian antics; the French were untrustworthy. England was only touched on casually. What the German professionals wanted more than all else, their Führer would not accede to: the organization of a joint headquarters in each arm under German command. Hitler held out for restraint and consideration of Latin feelings; he insisted that even advices on techniques and training should be conveyed through him to the Duce. Some such items he added to his long discourse on Monday 20 January. It began at noon and held on into the evening.[4]

"I must admit," wrote Ciano, "he does this with unusual mastery." The Master tramped from Finland's nickel mines in the far north to the Balkans, where for the first time, Partner Mussolini was let in on *Marita* a bit; back through unreliable France, on to Spain and Gibraltar and over to French Morocco. Through it all he wove a thread of Russian menace. Yet the East as a whole could only be "correctly evaluated in relationship to the West," which, of course, meant Britain. "Assault on the British Isles is the final aim." Surely this was what his rapt listeners wanted to hear. But at present the thing was complex. "Germany is in the position of someone who has but one shot left in his gun; if he misses, then the situation is much worse than before. One could not repeat the landing. . . . On the other hand, so long as the attack has not taken place, the British will have to reckon on one." It fitted so neatly; the Italians were delighted with the apt illustration. Had he hit on a new strategic truth, or did this latest excuse—the last before had characterized landing as "criminal" unless victory was certain—epitomize Hitler's failure before England? He never could face up to All or Nothing over the water, or for that matter, over land either; but there it was easier to conceal. He maneuvered or talked his way around such confrontations.

Defense of the Continent against Britain, Hitler explained, was

4. Ciano D and Ciano DP report on the meeting from the Italian side; OKW Ops War Diary (by H. Greiner) and Documents GFP, vol. 10, Doc. 672, from the German side. The two versions complement each other, though Greiner made the more exhaustive record of Hitler's speech. On Italian feelings, Hitler backed up his stand by issuing on 5 February a directive for the conduct of German troops in Italian theaters of operation: they were to earn Italian respect through their own discipline and courage. At the same time he prescribed command principles: the Italian theater commander would have operational control of the troops provided he committed them in concentrated divisional strength. A German commander would have recourse to the Führer. Göring retained exclusive command over the 10th Air Corps.

integral to the whole situation in the west from "Kirkenes in the north to the Spanish border," and on to Portugal, Southern France, and the Strait of Sicily. The Luftwaffe's present bar to that strait "is a weak substitute for possession of Gibraltar. . . . If Italy still could move the Caudillo to enter the war it would mean a great success and would in a short time fundamentally alter the Mediterranean situation." America, even if she entered the war, would be no great danger; "the gigantic block of Russia is much more dangerous." In this era of air power, attack out of Russia or from the Mediterranean "could reduce the petroleum district of Rumania to a smoking ruin; these preserves are vital to the Axis." Even so, commitments of valuable materials must not be made to places in which they could bog down. This applied to Libya too, where "only a blocking force is to be sent." (The block soon grew into a major commitment.)

Mussolini threw in his contributions between the crests of Hitlerian hyperbole. He expressed agreement and pleasure over the plans for Albania and Libya and would try Franco anew. Hitler led toward a close with a recital of German technical and operational developments (which he dared not trust to his professionals). The Italian delegation went away reassured and happy.[5]

They had hardly got home when the Tobruk disaster broke. It fell on 22 January, and with it twenty thousand men and their gear. This wound up the total destruction of the force originally allocated for the conquest of all Egypt. Nor was the end in sight. British forces rolled on against Derna, and soon there were reports of probes at Italian tank units in El Mechili, deep inland. Envelopment of Bengasi from the south might follow and bring the loss of all Cirenaica. It was already too late for the German blocking plans, thought General von Rintelen in Rome. The situation demanded armor capable of taking the offensive. This was the view of General von Funk, who returned to Berlin from his reconnaissance of Libya. British action was again crowding German decision.

Yet for Germans of this time the month of January had to end in grand Party pageantry, parading and speechmaking, for 30 January was the anniversary of Hitler's accession to power. And this time again, he delivered himself in mid-1920s style. His review on this Thirtieth of January took note of the many proffers of friendship he had made toward Britain. But the British had spurned him; they

5. Mussolini did meet Franco on 12 February 1941 at Bordighera. He was unable to move the Caudillo one bit.

wanted no peace. He concluded with prophecy of great events during 1941.

Army planning for the east progressed, and misgivings grew. The scheme was too ambitious. The Luftwaffe could still make forays against England as weather and inclination permitted. None of the operations matched the ferocity of the blows delivered during the past fall. Göring had met with his Führer on 28 January to explain the actions in course and to ease the Luftwaffe's overcommitment in coming operations. It was settled that Lemnos would not be taken by the 11th Air Corps (Airborne) because paratroops might be needed to secure the French fleet should Operation *Attila* be ordered against France. At Navy on the Tirpitz-Ufer in Berlin, hopes were rising for submarine and big-ship operations out of newly stocked Biscayan ports. No longer did Britain have German sea power hemmed in! So ran the thought. During the past December the cruiser *Hipper* had tested the Biscay basing facilities, but achieved only mediocre success at sea. Berlin's chairman of the military end of the Axis, which now also included Tokyo, was Admiral Groos, naval theorizer and historian. Admiral Nomura, head of the Japanese naval mission, had raised several points for discussion:

1. Axis measures to prevent United States participation at present and the possibility of a United States–Japan war;
2. Establishment of a common Axis plan based on United States entry into the war;
3. German and Italian support to Japan for increasing Japanese war potential against the United States.

Groos held that *Barbarossa* would surely relieve Britain, particularly if she were not pinned down in the Mediterranean. On the other hand, the invasion of Russia would free Japan because America's low state of preparation offered no threat. If Japan then attacked Singapore, "such action would be decisive militarily, economically and psychologically significant." Exploration of this January 1941 line of thought was recommended. Substitute Pearl Harbor for Singapore and we have a story.[6]

---

6. Halder, 2:261; Heusinger, pp. 107, 108; OKW Ops SitConf, 15–31 Jan. 1941.

7. Operation Sonnenblume

Rommel Enters the Mediterranean Arena: February 1941

Generalmajor Freiherr Hans von Funk, speaking in the Führer's Berlin office on 1 February 1941, wasted few words in getting to the point: Libya was lost, and nothing could now be done to hold it. In the words of diarist Greiner "der ganze Ernst" of the situation came out. Hitler, with Keitel, Jodl, von Brauchitsch, and Halder, listened attentively to the story of Marshal Graziani's dispirited talk at Cirene and to Funk's own estimate of what should—but now hardly could— be done. He saw little chance of blocking the British. By driving cross-country inland toward Bengasi they could outflank all positions along the coast. There would go all of Cirenaica, leaving only the grim prospect of a position close about Tripoli for a do-or-die stand. The intended German blocking unit would be inadequate and late. It would take at least a panzer division acting on the offensive to stabilize things. But such a force could hardly arrive before the end of April. By then the British would be in Tripoli. Army Commander in Chief von Brauchitsch chimed in to support von Funk, saying that "the commitment of a German unit to Libya would have use only if it made possible going over to the offensive."[1]

Germany's supreme commander fenced, seemed to agree with Funk's ideas in general, and refrained from taking direct issue. Yet there were signs that he believed something could still be done: surely

1. OKW Ops War Diary, 1 Feb. 41, pp. 149–56; H. Greiner, pp. 214–16; Halder, 2:265, 1 Feb. 1941.

some way could be found. Procrastinating over North Africa had brought on the crisis. There the soldiers had him. It was unlikely that Hitler could tolerate the implication for long. He would find a way.

With machinelike precision Hitler fixed on the nub of the problem—Italian submission to his command. Before deciding on a course, he needed to have the Italian attitude clarified, he declared. Under what directives did Graziani operate? How long could he hold out? How soon could Italian Air in North Africa be reinforced? What about delaying the British coastal advance by Italian naval forces? Would the remaining armored and motorized Italian division, plus the German blocking unit, suffice, or would it take more German panzers? General von Rintelen was to bring the answers from Rome to Berlin in person. "Until then the transports bound for Naples and from there to Libya [with German support aboard] are to be stopped." That should smoke something out, including agreeable command arrangements. The British might be halted by dive bombers and twin-engine fighters from the Luftwaffe's celebrated 10th Air Corps, which had shaken Admiral Cunningham's sea control so hard. The chief of the Air General Staff, Jeschonnek, was to report on this question as soon as possible. The Führer departed for the Berghof.

The following day, a Sunday, must have found him poring over maps and figures—breaking away to stride up and down in self-debate, then back to his chart table. For by Monday when he met the Army chiefs for another conclave on *Barbarossa*, he was well on his way toward definite and detailed conclusions about the Libyan impasse.

If he needed further spur to decision, Hitler got it on that Monday, 3 February 1941, through General Halder's prior portrayal of the moving *Barbarossa* drama. A screen of vast field actions came alive in an orgy of soldier play—dozens and dozens of divisions (infantry, motorized, and armored) moved over hundreds of miles with gun, cannon, tank, and plane. To the head player it was utter joy. He entered right in with approving comment and burst out at the end, "The world will hold its breath when Operation *Barbarossa* is carried out." The picture has swollen; 9 January's boast of "Europe holding its breath" is too puny; here it reaches global proportions as the whole *world* clutches its breath in transfixed wonder. The power of decision is in him. He leaped into the thick of the Libyan crisis, and dispatched it.[2]

2. *Barbarossa* was to drive three prongs into Russia: one toward Leningrad, anoth-

Hitler had remarked on "a possibly dangerous moment, if all Libya should fall to the British," who, thus freed, could make trouble in Syria on the south flank of *Barbarossa*. This theme he now expounded as his talent for vivid word pictures about the Mediterranean took charge and produced unguarded verbal embellishments to his basic thinking. While the loss of North Africa might still prove bearable, he ventured, Italy might succumb to psychological aftereffects. "For then Britain could put a pistol to Italy's breast and confront her with the alternatives of either making peace . . . or submitting to the heaviest air attacks." He was applying his old air formula, used unsuccessfully against England, to an isolated Italy. The British in the Mediterranean would be free to use a dozen divisions against Syria, which would be very dangerous. Germany would have only the weak bases of southern France. "Therefore the defeat of the Italians in the Mediterranean must be prevented." In a measure, Operation *Marita* would provide against it, but beyond that indirect effect, the Italians had to be helped decisively in North Africa. The time had come.

A proposed defense stand close around Tripoli left no room for employing the Luftwaffe. Marshal Graziani had to be supported in a forward position, and since German army units would arrive too late, "the Luftwaffe is to be committed"—above all, dive bombers working from Libyan bases. Following this sequence through, Hitler saw that even if the British were halted, the intended German blocking unit would lack the power for counterattack. It needed reinforcement by a strong panzer force. Of course the British, after their long westward drive, would be weary and worn. The sudden appearance of fresh, well-equipped German forces might then and there tip the balance in the Axis favor.

The Führer paid small heed to Army remonstrances that armor committed here would be missed in *Barbarossa*. For him the crucial question was whether the Luftwaffe could *intervene immediately* in Libya. Indeed, was there time to transport help? General Jeschonnek spoke for vigorous Luftwaffe action, supported by air-transported supplies. Bengasi would be the only Libyan dive-bomber base close enough to the target. He also broached the question of Malta: rub-

---

er at Moscow, and the third against Kiev. Hitler again stressed cutting off Russian retreat. Further, the wing prongs were to "drive ahead while the center held, then operate on the flanks to maneuver the foe out of the middle." This was his set personal plan. OKW Ops War Diary, 3 Feb. 1941, p. 161.

bing it out was imperative. Though the 10th Air Corps had bombed the island steadily since 10 January, British air forces were still active. It was Army's turn. Field Marshal von Brauchitsch proposed reinforcement with only one panzer regiment, initially; the rest could follow. Moreover, he wanted a German corps headquarters in Libya to command, and to coordinate with the Luftwaffe. Hitler reacted at once in full agreement. This was the kind of talk he had waited for. On the spot he translated the proposals into verbal orders.

The enterprise still lacked one essential—an energetic and trustworthy commander. General von Funk, who had precipitated the action by speaking out, did not suit. He had offered no saving solution; perhaps he had no faith in one, for he rested his case on the problem's intransigence. This is never enough, nor was it for Hitler. Where to find a true leader? On this very day, 3 February 1941, an adjutant from Führer headquarters called on General Erwin Rommel to advise him that he was wanted in Berlin. Rommel reported on 6 February 1941, at first to Brauchitsch for preliminary briefing, and then to the Führer for prolonged indoctrination, including British and American press pictures of the British advance. Hitler had his man and told Rommel so; he knew him as the devoted energetic officer who had formerly commanded that crack battalion at Führer headquarters.[3]

Old infantryman Rommel—now turned tankman—took the new job in hand with a will. It "is very big and important," he hurriedly dashed off in a note to his wife, ". . . terrible lot to do in a few hours." The summons had caught him at home on leave; he had been spoiling for action. His last exploit of the French campaign included a 225-mile drive by his 7th Panzer Division to take Cherbourg. Always a strong believer in the initiative through shock and speed, he had led his division from the van, and from there carried the day. This doctrine he applied at once to the African gamble, for which the Führer assured him personal support and a free hand. Armed with the high blessings and fresh *Sonnenblume* directives, Rommel set out; he checked through and won approval for tentative ideas at the Italian Commando Supremo in Rome on 11 February, then flew on to Catania in Sicily to consult General Geissler, commander of Luftwaffe's 10th Air Corps.

The latest news from Africa was bad. Bengasi had fallen; routed Italians streamed back toward Tripolitania. "Something had to be

3. Halder, 2:270–73; Rommel, pp. 1–36; Liddell Hart RP, p. 98.

done at once," wrote Rommel, "to bring the British offensive to a halt." He asked General Geissler to attack Bengasi that same night. The astounded airman would have none of it. Apparently the Italians had asked him to spare Bengasi because many of them owned homes there. For such barter, soldier Rommel had no patience. He decided, here at the outset, to stake his prospective command on the issue. Colonel Schmundt, the Führer's chief adjutant, who was also there, got in touch with high headquarters and obtained immediate approval. The planes took off.

The next morning, 12 February, Rommel, ostensibly still only on reconnaissance, arrived in Tripoli. The gravity of the situation showed all around him—morale zero, bags packed for Abandon Ship to the home shores; command was vague. Graziani having abdicated, his chief of staff, General Gariboldi, attempted to keep the shaky structure together. He held out small hope. When General Rommel urged a stand at Sirte on the southern bulge of the Gulf of Sirte, about 250 miles east of Tripoli, "Gariboldi looked very dubious about it all," and suggested that the German first look over the unfavorable terrain. Rommel took him up, promised to reconnoiter by air and report back that evening, and at the same time reminded Gariboldi that German aid could come only if Sirte was held. "I was determined," he wrote, "to depart from my instructions—to reconnoiter only—and to take command at the front as soon as possible." That evening while he recounted his flight east, General Roatta checked in from Rome with the Duce's blessing for Rommel's ideas in fresh directives. This put things in order. The Italians fell in with the German Sirte plan; early on the morrow the last intact small Italian ground force moved out from Tripoli's seeming safety toward Sirte. Rommel had established himself, and just in the nick of time.

Or so it seemed in Tripoli. By all odds he should have been too late, should have found Tripoli abandoned. From such a misfortune the British government saved him through a remarkably coincident nick of time. The first German aid, a reconnaissance and antitank battalion, disembarked at Tripoli on 15 February and moved toward Sirte, where it dug in on the 18th. By that day, the British could have been rattling that outermost gate of Tripoli, that is, if the order to halt—out of London, conceived by Churchill, as early as 8 January—had not come in between. For Britain's ground forces entered Bengasi on 6 February, the day Rommel was appointed, and by the 7th had pushed a mile beyond, had cut off Italian army withdrawal, and had

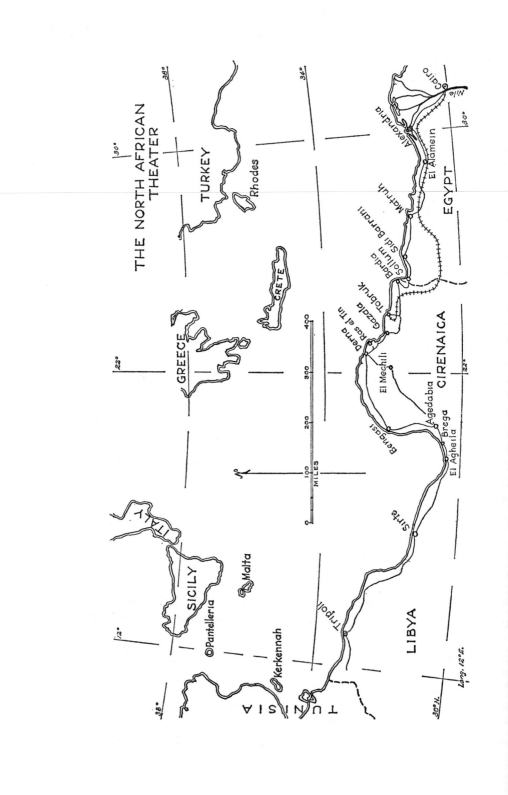

THE NORTH AFRICAN THEATER

moved toward Tripolitania. Cirenaica's defenses collapsed. The shock of it, plus the real and imagined pressure against Sirte, Tripoli's outermost gate, could have triggered Abandon Ship there by 10 February (two days before Rommel arrived). That loss would have run right up to the Tunisian border. A link-up of the conquering British and the dissident French of Tunisia would have opened incalculable dangers to the Axis out of Algeria and Morocco. And as for Italy, we can recall Hitler's apt picture of a British pistol poked in her ribs. Facing the British was a chance to rip the south flank of all Europe open and keep it so. Army leaders on the scene understood this.

But pursuit into Tripolitania stopped cold on London's orders because of a wishful switch to Greece. This major political decision, so named by Churchill himself, turned the local strategy upside down. The end effect was as harmful to operations in the Mediterranean as Hitler's tank-halt order before Dunkirk in May 1940 had been to war on the Channel. In both instances dubious political scheming dictated bad strategy.

Here we could celebrate a great moment of giving all credit to Hitler for dispatching Rommel just in the nick of time, and all blame to Churchill for stopping Wavell's forces in the same nick. In the field the two moments of change almost coincided. There can be no doubt that without Rommel and without Wavell's order to halt, British forces could have marched into Tripoli. At the very least Britain forfeited a showdown in a game and environment in which she held the trumps. She held what fighting men are willing to die for—a chance at the strategic initiative and victory—and gave it up. She chose instead to challenge at a disadvantage in Greece where men would die without such a chance. "The more we studied the problem," wrote General de Guingand, a member of General Wavell's staff, "the more unsound the [Greece] venture appeared." Even its name was unfortunate: Operation *Lustre*.[4]

4. Churchill, pp. 14–77; De Guingand, pp. 47–72; Spencer, pp. 13–30; Liddell Hart RP, p. 95; OKW Ops War Diary, 7 Feb. 1941, p. 184. This last source quotes a German Army General Staff intelligence report of 6 Feb.—No. 438, which covered the span 24 Jan. to 5 Feb.: "British will reach Agedabia [125 miles south of Bengasi] in a short time. . . . The weak Italian forces can hardly succeed in withdrawal. Whether the British command will continue the offensive across the desert to the south of the Gulf of Sirte is questionable . . . only possible after extensive preparation." General de Guingand, then a major on the Cairo planning staff, wrote: "We had convinced ourselves that once Tobruk and Bengasi were captured, after a pause of a week or two, we could advance to capture Tripoli. The prize was great. We would be in a position to avoid major campaigns in North Africa . . . link up with the French in Tunis . . . shipping routes through the Mediter-

By good fortune and vigorous action Operation *Sonnenblume* got off to a flying start and no one could have been happier over this than the project's gallant commander. "I hope I can pull it off," he wrote home. His impatient insistence on immediate air attack against Bengasi worked and found support in high places. On the day he left OKW, it issued the up-to-date directive that ordered the Luftwaffe "to eliminate British air forces on Malta; to attack supply shipments along the African coast; to combat the advance west in Cirenaica and to smash concentrations of tanks and advancing motorized units . . . using all available forces and the heaviest bombs." Moreover, for these vital actions, air force withdrawals were authorized from the high-priority air war against England. German sea transport from Italy to Libya was organized and its protection by air cover taken in hand, and air transport by the doughty Ju-52's was to supplement sea traffic. Rommel's phenomenal campaign was under way.

Even with these extraordinary logistic provisions, it was easy to see that *Sonnenblume* transport and supply was going to be no picnic. L Section of OKW recorded an initial requirement of 140 troop trains from Germany to an Italian port, and on top of such land problems, delays at sea interfered at once. On 9 February Britain's Force H, based at Gibraltar, bobbed up off Genoa, lobbed shells into the port, turned to let nearby Savona have a few, and departed un-molested. Such sea bulls at large were a menace to three deep-laden German streamers under way from Naples to Tripoli. They turned into Palermo, Sicily, to await an all clear, then continued to become the important first German arrivals that mattered so much for the precious nick of time.

Elsewhere, too, deep-loaded ships mattered crucially—those plying the Atlantic with sustenance for England. The two theaters, Atlantic and Mediterranean, would interact. The planned German battleship entry into Britain's Battle of the Atlantic, for example, was bound to suck British naval strength away from Germany's Battle of the Mediterranean, an effect which meant that a measure of security for Rommel's supply could be won in the Atlantic. The relationship was not fully comprehended until much later. What hindered Ger-

---

ranean easily kept open. . . . An orderly arrived with a 'Most Urgent' signal. We read it together and our faces fell." The day was 10 January 1941. "The message changed the whole framework of strategy. Greece was now to become top priority." London's complex strategic intention may have been to keep the Germans diverted in the southeast away from the Channel on the chance of encouraging Russia to attack them in the rear before the Germans themselves drove into Russia.

many's war in the Atlantic most, her sailors thought, was the weakness in naval air strength over the sea and the air failure to hit the proper naval targets, such as ports and shipyards, ashore. These thoughts, and Navy plans for *Marita* and *Barbarossa*, Admiral Raeder presented at the Führer conference on 4 February, the day after Hitler had been moved by the Army's *Barbarossa* to declare that the world "will hold its breath."

First the admiral reported on the long-planned entry of the heavy ships into the Atlantic fray. Superbattleships *Bismarck* and *Tirpitz* would soon be ready, but for the present it was the fast battleships *Scharnhorst* and *Gneisenau* that would sortie from Norwegian waters for a break into the Atlantic either side of Iceland; heavy cruiser *Hipper* would join in, out of Brest. Twenty-one submarines were being added also. Raeder plodded on with his *Marita* and *Barbarossa* plans, having said that he was to meet Admiral Riccardi, his opposite number in Italy's navy, soon to urge offensive operations on the Italian Navy in the south. He offered nothing about possible German naval transfers to that area by way of encouragement, no thought of submarines or of transferable small craft, despite the Mediterranean's increasing significance. No, the Atlantic was the German Navy's true fulfillment, and her sailors could see it no other way. A final item in Naval strategy was transmitted in an eight-page Skl study about the prospective entry of Japan and the United States into the war. The study is noteworthy for appalling ignorance and wishful thinking. It concluded: "To encourage Japan to take any initiative . . . in the far eastern area, as this would . . . keep American forces from the European theater. . . . Such action might bring America's entry into the war, a risk which can be accepted, since the total advantages outweigh the disadvantages." German naval theoreticians erred about war with the United States as badly as their Führer erred about war with Russia. If World War I should have taught them anything, it was to avoid embroilment with the United States. Nothing could change these perversities, not in Hitler or in his sailors.[5]

This conference of 4 February 1941 between Hitler and Raeder

5. How far theorizing over a chart or globe can get adrift! The Skl study held forth on control of the Pacific: "Without this basis [control over a sea triangle Hawaii-Upola (Samoa)–Guam], politics is unthinkable in East Asia." Another earnest Navy study was about the implacable contest of Navy versus Air Force. East Plan would pinch air support in reconnaissance and attack against important shore facilities; Navy wanted assurance of air support in the siege of England; it was already growing weaker because of *Barbarossa*.

apparently spurred the issuance of three significant papers: Führer Directive No. 23 of 6 February, "The Conduct of War Against the British War Economy," Führer "orders" of 28 February to settle "differences in opinion prevailing in the Navy and Air Force," and Führer Directive No. 24 of 5 March, "Cooperation with Japan." To close out (for a time) the last topic first: Directive No. 24's general purpose, as has already been foreshadowed, was to induce Japan to act soon in the Far East in order to shift American interest to the Pacific and keep it there. German know-how in war making would be shared "generously," and items that could influence the war "at an early date" were to have top priority. The fictitious *common aim* supported the Navy's own ideas: conquer Britain quickly before the United States could get into the war. *Capture of Singapore* would be a decisive step in that direction. "American naval bases," said the directive, "should be attacked only if the U.S.A. cannot be prevented from entering the war." Events and repeated orders to the same effect will bear out the presumption that this last admonition was Hitler's own. Contrary to Navy, he wanted no involvement with the United States before the conquest of Russia was a fact. "Coordination of the operational plans" of Germany and Japan he assigned to his Navy, so that whatever background images he may have built for the Pacific during the next nine months probably came from Navy sources. If the papers on hand at the 4 February conference are fair samples of Hitler's advices on the subject from the Navy, he was indeed poorly briefed at decision time in December 1941 when, out of hand and on his own, he declared war on the United States.

Raeder had stressed the need of pursuing the Navy's paramount war doctrine of siege of England by air and sea with steadily increasing power, especially by the Luftwaffe, and despite demands of the East Plan. Directive No. 23 reviewed the results thus far achieved and concluded that Navy's tonnage war was far more effective than Luftwaffe's erratic strikes at industry and England's morale. The British had refused to take fright, as half-expected, but the belt-cinching occasioned by lack of overseas supply was growing tight. It was to be made tighter by revised target priorities, and along with this, the renewed threat of imminent Invasion. Göring and his Luftwaffe found means of getting around or sabotaging most of these newest orders for cooperation, as they did with the lengthier Führer supporting orders of 28 February, which attempted to redivide and reassign air tasks that went overseas. In the existing circumstances there was no cure for the bitter internecine Air-Navy war.

In England *Sea Lion* died hard. At times it seemed as if the British government was deliberately fostering invasion fright; it reached to America. A fresh batch of civil instructions about landings descended on the public during February. Yet Churchill reported on the state of the war in reassuring terms. No Invasion so far—a good sign that paralleled the encouraging news from Libya. He warned of a German thrust into the Balkans and assured Turkey of aid. It was difficult, the old warrior complained, to convince uncommitted governments of Britain's ultimate victory, and he signed off with a cheering forecast that the war would be decided at sea and on the island of England. Invasion, let it come.

British news estimates of German migrations toward the Balkans hit close to the true figures; rail traffic eastward also received close scrutiny. By German records the daily train allocation began at twelve and doubled each month until it reached a maximum of forty-eight trains per day. Squirming, sprawling *Barbarossa* swelled enormously, not only physically but in possessing the minds of his masters. While his validity was on occasion questioned, this became harder and harder to do. What indeed was the true why? On 17 February, in the course of a report to General Halder, the Foreign Office liaison man at OKH, von Etzdorf, repeated an old and early byword, recently heard again from the Führer: "A reckoning [with Russia] is inevitable. Were Britain eliminated I might not be able to rerouse the German people against Russia; therefore Russia must be eliminated first." These very words went back over six months to July 1940 when General Jodl first disclosed the Führer's eastern intent to his amazed L Section men. He had tried to mollify them with the same deceptively candid reason. The din of such sloganized reasoning was a part of the selling job that eventually made *Barbarossa* as unassailable as Hitler himself.

The Master still kept his vigil on the Berghof, where on 14 February Yugoslav representatives came to exchange views. He reacted favorably to their proposal to serve as intermediary between Italy and Greece. Did this mean that Greece would have been spared German occupation if mediation had succeeded? Not at all. It would have cleared the Italians out of the way for Hitler's own occupation of all Greece, to which he was by now fully committed.

Sooner or later in any operational planning, logistics close in to pose final doubts and queries. *Marita's* readiness now tended that way, and more heavily, *Barbarossa's* too. Another forward question was how far and deep this new *Sunflower* could infringe on older plants and their stored nutrients. Or could any juggling of resources be tolerated? In pace with Rommel's explosive start, the requirements jumped higher and higher. It had 6000 tons of supply on demand and orders for huge fuel stocks that were nowhere in sight. "Quartermaster business," fumed Rommel, and went about winning his private war, as a fighting man must.[6]

We left Rommel in Tripoli exceeding his orders and breaking speed records for unloading ships. The first record fell when the troops worked round the clock on 14 February to get their gear out of the ship that brought them—the 3d Reconnaissance Battalion and an antitank group. In smart new kit they marched past their commander at the plaza the following morning. Tripoli's morale took an upturn. The troops kept on along the Via Balbia toward Sirte and arrived on 16 February. Rommel closed up behind and recorded, "I took over command at the front."

Lying 240 miles southeast of Tripoli, Sirte is an inconspicuous cluster of low white buildings that are pressed toward seashore by an inland salt marsh. The last cohesive Italian force of about a regiment held the place against expected British advance from El Agheila, 160 miles beyond. Distances were expansive. Day on day German and Italian troops streamed forward from Tripoli, while coastal craft brought supply by sea. By 18 February scout units probed forward for contact, and so on the 24th the first clash occurred 75 miles in front of Sirte. Several British vehicles and three men were taken. A new African campaign had begun (p. 104).

Rommel consolidated along the lowest turn of the gulf. Forward elements of the 5th Panzer Regiment joined on 11 March with news of more to follow. Power for an offensive grew each day, and General Rommel could plan and set up units for attack on El Agheila for 24 March by his 5th Light Division. With this in order, the commander of the German Afrikakorps, so dubbed by the Führer himself, flew home to report on his reconnaissance and to promote approval for his

6. Not only was there a logistics problem of allocations but a problem of rail transport to an Italian seaport, thence by sea to Tripoli, and from there by truck and coastal craft forward to the Sirte. Tripoli could accommodate only four ships. Even if four or five ships sailed from Italy every other day, it would not be enough. And what of British counter action at sea?

expanding plans. With the help of London the crisis had been surmounted.

Rommel arrived in Germany on 9 March, bursting with plans for the reconquest of Cirenaica, or even the invasion of Egypt. Who could tell what might develop? He began sounding out his superiors for support. Neither they nor he could know that a thrust through Cirenaica would complement the Balkan drive that was to end on Crete, thus creating an opportunity to cut off the East Basin and put it under Axis control.

Another thought that entered only hazily into his calculations at this time was that the island of Malta sat on the flank of his supply route. On the day the first reinforcements arrived in Tripoli, 14 February 1941, the Führer directed Göring to determine if the 11th Air Corps (airborne) could take Malta through the air before *Barbarossa* time. Göring's negative answer quashed a contrary recommendation by L Section and the Navy. The project was put off, only to revive from time to time when the need pressed.

8. Yugoslavia

The Decision to Destroy Her: March 1941

In Europe, eventful 1941 began its long season of war with the long-expected German thrust into the Balkan Peninsula. The move implied the doom of Yugoslavia, a country that had tried to steer clear of Axis entanglement.

Crossing the Danube from Rumania into Bulgaria presented the natural hurdle on which so much depended, but the German advance guards cleared it exactly on schedule. Working around the clock from nightfall 27 February 1941, their bridging gangs heaved the last truss into place and jumped clear as the poised advanced units rushed over. It was the last day of February. Two days later General Halder could open his record for 2 March with the significant entry: "12th Army (List) marches into Bulgaria." This was a relief in many ways and, contrary to the fears of some, the unmasking of another German design set up in world commentary only a few extra ripples. Moscow gave off nothing stronger than news mention; London had already forecast it in rumors that were now fact. It was different from a year ago when news of the leap into Norway exploded.

Unfriendly comment emanated only from Belgrade, Yugoslavia's capital, when neighboring Bulgaria on 1 March proclaimed her accession to the Tripartite Pact. What troubled the Yugoslavs was that they sat on the west flank of the marching Germans. They pondered what the object might be. Moreover, the Yugoslavs had parallel roads and rails which could come in very handy. Hitler invited Prince Regent Paul of Yugoslavia to the Mountain for a secret session on 4 March.

The Prince arrived full of good will, which he maintained throughout; yet his easy demeanor betokened no joining up. Military support to the Axis, he declared, ran counter to the feeling of his people: they wanted none of it. As with Franco, Hitler restated the attractive case in extenso, sympathized with the Yugoslav feeling, and gave assurance that he wanted no military participation; he even renounced any wish for troop passage. All he sought was friendship sealed by accession to the Tripartite Pact. Apparently agreeable himself, the prince expressed doubts about cabinet consent—he would see what could be done—and departed. On 8 March he replied with three strings attached to accession: no troop transit, no commitment to war, and an outlet on the Aegean. These seemed agreeable to Hitler, and the play turned to pressing a pen into the reluctant Slav hand; it still took time.

On the opposite flank in the east, Turkey turned out to be less of a problem. General Rohde, the German military attaché, counseled soft treading, through a private letter by the Führer to President Inönu with assurances of peace and security. The scheme flattered Hitler, and its advance billing soothed the Turks. Meanwhile, Britain severed relations with Bulgaria, and Foreign Secretary Eden, accompanied by Sir John Dill, chief of the Imperial General Staff, came south to woo the Turks. In the midst of Eden's talks Hitler's letter, loaded with fond recollections of World War I bonds and reference to current British machinations in Greece, arrived. He promised to remain 60 kilometers from the Turk-Bulgar border. Turkey and the Dardanelles would be secure. The German approach won. President Inönu replied in the spirit of a friendly neutral.

German columns ground south over bad Bulgarian roads, hub deep in mud. In the van, construction gangs cleared the twists and turns, reinforced the flimsy bridging, and eased the steepest heights. Steady progress continued each day; so, in the tradition of their fathers, the staffs plotted advances happily and recorded the threadbare phrase: "All proceeding according to plan." By 9 March the van had reached the frontier of Greece. But attack on her was not yet due. It was still an open question, according to OKW in Germany. Faced with this overpowering force, the British might abandon

Greece. Or was it uncertain Yugoslavia on the west flank that stayed the Führer's decision?

On the scene in Albania, Mussolini raised a flurry. He lacked precise intelligence about German timing for Greece, yet he had to be in time for the spoils. During the German attack on France the same problem had bothered him. This time he was going to be on hand: reports of 11 March from the Albanian front had the Duce commanding in person. This only incited the Yugoslavs to stiffen their anti-Axis attitude. They backtracked from their early March willingness to sign up and began throwing out provocative jibes against the Italians on their south. On 14 March Mussolini found it prudent to reinforce his Yugoslavian border from units opposing the Greek Army, whereupon that army attacked in force frontally and routed the Italians before them. Another disaster! General Papagos of Greece celebrated it with a special order of the day. A disconsolate Duce headed back for Rome.

If Hitler cherished one doctrine above all others, it was "No Britons on the Continent!" He had chased them out at Dunkirk; he wanted to chase them out of Gibraltar; this was the main preventive motive behind *Marita*, indeed behind *Barbarossa* (he claimed). They must not return, either in the flesh as in Greece or in the spirit as in Russia. Nothing could get him upset quicker than a British probe into his Continent (a hypertension which was not fully grasped in England), as now happened in the far north on 4 March 1941. A British force raided the Lofoten Islands off Narvik, Norway. Royal Navy ships jabbed into the port of Solvaer, landed troops, shot up supply and oil storages, and carried off 200 prisoners. Hitler exploded. He summoned General Dietl, the victor of Narvik, his superior General von Falkenhorst, and their Air and Navy running mates. The Army was told to ready immediately 160 additional batteries of artillery to make Norway absolutely impregnable. A disproportionate share of men and materials stayed tied down there. Hitler believed in forts and fortresses—Festung Europa—and some of this must have been personal insecurity. The Lofoten raid stirred more world notice than the momentous events working up in the south on the shores of the Mediterranean.

Alongside signs of a refractory Yugoslavia, there sprouted fresh German rumors of continued peace with Greece. The stories were strong enough to hasten Admiral Raeder's submission of what he wanted as spoils out of any settlement with Greece: a few ships for his Mediterranean tasks and coastal defense works. The chief of L Section OKW, Warlimont, finally braved Jodl on the disarray: Would *Marita* go even though Greece offered no resistance? It took days before an answer came on 18 March, after Jodl reviewed the Führer's definitive *Barbarossa* conference of the day before. He said, "The Führer has fully determined that the operations against Greece are to continue until the British have been driven from the continental mainland." Reports of British troop landings had been confirmed. But Jodl failed to define the system of high command that would govern: whether like Norway through OKW, or like France through OKH. On 21 March, L Section recorded, "How Operation *Marita* is to be conducted is unknown. . . . OKH does not know either." The truth was, Hitler himself was unsure: Should the thing go at all?

Queries kept recurring about the offshore islands. It turned out that *Barbarossa* was the key: How did the islands, how did anything affect him? That made one pertinent question, but more binding still, was he really going? Much was at stake! Reconnaissance messages were crammed with news of RAF flights from Crete, of convoy traffic to Suda Bay and to the Greek mainland. Belatedly, British troop landings in Greece were confirmed, and at Führer direction, reconfirmed. A review of these uncomfortable developments on 13 March, followed by another on the 15th, and then the inspirational life of *Barbarossa* review on the 17th, clinched decision for a hesitant Hitler. He was sailing in unfamiliar waters, but there was the Air. He redecided that Luftwaffe should prepare the airborne seizure of Lemnos, Operation *Hannibal*; Army, supported by Air, should land by sea and take the Cyclades and the steppingstones Kithira and Antikithira, stretching southeast toward Crete. But Crete herself, of such avid interest early in the game, dropped out. Not a word on her. By 22 March a reinforced paratroop regiment under General Süssmann, commander of the 7th Paratroop Division, moved into readiness in the Bulgarian department of Plovdiv. On 24 March General Jodl signed a paper that "ordered reconnaissance and attack [by air] on all naval forces (including those of Greece) in territorial waters around Crete."[1]

One man alone, beset by a monstrous private compulsion, ruled

1. FD, p. 161; OKW Ops War Diary, March 1941; OKW Ops SitConf, pp. 177–204; GCB; Warlimont KFA, pp. 147–49. These sources apply also to what follows immediately.

Germany, her strategy and policy. Professional strategy and thought on policy lapsed more and more into efforts to outmaneuver his fixations and to save what could be saved of sound action. Though *Barbarossa* rode high, behind pressed block after block of post-Russia actions. Already in mid-February 1941 L Section was charged with a deployment into Afghanistan for the conquest of India. Britain would be driven from the Mediterranean. And then England would find herself under the guns again, and alone. "After Russia!" became a cover for myriads of evasions, a sort of mañana storage for all things yet to come. There were many!

The political arena exhibited peculiar variants of calm and evasion in the west, contrasted against tension and pressure in the southeast. Toward the United States, for example, a forced German calm prevailed, while toward Yugoslavia aggressive pressure mounted. The divergent actions were related, and they got their responses. On 11 March President Roosevelt signed Lease-Lend into law and promised to implement it with seven billion dollars. On the following day Prime Minister Churchill hailed the American bill as "the new Magna Carta." On 15 March Roosevelt plumped for a united American drive to "defeat dictatorships . . . in an all-out effort for victory." Although the German press refrained from comment, top political and military circles rated the speech as another and clearer "declaration of war." Between noon and 1213 on 16 March Hitler delivered himself of a veiled answer at the annual Memorial Day exercises: he replayed the war glories of the past year, poured venom on Churchill, and circumspectly omitted mention of Roosevelt or his country. He had to have quiet in the west, while he turned east. The West had spoken, and in his way he had answered.

Ah the decadent West. In this very time of March 1941, Hitler made his culminating drive for his grand design. It deserves special mention here for its first clear evidence of the whole East Plan's outright criminality. Recall the whipping up of the military before Poland and before France. The lash was out again, now for Russia. The tremendous expanses, separated theaters, and powerful forces passed in review, and as they passed, unthinkable thoughts occurred to his soldiers and sailors. What if this and what if that . . . ? Brauchitsch came in the forenoon of 17 March and his chief of staff, Halder, in the afternoon. Raeder reported a day later; then Rommel in another day; Göring had as usual maintained the closest personal touch. The lash?

There was no need for it. Rommel alone left with promise of some freedom of action. The others had given in to ineluctable *Barbarossa*. They had got used to the beast.

The fact was *Barbarossa* had come of age; growth had been countenanced by the professionals in the thought of taking care of things as they developed in the field. But the massive bulk had crept up on them, and now at full-blown maturity and power it was too late to turn and kill the monster. Having passed through prolonged preachment, searching scrutiny in strategy, operating, and tactics, the plan had become established as an article of faith. Hitler's closely calculated selling job seemed complete. An inspirational rally or two would supply the final spiritual fillips that would commit the military converts to the crusade's true political and ideological goals of enslaving the Russians in the service of a Nazi European empire. The excess infidels would be put to the sword or the bullet. This queer bedrock object of the grand design had remained pretty well hidden.

Warning of a pogrom policy had first emerged in official writing two weeks before, on 3 March, when General Jodl turned back for revision a draft of special security measures to follow Directive No. 21 (*Barbarossa*) of December 1940. In revision he now instructed Warlimont, direct from the Führer, in the political and social transformation of Russia. The result described a sinister Nazi colonial empire which was to succeed the Russian state. It was simply the irrational Hitler scheme of pacification that was to follow the fighting:

This coming campaign is more than a mere passage of arms; it is also a decision between two philosophies of life. Because of the wide spaces, it will not suffice to defeat the enemy armed forces to end the war. The whole space will have to be broken up into independent states, each with its own government with which we can conclude peace.

Formation of these governments requires a great deal of political skill and general, carefully thought-out fundamentals.

Every great revolution creates things that cannot be erased. The socialistic idea can no longer be spirited away in present-day Russia. It alone can serve as the political base for building new governments and states. Jewish-Bolshevik intellectuals, up to now the oppressors of the peoples, must be eliminated. Former middle-class aristocratic intellectuals . . . will drop out too. They would be rejected by the Russian people and in the end would be anti-German. This applies especially to the Baltic states.

Moreover, we must under all circumstances avoid having nationalistic Russian states rise in place of the Bolshevik predecessors; history proves they would turn out anti-German in the long run.

Our task is to build up as soon as possible, with a minimum of military force, socialistic political structures which will be dependent on us.

These tasks are so difficult that they cannot be expected of the Army.

Jodl's guidance was obviously no offhand staff scribble to rework a submitted paper, but a carefully worded, practiced writing (entered in full in the War Diary) that expressed, in a sort of preamble form, Hitler's true objective for invading Russia in the first place and forecast the end goal of his mad private mythology. It explained much, for it was the basic reason for everything—the wellspring. More would follow in the sales words and operations of this policy, but for the present only three implemental directions were given:

(1) The army requires an operational zone. Its depth must be limited as much as possible. Behind it no military administration should be instituted. Rather, in its place National Commissioners (*Reichskommissaren*) are to take over in specific nationality-bounded great spaces and quickly build up new state governments. Armed forces commands should function alongside only for military problems under the commander in chief Army or OKW. . . . The bulk of the police forces should belong to the National Commissioners.

(2) Boundaries can only expand in the forward direction with the operations. Whether it is necessary to commit in those expanded spaces SS units besides the secret field police must be checked with the *Reichsführer* SS [Himmler]. The immediate urgency of rendering all Bolshevist leaders and commissars harmless speaks for such a need. Military courts must be kept out of all of these matters. . . .

(3) In the third section of the draft (guides for Rumania, Slovakia, Hungary, and Finland) matters will be handled through the commanders in chief of each country. . . .

Pacification has often proved to be harder than fighting and dying. It proved to be so in Europe after World Wars I and II. Yet it remains the forward object of all violence: to produce a viable peace favorable to the victor's policy. If Hitler's projected conquest of Russia was to stick, a scheme had to be on hand for swift and effective pacification. He knew this well, perhaps better than many of his warriors. The trouble came in the nature and conduct of his war. Here in the first specific signals we begin to comprehend the depth of the German political leadership's depravity.

Internal evidence of Hitler's own hand in these precepts already showed through to Warlimont, and all the more in the repeated changes that occupied ten days of rewriting and resubmission by L Section before approval of a draft that, while omitting specific mention of mass executions, merely entrusted "the Reichsführer SS [Himmler] with *special Führer-ordered tasks* which would rise out of the conflict between two opposed political systems." Thus Himmler was assured of a free hand in an operational area. On 13 March Keitel signed and released the long, rambling Supplement to Führer Directive No. 21, containing the above first version of that cause célèbre—*criminal orders*. Its labored production seems to have persuaded Hitler that he must personally do more to get his extermination thesis over. He pursued it in brutal terms with the Army leaders on 17 March, and culminated his drive on 30 March in a carefully staged 2½-hour challenge to 200 higher officers of the services in the Reichskanzlei.[2]

Führer conferences of the period lacked the old professional independence of the chiefs about what should and could be done in the field; the question had become more one of *how* something already fixed would be eroded or evaded. The Army immersed itself in the minutiae of operational planning; it encouraged an easier rapport with the supreme commander, and anyhow, this unlimited field operating was unbelievable and fascinating. No previous experience had ever approached its exhilaration.

Operation *Marita*, the forerunner, expanded in turn as Hitler again explained his wish to chase the British from the Continent. That this might require reinforcement of the 12th Army at *Barbarossa*'s expense worried him not one whit. Brauchitsch on 17 March reported his readiness for *Marita* Day, 1 April: Good, make it so! He and Hitler had rarely got on so well. The Führer even confided the contents of a personal letter from the president of Turkey. Nothing to fear from that flank; and as for Yugoslavia on the opposite flank, he gave no sign of uneasiness—never even mentioning her. Later in the day in a 3½-hour session with General Halder he mentioned Yugoslavia only to say that Turkey might be rewarded by a slice of

2. OKW Ops War Diary, pp. 233, 242, Beilage zum Parlament; H. Greiner, pp. 369–72; Halder, 2:317–38; Philippi and Heim, pp. 50–53; "Der verbrecherische Befehl," *Aus Politik und Zeitgeschichte* 27 (17 July 1957):431–46; Warlimont KFA, pp. 161–87. Warlimont was stuck with the unpleasant duty of authenticating on 6 June 1941 the transmittal of the document (meliorated, and provided with escape hatches by him) containing guidelines for the handling of Russian political commissars when met on the field of combat. For his connection therewith he stood trial at Nuremberg and was punished. His accounting of the circumstances, their development, and his part in them has the feel that comes only to a man "who has been there," which his judges and prosecutors obviously could not have. It is a feel for how things go on, and usually must, in staffs when its members have to implement or try to soften repugnant directions from on high.

land from Yugoslavia. *Marita* was to be carried through until a basis for "air control over the eastern Mediterranean is achieved." Plainly it was a matter of security for *Barbarossa*'s south flank. The line of thought confirmed itself when Hitler next plunged joyously into Russia. This had to go with stunning success from the start. He ranged from Finland to Rumania in detailing the deployment of the German forces. On he raced, to conclude with the picture that we have already noted of postwar Russia pacified: *"We must establish Stalin-free republics* [a new word] *. . . intelligentsia to be destroyed . . . leadership machinery of Russian state smashed . . . use of brutal force is demanded. . . .* Philosophical bonds do not bind the Russian people strongly together. They will break away when the officials are eliminated. The Caucasus, after exploitation by us, should be given to Turkey." The Führer was soaring again, as he always did when once worked up, and he revealed one of his pet delusions—that the Russian people would break away from their Bolshevik masters. Late into the night General Halder talked to his assistant General Paulus about the Führer conference (Halder, 2:318). Hitler was obviously stepping up his post-Russia drive toward climax. But who would know when it came?

Far removed from these disturbing goings-on, the Navy moved ahead at sea. To bring that war closer, Admiral Raeder came in the afternoon of 18 March just as fresh news from Belgrade arrived to sweeten the Führer's mood. Yugoslav representatives would come to Vienna for the signing of the Tripartite Pact on 24 March—a week hence and in good time for *Marita* Day. At last things were working out in that quarter exactly as hoped.

Though Raeder could then share the Führer's good cheer, his own thoughts ranged far to sea—to the western reaches of the Atlantic where the first heavy ship operations had scored; submarines alone had sunk a record 200,000 tons in two weeks. What galled, though, were the sanctuary zones enjoyed by American ships. Despite this, the war at sea was succeeding, there was no doubt; but the Luftwaffe was still off target: both Tokyo and Paris had reports that the "random bombing of nonstrategic targets did nothing but strengthen the British will to resist." Attacks on ships at sea, on shipyards, warehouses, armament factories, and transport facilities were what could hurt.

Apart from these failures, the Navy itself ought to have greater freedom at sea: Iceland and the Denmark Strait should be included in the closed zone. "American ships should be treated like all other neutrals . . . in accordance with prize law." Raeder was back in the errors of Warld War I, blindly pursuing war with the United States because he could think of no other solution. Hitler wanted to avoid such involvement as long as at all practicable. Then when a bit later the Navy chief repeated his plea for measures to counter an American beachhead in Northwest Africa by suggesting that the problem should be clarified "after *Barbarossa*" Hitler heartily agreed. In the autumn, he said, we will also force a decision on the Spanish Gibraltar question. The phrase "after *Barbarossa*" was gathering magical power, to which the sober sailor had succumbed.

One more point that Raeder raised has special meaning: the problem of Malta. At this meeting he made his first strong case for taking the island. By now it had been recognized that the Atlantic battleship operations had eased the British pressure on Mediterranean supply to North Africa. Seizure of Malta would complete the job. "The Navy favors its airborne capture as soon as possible," he ventured and assured the Führer of Luftwaffe concurrence. Hitler protested that more recent advice from Göring said the contrary. Malta had by this time come under fire from Army, Navy, Hitler, and Göring. The last two had made the decision negative. Crete received no mention whatever as Raeder ticked off the Navy plans for *Marita,* and Hitler confirmed that Greece would be occupied to the southernmost tip. Nevertheless, both Malta and Crete had by now been considered for airborne seizure, and thus the groundwork was laid in the German mind for a choice between the two.

Navy interest in *Marita* was of necessity shore-bound. The opportunity of coordinated employment of German air and submarine power in the Mediterranean against British sea power was there, but up to this time never tested.[3]

Over half a million Germans stood on the Bulgarian side of the Greek border. Only foul weather and Hitler could delay the strike

3. FC, pp. 27–36; Skl War Diary, 19 and 22 March 1941. An entry on the latter day ran: "The Führer-directed evaluation . . . of surprise U-boat attack against the American fleet in U.S. harbors has been carried out and reveals that . . . entry into American fleet bases and anchorages offers small prospect for success because of net barriers and counterbatteries." Admiral Raeder's meeting with Admiral Riccardi of Italy at Merano had not been very productive. Italy needed fuel for the expanded fleet operations that Raeder urged. He acquainted Riccardi with *Marita* plans which might increase Italian freedom of action. To Hitler, Raeder had also suggested that Foreign Minister Matsuoka during his coming visit should be apprised of *Barbarossa* plans. Interest in Japanese cooperation in the war was growing.

south into the land of the Hellenes. Yugoslavia on the exposed right flank was falling into line. On 19 March General Halder noted, "Yugoslavia to join Three Power Pact. British in Greece 18,000 to 20,000 men." Nothing to bother about.

This quiet content at OKH was jolted on the following day by an apparition from far-off Africa. It was General Rommel, bursting with expansive plans that ranged far beyond those of his superiors. Only three days before, the Führer had rejected von Brauchitsch's suggestion to reinforce the newly named Afrikakorps. Its mission was to fend off and buy time; certainly no offensive move until the end of May, when the whole of the 15th Panzer Division should be available. But Rommel thought far ahead; he wanted to open new possibilities in this new theater. His idea was to press for decision and he said so— not only Bengasi but all Cirenaica had to be retaken. He got little comfort and left to report to the Führer.

One role in which Adolf Hitler fancied himself truly at home was that of benefactor and rewarder of the faithful. So he held a pleasant surprise in store for the commander of the Afrikakorps. Shortly after Rommel's entry, the Führer decorated him with the oak leaf cluster for his leadership of the 7th Panzer Division in France. The exchanges stimulated by this opening were all in the general's favor. He returned to Africa buoyant and safe in his plans for branching out on his own.

This he did by producing victories, which exacted swift approval. He persistently exceeded his orders, and in a short two weeks his series of bold actions landed him in Bengasi and sent the weakened British into full retreat.

Rommel's reports were music to Hitler. That he grasped their influence on a new strategy a-building is doubtful; what he had was new victories! "His congratulatory message was accompanied by a directive for further operations," wrote the happy recipient to his family, "in full accord with my own ideas." It was April 1941. Much had also happened at home. Yugoslavia was in turmoil! Three cabinet ministers had resigned in protest over the pro-German stance. Serbia threatened rebellion, and British interest was reported on the rise. Still no official sign appeared to jeopardize the agreed schedule of signing in Vienna. German press reports offered nothing but cheerful notice of the approaching event at the Schloss Belvedere; one paper gave the time of signing as high noon on 25 March 1941.

True to the billing, toward midday of that Tuesday the many interested parties assembled. Hitler presided as the friendly, engaging host: Count Ciano stood in for Italy, General Hiroshi Oshima for Japan. In the background ring lurked four ministers from junior partners. Premier Cvetković and Foreign Minister Cincar-Marcović signed for Yugoslavia, under the wing of their German ambassador, von Heeren. Advice to his own government to wait had not prevailed, but Germany and Italy tendered notes affirming respect for Yugoslavia's sovereignty and boundaries and promised, moreover, to refrain from requesting troop passage. The beaming Führer led his guests into the adjoining hall to celebrate the event at lunch. Five junior members now had joined: Yugoslavia, Slovakia, Rumania, Hungary, Bulgaria. Only Greece trembled outside.

The German press trumpeted the news to the world: from Biscay to the Black Sea stretched a solid bloc allied to Grossdeutschland. Fundamentally, she was continental and land-bound, like her Führer, in thought and spirit. Nowhere did a press notice speak of the great Middle Sea that could bind the bloc together. Yet on the day before, Jodl had released a Führer directive "to attack all non-Axis naval forces (including those of Greece) in the waters around Crete." Here began the air-sea battle for the East Basin.[4]

Over the whole signing ceremony, Ciano reported, a benign humor had prevailed and time even permitted the Führer to review the favorable events with him. Then Hitler set off for Berlin to receive Japan's foreign minister, Matsuoka. Within hours the fair Vienna picture turned dark and stormy. Germany's Führer found himself crossed by his newest ally and put on a big show of Olympian rage.

What Ambassador von Heeren had feared came about. Belgrade seethed in disapproval. During the night of 26 March the government resigned and was succeeded by one under General Simović. Seventeen-year-old Prince Peter was induced to ascend the throne after Prince Regent Paul fled to Athens. Then the government sealed the borders and called the army to the colors. Early on 27 March the new foreign minister assured von Heeren that the signed protocol would not be repudiated, though he could not promise ratification of the Tripartite Pact. In Berlin the assurances proved of no avail, for by this day Hitler had pumped up a rage that had to be vented in crashing destruction.

4. At this time the German battleships *Gneisenau* and *Scharnhorst* entered Brest from their historic Atlantic sweep after sinking 116,000 tons of shipping. It was this sweep that had helped ease the pressure on the North African supply convoys in the Mediterranean.

All the energy, all the drive dammed up while patiently waiting and persuading the Yugoslavs burst forth to reveal Hitler the raw savage. It looked as if this turn was the one waited for, so swiftly and surely did he move. Quandary and self-debate were long since over: the setting, the chain of events, including *Barbarossa* in the offing, the victim—a miniature Russia—were cut to his order: no riddle England, hazardous Norway, or slippery Spain, but a sharp-cut, profitable drill on the way to Russia. The Führer passed out the orders. By mid-morning on Thursday 27 March 1941 he told his keeper of the thunderbolts, Göring, where and when the bolts should land. Had they talked before? Undoubtedly.

Göring, Keitel, Jodl sat before him, adjutants in the background, as Hitler sketched the picture. Keitel recorded:

Yugoslavia is a doubtful factor for *Marita* and even more for *Barbarossa*.

Serbs and Slovenes were never German friends; government was never firm in saddle.

The present moment is a favorable one for recognizing the state of affairs politically and militarily.

Had the governmental overthrow occurred later during *Barbarossa*, consequences would be fundamentally more difficult.

The Führer is resolved, without awaiting professions of loyalty from the new government, to make all necessary preparations to destroy Yugoslavia militarily and as a state. The attack will begin as soon as suitable means and troops stand ready.[5]

How far ahead of his day this man ranged in imagery of nuclear holocaust! The blows must fall with pitiless severity in blitz fashion. Turkey would thereby be held in added check, and thus the campaign into Greece would be favorably advanced. The services must meet all measures promptly in a commitment of such overwhelming power that Yugoslavia would at once collapse.

Time was of the essence for more reasons than one: the digression into Yugoslavia could retard *Barbarossa*. Without a quibble Hitler faced up to a four-week delay. This alone established *Marita*'s importance as a part of *Barbarossa*: elimination of Yugoslavia had become essential. A delay of nearly six weeks did result from all causes—Yugoslavia, weather, and others. In fact, *Barbarossa* could not have gained these weeks by starting earlier because during this period bad weather in the east would have mired any start. A goad

5. IMT, Doc. 1746 PS; see also OKW Ops SitConf, pp. 205–9; H. Greiner, pp. 271–78; Halder, 2:331; Jacobsen, pp. 227–29; GCB, pp. 20–24.

from across the Channel spurred Hitler on. Churchill hailed the change in Yugoslavia with pledges of full aid. She, he declared, "has found her soul." How aid could be brought to the distraught land he left unclear; but his assurance roiled Hitler against Yugoslavia the more.

At noon this same day, 27 March 1941, the Army chiefs were called in and Jodl alerted his L Section to stand by: "The Führer is resolved to destroy Yugoslavia," he said simply; "a directive is to be drawn up so the Führer can sign it this evening." It got signed. The day turned into another of those exciting postdecision heydays, whose repetition confirmed so much. All ingredients were on hand: power, spite, easy victim, and promise of maximum profit. Hitler fairly flashed and crackled with the brilliance of a well-laid fire.

He ticked off the detailed actions to his assembled military in one, two, three order:

(1) Speed up *Marita*.
(2) Thrust from Bulgaria toward Yugoslavia's Skoplje, to relieve the Albanian front.
(3) Thrust via Nis toward Belgrade.
(4) Divert necessary forces from *Barbarossa*.

The thunderbolt he held for the last:

(5) Main effort falls to Luftwaffe. At the very earliest possible time, knock out Yugoslav air-ground organization, and annihilate the capital city Belgrade by successive waves of air attack.

With his unfailing swagger Göring at once piped up: The 8th Air Corps can begin immediately from Bulgaria. Planning and readying such a strike takes time and precise verbal drill; he must have had foreknowledge. In a more modest, solid vein, the commander in chief of the Army promised written plans by three in the morning. Thereupon gang leader Adolf packed his boys off with the admonition: operation plans had to be in this very evening for signing. Somehow the trick got done. Late in the day Jodl issued the signed Directive No. 25; the number became the project's name—*Op 25*, one of the must ignoble of the war. For his brutal kickoff Göring had found time to affix the code name—Operation *Punishment*. The meeting broke up at 1430, so that the Führer could receive the Japanese foreign minister, Matsuoka, whom von Ribbentrop had been diverting in talk about sacking Singapore.

Hitler's interpreter reports how the ebullient Führer came through in fine form, cascading over his diminutive Oriental visitor in a shower of facts, figures, and boasts about German war success, especially against Britain, even in the Mediterranean where the Italians had experienced a little trouble, now corrected. The war was lost to Britain. She was looking to the U.S.A. and Russia for help. Germany aimed to destroy British hegemony over the Continent. Japan's opportunities to attack her in the east had never been so good—which thought, mixed with hints of German-Russian conflict, became the predominant note of the whole visit. Matsuoka admitted Japanese interest in Singapore—"attack would be only a matter of time"—yet throughout, he steered clear of firm commitment, while speaking his piece at length, informing the Germans of his talk with Stalin en route and of dickering with him for a neutrality pact. Hitler he praised Asiatically in response to a self-portrait offered by the Führer:

He [Hitler] had complete confidence in himself, and the German nation stood united behind him as it had been behind no one in its previous history. He had the necessary power of decision in critical situations; Germany had had an unparalleled series of successes such as occurred only once in world history. . . .

Matsuoka journeyed to Rome and returned to Berlin for final adieus. At these farewells Hitler came out with his strongest hint of trouble with Russia, as his visitor pushed off for Moscow. Accordingly, on arrival there, the Japanese took out counterinsurance with Stalin in a neutrality pact. It led to the curious anomaly of Russian freedom to transfer groups facing Japan in the east to the west for the relief of Moscow.[6]

Thus the Matsuoka visit, through linkage with Russia, also tied in Yugoslavia. Directive No. 25 for her destruction added little to what we know: *Op 25* would simply go alongside *Marita*. Two stipulations shed light on basic profits that surely counted from the beginning: (1) The southern segment of Yugoslavia was to be cut off to serve as base for the offensive into Greece. (2) Resumption of Danube barge traffic and output of the Bor Yugoslav copper mines were to be

6. Documents GFP, vol. 12, Doc. 222, p. 386–90; *ibid.*, Doc. 230, p. 405; *ibid.*, Doc. 233, p. 413; Schmidt, pp. 220–33. Schmidt was also the recorder of the preceding documents. Ribbentrop bombarded Matsuoka in several sessions and Göring added his bit at Karin Hall. Ribbentrop went so far as to say, "At any rate on your return to Japan you cannot report to the Japanese Emperor . . . that conflict between Germany and Russia is out of the question." These were almost the same phrases as Hitler used on seeing Matsuoka off.

expedited. In the field, the 12th Army, under Field Marshal List in Bulgaria, would have to carry the extra western (Yugoslav) and southwestern load until General von Weichs of the 2d Army struck southeast from lower Austria to join up.

The latest blitz brew was all but complete. One final touch did it: psychopolitical harassment. Hitler dropped it in the pot last, but ordered its telephonic release first so that it might become productive before the field operating got serious. He prescribed generously not from an honest soldier's book, but from his own cheap tricks of mob conquest by voice and suspicion. Every device for sowing division, panic, and terror by radio, loud-speaker, placard, and press was to be marshaled to the very front line: the German opponent was actually the pro-Serbian government, which in the service of England had loosed the fight against her. . . . German troops did not come as enemies of the Bosnians and Croats. Of course Churchill and Eden received special mention. A Führer letter apprised Mussolini, and other messages baited junior partners with promises of territorial rewards. Field forces reconciled their field objectives, so that by 31 March 1941, OKW could issue a final catch-all directive and timetable:

5 April: Attack into Greece—*Marita*;
Attack into Yugoslavia toward Skoplje—*Op 25*;
Air attack on Yugoslav air-ground organization and Belgrade—Op *Punishment.*
8 April: Attack into Yugoslavia toward Nis.
12 April: Attack toward Belgrade from region of Graz, Austria.

There was no good reason for this violence, strategic or other. For Hitler this probably was among his greatest hours, for it cleared up the last remaining doubts about *Barbarossa*. If to this point history lacked a gauge of his criminality, the timetable, built around Belgrade's extinction, furnished it. Up through mid-March he had wandered in private quandary, unsure. As *Marita* matured, the earlier advertised preference for quiet in the Balkans wore away and he managed to say the operation would go, but not how or exactly when. Operational problems that remained unsolved were left for his staff and the Army staff at OKH. Both were in the dark, and so was the Master. Events closed in to free him. British troops violated his continental doctrine by landing in Greece, and then came the Belgrade coup as an opportunity to decide for and act out a miniature *Bar-*

barossa in Yugoslavia. It was enough; he had stood the test. After 27 March he was firmly on his way to glorious fulfillment!

One more item of preparation remained: the grooming of his generals for their tasks. Savagery ordered against the Yugoslavs would test his officers for orders of an even uglier content against Russians. These orders appeared, as already noted, in the making as early as 3 March. He now gave them verbally in a lengthy tirade to top field commanders on 30 March 1941.

Criminal Orders: 30 March 1941

As a final journal entry for 29 March, General Halder could record, "Finish with deployment directive for Operation 25." Yugoslavia's destruction was all set. Early the following morning of 30 March he departed for Berlin to attend the Führer's *Barbarossa* indoctrinal assembly of high field commanders, over 200 of them. They began to arrive toward 1100 at the roomy assembly hall of the Kanzlei and took their seats in rows according to rank and command. A hush settled over the hall, an air of expectancy, though everyone knew East Plan was up for almost final review. These men had attended pep rallies of this sort before and were aware of their spirit and intent as a part of the Hitler system. The quiet was broken when they rose as he entered through a door back of the lectern in front center. The officers settled themselves and the supreme commander began his two-and-a-half-hour lecture.

As a point of departure he picked the favorable time after the fall of France, when Germany wondered why England refused to make peace. Hitler pointed out how foolish Britain had been: she had passed up her chance. He swept on with the course of the war: the poor Italian performance, and its help to Britain; then the tired old saw: her hopes rested in America and Russia, which could only mean she had to be struck down through Russian collapse. Since United States help could not reach a peak for four years, this was the time to clean up Europe. "Only so, if we first solve the land problems," recorded General Halder, in the only direct record, "shall we be ready two years hence with material and personnel to master our tasks in the air and on the world's seas." The present task was twofold: smash Russia's armed forces and do away with her as a state.

The speaker's build-up led purposefully to the main question:

What to do with the Russians? But for a bit he went on about their strength, or weakness, in tanks, in aircraft; about their limitless land, which would require concentration on those objectives that were truly decisive. "The Russian will quit," he said, "in the face of mass attacks by tanks and aircraft." Now he broke into the thick of the fight, knocking over one barrier after another, outsmarting the Pripet Marshes (in the center of the front) and foiling Russian withdrawal. The fight was finished. He got on with the why and what of the Russians themselves.

The answers came out with much the same sense as Jodl had imparted in words fresh from the Führer to Warlimont on 3 March (p. 117), but here extensively elaborated for the benefit of the field forces:

> This is a fight between two opposed philosophies. Since Bolshevism is a criminal society, it must be destroyed. Communism poses a dreadful peril for the future. We must make a break with soldierly comradery. The Communist never has been a comrade and never will be one. This business turns about a fight of extermination. If we do not take this in, we may indeed, beat the enemy, but in thirty years he will be back against us. We are not waging war to conserve the enemy.
>
> *Future Scheme of States*—Northern Russia will go to Finland; protectorates over the Baltic States, Ukraine, White Russia.
>
> *The Fight Against Russia*—Annihilation of Bolshevik commissars and the Communist intelligentsia. . . . A fight must be waged against the poison of seditious resistance to authority. It is not a question of courts martial. The troops must know what they have hold of. . . . Commissars and GPU people are criminals and are so to be treated. This will be far different from the fight in the west. In the east harshness will mean mildness for the future. [Parts of the last two sentences were annotated in the margins of General Halder's record.]
>
> Leaders must demand from themselves this sacrifice of overcoming their scruples.

Hitler thus raised two questions which involved the Geneva and Hague Conventions: (1) treatment of prisoners of war, and (2) treatment of noncombatants. In the verbal orders just given he sought to abrogate both conventions in the field of operations and for a private political reason. A punch line summed up his basic message with a favorite phrase of finality, *aller Zeiten* (for all time). This is a fight in which not only must the Red Army be knocked out in the field, but Communism must be eradicated for all time.[7]

7. Warlimont KFA, pp. 175–78, offers his recollections and probably deeper familiarity with the subject than any other person. His account agrees with Halder, 2:335–38, but Warlimont is more specific in Hitlerian terminology. The scene and

The Führer has shot his bolt. His listeners rise; without a word, he turns on his heel and disappears through the same lectern door. For more than two and a half hours no one in the hall has moved; no sound has been heard but his voice. These men have sat through his tirades before; they know his ranting. How much do they discount it? How clearly can they discern the enormity of today's discourse and its cause? An ugly cause that will become Germany's national cause—unless they renounce it, and to him, today!

At first, the listeners must have stretched, yawned, and glanced at each other, maybe sidelong for sizing up. Any professional who attempts to reconstruct and judge this event is bound to put himself in the shoes or the tired pants of these officers. What would he, himself, think or do in these circumstances? Would he rise up in anger? He has been listening with no great concentration as part of a captive audience on the defense, while the speaker has thundered on the offense. Let him thunder; that's his business. Action is still a long way off; who can tell how things will change by then, perhaps through professional command channels? Besides, who will control in the fighting field? Usually each battlefield develops its own rules. In the rough and tumble of combat the Laws of Wars suffer when both sides indulge in pot calling the kettle black—as here. There is little time for soul searching. By and large it appears unlikely that a spontaneous

its feeling have been discussed with him. He writes (p. 176): "Certainly it was Hitler's premeditated purpose to point up . . . the particular demands of a fight between two philosophies. . . . From this speech derived the Commissar Order (Kommissar Befehl) and the Decree (*Barbarossa* Befehl) about the exercise of martial law. For the former Hitler set guidelines [in his speech] that designated Soviet Commissars criminals and therefore not to be treated as soldiers or as prisoners of war; they were to be turned over to the SD [Himmler Security Units] or if this was impossible, to be shot on the spot. For the latter (martial law) Hitler elaborated his remarks to Jodl of 3 March; courts martial were to deal solely with troop matters. In his behavior toward enemy civilians the German soldier was not to be bound by strict interpretation of martial law or military discipline; on the contrary 'attacks of every kind by enemy inhabitants were to be punished by the harshest means, including immediate shooting without reference to courts.' He based his orders on Russia's failure to sign the Geneva Conventions, and anyhow, Bolshevism was on the whole a criminal society, as shown by the inhuman cruelties committed by the commissars and officials in Poland, the Baltic states, Finland, and Rumania. In repetitive terms he drove to convince his listeners that 'chivalry and worn-out concepts of military comradeship cannot be tolerated. This is a fight in which not only the Red Army has to be knocked out of the field, but communism must be eradicated' for all time!" On 13 May a decree issued on the relaxation of the rules of martial law and troop discipline in *Barbarossa*. On 6 June 1941 a supplement to this decree set forth the handling of commissars. They were not to be treated as prisoners of war, and noncombatants were placed at the mercy of the individual soldier. The decree came to be known as the *Barbarossa* Order and its supplement of 6 June as the Commissar Order.

mass rising against these verbal orders would take place. It just does not happen in a service gathering of this calibre. Who wants to instigate mutiny?

Evidence of protest rises from several sources. After Hitler departed three army group commanders and some army commanders—in short the top field commanders—approached Field Marshal von Brauchitsch, their commander in chief. They told him such a war would be intolerable. Brauchitsch so testified at Nuremberg, and said he replied that, while he agreed and could assure his officers no implementing written orders would issue from OKH, he would have to consider what the best course might be to induce the Führer to change his mind. From what he had learned about him, once his decision had been made and promulgated, nothing on earth could right-off induce him to retract it. Meanwhile General Halder proposed that occasion be taken during the afternoon session to acquaint Hitler with the unfavorable feeling, request he rescind the orders, and failing that, request that they (Brauchitsch and Halder) be relieved. This was the call. It went unanswered. The subject was never brought up during the afternoon. There are reports of heated arguments on the subject later between Hitler and his Army commander in chief. In most commands the objectionable orders were either ignored or evaded.

The peak of Hitler's drive to put *Barbarossa*, in all his colors, over to the professionals came here on 30 March 1941. The occasion's true meaning escaped the soldiers. He had challenged, and they, through silence, became committed, not alone to barbarous, unstrategic demolition of Belgrade, but to total annihilation of Russia. Apart from that, he had tested his own mettle, which to him, as to all men, mattered more than all else.[8]

8. OKW Ops War Diary, Beilage zum Parlament, p. 432, "Der verbrecherische Befehl"; Philippi and Heim, pp. 50, 51. To an outsider it seems as if Hitler, while testing himself, was here testing his men. A strong response from them might at least have placed him on notice that their warrior honor was at stake, something he had in the past shown deep respect for. On the other hand, his criminal tendencies had cropped up repeatedly. The most recent mass example was the sack of Poland and the brutalities visited on her people by the same Nazi system that he was now readying for Russia. The Army, in the critical days of 1933, had stood by Hitler. He would never have reached power without this support. From then until now in 1941 the Army remained the only powerhouse equal to calling a halt. But there is a war on. It is too late.

9. Power Balance in the East Basin

While Berlin plotted against the Balkans and Russia by land, major combat was occurring at sea in their Mediterranean approaches. Italy tested her power, at the very limit of her sea range, against Britain's Royal Navy. Superbly sited as Italy is for looking to the sea and acting upon it, in modern times she has never truly comprehended the opportunity or taken it. Her development of sea power revealed the usual myopic tendency of an inferior that tries to pull ahead through surprising performances of individual craft or specialized weapons—extremely high-speed destroyers or new magic with mines or torpedoes. France was the perennial rival, not Britain. Technology and training in large ships lagged far behind. But here again, prestige demanded big ships and ancillary craft, so that when Italy entered the war she had a fairly well balanced fleet of seven battleships (five from 1913, two new ones of the *Littorio* class), nine modern heavy and ten light cruisers, and destroyers, submarines, small craft in generous proportion. Mussolini had decided his fine shore-based air force needed no aircraft carriers at sea. Strategy for this fleet remained fuzzy.

Britain's Royal Navy and its tradition were greatly admired. While its presence in the Mediterranean must have entered Italian calculations, no countering solution even for Italy's home waters, had been worked out. Her sailors looked up to the British Navy, and the extreme thought of tackling it directly to wrest away control of the sea was as alien to the Italian mind and spirit as a like thought about the North Sea was to the German mind. Yet fate, prodded by Hitler and Mussolini, worked toward just such a predicament. Signs of it appeared after France fell: Italy found herself pitted against the most powerful navy in the world. Her sailors naturally took defensive refuge in an ill-defined policy of a "Fleet in Being."

Britain had posted herself as gatekeeper at either end of the sea: at Gibraltar and at Alexandria. The two strong points were about 1800 miles apart, a little less than the run from Honolulu to San Diego, or about four days' steaming at twenty knots. About halfway, Sicily and Tunisia squeeze the sea to its narrowest gap between Europe and Africa in the Strait of Sicily. Forces steaming from either end toward contact there would take about two days. One hundred and forty miles east of the gap and about fifty-five south of Sicily lay the tiny, indispensable British island base, Malta, doing its best to link east and west. Force H at Gibraltar and the Mediterranean Fleet at Alexandria each had two or three battleships, a carrier, cruisers, and destroyers to match. The two commands frequently made contact near the center to turn over convoys. The Taranto strike of November 1940 had established Britain's undoubted freedom to do this and to control the sea generally. But this surety was interrupted in January when Germany's 10th Air Corps began counteroperations out of Sicily against Malta and British fleet units near the strait. The Axis project of cutting the sea in two at the midriff and assuring combat supply to North Africa revived.

Relations between the partners were far from pure. Teutons were always telling Latins what to do and what they had missed doing; Latins were recoiling in resentment against Teuton condescension and criticism. The dominant note was mistrust. In February Admirals Raeder and Riccardi had met to establish a congenial rapport. Raeder sought to improve his leverage through his liaison chief at Rome, Admiral Weichold.

As Britain's Operation *Lustre* in support of Greece worked into heavy convoy traffic across the East Basin, German pressure for Italian naval counter-convoy action mounted. Admiral Iachino, commander in chief of the Italian fleet, himself wrote, "Something had absolutely to be done to counter British intervention on the Balkan Peninsula." Over and over the Germans pressed for attack. The refrain rose steadily through 15–17 March 1941, and culminated on the 19th. For on the 16th the 10th Air Corps reported an air torpedo hit on a British battleship west of Crete; on the 17th it not only confirmed the hit by a detailed description, but added a hit on a second battleship, making two disabled battleships. The reports indicated that the ships were disabled on 14 March, yet there was no follow-up to sink them. On 19 March Admiral Weichold, instructed by Skl, Berlin, submitted a conclusive memorandum to the Rome authorities to "set forth the views of the commander in chief of the German Navy" as follows:

Skl holds that only one British battleship (the *Valiant*) is fully operable in the eastern Mediterranean. Immediate transfer of any British battleships from the Atlantic is not expected. Nor is there probability of intervention in the Mediterranean by Force H. The state of British strength is thus favorable to the Italian Navy at this moment as never before.

The intensive traffic from Alexandria to Greek ports, through which the Greek forces [fighting Italian forces in Albania] receive reinforcement of men and materials, offers targets for attack of particular interest to Italian naval forces. Skl is of the opinion that the presence of an Italian unit . . . south of Crete would greatly disturb the movements of British transports, at least of troop transports, since adequate escort is actually not available.[1]

The memorandum nailed down that Italian action at sea had grown to major political significance. Here might be a chance to retrieve some of the prestige squandered in Albania and Libya.

In fact Italy's Supermarina (Supreme Command Navy) had already received the policy instruction from on high and begun formulating plans for a sweep south of Crete. So early as 15 March (the day after the torpedoes were supposed to have hit) Admiral Iachino was summoned to Rome from the fleet base at La Spezia for initiation into the latest version of a scheme discussed with him previously. On arrival, on 16 March, Iachino fell in at once with the new trend and departed for his command the next day, bent on overhauling his earlier designs. It is to be noted that he left Rome when Supermarina must have had news of the torpedo hits, but before Weichold delivered his memorandum. The plan he started developing postulated only one

1. Detailed to me from his own notes of the time and his private manuscript by Admiral Weichold in Germany, 1960 (Weichold WM). Besides his rich material and comment, the following sources bear: Iachino GM; Iachino SM; Pack; Skl War Diary, March 1941; Seth; Cunningham, pp. 325–37. It is noted that no battleship sinkings were reported, by the Luftwaffe presumably; only disablement was meant. Why did no follow-up attacks ensure sinkings?

opposed battleship, and she less powerful and slower than his flagship, *Vittorio Veneto*. On 20 March Iachino sent the older battleships *Doria* and *Caesar* out to exercise with *Veneto*, who had some test shots to fire out of her 15-inch main-battery guns. Skl noted the rising activity in self-congratulation; also that cruisers *Zara*, *Pola*, *Fiume* were maneuvering off Taranto. It all made wonderful news, eagerly devoured in Berlin. The Italian battleships shifted to Naples while their commander in chief made final arrangements in Rome. In this hum of excitement, 23 and 24 March passed easily; something truly big was under way.

During the early morning of 24 March a German plane shadowed and photographed the British Mediterranean Fleet, including three battleships, plowing its way toward Alexandria from a convoy-covering operation in the west. The ships took the plane under fire without success; it reached base safely the same day and so did the fleet. For the ships it meant simply a routine end of a convoy job, but for the plane, far more. Its camera contained precise information on the number of battleships at large. The operation just finished had begun on the 19th and must have been under planning and preparation in port during the period 14 to 16 March. So the three battleships must have been snugly moored in Alexandria instead of floundering with two of them disabled west of Crete. Pictures taken by the plane showed three battleships steaming smartly along in full combat readiness; indeed, they had fired at the snooper. Admiral Iachino wrote later (*La Sorpresa di Matapan*, pp. 51–57), "reports about disabled battleships, unfortunately, had no foundation."

On the evening of 26 March he "departed Naples . . . still under the impression that at Alexandria only one British battleship was ready for sea, though at Rome it was known that this view stood contradicted by precise evidence of 10th Air Corps photography." Although Supermarina forwarded the fresh news, which arrived tardily in the afternoon of 26 March, to the Italian officer in liaison with the German Navy, it failed to inform its own fleet. Admiral Riccardi seems to have believed that a flyer had erred in identification of battleships, because previous reports had twice indicated there could be only one at sea. So the report was not forwarded to Iachino. Possibly the operation was meant to go in any case. First, get the fleet to sea and let the situation develop! The pressure had been massive. Yet, left as it was, the fleet was cursed with a phony backdrop upon which it had to base its further action. The result was an increasingly unreal grasp of what was going on.

Intensified German overflights of Alexandria had aroused British suspicions by 25 March. "The unusual persistence . . . caused us to believe," Admiral Cunningham remarked (Cunningham, p. 325), "that some important operation by the Italian fleet might also be intended." Thus the two contestants plotted toward action at the same point—the Italians for intercepting a fat *Lustre* convoy south of Gavdos, an island 20 miles south of western Crete, the British for intercepting the Italian fleet at the same point. Far off in Berlin Skl's Diarist could happily record for 27 March: "situation appears particularly favorable for carrying out operations . . . against British convoy movements. . . . An Italian force (*Vittorio Veneto*, cruisers *Zara, Pola, Fiume,* two *Garibaldis* and three destroyer flotillas) sailed on . . . the 26th for the intended operation. . . . Intention on 28 March to operate in the morning twenty miles south of Gavdos. . . ." German radio listeners reported a volume jump in British radio traffic after deciphering a British air-reconnaissance message that virtually cried out: Italian fleet at sea! The Royal Navy's Mediterranean Fleet stood alerted. On the other side, Iachino could have reflected that off Gavdos he would be 450 miles from home waters, while Cunningham, if he came to do battle, would be in home waters, with the Libyan coast only 120 miles under his lee, and home base 300 more. The Italian was the invader, far from home. To him the East Basin had grown almost as remote as the Atlantic.

Though steaming into the Ionian Sea between lower Italy and Greece presented no novelty or worry to Cunningham with aircraft cover from Malta and his carrier, entering the East Basin was a decidedly new and dangerous departure for Iachino. He settled on two controlling needs for success: naval superiority at the point of contact, and adequate air support in reconnaissance and fighter cover.

For the first he depended on the 30-knot, 15-inch-gunned flagship *Vittorio Veneto*, supported by:

> *3d Cruiser Division* (heavy) with 8-inch guns: *Trieste*, flagship Admiral Sansonetti, *Trento, Bolzano*; and screening destroyers;
>
> *Cruiser Diversion Group Zara* (heavy), 8-inch guns: *Zara*, flagship Admiral Cattaneo, *Pola, Fiume*; and destroyers;

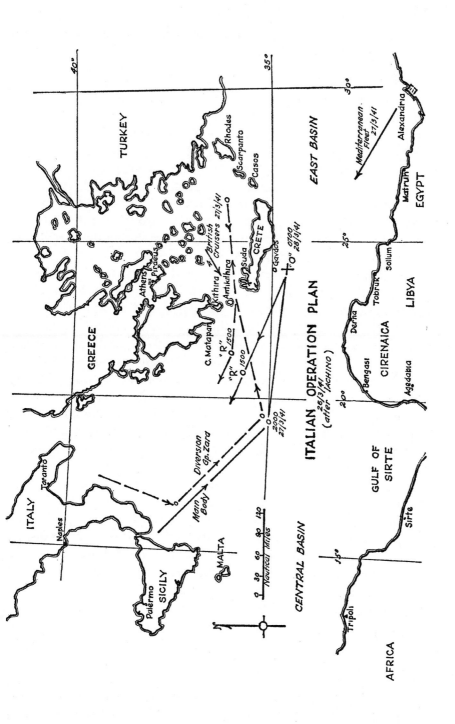

ITALIAN OPERATION PLAN
26/3/41
(after IACHINO)

> *8th Cruiser Division* (light), 6-inch guns: *Abruzzi*, flagship Admiral Legnani, *Garibaldi*; and two destroyers.

Veneto and the 3d Cruiser Division constituted the main body.

For the second need, air support, Iachino's situation was not at all encouraging. The unsatisfactory air support problem seesawed back and forth by telephone between the commander in chief and Rome right up to the time of casting off *Veneto*'s moorings in Naples at 2100 on 26 March. Apart from the inadequate short-ranged shore-based fighters themselves, their pilots lacked experience in ship-to-air communication and combined action. An attempt to improvise a system and drill it with German planes, through the detail of two Luftwaffe officers to the flagship, got nowhere during the early hours, and after that, poor visibility interfered.

The task force steamed at high speed toward Gavdos. Would it just stumble on a convoy? Or how was one to find such a prize? It seemed to be a forced effort without a target and no way of searching for one. In Iachino's plan the main body was to make for point "O" [Origin] off Gavdos so as to arrive there by 0700 on 28 March 1941, then reverse to pass through "R" 100 miles west of Crete at 1500, and thence return to base. Group *Zara* was to make a sweep into the Cretan Sea north of the island to its easternmost meridian, reverse, and come out through a point 40 miles northeast of the main body's expected position (point R) at the same hour—that is, establish distant contact with the flagship after the sweep. The orders intended attack on enemy traffic south of Gavdos and in the Cretan sea, but "in case of contact with an enemy unit, attack only under favorable conditions of relative strength."

Other things being equal, the cover of mist or dust would be a boon to Admiral Iachino as he steamed on southeast at 20 knots. At 0700 on 27 March, the 3d Cruiser Division, with Admiral Sansonetti, joined from Messina. The head sea grew heavy under a force-4 scirocco wind; visibility shut down to about 7 miles. The escorting destroyers labored in the heavy seas; Iachino wondered about them and possible retardation of his program by weather. What would that do? Were there fresh reports from the submarines stationed in the area to be entered? He signaled to Sansonetti for late news, his command having been the last in touch with Rome by shore wire. No, nothing at all from Rome. But by 1225 there was crucial news: Sansonetti observed a British Sunderland flying-boat shadow to the south for half an hour and then disappear in the east. It may have been the Malta aircraft that made the first positive contact report of the cruisers to Cunningham. In this poor visibility the plane was either lucky or well informed in advance, for it failed to sight the Italian main body farther astern.

Exactly this point puzzled Cunningham. What could cruisers be doing out alone? The message from the plane had three Italian cruisers and destroyers 80 miles east of Sicily steering southeast, roughly toward Crete (Cunningham, p. 325). Cruisers there might mean heavy ships near, bound for "the tempting bait of lightly escorted convoys to Greece." The admiral professed doubt of serious Italian commitment. Nevertheless he decided to sortie with the whole battle fleet that day of 27 March after dark. That he could wait so long was a mark of his advantage in time and space, and also of his superior Intelligence. He engineered a private cover plan by which he now went ashore in the afternoon armed with golf and overnight bags. The local Japanese consul general would be sure to observe this and make a safe report. In the dark of the evening Cunningham regained his flagship *Warspite* and sailed at 1900. She crowded a shore bank in getting out and picked up a condenser full of mud, which reduced her maximum speed to 20 knots. It irked the old sailor as he crowded on speed toward contact.[2]

Another cause for short temper was weak air coordination. On the day before at Suda Bay the fine cruiser H.M.S. *York* was knocked out by Italian explosive boats. She had to beach at the head of the bay. When her electrical systems then failed, control of the fleet air units in Crete failed too. Air operations at sea would suffer; surface craft would have to scout ahead. In such a mood Admiral Cunningham ordered Vice-Admiral Pridham-Wippell with cruisers *Orion* (flag), *Ajax*, *Perth*, *Gloucester*, and accompanying destroyers out of the Aegean to meet the battle fleet southwest of Gavdos at first light 28 March. Battleships *Warspite* (flag), *Valiant*, *Barham*, carrier *Formidable*, and screen were to steam northwest toward that same fateful meeting point off Gavdos. The resulting action might better have been named for the island. Once out of port, the fleet passed the night of 27–28 March peaceably enough under the beneficent influence of a quartering wind and sea. In our postknowledge grandstand seat we

2. Iachino SM, pp. 67–69, maintains that Cunningham had intelligence of the Italian sortie before the Sunderland report, which then merely confirmed data already on hand and persuaded Cunningham to take his fleet to sea.

can wonder if *Orion* Group will tangle with Group *Zara*—one inbound to the Cretan Sea, the other outbound. Supermarina Rome cut short any speculating. It told Cattaneo of *Zara* to join the main body. (He and hundreds of his men would have done much better in the Cretan Sea.)

Soon after Sansonetti's alert, the cryptanalysts aboard *Veneto* dashed Admiral Iachino's hope of catching the British off guard. They had deciphered the Sunderland contact report and amplifying data on his course and speed to CincMed. Therefore at 1400 Iachino changed to a more southerly course in the hope of eliciting from the snooper a report of this change in course toward Cirenaica. But the snooper failed to react. The main body and company resumed the old course and at 1930 increased speed to 23 knots on an easterly course. During the evening the admiral restudied all data, including the news that three battleships still idled in Alexandria as late as 1445. They could still get out in time to meet him. Surprise, he saw, was out, though *Veneto* remained unreported. What would they do? What should he do? He concluded that his sole recourse was to continue, despite loss of surprise and a "vanishing prospect of success." Far back in his mind lurked a yearning to call the whole thing off. Yet how could he judge all factors, above all, "political considerations?" At 2200 Supermarina took him off the hook by directing that his "program remains unchanged," that Group *Zara* (Cattaneo) was to join him at daybreak. Iachino was being maneuvered on a shore-oriented game board. Nearly all of Italy's modern sea power could be at stake, and for what? If not wholly political, the foray seemed like that fearless German battleship drive into the Atlantic—steam out and see what you can find. The Med was tighter and tougher. Everything now hung on Iachino; he was far from happy.

First light should reveal his entire fleet reunited. Reunited? Never before had it steamed as a united fleet at sea. Neither Cattaneo nor Legnani had ever operated under him at sea, and Sansonetti, 7 miles ahead, had steamed with him only once. Confusing reports begin to multiply. Iachino's obsessive thought is that daylight will find him in "the area assigned to be probed offensively." He thinks out his moves. Cattaneo he will put to port 10 miles off; Sansonetti can continue in the van. *Veneto* shall launch an observation plane, and cruiser *Bolzano* another, to scout out the area. Unless they sight some quarry promptly, the fleet will return to home waters. Finish. There was the plan.

Perhaps it was not so much superior Intelligence as confidence in a command of superior, well-indoctrinated ships in their own waters that gave Admiral Cunningham the edge. He plowed confidently through the night in the hope of losing ten shillings to his operations officer on a bet that nothing would develop from the Sunderland report. Just after 0800 on Friday 28 March he paid up cheerfully. His target had been sighted. *Orion* Group positively confirmed the shifting air reports of "the Italian fleet at sea."

At dawn Admiral Iachino had not a blessed thing in sight, not Sansonetti nor even the escorts. Nevertheless, shortly before 0600 *Veneto* launched her plane into the murk. A half-hour of breaking light brought the van and Group *Trieste* into view, and shortly Cattaneo with Group *Zara* in the northeast. The sea was calm. Fleet speed increased to 25 knots on an easterly course. The great probe was on. Almost at once, as though to gratify the hungry suspense, Lieutenant Micali in *Veneto*'s plane tapped out an urgent message. "Everyone crowded around the flag bridge," wrote Iachino, "to speed decipherment and to learn the news." "At 0635," Micali reported, "four cruisers and four destroyers in sight on course 135 [southeast] at 18 knots." His grid position placed the foe 50 miles southeast of the main body. Cruisers and destroyers lent color to the wishful thought of convoy prey in the vicinity (although good escort practice normally kept escort and convoy together). No one seems to have thought it might rather indicate heavy ships in the offing; only wishfully that here might be a real juicy target.

At 0657 Iachino directed Sansonetti to reconnoiter the contact at 30 knots and increased *Veneto*'s speed to 28 knots on course 135. He noted how these orders galvanized the men around him. Half an hour passed in silence. At 0734 he signaled the van: Upon sighting enemy retire on us. Ten minutes later he ordered battle stations, for 0800 should bring the target within range.

The ships Micali had in sight were, of course, *Orion* Group, fresh out of the Aegean. This young man knew what he was about. He found the target, made an accurate contact report, scouted out the supposed combat area to make sure he had them all, and returned to his contact, this time greeted by fire. He held fast to pass on course and speed changes and vectored Group *Trieste* onto the target. Yet at this crucial moment of almost "commence fire" he had to depart for a shore base in the Dodecanese because of low fuel. There was no provision for plane recovery at sea, and no effective provision was made for Micali's relief. The failure was decisive. A half-hour more of a main-body plane on the job, spotting the fall of shot, should certainly have told Admiral Sansonetti that he needed to close the range radically.[3]

Steaming in column for all he was worth on a southeasterly course, Sansonetti opened fire at 0812 on *Orion* Group, a little forward of his starboard beam on a near parallel course. At 26,000 yards the shells fell short; the target bore off and made smoke furiously. The Italians

3. *Bolzano,* of the Sansonetti division, apparently launched no plane; *Abruzzi* of *Zara* Group did, and the plane kept the target in sight for an hour. Spotting for strange ships in mediocre visibility failed. Iachino gives his reason for failure to relieve Micali. He wrote (Iachino SM, p. 94), "In reality, I should have been able to catapult them [planes] later . . . at opening fire."

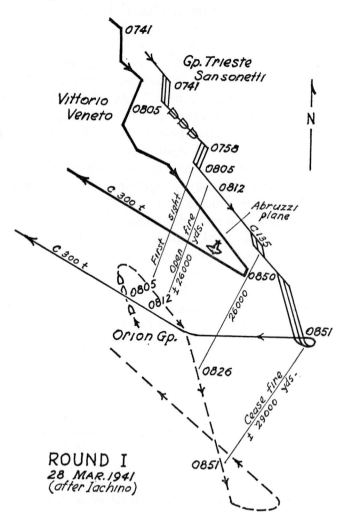

ROUND I
28 MAR. 1941
(after Iachino)

attempted to concentrate on the nearest tail-end British cruiser, little *Gloucester*, who snaked her course to escape hits in a sudden burst of 30 knots (a remarkable recovery from reported engineering troubles which were supposed to limit her to 24 knots). When the range had closed a bit, she steadied and let go three salvos; they too fell short. Courses were almost south, with *Orion* Group bearing off farther and Group *Trieste* still firing futilely. At this point, about 0830, Iachino realized he could not close fast enough to force decision. Why Group *Trieste* had not scored puzzled him, yet he could not have it rush headlong deeper and deeper into hostile waters. He wondered why British cruisers, contrary to tradition, had retired at all (if not to trap him). He ordered Sansonetti to break off and come around to 300 (northwest) "if unable to bring the target within range." Eager for first blood, Sansonetti hung on for a little while, then at 0850 ceased fire and turned off as directed. So ended Round I, a shoot of almost forty minutes without a hit.

When initial contacts fail to agree with preconceptions, they cause uneasiness. The Italians' initiative had netted them nothing. The British, on the other hand, had positive proof of Italian forces, but the chart plot was still badly fouled. For RAF planes mistook cruisers for battleships and British cruisers for Italians; they gave positions that refused to coincide. Cunningham, 70 miles astern and as puzzled as Iachino, increased speed to 22 knots and told *Formidable* to ready an air torpedo strike to relieve the pressure on *Orion* Group. When the smoke had cleared with nothing in sight, that Group turned northwest and reestablished contact on the three Italian cruisers at 16 miles. Just before 1000 *Formidable* launched her torpedo strike. Britain's sea power streamed northwest, unaware of battleship power just over the horizon. The truth struck in at 1059. Huge shell geysers splashed around *Orion*. She turned south sharply under smoke; a dim shape loomed in the north. Only 15-inch shells could kick up that much water, and they could come from only one ship: *Vittorio Veneto*. Round II began.

Likewise innocent of knowledge of the true British strength, Admiral Iachino had determined to try a little trapping of his own. At 1017 he initiated the first moves to catch *Orion* Group between Group *Trieste* and *Veneto*: the flagship circled gradually to course 150 (nearly southeast); Sansonetti was told to keep on northwestward "until further orders and be ready for action."

Much sooner than expected, *Orion* Group rose out of the sea to starboard just forward of *Veneto*'s beam. *Veneto*'s radio experts mean-while intercepted a British transmission: "Sighted unknown ship, in-vestigating." And *Orion* actually steered over for a look, flashing the day's recognition letters, OBI. To hold fire for the optimum range was Iachino's secret. At 25,300 yards he passed the word, "Viva il Re!" and let fly three fast ranging salvos. 1059 Friday 28 March 1941 should mark a high point of Italian sea power. Visibility was only fair under light northeast airs.

In one respect the shells that landed around the British ships scored a bull's eye without hitting—they achieved complete and fright-ening surprise. The flabbergasted British commander made three ur-gent signals and executed them at once: "Turn together to 180 [south]. Make smoke. Proceed at maximum speed." The maneuver produced an echeloned line abreast that again left poor *Gloucester* naked on the tag end. She soon became the object of Italian attention, and again in World War I fashion, she steered a snaky course and strained to keep up. Destroyer *Hasty* came over to windward to cover with smoke. *Orion* Group was in a tight bind, for Sansonetti had by now turned back to attack from the other flank. Soon heavy fire would come from both quarters. So far only uncomfortable near misses had splashed water aboard several ships. It was just a matter of time until some shells must crash aboard.

In Flagconn of *Veneto*, Iachino has reason to exult, even if his trap was sprung too soon. The foe must not slip out. One British ship disabled would boost the homeland prestige. Time passes and no change, except the range has opened. Sansonetti is still far back. *Orion* Group has turned into column and headed off southeast. Small chance of overhauling them! A new alarm, "Torpedo planes in sight." Air Force Lt. Colonel Farina, on board for the trip, identifies the planes as British torpedo carriers (Cunningham's relief strike from *For-midable*). They parallel *Veneto* to get ahead; the main battery ceases fire, while antiaircraft batteries concentrate on the passing planes, without effect. The planes circle and bide a time, and then suddenly break into two sections, diving low to come in on either bow. On they come. At 2000 yards they launch their fish. Fat, heavy *Veneto* lurches slowly into a tight turn, then picks up the swing with all 28 knots. The admiral struggles through the obstinate battle doors of his con-ning tower to regain his open flag bridge, where he can see. Ah, there they go, six torpedoes, all churning away from the ship. What a re-lief! He felicitates Captain Sparzani, who responds with feeling and, as ordered, sets his ship on the old retirement course, 300. It is 1130 and the game is up—at least for this side. Round II is over.[4]

But all rounds are not over for Cunningham, stomping the flag-bridge of *Warspite*. He readies for action, destroyers toward the van, observation planes to take the air, and more—all under the misapprehension that *Veneto* and *Warspite* are closing at 50 knots. Visual contact is due at 1240. But it fails. Navigational discrepancies between the flag and *Orion* have fogged the composite picture. The actual range to *Veneto*, when back-plotted, comes out 70 miles. The error begins to register about 1230, when *Orion* heaves into sight far off to port where, by flag reckoning, she has no business to be. A long stern chase is in prospect. With such dull promise the final round takes shape.

The sole hope is to slow *Veneto* by air attack to bring her under the guns. A second *Formidable* torpedo strike flies off. RAF bombers from Greece, even Fleet Air Arm at Maleme, get the word to join in. Shortly after 1500 shadowers from *Formidable* make firm contact on *Veneto*. Lieutenant Haworth arrives in time to report on the second,

4. Granted poor visibility and target maneuvers, hits were still due in the two shoots of 40 and 20 minutes against *Orion* Group. Group *Trieste* was at the edge of good hitting gun range. One critic blames an overlarge fall of shot patterns—straddles without hits. Iachino SM blames the British escape on his mistakes in establishing *Orion's* position for setting his trap. It thus sprung itself too early. The basic failure, however, was poor gunnery—no hits.

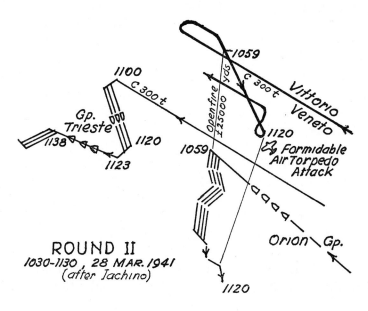

ROUND II
1030-1130, 28 MAR. 1941
(after Iachino)

the crucial, torpedo strike in accidental concert with bombers from Greece.

When the excitement of the foiled torpedo attack has subsided, Admiral Iachino calls it a day. His current cruising disposition would do for return. Group *Zara* out of sight 40 miles ahead, Group *Trieste* barely visible at 14 miles off the port beam, course 300 at 28 knots. After a couple of peaceful hours, speed is slowed to 25 knots to conserve fuel. All units have plenty of maneuver room against all forms of attack.

But what and where is the foe? Iachino had come to the conclusion that only one heavy British unit was at sea. For its location there were two answers: 80 miles astern and 170. He favors the latter, established by radio fixes, and pays scant heed to his adversary's probable intent, especially that of Cunningham. Iachino estimates the opposed force still as one battleship capable of 22 knots, one carrier, cruisers, and destroyers. The chances of reaching home port are good.

Then soon after speed is dropped to 25 knots the pace of action quickens. For from 1420 on, RAF bombers from Greece begin to work the Italian main body over. Without hitting, the bombs divert attention from a far more dangerous attack by *Formidable*'s second torpedo strike. It comes toward *Veneto* out of the sun on a quartering approach. All hell breaks loose when British fighters begin strafing the Italian formation.

The three torpedo planes dive toward the van while a pair of fighters clatter and bang their way over *Veneto* and escorting destroyers at masthead height. Taken completely aback, the ship gunners freeze dead under the strafing. The torpedo planes keep on ahead to about 3500 yards, there they reverse—two to port, the third to starboard—and then from three directions dive ever lower at the fat one. Admiral Iachino sees "the attack reveal its sudden and extreme danger." He lunges for the bridge voice tube; Captain Sparzani answers instantly, "Rudder already hard right." Again that eternity until the ship gets into her swing, gun crews still paralyzed, planes coming on. Hearts in throats, here is a high point. The three torpedoes hit the water; the lead plane "almost precisely on the bow" swerves a bit as it makes the first drop. "He demonstrates the greatest skill and highest courage." It is Lt. Commander Dalyell-Stead, squadron commander. A bubbly wake marks the track of his torpedo, running hot down the port side of *Veneto*, and like any sailor, Iachino casts a hasty glance aft. Will the stern clear? It is now swinging rapidly to port, as if to meet the torpedo. Heavy fire picks up against Stead close on the bow; to shake free he pulls up in a tight chandelle across the ship's bows, is caught broadside and blasted down. His plane lurches out of control, plunk into the sea. Almost at the same instant a deeper plunk from aft rocks the ship—the stern has met Dalyell-Stead's torpedo. Could he but have seen it!

Wounded *Veneto* turned slowly back to 300, straining hard. No one aboard noticed drops by the remaining planes. The one hit sufficed to throw out steering control and main propulsion. The engines turned slower and slower. Gradually a list to port and a trim by the stern showed; she was helpless. How could she last the night out?

Lieutenant Haworth, shadowing *Veneto* from aloft reported at 1552 "a large reduction in speed." Almost three hours of good daylight remained. The British command jumped at the chance: surface ship contact had to be restored, a third torpedo strike prepared, destroyers formed for attack. Orders spat out accordingly. *Orion* Group pushed ahead; *Formidable* readied a third strike, and Maleme Field too. But what might the chase lead into? Lt. Commander Bolt, the staff air observer, was relaunched from *Warspite* at 1745 to find out.

Time pressed harder and harder. The caged commander in chief would wait no longer. Without news from Bolt he released his plan for the night at 1810: "If cruisers gain touch with damaged battleship . . . destroyer flotillas will be sent in to attack. If she is not then sunk, Battle Fleet will follow in. If not located by cruisers I intend to work around north . . . then west and regain touch in the morning." The staff did not favor the plan.

Even before the signal got out, Bolt had his signal book crackling with images of the prey ahead, yet not without hazards. His first report (1820–30) had *Veneto* and destroyers on course 300 at 14 knots, 50 miles ahead of *Warspite*, or five hours until gun contact. Five hours? Two would be too many! Near 1900 with the sun setting he reported the ships bunching around the flagship in five compact columns. The bold plan for the night was under warm discussion on *Warspite*'s flag bridge. Was the plan indeed practicable?

Its bare words fell far short of telling the whole story: "Battle fleet will follow in . . . regain touch in the morning." But how? There hung the leap into the dark and into a melee that would make friend and foe alike. Then at dawn, to have the skies dark with German and Italian dive bombers! What about vulnerable *Formidable*? Would she be overwhelmed like *Illustrious* in January? In staff opinion the pros and cons balanced out strongly con. The admiral alone stood pro, and there he stuck. It was time for food. He went below, promising to test his morale during dinner. The thought kept recurring to him: "Having got this far, it would be foolish (or worse) not to make every effort to complete *Vittorio Veneto*'s destruction." She was the strategic objective. These are the musings that raise a great leader above the ruck. Decision for the night action held. The destroyers were ordered in to "find and attack the enemy," who was estimated to be steaming at 13 knots 33 miles ahead.[5]

At last light *Orion* and company sighted the Italian main body, hull down about 12 miles off. The cruisers watched the fireworks of *Formidable*'s final dusk attack. It was the time to hold contact; instead, the cruisers slowed and sheered off. Near this critical moment *Veneto* increased speed to 19 knots and slipped away into the night. By 2040 *Orion* had radar contact on a large ship lying dead in the water 5 miles away and a little to the left of the fleet track. The cruisers went on ahead. Of course, the dead ship could have been *Veneto*. (There was no way of knowing it was actually cruiser *Pola*, disabled at dusk by an air torpedo. As the middle ship in the starboard column guarding *Veneto*, *Pola* had absorbed a hit intended for the flagship.) The British battle line altered course toward the radar target, hoping to have the prize at last at bay.

Before sundown, when the hubbub over *Veneto*'s hit had somewhat subsided and she had resumed course at a reduced speed, Admiral Iachino decided on a compact disposition to shield her and to mass fire against planes and destroyers. But the concentration would also present an unmissable large target; some ship would have to get hit. And so it came about. Sansonetti's three cruisers took station 1000 yards to port of the flag, in column, Cattaneo's three at the same interval to starboard, and a destroyer column outboard of each cruiser column. The two *Garibaldi*s (Admiral Legnani) had gone home earlier. In the uproar of the dusk attack, followed by an increase of speed to 19 knots, no one noted that *Pola* on *Veneto*'s starboard beam had dropped out with a hit. A good half-hour later the commander in chief learned of her plight by accident. It was 2018 before he could order Admiral Cattaneo to reverse and stand by her

5. The Cunningham decision and what went before and came after have been talked out with my old friend of Asiatic destroyer days, Rear Admiral Royer M. Dick, R.N. He was on the *Warspite*'s bridge at this time and later became chief of staff to Admiral Cunningham. The decision was the admiral's alone. Whereas on previous occasions he had acceded to staff proposals, "This time No!"

with *Zara* and *Fiume*. Cattaneo skillfully maneuvered out and to the rear and with four destroyers stood down toward *Pola*, as ignorant of the pursuing British as his commander in chief. It could have been a peacetime exercise of bringing aid to a faltering comrade. Not a heavy gun was manned.

The evidence indicates that *Pola* was struck by the last torpedo fired from *Formidable* planes, the one from plane 5-A, piloted by Sub-Lieutenant C. P. C. Williams. Surely neither young Williams nor his younger observer, Midshipman Davis, could have had more than a dog's watch behind them in the Navy, or for that matter, in life. But they did their trick, and well. Blinded by searchlights, Williams dove in on the Italian starboard side through heavy fire. Smoke obscured the targets, yet he got steadied on his, the big middle ship, and let go at 1946, low and close aboard. His fish cleared the destroyer screen and struck *Pola* at the tender junction of boiler and engine rooms. Several planes reported the big middle ship hit— *Veneto*, of course. Another high performance was that of two boy pilots from Maleme. Only persistence and courage got them to the scene at all, and in on the kill—250 miles at sea in the dead of night. Afterwards they and all *Formidable* planes, except Williams, got down at Crete. After many high and low moments, Williams had the final low one: he ran out of fuel. Fortunately destroyer *Juno* was near; he ditched alongside and got aboard with his crew.

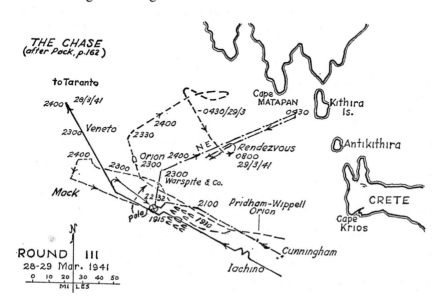

Meanwhile the battleline thought it had *Veneto*. It was 2111 when Admiral Cunningham turned his column toward *Orion*'s radar contact. Ships in column ran *Warspite*, *Valiant* (with her priceless radar), *Formidable*, *Barham*; two destroyers screened on either bow. Course was westerly, speed 20 knots. In less than an hour *Valiant* latched onto the target by radar and by 2210 identified it as over 600 feet long, lying dead 6 miles off the port bow. Old destroyer sailor Cunningham turned the ships together 40 degrees toward the target and ordered the port destroyer to clear the range. Climax was at hand.

Onto *Warspite*'s open bridge crowded an unwelcome company of CincMed and staff the better to see. No stars shone through the light mist; visibility varied around two miles in light airs. But wait: even in this crush a sound destroyer practice requires a sharp lookout by the No. 2 on the disengaged bow. Commodore Edelsten, the new chief of staff, kept just such a watch on the starboard wing of the bridge. He was not long at it when large shapes crept across his vision from right to left. Quietly he drew the admiral over, then Commander Power, an ace at ship recognition. He at once pronounced the second and third shapes 8-inch-gun Italian cruisers. Destroyer *Stuart* saw too, and broke the night alarm. A voice radio command to turn back into column (on course 280) was Admiral Cunningham's instant reaction. All targets were thus brought into a favorable arc of fire to port. Frantic moments while "Fleet Gunner" Barnard got all targets covered. They were Admiral Cattaneo's Group *Zara*, led by destroyer leader *Alfieri*, and followed by the others, *Gioberti*, *Carducci*, *Oriani*, all come to succor poor *Pola*. As the range shrank to 3500 and fire commenced, another helpless ship, *Formidable*, hauled out of column to starboard.

It was Cunningham's big moment, this one of high suspense. He does it justice in recounting how "in dead silence . . . one heard only the voices of the gun control personnel, saw the turrets swing and steady when the 15 inch guns pointed at the enemy cruisers . . . a calm voice . . . 'Director layer sees target,' a sure sign of his itching finger on the trigger." He presses it and flashless powder flashes red; the ship quakes; five big shells roar into *Fiume*'s guts. She is the third, takes the early brunt from *Warspite* and *Valiant*. With the first salvo, destroyer *Greyhound*'s searchlight falls on *Fiume*, shows a sleek silvery ship caught completely unready, guns trained fore and aft. The time is 2227 on 28 March 1941.

Zara and *Alfieri* come next, but live little longer. In five minutes, or less, these fine ships are blasted into hopeless fiery hulks; searchlights light up a welter of slaughter—men and ships overwhelmed by shock and fire. Elation gives way to compassion. *Zara* thrashes south in a full circle. *Fiume*, burning furiously aft, hauls right, stops, and soon goes under. Destroyer *Alfieri* (who appeared to be leading, but may have been coming up on the south flank to reconnoiter toward *Pola*), heavily hit, turns to starboard listed over, begins to make smoke to cover. Then comes her mate *Carducci*, also badly hurt, trying to screen with smoke.

These oncoming destroyers could intend torpedo attack. CincMed turns the battleships away together 90 degrees, spang in the path of *Formidable*. She squeaks clear as the battle line resumes column. Captain Waller in screen leader *Stuart* receives orders to finish off what is left with his *Havock*, *Greyhound*, and *Griffin*. The big ships haul out of the way to the north and then northeast as ordered by a

THE MISTAKEN KILL

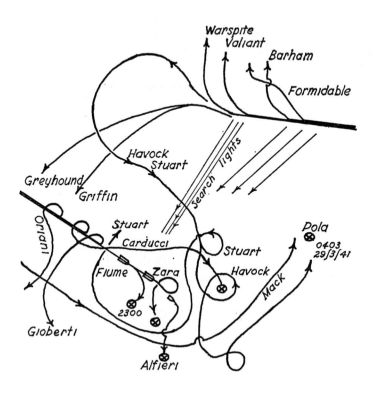

fleet-wide signal. Matapan's peak action had lasted five or six minutes, total.

Night destroyer actions are among the hardest to keep in hand. "Finishing off" here would require taut coordination. By the time the four destroyers received the fleet-wide signal of 2312—"All ships not engaged in sinking the enemy steer northeast"—they had been at their finishing job for more than half an hour, were widely scattered and ready to believe the job about done. The intent of CincMed's signal was simple: to clear the combat area for the destroyers and avoid their own ship tangles in gunfire and maneuver. Several close calls had already occurred—*Griffin* and *Havock* straddled by *Warspite* shells, then her searchlights and guns locked on *Formidable*. A common practice for clearing a foul-up is to order all ships to take the same course and speed, then to go about sorting them out and coordinating effort. The system failed here. *Greyhound* and *Griffin* chased phantom Italian destroyers westward, and finding none, took course northeast. *Stuart* and *Havock* made for the Italian cruisers. The leader fired all eight torpedoes at *Fiume* and *Zara*, thought one torpedo hit, and thereupon was forced to turn off by a charging Italian destroyer (possibly *Carducci*); *Stuart* then returned to *Zara*, decided she could wait until daylight, and took course northeast. Meanwhile *Havock* steamed off to get after the supposed *Carducci* (she may have been *Alfieri*). It is the way of destroyer night action.

Sub-Lieutenant Sansonetti, son of the admiral, served as *Alfieri*'s torpedo officer. He tells of his ship's combat and death at the hands of a British destroyer in terms that fit *Havock*. According to Iachino, *Alfieri* alone fired her torpedoes and guns. She was sinking. Her commander, Captain Toscano, assembled his crew aft, led a cheer for king and country, ordered Abandon Ship, borrowed a cigarette, and returned to his bridge to die with his ship.

Thus, further clean-up fell to *Havock*, Lieutenant Watkins, circling, on the rim of the arena. He had sunk the *Carducci* (or *Alfieri*) then headed south, away from the melee, and came on *Zara*. Four torpedoes failed to hit. Watkins then reversed course to the north to take the target under gunfire with starshell illumination. Instead of lighting up *Zara* to port, the stars disclosed a totally new target to starboard, large and inert. In a bridge atmosphere surely charged with excitement and haste, *Havock* broadcasted contact on a *Littorio* class battleship. Who could she be but the long sought *Veneto*? Near midnight the alarm rang through the fleet. Watkins then brought *Havock* to course northeast, maybe with the thought of awaiting further orders; he must have had misgivings, for he became convinced the contact was an 8-inch-gun cruiser. Perhaps some sharp-eyed *Havock* signalman had read the name lettered on her hull—*Pola*. Anyhow, a correcting message changed "battleship" to "8-inch-gun cruiser," added *Havock*'s own position and intention of regaining contact on the now less formidable target. When, after an hour, contact was reestablished, there were *Greyhound* and *Griffin* circling *Pola*, wondering what should be done. They had rallied toward *Havock*'s first alarm.

But these two were not alone. Captain Mack, far up front seeking *Veneto* with his destroyer strike force, reacted the same way. He charged southeast. That either he or *Orion* Group might feel bound to steer northeast before the job in hand got done never entered a staff or command head on *Warspite*'s bridge. Indeed, an intercepted night alarm from up front with *Orion* gave an impression that Pridham-Wippell and Mack were deep in their *Veneto* business. They nevertheless both turned northeast. The cruisers stayed on it; the destroyer boss queried the northeast signal and was told it applied to him only after he had attacked. He turned back west to his pursuit course, but only for a short time. By midnight he estimated his advance had outdistanced *Veneto* and that a southerly course to cut in toward her supposed position was in order. Hardly had this been set when *Havock*'s first alarm broke in. Captain Mack raced southeast. With every turn of his wheels he was leaving the Italian main body; at midnight it had been 30 miles north of him. Lost to mind in the cruiser carnage, the big prize had plowed placidly on toward Taranto. It was the British turn at lost opportunity.

Searchlights stabbed the dark ahead; about half an hour more and Mack's destroyers were threading waters that teemed with rafts, ship debris, and struggling men. It was the battleline arena. There was *Zara*'s hulk, apparently abandoned, burning feebly at two or three spots along the weather deck. The ships began picking up survivors from the sea on lines trailed over the sides. At 0240 *Jervis*, Captain Mack's leader, squared off and drove five torpedoes into *Zara* at a thousand yards: an explosive flame illumined the dreadful litter round about; a rumble, and she heaved over slowly, then submerged. Rescue work resumed and continued until just before 0300, when a recognition signal flashed in the east from the ships around *Pola*, about two miles off. Mack stood over. *Havock* greeted him halfway there and attempted to explain *Pola*'s situation: on an even keel, decks littered, demoralized men forward, some naked, some screaming in the water. Mack went close, looker her over, astounded his officers with the word to prepare to go alongside. As soon as the mooring lines were ready he put *Jervis* alongside. His terse signal to CincMed said, "Have sunk *Zara*, am about to sink *Pola*. Large amount of survivors which I shall be unable to pick up." Yet in twenty minutes *Jervis* took off all aboard, 257. Commander Scott, *Jervis*, first lieutenant, aptly described the closing scene (Pack, p. 151):

Casting off, *Jervis* steamed slowly round and illuminated the dead cruiser. . . . *Jervis* had had more than her fair share of the fun, Captain D [Mack] ordered *Nubian* to finish off the enemy . . . with a torpedo after toying with the idea of towing the cruiser back to Alexandria, some 500 miles or so. He reluctantly dismissed it owing to the certainty of heavy air attack next day.

Nubian made it with two torpedoes at 0403 on 29 March 1941. The Battle of Matapan ended.

Perhaps the battle took its name from CincMed's first landfall after the action on Cape Matapan at 0430. It is the middle finger which the Peloponnese thrusts south toward the islands Kithira and Crete. The battleline sighted both Cape and Kithira, took a fix, and reversed toward the appointed fleet rendezvous set for 0700 to the southwest.

The happy ships streamed thither, flashing signals and wisecracks; *Warspite*'s flagbridge joyously checked them off as they rallied round, signaling: no damage, no casualties, absolutely none! The flagship had not blasted one of her own destroyers after all. Their commander in chief exulted, "To our inexpressible relief all twelve destroyers were present. My heart was glad again." This may explain better than anything the plagued northeast signal.

The day was fine, course set for battle waters. They were easy to find: from horizon to horizon stretched a graveyard sea in a gloss of oil and litter. Rescue of survivors began anew and progressed well until about 1100, when a hostile plane sprang the air alert. That was enough; the fleet cleared out for Alexandria. All told, over 900 men were saved; Greek destroyers added 110, and a day or two later an Italian hospital ship 160. Her sailing directions to the spot came from a chivalrous message sent by Cunningham. He dispatched the message to Supermarina, Rome, via a plane from the fleet to Suda, thence to

Malta and to Rome in a broadcast. Over 2400 Italian sailors lost their lives, among them Admiral Cattaneo and three of his captains. The ship casualties we know: heavy cruisers *Fiume, Zara, Pola,* and destroyers *Carducci* and *Alfieri.*[6]

Lapses occurred on both sides. *Pola* was dropped, then rediscovered by accident. The presence of *Zara* and *Fiume* was not evaluated, and *Veneto,* the prize, was allowed to fade out of mind. Misinterpretation of intelligence and preconceptions took a heavy toll. Looking back on the action, Admiral Cunningham gave his appreciation of the difficulties:

Several things might have been done better. . . . Calm reflection in full knowledge of what happened is a very different matter to conducting an operation from the bridge at night in the presence of the enemy. Instant decisions. . . . In no other circumstances than in night action at sea does the fog of war so completely descend to blind one to a true realization of what is happening. '

Modern radar has ameliorated some of these troubles.

The Italian tally was grim—a tally to cap what seemed an irreversible trend: from Albania through Libya toward the Italian homeland, one stark catastrophe after another. Now the Navy sounded as phony as their Duce's bombast. The political foray that sent the fleet to sea led to Matapan and ended by publicizing Italy's total strategical impotence. What puzzled the Italians and Germans was the accuracy with which the British located the Italian forces at sea. Iachino believed word of his sortie had been passed to the British. Putting this together with evidence of fakery in the Luftwaffe claim of two British battleships disabled, he could find himself first tricked into going to sea and then betrayed to the foe by revelation of his going.[7]

6. Naturally, Italian and British accounts differ. One difference turned about a seaman's honor that requires him to sink his ship rather than let the enemy do it. Italian sources claim they scuttled their ships; British reports claim British guns and torpedoes did the scuttling. Undoubtedly, both contributed. The ships took too long to sink. On *Pola* and *Zara* men went overboard after a ceremony of salute and a cheer and scuttling measures. When the ships still floated after a long time, the men climbed back aboard, wrung out their clothes and in some cases warmed their innards from the broken wine lockers. Eager Britons who found them in searchlight beams, naked and uncontrolled, did not know the whole story.

7. Admiral Iachino (Iachino GM, pp. 186–87) tells of Mussolini's frank admission of the disastrous operation's political aim. The Duce's immediate, sympathetic understanding for the need of a fleet air arm gratified Iachino. Until one could be readied, Mussolini directed, "naval operations were to confine themselves to sea areas under Italian control . . . within range of our own fighter aircraft." To Hitler the result confirmed his own low opinion of Italian war capability. And for its part,

Matapan confirmed the growing realization that action at sea had to become an integral sea-air undertaking. For the moment the battle tipped the prestige balance in Britain's favor. Her position at sea seemed assured. Yet the Luftwaffe's power was on the rise, and its command was more convinced than ever that from shore bases air could control the East Basin.

A week after Matapan, on land in the North African rim, Rommel added his challenge by taking Bengasi. Cunningham stretched his fresh freedom at sea to the limit when in reply he dispatched Captain Mack to Malta with his four destroyers for action against Africa supply convoys. Mack's first opportunity came on the night of 15–16 April. He killed a convoy of five deep-laden ships and three Italian destroyers. One British destroyer was lost. On top of Matapan, this stroke brought the convoy traffic to a full stop. Among German staff-men, Mack's work roused demands for the elimination of Malta. Coincidentally, another island came under reconsideration—Crete. Which of the two meant the most to the power balance of the key Basin?

Skl, the chief proponent of action at sea, recorded in its War Diary, "In view of the complete failure of the Italian Navy, Skl finds it necessary to refrain in the future from any suggestion of offensive operating."

10. The Balkan Campaign

Yugoslavia (Operation 25) and Greece (Operation Marita): April 1941

At the other end of Greece from Matapan, on the Bulgar border, stood twelve crack German divisions, strong in armor and mountain troops, supported by a complete air fleet. They constituted the continental German answer to such things as ships, men, and seawater. Their might would go by land. And no doubt whatever existed in the mind of British leadership that the intent was to overwhelm Greece. Yet that leadership thought it best to persist in diplomatic agitation for a united Balkan front to scare the Germans off, or to do something more obscure. The end purpose was hazy. It could have been to encourage Stalin to join against Hitler or to encourage him to turn off into Russia and thereby save Greece—and, of course, England. For once, Churchill and Hitler agreed—Russia held the answer to the Continent.

During March 1941 Churchill wired Eden in Athens (he was by this time foreign minister), "Is it not possible that if a united front were formed in the Balkan peninsula, Germany might think it better business to take it out of Russia . . .?" Fronts and numbers of divisions fascinated him as though they represented real power. Eden had already been told, "Together Yugoslavia, Greece, Turkey, and ourselves have seventy divisions mobilized in this theater. Germans have not got more than thirty." But how could a Hitler bound for Russia tolerate a British beachhead on his south flank? Would it not incite

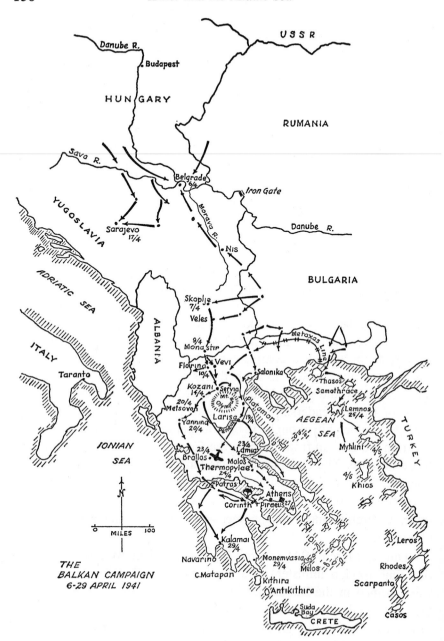

THE
BALKAN CAMPAIGN
6-29 APRIL 1941

German entry the more? Eden's mission had begun six weeks earlier: to sell the United Front in Ankara, Belgrade, Athens, and of course, Cairo to his own forces. He got a halting commitment from Athens, none from Belgrade or Ankara, and misgivings from Middle East Command in Cairo. He persisted.[1]

Hitler's target in the southeast had long been Greece. Her subversion or conquest would fill out his continental security in the south even as Norway did in the north. When the Balkan campaign plans at this time culminated in the welcome inclusion of Yugoslavia, a southern corridor giving perfect access into the heartland of Greece became available, as well as routes by which the Metaxas Line on her north boundary could be circumvented. This formidable monument to the general and premier who had died in January took off from the head of the Aegean Sea, ran inland a piece, then curved west for 132 miles to end at the sensitive junction of three countries—Greece, Bulgaria, and Yugoslavia. A lack of effective mutual defense arrangements could vitiate all of the sturdy Metaxas defensive strength. The Germans counted on cracking it by special troops and outflanking it as well through Yugoslavia. This was done when Germany ushered in the fresh 1941 season of continental war on a drizzly, cold Palm Sunday of 6 April.

Blows fell at several points, the most telling on unsuspecting Belgrade. From 0530 until 0700 bombs and bullets from screaming aircraft rained down on the city and paralyzed it. In successive waves Operation *Punishment* blasted the government buildings to bits. Left behind by nearly 150 planes of General von Richthofen's 8th Air Corps lay a mangled, nerveless mass of humanity in rubble. The toll came to over 17,000 dead, thrice that number injured, and a country decapitated in nuclear fashion. The outer cordons of defense quickly crumbled.

German ground forces exploited the paralysis to occupy the country and seize the springboards into Greece. From southwest Bulgaria, panzer forces drove up the Struma Valley to Strumica, beat off a weak counterattack, and early on the second day turned south toward Salonika, the key port of northern Greece. The German vanguard entered it a day later. In the rugged Metaxas Line they met tough resistance. The 5th Mountain Division, under General Julius

1. Churchill, pp. 4–21, 28–37, 56–77, 94–110, 168–75, 196–237; De Guingand, pp. 55–80; Long GCS, pp. 11–17.

Ringel, penetrated the Struma Valley, turned, and freed the important Rupel Gorge from the rear.

These specialist mountain troops will be heard again. At a few points the Metaxas defenders held against them for a week; yet with Germans in the rear and at the Greek supply base of Salonika, the defense grew hopeless. On the third day of hostilities, the 2d Greek Army, including all forces in eastern Macedonia, capitulated. Loss of the port and supply depot became fatal when the truly main source, Piraeus, the port of Athens, was wrecked in the night of 6–7 April. Luftwaffe attacks that night exploded the munitions ship *Clan Fraser* in Piraeus; the port's capacity was cut in half. Supply to Britain's still incomplete expeditionary force and to the Greek Army was cut in the same measure.[2]

On 8 April a race began by three armored forces, from northwest, northeast, and southeast toward stricken Belgrade. In the young tradition of German panzers, they charged on through two days and nights, stopping at nothing, putting wild miles behind them. The finish was close enough to a dead heat for each contender to claim a win. Actually, the northeast thrust out of Rumania, an independent armored corps under General Reinhardt, pushed the first contingent under the wire. It was a mobile SS patrol commanded by Leutnant Klingenberg that arrived on the north shore of the Danube across from Belgrade in the afternoon of 12 April. By great good fortune he found some pneumatic pontoons on the water front, loaded his men aboard, paddled over to the city, re-formed, and picked a way to the German legation building. There at 1700 on 12 April 1941 he hoisted the swastika colors. SS units were the Führer's own; their exploits had to be reported promptly or explosion followed. Failure of report about the Klingenberg feat to get through to Hitler immediately raised a hue and cry around OKH and the Führer battle headquarters, where he had arrived only the evening before. Already he was getting inside each unit's action.

From Berlin Hitler had sounded his battle cry on 6 April to the field forces and to his *Volk*, then delayed departure for the front until the evening of 10 April. By the following evening his headquarters train arrived at station Tauschen-Schauereck, near a tunnel, 35 miles northeast of Graz, Austria. There it rested at one end of the protective tunnel, while train "Atlas" housing the field echelon of L Section,

2. This reporting is based on GCB; OKW Ops SitConf; Halder; H. Greiner; Skl War Diary; Long; OKW Ops War Diary; Clark; Papagos; Spencer.

OKW, took up the other end. Army and Luftwaffe posted themselves nearby. Navy remained in Berlin.

Political disquiet accounted for the late departure from Berlin; also, self-debate over rubbing out a capital city declared open. Russian strategic reaction had importance. A tally at OKH showed the Red posture still defensive, yet capable of swift shift to the offensive. On the peninsula things were going remarkably well, and in Libya so was Rommel's drive. For diversion Hitler renewed talk of French collaboration, linking it to attack on Gibraltar, soon to come. The truth was, Belgrade's desecration could be evaluated best at the Berlin nerve center.

There were repercussions. A German surge on both sides of the East Basin shook United States thinking. Was it another total takeover? President and secretary of state denounced "the barbaric invasion of Yugoslavia" and promised aid (likewise undeliverable). In practice, the fresh emotions spurred aid to Britain. "The Battle of the Atlantic," superseding the Battle of Britain, would be won by a "bridge of ships," vowed the President. Transshipment of war supplies in Halifax became real; soon U.S. shipping discharged war materials in the Red Sea to stop Rommel.

In London, Churchill could do little more than flay Hitler and hope for the best. On 9 April he accounted to the House in a somber strain, though without loss of verbal imagery against prime target Adolf. "A boa-constrictor who has already covered his prey with his foul saliva, and then had it suddenly wrested from his coils would be in an amiable mood compared with Hitler, Göring, Ribbentrop, and the rest of the Nazi crowd." But what was wrested from whom? Again Churchill forecast a German turn on Russia; for good measure he threw in the pressing need for winning the Battle of the Atlantic. About Greece, could she truly be saved? He never said, though it was a strategic impossibility. Uneasy thoughts of another Dunkirk tormented Britain's spirit. Yet the possibility, even probability, of failure and evacuation had already by mid-February been accepted as Eden prepared to make the Middle East round. No professional leader could wholeheartedly subscribe to such a political solution of a strategic problem. It was bankrupt strategy, if it was strategy at all. What seemed to have been further ignored was the effect a double reverse, one in Libya and a second in Greece, might have on the world, and especially United States, opinion.[3]

3. Long, p. 9, paraphrases a 21 February dispatch report from Eden in Cairo on

Deployment into Greece looked more and more like a sorry botch—like Norway, except that there at least the offense was in mind. All the folly here would eventually tell in Crete. Greece could in no way be held, and no one knew so better than her leaders. They tried to say so. Their military balance, they realized, was far lower than the brave performance in Albania implied. Their courageous leaders, desperately short of war materials, plagued by primitive communications over wretched terrain, surrounded by neighbors yet more helpless, could hardly see how British aid, far inferior to the massed German power, could do better than invite disaster. Reluctantly they gave in to British importunities and even sanctioned an appearance of having requested help. The mix of propaganda, in the name of policy, backed by a strategy of withdrawal, passed its vagaries on to the operational field.

First where should a stand be made? Could the Metaxas Line be held to save Salonika? Since this port supplied the war in Albania (by routes across the top of Greece) and its own defenses in Macedonia, how could the Metaxas bulwark in the north be abandoned for a line the British preferred in the Vermion Mountains farther South? Such questions quickly became idle when the Germans by 9 April breached the Metaxas Line and took Salonika. Farther west a dangerous advance on Monastir Pass in southern Yugoslavia began. On this same day General Maitland Wilson, commanding Group W, ordered a switch to a "rear defensive line" running from the Aegean coast north around Olympus and west along the Aliakmon River, for a "protracted defense." General Papagos, who commanded in chief, agreed. Yet agreement on a line was merely map work; the real peril was north of it—a German threat to central Greece from Monastir through Vevi Gap at the Yugoslav border. As had been known all along, poor Yugoslavia had become decisive.

General Wilson's Group W included two inexperienced, undermanned Greek Army divisions and the latest BEF. Talked about for months, this British Expeditionary Force was still a hasty pick-up assemblage of Dominion formations, never before together, commanded

---

the sentiment of the service leaders; that it was better to suffer with the Greeks than to make no attempt to help them, though none could guarantee that they might not have "*to play the card of our evacuation strong suit*" (italics added). Churchill, pp. 72–73, quotes the same dispatch but omits the dirty word "evacuation." His phrase reads, "*May not have to play trump cards.*" Though sold by Eden, the professional leaders were unenthusiastic about the whole venture. By side remarks they leave the impression of having been pressured into bad strategy.

by a comparative stranger. Its order of battle ran: 6th Australian Division (Blamey), 2d New Zealand Division (Freyberg), each with some artillery, a British armored brigade, and an antitank unit. RAF squadrons already in Greece were to give air support. Planning, communications, supply, and general administration were heavily British Army. The overriding problem was command: over the Greek Army units, of course, but more important, over the BEF itself. Air, Navy, and Ground were three separate, inviolate empires. General Wilson's staff was the best he could grab as he shoved off for Athens on 3 March from his post as military governor of Cirenaica. His appointment to the BEF came only late in February. The Dominion forces thought that one of their own should have been appointed. General Blamey by seniority and experience rated the post and said so himself. Neither he nor Freyberg, also an old hand (as, of course, Wilson was too), was drawn in on the planning. When called in, they felt it was to be told, rather than consulted.

The threat of Yugoslavia came from the armored drive of the 40th Panzer Corps under General Stumme. He had cut west out of Bulgaria, took Skoplje and Veles, then headed south toward the passes. From Monastir, which his van reached on 9 April, usable roads led south 16 miles to Vevi and on to Kozani behind the once-manned Vermion Hills positions.

A few unhappy words will suffice to finish Yugoslavia. Her provincial patchwork fell apart piece by piece. In the northwestern lands of the Slovenes and Croats, key points tumbled before the advance of General von Weich's 2d Army out of Austria and Hungary. Zagreb, the Croat center, fell to the convergence of German columns. A separatist Croat government, which had already been formed, called for a cessation of resistance. Neighboring Slovenia followed suit. German forces regrouped to pursue the few remaining bands of Serbian resistance toward World War I's Sarajevo. It fell on 15 April. At Belgrade survivors of the blitz concluded an armistice with General von Weichs, to begin on 18 April. Twelve days had done it.

The lightning pace offered no chance for OKH or the Führer headquarters to take a hand, though both tried. Anticipation of speedy runoff had included authority for field commanders to accept bulk surrenders in order to spread area decisions wide. Forward units frequently fell enough out of touch to raise the tension index at the Tunnel. An unforeseen commotion superimposed itself on these disturbances and caused a much greater to-do. It was Rommel in Libya.

On his own he had veritably raised hell down there. OKH complained that he would scare the British command so badly it would cut troop transport to Greece adversely and reduce the prisoner bag there and its propaganda impact. The complaint carried some truth. Before Salonika fell on 8–9 April, Rommel had Mechili, inland of Derna on the coast, which he soon took, as well as a clutch of high-ranking British officers. Now he laid siege to Tobruk. In ten days Rommel had retaken almost all of Cirenaica, a big bag of war materials, and 1700 prisoners. The British command was deeply disturbed, and London too.

At the center of interest in Greece these southern alarms were remote foreign news. Locally, in Athens and on up the line, people worried over the German advance through Monastir Gap. Field Marshal List's two powerful prongs exploited their opportunities. General Böhme's East Force, already known from the Metaxas Line and Salonika, included the 8th Mountain Corps (with the 5th and 6th Mountain Divisions), the first such, in addition to the 2d Panzer and 72d Infantry Divisions. Just as renowned, General Stumme's center force, intent on Vevi, included the 40th Panzer Corps, the 73d Infantry Division, and the 1st SS Infantry Regiment reinforced and would be joined soon by the 5th and 9th Panzer Divisions. These two forces (Böhme—east, Stumme—center) packed three times the punch anything Britain and Greece together could muster. The comparison demonstrates the British folly. List had directed Stumme to cut off the 1st Greek Army in Albania from egress eastward and to drive south into central Greece. Böhme, in the east, would push south past Salonika along the Aegean coast toward critical Platamon and the Peneus Gorge beyond. Both drives would make marks, but Stumme's in the center carried the real shocker.

With luck Stumme could outflank any reasonable defense position facing Böhme on the east coast and at the same time rip central Greece wide open. By the morning of 10 April, he had a reconnaissance battalion of the SS Regiment forward in Greece. The troops poked at Florina to the west against light Greek opposition; farther east they approached the village of Vevi and met artillery fire from a south defile. The shells came from British guns. The first pitched battle was in the making.

General Wilson dispatched a hastily gathered force under Australia's General Mackay to counter. He directed his countryman, Brigadier Vasey of 19 Brigade, to organize a stand athwart the defile, just south of Vevi village. Vasey placed his 2/4 Battalion on the 3000-foot ridge that dominated the gap from the west, 1 Ranger Battalion astride the road in the center, and his 2/8 Battalion, still en route, on the heights to the east. Greek Army formations adjoined either flank. In support was an incomplete New Zealand machine-gun battalion, backing the Rangers, and farther south an antitank and the 52d Tank Regiment, plus some mixed artillery, which lobbed the first shells at the Germans in the north.

"Hold the positions as long as possible," said the Mission—"in any case for three days," in order to enable other formations to establish themselves on the basic Olympus-Aliakmon line for "protracted defense." A cold, snowy 9 April broke on the heights as march-weary Australians scratched and picked at their inhospitable hillsides. To judge the "possible" here or the tenure of "protracted defense" later was going to be hard. Provision for counterattack found no mention. These men had pushed farthest north of all—from ship to packed rail transport, to truck, and on foot without respite; and before the individual soldier fired his first shot of the war, he knew pretty well his end object was pullback. By morning of 10 April he could spy General Stumme's columns weaving south toward Vevi to throw him out. No relieving victory goal of this kind encouraged him. True, his position astride the gap was strong, but it was static.

In mist and snow of the next day, 11 April, German troops entered Vevi and probed forward. British artillery tried to interdict

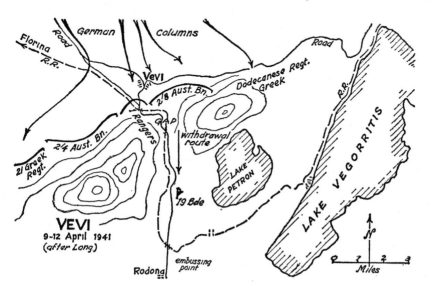

movement, but supported by their own artillery, the Germans continued jabbing. A late afternoon test assault in battalion strength halted under shellfire just before the outer posts. The probing measure held on into the night. Two of the equivocal three days were gone.

A definitive challenge started in the forenoon of the 12th against the already tested weak eastern side. After heavy mortar barrages and machine-gun fire, the gray infantry of the SS Regiment struck in compact squad tactics at the junction of Rangers and 2/8 Battalion. Both gave ground, and on the far right Greek units drew back up the hill. The defenders saw tanks and armored cars mill around in deployment back of the assault wave. At midafternoon the blow for decision fell. Hundreds of attackers, tank-supported, swarmed over the British right. Others came straight down the road. The British left stayed put, but the gap burst open, and the right gave ground. Artillery and antitank support interdicted the gap pretty well until evening. Then the right disintegrated, so that under renewed assaults all along the front, the Germans surged through. Confused British withdrawal began; remnants of 2/8 Battalion (about 250 men), all but one company of 2/4 Battalion (the missing company was ambushed and taken), the Rangers, and the machine gunners, all collected at the designated embussing point, seven miles in the rear. For British arms the baleful influence of withdrawal had set in.[4]

Pleased at the progress, Stumme turned the SS formation west toward Kastoria to block Greek Army egress eastward and ordered the newly arrived 9th Panzer Division to take over pursuit through Vevi toward Kozani in the south. Evidence of the British intent was in hand. It registered at the Tunnel too.

Two rearguard brushes on the road south during 13 April led to a furious tank battle, the first and last. Beyond Ptolemais, a sizable town halfway between Vevi and Kozani, prepared defenses had a natural strength on high ground flanking the southbound road; they included a tank ditch 500 yards south of the town and a blown bridge in a bottom farther along. The bridge site lay under the guns of Rangers, New Zealand machine gunners, and an antitank battery manning a line athwart the road. Brigadier Charrington with thirty some tanks in support commanded from a post three miles farther south.

4. Long, pp. 56–69; GCB, pp. 89–94. Both sources apply to the passages that follow.

When the commander of the 33d Panzer Regiment arrived in Ptolemais near midafternoon, his scouts reported the tank trap and the wrecked bridge. He decided to make an end run to his right for the main attack. The soggy ground dropped the tank advance, in full sight of the British, to a slow walk. Seven tanks stuck, but more got through to hard ground and brush cover. It was growing late. British armor started moving to its left to counter when of a sudden the panzers broke from their cover, guns blazing. Their course from the flank headed straight for Charrington's command post. Tanks of both sides milled around, blasting each other at close range; Bren-gun carriers joined in. Artillery flashes and tracers lighted the sky, when out of it dove German planes, strafing and bombing with a deafening clatter. It was the first air encounter.

Defense fire slackened; both sides were almost shot out. Under smoke and the lowering dark the defenders withdrew to the south. First Armored Brigade had expended itself; thirty-two tanks, some antitank guns and a number of trucks were left on the field of battle. Yet the German drive had been arrested: four tanks were out of operation, fuel was low, a halt was in order. That halt sufficed for redeployment of Greek Army units and the consolidation of Group W's Olympus-Aliakmon defenses. Consolidation may, however, be too strong a word, for by 14 April the feasibility of a "protracted defense" was in doubt.

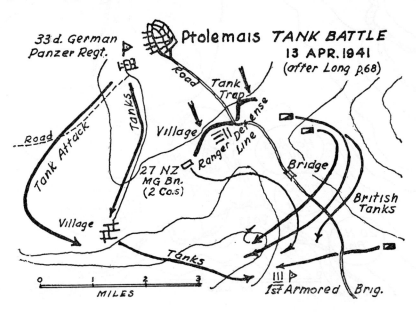

So early as 13 April General Wilson had made up his mind for an independent withdrawal to a Thermopylae line to cover evacuation. His command had only begun to make a little sense; casualties were bearable; hardly a half of the contemplated strength had arrived in Greece. No more was coming. The dream of a strong front in the Balkans was proving to be just a dream, as the unstrategic trump card of withdrawal began to take over. An unfortunate result was that many fine troops got their combat blooding not in forward movement to conquest, but in the degrading maneuver of hold, give up, and pull out. The troops had been given nothing to fight for. On 15 April Wil-

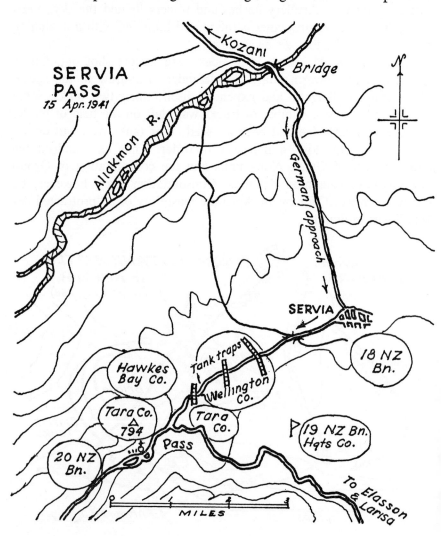

son ordered the commander of the Anzac Corps (Blamey) to conduct the retirement to Thermopylae. (We get ahead of our story.)

After the tank battle of 13 April, elements of General Stumme's 9th Panzer Division cleared Kozani and angled left toward the village of Servia and its mountain pass. At the Aliakmon River these troops came under artillery fire, but got over. Just beyond in the hills Anzac battalions were deployed to bar the way: 19 New Zealand Battalion in the center at the pass, 18 Battalion on its right, and 20 Battalion on the left. A determined German drive on 15 April failed to get through after heavy losses at the hands of 19 Battalion. These casualties betokened the first and biggest British bag of the campaign. It was an important action and went as follows.

Having crossed the Aliakmon, the Austrian troops of the 11th Infantry Regiment, 9th Panzer Division, took up the four-mile uphill march to Servia; on the road were knots of plodding refugees and retiring Greek soldiers. At the village a turn southwest heads the road for the pass three miles farther up. At about half of this way the New Zealand defense works began in the form of three tank traps athwart the road; they were covered by troop sections of Lt. Colonel Varnham's 19 Battalion. The troops had labored over these works in rain and cold since 10 April. They and the works were in good order on 15 April when in the breaking day the sentries at the first tank ditch heard the shuffle of trudging feet from below on the road. To a challenge the answer came back, "Greko! Greko!" More refugees. In the dim light Private Jack Barley found what he expected at the first tank trap—a Greek soldier leading a party of straggling refugees. Barley signaled them through. But once they arrived at the second and got down in its cover, fire broke out against the defense posts from the low ground in front of the first trap. The defenders had been tricked; they fired back and added a Bren gun and grenades. While this quieted the fire from forward, the fake refugees in the rear cut loose. Wellington Company's forward platoons closed in with tommy guns and rifles. The intruders began to surrender.

It took two hours before it became clear that the attack had been broken: an estimated 300 Germans had taken part and only about 30 escaped. Besides Wellington, Hawkes Bay Company (Captain Bedding) on the left had contributed importantly. Near midday another attack by a party of about 70 straight up the road was repelled in confusion, leaving some 20 casualties behind. And again later, after almost an hour of preparatory bombing, the 11th Infantry Regiment sent in a final bid to take the pass and failed: 19 Battalion had stopped the German thrust by the center task force at a decisive point.[5]

So General Stumme had to look elsewhere for an opening. He sent the 5th Panzer Division on a detour to the west via Gravena and Kalabaka toward Lamia in the south. For the moment, Larisa had to be left to Böhme's eastern task force. The western detour turned out rough and costly in time; not until 19 April did the van break into the open at Gravena. In another day it was knocking at Lamia's gates 45 miles south of Larisa. From Brallos Heights beyond, British defenders of the last stand watched the arrival and tightened their belts.

The eastern threat to Larisa by Böhme's forces was arrested at Platamon on the Aegean coast. It gave access to the Peneus River Gorge, which if pursued upstream, led directly to Larisa. The rail and road station of Platamon lies on the ancient route down along the coast from Salonika; it tunnels under Platamon ridge, whose rough brush-covered crest climbs inland toward Olympus from the ruins of a Turkish fort above the sea. From this elevation everything to the north is laid out—the approaching routes, the leveling land they pass through, and its fine curved beach. Lt. Colonel Macky, commanding 21 New Zealand Battalion, was to hold it against any Böhme intruders. Macky deployed his A and B Companies inland up the ridge from the Turkish ruin and his C Company still farther along, short of Pandeleimon village; D Company was in reserve, back of A and B. The men settled into their territories and defense works. Surely nothing but foot soldiers would try to get through here.

In midafternoon of 14 April 1941, General Freyberg visited 21 Battalion. He wanted to make sure the mission's importance was well understood: at stake was the security of Anzac Corps during withdrawal to the final stand at Thermopylae and eventual evacuation. That was the situation, but the general could hardly say so. Platamon had to be held. He wished good luck all around and headed south by rail for Larisa.

Hardly had he got out of sight when 21 Battalion's battery of supporting field pieces fired the first shots of the action. Germans were streaming over the rise into the level lands in the north. Böhme's eastern task force, had taken Katerini, 18 miles north of Platamon; thence one branch turned west and south for Olympus pass, and an

---

5. The account above is taken from Sinclair, pp. 71–85; see also Kippenberger, pp. 22–24, and Long, pp. 74–93; also GCB, pp. 90–120. German casualties at Servia were 36 killed, 72 wounded, 190 missing; 19 New Zealand Battalion lost 2 killed, 6 wounded.

eastern branch moved due south for Platamon and the Peneus Gorge. In the van putted a motorcycle battalion—unbelievable in this terrain, but there the noisy things were, deploying in front of Platamon ridge for attack on the morrow.

The dawn of 15 April was broken by artillery shells. They swept the length of the New Zealand defenses. German infantrymen followed and were repulsed everywhere but in the extreme west. There they lodged in Pandeleimon beyond C Company's farthest outpost. Nine tanks tried frontal assault up the steep slope in the center and failed. The position remained secure. The pressures of constant probing continued during the night; by morning freshly arrived German troops and equipment more than doubled the assault power.

Early on this new day, 16 April 1941, four loose columns of German infantry stormed out of Pandeleimon on the left flank, toward C Company. Under outpost fire the columns scattered, but quickly re-formed for renewed advance; the gray figures kept edging closer. They overran the outer posts one after the other. C Company fell back to take stock. Then tanks reached the top of the ridge to follow the infantry down its length. They soon ran on mines and stuck. "Every tank," noted the 3d Panzer Regiment's war diary "be-

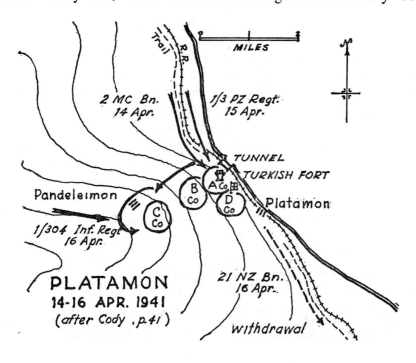

MILES

2 MC Bn.
14 Apr.

1/3 PZ Regt.
15 Apr.

TUNNEL

TURKISH FORT

Pandeleimon

B Co

A Co

D Co

Platamon

C Co

1/304 Inf. Regt.
16 Apr.

PLATAMON
14-16 APR. 1941
(after Cody, p.41)

21 NZ Bn.
16 Apr.

withdrawal

came a casualty and completely blocked the path." But the infantry columns kept on against C and B Companies. The field pieces that supported 21 Battalion were running out of ammunition. The odds were growing overpowering. About 1000 Macky found his position untenable. He ordered withdrawal. It proceeded as arranged toward the Peneus River mouth. Over the south side of the ridge the German troops saw the last defenders disappear into the brush. Before long the lofty battlements of the Turkish castle flew the swastika.[6]

The Germans had even found Platamon worth an attempt to outflank it by sea in small craft; they were to sail past Platamon and up the Peneus River to seize the only bridge crossing by the railroad at Tempe village. Heavy swells turned the soldier-sailors back. The railroad bridge remained an objective for both sides.

When Macky retired, he hoped to make a stand on the coast a mile below the ridge; it proved impracticable. Soon Brigadier Clowes appeared from headquarters and decided with him that a position on the south side of Peneus Gorge could oppose a thrust along the coast and up the river as well as one over the hill inland. Actually the Germans used both routes. Macky posted his companies on the steep south bank and established his command post in Tempe village at the upstream end of the gorge. The rail line ran along the north shore and crossed just above Tempe; one tunnel on it was blocked and a culvert blown. The road route ran upriver along the south bank after a ferry transit near the mouth. The historian of 21 Battalion tells how at the mouth the rope-hauled ferry had just got everybody over and the pioneers were about to destroy it, when, of all things serious or comic, "two shepherdesses arrived at the crossing with small flocks . . . and requested passage. The pioneer platoon took time off from the war to haul them over" and then dealt with the barge. Farther upstream on the south bank, opposite the blocked rail tunnel on the north side, the road was cratered to block tank passage, and a bit farther along, 10 Platoon of B Company took its stand to see that no tanks forded the river or passed through the road craters. Yet later, on 17 April, tanks did pass; they found a ford. Two stuck in the river, others in the soft ground alongside; yet many more made it across.

By that time 21 Battalion was well deployed to dispute the gorge. B Company's other platoons backed the road block and patrolled the

6. Cody, pp. 30–70; GCB, pp. 96–102. The 3d Panzer Regiment War Diary had noted further, "English shells crash all round . . . but the English do not counterattack." Thirty tanks were finally laboriously towed over Platamon ridge.

bank higher on the slope. Also higher on it, C and D Companies dug in on a line with the battalion command post at Tempe; A Company took an all-round defense posture just in the rear. When the near span of the railroad bridge was then blown into the river bottom, Macky could regard his position as strong and his men as ready.

But while it was still light on 17 April, a Platamon tank, accompanied by the ubiquitous cyclers, poked along the rail tracks as far as the blocked tunnel. Shots were exchanged. At about the same time the north bank far above the river came alive with small groups of mountain troops. As anticipated, they had come over the hill from Pan-

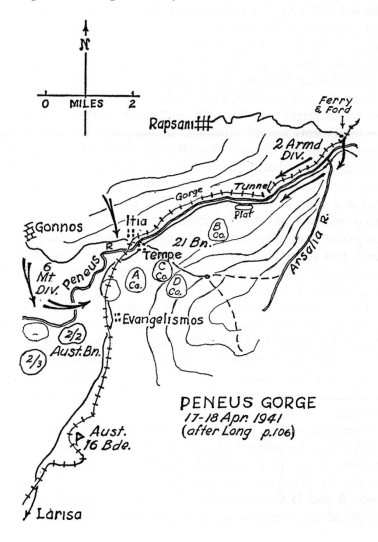

PENEUS GORGE
17-18 Apr. 1941
(after Long p.106)

deleimon. They took Gonnos town, a mile and a half up the north bank, west of Tempe. Lugging their gear and mule-hauling it, more and more of them arrived. Downstream they could make out a lone tank trying to cross. They prepared to cross over too.

Thus two heavy German threats developed, one upriver, the other cross-river. But defense reinforcements had begun to arrive: 2/2 Australian Battalion (Lt. Colonel Chilton), 2/3 Battalion (Lt. Colonel Lamb), and finally, Brigadier Allen, who had orders to combine with Macky in halting the astounding German stroke along the coast. If it should get through the gorge or over the river directly and on to Larisa before 19 April, a substantial part of Anzac Corps in the north would be trapped. The Australian battalions took up the defense of the river line upstream; 21 Battalion stuck to denial of the gorge and its road. A battery of field artillery and a troop of antitank guns joined. Brigadier Allen set up his command post at Makhrikhori rail station on the exit toward Larisa. 18 April would tell the story.

It broke bright and fair with artillery exchanges and mountain troop movements toward crossings. In the gorge the roar of battle mounted higher and higher with shell bursts, mortar bombs, musketry, and machine-gun chatter. Smothering the defenses was the obvious prelude to attack. About 1100 the initial probe across the river started at a sharp bend above Tempe. The mountaineers, wading and pushing inflated boats, tried to land. Bren-gun carriers from 21 Battalion joined Australian carriers in a charge toward the danger point between two Australian companies. Some Germans were stopped in the water, others after landing. The effort got nowhere; it may have been a feint for a higher-powered thrust farther up the river.

Thereupon more powerful drives in concert developed across the river and up the river road; for the latter, tanks and infantry had already negotiated the ford below B Company's crater block. Artillery preparation for a crossing at Tempe redoubled. Defense carriers again beat back the lead landings; yet others kept coming, and soon the tank advances along the gorge road crushed through. The landing succeeded.

Three tanks had got through the roadblock initially. The defending gunners waited for point-blank range and then let them have it. Two tanks fell out, the third continued, badly hit; others followed, but indirect fire by field guns "stopped them for some time." It was not enough. B and D Company defenders had been forced uphill, and when the advance resumed, C Company, next in line, could do little with rifles against armored cruisers. Here at crisis time seventeen of them drove on C Company; its survivors withdrew up the hill. Meanwhile the cross-river attackers had lodged between C Company territory and Tempe; another landing against the Australians upriver opposite Evangelismos got under way. Artillery now forced another pause, but the decision had fallen. The tanks made the difference.

A cratered road before Tempe still hampered the tank debouchment; tanks blasted the village in support of mountain troops clambering over the damaged bridge. A poor handful of men from the one New Zealand platoon still in Tempe got out to join A Company farther back. Battalion headquarters moved up into the southern hills where it could see the lead tanks overrun A Company and thus clear the gorge. The Germans were free to fan out behind the Australians. Yet Sergeant-Major Lockett in his Bren carrier rammed the lead tank off the road. The time was 1630 of critical 18 April. German entry into Larisa still had to be fended off. It was Australia's turn.[7]

About noon Brigade communication with Macky failed, and thereafter for over two hours the Australian positions were not heavily pressed. German tanks and soldiery had need of a pause. Near 1500 they fired up again in time for air support by about thirty planes; Allen's headquarters received special attention. He moved his post to the rear later. The tanks held through, towing their own infantry out of the gorge defile along the road and flats to the south. New Zealand 25-pounders knocked out several as they "milled around firing madly." One report counted ten of the monsters, then eighteen. There were plenty. "A group of fifteen or twenty men were round a tank firing rifles and LMG's to no effect. . . . The tank crushed two men. . . . The feeling of helplessness against them. . . ." Since 1700 retirement by companies had been under way. By now Allen's command consisted of odds and ends of infantry from three reduced companies, many carriers, some armored car troops, and two New Zealand 25-pounders. Around 1930 in failing light, five tanks plowed down the road. The two 25-pounders got busy:

The officer stood in the open directing fire, crews crouched behind the shields and fed and fired the guns while everything the enemy had was

---

7. Of course the Australians had already been engaged, but not as heavily and decisively as the New Zealanders. One reason 21 Battalion was "losing cohesion" was the lack of intercommunication. Each company, each platoon, was on its own. The wire means of command were left on Platamon. Cody, pp. 66–73; Long, pp. 113–25.

being pelted at them . . . a drawing by someone who had never been to war . . . the whole thing unreal. They got two tanks, lost one gun . . . pulled the other and their wounded out. . . . There was nothing to stop the tanks.

But approaching darkness did. On both sides casualties had been severe.

The toll for this day has not finished. If the Allen force felt good about keeping the Larisa road clear for others, German skulduggery was still able to block the British retirement. Men of the 2d Company, 143d Mountain Regiment, under Leutnant Jacob, crossed the Peneus on the battlefield's west edge in midmorning of the day and began a wide detour farther west and then south. By 2000 they found their spot on the Larisa road at a rail crossing about two miles north of the town. Abandoned railway cars, conveniently at hand, were pushed across to block the road; flank positions were established, and in them the troops bided their time. It came about 2230 in stiff fighting with the retiring Allen force and lasted past midnight. Casualties were suffered on both sides. One of Jacob's posts was taken out, but no one got through. The retiring troops had to find their way cross-country east around Larisa; a bad end to a good job. Jacob and what he had left boarded the van vehicles of the 2d Panzer Division and at 0700 on 19 April rolled into Larisa.

Mountain and panzer soldiery made itself at home with the generous British stocks. Units regrouped while revictualing and refueling proceeded. There was no hurry for the infantrymen, because from here on, mobile forces were to press the pursuit under close support of greatly expanded air power working from local fields. Infantry could hang back and take it easy. Böhme's eastern task force thus achieved its prime objective of opening central Greece. Farther west great advances were likewise being scored by the task force under Stumme.

It can be recalled that the 73d Infantry Division of that task force had orders to cut off the egress of the 1st Greek Army from Albania. From Kastoria in the north a long Greek Army column reached far back to the rear, where Italian troops hesitantly followed. In heavy fighting by the 73d Division, passage farther east was blocked. There was another possible outlet farther south in the Gravena region, which the SS Regiment reached on 19 April. It pushed on toward the mountain pass at Metzovon. There at 5000 feet a pitched battle developed. On 20 April the SS troops broke through and ended Greek resistance.

It was their Führer's birthday. A self-elevated general of the "Armies of Macedonia," General Tsolakoglou, opened parleys toward capitulation. The news flashed to Hitler's tunnel. Field Marshal List guided the surrender signing at Larisa the following day.

Even this pitiable ceremony in beat-up Larisa had to be run at blitz tempo because Hitler wanted no Italian involvement. Tsolakoglou helpfully made known that he would capitulate only to Germans. No Italian troops were in contact, and, said Rome, for the very good reason that German forces blocked Italian close-up. The Duce held forth to the Führer by wire and letter, and his language must have had effect, for Hitler began to hedge over approval of List's signed terms. List blew up. Hot words flew back and forth. In the field, Greek soldiers turned to killing Italians in their rear. At length on 23 April in Salonika the signing was reenacted with Jodl and Italians in attendance. British sources reported that Tsolakoglou, backed by his corps commanders, had deposed General Pitsikas, commander of the Epirus Army, which had done most of the fighting, in order to get talks started. General Papagos attempted to have Pitsikas dismiss Tsolakoglou; it was too late (Long, pp. 91, 92, 133). German records credit List with terms that included capitulation of both leaders of the Army of Thessaly (or Macedonia) and Epirus. The Greek soldiers, at Hitler's direction, were quickly released and allowed to go home; he admired their bravery.

On 18 April anxiety reached London too. The prime minister attempted to guide the actions from afar. He wired to the Middle East Command:

> . . . not possible to lay down precise sequence and priority . . . but the following may be a guide . . . extrication of New Zealand, Australian, and British troops from Greece affects the whole empire. . . . You must divide between protecting evacuation and sustaining Libya. . . . Crete will at first be only a receptacle of whatever can get there from Greece. Its fuller defense must be organized later. . . . All forces must protect themselves from air bombing by dispersion and use of their bayonets against parachutists or airborne intruders, if any.

These words make an amazing document, one almost good enough for a deep belly laugh, if it were not for the many lives at stake. Apart from frivolous meddling, the message reveals what a mania besting paratroops had become—a sort of bird-shooting sport in tall talk. Even in Greece, British commanders told off special reserves to deal with the birdmen. No sensible system developed. Another

Churchill dispatch a day earlier had cautioned, "We shall aid and maintain Crete to the utmost." In this context, he soon saw the advantages of holding a line at Thermopylae for two or three weeks to give Crete more time. Wavell transliterated this whimsy to the command in Greece: "If you can establish yourself at Thermopylae . . . no reason to hurry evacuation. Force enemy to fight . . . prepare to hold Thermopylae for some time. Will give more time for defense of Crete . . . and arrangements for evacuation." The thought from London through Cairo seems to have been that the ancient pass (gate) was still there to ease crucial 18 April 1941 along into another stand.

Of course, the narrow pass had disappeared long ago, and simply clearing Larisa on 18 April was not an end to the running fight. At midmorning of that day a 10-mile-long British truck column sat bumper to bumper on the road leading south, motionless, helpless. A bomb crater ahead was the cause. It was 70 miles to Lamia; if air attack intensified, the whole stretch could become one jumble of battered trucks and bloody flesh. Air attacks against the halted column did build up, but not with planned sense; some trucks were hit, some burned. After two hours a detour was devised; the column moved. Craters and renewed plane harassment continued, but inflicted no great damage. The attacks seemed individual and went on without creating a permanent block. The dangerous open road was cleared. What should the British do now?

Wavell arrived in Athens on 19 April just to settle this. The talk favored dispersal to evacuation points; yet it took two more days, during which the events at Metzovon culminated, to bring a firm decision. Evacuation was to begin, while a last stand was made before Molos, near what may once have been Thermopylae, and another directly inland before Brallos Heights.

On his fifty-second anniversary, 20 April, near the High Command tunnel, Germany's Führer received felicitations from Admiral Raeder and Count Ciano. Raeder made his Führer conference report for the period in these happy circumstances and extracted approval for keeping submarines out of the Mediterranean (there had been pressure to get them in); further, that the *Bismarck*'s planned dash into the Atlantic could proceed; that the mining of Britain's waters was to be stepped up by the Luftwaffe. Raeder explained the prospective division of Greek waters: the Italians would take over the west coast and Peloponnesus, while under Admiral Southeast (Admiral Schuster) the Germans were to control the east coast and Aegean. The Italian Navy had agreed to furnish ships and craft to Admiral Southeast for the discharge of his tasks. Crete, though not mentioned here, had crept into Luftwaffe gossip and would be the subject of a Führer conference on the following day. Hitler showed Raeder (War Diary Skl, 21 April 1941) that Russia remained the prime target, though he admitted she was friendlier since signing a treaty of friendship with Japan. This subject arose also with Ciano, as reported in his diplomatic papers. In Hitler's view, the Russo-Japanese treaty "completely counterbalanced any possible American action." As for the Mediterranean war, it could wait until October, which, like so many other things, meant "after Russia."

These pleasantries were firm convictions to the happy birthday child. Local evidence accumulated to show that in the Führer's view, the Balkan Campaign would end at the lower end of the Peloponnese, Cape Matapan. In the 12th Army, mobile forces rolled on faster and faster and their gratifying speed tore the Master along. He busied himself with making sure that adequate forces would get into Peloponnesus in time. His eye lit on the Corinth Canal and hovered there over the canal bridge. What was to happen to it?

Talk picked up. Could the Peloponnese become British sanctuary, even a bridgehead, if they blew the span behind them? Moreover the wreckage could later block the canal to *Barbarossa* logistic traffic. Records of OKW and service headquarters show Führer pressure for an air drop to secure the bridge intact. Admiral Southeast rated such a drop superfluous, but already by 19 April he recorded a Luftwaffe coolness to the plan, because it might jeopardize the airborne seizure of Crete—a suddenly revived idea. Here it is casually mentioned as though Crete were a current topic in the Luftwaffe. Army too was cool about Corinth; it took no stock in sharing honors with the single Luftwaffe airborne regiment deployed in Bulgaria. There the 2d Parachute Regiment reinforced, under General Süssmann, had idled disconsolate all through the campaign, waiting for a chance to light on Lemnos island in Operation *Hannibal*, which turned out to be unnecessary. General Löhr and his staff of Air Fleet 4, the campaign's total air support, favored the Corinth job, especially the chief of staff, Korten. Greece's collapse heightened interest yet more, and then, at a stroke, on 21 April, Operation *Crete* officially entered the arena. General Kurt Student, the Airborne leader, presented to Hitler his own scheme for the island's swift conquest. Approval of Student's plan may have made a Corinth drop all the more attractive to Hitler as a convenient test of Airborne capability. The next day, 22 April, without notice to Student, Hitler had Keitel order the Corinth operation to be prepared.[8]

Despite the lapse of Operation *Hannibal*, interest in islands climbed high, as it always does for soldiers in sight of the sea. Close reconnaissance revealed those of the Aegean free and ungarrisoned. About 10 April the 164th Infantry Division, charged with the Aegean coastal defense, initiated a mass march down to the sea in ships. Its troops commandeered all manner of craft from the Thracian shore south and organized them into flotillas. On 16 April this brand-new navy descended on Thasos and Samothrace and took over. By 25 April the flotillas were sailing against Lemnos, the cause of it all, then Mytilene and Chios, close off Turkey. With Airborne aid, a little later the larger Cyclades and Sporades were occupied, and eventually those steppingstones to Crete, Kithira and Antikithira. Fabled Melos at the top of the Cretan Sea roused enough publicity as a takeoff point toward Crete to rival its fame of old.

Back on the mainland at the origin of another great name, Thermopylae, Anzac forces gathered to make a last stand above Athens. But there could be no gateway defense on the sea in the ancient tradition, for the land had filled into the sea and greatly widened the gate. Access south had nevertheless to be blocked for a time. The designated troops passed through Lamia, below Larisa, on the north-south road. It splits just south of the town into a main and a coastal branch. The main branch with its paralleling rail track mounts due south into the central hills through 14 miles to Brallos Pass. One blocking position would be nearby at Skamnos, 3 miles short of Brallos. The coastal road branch runs south 10 miles and then east another 8 miles along the coast to Molos town, where the other wing block was to be thrown up. For a little while the two wings, hill and coastal, had been connected by a continuous defense line up through the foothills. Freyberg with his 5 and 6 Brigades was to hold from Molos up to Skamnos, which Brigadier Vasey of 19 Australian Brigade would hold. By 19 April the line was manned; but 5 Brigade's departure for embarkation on 23 April left the foothills in the middle bare. The two wing rearguard blocks (Vasey in the hills and Barrow-

8. Student to Ansel (Germany, 1960) and in later correspondence; OKW Ops SitConf, p. 237; Admiral Southeast to Skl, 19 April 1941; Halder, 2:376, 380.

clough of 6 New Zealand Brigade on the shore) remained, and so did General Freyberg. He maintained his headquarters on the coastal branch 10 miles south of Molos.

Luftwaffe reports of late 21 April designated the Anzac positions as "light fieldworks still building, supported by very strong artillery." More newsworthy, the planes also reported evacuation activity; twenty-four large and over forty small vessels were standing by to load, off the southern ports. Thus on 22 April from captured Greek airfields a long-overdue air offensive against ships and ports erupted. In perfect visibility, unhindered by opposition, bombs and bullets poured down from 8th Air Corps planes on the hapless targets in Piraeus (already a shambles from the ammunition ship explosion), in Salamis, and in Chalcis. Twenty-three ships sank, and the RAF was reduced to impotence. This was of the greatest strategic consequence. The battered RAF remnants first withdrew to Argos in the Peloponnese. There German planes caught them on the ground and scored the second big bag of the week, thirteen fighters. A few survivors flew out to Crete. Overwhelming German air power could now assert it-

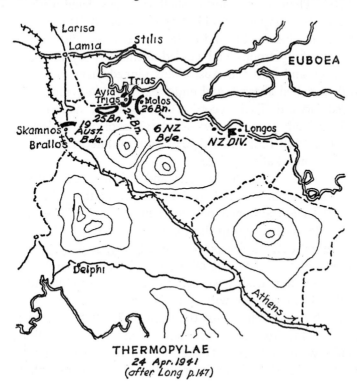

THERMOPYLAE
24 Apr. 1941
(after Long p.147)

self with mounting success. Another turn in Mediterranean fortunes had been decided. At the time this hint of finality passed unnoticed.

The Luftwaffe planes had also struck at the rearguard stands, in Skamnos and Molos. Meanwhile, detachments of the 5th Panzer Division moved down the main road; but defense artillery held them off. The German trouble was one of overcrowding in Lamia; the town was so jammed with armor, artillery, and troops that nothing could move. Somehow four medium guns got clear to duel with the defense artillery. Then, slowly, offensive moves in the pattern of Platamon and Peneus Gorge took shape. Two battalions of Colonel Jais's 141st Mountain Regiment, supported by the 55th Cyclers, approached the Skamnos position, while the familiar combination of tanks and cyclers advanced on Molos. The final pitched battles in Greece were about to begin. It was 23 April.

Early in the day 65 Stukas made 125 bombing dives at Skamnos where Major Sandover's 2/11 Battalion was dug in; Lt. Colonel Campbell's 2/1 Battalion secured either flank. But the air show, which had done no particular damage, was not followed by ground attack until 1700. Then heavy mortar shelling struck Sandover's left, and soon the center company was blasting Germans at 30 yards. Sandover moved his line back a bit and called up reserves. The position held.

The attacking troops had guided themselves by the sunken rail right-of-way, and in it the Australians pinned them; other mountain troops then pulled abreast, and under extra mortar support the whole lot moved forward. Their records claim Skamnos taken at 1800. Actually, 19 Brigade executed a well-ordered leapfrog withdrawal, which began about 1900 (corrected time). An hour later it moved out from Brallos for embarkation points.

On the other wing, 6 New Zealand Brigade's 25 Battalion held the south side of the coastal road branch from the point of turning east; 24 Battalion adjoined on the right, around village Ayia Tria; and 26 Battalion backed up the forward two from Molos.

"The great defense fire power" in artillery, said the German records, hindered their lowland effort. On the afternoon of 24 April, however, mountain troops worked through the foothills toward the unclosed hole in concert with a tank-supported cycler thrust along the coastal branch, right across the front of 25 Battalion. At the halfway mark of the front the attack stalled under heavy shelling. Fourteen tanks were in flames. Higher up on the open flank the wing companies of 25 Battalion felt enfilading fire from mountain troops creeping around the flank. The defenders swung back in an elbow, and there they held. The other two battalions hardly fired a shot. It was growing dark. Amidst these actions, General Freyberg received personal orders to proceed to an embarkation point. He replied he was "being attacked by tanks, while fighting a battle on a two-brigade front" and ignored the orders. Shortly before midnight 6 Brigade's convoy with the general aboard moved out of Molos for embarkation; just where this might be, was uncertain.[9]

The trump card has fallen. All Anzac is now evacuation bound. Official word to the troops did not circulate until 22 April. Various sources speak of troop chagrin and even surprise. Various explanations are offered: a wish to spare Greece more havoc, Greek failure in the field, Greek surrender in the west—thereafter what is left but to get out? All of it was unfair to Greece. The true reason for pullout was more British than Greek. At root lay a British political adventure that began long before 22 April 1941.

By this time (22 April) Hitler had already ordered the airborne seizure of the Corinth Canal bridge. Swift execution could throw a giant monkey wrench into the evacuation program. Genial General Süssmann, commander of the 7th Parachute Troop Division—he was an army convert to airborne—had at his disposal in lower Bulgaria a forward echelon of two parachute troop battalions under Colonel Sturm, a few engineers, and other support units. For transport, about 300 three-engined Ju-52's stood ready. When Operation *Hannibal* fell out, this task group lost its only chance for distinction. Süssmann jumped into the new chance with a will. There had been rumors and some just-in-case planning. He pushed this quickly to a finish. At dawn 25 April the Ju's in Bulgaria revved up with full troop loads and gear aboard; they took off and landed in Larisa. Now a wait for the final word, which came that night. This stodgy army campaign— at last a break for airborne!

To meet an H-hour of 0700 over the bridge, some 170 miles south, takeoff on 26 April had to begin at 0500 with first light. All planes got off in swirling clouds of dust, formed a loose column of threes (V's) and headed southwest. A few specially rigged craft towed gliders for pinpoint targets, such as antiaircraft batteries. Forty minutes out, the ponderous crates labor over the south end of the Pindus

9. Puttick, pp. 49–64; Burdon, pp. 30–53; OKW Ops SitConf, pp. 238–43; Halder, 2:373–77.

Range. They are making good a little over 110 miles per hour. The reckoning still shows it over an hour to the drop zone.

Squally gusts rise from the mountains; one plane is caught in a downdraft, crashes into the hills with all aboard. Over the crest the Transport Squadron commander, Colonel Rüdiger von Heyking, takes a southerly course and soon sights what he wants, the Gulf of Corinth, for the final over-water approach from the west. Altitude sinks to wave-skipping level along the gulf's southern shore. Aim is the canal cut. Its marks are unmistakable: a high-sided straight and narrow canyon about 2½ miles long. At a little over halfway through, the bridging for rail and road traffic spans the gap. Mist up from the water covers against the feeble antiaircraft fire beginning to spurt up. It won't be long.

The presence of transport planes in the area had been well established by the defenders, and the hazards of air drops had been widely preached, even by the prime minister. But here where the problem tapered down to tired men and a simple single command defense of a bridge, the thing is badly flubbed. A random mix of English, Australian, New Zealand, and Greek units, each under its own command, had been told off to save the bridge from paratroops. They posted both sides of the canal. The 8th Air Corps gave the defenses a thorough going-over at dusk 25 April and followed up with an intense neutralization fire in the morning. At about 0630 on 26 April bombs again hit the antiaircraft guns. . . . At 0700, over 100 dive bombers and fighters plaster selected targets with strafing and bombing. Nothing can move. Then comes the deep drone of many motors. . . . Here they come! The first airborne strike since Rotterdam, almost a year ago.

The mist has cleared; there is the target in plain sight. Up and up in a fresh, final surge of transport power, but only to 400 feet, where the jump command sounds through each plane to its ten or twelve jumpers crowding the open door—"Ready to jump!" (*Springen fertig!*) and the forced robust response, "Ready!" (*Fertig!*) Gliders can be seen casting off and swooping down. In perfect drill rhythm just before their drop zones, the Ju pilots slow, pull up in a semistall, and at last the jump command, "*Raus!*" Out they dive, cluthching forward at the plane's wing, never expecting to catch it. The wing planes of each trio first show the descending strings of men, parachutes opening, men swinging to earth. The time is short; maybe one can count to 22 or 26. Middle planes unload canisters and packages. All of the first are down, more keep coming and coming. In less than half an hour 1400 troops reach the ground, scramble to collect gear, to link up in groups, and begin shooting. They quickly take the bridge and post each end, round up prisoners, mostly British depot troops.[10]

German control over the bridge was short. It blew up and fell into the canal, carrying paratroops along. The wreckage completely blocked the waterway as Hitler had feared. British accounts credit detonation of the set charges to the rifle marksmanship of two British officers who had placed them; German reports blamed the blasts on a demolition charge hit by a stray antiair shell, and add that their engineers shoved a substitute bridge across the gap before the end of the day so that pursuit into the Peloponnese could flow uninterrupted. On the canal scene, resistance by British groups held on until near noon. This short delay made little difference to the final drive into the Peloponnese and its outcome. But the waterway was blocked.

In the achievement, then, of a specific strategic purpose, Airborne failed, though only by a hair, so that prestige suffered not a bit and indeed rose. The bridge was lost, the canal blocked. Army engineers quickly proved that there really was no need for the old bridge, and British provision for demolition indicated that the retreating forces would soon have blown it up in any case. Broader effects can be argued. For this study two questions have significance: the effect on evacuation and on the coming airborne seizure of Crete.

Evacuation jumped into high gear on 24 April in accord with Admiral Cunningham's signaled directive:

Object is to embark men, if possible, with arms; but no material . . . to take precedence to men. . . . Troop ships direct to Alexandria except Glen ships [landing ships] which unload Soudha Bay and do a second embarkation. Destroyers to take troops to Crete, [from] where they will be transferred later.

To hundreds, no, thousands of these men, "later" never came; they had to stay on Crete, as now happened also to many in Greece. The evacuation's unsuitable operational name was *Demon*; the last such

10. Long, pp. 163–68; GCB; Heyking. Heyking wrote that immediately after the drop, his squadron, in accordance with established procedure of General Conrad of 11th Air Corps transports, dispersed to overhaul bases in Germany. Planes were re-engined and overhauled and returned to airfields around Vienna within a week, in readiness for Crete or any other job. General Ulrich Buchholz commanded Squadron 3, which later made the first air-transport landings on Crete. Conversation and correspondence with him has helped fill out airborne procedures.

operation had been *Dynamo* at Dunkirk, a month short of a year ago. No rain or mist covered here; no Spits disputed the sky. Through a four-day advancement of his schedule *Demon* suffered a bad setback. Ships assembled earlier and unprepared in Greek waters; they were unused to their daylight hazards. Despite the ship losses of 22 April, 21 troopships, 7 cruisers, 20 destroyers, some landing craft, chartered Levantine caïques, and bumboats had survived. Small boats did a big business; whereas only 14,000 soldiers embarked over docks, three times as many boarded via small craft. Instead of the three days allowed in the beginning, the evacuation grind lasted six days and nights.

Ships learned to approach selected ports or beaches by night—four in Attica, four in the Peloponnese—and to load madly until 0300 of the new day, then to clear out beyond easy dive-bombing range. By broad day Crete would heave into sight as a mark on the way to Alex or as a speedy discharge point for a turn-around and another packed load. Never once did the Luftwaffe or the Italian Navy disturb the nightwork. During daylight, planes constantly dived and sprayed; air alert stayed on. More ships and men went down. A dirty job, Operation *Demon*, but with its own peculiar rewards.

Anzac Day—25 April—of 1941 differed ironically, sorrowfully from the first one at the Gallipoli end of the Aegean for General Freyberg, bumping along the road to Athens with his 6 Brigade after closing out at Molos. This day was fine and bright, and what cheered a little was the impromptu reception of the Athenians. They turned out in mass, crowded the dirty trucks, cheered, tossed greenery and flowers: Goodbye! Good Luck! "They seemed heartbroken," he wrote. Only a few more British troops would pass after this beat-up column; nor would many more cross the bridge into Corinth. The airdrop split the British forces between mainland and Peloponnesus. Still north of the canal were parts of 4 New Zealand Brigade and 1st Armored Brigade northwest of Athens; and some artillerymen were waiting to embark at Rafina. The milling main body was in the Peloponnese. General Freyberg decided to base near Navplion, at the head of the Gulf of Argos. On the morning of 27 April he became the only British general officer in Greece, commanding the chaos of large remnants north and south.

How much grimmer, had the Hitler agitation for his airdrop become effective earlier, when the evacuation game was snarled generally and plans were changing hour by hour. Disaster! Another one of those uncontrollable might-have-beens that seek a place in history, but succeed only in pointing out the unique significance of certain events. Corinth was *Demon's* tightest squeak.

To do the airdrop justice, it did beat its German ground competitors in reaching the bridge first. Like others, this blitz campaign lived on races for a prize, a grand prize that shifted constantly: when one was captured, another bobbed up. On the Continent, Corinth Bridge was such a one—the last trophy for this campaign. From Yannina in western Greece, the redoubtable SS Regiment set out on a strong but late bid along the gulf's south shore to seize the bridge. First it drove to the gulf, crossed in local craft, and then at Patras entrained an advance guard and sent it hell for leather toward Corinth—at ten miles per hour. Upon arrival in the evening of the 27th, Germans at once came into sight. The crestfallen party found their own troops, already in possession. These had entered the capital city that very forenoon from the north and had been dispatched to relieve the paratroops. There was nothing for it; the losers chugged back the way they had come, armed with fresh orders to help their own forces at Kalamata (or Kalamai) in the far south.

They proceeded by rail along the west Peloponnesian route. Cape Matapan (or Tainaron) forms the eastern shore of a deep north-reaching gulf at whose head lies Kalamata. There, before dawn of 29 April 1941, organized British resistance on the Continent ceased in a heartbreaking mistake which left some 8000 British, Greek, and Yugoslav soldiers and Cypriot and Palestinian labor forces stranded on the shore. The SS Regiment arrived only in time to help the 5th Panzer Division make the campaign's biggest haul of prisoners. The tragedy had run its course the night before.

In that early evening (28 April) a 5th Panzer flying column of two reinforced companies broke into Kalamata, while to the southeast, orderly columns of evacuees were moving off toward the beach. The Germans took the small quay and the Royal Navy beachmaster. Furious fighting broke out. Australians and New Zealanders mounted a counterattack along the waterfront that cleared the quay by 2130 at a cost of 40 dead Germans and 100 prisoners. But by this hour a fatal decision to give up embarkation had just been made at sea. Two approaching cruisers and six destroyers learned by signal that Germans were in the town. The destroyer closest-in landed her executive officer; he reported Germans in town, but British troops to the southeast, and at 2130 that the beach "was suitable for embarkation" (Long, p. 180). The message failed of delivery to the senior cruiser (H.M.A.S. *Perth*) until 2210, by which time she and her mates were well on their way out of the gulf at high speed (*Perth, Phoebe,* and destroyers). Destroyer *Hero,* joined by mates *Kandahar, Kimberley, Kingston,* tarried until about 0300, took off wounded and about 300 others. The anguish of it must have come in a realization that all might have been saved.[11]

The departure of the destroyers at 0300 on 29 April 1941 was not Operation *Demon's* last move out of Greece. Cruiser *Ajax* and four destroyers were still loading at Monemvasia, the last top British command post on the Continent, in a small port on the Peloponnese's eastern finger. General Freyberg and Navy's head beachmaster, Rear Admiral Baillie-Grohman, had moved headquarters there with 6 New Zealand Brigade and a few odds and ends. Embarkation completed at 0400 on 29 April 1941, the task unit stood out southeast for Suda to drop General Freyberg there. Since his 5 Brigade (and as it turned out, also 4 Brigade) had earlier been set down at Suda, the general thought to check on them, impart his plans and then fly on to Egypt. He hoped the whole division could soon rally there and prepare for the next project.

Thousands of eager Germans stuffed Greece's thin road and rail nets, her countryside, and much of her air overhead. The Teuton tide still ran full flood; it was about to hesitate before pushing up to a crest of men, machines, and spirit on Crete. During the lull we can look back the length of Greece and the Mediterranean, even to London, to recapitulate.

Usually the sobering shock of losses in men and material makes the first headlines, followed by strategic results, and finally by the more subtle, hard-to-weigh political and spiritual effects. Taken together, all these factors created the new situation now at hand. The Germans acquired considerable war booty; the British sustained

11. Brigadier Parrington commanded at Kalamata. It became his melancholy duty to collect the men on the beach, summon their officers, and say that no further chance of leaving by sea would offer. Then he sent an officer, accompanied by an English-speaking prisoner of war, to contact the German command. Besides those at Kalamata, about 2000 troops were left in Navplion-Tolos in the Gulf of Argos. In the one remaining embarkation point of Peloponnesus, Monemvasia, ships were still loading. The points used earlier in Attica were Megara, Piraeus, Porto Rafti, and Rafina. Vice-Admiral Pridham-Wippell (commander cruisers) had directed Operation *Demon* from Suda Bay.

serious material loss. They were out a full corps's worth of ground fighting gear, from rapid-fire weapons through heavy artillery, transport, munitions, communications to basic organic office stuff, and the same for an armored brigade. At the end of a long sea supply line, replacement would be hard. For some time the Middle East Command's fighting power would be weaker. On the water the British suffered an outright cut in sea power to the tune of twenty-six merchantmen and two destroyers. RAF losses were, however, the worst material calamity, for they reduced that arm to impotence and assured the Luftwaffe of undisputed air control.

Worse still for Britain was the political story implicit in her lopsided personnel casualties. By and large, loss of life was light on both sides, but the British loss of manpower in prisoners of war was disproportionate. The figures ran: German killed 1100, wounded 3700, missing 330; British killed 900 (many lost during evacuation), wounded 1200, missing as prisoners of war 11,000. Greek killed and wounded after 10 April were fewer than British; 270,000 Greek soldiers became prisoners of war, but were soon released. Thus about 12,000 British soldiers were taken out of the war, not because they missed the last boats at Kalamata or Navplion, but because their strategic tasks in Greece were beyond them. They should never have had to flee to Kalamata.

The above figures reflect the decisive strategical disparity between the contenders, as well as the severe impediments to joint Greek-British operation under one command; but most noteworthy, they condemn the dubious British attempt to squeeze a direct political result out of an impossible strategical situation. In the face of known handicaps, Britain challenged to combat without a feasible strategic objective in sight—only a chance that some political half-loaf might come out. No one knew precisely what. It amounted to a breach of faith with the fighting man. Who wants to die for half a loaf?

But German soldiers too were perplexed. They stand again on the shores of a great sea arm at a loss, unsure of what it means and of how the immense strategic momentum they have once more rolled up against their prime foe, Britain, should be used. She has sunk low from only a month ago, when Matapan seemed to give her rule over the sea and her positions in Libya established her power on land. The power lines have shifted out of all recognition. A solid German bloc from the Atlantic to the Black Sea, with lines into the East Basin, provides a secure continental base. The shocking days of spring 1940 return, and people wonder. A conclusion emerges the world over that the Germans will surely exploit the sea void before them. This would make the 1941 offensive the final fight for the Middle Sea.

And for a while action toward Crete made it look that way. But Germany's Führer seemed content with his Balkan Dunkirk, the British chased off his Continent for good. On to *Barbarossa*! There were people near him who still hoped to turn this urge off, possibly into the East Basin. Hitler's fears over the Aegean islands were being assuaged by their easy seizure; he was impressed and gained a new confidence about overwater leaps. Göring, who privately was against *Barbarossa*, stood in constant attendance to egg the mood on, exulting to his Führer over the Luftwaffe's brilliant performance and the opportunities still remaining in the East Basin. In the tumult of order for the Corinth drop, the OKW recorder noted, significantly, "Luftwaffe will be informed from here," which meant Göring was close at hand, conning his Führer with ideas for Luftwaffe glory. On 21 April he arranged for his ace Airborne leader, General Kurt Student, at his own request, to lay before Hitler a fresh version of his own lapsed project, airborne seizure of Crete.

If the Führer could be convinced of the fresh opportunities, *Barbarossa* might recede in importance. Signs showed that Air Fleet 4's command hoped for this. General Löhr himself believed strongly enough in a drop on Crete, as a beginning, to urge it on Göring. Löhr's chief of staff, General Günther Korten, an ebullient young man who knew how to get along and how to push his ideas, seemed even more enthusiastic. He stood close to Jeschonnek, chief of the Air General Staff, and to Göring. The Corinth drop had Korten's full support; it convinced him Crete and other East Basin targets should be won the same way. Thus, talk about Crete grew earnest. Navy, having heard about it just after mid-April, evaluated the strategic merits. Army, supported by L section of OKW, favored Malta over Crete. Irrespective of possible diversion effect on *Barbarossa*, both island targets had strategic merit. Which shall it be, then, at this time: Crete or Malta?

11. Crete or Malta?

Which Shall It Be?

When Mussolini reached across the Mediterranean for African conquest in 1935, Britain's Malta warmed up to Italy as a strategic problem. The island could get in the way; its reduction was studied; but typically, the results were never given operational planning status. Instead, Italy's sailors fooled around with new tactics or even new strategy, based on the world's fastest small torpedo craft; these, with the help of shore-based air power, would obviate the need of taking Malta. New craft and new tricks could easily keep the lines to Africa safe. Moreover, the island itself could be neutralized from the air. On 18 June 1940 the Italian Navy documented such conclusions in writing. But this came after German victory in France seemed assured and one could guess that Britain might even cede Malta to have peace in the Mediterranean.

As already recorded, by September 1940, midst waning hopes for peace, the chief of German naval liaison in Rome, Admiral Weichold, tried to interest the Italian Navy, and his own Navy superiors, in Malta. "Malta is a thorn in the flesh of Italy's sea war," he wrote, and urged her seizure. At the same time he mentioned Crete. On 10 September 1940 he entered in his War Diary, "If the Italian Navy wants to carry out its primary task . . . it must act now . . . eliminate Malta, occupy Crete as a preventive measure." Thus even in the earliest German thinking about the Mediterranean Sea, Crete and Malta were linked.[1]

1. Warlimont IM; Weichold DF. The Mediterranean problem of Crete and Malta has been discussed with both officers.

It will be recalled how failing Italian fortunes on all fronts after December 1940 threw a scare into the German High Command over Malta. General Jeschonnek of the Luftwaffe called for its reduction. The Führer dispatched another of his letters to the Duce: Malta had to be totally destroyed, he said. L Section in OKW undertook a study. The needs of the new Afrikakorps added pressure. Yet so far, all talk, all movements, were made of defensive stuff to save or buy time. Events had forced the pace, not perceptive German offensive planning.

The bright young men in L Section found the only long-term solution to be the seizure of Malta by Axis landing attack. They reckoned very sensibly from a premise of the worst eventuality: that Italy had lost North Africa. In that case Malta could provide a fair springboard for British attack on Sicily and thence the Continent (there was such a British plan, called *Influx*). If, on the other hand, the Luftwaffe could base air units on Malta and Sicily, the Mediterranean could be cut and all British sea traffic forced around the Cape of Good Hope. A safe balance of power might thereby be established in the East Basin, even while the bulk of the German war machine was busy in Russia. To invoke the East Plan at this early date (February 1941) must have been a play for approval of the Malta project; yet it failed. The Master shied away from such overseas commitment. Göring had begun to object, and Hitler allowed Keitel to include Malta in a lengthy summary of *Barbarossa* preparatory measures, only with a request for a Luftwaffe opinion about feasibility of seizure from the air (if all Africa had already been lost). Shortly, the Luftwaffe answered with an emphatic no; the island was crisscrossed by too many stone and earthen walls which would serve as defense works and foil all assembly for attacks. The Rotterdam airborne technique—paralyzing key points at a stroke and then taking over—did not fit.[2]

Two events thereupon radically altered matters: Rommel entered the scene and the British departed. The heat went off. After 15 March 1941, Axis disaster in Africa no longer impended. Though Malta's setting and potential for trouble had not changed, she sank out of sight once again. Then came Crete's latest turn.

Again Crete came on the horizon as an afterthought to events. Operations tore strategy along into new channels toward unanticipated goals. The Balkan blitz brought the Germans to the edge of

2. Keitel's paper does not admit Africa lost. This only becomes clear from Warlimont's evidence. While rejecting the operation for his own forces, Hitler hesitated not at all in recommending Malta's seizure by Italian forces to Mussolini.

another blue water. A long-ranged sight southward could imagine Rommel hammering on Egypt's gates. In between rose Crete. Luftwaffe flyers were becoming more and more familiar with the long island. As noticed above, the idea of taking over formed in several heads: in Göring's headquarters near the Tunnel; at Air Fleet 4 (Löhr and Korten) in Greece; at Süssmann's headquarters in Bulgaria; and at Student's top Airborne command near Berlin. Führer headquarters at the Tunnel took note. The earliest thoughts about Crete, first by Hitler in the summer of 1940, left an affiliation, almost a destiny, between Crete and Airborne. This bond now revived during the Balkan campaign with renewed vigor. In the quiet of General Student's Berlin headquarters, employment of Airborne before the campaign should run out was a natural staff concern. To the flight formations over Greece and the Aegean, Crete demonstrated her importance graphically. The voices of young flyers, wanting to end the campaign as an all-air show, the way it had begun over Belgrade, leap from the pages of General von Richthofen's 8th Air Corps daily record. He calls on Army for swifter ground action, and Army takes resentful exception. In this ideal natural environment, air power strove to come into its own.

Exchanges about Crete were undertaken by Air Fleet 4 with Student, with his subordinate Süssmann, and with the chief of the Air General Staff, Jeschonnek, before 15 April, for on that day General Löhr felt well enough heeled to urge the seizure of Crete by air on Göring directly. The idea caught on. As early as the previous January Göring had directed Student to study the air opportunities for island-hopping toward Suez. Thus various individuals and their commands invented a Crete project each considered his very own brainchild. Some later jealousies and actual conflicts in planning and operation can be traced back to the early rivalry for fatherhood.[3]

From start to finish German Airborne belonged to Kurt Student; it was his baby. An indispensable assist, however, came from Adolf Hitler. One story of 1936 has Hitler and a few cronies, including Göring, chatting in a Munich park. Newspapers strewn around pictured a gigantic Russian air drop of troops and equipment. The company scanned the pictures from the park benches and made merry over the crazy Russians. What would they think of next for propaganda? But not Hitler. He pointed out to Göring the masses of troops, the tactical applications, even the strategic possibilities, and advised

3. LF4 Kreta; Warlimont KFA, pp. 364-69; Student to Ansel, Germany, 1960.

him to look into it. Old fighter pilot Göring complied, with no great enthusiasm. A parachute troop training center was established at Stendal. It loafed along easily on its own. But in 1938, according to Student, a spectacular task for the new secret weapon appeared: seizure of the Czech frontier bunkers to clear the way into the heart of the land. A crash paratroop program got under way. To head it, Göring chose a man already familiar with the techniques and objectives, the recently promoted Major General Student. He had witnessed the mass drops in Russia in 1936.

A Lichterfelde boy of 1910, Student had entered the Graf Yorck Battalion No. 1 in East Prussia, finished flight training before World War I, and in it eventually led Fighter Group 3. Afterwards he joined the air technical branch and contributed much to the development of the new Luftwaffe. By late 1937 Student had become Commander Air West at Münster, where he was promoted to major general. Then came Czechoslovakia. On 6 July 1938 at Stendal he assumed command of Germany's Airborne might: one infantry company of air-transported landing troops. A German airborne strike capability was on its way. Although the test in Czechoslovakia never came off, other projects, even more exciting, beckoned. Student stayed with Airborne.

A year and ten months passed before the growing arm passed its first real test on 10 May 1940 by opening the gates of Belgium and Holland to German invasion. Glider descents on Fort Eben Emael and nearby bridges over the Albert Canal were followed by parachute drops around Rotterdam aerodrome and at vital Dutch control points. Eben Emael opened Belgium; the rest insured the collapse of Holland. The feats counted as triumphs for the new force, but above all for Hitler, who had taken a direct part in their planning. The tricky operations met his penchant for stealth, surprise, and fright. While Student's own theory preached strategic effect by deep paratroop penetrations to paralyze the foe's command and permit swift takeover with the help of air-transported reinforcements, his actual operational planning leaned heavily on psychological effect.

In its final phase Rotterdam taught a lesson that was later neglected. The old capital of the Netherlands, The Hague, was the final objective to be taken by troops air-landed on the region's broad concrete highways. In an eleventh-hour counter, the Dutch cluttered the highways with vehicles. They foiled the air transport plane landings, but failed to save The Hague, which fell to closing German ground forces. Overall success may have swallowed up the important lesson that to insure success, alternative air landing places must be designated for reinforcements. Before Rotterdam, small drops had been made in Norway. All of them impressed an invasion-conscious England far beyond reality; the Germans exploited the tension with drops of fake paratroop gear into England. "Paratrooper" became a name for terror (or glamor) that still speaks in news media today, though at a lowering pitch.

So German Airborne came of age and took its place in the arsenal. During the summer of 1940 plans called for air drops back of Hythe on the right wing of *Sea Lion*'s thrust into England. The leadership was split and unsure, for General Student lay disabled from a severe wound received at Rotterdam. Fully restored by the spring of 1941, he agreed with troops and staff that something big in airborne action should happen before the current campaign ended. Vague hints and questions had come up from Air Fleet 4, and some from Air headquarters. Whether at Göring's instance or his own, Student gathered up his plans against Crete and, accompanied by his operations officer, took off on 20 April for Semmering Pass below Vienna to report to Göring and win approval. His 11th Air Corps at the time was the most powerful airborne formation known; a paratroop *Sturmregiment* (shock regiment) reinforced (commanded by General Meindl), a full paratroop division (the 7th, commanded by General Süssmann), and an air field-landing division (the 22d, on loan from the Army). Ten transport plane groups (about 500 Ju-52's) and a few reconnaissance planes were at his disposal.[4]

Upon arrival at Air headquarters a few exchanges with Jeschonnek apprised Student of the depth and breadth of talk about Crete already in course, and of Hitler's inclination to consider arrival at the south

4. Kurt Student typifies the sincere, studious, and able soldier rather than the tough paratrooper. For hours over his study table he expounded airborne, its development, and its use on Crete. He prompted himself by reference to his own writings. Airborne was a strategic weapon rather than an instrument of sabotage and raiding. Air drops were to reach far behind the main body's front, seize strategic land islands or strongpoints, and hold them until the main body closed up. His execution banked heavily on surprise, fright, and panic. The rule was, pounce down and take over before the foe knows what is going on. *Handstreich* (coup de main), *Überraschung* (surprise), *schlagartig* (paralyzing) filled his doctrine. In the contest for Crete two top officers of the opposed sides had witnessed the 1936 Russian airborne demonstration as foreign observers—Archibald Wavell, in 1941 Britain's Army commander in chief Middle East, and Kurt Student, commander of the 11th Air Corps in the assault on Crete. Student's operations officer was Major Heinz Trettner, who grew up with airborne under Student, became his chief of staff, and eventually commanded the 4th Paratroop Division. The information given by these officers in conversation and in correspondence has contributed much to this report. See also Bashmore; Air Ministry RFGA.

end of the Peloponnese the definitive close of the Balkan Campaign. The British would again have been driven from his Continent, and he was willing to let it go at that. All the same, in the eyes of his chief of Airborne, whose horizon was still unclouded by the East Plan, such a view not only ignored long-range strategic possibilities in the Eastern Mediterranean but likewise the strategic instability of the area if Britain's air and sea forces remained established on Crete. In the course of the discussion Student was struck by the progress the project had already made; undoubtedly it had reached Hitler, who had, Student surmised, "shied off once more, as before England, from the risk of a leap over water." His 11th Air Corps could do the job, Student insisted; he showed where and how, in steady, resolute reasoning. Jeschonnek closed in with strong support. Göring held back for more questions about the result, about the conquest of the East Basin and Suez via Crete and Cyprus, of which they had talked long ago in January. After an hour of these lures Göring joined in wholehearted approval. He arranged a meeting with the Führer for Student on the following day.

Few people and few causes could be granted audience on such short notice. Göring had probably oiled the way in advance. He certainly had cased the plan for his Führer and could assure him that Student should be heard. It was arranged that he, accompanied by Jeschonnek and Trettner, would go the next day to the Tunnel to deliver the clinching argument. For this evening at the Hotel Panhans, which quartered the Air chief and his immediate staff, a special *Festessen* was laid on, perhaps in anticipation of Führer approval or in celebration of his fifty-second anniversary. Staff underlings wondered uneasily about what was up, especially those in Operations, because the appearance of General Student usually portended a promotional drive for an Airborne project to win the war. What could it be this time?

Student could scarcely have timed it better, for British action out of Malta was forcing an issue; Rommel was driving toward Egypt; German success in Greece was assured. He recalled the fine day and the pleasant countryside through which a staff car drove them the 20 kilometers to the Tunnel. Happy talk made the case for Crete still stronger. The party climbed aboard the OKW *Vortragswagen* (conference car) and were made welcome by Jodl. Since the Führer was resting, there would be a little while to iron out any moot points. Student, who had no such points, wondered what could be meant as he unrolled his scheme to Jodl. Hardly had he begun when Jodl broke in about the need to take Malta. Only a few days before, Captain Mack had sortied from there to polish off an entire Rommel convoy, and this very morning the British fleet had pounded Tripoli harbor—reasons enough for Jodl's suggestion.

Even now confirmatory wails about Tripoli were coming off the air. Unheralded, unhindered, the British ships had steamed in close aboard the port and blasted ships and gear up and under. In the wake of Mack's exploit, this was bad, in some ways worse than his action, for stuff already safely delivered and laboriously unloaded was gone and Tripoli reduced to impotence. How to get around the sea-going menace, how to keep Rommel strong? This was Jodl's growing anguish. He could recall a Führer query of some days ago when *Marita* first found her pace, "whether Crete or Malta would be of greater significance for Axis war waging in the Eastern Mediterranean through control of the air?" (Warlimont KFA, p. 365). It was a loaded question, for Malta bore on the East principally through Rommel and could have little influence on air control there; but Crete obviously could have just such influence. Göring had surely been working on his Führer to take Crete.

Jodl well understood how the 12th Army's crashing campaign, together with Rommel's dash through Libya, raised unexpected, almost unwanted, strategic possibilities; and how the spirit of Hitler's question matched his own at arrival on the Channel a year ago: Should England be invaded, or what? Then as now, operating had developed such questions of strategy. But here, under the compulsive priority of *Barbarossa*, Jodl's narrowed question became: How can the situation (which included Rommel) be helped most in buying time until after *Barbarossa*? By taking Crete or taking Malta? He had put the question to L section. A little while before also, OKH had produced its own Malta project and forwarded it to OKW and Skl on 15 April. Perhaps the Army was trying to outwit the Luftwaffe on Crete. Certainly Jodl was aware of its strong preference for Malta, and his own L section registered an equally strong unanimous service opinion (Air included) for Malta. Jodl was of the same mind.

Neither study has survived, thanks to the efforts of Hitler's chief adjutant, Colonel Schmundt, to be reviewed later. But Skl's War Diary comment on the OKH study describes it as a bold strike to take Malta by a landing attack, in order to keep Rommel strong until after *Barbarossa*, at which time the fight for the Middle Sea could begin in earnest. For its part, the Navy made reservations about total command of the sea through air power in the Malta landing assault area and the continued neutralization of British sea interference. Italian sea support would be weak and unreliable. On the whole, thought Skl, it would be advisable "to let the execution of Malta await evidence of how the campaign in Greece, including Crete, and the threat to Egypt work out over the whole Middle East position." Crete's seizure had clearly been widely discussed in this period of 15–22 April. Crete or Malta degenerated to a simple problem of timing. Both might have to be taken. Which should come first?

About the L Section study, evidence of participants suggests that it was based on a study of the same subject by the same people in February. Then, in extremis, the purpose was to offset the probable loss of North Africa by taking Malta. Since then the situation had improved, yet L Section still favored Malta, to "eliminate the threat to Africa-bound sea transport. . . . Moreover, a secure foothold on the far shore would contribute to long-term and sounder air basing, from which to control the Middle East, than could ever be offered by Crete." Additionally, possession of Malta would force Britain the long way around, while Crete would not improve German supply by sea or even maintain it at an adequate level. "Once the East campaign is under way, elements of the 10th Air Corps left behind in the Mediterranean would be so fully tied down to convoy escorting and combat support in Libya that maintenance of air control over the wide reaches of the eastern Mediterranean would fall out." This conclusion, like that of Skl about Crete before Malta, proved prophetic.[5]

The case for Crete was yet to be fully argued from the outside. The above studies and commentary suggest two approaches: that of the soldiers, who wanted to drive the British out of their main positions by land, and that of the sailors or flyers, who wanted to get at the bulwark of the British hegemony that made the positions possible in the first place: her power on the sea. OKH and L Section argued for the soldier cause: eliminating Malta would insure Rommel's supply. It was the view fed by the turmoil of daily events and their crises. Rommel had, however, proved he could buy enough time and keep Italy in the war in spite of Malta. An invasion of Crete could exploit the

5. Primary sources are Warlimont IH, IM, and KFA (pp. 365–70) as elaborated in discussion with him in Germany, 1960; Skl War Diary, 22 April 1941, and Skl Malta; Halder, 2:364–84, extended in discussion; Gundelach, pp. 98–99, and talks with him and General Student.

initiative rolled up by the Balkan campaign and would permit concurrent strikes at British sea power. Fundamentally the Mediterranean was a sea problem; intrinsically the two islands were sea problems. Their difference came in the end goal that each supported: attack on Malta supported Rommel and offered a chance to cut the sea in two; attack on Crete meant direct attack on the British power that controlled the sea and offered a chance to use the initiative already on hand. Finally, Crete offered a decisive trump: she could even contribute substantially to *Barbarossa*'s security and the continuity of the East Plan. So early as 17 March Hitler had ordered operations in Greece to be pushed "until a base has been gained for control of the air over the eastern Mediterranean" (Warlimont KFA, p. 367).

These were the bare essentials of Hitler's choice. The chances to get at England, or even at such fragments of her as Malta or her troops on Crete and in the Middle East, were dwindling. The choice here had about it a hint of a last chance to decide between England and Russia. Hitler stood again on a threshold, and confidently. Maybe a cheap and rousing victory over the British on Crete would turn him back to conquest of the Middle Sea?

At the time the stakes at issue rarely stand out stark and clear; a background of irrelevance, clamor, and personal compulsion garbles the true signal. Hitler broke into the conference car session; talk ceased. Looking fit, he greeted the company and sat down. Earlier in the day he had revised Greece's surrender terms, so there was little left to the campaign. He was ready for the next job. Talk resumed. Student, as first up, began to explain his proposition and its origins: how he felt a "duty as commander of Airborne to speak out about Crete in the current situation; the island could and should be taken through the air." Again, he barely got into the why and how, when someone, probably Jodl, injected Malta. But it never had a chance, for the Führer, in Student's words, "at once declared for Crete," and added as a pacifying afterthought, *Malta hat später noch Zeit* [There'll be time for Malta later]." Yet in the subsequent exchanges he showed pessimism about the chances against either island, saying, among other things, "Crete is too big for this." Then Student cut loose with his detailed plans: surprise drops in many key places to foster paralysis and takeover, and so on. Well, if he was sure, Hitler then conceded, "Conquest of Crete will make a good wind-up of the Balkan campaign (*einen guten Abschluss*)." Crete had become an extension of his Continent. Expansion of the Mediterranean strategy received no mention. A few words may have passed about Rumanian oil or British air and naval menace. The meeting closed after Hitler told how he would commit paratroopers: drop them as surprise packages (*Paketen*) at many places to confound the enemy, so that he would not know where to turn. The scheme fitted Student's plan to a tee. The Führer thereupon gave his verbal directive to prepare everything by 10–15 May, without inquiring about the practicability of the short time. But Student assented readily. Indeed, his airborne blitz of the day had succeeded beyond all expectation. He felt fine as he drove off to board a plane for return to Berlin headquarters bearing the best news ever for his Airborne.[6]

Hitler chose Crete; spoke only of it as the close of the Balkan campaign, meaning a well-finished job of continental security; not a word about getting at Britain's sea power. No, the stage and the actors suggest rather a superficial pre-Dunkirk rerun. Recall the Hitler-Göring connivance by telephone in May 1940 before Dunkirk! Like all men, Adolf Hitler was an inveterate repeater. But his repetitions mattered. His brisk, forthright decision for Crete came out too pat and ready to be anything but a studied answer planned beforehand. Time over his decision process exhibited this trait: the response would come out as though on the spur of that very moment in a marked show of decisive command. Normal command decisions of such an order emerge slowly, are more studied and deliberate. This answer bore every indication of having been firmed previously with Göring, the indispensable jumper-into-the-breach, the great consoler and resolver of his Führer's dilemmas, who in this instance was known to be against Malta but for Crete. Such an infusion showed here (Warlimont KFA, p. 368). The two had talked the thing out before Student arrived. Air Fleet 4 reported Göring had summoned Student after General Löhr had himself proposed Crete's seizure. All the same, Student on his own could have been busy with the identical idea. He was asked no pros and cons by his Führer; there was no weighing or quibbling about extras. He had only to declare himself. It is noteworthy that Hitler consulted no service head except the biased Göring. It is an old routine that can be recognized before Dunkirk, before ordering to prepare Invasion England (this time at Jodl's prompting), before Invasion's call-off (Göring), and before many smaller decisions. Their common traits traced a pattern whose lines no one knew better than Alfred Jodl. He noted that when Göring conferred at length

6. Student and Trettner to Ansel in separate interviews, Germany, 1960.

or repeatedly, it was a time to stand by for a ram. The decision atmosphere on this occasion reeks of the "special task" for the Luftwaffe and its commander in chief.

A crashing descent on the island would indeed end the Balkan drive with a bang; the south flank and its vulnerable oil preserves would be secure behind a screen that would help hide *Barbarossa*. After Russia Crete could provide the springboard for wider operations in the Mediterranean. Not a bad sequence to contemplate. Side effects seemed equally engaging: a channel-like jolt to British prestige and security. This time the enemy would already have gone over the water to be trapped on a foreign island. Victory over a sea stretch thrice the width of the Channel would tense the challenge on the Channel like nothing else. The slogan, "There are no more islands!" may have been invented here. Air attacks on England rose in power and number to remind her of her island status and how much safer she would feel if the RAF stayed at home.

But poor little Malta's rejection failed to eliminate her as a "thorn in the flesh of Axis effort"; another crisis blew around her a year hence. But for now her rejection brought a curious sequel that might have been the most significant result of the whole episode for the light it shed on the wellsprings of Hitler's personal power to command.

This power faltered before the Maltese fragment of England in much the same way as it had before the home island. His worry was, Might he not lose control? He mistrusted his own capacity to command this mysterious overseas venture. No private mythology could he call on and no deputy could he trust to take over except Göring, who had already counseled against the Malta attempt. Peculiar side effects of such inner disquiet showed a few days after Malta's rejection.

L Section's War Diary summarized the case that the service representatives had argued for Malta and against Crete. What naturally received no mention was private misgivings about *Barbarossa*. These men were for Malta, *Barbarossa* or no. In a day or so, Colonel Schmundt, senior adjutant to the Führer and his devoted disciple, queried Lt. Colonel von Lossberg, the Army L Section man and deputy to Warlimont, about the diary summary. Lossberg had guided the study and presumably seen to the diary write-up, including dissent from Crete. Schmundt thereupon invoked the Führer's authority to order deletion of the entry and moreover destruction of the basic L Section study. For the future, no dissent from Führer decisions was ever to be recorded. The extraordinary command and left-handed method of its promulgation evoked unfavorable undercover comment. But Schmundt was far from through. He went on to purge all files of any evidence of dissenting views. All copies of the companion OKH study of Malta were destroyed. It does not appear in the Army files nor does the copy OKH sent to Navy appear there. What Schmundt failed to catch was Skl's detailed analysis of the Army paper and a summary logged in Skl's War Diary on 22 April. The extreme measures employed to kill this record of Malta suggest cover-up of a Hitler weakness. But a dictator may have none. A year later, during a resurgence of the same problem, we shall see the same peculiar signals. The growing post-Russia plans already a-building in the spring of 1941 held no designs on Malta. In a murky, twisted way the tiny island at sea stood for an unconquerable Mediterranean England, while Crete stood for freedom to conquer Russia. One effect the Schmundt hubbub did have: it focused attention on the question: Crete or Malta? Now Hitler's commitment to Crete had to make good.[7]

7. Sources listed in note 5 apply here too. See also Ms B–250; Warlimont IH, pp. 145–50, and discussion with him. The interpretation of the Schmundt incident is my own. Staff life can readily produce a scenario that approximates it. Schmundt repeated with similar action later, on a higher level, in the role of guardian of Führer infallibility. Imagine him in the present scene—an affable, not too bright worshiper of his Führer, given to drink, none too well thought of professionally. He leafs through the L Section War Diary (OKW Ops War Diary) in search of up-to-dateness and juicy bits, and falls on the Malta entry of dissent on Crete. What is this heresy, and from that von Lossberg? He is an old offender. Diary in hand he stomps in to the Führer, shows him his find: Look what von Lossberg is up to now! His place on the blacklist stemmed from two notable earlier occasions of dissent: (1) The Narvik Dietl (Norway) episode when Hitler in despair directed the hard-pressed Dietl to intern in Sweden; Lossberg was instrumental in getting the hasty order nullified. Dietl pulled through. (2) The tank halt order by Hitler before Dunkirk. Lossberg again seemed to have the staff duty. He shouted objection to Jodl and Keitel loud enough for all to hear. The halt order stood, and facilitated the BEF's escape to England. There were other less striking occasions that lowered Lossberg's popularity on high. He was unlucky in catching the Führer in the wrong. This could not do. Dictators must be infallible. By the end of 1941 Lossberg was out of OKW.

12. Operation Merkur

German Practical Preliminaries: April, May 1941

One final function fell to Crete's Operation *Merkur*, as it did during this period to everything German: every manifestation, each sound or act by voice or body, had to divert world attention from Hitler's eastern intent. And this meant that preparations for the conquest of Crete should draw attention too. England had moreover to be kept uneasy while the sensational attack on Russia got ready and well under way. A revived *Sea Lion* under the names *Haifisch* and *Harpune* began thrashing about in the Channel and North Sea ports. Intensified air bombardment of England paralleled the amphibious antics. Now the airborne concentration toward the East Basin, complemented by Rommel's Libyan threat, added confusion to the query, What next? Further commitment to the East Basin could fortify the suspicion that further Mediterranean action was in prospect. The opening lines of Führer Directive No. 28 (Operation *Merkur*) of 25 April 1941 gave a specific purpose of deeper involvement there. Moreover, it made strategic sense: "As a base for the conduct of the air war against Britain in the Eastern Mediterranean, the occupation of the island of Crete is *to be prepared*." Final word was to follow. A maze of plots within plots to deceive grew too thick for the plotters themselves. For the Army, fakes on the Channel took on enough validity to threaten a takeover as the real thing.[1]

1. German Army leaders still believed in Invasion England as the best means of removing a hostile base against the Continent. Therefore remnants of *Sea Lion*

At the crest of the hullabaloo over the Corinth drop and a day after *Merkur* directive issued, Hitler left his tunnel for Berlin by a roundabout rail route. Mulling over the unbelievable fresh triumphs, he found the going fine in this lovely countryside full of spring. He would expound things to his *Volk* in a Reichstag speech on 4 May. What a joy to compose it, even act it out!

But Churchill again beat him to the punch. On 29 April before a cheering House he extolled the rescue of 45,000 soldiers from Greece, warned of reviving German-French collaboration, reviled Hitler over and over, and launched a trial balloon about a coming German attack on Gibraltar. A day earlier Hitler had accosted the Spanish ambassador about such widespread rumors; they seemed to signal British designs on Spain. OKH was told to earmark ten divisions for her defense (Operation *Isabella*). In his speech Hitler scored fifteen specific mentions of Churchill. He became guilty of every crime from Yugoslavia's perfidy to Greece's objection to occupation by the Germans, who had had to forfend "British entrenchment . . . at Salonika as in the World War." He gave the final green light for *Merkur* the day after Churchill's speech. Maybe the war of words accelerated action on both sides. On the German side it meant commitment to Crete[2]

The positive word that *Merkur* would go left only two weeks until X-Day; Mercury would indeed have to fly. The operation's high distinction for German arms came in the command structure. By the directive's second paragraph Hitler, for the first and only time, delegated

---

stuck with development of landing power. By April 1941 these efforts were well along. Klee, p. 226; and Skl Seelöwe, 1:15, Haifisch and Harpune. On 23 and 24 April 1941, OKH issued orders for three landing operations against England: a diversion called *Harpune Nord*, from Norway and Denmark, would attack east England, and another diversion, *Harpune Süd*, from west France, would go against southwest England; then the main dish *Haifisch* (for shark) from France was to work directly cross-channel against England's south coast—all to be ready by early August. While Army admitted that the *Harpunes* were fakes, it tried hard to make *Haifisch* the real McCoy. Yet Navy in a paralleling directive (Skl I Op 573) included a sealed annex for high commanders telling them that all were fakes. Army plugged away seriously, leaked stories to the public about the *Harpunes*, and took note of improved techniques and doctrines, especially in command relations among the three services. Toward the end of May, Army's *Haifisch* command (commander in chief West) pressed for a streamlined *Haifisch II* to take over as a sort of police action in England if she cracked under the current intensified bombing. Fake tried to steal the show by becoming real, and failed.

2. Estimates have claimed that the Balkan and Crete campaigns cost *Barbarossa* decisive weeks of fighting weather later in Russia. But bad weather in May and June of 1941 would in any case have precluded an earlier start for *Barbarossa*. The heaviest handicaps, already noticeable, came from Hitler. Among the best sources to establish this is Philippi and Heim, pp. 102–5. It is a first-class professional presentation.

absolute command to one service over the other two in a unified project and therewith divested himself of direct responsibility. While personal command is important to dictators, victory is vital. Norway, England, North Africa, Malta, and Crete reveal a Hitler nervous about commanding over water. He gave command of this supposedly easy closing of the Aegean boom to one person he could unreservedly trust—Göring. Except for some boasts about a total air show and roughshod kicks at the other services, Göring from his Berlin headquarters did very little commanding; he appointed General Löhr of Air Fleet 4 to command in chief.

Yet Göring did enough to get under the skin of the other services. OKH and Skl interest in *Merkur* therefore dwindled off to perfunctory notice. The Navy liaison office at Air headquarters was able to forward a precise general plan for *Merkur* by 22 April; it had been worked out between chiefs of staff of Air Fleet 4 (Korten) and the 11th Air Corps Airborne (Schlemm). The plan went so far as to include provision for the 10th Air Corps in Italy and Sicily "to take over conduct of the air war in the eastern Mediterranean" on an expanded scale from bases to be won in Crete. The airborne assault and conquest was to follow the pattern of Rotterdam in 1940. The solitary Navy task was safe conduct of sea transport to and from Crete. The keen eye of Skl's operational head, Admiral Fricke, saw that all of Crete would have to be taken, not just the airfields and Suda Bay. In a short time he wired his conclusions to naval liaison in Rome and Admiral Southeast: "The undertaking has the greatest significance for the war in the Eastern Mediterranean. . . . The task is to achieve momentary command of the sea around Crete . . . through the air." Over such detail commander in chief Air bothered little. Göring issued a weak implementing directive to Air Fleet 4 on 1 May, but thereafter he left the directing to his chief of staff Jeschonnek and to the commander of Air Fleet 4, Löhr. Early differences played themselves out down the chain of command and left General Löhr in firm control, ably supported by Field Marshal List of the 12th Army and Admiral Schuster of Naval Command Southeast—"Admiral Southeast." The work got done because there was so much to do in which everyone had a stake.[3]

Mounting this first air conquest of an island ran concurrent with

3. Halder (of OKH) and Schniewind (of Skl) to Ansel in Germany, 1960; also Heye and Student to Ansel (Admiral Heye was chief of staff to Admiral Schuster at Naval Command Southeast); and Skl *Merkur*.

the planning of it. Student recalls his happy return from the Tunnel to his own headquarters with the bacon in his bag. His staff began exchanges with Air Fleet 4. He realized he would be subordinate to that command in a general area way, but that he, supported by the 8th Air Corps under von Richthofen, should not command the assault never occurred to him. Crete was his very own. He planned to drop his force into the thick of the defenses at many points, demoralize the foe through the shock of surprise, link up the drops around airfields, and on them land airborne infantry as *das Gros*, the main body, to mop up. From first to last he planned to take all Crete by air. This radical doctrine had little patience for landing-from-sea theories explored with such pain and labor on the Channel, which based, and still base, on the cardinal principle of early establishment of a beachhead from which to expand the fight. If the principle was comprehended or countenanced by German Airborne planners, they never expressed its primacy. Rather, in record and talk their thought ran: "Once we command the air we can throw into Crete whatever we want wherever needed." They felt confident. For the moment such planning voids were covered by the tumult of deployment. Said General Student ruefully, "Then came one disappointment after another." In the middle of the uproar he first heard about the Corinth drop. The bacon he had brought home collapsed around his neck.

To this point the plan had been hardly more than an engaging travelogue, founded on hazy geography, sketchy intelligence, scattered own forces, unexplored logistics, and vague time and space factors. All manner of bottlenecks developed: equipment stored in France for drops on England, munitions short, no proper clothing; one important unit was up in the wilds of freezing Norway. There were absolute material lacks, but lack of time pressed the hardest. Up forward in Rumania, the 22d Air Landing Division sent bad news. Its movement into Greece was stalled because it ran counter to East Plan traffic. OKH stood firm and cold on *Barbarossa*'s right of way as provided by Directive No. 28; not even an essential cadre from the

4. Terms like "beachhead" and "airhead," which articulate the principle of a base so well, appear nowhere in the Luftwaffe literature or record. Later they gained currency through exposure to the Army. The 5th Mountain Division records the apt term *Landekopf*, "landing head." It expresses the thought perfectly. Maybe it took the Crete Campaign to coin the term. When queried, German Airborne men held that in practice, seizure of an airfield meant the same thing, though at the time they never seemed to regard it as establishment of a base, which an airfield actually is. "Landing head" can now be refined to "seahead." Logistics can go from sea (ships offshore) direct to the needy fighters ashore under the Fast Deployment Logistics (FDL) doctrine.

22d Division to initiate novice replacements could Student break through, nothing. At OKW Jodl examined the Cretan terrain; it looked remarkably rugged and wild, ideal mountain troop country, he mused and, Aha! There flashed a solution. The 5th and 6th Mountain Divisions received orders to remain in bivouac near Athens. The 5th Mountain Division substituted for the 22d Air Landing Division; the 6th Mountain would stand by in reserve. The arrangement brought an alien outfit into the tricky game, and into the top echelon of command a total stranger, General Julius Ringel of the 5th Mountain Division. He heard of this newest assignment by accident on 3 May, a short week before the earliest hop-off. He tells his story of receiving the news in Athens.

A grand victory parade had been scheduled for Saturday 3 May. A buffet lunch was to follow at Field Marshal List's quarters. General Ringel decided he must be present; his troops would be marching, and besides, he could get in a little ancient history sightseeing. The scene was one to remember. Wrote General Ringel later, "Summergreen trees surrounding the plaza before the old palace bend slightly to the breeze. Mixed architectural styles of Paris and Greece merge . . . the walls reflect the bright sunlight." Field-gray German soldiers, released Greek troops, and civilians mingle in the crowd around the square. The clock strikes nine as the Field Marshal ascends the reviewing stand; distant music heralds the marching columns. A battalion of the 5th Mountain passes; then come paratroops and to German and Greek embarrassment a battalion of Italian troops. The word is that the Field Marshal has refused to invite an Italian representative to the stand. Still, for Ringel it is a glorious day; a day in History— German troops parading in Athens! As the parade ends and the throng melts away, a figure pushes out of it toward him with outstretched hand. It is Generalleutnant Süssmann, a companion of Norway days. He clasps Ringel's hand in a firm grip and shouts, genially, "To good comradeship and cooperation in our next undertaking!" At no response, he asks, "Don't you know?" and at another blank, he says, "Why the Fifth Mountain has been selected for Operation *Merkur*—the conquest of Crete." He chuckled good naturedly at his old friend, whose words failed him, and went on.

For the commander of the 5th Mountain Division the marvels of ancient Greece fell out of mind and the Field Marshal's buffet too. Kerplunk! Ringel found his driver and rattled homeward to his new headquarters in Chalcis on Euboea (Evvoia). What would the orders say? And his hill boys, how many had ever been in a flying machine, to say nothing about bursting from one shooting? Heights they knew all right, and flight too, but on skis; this air-landing stuff. . . . So this was why his division had been ordered to hang around.[5]

On 1 May Göring's operations officer signed and released a "Commander in Chief Air Force DIRECTIVE FOR AIR FLEET 4 (No. 6524)." The first three paragraphs simply parroted Führer Directive No. 28, which this new paper was to implement. Paragraph 4 then redelegated *Merkur* command down the line from Göring to Löhr. What followed was no statement of General Plan by which an operation could be guided, but a hodgepodge of tasks and warnings off the top of the issuer's head. Paragraph 5 listed seven items "of particular importance": cover the sea around Crete; safeguard air and sea transport; fight down British sea forces, including attack by air-launched torpedoes (this one served as excuse to demand the last five torpedoes in stock from the Navy; it thus finished the Navy-Air fight and the air-launched torpedo too); transfer dive bombers and fighters to Crete as soon as possible; land mountain and infantry troops for occupation of Suda and Heraklion; protect occupied airfields; prepare transfer of fighters to Scarpanto island. The remaining paragraphs 6 to 11 listed administrative trivia, in which paragraph 11, at the end, in common staff buckpassing, made the impossible requirement that Air Fleet 4 report in four days: the date preparations would be complete, the operational details of execution, arrangements with the 12th Army and with Naval Command Southeast.

The Commander in Chief Air Force   *Air Headquarters, 1 May 1941*
No. 6524/41

DIRECTIVE FOR AIR FLEET 4

1. As a base for air war against Great Britain in the eastern Mediterranean, the occupation of . . . Crete is to be prepared (Operation *Merkur*).

2. Command of the undertaking the Führer and Commander in Chief of the Armed Forces has assigned to the Commander in Chief Air.

3. Army, besides forces named in Annex 1, will make available suitable reinforcements, including a mixed armored combat unit in Greece so that they can be transferred overseas to Crete. Navy will secure overseas communications to the island. . . .

4. Preparation and execution of the operation is assigned to Air Fleet 4 (Forces Annex).

5. It is of particular importance:

    (*a*) to continuously *cover the sea around Crete* before and during the air landing and the transport movements of the Navy;

5. Ringel Ms, as elaborated in discussion with General Ringel in Germany, 1960.

(*b*) to *safeguard the air and sea transport* by commitment of fighter-bombers and to hold bombers in readiness;

(*c*) to *put British sea forces out of action, including attack by air-launched torpedoes*;

(*d*) to *transfer dive bombers and fighters as soon as possible* after complete conquest of airfields (on Crete) for the purpose of combatting hostile sea forces;

(*e*) to land the attached 6th Mountain Division and the 125th Infantry Regiment for the rapid occupation of Suda and Heraklion bays [5th Mt. was correct, 6th in reserve; the 125th Infantry Division dropped out];

(*f*) to *protect the occupied airfields with antiaircraft artillery fire*;

(*g*) to prepare the *transfer of fighters to the island of Scarpanto*.

6. Units of the 10th Air Corps . . . are to be transferred to airfields at which they will base.

7. Designated Army units are to be relocated near takeoff bases.

8. Air Fleet 4 can draw on the 12th Army for antiaircraft protection of Greece and Crete. . . .

9. After occupation of the island, the 11th Air Corps will be replaced by 12th Army forces as soon as possible. . . .

10. After occupation . . . the 8th Air Corps will be withdrawn from Greece and will be relieved by the 10th Air Corps.

11. Air Fleet 4 is to submit by 5 May 1941:

(*a*) prospective date for the completion of preparations;

(*b*) intended runoff of the operation;

(*c*) arrangements reached with the 12th Army;

(*d*) arrangements reached with Admiral Southeast.

SIGNED . . . . Ia [Operations Officer]

ANNEX 1 (PROVISIONAL)

11th Air Corps (less 22d Division)

Placed under command by Army, 6th Mountain Division, one infantry regiment of 5th Mountain Division. [Note: By 3 May this became 5th Mountain Division, one regiment of 6th Mountain Division. Troops 23,000 + transport planes 503, gliders 71.]

Staff VIII Air Corps, 4.LG 2 [bombers]

Staff KG 2, I.KG 2, III.KG 3, II.KG 26 (from X Air Corps)

[KG = Kampfgruppe bomber group or wing; i.e., 2d Bombing Wing.]

Staff KG 51, I.KG 51 [5 echelons from X Air Corps], I.LG 1, II.LG 1 (from X Air Corps) [bombers]

Staff G 2, I.St G 2, III.St G 2, I.St G 3 [dive bombers]

Staff ZG 26, I.ZG 26, II.ZG 26, II.ZG 76 [fighter bombers]

Staff JG 77, II.JG 77, III.JG 77, I.LG 2 [fighters]

[Note: Combat air strength thus approximated: Bombers 280, dive bombers 150 plus, fighters 180–200, reconnaissance 40.]

The point of high interest is that no Landing Attack Commander was designated. That the question had not been settled is revealed in an Annex 1, marked "Provisional." General Student took for granted he would be the one, with von Richthofen and his 8th Air Corps in combat support. Richthofen thought otherwise. Annex 1 begins with "11th Air Corps (less 22d Air Landing Div.)" and under this heading, as though everything below belonged to it, the forces available are listed in an indented column; Staff 8th Air Corps is among them. The command fight continued.

Differences between the 8th and the 11th Air Corps developed over various arrangements, first over sharing the crowded Greek airfields. Eleventh's 500 transport planes required room. Then there was unloading munitions and fuel from ships, setting up communications—all produced friction, which soon began to show in operational planning. Near 8 May Jeschonnek flew down from Air headquarters "Robinson" in Wildpark, Berlin, and put up with his friend von Richthofen at 8th Corps. Not far away was another friend and contemporary, Korten, chief of staff of Air Fleet 4. The cards seemed stacked against Student, who was years senior to these youngsters, except for Löhr, an Austrian. Though they knew combat flying and were well flown-in in this theater, they knew virtually nothing about airborne landing attack. Student's assumption that he would command the landing attack because of Airborne's decisive role was soundly based. No matter how daring, combat flyers could not take Crete. Over precisely this: Who would command? Jeschonnek decided. He decided it would be Löhr and enforced it by requiring both Student and Richthofen as coequals to report to Löhr. Midst all his other troubles, this was a heavy blow to the 11th Corps's commander. Neither the manner nor the weight of 8th Air Corps support, nor even his own assault plan, was to be left to him in this, his grand hour.[6]

To settle an attack plan, Göring and Jeschonnek relied on their familiar routine of requiring a fresh solution from each operational head. This system put the commands on record, offered a comparison of ideas and opportunity to select the best of each; in any case, the

---

6. To this day General Student and his associates think the solution was faulty. They ascribe various failures to it and plenty of operational troubles. Worst was Richthofen's freedom to reject Student's calls for support on the basis of insufficient planes. A manuscript on the 8th Air Corps's chronology (8th FK Chrono) is the most direct source for the 8th Air Corps side. On the 11th Air Corps side the problem has been discussed with General Student and General Trettner, his former operations officer.

device saved the top staff great labor. As chief executor Löhr had to submit his ideas; as packer of the main punch, so had Student, and as his preparer and supporter, von Richthofen. General Löhr proposed simply to fight Crete free from west to east: land and occupy Kastelli Kisamou between the dragon horns in the west, work east toward Maleme Airfield through attacks, then straight along the coast. He professed a belief in "balling of force" to insure superiority at any point of attack, yet he seemed to rely chiefly on the 8th Air Corps overhead to provide the decisive edge. Thus while his thrust was to issue from an ill-defined beach or airhead base, its power was vested in air supremacy rather than in troop combat supremacy on the ground.

Old flyer Student—since 1913—ranged much farther afield. He wanted seven simultaneous air drops—at Maleme, Canea, Retimo, Heraklion, and on three settlements in the east, one on the south coast. At one mighty shotgun blast these key points would be paralyzed so that air-transport-landed reinforcement could easily mop up. Moreover, fixed defenses on the coasts Student thought to take in reverse from inland drops "where they ain't" (as amphibians say). Of course the wide spread forebode troubles in combat support, logistics, and communication, but he was ready to chance them. The other top leaders were not. The counts against prevailed; the plan was ground down to what were thought easier dimensions, while the germ of it remained in attempted shock effect at several points.

In Athens the Hôtel de Grande Bretagne became the throbbing beehive of *Merkur* planning and Student the queen bee; they came to him. Formerly the headquarters of Greece's defenses, the hotel now swarmed with eager German staffers and commanders, each pleading a special war-decisive cause. Student took quarters there; Jeschonnek, Löhr, von Richthofen, Ringel came and went. Meager communication nets were glutted with enormous overloads; paper orders fell badly behind reality, which had to depend on talk and verbal orders. Decisions, said General Löhr's later report, were hammered out in debate and transmitted verbally, and only because all commands could enter the war of words at one place did *Merkur* ever get off the ground.

Richthofen had said he lacked the support for seven simultaneous drops. When Student then cut out the three eastern drops, the choice had still to be made between his four drops in central and western Crete and Löhr's unchanged wish to work east from the west end, where Greek bases and their direct air support were closer. This progression, said Student, would take too long; besides, such a standard, humdrum ground plan had no place in Airborne Doctrine. But even his own reduced plan encountered further objections from Richthofen because of overload. The choice became Göring's: Should von Richthofen be required to do as much as he could, or should the plan be whittled down still more? The settlement was for four drops in two waves, morning and afternoon. X-Day's break-in drops would fall on the western complex of Maleme-Suda in the forenoon, and the second wave on Retimo and Heraklion in the afternoon. Three air facilities and the principal centers should thus be safely in hand by the end of the day. It had a satisfying sound. Göring and staff had managed a debilitating three-way compromise, having left some room for Löhr's emphasis on the west (but not enough) and some of Student's wide effect, and having spread Richthofen's onerous missions over the whole day. The solution telegraphed its piecemeal punches over an 80-mile front without adequate provision for exploitation of success. A similar amateurish lack of concentration had marked Luftwaffe failure in the Battle of Britain.

The term *wave* was confusing, for these air-transport waves were determined by Ju-52 takeoff schedules in Greece rather than by the decisive target priorities in Crete, where the front stretched 80 miles. Two targets of two commands were to be served by each so-called wave (*strike* would express more). Ten miles split the targets of the forenoon wave between the commands of General Meindl (Maleme) and General Süssmann (Canea-Suda), while 40 miles separated the afternoon targets of Süssmann (Retimo, to which he overlapped from Suda) and General Ringel (Heraklion in the east). To the flyer in the air, such ground separations may seem minute and inconsequential; to the falling paratrooper in a belated, inaccurate drop, they can be fatal.

On touching down in a rough alien terrain of hilly olive groves and vineyards, bristling with defenders, one mile (or even one-tenth of a mile) might as well be a hundred for jump commander and trooper alike. The misery of the falling trooper is isolation on touchdown. He needs the company of his fire team. At touchdown in defended territory his chances of company are slim. The fragmented expanse of the Crete front promised severe isolation trials. This was no populous, well-marked Rotterdam. Of course to start with, getting off the ground took priority, yet this was merely loading the weapon for a later solid hit on the target.

Frequently not all requirements can be fully met, but here the wretched basing facilities in Greece forced everything but takeoff to fringe attention. When on 21 April Hitler gave Student the first nod, German ground forces were still fighting 100 miles north of Athens. The Balkan Campaign was going well, and wishful eyes could easily range over a map to select likely sites for airfields; they seemed to abound in flat, dry wastes. But once the RAF had cleared out, the few sites that could hold more than one squadron were occupied by the 8th Air Corps, with no thought for 503 transport planes. Handicaps rising from basing and logistic deliveries threatened operational capability.

Even with the air combat tasks arranged in a forenoon and afternoon sequence, the 8th Corps mission remained heavily overloaded. Löhr nevertheless ordered von Richthofen to intensify his softening-up attacks and to work up to "preparatory" barrages for first light of X-Day's break-in drops on high-priority targets. In addition, the transport "waves" and sea convoys had to be air-escorted to their objectives. Any British naval forces encountered were to be sunk. These flyers, veterans of the English Channel, could have thought back to those days of a year ago, when bad weather shut down operations. Here flying weather was perfect and opposition weak; the flights, however, were much longer, and when you got back to base in Greece, where were you?

Basing on the waterfront was equally discouraging. The battered Athenian ports boiled with their own peculiar sailor crises. Only two or three true seamen were on hand, and they were submerged under demands for troop lift to Crete, a supply lift from home for the entire operation, and a multitude of impossible minor water chores. Sea transport took over for all supply from the Italian boot and the Balkan Black Sea ports to Greece when the job very early got beyond air-transport capability. The mountain troops, just learning of their new destination, quickly developed a special preference for reinforcement to Crete by water instead of air. Aided by the 12th Army, the staff of Admiral Southeast sent scouts into every nook and corner of the Aegean to dredge up any hulk that might float: yachts, caïques, motor sailers, coastal steamers, ferryboats—all were chartered or commandeered, sorted out somewhat, and enrolled in Sea Transport echelons. Air Fleet 4 directed Southeast Command to load and sail the first (or light) echelon of caïque motor sailers so as to arrive off Maleme by the evening of X-plus-1 Day; and the second echelon to arrive off Heraklion on X-plus-2 Day. A mild reservation requested that the third echelon of steamers, loaded with precious tanks, should be held until Suda Bay could be safely entered.

If sailor help to *Merkur* was earnest but limited, soldier help through 12th Army headquarters was able to offer basic communications nets, billets, trucks, rations, and route clearance for the 11th Corps's onward rush from Germany. Not only in services but in operations, the Army got busy. The island links from the mainland to Crete were secured by Army landings on Kithira and Antikithira, while Melos at the top of the Cretan Sea was delivered by Luftwaffe Major Waldenga as a way-station for the Sea Transport echelons. He landed on the island in a Piper Cub type and took over from the civil authorities. When thereafter Luftwaffe planes should establish themselves, as planned, on the Italian island Scarpanto to the east, the barrier to the Aegean, except for Crete, would be complete.

Over on another island, hugging close to the mainland, the island of Euboea, General Ringel fretted about getting no word. What was his rumored objective like anyhow—like the island he was on or what? Surely there must be something special in it for a mountain division. He dug into his maps; Crete's rough spine, rising in four lumps connected by the thin coastal road, soon told the ground story. But there was the sea. What about getting over? This became the prime worry. In the afternoon of 8 May a two-man team from the 11th Air Corps arrived "to explain the coming operation order to the division," recorded the 5th Mountain Division War Diary in precise old German script. It was Colonel Bernhard Ramcke with a young captain in tow; they had come at General Student's behest as experts from the Parachute Troop Training School to indoctrinate and hearten the mountaineers. Ramcke, once a bosun's mate in the Navy, had spent most of his life fighting, and always in the thick of it. Here he could do little more than touch a few high spots of the operation. Yet he at once hit on the prime problems of crossing the water and getting in and out of planes. Ringel and staff found that corps plans were well along. Ramcke was to jump ahead of the mountaineers with a force of paratroops to break a way into Heraklion. This last must have been the best news.[7]

7. Ramcke VSJ gives an account of the wide career of General der Flieger Bernhard Ramcke *From Ship's Apprentice Boy to General of Paratroops.* Pp. 194–222 are pertinent to his Crete experience. During 1960, opportunity offered to discuss his experiences with him. His obvious resourcefulness and initiative show through— a short, wiry figure of a fighter. He would make a go of things, and did so on Crete.

Plans were maturing at the Grande Bretagne; the hum and hurry of their production mounted higher. By 5 May all commands but the mountain division were represented. Familiarity with Crete was growing, especially with her hazards; little became known of her hardy people. General Student recalled how the chief of counterintelligence, Admiral Canaris, came in on 7 May to pass the word that almost all Englanders had cleared out of Crete and that the people would themselves help disarm those who remained. A password, "Major Bock," for greeting the friendly natives was circulated. On hearing it any Cretan would be sure to lower his fowling piece and come over to shake hands. Student remained unconvinced, yet in action reports both he and Löhr took note of this intelligence. While Student busied himself in northern Greece to see his men through critical transport bottlenecks, his chief of staff, Colonel Schlemm, carried on with the plans. He had the final corps plan ready for a meeting of principal commanders on 11 May. On the 12th he issued the operation order.

The corps mission led off: "The 11th Air Corps, supported by the 8th Air Corps, has the task of taking the island of Crete into possession as a base for the conduct of air war in the Eastern Mediterranean. . . ." A short second paragraph gave a weak summary of the opposed strength and then followed the General Plan, to which all else had to contribute: "The 11th Air Corps with strong advance parachute troop elements and other shock troops . . . will take possession of the airfields and important towns of the island by surprise attack from the air." In this burst of confidence, victory was hung on the break-in drops. A spirit of "this time we'll show them" breathed from the order; and this spirit held through on Crete. Often it proved decisive.

A thoughtful breakdown into Task Organization and Task Assignment followed to fill out the bones of an enterprising combat scheme with the flesh of detail. The three principal task groups already cited, each commanded by a general, would carry the scheme along: Meindl had Group West (Maleme), Süssmann Group Center (Canea-Retimo), Ringel Group East (Heraklion and eastern Crete). In the first wave Meindl was to glide and jump his reinforced Sturm regiment against Maleme Airfield defenses, take the field at a stroke (*handstreichartig*), clear the runway, and hold it against all counter action, including artillery, for the landing of transport planes. After

---

The 5th Mountain Division's War Diary, handwritten, is a very valuable source (5th MD War Diary).

reconnoitering west and south and linking up with Group Center, east of him, he was to place a reinforced battalion at the Corps's disposal at Spilia village, 3 miles southwest of the air field.

This provision for corps on top of Student's strict injunction to notify him at once of the initial results, stresses his wish to take command in the field as soon as at all feasible and useful. It speaks also for his faith in a decisive first blow by his crack, quasi-corps formation, the Sturmregiment. It had grown to regimental size with a general in command from the elite nucleus called Sturmabteilung Koch that had won fame at Eben Emael in May 1940 by opening the way into Belgium. Even as a regiment it was still meant for special jobs directly under corps.[8]

Thus, with Maleme in hand, Student planned to strike east in support of the main effort under Süssmann against Canea and the British island command. He would have glide-landed and jumped his 7th Paratroop Division Headquarters and 3d Regiment, reinforced, and attached specialists from the Sturmregiment into Prison Valley for action against the defenses of Canea-Suda. "The chief object of attack," said the order, "is the elimination of the highest island military command and the destruction of the defense forces there." But a couple of inside blows were provided by the Sturmregiment specialists. One glider detachment was to land on an antiaircraft battery at a radio tower, take it, and nearby the supposed primary British communication and command center; a second detachment would meanwhile have landed farther north on Akrotiri Peninsula, the dragon's head tassel, against an antiaircraft battery and Canea. These two may have been the closest counterparts to the Eben Emael and the neighboring bridge drops that did so much in May 1940 to open Belgium and Holland to conquest. Could they now do the same for Crete? Close and heavy air combat support was to seal off the two targets and make them soft. The pretentious goals evidence a low-grade evaluation of British defenses and an inflated confidence in daylight airborne. In the second wave, during the afternoon, the 2d Regiment of Group Center was to take Retimo and its airstrip, 30 miles east of Canea, which could provide a reserve landing spot for Group East at Heraklion.

8. Merkur B, and discussion with Generals Student and Trettner in Germany, 1960. The German records reveal an unfamiliarity with the terrain and some confusion of Greek place names. Spilia was an old village deep up a valley, quite remote from the scene of action, but on some outline maps it was the only name shown, perhaps because of its age. Even if reserve elements could have found it, they would have been far out of touch.

Succeeding waves were then to land the 100th Regiment of the 5th Mountain Division at Maleme, whence it would join Group Center. Added was an interesting note about reconnaissance of a "high plateau Alikianou" (at the head of Prison Valley) for airlift landings. Alternative spots for this purpose had always to be kept in mind in case landings on the airfield proved impossible. The spot was conspicuous because it lay alongside the only water reservoir and power-producing facility. Group Center had an ambitious assignment of tasks.

If Ringel in the east was thus to lose his 100th Regiment to Süssmann, he would be recompensed by having Ramcke and the 1st Parachute Regiment, reinforced, blaze a way onto Heraklion's airport. Tasks assigned to Ramcke were repetitions of Meindl's at the opposite end of the front, with emphasis again on clearance of a runway and report of its readiness to receive troop airlifts. This done, the paratroops were to go over to the defensive until the third and following waves should land the 5th Mountain Division so that the occupation of eastern Crete could begin.

Student's drive for airfields was plainly directed at a flexibility that could enable him to throw stuff and bodies wherever most needed, rather than at creating strategic bases from which the ground fight could expand. For him the main base remained in Greece, while his paratroops in the van on Crete led the assault that would force the decision. He tried hard to make it appear strategically sound. Some support in men and machines might come by sea, but more direct support would come from combat planes acting as artillery. Sea support received only cursory notice in one sentence: "(7) *By sea*—Troops and follow-up supply not transported by air will be brought over by sea." The other, air combat support, filled almost a page of what Richthofen was expected to do:

(*a*) *Fighter Cover.* Protect [Air] Transport Groups against attack from the air during the approach of flights, drops, or landings and return. Main effort over target area.

(*b*) *Fight Down Ground Fire.*

        (*aa*) VIII Air Corps will subdue fire from hostile fleet units in Suda Bay or other island anchorages.

        (*bb*) It will concentrate attacks by bombers and dive bombers to eliminate antiaircraft batteries and troop massing immediately before the air drops of advance forces.

(*c*) *Further Support.* VIII Air Corps will support the advance of XI Corps against recognized hostile forces on call by ground forces after own reconnaissance. It will prevent encroachment of hostile fleet units by constant surveillance of the sea around Crete and attack all hostile warships of whatever kind.

(*d*) VIII Air Corps will assume responsibility for security of sea transport against hostile sea and air forces.

(*e*) Details will be settled mutually.

(*f*) Cooperation with ground forces will be regulated by a separate order.

(*g*) Early transfer of fighter and dive-bomber echelons to Maleme and Heraklion is counted upon.

Our earlier impression seems borne out—that Student held to his original basic plan and committed the bulk of his paratroop power to the initial two break-in waves, retaining behind only a minor capability for at once exploiting success. In the face of an imposed unfavorable spread in timing and space, he depended on mass paralysis by fright. As with England, the lever was psychological rather than strategic.

So the original basic theory was stuck to and hammered out operationally around the imposed unsuitable conditions. Yet, without men and material at the right spot at the right time, there could be no operation at all. Logistics and the press of time took over. Could the men be got to the still undetermined hop-off fields in time? Could the planes arrive and be fueled to lift them? Would each squatting trooper have his combat gear in hand and around his body? A fight for affirmative answers was led by the 11th Corps's versatile quartermaster, Lt. Colonel Conrad Seibt. Labors and mysteries of this new airborne realm descended upon him in March of 1941 during the long-ranged leap of General Süssmann's 2d Regiment into Bulgaria. The move demonstrated that for such operations the corps's organization and resources were in nowise adequate. For *Merkur*, then, supply by sea from Italy was soon adopted, but unexpected blocks turned up there too, notably in transport of petroleum.

The deeper Seibt dug, the longer his list of impossibles grew. First the troop lift: most of the 7th Paratroop Division had to move 1500 miles from Germany. The overhaul of Ju planes and need to avoid disclosure by mass plane movements ruled out air transport. Then came problems of general supply, munitions of undetermined calibers for ten days' combat (his guess) on Crete. Where in Greece could 503 planes be based and their crews, their troop cargoes, and commands be billeted? Over all sputtered the absurd local communications system. To have raised such minor irritations as drinking water, life jackets, air-drop harnesses, tropical clothing, or even armament for caïques in a rapidly growing soldier-navy would have been nit-picking. By and large petroleum—POL, three million gallons of plane fuel and lubricants—was the big bogey.[9]

But for the 11th Corps's commander, what counted most was his troops' arrival. A mass lift from home bases, and even from Norway, had to get under way at once; it coined its own name as it trundled through the countries—the Flying Dutchman. Rail transport stopped at Arad and Craiova in Rumania, whence columns of 3000 trucks hauled the men and gear over mountains and demolitions toward Attica. A single tangle occurred at Kozani with a *Barbarossa* convoy. Eight running days did it, so that by the evening of 14 May, one day before the first X-Day, all units had checked in at corps command. General Student breathed easier, but only for minutes.

The 8th Corps, already busy softening *Merkur* targets, grudged every bit of room for General Conrad's 11th Corps transport planes on fields in Greece. He had ten groups, fifty planes to a group, to be accommodated, nearly as many as the 8th Corps had altogether, and these heavy transports needed a good takeoff run. Ideally, a transport group and its organic troop cargo stayed together at one field; here lack of space imposed the splitting of groups and fighting teams among several takeoff points. The most dangerous disorganizer, though, was dust. No matter how hard Seibt's hired and enslaved labor crews sprayed and sprinkled, an impenetrable cloud of dust fouled each takeoff. Whereas the standard for two groups to get off and form for flight was a few minutes, it now took over an hour. Serious operational fragmenting and retardation threatened. The final seven fields in use by Conrad's planes were scattered over 150 miles, from Corinth along the isthmus to Megara, Eleusis (where the 8th Corps headquarters based), Phaleron (along the shore beyond Athens), then northward to Tanagra, Topolia, and finally, Dadion. Plane crews and improvised ground crews growled about their miserable lot; short supply, catch-as-catch-can quarters and messing—but worst, no fuel. It remained the crisis item. Not a transport could fly.[10]

Corinth's blown bridge still blocked the canal. A gasoline tanker

9. Seibt.

10. Colonel von Heyking, commander of the 2d Transport Squadron and a vet-eran of Corinth, held a dry run of his squadron's takeoff on 18 May. Seventeen-minute lapses to let the dust settle between echelon launches dragged out the time for the squadron to form in the air to over an hour. Heyking reported this loss of time, but no change in scheduling resulted. Heyking Ms.

and another ship loaded with 8000 drums of fuel from Italy waited at the western entrance of the Gulf of Corinth. Discharge would have to be made beyond the eastern canal exit and going roundabout the Peloponnese would take too long. Since the day after the air drop, 27 April, local divers had toiled to move the tangled metal in the bottom without success. On 15 May German divers from Kiel began a frantic fight against the clock. Little by little their equipment bumped and yanked away. By 17 May they had got a narrow pass sufficiently

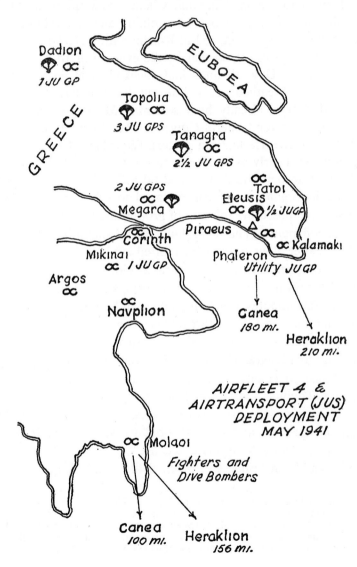

clear to squeeze the waiting vessels through. The latest X-Day was put off for one day. It would not do, for the shipmasters refused to move without mine sweeping to precede them. Seibt wrote, "in case of need, force must be used." Time was up. Two armed persuaders boarded each ship, and slowly the ships began to move. Late on the seventeenth the ships docked at the east exit. Trucks rolled alongside from the Corinth airfield; unloading began. Early the next morning the ships fueled Megara, and by noon they were in Piraeus to finish the remaining five fields. X-Day was now set for 20 May 1941.

Fuel for three sorties was the initial demand, one million gallons per sortie. Converted to conventional drums it meant 12,000 drums would be bouncing over the Grecian landscape in trucks to fill one sortie; the other two had to be pieced out in part by raw uncrated five-gallon tins, thousands of them, recently liberated from an Athenian factory. The crazy fuel stream ran from ship to shore tankage to drum by hose to truck to plane by hand pump at 92° in the blazing sun. Late on 19 May, Colonel Seibt reported that the final truck column was rolling. First wave was sure of takeoff.[11]

Other crises rose and fell in this fevered climate of impossibles. Logistics achieved a new urgency and authority even with the flyers. Every act took on operational meaning. The uproar preempted the command mind and energy to the exclusion of operational problems still unexplored. On the evening of 19 May, General Student on the near shore knew that his corps could make the takeoff deadline, but what it would meet on the far shore he knew little about. Combined sketchy intelligence and wishful preconceptions produced a badly distorted picture of the opposing ground forces. If they had not cleared out, they should be near one division—a security garrison, Student called it—of two infantry regiments and one of artillery, plus an uncertain number of evacuees from Greece. British air he overestimated at twenty-five to forty fighters and bombers. In consequence German air strikes were wasted against a nonexistent air power. Yet at this hot stage who cared? Certainly no one in the 11th Air Corps. It was time to ignore any new or resurrected handicaps, and go, which is the way it usually happens when the chips are down. If it were not so, there never would be a battle. If *Merkur* was impetuous, he was also over-hasty.

11. Eighth Air Corps men unloaded a ship of bombs, but took out only enough for the moment; more could be unloaded when needed. Their command refused to move the ship for the 11th Air Corps unloading of another ship. Time was wasted in intraservice bickering—combat flyers versus paratroops.

On the island no one could guess the ultimate weight of those chips, least of all the latest defense commander, General Bernard Freyberg of New Zealand. He had received wholly unexpected orders to take over Crete's chaos while stopping there en route from abandoned Greece to Egypt. He had wanted to check on the needs of New Zealanders already on Crete for re-equipping and re-forming in Egypt, where they were soon to have joined him. General Freyberg was an old hand in this region of the East Basin and Aegean from World War I. Could that have been behind this surprising assignment to the defense of Crete?

13. Crete's Defenses

British Deployment: May 1941

In the year 1915 above Gallipoli, on the north rim of the Aegean, a brawny leader in Hood Battalion, Royal Naval Division, brought distinction to the division and himself. Lt. Commander Bernard Freyberg was to lead a troop ashore in a feigned night landing attack to divert and confuse Turkish defenders. It occurred to him that one man ashore lighting flares could create as much diversion as the whole party. He rigged himself out accordingly and went over the side of a destroyer's boat off the beach, swam in to "make like" a big landing, padded up on the beach, lit his first flare, and ducked back into the water to watch results. Nothing happened. He swam along the short a piece, lit another flare, and this time took cover on shore. Again no response. Where could they be? Poking around, he found defense works, vacant ones—not a sign of a soldier. After a third flare burned out, the one-man diversion force swam out to sea. Eventually his boat picked him up. His activity had nevertheless affected the Turkish deployment. For his contribution, Tiny (for Big) Freyberg received the D.S.O. As the Gallipoli actions dragged out, he also received a thorough grounding in the landing game and went on to the Western Front to earn three bars to his D.S.O. and a Victoria Cross.

Born in England, brought up in New Zealand, Freyberg had fought on foreign soil before World War I drew him to England. There a novel Naval Division was forming, under the eye of Winston Churchill at the Admiralty, for special service. It stirred Freyberg's interest. He had a letter to Churchill, and the two venturesome spirits hit it off well. A commission for Freyberg in the Naval Division soon followed, and with it he went off to Gallipoli. When World War II broke, he was appointed to command the Second New Zealand Expeditionary Force, part of which was to be the Second Division, for service in England. Some New Zealanders at home would rather have seen one of their home-born soldiers get the command, someone who knew the battalions and their men, for Freyberg had spent so much of his time away. During the Battle of Britain of 1940 he was in England with 5 Brigade; he took it to Egypt, where it joined the other two brigades, 4 and 6. In March and April, then, the whole division took part in the Greek campaign. After H.M.S. *Ajax* evacuated General Freyberg as the last general officer of the BEF out of Greece, she brought him in the early hours of 29 April to Suda Bay. With members of his staff he went ashore to confer with officers of New Zealand formations already on Crete. Besides 5 Brigade, he found 4 Brigade there, which made two-thirds of the division. These two were to stay on Crete for a time as part of Crete's defense force. Then 6 Brigade went on to Egypt. The general talked things out with his people and arranged for an early morning flight to Egypt. There he hoped the division would soon be reunited and rehabilitated, after Greece. He undoubtedly heard something about defense plans for Crete and the involvement of his troops.

Shortly before his plane was to take off, word came for him to wait; a conference with General Wavell, just in from Cairo, impended. Toward noon the senior officers gathered on the terrace of a small villa in Platanias village, halfway between Maleme Airfield and Canea. Present were General Wilson, commander of the BEF in Greece; General Weston of the Royal Marines, newly arrived and appointed commander of defense forces on Crete (Commander Creforce) only three days before; Air Commodore d'Albiac, commander of the air forces in Greece; Wing Commander Beamish, also a recent arrival, to command the RAF on Crete; General Heywood, the head of Britain's military mission in Greece; General Freyberg; and Sir Michael Palairet, Britain's ambassador to Greece. That in this sea-bound problem no Navy representative was present is remarkable. Freyberg recorded that Wavell came in last, looking drawn and tired. He was just back from Palestine. Immediately he took Wilson aside for some earnest words. As the next senior to Wavell and the BEF commander, Wilson would normally take over any command on Crete, since his forces gathered there and took part in building the defenses. For this very reason Wavell had wired him a day earlier to ask about Crete's defense chances. Wilson's able reply, in which Weston concurred, postulated that sea and airborne invasion from Greece was likely and that with their well-known power, the Germans could mount whatever kind of landing attack they wanted and reduce the garrison defenses in short order. He cautioned that unless adequate forces from all services were made available, "holding the island would be a dangerous commitment." While this view could hardly have been what Wavell wanted, events proved the prescience of Wilson's judgment. The commander in chief had to sell Crete's defense. That was why he had come.[1]

In the private talk with Wilson he apparently made his point (which was to shift him to Palestine), for the two men broke off, and Wavell motioned Freyberg over, took his arm, and launched into a welcome tribute to New Zealand Division: no other formation, he said, could have carried out those withdrawals so well, Freyberg recorded, and continued, "His next words came as a complete surprise. . . . He wanted me to take command of the forces in Crete . . . it would be attacked in the next few days." On the heels of the flattering compliments, midst the visible confusion on Crete, the proffer bore all the signs of a quick sale to a Dominion commander, one who had never been consulted about plans for him or his forces. He responded with the need of keeping New Zealand Division together; his government would surely have misgivings over splitting the division. Wavell sounded a call to duty. "I could do nothing but accept," said Freyberg. It seems he understood the assignment to be a temporary affair that would soon be over, and Wavell promised opportunity for reuniting the division. The Terrace conferees then gathered around the table to discuss Crete's unhappy lot. Had Wavell confided what soon came out, that the newest Commander Creforce had been nominated by his friend Winston Churchill, the going might have been easier. Freyberg's record added, "There was not much to discuss." The island was to be held with *the main object to deny the enemy the use of Crete as an air and submarine base.* No reservation of own offensive use was made, and as for the opposing order of battle and probable

1. Davin, pp. 12–43; NZ Docs, 389, 390; Churchill, pp. 218–304; Long, pp. 152, 179, 206–14.

plans, according to Wavell, 6000 airborne troops, backed by a seaborne effort, were expected to attack Heraklion and Maleme airfields. British air power to repulse the attack was in doubt, but the sea menace he would pursue with Navy. Guesses about own ground strength varied widely. A day earlier Wavell had cabled Churchill optimistic statistics about the permanent garrison of three British battalions, two heavy and three light antiaircraft and coastal artillery batteries, 30,000 evacuees from Greece with rifles and some machine guns, and Greek formations. MNBDO (Mobile Naval Bases Defense Organization) was to arrive by 14 May. No one was prepared to talk about plans or about what was most urgently needed from Egypt. Command over the whole strange mix on the island was sure to be bothered by national diversities of New Zealanders, Australians, Britons, and Greeks. The meeting broke up. All it had accomplished was to pass the buck for the unholy muddle on Crete to Freyberg. That had been Wavell's mission. The enormity of it must have worked in on the recipient, for at parting he expressed forebodings and took a stand for immediate reinforcement, especially in the air.

A review of the changing images of Crete entertained by Churchill and Wavell is informative. Fortress Suda as a "second Scapa" came first; it ignored the rest of the island. A directive during February to the fourth Commander Creforce, Brigadier Galloway, named him "Fortress Commander Suda Bay" and commander of all British personnel on Crete. He was to "defend the Bay as an advance fueling base, . . . to hurry administrative preparations for a garrison of Divisional strength." Though the early estimates counted on air and airborne threats, they failed to consider the whole island or the specific defense of the airfields.

When in March the German hosts crowded through Bulgaria to the Greek border, British counterplanning revolved around an Allied front across Greece. Notice of Crete grew from the needs of the front in Greece to which the island could contribute as a transit base. By 2 April Wavell regarded Suda Bay as a staging base for troops and planes. At about the same time he fell on a welcome solution for the island defense and command: both would be turned over to the prospective MNBDO commander, General Weston of the Royal Marines. Weston arrived ahead of his outfit in late March and went to reconnoiter his prospective island command. The image of Fortress Suda thus blended with that of a convenient way-point. Crete's own needs got no serious consideration.

When Greece crumbled, the image changed into a series of new forms dictated by events. On 16 April Wavell told London he assumed Crete would be held. Churchill agreed and added a few political complications that made Crete over into a surviving piece of Greece. "Crete must be held in force . . . strong elements of the Greek Army should establish themselves on Crete together with the King and his Government. We shall aid and maintain Crete to the utmost." In his post-mortem (Churchill, p. 269), he said that Middle East Command had neglected study of the island and had executed directions feebly as to road building from Sfakia on the south coast to the north to facilitate reinforcement. By 18 April, instead of a "bit of Greece," he renamed the island a "receptacle of whatever can get here from Greece . . . fuller defense later . . . Libya counts first, evacuation from Greece second, Tobruk fitted in as convenient . . . Crete later." The form kept shifting.

Rommel's drive diverted both Middle East Command and the prime minister. He busied himself with his Operation *Tiger*, steering a fast convoy full of tanks from Gibraltar to Egypt, with a sideshow bombardment of Tripoli en route. A joint intelligence estimate of the eastern Mediterranean jolted him back to Crete. He cabled a shifty, incongruous warning to Wavell: "Heavy airborne attack will soon be made on Crete. . . . Let me know what forces on island . . . and what your plans are. It ought to be a fine opportunity for killing parachute troops." Wavell replied with the optimistic guess already noticed at the Terrace Conference and added a new twist: attack on Crete might be a cover for the seizure of Syria or Cyprus. He also downgraded the joint intelligence estimate that had inspired the prime minister's inquiry and that was soon to disturb General Freyberg deeply. What good came from Churchill's direct exchanges with the operational leaders is questionable. He soon added the latest Commander Creforce to his list.

When Freyberg on 29 April looked up his men on Crete, he found Brigadier Hargest and troops of his 5 Brigade clustered thick around Platanias where the Terrace Conference had taken place. The day before, Brigadier Puttick had arrived from Greece with 4 Brigade and was now, as the senior, relieving Hargest as commander of all New Zealanders. Hargest would revert to his own 5 Brigade. Puttick at once examined the defense dispositions ordered by General Weston for Creforce. Thus Freyberg saw two-thirds of the Division being incorporated in an expanding defense scheme; he must have heard the brigadiers out about what was going on, and it is a fair guess that they painted no rosy picture. The upshot was plain—the two brigades, 4 and 5, were trapped. The surprise sprung by Wavell on the Terrace must have raised a question of loyalty to his men in Freyberg's mind: where could he best look after them, in Cairo seeking their relief, or working with them on Crete? He chose Crete, though his own record hardly says as much, and committed himself with his men. He determined at this time that Creforce must get what it needed or the job be given up. His predicament was well described by de Guingand of Wavell's staff when he wrote (De Guingand, p. 3), "Rarely have a commander and his troops been given a more difficult task."

Commander Creforce wasted no time: he at once relieved Weston, who remained Commander Suda Bay Sector, and set about taking stock while a headquarters was established and staffed in Canea. He was not aware of Churchill's backing. As an old hand he had a feeling for what his troops needed most and what he himself needed if he was to get hold of his ship. On the following morning he issued his noteworthy Special Order of the Day:

The withdrawal from Greece has now been completed. . . . A smaller force held a much larger one at bay for over a month and then withdrew from an open beach. This rearguard battle and withdrawal has been a great feat of arms. The fighting qualities and steadiness of the troops were beyond praise.

Today the British forces in Crete stand and face another threat, the possibility of invasion. The threat of a landing is not a new one. In England we have faced it for nearly a year. If it comes here it will be delivered with all the accustomed air activity. We have learned in the last month a certain amount about the enemy air methods. If he attacks us here on Crete the enemy will be meeting our troops on even terms, and those of us who met his infantry in the last month ask for no better chance. We are to stand now and fight back. Keep yourselves fit and ready for immediate action. I am confident that the force at our disposal will be adequate to defeat any attack that may be delivered on this island.

He could say this after seeing unkempt, disgruntled men eating from tin cans for lack of mess gear and sleeping without cover! And after hearing about a number who had taken to the hills with their rifles to roam on their own. How to get at all these men, strike fire in them as their leader? Tiny Freyberg knew how.

All Crete's grim prospects were now his. The unfortunate Greek campaign had been a harmful experience—retreat and re-retreat, ending in a struggle for escape. All of it, as the first exposure to real action, was bad soldier blooding. Withdrawal had become a habit. And the confused first haven of refuge, Suda Bay, inspired only more doubt; a pall of smoke hung over it from burning tankers; cruiser *York* lay beached high at bayhead; three disabled hulks were lying down bay. One ship was trying to unload at the quay that stuck out from the south shore at Suda village. Nearby were the Naval headquarters of Captain Morse, Naval Officer In Charge (NOIC). His sea power was weak and his troubles many. From high ground near Creforce headquarters, Suda Bay and its crippled sea power must have looked hopeless. From Suda Vice-Admiral Pridham-Wippell had conducted the evacuation of Greece, but he and his ships had cleared out for Alexandria. Naval action to foil German seaborne invasion became General Freyberg's painful anxiety. In his own dark seascape, he lacked a strong sailor voice of command alongside. What could the Navy do from over 400 miles away?

To recall how things got that way: from 25 to 29 April the human tide from Greece had swept over the quay and the shores of Suda. Feeding and bivouacking the men were high priorities, but sorting out was even more important. The command separated the Dominion soldiers by directing New Zealanders westward along the shore road from Suda, and the Australians east. This sorting out fitted the defense plan just now being implemented. General Weston's Creforce Operation Instruction No. 5 set it forth, starting with the decision of the commanders in chief in Egypt, "to hold Crete at all cost," and named "Maleme–Suda Bay and Heraklion as essential to the defense," Retimo as desirable. Airborne attack was a certainty, and invasion by sea a possibility. Lines of responsibility followed the natural division of troops: New Zealand west, Australia east, of the center, Canea-Suda. Retimo fell to the Cretan gendarmerie and Heraklion to the permanent garrison, 14 British Army Brigade of three plus battalions; it was the oldest and the fittest formation on the island. One regular British battalion, 1 Welch, remained to defend Canea and headquarters. Troops were executing this deployment when General Freyberg took over command on 30 April; he could do nothing but let them proceed.

On the day that he announced his assumption of command in Creforce Order No. 3, he confirmed the division of the defense organization into four sectors:

> Maleme-Galatas (Brigadier Puttick), New Zealand Division;
> Suda Bay Sector (General Weston), MNBDO, 1 Welch, assorted British units;
> Retimo Sector (Brigadier Vasey), 19 Australian Brigade;
> Heraklion Sector (Brigadier Chappel), 14 British Army Brigade reinforced.

So constituted, Creforce limped along, preoccupied with getting established and checking capabilities.

What in truth was this a command of, this Creforce: of terrain, of a theater, or of an all-arms force for a specific task? Freyberg's appointment was as General Officer Commanding Creforce. Whittled down to bare bones, he commanded only an unhomogeneous lot of marooned soldiers in a last-ditch stand on an island from which there was no escape. No one man commanded in chief over holding Crete as Löhr did over taking it. When ComCreforce applied to his Army commander in chief, Wavell in Cairo, for major interservice support, Wavell had to work the answer out with the other two chiefs through a cumbersome committee system of talk and deal. No one carried the overall responsibility for getting things done. By nature men dislike insoluble problems, and these men were no exceptions. They had a local glut of them. For a sustained drive of all arms as in Crete, the committee system was totally unsuited. For lack of any other, it had to do.

From any point of view, the worst situation was in the air. A few Fleet Air Arm fragments at Maleme enjoyed the longest tenure, but even they hardly felt at home under frequent changes, field construction, and unsure local command. RAF pieces flew in from Greece and Egypt, so that at the end of April the grand total came to thirty-six assorted aircraft. About half were fully operable. No locally integrated field defense policy of all arms, or even of grounded airmen, existed. While the RAF held that for lack of planes, defense by air combat should not be attempted, it said nothing about denial of the fields. The agreed mission of Creforce at the Terrace Conference was one of pure denial; no mention of field demolition, however, occurred, because of expected own use, by two hoped-for Crete-based RAF fighter squadrons. The figure 2 appeared in a 21 April estimate of the London Joint Planning Staff. But the RAF soon began to hedge; two full squadrons with a third ready as reinforcement degenerated to one squadron with 100 percent reserves and then slipped lower still. Wavell adopted the one squadron plus reserves idea, but Freyberg clung to his hope for two.[2]

A threat from both air and the sea troubled ComCreforce most. He knew the exacting requirements of the landing game well and felt no qualms about the land fight or about parachutists. Still, a sea landing, closely coordinated with airdrops around nearby airfields, was something else. From England Freyberg had watched the cross-channel threat of a few barges grow into a formidable landing fleet; he knew how the Luftwaffe had almost achieved supremacy over England and how vital Fighter Command had been to her survival. Indeed, just now reports spoke of revived Channel activity. Soon after taking command, he read an April summary for Crete prepared by London's Joint Intelligence Subcommittee. Its premise immediately arrested attention: "imminent simultaneous attack by Airborne and Seaborne expeditions." Timed and targeted together on the scale and dispersion postulated, the report struck home. The attack scheme approximated what nowadays is inaccurately called vertical envelopment. Freyberg on 1 May passed his concern on to Wavell and closed in these words: "The force here can and will fight, but cannot hope to repel Invasion without full support from the Navy and Airforce. If for other reasons these cannot be made available at once, I urge that the question of holding Crete should be reconsidered." Here was a strong courageous stand. Actually, it reflected the weakness of Freyberg's lone ground command in a three-service task. His conclusion paralleled the already noticed answer of General Wilson of 28–29

2. Major Davin, *Crete*, pp. 19–21 writes: "From the first Crete was envisaged as being an air base as well as a naval one . . . as early as 13 November 1940, the Chiefs of Staff accepted a policy of holding Crete 'whatever happens on the mainland.' . . . On 4 Jan. 1941 . . . the Joint Planning Staff accepted a memorandum from the Chief of the Air Staff which ran, 'The foundation on which we should base assistance to Greece is Crete, which must be held at all costs. . . .' By 21 April . . . JPS paper 49 . . . recommended retention of the existing two RAF Fighter Squadrons [on Crete] and their reinforcement by a third." On 24 April, Air Marshal Longmore, commander in chief of Air Middle East, after a visit to Crete reported that "one squadron of Hurricanes with 100 percent reserve . . . ought to be able to keep Suda Bay open for the Navy"—Davin, pp. 30, 31. But he doubted the squadron could be kept up to strength. He returned to England and by 8 May had strengthened the Air chief of staff, Air Marshal Portal, in his own belief that active air defense over Crete would be dangerous to Egypt's security through withdrawal of air protection. Therefore Crete's "ground organization [at the fields] should be kept to permit aircraft to fly in from Egypt if seaborne attack was attempted" —Davin, pp. 35–37. Meanwhile General Wavell had adopted the idea of one squadron plus 100 percent reserves for "keeping Suda Bay open for the Navy," which Longmore himself had now abandoned in favor of the Portal scheme to use Cretan fields "only as advanced landing grounds for fighters."

April. Thus the three top candidates for ComCreforce—Weston, Wilson, and Freyberg—were in agreement.[3]

At the Terrace, Wavell had said he was at his wit's end for aircraft. Now he replied to Freyberg's stand on 2 May with firm assurance of full fleet support. Air would be more difficult. Other deficiencies would be filled. He thought London's estimate exaggerated. An all-out effort was under way on the air question. Then came a deal. (Wavell seemed always to be talking of the future, as if Crete were merely a short, passing show.) He could be helped to fulfill his promise to relieve New Zealand troops in Crete for re-forming in Egypt if Freyberg would release the New Zealanders already in Egypt (6 Brigade) for communications guard duty. The long message closed on an uninspired note: "Have most definite instructions to hold Crete and even if the question were reconsidered, I am doubtful if the troops could be removed before the enemy attack. . . ." Small comfort to the man on the spot. What if the defense should fail? Would it be easier to remove the men then?

"Most definite instructions" may be inferred from the flood of Churchill messages. It seems that London, like Wavell, simply presumed Crete could be held, and thereafter events and last-minute thoughts hardened the presumption into a decision. In a cabinet meeting of 28 April the disturbing joint intelligence summary had come under scrutiny; the prime minister himself felt dubious about holding; yet later in the day he dispatched his jocular message to Wavell about (the sport of) killing parachutists and ended the admonition, "The island must be stubbornly defended." Had a formal question been put and a cabinet decision been taken, Winston Churchill would have seen to an eloquent notice of it for record and not have given it later by radio to the public for politics and propaganda. Rather, the London chiefs held off, pending advices from the scene by Navy (Cunningham), Weston, and Wavell. The dangerous presumption was fortified by Admiral Cunningham's reply of 1 May, which gave a confused double answer: need for a night fueling facility at Suda (well enough), yet more important, denial of the island as long as possible

3. NZ Docs 387, 389, 392. General Freyberg also cabled the New Zealand government in the same tenor: The island could not be held unless Air and Navy could bring full support. "There is no evidence of naval forces capable of guaranteeing us against seaborne invasion, and airforces consist of six Hurricanes and seventeen obsolete aircraft." He set forth the gaping ground-force shortages in artillery, tools, transport, reserve equipment, and ammunition. He suggested pressure should be brought on London "to supply us with sufficient means to defend the island or to review the decision that Crete must be held."

to postpone German Air against Navy and other ships operating in the East Basin. With the latter need—freedom of the seas—the chiefs seemed to agree. All Crete was to be denied. On 2 May Wavell's précis painted a grim picture of Creforce's appalling deficiencies and burdensome surpluses. He came out with it, "Crete is a difficult problem for all three services," but could not forgo the softening last word: "All these difficulties are being tackled and, if time allows, will be overcome." There was small basis for such hope.

Freyberg's call to reconsider was as sound in strategy as it was strong in loyalty to his men. It would be the individual soldier who would have to stand against the old unutterable, unanswerable query: Why must it be me? The fact was, no alternative but to stand any longer existed. This ComCreforce now knew. He knew also of Churchill's warm personal interest. It must have been welcome, for selection by the highest level adds stature to a job and to its commander. It pumps up prestige (witness Rommel) and challenges local sources to give support. So the impossible edged toward the possible.

Creforce spirits were rising. A Freyberg message to Middle East Command late on 3 May reflected a fresh confidence:

You can depend on all here. . . . We have now sorted out and reorganized . . . by this evening we will be as ready as can be within limits. . . . So long as Navy supports our efforts, I feel all will be well. . . . During the last forty-eight hours I have seen all officers and NCO's; they are in great heart and will do their utmost. . . . Every day we grow stronger [NZ Docs 395].

The "forty-eight hours" were those since his call for reconsideration. Wavell had replied and the above message then finished the matter. When Freyberg said "within limits" he knew the defense was short of air support, but he had high hopes of support by two fighter squadrons still to come. His troops could be seen settling into their new role; they had sighted their force commander and evinced a comforting reaction to his call. In much the same vein Freyberg responded two days later to Churchill's confidence mixed with uneasiness:

Many thanks for your cable. Cannot understand nervousness. I am not in the least anxious about airborne attack . . . have made my dispositions and feel that with troops now at my disposal can cope adequately. However, a combination of airborne and seaborne attack is different . . . even so, provided the Navy can help, I trust all will be well. When we get our equipment and transport and with a few extra Fighters it should be possible to hold Crete. Meanwhile there will be a period during which we shall be vulnerable. . . . Everybody in great form . . . [NZ Docs 398].

His "dispositions" had been ordered in Creforce Operation Instruction No. 10, released the day before.

Despite the direct and friendly Churchill-Freyberg liaison, London aggravated Crete's political problems and snarled them up with strategic necessities. The king of Greece, for instance, arrived on Crete 24 April and was followed by a skeleton government. London kept insisting on a fiction of Greek sovereignty over the island, which the British were merely assisting. The security of king and government made problems, as did the reorganization of his military forces on Crete of about 10,000 troops, short of arms, munitions, and training. Some 450,000 islanders required food, and so also did 14,000 Italian prisoners taken in Albania. In Creforce itself there were too many extra mouths to fill: about 10,000 specialist and service troops were in the way. Shipping space to bring arms, artillery, tanks, and munitions grew short. But the shortage that hurt most was still in communications and motor transport; every message, every move was affected.

Creforce Operational Instruction No. 10, which took effect 4 May 1941, carried forward the deployment and tasks assigned to the four sectors by Creforce order of 30 April. So established, this framework, adjusted in minor particulars as things shook down, held through to X-Day of 20 May 1941. In the accompanying table of Creforce Task Organization[4] the sectors are presented in the sequence of attack from the west at Kastelli Kisamou, between the dragon horns, toward the east—to Maleme, then Galatas and Canea-Suda, all in the forenoon; and on to Retimo and Heraklion in the afternoon of X-Day.

4. After Operation Instruction No. 10 and Order of Battle. Davin, p. 44 and app. 4; Long, pp. 215–20, 279–83.

CREFORCE TASK ORGANIZATION - MAY 1941.

MALEME SECTOR

NZ Div, Greek Army Regts (Brigadier Puttick).
Task - Repel air and sea invasion Maleme Sector.
    Boundaries: Western - West coast Crete.
            Eastern - South from sea at west edge Canea along Kladiso R
      to junction coastal and Prison Valley rds, thence SW along Prison
      Valley Rd 1200 yds, thence SSW through Turkish fort nr Pirgos.

1st Regt Greek Army (1030), (Major Bedding) NZ Liaison Party (14)   1044
Task - Hold Kastelli Kisamou area (between the dragon horns).

5 NZ Bde (Brigadier Hargest): 21, 22, 23, 28 Inf Bns, Engr Det (as
    Inf)   3183
    Support - 2 MG plats, 2-3.7 hows, 7-75's, 2 heavy tanks;
        (not under local Comd: AA 2-3", 10 Bofors, Coast Arty 2-4")
Task - Hold Maleme airfield, beaches and coast from Tavronitis R
    through Platanias.

10 NZ Bde (Col Kippenberger): Composite Bn (1043), Div Cavalry (194) 1237
    6th and 8th Greek Army Regts   2498
    Support - 1 MG plat, 2-3.7 hows, 3-75's   85
        in Reserve, for use only with Div approval - 20 Bn   637
Task - Hold Galatas Heights and Prison Valley.*

4 NZ Bde (Brigadier Inglis): 18, 19 Inf Bns
    Support - 1 MG plat, 4-3.7 hows, 10 Lt tanks;   1417
        on call, 1 Welch Bn from Suda Sector.
Task - Force Reserve, in position adjoining 10 Bde, for counter
    attack toward Maleme, Prison Valley, Retimo and the east.

        Troop Summary: Greek 3528, British 6573   10101
                     Hqts and services   1396

                   Maleme Sector total   11497

*The task of holding Prison Valley was hardly so clearly assigned to 10 Bde.
Command over the Valley was split between 10 Bde and 19 Bn of 4 Bde. Neither
Bde commander (Kippenberger or Inglis) could order a general counter attack to
clear the Valley. Apparently this authority was reserved to NZ Div command.

- -

SUDA SECTOR

Mobile Naval Base Defense Organization (MNBDO), Greek, British, Australian
    Army units (General Weston Royal Marines).
Task - Defend Suda Sector - Canea, Akrotiri, Suda Base - against sea, air,
    and ground attack.
    Boundaries: Western - eastern boundary Maleme Sector.
             Eastern - SW from the sea at Georgeoupolis (southeast of
      Suda Bay) to Askifos.

    2d Regt Greek Army (930)   930
    Royal Marines (364), 1 Welch Bn (854), 1 Ranger Bn (417), N. Hussars
        (279), Royal-Horse Arty (307), NZ Supply Col (145), Misc British
        (700)   3066

```
    2/2 Aust Fwd Regt (554), 2/3 Aust Fwd Regt (306), Parts of 16
        Aust Bde (443) and 17 Aust Bde (387)                            1690
        Support - 2-12 pdrs, 16-3.7 hows, Coast Arty 4-6", 2-4"; AA
        10-3", 16 Bofors, 22 search lts                                 2255

    Troop Summary:  Greek 930, British 7011                             7941
                    Hqts and services (Engrs, port labor, Ord)          7717
                    Suda Sector total                                  15658

Soon after battle began 2/7 and 2/8 Aust Bns under Brigadier Vasey at
Georgeoupolis joined Suda Sector with 1756 trs                          1756
                    bringing Suda Sector total to                      17414
```

- -

RETIMO SECTOR

2 Aust Bns, Cretan Gendarmerie, 2 Regts Greek Army (Lt Col Campbell)
Task - Hold airstrip, port, town of Retimo.
    Boundaries: Western - from the sea at west edge of Retimo south
        approximately 1 mile.
        Eastern - from Olive oil factory on sea at Stavromenos
        south 1 mile. (A 1-mile deep by 8-mile long coastal defense
        belt to include Retimo town and port, airstrip, and olive oil
        factory.)

```
    Cretan Gendarmes                                                    800
    Task - Hold town and port of Retimo.
        2/1 Aust Bn (620) (Lt Col Campbell), 2/11 Aust Bn (650)
        (Maj Sandover)                                                 1270
        4th, 5th Regts Greek Army (each 1200)                          2400
        Support - 2 MG plats, 8 field guns, 7 mortars, 2 hvy tanks      190
    Task - Hold airstrip and adjacent lands.

    Troop Summary:  Greek 3200, Australian 1460                        4660
                    Misc (Medic, Signals, RAF)                          175

                    Retimo Sector total                                4835
```

- -

HERAKLION SECTOR

British, Australian, Greek Army units (Brigadier Chappel).

Task - Defend Heraklion Sector against air, sea, and ground attack.
    Boundaries: Western - from sea at west edge of Heraklion south 2 miles.
        Eastern - from sea just east of airfield south 2 miles.
    (A 2-mile deep by 5-mile long coastal defense belt to include
    Heraklion town, seaport and airfield.)

```
    3d & 7th Regts and 1 Garrison Bn Greek Army                        2700
    Task - Hold town and seaport Heraklion.

    14 Inf Bde British Army (Brigadier Chappel):  2 Yorks & Lancs Bn (742)
        2 Black Watch Bn (867), 2 Leicester Bn (637), 4 Med Regt (450)
        2/4 Aust Bn (553)                                             3249
        Support - 13 field guns, 2-4" coastal guns, AA 4-3", 12 Bofors
        2 hvy, 6 lt tanks                                              675
    Task - Hold airfield and land between it and town.

    Troop Summary:  Greek 2700, British & Australian 3924             6624
                    Misc - Medic (245), Hqt & Navy (195)
                    RAF (192).  Engrs (190)                            822

                    Heraklion Sector total                            7446
On 24 May Argyll & Sutherland Bn joined 14 Bde from a landing
on the south coast                                                     655
                    bringing Heraklion Sector final total to          8101
```

- -

The total of all troops came to 41,847—a deceptive figure, since about 6,000 were service hands without arms or training. Discounted for these and other supernumeraries, the totals in fighting strength round out to the figures below. There should never have been so many supernumeraries. They became a weighty factor in the final outcome.

British Army	9,000
Royal Marines	1,900
New Zealand Division	7,400
Australian Imperial Force	6,200
Total	24,500
(the corresponding German figure was 23,000)	
Greek and Cretan forces	10,000
Grand total	34,500

If the Greek and Cretan forces were not on a British level of weapons, munitions, and training, they nevertheless fought better than is generally credited. They inflicted casualties on the invader and denied him passage and positions.

The oldest force on the island, 14 Brigade, felt at home on Crete, was fresh and fully equipped, and had suffered no withdrawal pains from Greece. This brigade could have been used to better advantage in Maleme Sector.

Sorted out, reorganized, and reoriented, the new Creforce deployed for battle, along old lines extended rather than fresh ones drawn by a fresh evaluation. It seemed to be all there was time for. Yet time held on and invasion held off. Under bright Cretan sunshine and clear skies in a warming island countryside, tensions eased; the nightmare of escape from Greece receded, like the privations and slackness of the first bitter days on Crete. Scouting expeditions discovered sources of eggs and poultry. Oranges abounded. The native wines and spirits in village and town proved a little heavy and heady. But life was good and things stabilized as the men took root in territories of their own. The sun warmed the days enough to encourage swimming on the fine north-shore beaches. Not many swimmers noted how suitable the beaches were for hostile landings, though every few days another ramshackle boat full of escapees from the mainland was welcomed with cheers and rejoicing. The menace of invasion by sea did nevertheless distort the defense deployment into attempting to face in two directions at once. While in far-off London the nagging worry for Crete was over parachutists, in the island command it was over amphibians.

Behind the quips about bird shoots and speculations about which day it would be, there lurked the true nub of the strategic issue: What was it that had to be saved or taken? Bodies, of course; but what loss or gain would make them give up? What vital feature meant victory or defeat? This is where sound planning had to begin.

If Student thought to do without an old-fashioned beachhead base, Freyberg was burdened with too much of one in Canea-Suda Sector. It was jammed with Government, 35,000 civilians, Creforce Headquarters, Sector Headquarters and its troops (plus 6000 service hands). From Canea across a two-mile neck to the bay, the sources of life and combat clustered around Suda village and its single unloading pier. If this supply base fell, the game would be up. Here was the prize of battle that Freyberg had to hold and Student had to take.

But before that, Student had to have won lodgment on Crete from which he could launch a decisive ground fight for the prize. His written plan followed such a sequence, though he personally believed the defense would collapse under the shock of many-sided airborne blows.

On the other hand, Freyberg had to repel all landings whatsoever and wheresoever, identify the main effort, and move at once to crush it. If he succeeded before it got out of its landing compartment of terrain, so much the better for him. But failing that, he had to base an expanded land fight on the integrity of a Final Force Protective Line before Canea-Suda. On that line, if last came to last, he had to stand.

For initial deployment the defense must choose between a *cordon* system of strong fixed works at each landable beach and an *elastic* system of limited power at the beaches, backed by strong mobile reserves held for decisive counterattack against the foe's main effort. Often both systems come into play, as in England.

Crete added a new wrinkle by its airfield-beach contiguity, which meant the three airfields might become airborne extensions of seaborne landings, or the other way round—beach landings might back up airdrops on the fields. Thus by striking in concert by sea and by air the Germans might effect lodgments at several points for later freedom to exploit the one of greatest promise. Such a bogey can grow on the lonely island defender, who possesses little latitude for maneuver and none at all for withdrawal to fight on another day. Island defense (or attack) is a one-shot affair.

Confusion of old and new threats and their supposed counters produced an odd mix on Crete. An established Final Force Protective Line never got its full due, while the tactic in local defense and counterattack fell back to the trench warfare practice of World War I. In such a system, the attacking paratroopers would have time to overcome their initial landing shock and to form for attack on positions which eventually could only become marked targets for Luftwaffe strafers and dive bombers. The early initiative could thus shift to the opponent when he was at his weakest. A final fundamental defense misfortune was that Maleme Sector and Canea-Suda Sector lay within convenient range of maximum Luftwaffe power. This made holding Maleme in the west all the more critical. Indeed, at Force Headquarters a feeling prevailed that Maleme on the front line was the key to Canea-Suda. But out in the rough country toward the airfield, the feeling seemed different. Canea-Suda in the rear became a citadel of refuge on which one could fall back to grow stronger.

Whatever the inner British differences, the opposed sides arrived at the same overriding finality that the main clash would take place in Maleme Sector. Probably because of his own like conclusion, Freyberg kept his New Zealand troops posted there to turn the brunt of attack; correspondingly Student committed his elite Sturmregiment there, to insure that the attack would succeed.

What were the terrain features and what routes led around them? Attack and defense eyes quickly fastened on two natural entries toward the prize. The obvious one, constantly in use, led along the coast, a fair two-way road. It squeezed to seaward around shore bluffs as it approached Canea's side door that led to the central marketplace behind the little Venetian port at the front door. The second access ran down Prison Valley from inland heights in the southwest toward the same side door, whence, besides the continuation direct into Canea, a switch road led across Canea plain south of the city directly toward Suda, the nub of Creforce life. Wedged between the two approaches bulged a massive hill feature, Mount Monodhendhri.

It hulked there, a tanglewooded mass, blocking off the west like an outwork guarding Canea. Both accesses were in plain view from its 850-foot summit, two miles in from the coast. There a visual signal station linked Canea with the west, and the defenders called the mount Signal Hill, just as they named Prison Valley after the prison

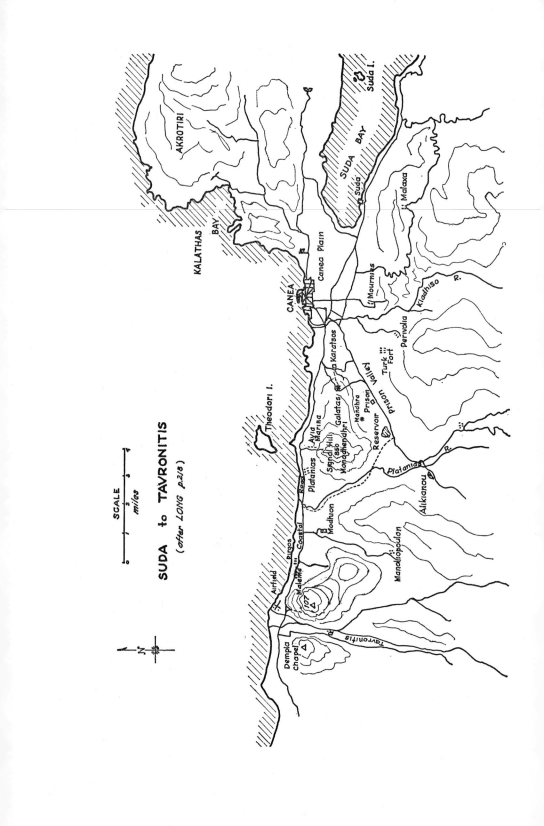

SCALE

miles

SUDA to TAVRONITIS

(after LONG p.218)

that marked the halfway point of its run northeast toward Canea and the sea. The run began at an inland plateau that supported a water reservoir and power plant, from which another valley—Platanias Valley—ran northwest to the sea. These two valleys formed two legs of Monodhendhri's triangular base; the third leg was provided by the sea and its coastal road on the north side. Halfway along it, a small cape jutted out to sea from the village of Ayia Marina on the Mount's lowering slope. A bluff ending of the slope crowded the road into a critical passage between land and sea. The road itself was fair, and so was that of Prison Valley, but Platanias Valley had only a two-tracked trail that emerged on the coast a little west of Platanias village. Brigadier James Hargest of 5 New Zealand Brigade established his command post there at the eastern end of his territory. Four miles in the opposite direction lay the brigade's chief concern, Maleme Airfield. A hostile advance from there on Canea would then have a choice at Platanias of sticking to the coastal route with its tight squeaks between shore and sea or proceeding up Platanias Valley to the reservoir and thence down Prison Valley toward the prize. The Germans took note of this choice; the British paid it little heed in defense planning, though they seemed to feel Monodhendhri's isolating effect. They based their linkage east and west on the coastal route. It will be noted that contrary to nature's division, Creforce's Maleme Sector included all of Signal Hill and Galatas right up to Canea's side door.

To the Germans the massive hill presented a formidable barrier to be stormed in force, for it should hold the final British defenses. They therefore planned to outflank it by airdrops into Prison Valley. The British planned to hold a position closer to Canea in the eastern foothills of Monodhendhri around the little village of Galatas. Some roomy trenches (dug by 1 Welch Battalion) were already available, yet more important, defenses at Galatas could dominate both approaches —coastal road and Prison Valley. Perfecting the defenses from 14 May on was entrusted to an able soldier, Colonel Howard Kippenberger, who on that day took command of the scratch New Zealand formation called 10 Brigade, deployed around Galatas.

On Prison Valley road near its junction with the coastal route, Brigadier Edward Puttick, commanding New Zealand Division and Maleme Sector, established his command post. The eastern margin of the valley road marked the beginning of his vast empire to the west; the road, all the land (including Monodhendhri), all the defenses, and the men who manned them westward clear to the end of Crete belonged to him. In his 25-mile domain 4, 10, and 5 New Zealand Infantry Brigades and three-plus Greek Army regiments deployed for battle. At Canea's side door about one-third of this power (4 Brigade, with 18, 19, 20 Battalions) was packed into the small triangle between Galatas and the junction of Prison Valley and coastal roads as force and divisional reserves.

When they first arrived, these battleworthy troops of 4 Brigade had occupied posts farther out to the west as "cover against attack from west, and to destroy any hostile troops dropped in Prison Valley."[5] As time passed, emphasis shifted from mere reserve to a concept of counterattack force. Power verbiage from Churchill about fierce "counterattacks by tanks and assault parties," after the Germans had been baited onto the airfields, took hold. The theory was insistently expounded to General Freyberg, not alone by dispatch but also through a special officer messenger. The vision was an obvious shade of England's mobile defense force against cross-channel invasion that now took paper form on Crete: 18, 19 New Zealand Battalions and 1 Welch (on call) were the shock troops, supported by light tanks, a troop of artillery, and a machine-gun platoon, all under Brigadier Inglis, who arrived from Egypt on 17 May just for this task. Prison Valley and Galatas defenses were enfeebled by the new concentration near the side-door triangle, although 20 Battalion (also divisional reserve) was on call to Kippenberger in 10 Brigade, and 19 Battalion backed the center of his line. But Crete was no England. Whether the counterattack force could ever develop the mobility and punch intended was highly doubtful; scarcity of motor transport alone made it questionable. The blanks left in the Galatas position gaped wide. Who would now crush a German airdrop deep in Prison Valley? This was Colonel Kippenberger's sorrow at 10 Brigade.[6]

5. Davin, pp. 58–62; Kippenberger, pp. 46–78. General Kippenberger had commanded 20 Batallion in Greece, then 4 Brigade briefly in Crete. On 14 May he moved on to command newly created 10 Brigade. Brigadier Inglis arrived from Egypt to take over 4 Brigade. It was to form as a strong, mobile counterattack reserve.

6. A trek over the area made by this reporter in 1960 filled out the map picture with ups and downs, boulders, cliffs, and just plain rough going; it was goat's work. A rock-strewn trail wound through 19 Batallion territory to emerge at Karatsos village, sitting in the clear on a rounded knoll. Farther along on another rise was Galatas. There the schoolmaster took us in, opened his classroom, and called in the oldsters of the neighborhood to lend a few words in reconstruction of the 1941 scene. Ah, those were the days of high excitement, stealthy action, and miracles! Men fell from the skies, bullets whistled through the trees and bounced off rocks.

When he took over on 14 May the brigade had only begun to function as one command. About a thousand New Zealanders—gunners and service and supply men acting as infantry—formed into a Composite Battalion that provided the nucleus. Then there was the Divisional Cavalry, dismounted, of 194 seasoned troops. Two Greek Army regiments, the 6th and the 8th, each of about 1200 men, were to operate under the brigade. Artillery consisted of three old pieces; one machine-gun platoon was in support. Of his mixed command Kippenberger wrote: "Composite Battalion was composed of good material, but both officers and men were wholly untrained in infantry work. Though reliable at first in defense, they were wholly incapable of maneuver or attack, and gradually lost confidence in themselves." He described the Greek contingents as "malaria ridden little chaps with four weeks service." Neither regiment, he concluded, "could be said to have any military value." That was 10 Brigade, holding Creforce's last-stand position.

The line of defense ran south from the sea through the foothills west of Galatas, thence east a bit, and southeast across the valley. Of course the old wired trenches faced generally west and southwest and upvalley. An old Turkish fort looked down on the left flank in the far south, and a steep shore bluff anchored the right flank above the sea. The left was weak, manned by green boys of the 6th Greek Army Regiment, each with an antique rifle and, if lucky, three shells that might fit. Their segment ran across the valley bottom—for them the worst possible place, where they would provide nothing but a sacrificial screen. The prison compound and its high, defensible walls posed another puzzle; it lay a thousand yards upvalley in front of the Greeks, totally undefended. On the right, Composite Battalion picked up the Greek line and carried it west around Galatas, then north to overlook the sea. Poor 10 Brigade! Its deployment reflected the mixed backgrounds of its units.

Two units were off by themselves up Prison Valley a mile and a half beyond the prison. The 8th Greek Army Regiment posted a ridge south of the Ayia reservoir on the plateau and the New Zealand

---

The old tasks of tillage and shepherding fell out. Chuckles and grimaces enriched the tales and breathed life into the penciled map (that was astoundingly accurate). Nothing was said about terrain difficulties. The road down the north side twists and turns steeply, but is passable to the sea; on the valley side it descends gently and straight south toward the prison compound, where it connects with the main artery in the valley bottom. In the west, Signal Hill (Monodhendhri) looks down the throat of Galatas and the whole valley.

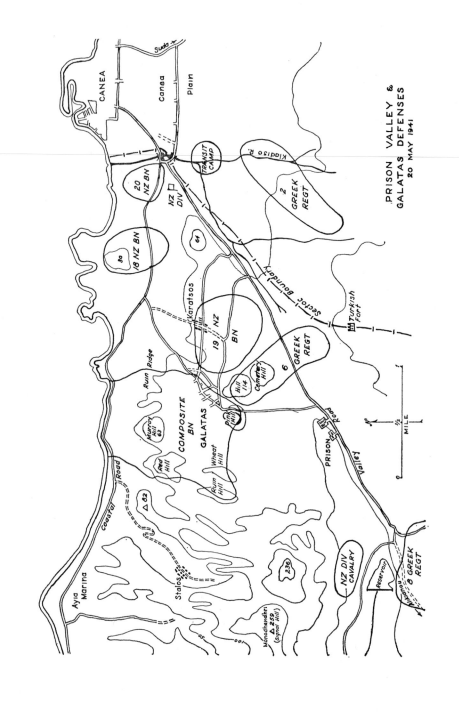

PRISON VALLEY &
GALATAS DEFENSES
20 MAY 1941

Divisional Cavalry was on the opposite rise of Signal Hill (Mono-dhendhri). If these formations were to bar western access to the valley or to counterattack paratroops dropped in it, the idea was sound but ambitious for the units committed. On 17 May Colonel Kippenberger trudged the length and breadth of his command (Kippenberger, pp. 50, 51). He reconnoitered "the ideal and expected place for parachute landings southwest of Galatas" in the valley bottom and stopped in on Major Russell, of Divisional Cavalry under Signal Hill, and Major Wilson, liaisoning on the opposite slope with the 8th Greek Army Regiment. He authorized Russell to move into the main Galatas line if the situation demanded; but for Wilson, what could he say? They made their farewells; the colonel returned to his Galatas headquarters. On 19 May, a day before The Day, he and Brigadier Inglis of the counterattack force compared notes. They agreed the impending attack would be "disastrously repulsed."

Between 10 Brigade around Galatas and 5 Brigade west of Platanias, Monodhendhri accomplished physically what no papers, talk, or deployment fully recognized: it separated 5 Brigade and Maleme Field from the rest of the sector and from the division; 5 Brigade's supply dump at Ayia Marina and its seaward-reaching cape marked the cleavage. The western defenses did not begin until a mile beyond, at Platanias, where on 28 April Brigadier Hargest had set up his temporary headquarters for the defense of Canea. A 4-mile passage farther west through bush and settlements of Pirgos and Maleme village breaks into the open at the Tavronitis River delta and its airfield. It shapes a sandy right triangle to seaward of the road, which parallels the east-west-tending hypotenuse. At the airfield's southwest corner the road turns onto the first section of the bridge over the shallow riverbed. From the vantage point of the turn a sweeping sight inland reveals how the delta, its airfield, the adjoining lowlands, and the bridge lie under the guns of an elongated knoll less than a mile to the south—Hill 107 ("meters"). One notes a twin eminence on the far bank of the river, also looking down on the whole scene.

By 10 May the New Zealanders felt at home here in their variegated territory of hills and sandy flats, groves and vineyards, rocky gullies and fine beaches. One is unprepared for this diversity and the general closed-in-ness. The road drives a canyon through leafy palisades; vineyards lie low, but olive and orange groves, protected by man-made and man-planted windbreaks, cut visibility and fields of fire drastically; control of troops in a fire fight would be complicated. At three hundred paces in from the sea it is often hard to sight more than a few yards.

5 Brigade had four line battalions—21, 22, 23, and 28 (Maori)—plus an engineer detachment of small battalion size acting as infantry. The deployment starting at Platanias toward the west ran: 28 (Maori) Battalion around Platanias, its beach, its mouth, and Brigade Headquarters (inland on a bluff) in order to repel attack from the sea or along the coastal road toward Canea and to act as Brigade Reserve. Next came the engineer detachment of 350 rifles in two companies astride the road; then just beyond, 23 and 21 Battalions, one back of the other on ground rising inland. They could rush downhill against beach assault or westward to support the last battalion, 22, in the post of honor. It was around the airfield and above it on Hill 107.

New Zealand responsibilities went farther than the Tavronitis east bank, however. Ten miles along, a stout band of brothers stood to their primitive arms to repel any assault. The 1st Greek Army Regiment held the port of Kastelli Kisamou at the base of the U-shaped Gulf of Kisamos between Capes Spatha and Vouxa. They are the two horns that jut from the dragon head, making perfect landfall marks for an invader from the north and shelter for his approach to fine landing beaches at the base of the U. In its middle is the little port Kastelli Kisamou, which received New Zealand Divisional Cavalry on evacuation from Greece. Now the port and adjacent beaches became the defense tasks of the 1st Greek Army Regiment under the guidance of a fourteen-man New Zealand team led by Major Bedding of 19 Battalion. He split the regiment into two 500-man battalions, posted them, and schooled them at their tasks. They were

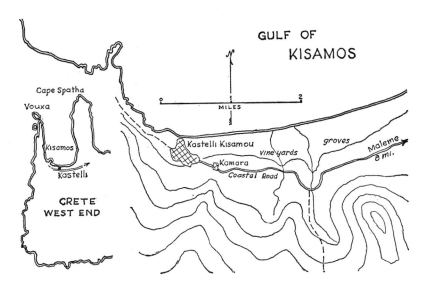

doing very well when word came of a possible move east toward the Tavronitis.

The yawning mouth of the Tavronitis River was one of 5 Brigade's crucial problems. No other approach to the airfield beckoned so wantonly as this flat dry riverbed. The low eastern bank gave directly onto the airfield's 300-yard baseline. At its inshore end the bridge crossed in two spans to a cluster of houses on the west bank; inland from them loomed a bulge of high land. Strategically its summit was important, for it commanded the scene of riverbed and airfield just as well as Hill 107 opposite. From 10 May on, Brigadier Hargest requested that this eminence be occupied; Bedding and his people came under consideration. Interest waned; Bedding stayed where he was at Kastelli Kisamou. The west bank of the Tavronitis was left open.[7]

No broad, hard runways crisscrossed the airfield in 1941 as they do today. Then, when General Student first saw it from the air, he thought of three clay tennis courts, all brown-red, within a private triangle. Yet on the ground the courts expanded and their surroundings pressed for notice. In the south, Hill 107 overpowered all else; possession of it was the obvious key to Maleme Field, a point on which attackers and defenders agreed. So sure were the Germans that they soon marked the map summit 107 as 5 Brigade command post. But in reality this spot belonged to Colonel L. W. Andrew of 22 New Zealand Infantry Battalion.

Andrew established his command post well forward on a northern flat within the perimeter of his A Company, whose duty it was to hold the summit. Looking to seaward, a spur road on the right descended toward junction with the coastal route. In and around the small contiguous settlements of Maleme and Pirgos, Andrew posted his Headquarters Company, and on the spur were his twelve Bren carriers. Across the spur and to his right rear, he placed B Company to back up A and to safeguard the rear. The airfield proper he assigned to C Company under Captain Johnson in a tight perimeter defense. In turn Johnson placed 13 Platoon on the seaward leg, himself with 14 Platoon on the opposite hypotenuse leg (above the coast-

7. Hargest wanted Division to place a battalion on the strategic tongue across the Tavronitis (Davin, p. 62). The time coincided with the counterattack force upsurge. That this urge crowded out Hargest's recommendations is only a guess. By 12 May, however, Wavell felt obliged to send to Freyberg an emissary to expound the prime minister's counterattack views, which would have baited the Germans onto the fields and worked them over with counterattack forces. There is no hint that demolition of field runways was included, although such a thought would seem to be the logical end provision in such planning.

al route) and 15 Platoon along the airfield's tender west baseline on the bank of the Tavronitis. That left Captain Campbell and D Company to look out for the western slope of Hill 107 down to the riverbank and upstream from the bridge.

A bad boundary problem faced Campbell where the near end of the bridge and the coastal route joined. There the approach route bent north around the base of the Hill, and just above the bend a sizable Air Force compound for headquarters and living had established itself. If an invader crossed the bridge from the west and kept straight on east instead of taking the bend, he would soon gain the cover of the Air Force shacks and entry to the Hill defenses. Campbell knew he had to deny the bridge; yet its close proximity to the boundary between him and C Company's 15 Platoon on the airfield's western baseline tended toward making the line of the bridge, extended east, the boundary. The Air compound became a foreign island dangerously in the way of proper defense lines. Its 350 airmen scarcely burned with the same eager ground defense zeal as the soldiers. Until X-Day the flyers evinced little interest in ground weaponry. Their line of command, mixed Fleet Air and RAF, was a loose one under Commander Beale; it admitted no accountability to Colonel Andrew for field defense. His request to Creforce superiors to place the compound under him for defense was refused.[8] A reasonable defense line ran through the choicest Air Force living facilities. In consequence the line was forced outside around the compound and too close to the river bank for fair fields of fire. No provision for blowing the bridge is recorded (though German attackers later reported defusing charges) nor is provision for coordinated denial action by D and C Companies at this tough corner. In the final deployment the bridge denial buck was passed to Sergeant Sargeson of 18 Platoon as a commonplace outpost task. He put two riflemen in pits on either side of the eastern bridge end and two on the road overhead as pickets. The rest of the platoon continued the line south along the bank, as did 17 Platoon; 16 Platoon covered the slope from higher up and in the rear. The critical entry was drifted with; no one raised hell about it, but hindsight made a story around it and thereby registered another failure in command relations.

Andrew found other chinks in his armor by flying over his dispositions and having the faults immediately corrected. Still other com-

8. Henderson, pp. 48, 56, 57; Davin, p. 100. Davin notes, "Requests by Andrew that these troops [the airmen] should come under his command had been refused."

mand failures bothered him. Two 4-inch coastal guns, emplaced almost on top of his command post, could take fire orders only from their own MNBDO controller in Canea ten miles away. Under mounting air activity the weak telephone connection to Control could only grow weaker; yet so it stood. Two 3-inch antiaircraft guns and ten AA Bofors around the airfield were likewise outside 22 Battalion's authority. But as final trumps under battalion command, two heavy infantry tanks were dug in near Captain Johnson above the coastal route. Tests or drills with the monsters by night or day are not on

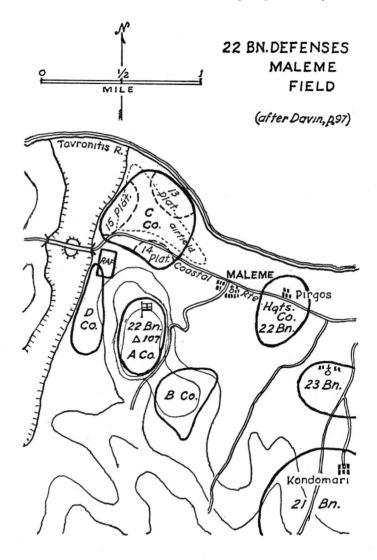

22 BN. DEFENSES
MALEME
FIELD

(after Davin, p.97)

record. The prime weakness in this subsector, recognized as pivotal, was not in men or material, but in ambiguous command.

Reserve combat support to 22 Battalion in troops was to come primarily from 23 Battalion, and if need be, from 21 Battalion; both of these adjoined on hills to the east. 23 Battalion had been assigned to support 22 from the very beginning on 1 May as a result of Brigadier Puttick's reconnaissance when he took divisional command. He thought that 5 Brigade lay too far back from Maleme Field. Accordingly 22 Battalion moved forward with 23 in support. This role for 23 was thus well established. A change of command on 13 May in 23 Battalion may have disturbed the relationship: Major Leckie moved up to command 23. In the past he and Andrew had had differences. To make added trouble, Brigadier Hargest's Operational Instruction of 18 May granted Leckie a wide choice of action: he was to maintain "present position and be prepared to counterattack if the enemy effects a landing (a) on the beach or at Maleme Aerodrome, (b) on the area occupied by NZE [Engineers]. . . ." No priority was accorded the airfield or support to 22 Battalion, whose own orders Hargest made more strictly maintenance of a static defense of the airfield. He did recommend immediate counterattack and return thereafter to original positions. Here in 22 Battalion's orders occurs the sole written mention of support from 23 Battalion: ". . . if necessary, support will be called for from 23 Battalion, and should telephonic means . . . fail here the call will be by verey signal (WHITE—GREEN—WHITE)." That put it up to Andrew; he could cry for help if he could bring himself to do it.[9]

Despite some queer quirks in his deployment, Brigadier Hargest seemed happy with his defenses. The deployment did not conform to his written directions as to front and command axis. The latter ran along the front instead of at right angles to it. His Instruction No. 4 of 18 May directed: "5 Brigade will maintain a defensive line running west and east from Platanias to Tavronitis river with special regard to the defense of Maleme Aerodrome." Yet instead of getting back of this defense line to command it, he remained on its inner flank at Platanias. In the beginning, such front as there was ran north and south just beyond Platanias; the battalions had simply faced west beyond the village in a sort of outpost role for Canea's defense. Then came the stretch ordered by Brigadier Puttick to include Maleme Field and the beaches in between. 5 Brigade pushed units west with-

9. Henderson, p. 37; Ross, pp. 57-63; Cody, pp. 80-86; Davin, pp. 54-56.

out adjusting its command axis or command post. The axis remained on the coastal route, and to it the forward battalions chained themselves for supply or withdrawal. That is, in thought and practice the front stayed as it had begun: north and south with a tender flank on the sea. Plotted on a map, the disposition suggests a delaying action or an outpost arrangement for falling back on one another to gain strength. One trouble was that Puttick had not closed up in the rear. He apparently did not realize, any more than did Hargest, that the stretch west implied the creation of a new Maleme sub-sector beyond Platanias and that Galatas should then come naturally and directly under himself as commander of a final protective line there. Maybe there were too many commanders. At any rate, 5 Brigade felt cheerful and Brigadier Hargest made note of it in his diary.

Creforce felt good too, for on 16 May, the eve of the estimated X-Day, which coincided with the original German intent, General Freyberg reassured his commander in chief in Cairo:

I have just returned from a final tour of the defenses. I feel greatly encouraged . . . all ranks are fit and morale is now high. All defenses have been strengthened and positions wired as much as possible. We have 45 field guns in action. . . . Two infantry tanks at each aerodrome. . . . I feel that at least we will give an excellent account of ourselves. With the help of the Royal Navy I trust Crete will be held.

About the Royal Air Force there was not much he could say, though he still hoped for its reinforcement. His battle station had been pitched on a flattened rise a mile and a half northeast of Canea. He could sight west along the shore over the water to Maleme or southwest over Canea's roofs to Prison Valley. Farther left the batteries on St. John's Hill could be seen firing at planes attacking Suda's ships. The struggle to unload them could now carry on only at night. Eight ships had been sunk; yet out of fifteen others, 15,000 tons of fighting stuff had reached the shore. It was enough to give Creforce a fair chance, thought her stalwart commander. His confidence did not necessarily mean that the defenses of Suda Sector itself were satisfactory.

In that sector General Weston's Mobile Naval Defense Organization (MNBDO) was a strictly Navy package of marines, guns, and gear to make Suda Bay a secure fleet facility in an old-fashioned way. He now also commanded a miscellany of 17,000 men, hardware, and supplies to hold and operate the Canea-Suda complex as a base for all Crete. What to do about Canea's 35,000 civilians or about Suda's 6000 idle service troops? His combat forces totaled about 4800 riflemen, 1400 artillerymen (on field and coastal guns), and 800 antiair gunners. The fittest infantry formation was 1 Welch Battalion, of 854 men. While they stood by for reserve action, Weston deployed them for close defense of Canea on a crescent off the city's southeastern border. A second concentration of about 700 men from various British sources held a transit camp on the sector's western boundary. What was left General Weston scattered about in fragments on Canea plain and around Suda Base. Four miles to the east of the village, near the entrance to the bay, three thin Australian battalions blocked entry from the east. North of the bay on Akrotiri, posts were manned by small British Army parties. Finally, the Greek Army's 2d Regiment looked down on this puzzle and into Prison Valley from hill positions in the south. Batteries of coastal and antiaircraft artillery rimmed the bay; heavy fire came from St. John's Hill at the bay head. As for command: the headquarters of Force, Sector, and Navy were far apart in this heart of the whole operation.

The two independent eastern sectors enjoyed a freedom from high headquarters worries. Beyond Suda Bay's entrance, the coastal road cuts inland through 8 miles of tough turns and defiles and regains the sea at the village of Georgeoupolis on Almiro Bay. Its north-south and then eastward curve on the shore forms the nape of Crete's dragon neck, which continues eastward in a series of superb landing beaches, backed by lowland flats suited to airdrops. The familiar combination, which resembled that in Maleme Sector, offered lodgment possibilities and an approach of sorts to Suda from the east. To cover this threat further, Brigadier Vasey, now Retimo Sector commander, stationed himself and two Australian battalions near Georgeoupolis village and sent Lt. Colonel Ian R. Campbell with his 2/1 Battalion on to Retimo proper, 18 miles farther along. In a few days another battalion, 2/11 Battalion under Major Sandover, joined Campbell. These two Australian battalions played out the Retimo Sector story alone, while Brigadier Vasey and his other two battalions soon joined Suda Sector.[10]

10. The boundary between Suda and Retimo sectors ran southwest from Georgeoupolis to the highland bowl of Askifos, a halfway point on the only cross-island road between Suda Bay and the south coast. The road ends 6½ miles south of the bowl, at the edge of an escarpment above and a little east of the fishing village, anchorage, and beach landing place of Sfakia. It is the second largest settlement on the south coast. The road and its southern terminus offered cross-island possibilities that Churchill (p. 269) later regretted had not been developed for supplying Creforce from Egypt. Much steaming around the ends of Crete to the northern ports might have been saved and Creforce made stronger via Sfakia. The cross-island route runs 24½ miles to Suda Bay and then another 7 miles along the shore to Suda base.

Halfway along the eastward trend of the Almiro Bay beaches, the road again dives deep into the interior; around wild gullies and wilder hills it twists and climbs. All at once it breaks for the sea, as though to check its bearings. There on the coast one looks down eastward upon a coastal plain and more beaches, interrupted at the near end by the fortlike promontory of Retimo. Smooth wide sea landing spots flank it on either hand; parallel to the farther one a flat space under some low hills can barely be made out today. This is the site of the 1941 airstrip. Campbell hurried there, leaving the town and port of Retimo to 800 efficient-looking Cretan gendarmes. At this date, 9500 people lived there, worked the coastal sea and land traffic, tended the vineyards and olive groves. The town and port reflect their Mediterranean character with minaret and mosque setting off the Bible picture of the heavy-laden donkey and his guiding master in turban and flowing robes. Country folk display produce at a crossroad, hawkers demonstrate newfangled kitchen wares, and youngsters pedal off to class in school caps. The town spills inland from the promontory and eastward toward Perivolia village two miles off. Behind it a low hill rises. Colonel Campbell named it Hill C in his plans of defense.

Four hills looked down on the coastal plain. In the front rank were Hill C on the left (west), and after another two miles, Hill B, and then Hill A on the right; alone in the rear rank, Hill D faced the airstrip through a gap between A and B. These hills are gentle elongated swellings separated by shallow wadis. Today the site of the airstrip is under cultivation and has been for so long that its war fame is forgotten. An aged farmer scratched his head and eventually recalled airplane landings; he jovially pointed out the inexact limits of the strip. Then his memory revived in a surge of bursting bombs, clouds of paratroopers, machine-gun fire from the hills. The terrain lent itself readily to defense of the strip.

Campbell had available his own 2/1 Australian Battalion of 620 rifles, Sandover's 2/11 of 650 plus, and the 4th and 5th Regiments of the Greek Army, totaling 2400. In addition to their personal arms, the Australians had a few armor-piercing rifles, light and medium machine guns, and a few mortars. The Greeks carried the usual assortment of obsolete rifles with a few rounds for each. Eight field pieces (but no antiaircraft guns) and two Matilda tanks were in support. From the neighborhood the troops soon filled out the dull standard rations with goat's milk, eggs, fruit, and poultry. A few evening brawls in town at the outset moved their commander to put Retimo town out of bounds. The men responded well in their own areas at wiring and strengthening the terraced hill positions. Each day they grew safer, stronger.

The final main line of defense ran from Hill A on the right through Hill B on the left. One company of Campbell's own battalion was posted on Hill A, supported by machine guns and field pieces that could enfilade the beach, the road, and the airstrip. The rest of 2/1 Battalion and Campbell's command post occupied the forward slope of Hill D, between A and B. The 4th Greek Army Regiment filled in on his left across wadi Piyi. Major Sandover's 2/11 Battalion occupied all of Hill B and, as on the right, had supporting machine and field guns that could rake the approaches. The 5th Greek Army Regiment went into reserve a mile and a half inland of the main line's center.[11]

Another bumpy passage eastward through forty twisted miles of rough hill country brings one into the clear with the same welcome surprise—to look down on Crete's thriving largest city and port, Heraklion. The modernized port is on the east, outside the thick Venetian walls of the old town; two miles farther along the coast lies the all-purpose, British-improved aerodrome. Everything of strategic value is thus within a compact belt of four miles along the shore. The inland country forms the end of a broad saddle land between two

11. Long, pp. 256–58; Davin, pp. 174–76; as filled out by this reporter's own reconnaissance and discussion with participants during 1960. The same sources apply to Heraklion.

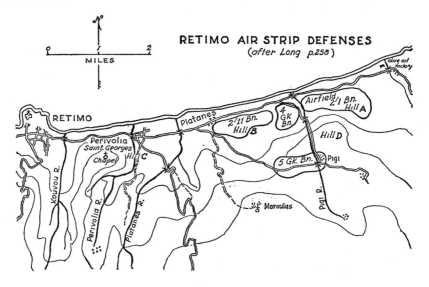

RETIMO AIR STRIP DEFENSES
(after Long p.258)

massive mountain clumps: Dhikti (where Zeus was born), the lower and less compact, 20 miles southeast, and Idhi (where his mother hid him from his hungry father), the higher and more impressive, 20 miles southwest. Country roads and trails follow the slope of the saddle through villages and vineyards, olive groves and grain plots, down to the shore. From Heraklion port to Suda Bay by sea is 55 miles.

Brigadier B. H. Chappel, a regular British soldier, commanded 14 Brigade of the British Army and Heraklion Sector with three regular battalions: 2 Yorks and Lancs, 2 Leicester (late arrivals to replace 1 Welch), 2 Black Watch—all fit and well equipped. After the evacuation from Greece, 2/4 Australian Battalion and 7 Medium Royal Artillery Regiment, as infantry, were added, and also three Greek Army formations. On 18–19 May, 2 Argyll and Sutherland Battalion landed on the south coast and marched over the saddle to join the fight. Sector support consisted of two heavy and six light tanks, thirteen field pieces, ten Bofors, and four 3-inch antiaircraft guns. Total troop numbers came to 6056 British, 2700 Greek.

Of all the sectors, this one, which was the freshest and best equipped, defended the smallest and strategically least vulnerable sector. The force deployed in a belt of positions 2 miles wide along the sea for 3¼ miles. On the flanks were Heraklion town in the west and the airport in the east. Greek formations, as at Retimo, took over the town and the west flank, while British battalions took all else:

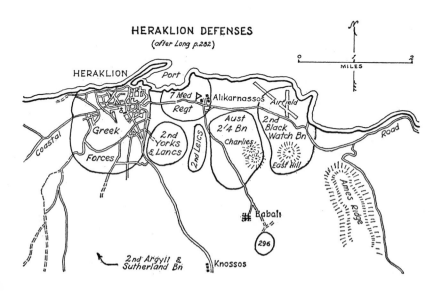

HERAKLION DEFENSES
(after Long p.282)

the center, the airfield, and its approaches on the east flank. Chappel set up his command post on the edge of suburban Nea Alikarnassos, a mile beyond Heraklion's eastern ramparts: 7 Medium Regiment covered the headquarters and an open space farther east, called Buttercup Field, that gave onto the airfield; then came 2 Black Watch in an east end rectangle to cover the airfield and its approaches; 2/4 Australian Battalion adjoined Black Watch's southern extension on the west; and in the center sat the recently arrived 2 Leicester Battalion as sector reserve. Finally, 2 Yorks and Lancs closed the gap to the Greek formations south of the town. A road there led inland to the bivouac of an ambulance company nestled alongside Knossos, the pre-ancient seat of Minoan power. There would be heavy fighting on this road and a hillside nearby, fighting for ground that other men kept safe ages ago by besting the invaders at sea. Now he was to come by air.[12]

Cruisers *Fiji* and *Gloucester* brought Leicester Battalion into Heraklion on the night of 15–16 May 1941. In the night of 14–15 May the fleet assumed stations in readiness around Crete. Admiral Cunningham wrote: "It appeared almost inconceivable that airborne invasion alone could succeed . . . some seaborne support was inevitable and . . . destruction of troops would win the day." He agreed with General Freyberg: the decisive German punch had to come by sea.

To counter it, five naval task groups came into being: a main body of battleships with screening destroyers, and four advance groups of cruisers and destroyers. The main body was to cruise west of Crete, block off the Italian fleet, and back up the advance groups, which would be working in close off the island's north coast at night to intercept invaders by sea. During daylight they would retire south of Crete to the rim of the German air reach. The deadly lack of air cover and prolonged steaming and fighting naked was beginning to tell. If the damned island could only be turned around to face south, many, many hours of steaming would be saved. When the ships moved up on 14 May, the German 8th Air Corps stepped up its softening process against the defenses in earnest. Thus while one con-

12. Another Minoan vestige is Phaestos near the south shore landing point, Timbakion, of Argyll and Sutherland Battalion. The site of Phaestos is naturally attractive, but the seat of Minoan power at Knossos is more stirring. One can wander through chamber after chamber to admire the artistry and ingenuity of construction, and let fingers brush mighty Ali Baba jars that other hands fashioned forty centuries ago.

tender leapt joyously over the sea at his open target, the other plowed doggedly through the sea to counter as best he could.

A day earlier (13 May) General Freyberg had reported that there were only six Hurricanes left and requested Cairo to take over air reconnaissance so that the six and the expected reinforcements of ten could concentrate on fighting off German air. But as the 8th Air Corps turned on more heat, the skies over all Crete grew more German than ever. On 17 May ten Hurricanes flew in from Egypt and were quickly whittled down to three. These, plus three Gladiators at Heraklion and a lone Hurricane at Maleme, made the airworthy grand total precisely seven. What could they do but die? On 18 May Freyberg agreed with Group Captain Beamish that the planes should fly out to Egypt. On 19 May the last plane rose from Maleme and vanished over the hills into the southern sky.

What Hitler and Göring wanted over England, but never got, they now had over distant Crete: complete and absolute control of the air. But for Britain, Crete was remote and little understood, left for marooned soldiers and tired sailors to save if they could. The action that followed would leave its own mark. How things got that way has been traced without asking the question plain to the soldiers: Why defend the airfields if no defending planes are to fly from them? Surely there could be a better way of prohibiting enemy use.

Gradually the airfields had become major liabilities. After Freyberg's call to reconsider, a figure of two active fighter squadrons had caught on at Creforce. It gave the command something to hang its arguments on. The figure soon shrank to one squadron plus 100 percent reserves, and finally to an RAF fantasy of having fighters swoop in from Egypt at the last desperate moment, land on their own fields, and fly from them to save the island from seaborne invasion. Actually, saving both fields and planes for the future grew stronger than interest in denying them now to save Crete. The whole made a bad case of eat your cake and have it too. The dire and irretrievable shortage of planes had been known all along.

Creforce's mission, derived at the Terrace, was "to deny the enemy the use of Crete as an air and submarine base." London tampered with this basic concept. Had it insisted only on keeping a runway operable on one field, say Heraklion, closest to Egypt and farthest from Greece, this might have been a tolerable idea—but not Maleme Field, right under the German bombs. If the Germans lodged there,

Crete could not be held. It should have been prepared for emergency demolition.

The root failure was the reluctance in London and Cairo to face the fact of no defensive air support. Both temporized and permitted events to decide. But not Freyberg. His hope for two fighter squadrons had become a part of him and his plan. On the side, the air dilemma receded somewhat under the marked improvement he saw in ground defenses. His hopes for both ground and air persisted. There is some evidence that in the end he did propose mining all fields and was turned down. One would expect a man of his stamp to proceed without asking, but that would have killed all chance of air reinforcement; besides, the Royal Air Force commanded the fields. Cairo and London would have to be informed. In all likelihood demolition never really became a clear-cut issue. Belatedly, General Freyberg may have explored the subject with higher authority and been dissuaded by the "Chiefs of Staff [who] wanted the airfields left intact against a time when they should be able to send aircraft" to use them (Davin, p. 460). By the time Maleme mining really got hot, it was just another goddam thing for which there was no time; and anyhow, no one likes to plan his own defeat. To hell with it![13]

If hindsight thus uncovers some British slips, there were lapses on the German side too, just as bad—first off, a fixed expectation that the airfields would be left intact for seizure. True, German intelligence exaggerated the defending air power and its need for operational fields; yet the plans provided no alternative landing spaces for transport planes, should the fields prove unusable. German success hinged irrevocably on capture of the existing fields by advance strikes of parachute forces. It looks as if the two sides conspired to make the fight for the airfields the first order of business, with Maleme the first prize.

13. Davin, pp. 27, 35–37, 50–51, 460; Long, p. 220; Hetherington, pp. 48–49. Hetherington quotes Major M. F. H. Hansen of New Zealand Division Engineers: "I still believe a major mistake was made in not making the aerodrome [Maleme] unsuitable for landing planes." Hetherington continues: "Hansen's suggestion was rejected because aircraft had to continue reconnaissance flights from Maleme. Yet these were taken over by Cairo on 14 May." If Major Hansen made his proposal early, this excuse might have applied, and anyhow, hope of air reinforcement was still strong. Later his proposal could not have received due consideration. The latest action dispatches from Crete, received in London and relayed to Washington, documented General Freyberg's abiding faith in two fighter squadrons up to the very last. He seemed to feel that they could have made all the difference, particularly against lumbering German transport planes. A British staff appreciation later noted: "A lesson learnt was that airfields not required by own forces, and which might be of use to the enemy, should be prepared for demolition."

In the world at large, news dispatches noted the 8th Air Corps's bombing crescendo toward Crete's reduction. A heavy blasting on 5 May stirred extra comment, which mounted higher on 7 May when Churchill cried out in the Commons for a stand to the death on Crete. The House came to its feet as he vowed no retreat: "All the more true is this while we defend, as we intend to do to the death, and without thought of retirement, the valuable and highly offensive outposts of Crete and Tobruk." The world press headlined "The Stand to the Death," which the Germans eagerly took up as a challenge.

Renewed Luftwaffe action against England then eclipsed Mediterranean interest for a time. Liverpool, Glasgow, and Hull were hard hit, but the strike that hurt most fell on London on 10 May. It rated as the worst night blitz ever. Three nights later the roof fell in again. Big Ben took a hit, yet kept on ticking, and London too, but shakily. United States Naval officers on duty there surveyed the countrywide ruin to judge Britain's powers of survival. If attacks of this magnitude continued, they reported to Washington, she could not last the summer through. Across the Channel, OKH assessed *Haifisch* effects and concluded that the British expected a landing attack momently. The commander in chief in the West (Oberbefehlshaber West—OB West) must have caught some of the same feeling which had also filtered down from the Führer and OKW. Hitler was becoming convinced that a British "collapse could occur suddenly." OB West (von Witzleben) conceived the idea of cutting *Haifisch* down to three divisions which would dash cross-channel at three points and take over in a quasi-police action. It was to be called *Haifisch II*, a superfake that wanted to become the real thing. The question was: Who was fooling who now, and what about? The heavy bombing stopped cold; like a miracle, the crisis passed. Tensions tapered off on both sides of the Channel.[14]

During the air storm, and partially screened by it, the freak story of the war broke. Minutes after midnight on Saturday 10 May 1941, Rudolf Hess made his singlehanded Invasion of England, but in the

14. Hitler constantly toyed with a wishful picture of Britain on the point of collapse. This time his vision may have held some substance. It is therefore tempting to single out this period of late May and early June 1941 as the most crucial of all for Invasion England, because the one man who could give the "Execute" thought he saw the long-looked-for prerequisite signs of disintegration. He erred. Britain's strategic forces—land, sea, and air—were nowhere near the brink of collapse. *Haifisch II* would have suffered the same fate as that promised to *Sea Lion*. Skl of the German Navy said as much in response to the Army's notions.—Halder, 2:311–479; Skl Seelöwe 1:15; Skl Haifisch; Skl Harpune; FC 1941, 1:96.

south of Scotland, as a political paratrooper. He came, said he, to bring peace on the basis of the Führer's hope of associating Germany and Britain. So united, the German Army and the British Navy could rule the world. Winston Churchill wrote later that he "never attached any serious importance to this escapade"; yet it stirred the people and brought out some of the best news stories, such as indignation over Hess's menu for lunch—chicken, mind you! The basic speculation settled down to a question: Was Hitler party to the transaction, and if so why? (Could this have been *Haifisch 1½*?) The government concluded that Hess had acted on his own; he changed not a thing "in the march of events," said Churchill; yet the public gabble did raise images of peace to wonder about, and then to stop short when the specter of Invasion stalked through the wings.[15]

Less obscure events on the Continent seemed to signal Franco-German rapprochement. Marshal Pétain's deputy, Admiral Darlan, conferred with von Ribbentrop at Salzburg on matters of accommodation that had been under joint reevaluation, and on the next day, 11 May, he proceeded to the Berghof for a lengthy exchange with the Führer. It was the day after Hess's takeoff, with attendant stir and conjecture. London burst out anew with cries of "collab-

15. Luftwaffe Headquarters sources say Hitler had second thoughts about success in Crete if air reinforcement from Britain should reach her. To keep the RAF at home was therefore one reason for the stepped-up bombing against England; the bombs would at the same time preoccupy Britain and screen *Barbarossa*. At the tail end, the wild Hess scheme may have been given the green light. The British side of that story is well told by Sir Ivone Kirkpatrick, who had known Hess in Berlin and was here the principal British adviser in sifting out Hess's mission. (Kirkpatrick.) He identified Hess, transmitted his message for accommodation with Germany, before it should become too late, to the British government, and otherwise filled out Churchill's account (pp. 48–55). Contrary to British conclusions, high German sources believe Hitler was party to the play at takeoff, and that he set a time limit for Hess to make good, after which he would be cut off. Kirkpatrick notes a marked downturn in Hess's spirits three days after arrival; his deterioration accelerated as time dragged on and established the failure of his mission. He finally attempted suicide. Another German observer raises Hitler's excessive protestations of innocence (a symptom always to be watched). A third source substantiates the transmission of an air alert, ordered by the highest level, immediately after Hess took off (timing checked back later), requiring all air installations to check on the whereabouts of plane number so and so, Hess's plane. It was a cover maneuver for what might, and did, happen—failure of his mission. Hitler's practice of prearranging repudiation of an envoy was well known. If one adds up these indicators with Hitler's Problem England, his impossible hopes, his illusions (currently, that England was on the point of collapse, which he vouched to Admiral Darlan the day after Hess's takeoff), his limitless methods, this episode could have included a last-minute approval of a Hess proposal to mitigate the air blasting and Invasion uproar with an offer of a last chance for Britain "to come around" before *Barbarossa*. It was something Hitler had always wanted. What a final fulfillment if Hess had succeeded, and what a lift to *Barbarossa*!

orator" against Darlan and Pétain, and sharp inquiries flashed out of Washington to Vichy. Darlan reexpressed the Marshal's earnest wish for rapprochement; he volunteered French support for a European confederation that Hitler as the conqueror should form. The spirit was amicable; Hitler got another chance to sum up the sins of France, elaborate his striving to end the war with Britain, and open the subject of French material help in Iraq through Syria. The French seemed to be willing. In fact, what was before Hitler may have been his final and most favorable opening, as to France, for European union. But he was preoccupied with *Barbarossa*; his leverage on France would be greater thereafter, and anyhow he still mistrusted her. He failed to pursue the opportunity.[16]

In the Middle East, German planes and agents persuaded Iraq's Rashid Ali to sever ties with Britain and install a pro-German regime. Hess had carefully stipulated, as an afterthought, that Rashid Ali must suffer no reprisal while Britain and Germany were getting together. Such a provision could hardly have originated with Hess. Elsewhere the ring seemed to be closing around the East Basin: Rommel laid siege to Tobruk and threatened Egypt from her western boundary at a point 200 miles due south of Crete, which he envisioned (Rommel, p. 53) as a prospective center of Luftwaffe power for bringing Tobruk down. Then it would be On to Alexandria!

Suddenly the spotlight switched back to England and crisis at sea—mighty *Bismarck* sighted off Norway. What if she broke out into the Atlantic to prey on Britain's lifeline? She delayed her sweep with cruiser *Prinz Eugen* as Britain's tension mounted with the cry, "Sink the Bismarck"; it blotted out all thought of approaching X-Day on Crete.

Britain's leadership had worked around to a stand on the island for lack of any alternative, while on the highest German level the true object of challenging the stand was merely to secure the south flank of *Barbarossa* and Rumanian oil against air attack. For Creforce, a repulse of the assault would mean Hitler's first outright defeat of the war. This alone was worth doing.

16. Documents GFP, Doc. 491; Warlimont IH, pp. 139 ff. Admiral Darlan and German Ambassador Abetz in Vichy had worked out areas of agreement whose strategic aspects General Huntzinger (for France) and General Warlimont (for Germany) reduced to protocol form. Provided for were French support in the conquest of the Nile region and the Middle East and guarantees about security of North and West Africa against British incursion. The German rear was thus covered and the south flank of Europe secured. The papers were not ratified.

STRENGTH OF OPPOSED FORCES IN CRETE, MAY 1941

GROUND POWER

Troops

DEFENSE	OFFENSE
24,500 English and Dominion troops	23,000 homogeneous seasoned parachute and mountain troops
Equipment in small arms fair, and fire power—strong	Excellent except on first touchdown contact, when fire power—weak

Terrain

Familiar, positions strong	Strange, individual positions weak

Support

Artillery, 49 second-hand field pieces, makeshift control gear; moderate ammo, some mortars	A few pieces of Pak and mortars. Ammo weak
10,000 Greek troops, green, poorly equipped, but fighters	
Armor, 9 heavy, 16 light tanks in only fair condition, but a matchless superiority	None until late; then 2 light tanks

SEA POWER

3 battleships, cruisers, destroyers, submarines—based on Alexandria 400 miles from the scene	Italian Navy escort forces, 8 destroyers, 8 minesweepers, 3 submarines. Amphibious makeshift force of 52 vessels, mostly caïque motor sailers in two flotillas, and 7 steamers

AIR POWER

None on Crete, weak in Egypt; moderate AA defenses	Over 7000 first-line assorted combat planes in Greece assured air control over Crete and air support to ground combat during daylight, 500 vulnerable transport planes for troop and supply support
Fighter support expected from Egypt when needed.	

LOGISTICS

Adequate, local availability	Totally dependent on air transport from Greece even for drinking water.

COMMUNICATIONS

Mostly wire and subject to interruption; some unreliable radio. Land transport 150 trucks, 117 Bren carriers, miscellaneous local vehicles

Radio Greece to Crete and between units. No wheeled motor transport

---

On paper it is plain that in combat, daylight should favor the attacker and darkness the defender; that the defender had the resources to outlast the attacker. Shore-based air power appears as a dangerous factor.

14. Last Moments in Greece

If Creforce required further signal of the approaching storm, 15 May's air fury from dawn till dark furnished it. General von Richthofen's 8th Corps flyers swarmed over Crete's airfields, streets, and barracks with bomb and bullet, over Suda Bay and even a convoy at sea. Nothing, fixed or stirring, was left out. This was a Friday, and the following Tuesday, 20 May, had still not established itself as The Day. Only after eleventh-hour bickering about the 8th Corps's final preassault barrages did X-Day firm up. Of course there were logistic problems too, but this one of preparatory fires that was being argued by Generals Student and von Richthofen was operational. On 16 May therefore Chief of Staff Luftwaffe Jeschonnek presided while the two presented their causes. Richthofen wanted four full days of softening attacks, followed by eight complete sorties in support of the ground action. Student, counting strongly on shock, seemed content, now that the great moment was at hand, to do altogether without such give-away notice and even without direct support. The 8th Corps's leader argued for a foe demoralized by prolonged smothering attacks that would also silence all antiaircraft response, sever all communications, and eliminate all enemy ships and planes. As he put it, "Gasoline and bombs are cheaper than blood of paratroops and a failure." Student gave in. But Jeschonnek objected; such full air support had an absolute terminal date because of *Barbarossa*; there was simply not enough time. Therefore the East Plan demanded that the earliest day permitted by all other requirements should be set, and this turned out to be 20 May 1941. In the interim Richthofen was to do what he could. Harassment from *Barbarossa*'s demands would keep on.[1]

What a journey German arms had come in the last six weeks! Now they fretted again in the familiar last-minute X-Day alarms over this, their first leap direct overseas at the foe. In the air, the contest had already begun and something queer about it emerged. Richthofen stepped up his strikes, but the old Channel index of progress, the number of RAF fighters killed, stayed disappointingly low at one or two a day. The unbelievable truth that there were virtually no fighters on Crete to kill failed to get through. In trying to puzzle it out, the Germans credited the RAF with the evasion tactic used over England, whereas to break up exactly such a rerun Richthofen had insisted on prolonged preassault bombing. When the British struck back at the airfields around Athens, the evasion theory seemed all the plainer. Early on 17 May, RAF planes caught a German fighter base in Greece fast asleep. Out of the rising sun they streaked to knock out twenty-two Me-110's on the ground. "They do it precisely as we do, dashing in close," exclaimed von Richthofen in admiration. Other bases caught it too, yet the prize, the most obvious strategic target, the unhidable Ju transports escaped unscathed. Apparently their vulnerability and massive numbers on improvised, unguarded fields did not register on Cairo.

So blows by air constituted the first exchanges for possession of Crete. The Germans had expected and strongly feared that the first clash would develop from the sea; Britain's sea power breathed down German planning necks from the start as they strove to prove air power would control from on high. Yet old-fashioned doubts persisted, and with the Führer too. Britannia had forever ruled the sea.

This was what engrossed Jeschonnek and Richthofen when they moved to lower the boom against British access to the Aegean. They flew down to the Dodecanese islands northeast of Crete to see for themselves. On Scarpanto Richthofen ordered a Stuka strike against Suda. (There had been reports of British ships passing inbound. They had delivered troops to Heraklion.) Returning pilots gleefully boasted about another tanker fired at Suda, two destroyers and two steamers sunk. Jeschonnek recommended a redoubled attack for the morrow. Smoke from hits obscured the targets, aiming became impossible, but

1. 8th FK Chrono.

bombing kept on. Claimed sinkages exceeded by far the number of ships present. The high density of dive bombs denoted an interlocked bombing capability between bases in the Peloponnese and Scarpanto. Open water in the Aegean island boom was shrinking.

During this time the 8th Air Corps did nothing against the sweeps of naval task groups out of Alexandria, or about safeguarding the prime object of the British fleet's activity—*Merkur's* amphibious flotilla chugging toward landing attack on Crete. News of this was another prelude to X-Day. On 19 May Richthofen's Chronology noted, "Already at sea are a number of Greek motor sailers with a battalion of 5th Mountain Division, antiair and antitank weapons, artillery, and armored cars for the support of the troops to be dropped. Under escort of Italian torpedo boats they are sailing to the island of Melos, there to wait out what the British fleet will undertake and until Crete is free for them." They were the first of the German soldiers to go forth to battle in the maddest assortment of landing craft ever assembled. Their sortie made an earnest beginning of assault from the sea that would climax in the war's fiercest trial of shore-based planes against ships at sea.

Tiny Melos sits on the north rim of the Cretan Sea, about halfway from Piraeus to Crete. To go there means 86 sea miles, and onward to Crete, due south, 74 miles more. Five islands mark the course, like huge channel buoys, from the mainland to Melos; but beyond, the sea is free and open to pirating or intercepting landing flotillas. The island offers a well-placed navigational mark, with its lofty peak, and shelter in a north-shore bay. The lowliest levantine caïque out of Piraeus could raise Melos in a night and a day, and from there, Crete by midafternoon of the next day, if its motor held through.

That *Merkur* should have the support of a sea landing at all was no brainchild of the operation's airborne progenitors. No, the idea sprang from soldier fundamentalists. It allied itself with ground combat doctrine and its sound soldier wish for a base on the foreign shore to sustain him. While the flyers accepted the need for sea transport as a sort of auxiliary service after air had won control of the sea, direct seaborne support to ground combat entered the calculations only belatedly. But these soldiers knew what a ground slugfest could be. From such anticipations and with Navy connivance, the plan for early reinforcement by sea took shape. "The thing must not stand on one leg alone," reasoned General Ringel. He attributed a like view to the Führer. His friend and countryman General Löhr agreed and directed the creation of a light seaborne combat echelon and a heavy echelon of steamers for tanks and artillery to follow. Two motor-sailer flotillas were contrived for landing on open beaches west of Maleme and east of Heraklion. General Student went along, lukewarm; he conceded that sea reinforcement to paratroops might thus be speeded, if the British destroyed the Cretan airfields. He said so in his postoperation report of *Merkur*: "Thereby [sea support] the supply of ample reinforcement would be secured, as well as provision for the case of delay in air-transport landings because the British had destroyed the airfields." This is a rare after-the-event mention of a possibility that the airfields might be demolished, to prevent (what was never mentioned) the building of an airhead. It was an old soldier-sailor concept of an orthodox beachhead trying to surface. Ground fighters have a faculty for coming up with serious soul searchings as The Day draws nigh.[2]

That is why General Ringel sent his officers scurrying through the reachable waterfronts in search of craft, and why Navy's Command Southeast sent for an old hand from the Channel. Commander Heinrich Bartels had been one of *Sea Lion*'s producers; he readied the Dunkirk flotilla for invading England in the summer of 1940. Now he was to ready a Maleme flotilla for invading Crete. It was late. Early on 17 May he stood on the only upright pier in the wrecked port of Piraeus and looked about him. Dunkirk had never been this bad. This single pier might do for loading, but loading into what? Where to magic up landing craft? Over there in the small-craft basin a few masts stuck up; perhaps something could be salvaged there and in the fisher and yacht harbors nearby. The 5th Mountain had found a few wrecks in Megara and Chalcis on Euboea.[3]

In Navy Lieutenant Albert Österlin, Bartels found a kindred spirit; both had been fetched up in the school of the ship aboard merchantmen, and here was an adventure that appealed to their talents and

2. 11th FK Kreta, 2 June 1941; LF4 Kreta; Ringel Ms; Ringel HG; discussion with Generals Student and Ringel, Germany, 1960. Although Führer Directive No. 28 implied a concern for adequate reinforcement by air alone, the idea failed to take hold until a vagrant thought about demolished airfields bobbed up while the soldiers were worrying about support over the beaches.
3. Vidua gives a lively account, as does Horbach. Lt. Colonel Horbach's official report, made immediately after the operation, and eight other reports of participants in the attempted sea landing—5th MD War Diary—have been consulted. Naval advices came from Admiral Südost (Schuster) and direct from Admiral Hellmuth Heye, Germany, 1960. He was chief of staff to Admiral Südost in 1941. The Crete operation was discussed with Captain Bartels in 1953. He still bubbled with enthusiasm for the undertaking.

tastes. They determined that Österlin would lead the first light echelon of Maleme Flotilla out of Piraeus, on one of the four auxiliary Italian motor minesweepers that had just joined the enterprise. Bartels in the role of beachmaster would fly over in an early air wave to select a suitable beach near Maleme, mark it with lights shining to seaward, and round up some paratroop help for unloading. It was all worked out with the keenest relish. How some of this bulky gear that already blocked the pierhead would be manhandled from ship to shore, over there, stopped nobody. By degrees the berths alongside the pier filled with the outlandish craft of Österlin's command. They were for the most part two-masted motor sailers of about 100 tons in wood hulls, built for fishing or coasting. All were past their prime in hull, sail, and machinery. A couple of small steamers together with the auxiliary minesweepers were the queens. For the immense load to be lifted, the total number remained short. Maleme Flotilla out of Piraeus had an uncertain twenty-four vessels, Heraklion Flotilla out of Lavrion at the tip of Attica (after junction there with a branch from Megara and one from Chalcis) a vague thirty. So lusty was the scramble of getting off and so loose the formation keeping under way that neither flotilla commander could ever be sure of what he had. But devil take the hindmost while "sailing 'gainst England," at least in spirit.

Now they are loading; it is Sunday 18 May, Mother's Day in Germany. Troop assembly, only just begun, halts. Appearance of Britain's Royal Naval forces north of Crete has convinced Admiral Schuster's staff in Athens that the Melos sea area at this time would be no place for these fragile craft. Postponement is ordered for the situation to clear. The British ships then withdraw (for refueling) and the all clear for flotilla sailing in the evening of 19 May is given by General Löhr. But Captain Heye at Navy objects. To him the situation is still clouded. He is overruled; the order stands. In an inaugural skirmish off Crete between Luftwaffe planes and British combatant ships, they seemed to cancel each other out. But will they always?

Another halt! Just before troop embarkation a radical change is ordered in the mission of Maleme Flotilla. Instead of transporting follow-up troops and gear, it is now to take combat troops and gear. The Maleme sea contingent becomes an assault group. Third Battalion of the 100th Mountain Regiment arrives at the pier to embark. The troops are happy over the transport switch. Something has happened, someone has won an argument. Perhaps confidence has slipped in success by paratroop assault alone at Maleme, or the possibility has rung through of finding nothing there but a cratered reminder of an airfield. Has Student given in to the ground fighters? Ringel had wanted provision for assault from the sea at Heraklion too. This 3d Mountain Battalion he had already designated to join General Süssmann in Group Center over Maleme; being more soldier than airman, Süssmann may have engineered the switch.

General Ringel reported completion of flotilla loading at Chalcis. His whole division was as ready as he could make it. On such occasions, when there could be no turning back, he was wont to close off his war diary with a cheer as he signed it. What could serve better than the division's battle cry, "Hurra die Gams"? He prefixed, "Ever onward to final victory," then "Hurra die Gams!" and signed with a flourish.[4]

Captain Bartels reported Maleme Flotilla stowed and ready for sea. What an odd assortment of stuff he had seen go aboard! Ammunition, rations, antitank and antiaircraft guns, motorcycles with sidecars, command cars, mules, horses, and even dogs—everything that could not get into a plane. Ships seemed more elastic to the soldiers, and here was the chance. Almost everything got loaded, well and good! Österlin and he, as they watched, were prepared for some soldier versatility at smuggling, for this was the Channel story all over again: each man, each clique had a private, secret solution for what lay ahead. Josef Vidua tells of the flak gunners who mounted their three pieces topside where arcs of fire were fine, only to be told to dismount two of their guns or the ship would roll over at sea. They complied, but not without producing their own solution. To the amazement of the sailors, the same little band paddled alongside in a little while on a raft, the two guns securely mounted, complete with a safety rail around and nails in it for hanging personal gear. One such contraption actually made it to sea in tow and was cut adrift only after its mother ship came under British shellfire.

They filed aboard lighthearted, these mountain lads from the Führer's favorite region on the Austrian border. Their 3d Battalion of Mountain Regiment 100, better known as the Reichenhaller Battalion after its home town, was commanded by Lt. Colonel Ehal, who embarked in Ship 105 (the vessels were numbered S-105 and

---

4. A *gams* is a chamois, able to go anywhere and do anything in the mountains. The cry became the title of General Ringel's book which recounts the exploits of his division, the Gams Division.

so on). Counting reinforcements, flak units, and leftover paratroops, he commanded 2331 fresh-caught amphibians playing a role as alien to them as space travel. Troop lifts per craft varied from 66 to 124, all packed in tight. The auxiliary minesweepers carried Italian crews of twenty, the rest of the craft only two or three Greek hands; each had a German sailor or two abroad. The Maleme-bound assemblage made the better half of *Merkur's* sea landing force that so deeply affected the British defense deployment.

Heraklion Flotilla was more nondescript because of the split between Chalcis and Megara. For Major Treck, commander of the embarked 2d Battalion, Mountain Regiment 85, control under changing circumstances and orders became impossible. Junction of the two branches never came about, nor could it be established on arrival at Melos. In an early scheme, Captain Lipinski, Treck's Navy opposite, was to command a union of the Maleme and Heraklion flotillas in one grand armada. That dream fell out. He was to sail both branches as best he could, a day after Maleme Flotilla, for Melos. This was attempted. A later report of his colleague Treck reads like the wildest nightmare: ships too small, unseaworthy, during embarkation a constant shifting by individual units from one vessel to another in the hope of ship improvement, unreliable communications, unmanageable unloading pontoons to be stowed or towed, foul drinking water, and on and on. At departure from Chalcis he considered that "battle readiness could not even be spoken of."

In the dusk of 19 May as Maleme Flotilla chugged placidly to sea, the minesweepers took the van. Österlin led the two-columns-abreast formation from the starboard column lead ship. Italian torpedo boat *Sirio* escorted at a station well advanced. Since she alone had radio touch with Naval headquarters, she exercised operational control over her charges by blinker, and when necessary, by megaphone. Word of mouth, not always polite, likewise served the individual motor sailers amongst themselves. Dark was falling; each craft lit a stern light, and sea routine took over in posting of lookouts, checking of gear stowage. The boats rose and fell in the easy swell while the mountain boys made themselves comfortable. Some three hundred of them were embarking on their first and last sailing to sea.

In the annals of landing warfare, this venture makes a mark. Operation Order No. 1 from Admiral Schuster set the following timetable:

(*a*) Sortie Piraeus X-minus-1 Day. Depart Melos X-Day. Land Maleme X-plus-1 Day.

(*b*) Close security requested of Luftwaffe. . . .

(*c*) At a point 25 miles off Maleme, stand by in readiness at 1000 on X-plus-1 Day until ordered to land.

In effect the orders said: Go to Maleme, lie to off shore, land some way or other when ordered. This was the hurdle—some way or other. How to get the stuff out? The motor sailers could beach, topple over, and fill; or if they grounded deep and evenly, how could the troops wade ashore laden with heavy gear? Inflatable and improvised rafts and pontons had been loaded for bridging the gap. Would they do? It was worth the gamble. To have put two battalions, reinforced, of over 4500 troops afloat was an achievement; to have stuck by sending them forth to battle is most arresting of all. This zeal to go pervaded all *Merkur* and made the operation remarkable.

But the mood of this carefree scramble on the waterfront petered out as one went inland to the improvised air fronts. Their corresponding bustle called forth only bitter blasphemy. Instead of a handful of boats trying to get to sea, there were hundreds on hundreds of heavy planes trying to get into the dusty air. Two major deficiencies galled the transport pilots: visibility and fuel. Hot sand swirled everywhere to begrime everybody and everything. On 18 May Colonel von Heyking held his rehearsal of squadron takeoff at Topolia, 50 miles north of Athens. The time to get the squadron airborne ran to over an hour, and landing to much more. All through the night of 19 May sprinklers sprayed various concoctions over the fields. The squadron of Colonel Ulrich Buchholz at Tanagra suffered the same troubles; in fuel shortage still more. To the last moment before takeoff on X-Day, hand-pumping from truck to plane continued. It was an unhappy time.

Among the ground and airborne troops the mood was easier. Campsites were good, some on the sea even pleasant. Near Topolia Captain von der Heydte watched his men of the 1st Battalion, 3d Parachute Regiment, relax on the shore in sunbathing and swimming. They felt fine. Excitement filled the air as briefing and packing up took over. Eager mountaineers tried to absorb the mysteries of Airborne. They had practiced emplaning, anxiously squeezing in each favorite weapon, and deplaning ready to fight. Paratroopers brought out their brimless helmets, girded and ungirded their comic short rompers, buckled on life jackets for the first time, packed weapons containers and during all, scandalized the mountaineers with their abandon. They joined plane crews in the vexatious fueling job. Units huddled for final briefing: vital ground actions were pounded home again—and then the objective for X-Day was announced: Crete, Tuesday 20 May, Y-Hour over target 0715. Start time would be 0430 (or later, up to 0530, depending on the field). The password came last. It honored their chieftain Hermann Göring by invoking his title: Reichsmarschall![5]

General Student must have felt his battle half-won or more. How he had had to fight to get his ideas over, his plan and technique! This was now behind him. Five days ago he had expounded the elements of the project personally with earnest care and confidence to his leaders down through battalion commanders in that shuttered, steaming room of the Grande Bretagne. In the crucial first strike, Meindl was to pounce on Maleme's defenders and drive them from the field; Süssman was to drop on Canea's approaches, take the city, and knock out the British high command. Meanwhile the two forces would have linked up and together would clean out all resistance.

Süssmann's threshold story suffers from lack of record, for soon after takeoff the glider carrying him and his immediate staff crashed in total loss. He had planned to land by glider at the head of Prison Valley after Colonel Heidrich with his 3d Paratroop Regiment had jumped into the valley approaches to Galatas, just as the defending Colonel Kippenberger anticipated. The ground fight would then open—Heidrich versus Kippenberger.

Meindl summoned his staff, headquarters people, and leaders of the 4th Battalion, which was also at Megara Field, to review the regimental plan until "every soldier felt prepared in the exact requirements of his individual task." He stuck fast by the doctrine of shock and surprise when he expected the most troublesome spots to be taken by advance-party glider descents in company strength on the west edge of the airfield and another on the lower slopes of Hill 107, facing the field. Major Koch, hero of Eben Emael and now commander of the 2d Battalion, was to deliver these shocks fifteen minutes before zero hour. He himself would lead the 4th Company on lower Hill 107, while Leutnant Plessen took the 3d Company against the west rim of the airfield. Also, Major Braun, the senior officer of Meindl's staff, with 80 troops in gliders, would land alongside the Tavronitis bridge

5. Lt. Colonel von der Heydte has described his experiences in Operation *Merkur* in his lively and perceptive book *Daedalus Returned* (Heydte).

and secure it. At 0730 the 3d Battalion would jump east of the air-field, cut it off, and insure its seizure by the 4th Battalion, which would have jumped just west of the Tavronitis. The 2d Battalion (Stentzler) would meanwhile have jumped in farther west to secure the rear, with special emphasis on Kastelli Kisamou and approaches from the south. General Meindl and his headquarters staff were to drop and glide down west of the bridge end to establish the command post on the very strategic high ground left vacant by the defenders. It would be Meindl against Andrew.[6]

Last-minute checks with the transport pilots revealed that they had no aerial photos of the drop zones. After all, being set down in the right place was an absolute first priority. Staffers scurried out to pry off extra copies from the troop units. A War Diary entry about readiness finished on a wistful note: "Home baggage is being packed and assembled. The feeling of all soldiers is good and happy." The word went out: "Knockoff and rest! Reveille 0330." It was to come quietly and individually to each man through the men left on watch, but loaded with unanswerable questions.

Before then, 8th Corps pilots would be in their saddles ready for dawn takeoff to break the last little way into Crete. Though not unsung, the combat pilots have been lost to our sight in the hurlyburly of landing-attack preparations, whose success will hang on the efficacy of these final 8th Corps barrages. At Eleusis Field on 19 May General von Richthofen struck his eleventh-hour balance with his leaders. He canvassed the scheduled strikes, tied up loose ends, checked on the fresh experiences to be applied and the state of resources that would be left available. Bombs showed a critical shortage; henceforth each bomb had to do a specific job. At 0530 the two main strikes would begin their final round of a half-hour duration. Further attacks would follow only if desired by the Airborne chief. General Student did not believe he would need them.[7]

Indeed, Student had turned in, secure in his faith in an Airborne triumph. Later he wrote in his action report: "On 19 May in the evening all preparations for attack on Crete were complete. Leaders and troops had been carefully indoctrinated in their tasks and stood ready at the airfields, eager for action. The command reckoned on a swift and decisive success."

Before seeking his couch, Student checked one weighty last item—

6. Sturmregt TB, 23 April–20 May 1941, and Sturmregt B, 20 May–28 May 1941.
7. 8th FK Chrono; LF4 Kreta.

weather for the morrow. Against Air Fleet 4's weatherman he agreed with his own, who minimized the influence of a disturbance over Italy and prophesied clear flying and sailing for Crete—and what was more important to paratroopers, light surface winds over the touchdown areas. All clear. He could sleep.

Lt. Colonel Trettner, operations officer of the 11th Air Corps, still busied himself over last-minute crises; he stared at a message just in; the intelligence officer had brought it himself: "Alexandria squadron of two battleships, one carrier, four cruisers, fifteen destroyers approaching Crete." What in hell could that mean? A horrible thought struck him as his eyes wandered over a chart: What if by daylight this force stationed itself off Kithira Island on the Greece-Crete approach route of the massed low-flying troop-lift columns of Ju's and methodically shot the lot of them out of the air? Troubled and uneasy, Trettner sought out the counsel of Captain Heye, chief of staff to Admiral Southeast. Could the ships reach such a position? This was the fearsome question. Yes, they could. Time and space factors quickly proved it, as Heye demonstrated. Together they went to General Korten, chief of staff Air Fleet 4; he agreed it made a grim picture. They went on to brace the prime mover of Operation *Merkur*, General Student. It was getting late to halt the operation. The general roused, heard them out, looked over the plot, and forthrightly rejected all thought of change. *Merkur* would go; these apparitions he had faced long before and faced them down; and he added, "Waking me was really unnecessary." So spoke the spirited leader of *Merkur*. Without that spirit it would never have gone.[8]

German Airborne Practices of 1941[9]

Troop lift. The Ju, the three-engined Junker-52, was the workhorse transport plane for jumpers, towed gliders, and field-landed troops and for equipment and supply to the landees. Some 1000 Ju's were kept in commission for war needs. About half of these, organized in ten plane-groups, participated in *Merkur*. Shortly before the operation they were overhauled and reengined in the vicinity of Vienna. Each was capable of lifting 1280 kilograms, i.e., 12 to 13 fully

8. Trettner and Heye to Ansel in separate conversations in Germany, 1960.
9. The following brief of German Airborne practices has been read over by General Trettner, who gave advice.

equipped troops at 100 kilograms or an equivalent weight of cargo in munitions and supply—about 1¼ tons.

One *Staffel* (echelon) of 12 Ju's accommodated a company of 156 paratroops. One plane group—4 echelons of 50 planes—accommodated a battalion of about 600. And one squadron of two or more groups accommodated a reinforced regiment.

Troop assignment to planes, loading, and launching corresponded closely to boat diagraming, scheduling, and dispatching in amphibious operations. Three plane groups could be compared to one attack waterborne transport (APA) in seaborne landings. As a landing boat, the Ju cruised at 130 knots, landed at 50 to 60 knots.

Approach and drop. The run to Crete from fields in Attica required about 1.6 hours. The basic cruising unit was a V of three (*Kette*) and the group cruised in columns of V's abreast, usually at low altitude (*Tiefstflug*). On approaching the drop zone, the formation adjusted to the landing and combat problem being undertaken. Drops aimed at 120 meters (350–400 feet), and at this point the plane was usually in a climb that was throttled down to a near stall for the drop. An *Absetzer* (or in the vernacular *Abschmeisser*—off-thrower) regulated the jumps by well-known commands. Officers and squad leaders leaped first and all headforemost through the door that had been kept open. Accompanying gear, each piece with its identifying colored chute, was kicked out by the plane crew after the troop drop. In the Crete operation troops used white or lightly mottled chutes, equipment solid-colored ones.

Gliders. While specially fitted Ju's had towed two or three gliders, each holding eight men, at Crete each Ju was still to tow only one glider. The gliders were cast off at 1200 and 1500 meters altitude about 6 miles from their target. Gliders retained some small choice of landing spot and were therefore favored for targets requiring a noiseless approach, precise targetry, and instant combat readiness on touching down. In *Merkur's* initial break-in strikes, 78 gliders were used.

Paratroops and armament. Individual paratroops carried 4 to 6 grenades, a Schmeisser automatic pistol with a stock, and in some cases a machine-gun pistol, which approximated a light tommy gun. Regular rifles, automatic rifles, machine guns, and mortars had to be retrieved from containers dropped from the mother plane. The individual also carried extra ammunition and rations for three days. He wore a brimless cloth helmet, abbreviated coveralls of many pockets, knee and elbow pads, and stout high shoes. A company all told mustered 156, but for select jobs this could be scaled to 108 fighters. Usually a battalion had four companies, No. 4 being a machine-gun–mortar combination; three battalions made a regiment except for the Sturmregiment, which had four. It was a quasi-corps formation, as were antitank and mortar companies, a light and heavy antiair machine-gun battalion, several light-artillery sections and an engineer battalion. Most of the equipment for these corps organizations (except the Sturmregiment) had to be lifted by transport plane to fields. From these units, those in combat could be reinforced as the job in hand demanded.

15. Vertical Envelopment—
Fact or Fancy?

The Break-in: To Noon, 20 May 1941

General Student went back to sleep, safe in his deep conviction of swift and certain success. By this time tomorrow all would be over, his paratroop spears dug deep into the vitals of Crete. There was the key: panic the Britons at the airfields and the main command posts and take over. If only simultaneous drops at all four points could have been put over! Yet a quick forenoon strike in the west might do. Victory would be in easy sight.

Possibly so; just the same, the departing staffers made sure that word from the dawn reconnaissance flights should be channeled through instantly. The 8th Corps's own reaction to the original sighting of the fleet had been the frank but helpless entry: "Unfortunately, today no attack is any longer possible." Nothing had been saved for this jam. But now, early on 20 May, Scarpanto and the mainland fields stood ready with attack groups to respond at the very first light, which came on this day at 0418 German time (0518 British time). They waited in vain; no fleet could be sighted. Where could the British be lurking? At Admiral Southeast headquarters the guess was that the fleet had judiciously assumed stations in readiness to the westward against the only opposing sea forces, those of Italy. This was correct. If General Freyberg and his staff, waiting on Crete, worried about assault from the sea, so did his German opposites.

20 May 1941 broke into light perfect. At Maleme, 22 Battalion's War Diary noted: "20th May. Usual Mediterranean summer day. Cloudless, no wind, extreme visibility: e.g., details on the mountains to the southeast easily discernible." For a short time, before bursting bombs cut off the serenity and vision, the regular morning tattoo went on. But was it regular? So sharp and short, ceasing as abruptly as it started. No one was hit; 22 Battalion, falling out for breakfast, took no note of anything special; most of the men felt this to be merely the same beginning of another day, as per routine. And such belief accorded with German intentions, for General Student had explicitly requested "no further introductory attacks in order to avoid alarming the island prematurely." Lull them with the standard breakfast pause,

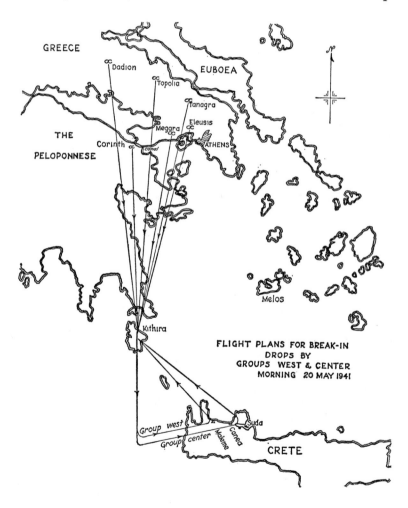

FLIGHT PLANS FOR BREAK-IN
DROPS BY
GROUPS WEST & CENTER
MORNING 20 MAY 1941

then let the heavens fall. Preassault barrages from every plane on hand were to break the lull at 0635.[1]

By this time every Ju that was going to make it was in the air. *Merkur*'s initial Airborne sortie came closest to achieving the planned execution; later sorties were overhauled by events. This first, most ambitious one sailed off free, carrying in its cumbered airhulls the high hopes of Airborne. They would never be so high again. A few foundered on the fields at takeoff; dust took a toll; one complete group delayed a full hour. Never mind! The 493 lumbering transports thundered toward Crete, low over the water, bearing into combat 6002 deflated young men of the first wave.

Among them a battalion commander, a captain of scholarly mien, eyed his planemates squatting along the sides of the Ju and wondered. They were young too:

Not one of the thirteen men seated in the plane uttered a word. Everyone was preoccupied with his own thoughts. When there is no going back, most men experience a strange sinking feeling, as if their stomachs had remained on the ground. Suddenly the bright light of the morning sun broke through. The plane had risen beyond the layer of dust and fog. One of the men started singing. It was the "Song of the Paratroopers"—and in a moment we all joined in:

> Fly on this day against the enemy!
> Into the planes, into the planes!
> Comrade there is no going back![2]

Ah, a deep breath; the spell is broken. They were ready to carry on, loud and eager.

To catch the first glimpse of Crete, that possessed them now. What would it look like, this island? They had only heard of it as the target positively yesterday. How does an island look in the sea anyway? Who has ever seen one, or for that matter, ever flown overseas? Not many. A new and enthralling adventure, this pounding over the water just above the swells. One sees how endlessly they reach, surely almost to Crete.

But rather than lengthwise, they sighted the island end-on from the west. The flight plan detoured westward to free Crete's direct approaches for the 8th Air Corps's planes, busy at their final blasting. The transport route led over the island of Kithira—it provided the guiding "point of departure." Meindl's Maleme column flew on the left, Süssmann's Prison Valley group paralleled outside on the right.

1. Henderson, p. 41; Davin, p. 92; LF4 Kreta.
2. Heydte, p. 52.

Due west of the drop zones the columns swung east to bring Crete's western face, still 30 miles away, into uncertain focus. The sun blinded, but there lay the target in hazy outline, narrow but lofty. The Ju's began a slow climb. Only minutes more, unending minutes, up over the etched shoreline, the mountains, and on to the drop zones beyond. Then the jump commands ring out: Make ready! (hook on, close up); Ready! And at last the piercing squawk of the go signal: *Raus!* Overhead the escorting fighters crept ahead.

At 0645 renewed violence overwhelmed Maleme Field and its breakfasting defenders. By German scheduling the barrage was ten minutes late, but none the less awesome, frightening. Such sound and fury the New Zealanders had never before experienced. Two dozen heavy bombers thundered out of the east, a signal of something extraordinary; in their wake Stukas dived on the field's perimeter; fighters swooped in and out, strafing furiously. Each earthbound soldier can feel sure he is singled out as the target—and he is. He is to be demoralized. The ground shakes, his ears bleed, smoke and dust are everywhere. It clears enough to reveal a pocked no man's land, stripped of vine and olive cover. Hill 107 bulges high and naked. The time has come—Airborne's big moment.

For this loaded moment, finding and timing are the twin anxieties of all landing projects, whether by air or by sea: the right place at the right time. In this air landing, these two bugbears were magnified out of all proportion because of high speeds. A slip in one or the other could spell disaster, and all the more when the final barrage falls late and leaves behind a terrain beaten into unrecognizable chaos fogged by smoke and dust. It is remarkable that the first-wave drops fared as well as they did. But then, initiating actions always enjoy a free start and extra prepping. Here the break-in batted about 60 percent. For its ambitious objectives it was not enough.

We know that Meindl's order pointed three glider punches at key targets. He picked them right: the antiaircraft batteries on the Tavronitis delta, the bridge, and Hill 107; his orders were:

(1) At 0715, fifteen minutes before all others, Leutnant Plessen with his 3d Company of 108 men in 14 gliders, land on Tavronitis delta, take out the Bofors AA guns hard west of the field, then attack the tentage and defense works on the west edge of the field [Lt. Sinclair and his 15 Platoon].

(2) Also at 0715, Major Koch, commander 1st Battalion, with 4th Company plus his Headquarters, all told 120, in 15 gliders, land on either

side of Hill 107, take it, the munitions dump and tentage on it, and attack the field from the south. [His 1st and 2d Companies were with Altmann and Genz in the Canea area.]

(3) At 0730, Major Braun [the second man in Headquarters] with 80 men [from Headquarters and the 3d Battalion] in 9 gliders, land alongside Tavronitis bridge, seize it, prevent demolition and support Plessen.

A fourth shock wave, Captain Witzig and his 9th Company, reinforced by machine guns—would meanwhile jump on the east rim of the airfield to spearhead the 3d Battalion's assault from that quarter. Meindl fully expected quick and easy success from these blows; they were to enable him to close the sound of the strife with his remaining forces dropped west of the Tavronitis, and to begin thinking about contact with Süssmann in Prison Valley.

To recapitulate, the basic tasks by Battalions were

1st Bn (Koch): Seize Hill 107 and the west rim of the airfield.
2d Bn (Stentzler): Guard the rear, seize Kastelli Kisamou (Mürbe).
3d Bn (Scherber): Attack airfield from east; link up with Prison Valley.
4th Bn (Gericke): Support bridge and airfield seizure from west of the Tavronitis.

The attack orders make repeated reference to seizure of tented camps (*Zeltlager*), as though the defenders might be found lounging in them. Action reports acknowledge disappointedly that the camps were empty. Probably tentage was one set of identifiable objects on aerial reconn, and it was assumed that important defenses would be nearby. If so, it is a mark of the sketchy intelligence available to the Germans.

Leutnant Göttsche, regimental signals officer, recounts how the general and his headquarters got off from Megara in seven Ju's and five gliders, how they proceeded in ideal flying conditions by a direct route into Kisamos Gulf, how there at 5000 feet the gliders unlatched to sail along on their own, while the Ju's continued eastward at lowered altitude to drop their jumpers, Meindl included, but a bit farther east than planned. By this time the sky around boiled with great droning birds, and of a sudden, petals of many colors showered down from their bellies, hundreds of them.

Plessen is already at work on the delta. In all *Merkur*, he is the first down, followed closely by Koch on Hill 107. His gliders swish in under cover of the last bomb blast, which helps Plessen too. After overwhelming the four Bofors guns farthest west, Koch is stopped by fire at the airfield edge and shortly falls a casualty while trying to make contact with Braun under the bridge. Braun too has been drilled through the head as he steps out of his glider; his second is injured in landing; the third man, Leutnant Trebes, carries on. He and a depleted party reach the bridge, claw their way under the structure, and force back Sargeson's pickets on the British end, but get no farther. The fire from Hill 107 is intense. Plessen's party is stopped too, but establishes touch with Trebe's handful. And Koch, where could he be? He raises no flag of victory on the Hill; he lies low, critically wounded; his men manage only a frantic wave or two from the hill-side.[3]

No one person can know all this. Most men know only what is closest and act accordingly. So it may be for Trebes under the bridge, Meindl on the west bank, and Andrew on the Hill. They strain to see through, to hear through, to make sense. Yet Trebes and Meindl have the advantage. Their objective for the moment is clear-cut—the bridge; they know they must have it, and they go after it. The rest may wait.

So Meindl concentrates on the bridge. He dropped from his Ju into a grain field south of the coastal road, a short way from the riverbed, and at once pressed forward with headquarters combat squads as they rallied round to report. The machine-gun section he sends to cover the bridge as far as the little island in the center and to give fire support to the attack on Hill 107; the others scuttle over the dry bed from one gravel runnel to the next to join the fight for a bridgehead on the far side. Meindl's own reception on Tavronitis bank is a warm one. He wants to know about Koch, and as he attempts to signal him by ground panel, a bullet creases his hand. Signalers and he lie low. Other men appear on the bridge roadway erect, ready to dash over; exasperated, the general jumps up to wave them down and is struck by a bullet in the chest. The men get over, dodging from one bridge pile to another. A mortar joins their cover. A start is under way, but a far harder one than expected. It is 0900 o'clock.[4]

Things are pretty much adrift. There lies the general, his devoted men hovering about, making him comfortable in a little shelter; yet

3. The action report of General Student (11th FK Kreta) mentions the severing of a demolition-charge wire under the bridge. This was one of Braun's tasks. It was logical that the bridge should be wired, and from Corinth on, all German commanders must have been doubly bridge-conscious. No evidence comes to hand from British sources that the bridge was charged or wired. It is the way of action reports; they often carry forethoughts over to events, often inflate difficulties to enhance their conquests. The Germans encountered "heavy resistance" from unoccupied points. The British lost points that were "heavily attacked" by no forces.

4. Told to me by General Student, and also in 11th FK Kreta, Sturmregt TB,

he is very much alone, without a single staff officer (this is Airborne). He sends word to Captain Gericke of the 4th Battalion to take over the cross-river fight. After a while the regimental signals officer, Leutnant Göttsche, hustles up to report. He has with him on wheels the one 80-watt radio transmitter salvaged from a wrecked glider landing. (Of four gliders devoted to communication gear and operators, only half survived.) Young Göttsche thereupon finds himself alone at the helm. He sets about establishing a command post and gingerly takes charge. A prepared British defense post in an olive grove on the neglected strategic hillside serves perfectly. What a find—complete with cover and gun ports! By 1000, radio touch is made with Gericke's 4th Battalion and with Major Stentzler's 2d Battalion in the west, the next senior in the regiment. From Major Scherber and the 3d Battalion east of the airfield, nothing comes through, nor from Koch (1st Battalion) on the hill. The Sturmregiment is operating under an able lieutenant, guided by an ailing general.

"So ran the situation at regiment after the break-in," says the later combat report of this time, after piously reciting that the enemy is decidedly stronger than expected, that Koch of the 1st Battalion has failed, that the 3d Battalion east of the airfield has been rubbed out, that Braun is dead and his project stalled, that the 16th Company, high upstream on the Tavronitis, has secured the south flank, that Leutnant Mürbe is in trouble [with Bedding and his Greeks] at Kastelli Kisamou, but that Major Stentzler of the 2d Battalion has the rear well secured. All three glider strikes have failed. This is all true, but fortunately for them, neither Göttsche nor his general knows the half of it. They must plug away at what presses hardest in front of them. The riverbed fight goes on; it becomes the true arena. Gericke's men of the 4th Battalion enter the badly mixed free-for-all of individual surges. Control is nil, but spirit is high. More and more men get over the Tavronitis, as do a mortar and a couple of machine guns.

Thank heaven again for this radio operator Erich! He sets up shop in a corner of the trench, fusses over the damaged radio pieces, ties them together. In no time there comes a sputtering, and by 1100 businesslike buzzes. He has raised the 11th Air Corps in Athens!

---

and Sturmregt B. Major Braun was regimental major, that is, Meindl's chief of staff. The scheme to take the bridge was concocted the day before X-Day. It may have come after a switch of nine reserve gliders to this assault mission. Apparently, then, Braun's project became a last-minute extension of a bridge action already laid on for Headquarters troops. Thus Braun would spearhead the bridge effort by glider while Meindl would move support by Headquarters combat parties. It is noteworthy that each paratrooper is a fighter, even the Headquarters people, including the doctor.

The day is saved, help within hail! Surely this man must be decorated. Göttsche hastens to transmit a summary of the situation. It is no glowing report. Messages fly back and forth. Over Athens, over the Grande Bretagne, the clouds gather.

Major Stentzler arrives with two companies (the 5th and 7th) from the west. "During the noon hour" (there must have been a pause, for it is mentioned) General Meindl goes over the situation with the major. His fresh, well-gathered companies are to work around the south flank of Hill 107, force the defenders toward the sea while Gericke continues to press them frontally on the bridge and the coastal road. Heavy weapons from Stentzler are added to Gericke for storming the north slope of Hill 107. Stentzler is to command in the field, but "conduct for the operation as a whole remains otherwise in the hands of Generalmajor Meindl."

What of his opposite, Lt. Colonel Andrew on Hill 107? Is he forming for counterattack to clear the Tavronitis? A concerted effort from there is something that the German command feared. But Andrew is chained to the hill, a victim of trench warfare without another trench opposite to mark the no man's land between. The furious pace of the day's work demands that Meindl's force move forward, and it does. It could have been wiped out.

A Company of 22 Battalion is dug in on the flat top of Hill 107. Colonel Andrew and staff, plus a small reserve, are forward within the company perimeter. B Company is in back of A on the hilltop's extension; Headquarters Company is around Pirgos village east of the airfield; C Company around its three sides; D Company on the hill's west slope overlooking the Tavronitis. This means that D Company is engaged with what is left of Braun's party at the bridge entry, and C Company's 15 Platoon with Plessen's party on the airfield's west rim. A Company receives and dispatches about twenty paratroops; B has more—Witzig and his 9th Company have touched down here, badly out of place. They should be storming the airfield from Pirgos in the east, where Andrew's Headquarters Company has its hands full with members of Koch's group.

Counterattack proposal comes from C Company by nine o'clock (the very time that Meindl drops out of action), yet Andrew for reasons of his own rejects it. The moment's meaning eludes him; the significance of Tavronitis and the bridge elude him. He cannot see or hear his companies. Though runners skip back and forth, the distances are long, the hazards great. Command is at a minimum, and no designated goal rises to take its place, only the negative hope of holding the hill and thus saving the airfield. Fierce air violence has scourged 107. It is bare. Andrew is nipped in the temple, his communications severed, his vision fogged. He too must feel weighed down and alone, unable to distinguish his best chances and gravest peril.[5]

Glider landings toward Headquarters Company at Pirgos worry Andrew so much that he tries to break a contact through and finds the same hard line as his runners, failure. He manages to get through to B Company for a check. In a little while, radio touch to Brigade is restored; he requests that 23 Battalion make contact with his Headquarters Company. A German barrier in that region could cut 22 Battalion off, and the airfield with it. This seems to be Andrew's engrossment.

Near this time, about 0900, Captain Johnson of C Company opposite the south edge of the airfield makes the bid for counterattack. He recognizes the dangerous threat from Plessen's men in the riverbed; he sees paratroops filtering through between 13 Platoon on the seaward edge of the airfield and hard-pressed 15 Platoon (Lieutenant Sinclair) on Tavronitis bank. Counterattack by the two tanks and accompanying infantry is what he wants and so recommends to his colonel, who feels bound to refuse because a greater crisis may come. (Waiting for a bigger crisis recurs again and again.) Nevertheless, Johnson's bid influenced Andrew to ask Brigade to search the Tavronitis and westward with artillery shells. It is done, but too late. Meanwhile the Germans rivet attention on the bridge entry to the RAF "island," the tenderest point of all.

Trebes's party, reinforced by the men Meindl started over, gain entrance to the RAF compound and in an act of "cats among pigeons" (wrote Jim Henderson) they round up unhappy airmen, prod them ahead of themselves up the hill. Gun crews and men from 22 Battalion staff halt this sally. Johnson from the south edge of the airfield dispatches a section from 14 Platoon to take the Germans in flank. But Andrew, from above, waves the flankers off with a shout; he will "tend to his own backyard." He seems intent on having Johnson stick close to defense of the airfield—an obsession that leaves no room for a situation to change. The defenders remain content to stall the attackers and do nothing about going over to the offensive to clean them out. The opportunity passes. Others will occur, but none so good. The

5. Davin, p. 111; Henderson, pp. 41–70. The final blitz put out all wire communication. Contact with Brigade was not reestablished until 0900 over an unreliable radio set. Runners had to do for all messages.

Germans keep their bridgehead and consolidate it. Just this may have made all the difference: they had to move and did. They are in.

On the far side of the Tavronitis, Göttsche's star radio operator keeps calling the 3d Battalion and keeps shaking his head. No answer, not a peep. It had fared badly at the hands of 21 and 23 New Zealand Battalions; this preoccupation may have reduced interest in 22 Battalion's predicament. In contrast to Meindl's 3d Battalion and the 1st, which was to make for Hill 107, the 2d and 4th, under Stentzler and Gericke, had landed free, west of the Tavronitis, and at once closed toward the riverbank for the main effort against the airfield.

Colonels Leckie (23 Battalion) and Allen (21) have the advantage of tight control over their smaller hillside defense territories straddling a spur road up from the coastal route. Distances are short and direct; communication is easy and effective. They could almost command by shouts and gestures through the olive trees that helped hide the strongpoints. Into these positions Meindl's 3d Battalion fell and was slaughtered.

Major Scherber commanded the 3d Battalion. It had paralleled Meindl's approach on an easterly course, passed over the Tavronitis, and headed for a point south of Platanias. The detailed flight plan prescribed a turn north and then west to skirt the coast and drop on Pirgos in order to cut Maleme off on the east side. Repeated talk about the risk of falling in the sea had impressed Scherber. Anxious to minimize the chance, he acceded to drops on a northerly course short of the sea instead of on a westerly course along it. So the Ju group turned north early and began dropping raggedly right into the populous hill sites of 21 and 23 New Zealand Battalions. The New Zealanders had a turkey shoot, but the 3d Battalion had a disaster.

The first three V's dropped their loads on 21 Battalion. Colonel Allen had all four companies on Vineyard Ridge near his west boundary, where vision was fine all around. There D Company received the first lot in plain sight and dispatched it before a single member touched ground, Major Scherber and staff included. The next lot fell on Kondomori village at the north rim of the territory. Only three survivors lived to become prisoners of war. Inside an hour the commotion had ceased; 21 Battalion stood easy. Its day ended in waiting.[6]

The ill-fated drops continued on down the hill; they spilled all over 23 Battalion, whose men had been ohing and ahing at the action

6. Davin, pp. 121–27; Ross, pp. 64–67; Cody, pp. 85–87. These sources also apply to the account below of 23 Battalion.

farther west toward Hill 107. All at once their own overhead became agitated; human forms crashing down, legs sticking out of trees, bodies rolling on the ground. The carnage was on. Individual bags were counted and later contested. Not moving an inch from his field desk, the adjutant knocked two forms out of the sky. Was this the sport that Churchill had imagined, and many people in Creforce? Paratroopers had never been a great worry. Companies fanned out to mop up their neighborhoods. One patrol killed twenty-nine and took three prisoners; others made comparable scores.

How different Andrew's lonely lot was! His wire contact with 23 Battalion went off at the start and stayed so. Attempts at visual signaling failed; no WHITE–GREEN–WHITE lights appeared. From 23 Battalion Andrew's Headquarters Company of 22 was in good sight and holding well, after dealing with Major Koch's party. When Leckie sent a patrol to make direct contact, as Andrew had requested through Brigade, the patrol was turned back by fire, probably from Headquarters Company itself. Thus Leckie had reason to believe that Andrew had been as fully and fruitfully occupied as himself. At 1040 he signaled his own busy yet satisfactory situation to Brigade at Platanias, and after midday received an encouraging reply, which said in part, "Will not call on you for counterattacking unless position very serious. So far everything is in hand and reports from other unit satisfactory" (Davin, p. 124). The message must have confirmed Leckie in his own evaluation.

Brigadier Hargest saw some Germans brought in by 28 Battalion at his headquarters and had exciting news of more being mopped up by adjoining units; then came good news from Leckie and Allen to clinch his confidence. He found much to feed the general turkey-shoot expectation. This had apparently become firmly established. So any idea of orthodox ground fighting, such as faced Andrew, failed to surface. By the time Leckie received an answer from Hargest, about noon, signs of Maleme in peril were unmistakable—yet not to him. Break-in at 5 Brigade left the curious paradox of Meindl in crisis on the west bank of the Tavronitis and cheerful Hargest at ease in Platanias, far from the decisive action.

Farther east in Prison Valley (Heidrich of the 3d Parachute Regiment) and beyond on Canea plain (Genz) and Akrotiri (Altmann), German fortune was still worse. Gliders, huge ones sailing slowly right overhead, widely heralded the break-in. In two groups of nine to fifteen craft they swooshed toward Canea and Akrotiri in plain sight on obscure missions. Oberleutnant Genz's targets on the Canea plain lay close enough to the Prison Valley drops to make sense for linking up. His secondary target, near the primary one, an antiaircraft battery, was the radio station, thought to be a critical Creforce communication link. Captain Altmann's antiaircraft battery target on Akrotiri peninsula, on the other hand, was off by itself, but close enough to Creforce's battle headquarters to raise the suspicion that this might have been Altmann's primary object. Airborne command could have dreamed of a lucky strike whereby Creforce and its communications were to be taken out by these two bands of brigands. If this was the hope, it had a short life. In the approach, Altmann's Ju tow formation was broken up; withering antiair fire caused the gliders to unlatch early and to land scattered far and wide. After several days, hungry and thirsty survivors surrendered; forty-eight had died, and half of the remaining sixty bore wounds. Genz fared a little better. He took out the four 3.7″ antiaircraft guns, but could not get at the radio tower. During the night of 20 May, by answering hails in English he skulked past a Royal Navy Hospital Detachment and numerous Cretan defenders to German jumpers in Prison Valley. He had only twenty-four of his ninety-man team with him.

At Creforce the appearance of the Genz party to the south produced one significant reaction: before 0800 General Freyberg ordered Force Reserve to send a battalion to deal with it. Since all of Force Reserve was busy with paratroopers locally, Brigadier Inglis found it impossible to comply; yet the prompt order shows Freyberg's reaction of swift and vigorous counterattack. Soon after, he confirmed this by releasing 4 Brigade altogether. From his hillside he had watched the parachute descents in Prison Valley and in the west toward Maleme. An enthralling sight, he remarked, and added a speculation about the havoc that the two promised fighter squadrons could have inflicted on the lumbering Ju's. He had hoped for the fighters to the last. Now the troops were down and would have to be fought on the ground. This he was ready for.

Generalleutnant Wilhelm Süssmann, General Freyberg's prospective opposite as senior German officer present, had the worst possible luck. Cheerful, carefree, no "plank owner" in Airborne, he elected to land with his staff by glider at the head of Prison Valley when the 3d Parachute Regiment broke in. His tow took off well from Eleusis near Athens. When scarcely twenty minutes out, a Heinkel III bomber overtook the formation and passed overhead at close quarters—so

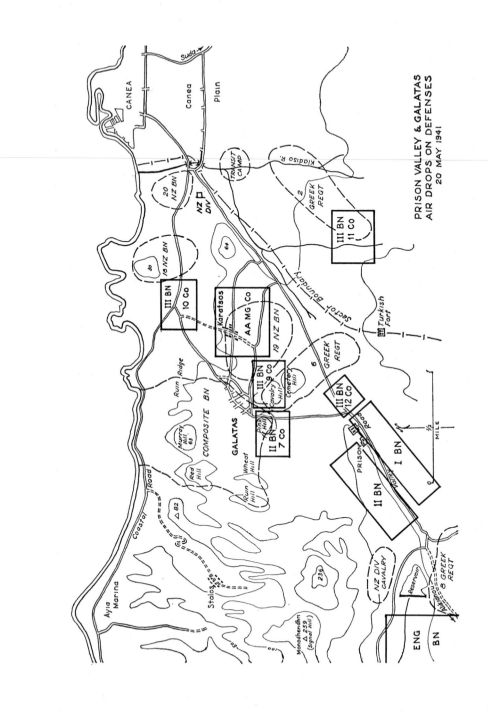

PRISON VALLEY & GALATAS
AIR DROPS ON DEFENSES
20 MAY 1941

close its propeller turbulence caught the Süssmann glider and ripped its wings off. The loaded fuselage plummeted down on rocky Aegina Island. Over a third of the gliders ended in total casualty. When no general appeared in Prison Valley, Colonel Heidrich of the 3d Regiment took command.

So far, tough soldier Heidrich has managed. On picking himself up from the jump, minutes after 0800, he sees the white walls of the prison close ahead; men of his signal detachment join him. They quickly establish headquarters behind the prison at Mandhra and begin testing to contact the battalions; some must already be hotly engaged, to judge from the crackling up toward Galatas. That height looks higher than it should; likewise the hills on either hand hemming in the valley and its road to Canea. Heidrich realizes he is in a tight *Kessel* (kettle). The strong British showing at Galatas has upset the plan. The 3d Battalion was to land on the saddle between Galatas and Karatsos, seize both and the nearby tented camp. (What fatal fascination these tents held for the Germans—this one a hospital!) The 1st and 2d Battalions were to land down valley, link up with the 3d Battalion, crush through south of Canea to link up with Genz on the plain, and rush on to take Suda. Heidrich could see things were turning out otherwise. Even to stay in the valley, he must knock the British off Galatas.

These telling first moments! Nothing from Major Heilmann of the 3d Battalion on the saddle (for he is hemmed in too, having landed out of place in the valley bottom with his staff and his 9th Company on top of the 6th Greek Army Regiment and in front of 19 New Zealand Battalion). Nearer at hand, Major Derpa of the 2d Battalion is in touch with three companies and has them ready. Captain Heydte of the 1st Battalion is best situated; he has all four companies making down the south side of the valley. Let him go! But Derpa Heidrich decides to keep as reserve to guard the rear and south flank: who can tell what might charge down from those hills? At length word comes from Heilmann: he has extricated himself with survivors of his 9th Company and retains a slim hold on a knoll in the Greek position (Cemetery Hill 103). Heidrich adds the 5th Company from Derpa's battalion to Heilmann for storming Galatas. The attack launches forth at 0800, up and up on either side of the road from Prison Valley to Galatas. Now it is Heidrich against Kippenberger of 10 New Zealand Brigade.[7]

7. Too much German confidence was staked on pinpointing drop targets. It went

Genz's gliders skimming the trees close overhead alerted Colonel Kippenberger at breakfast in Galatas on 20 May 1941. He jumped up, shouting "Stand to," and lit out down the road toward the prison for his battle station. Hundreds of parachutes were settling in the valley before him, some within the defenses. Of the same moment Captain von der Heydte of the 1st Battalion remarked on landing near the prison, "On every side during the drop, parachutes surrounded me, but now on landing I am absolutely alone. It is a strange feeling to be dropped suddenly into an alien land with orders to conquer it. Every tree, every bush, every blade of grass holds its secret." Each man set about his separate business, German captain and British colonel.[8]

Right on the doorstep of his own command post, the colonel ran afoul of a lone paratrooper. A blast of bullets greeted him as he lunged through the cactus hedge toward the house. It is now private against colonel, which neither can know. The German boy must have noted field telephones and headquarters fittings. Could he have imagined that single-handed he had captured the British command post for all the valley, that he alone had made the perfect break-in and quick takeover? On all Crete it proved the sole recorded instance of hoped-for airborne success. Now he thinks only to fire a blast at movement in the hedge and hope that it will go away. And the colonel on the receiving end thinks only to jump aside and roll down the bank. No hits on him, but a turned ankle. Back up the bank he crawls unobserved and continues through the hedge into the house. He can see the German outside, still intent on the gap in the hedge. So it's out of the house again by the backdoor for Kippenberger, where he "stalks him round the side of the house and shoots him cleanly through the head at ten yards." So it must have ended for many a lone soldier this day. Brigade Major Bassett and signalers arrive and together they consider what to do. This command post is surely too exposed for usefulness. They move it north of Galatas and set up with Composite Battalion. Pink Hill received the expected attention.

Composite Battalion had thinned out into five companies: Transport Company, farthest north toward the sea, faced west on the slopes of Red Hill; 4 Field Company adjoined on Red Hill's southern ex-

---

beyond practicalities. Another curiosity was the freedom exercised by commanders, after being airborne, to change their targets. We have seen this in Meindl's 3d Battalion, and here Leutnant Neuhof of the 7th Company shifted his drop northeast. He and his company were rubbed out before Pink Hill.

8. Kippenberger, pp. 52–54; Heydte, pp. 61–62.

tension; then came Supply Company, on Ruin Hill at the eastward turn of the line; next 5 Field Company, facing south on Wheat Hill; and finally Petrol Company, a bit farther east, straddling the Galatas-Prison road on the southern slope of Pink Hill. This 109-meter knoll bulwarked Galatas and offered perfect observation over the whole valley. Leutnant Neuhof requested that his Ju leader drop him and his 7th Campany on the southern approaches of the hill.

Neuhof bore out this independent spirit by a fierce attack on Petrol Company defenses immediately after landing; but the defenders held; he and most of his company became casualties. This was the noise and sign of combat to which Heidrich reacted when he ordered Heilmann to renew attack with the reinforcement of the 5th Company. Colonel Kippenberger speaks of "a tremendous racket . . . on the Galatas-Prison road," and how the Germans made headway and got beyond his old command post, but there they stalled. If Heidrich was straining through his binoculars for a break, it was in vain. By noon the fighting died out and he took stock, for soon the 11th Air Corps in Athens received his disquieting report that he stood stalled below Galatas, which must be taken before the 1st Battalion (Heydte) could move toward the Canea plain.

For his part, Kippenberger rails at Composite Battalion's failure to counterattack. Otherwise he can take comfort that the Greek regiment has in part rallied and a thin connection between Petrol Company and 19 Battalion has been fashioned. Except for a few snipers, the brigade territory is clear. Yet the Germans are still in the valley, and on the south slope they progress.

They are von der Heydte and his 1st Battalion. From the start its luck and planning have been superior: all companies landed together, which had been his sole request. The men quickly occupied the prison. There Heydte composed sensible orders and exacted prompt execution of the drive down valley. Their ranks begin to swell from misdropped troopers. His 2d, 1st, and 3d Companies deploy abreast south of the road, while the 4th Company (heavy weapons) remains in reserve with the battalion commander as he moves up. Forward the men pick "their way in lifeless silence" and oppressive heat. They can see little for trees and hillocks; rifle and machine-gun fire up front may mark advances. On the right, a height is gained, but still the restricted sight tells nothing. The looked-for confrontation—where is it? It seems clear that junction with the forces engaged below Galatas must wait for some time. Heydte returned to the valley bottom to set up a forward command post; he pieced together, from company reports, that on his left resistance was stiffening, but up the south slope, on the right, scarcely any opposition showed. The 2d Company had a coup to report: a British field piece taken, another hauled off under fire (probably 1 Light Troop Royal Artillery on Kladiso run, south of 19 New Zealand Battalion). The captured gun is turned on a strongpoint and it is taken. It is getting on toward noon.[9]

The decisive break-in strikes at Maleme and Prison Valley are over. They have failed in both places. Nowhere has quick takeover eventuated. Heidrich is locked in a stiff fight for Galatas; Meindl lies wounded, while his men press desperately for a bridgehead at the base of Hill 107. Mürbe at Kastelli Kisamou does not answer; all glider quickies—Koch, Plessen, Altmann, Genz—have fallen short of their goals. By their own reckoning the Germans are stalled. They know one thing the British cannot know: that the heaviest punch has missed. Group West and Group Center are in trouble.

The defenders, on the other hand, stand by for more—Andrew at the crucial spot, in particular. Alone and infiltrated, he must feel almost abandoned. His communications are unreliable. If he has fired his WHITE–GREEN–WHITE signal for help, no one has answered by signal or reinforcement.[10] His immediate superior, Hargest, glad of the big troop bags being reported by other battalions, entertains no thought of reinforcing him. Puttick at Division developed no interest in counterattack toward Prison Valley when General Freyberg released Force Reserve. He was the first to react with counterattack order; the others, except for Kippenberger and later Inglis, seemed content with a vague status quo. The mood is mistakenly cheerful and contrasts sharply with the changing mood in Athens.

At the Grande Bretagne spirits had been high, even gleeful, through midmorning, under the influence of that age-old and dangerous disease of impossible expectations feeding on flimsy incoming data; the Ju's returned with small losses (only 7 out of 493) and their report of perfect drops; the 8th Corps flyers claimed to have silenced defenses; and so it went, with nothing concrete about the drops. De-

9. Heydte, pp. 66–74.

10. Inconclusive evidence indicates that the signal may have been made about noon (1300 British time). There is no direct evidence of exact time, of the circumstances, or of Andrew's order to make the signal. Actually, the question of whether or not the signal was made has no bearing on the outcome. The brigade commander believed that 23 Battalion, which was to respond, had enough on its hands.

lusions thickened. By 1000 Generals Jeschonnek and von Richthofen recorded favorable prognosis. Süssmann's crash was among the early dampers to the congratulatory exchanges. Then radio touch with Crete turned euphoria into depression. Göttsche reported Meindl's wounding; no one any longer commanded in the west; many jump casualties on rocky terrain; everywhere the Englander bobs up from hidden works and shoots, also with artillery. He attacks in armored cars (Bren carriers) and in infantry formations, notably in Prison Valley. The downtrend lurched deep when Heidrich reported: "After heavy casualties in fighting, the attack on Canea is discontinued." A whole regiment trapped! This shocker led General Student to weigh the advisability of diverting Retimo drops (believed to be still on the mainland) to Prison Valley, and he decided to do so, for Richthofen reports that the decision came too late (*zu spät*). The Ju's had begun to take off for Retimo and Heraklion.[11] Thus the German leadership barely escaped the pitfall of reinforcing failure. Before the day was out, other crises more gripping would put Prison Valley in perspective. In Athens the forenoon of fateful 20 May 1941 wound up on an underdog note of fervent hope for Retimo and Heraklion.

Retimo and Heraklion I: Afternoon of 20 May

In record and recollection, alongside the decisive events in the west the actions at Retimo and Heraklion tend to recede into irrelevance. But such is far from the fact and feeling of 1941, especially on the German side, and far from giving credit due to some of the best fighting on the island. Of course, air blasting there was weaker, but so was defending antiaircraft fire. These afternoon strikes of 20 May carried for the Germans ardent prayers for a quick win in a game that already at half-time of the critical break-in bade fair to end in disaster. For the British, Retimo and Heraklion demonstrated what independent task forces can do with resolute fighting and timely counterattack. Retimo presents an inspiring story.

A ragged, retarded second German start made a poor beginning of retrieving Lady Luck. Scheduled time was 1300; the transport planes were unable to start until after 1400 and from then on struggled into the air, bearing out the direst forebodings of Colonel von Hey-

11. 11th FK Kreta; consultation with General Student, Germany, 1960; 8th FK Chrono.

king at Topolia Field. At about 1000, after a labored dusty landing from the morning drops, he had taken prompt steps to alert the higher commands about inevitable delay. Failing to reach his immediate superior, he got through to the 11th Air Corps's chief of staff, warned him of retardation, and requested adjustment of 8th Corps support fires accordingly. No corrective action followed. Off he went, piecemeal and late, trying by a direct approach to Retimo to save a little time. Between 1545 and 1700 some 160 Ju's unloaded about 1500 paratroops over the target area in scrambled and straggling lots, without fire support.[12]

They belonged to the 1st and 3d Battalions of the 2d Paratroop Regiment under one of Airborne's senior veterans, Colonel Sturm, whose latest exploit was the seizure of the Corinth Canal bridging on 26 April 1941. Although minus his 2d Battalion (sent to Heraklion force) he gained in exchange two machine-gun companies, two heavy-weapons platoons, and an artillery section. His plan called for three simultaneous drops: West, Center, and East. Center, which he would lead, was to have Headquarters Company and the 2d Company, reinforced, land just to the west of the airstrip. East, under Major Kroh, was to have its three companies, reinforced, land just east of the strip. Its task was to take the strip while closing toward Center. West force, under Captain Wiedemann of the 3d Battalion, reinforced, was to land between Center and Perivolia village, turn west, and take Retimo town and port. For these veterans of Corinth it was a cinch.

On schedule as first set up, the 8th Corps's bombers and fighters began at about 1500 to rake the airstrip and surroundings with intense fires of bombs and bullets. The planes scurried up and down, but found few real targets because of Lt. Colonel Campbell's superior camouflage. The bombers departed; the fighters lingered for a time in aimless repetition. Two planes crashed. The premature delivery did nothing but signal the delayed approach of the transport planes, which had made their landfall far east of the strip about 1530. Thence they coasted westward ponderously at 400 feet and let go their loads in a half-mile-deep strip along the coast from 3½ miles east of the airstrip almost to Retimo town. Even without antiaircraft guns the defenders took a heavy toll: seven transports fell; others went away flaming. The paratroopers suffered seriously in the air and as soon as they hit the ground.

Instead of landing close east of the airfield, Major Kroh, the first

12. Heyking Ms.

down, found himself in a barren, rocky coastal terrain with a few men from the 3d Company, many of them injured in landing; the chimney landmark of the olive factory close to the airstrip was barely discernible far in the west. He rallied the able-bodied around him and set out for the landmark. En route this contingent picked up parts of Wiedemann's 10th and 12th Companies. As at Maleme, the main effort for the strip was without its designated leader, Kroh.

But Kroh's 1st and 4th Companies, down in the midst of Captain Channell's troops on the eastern slope of Hill A, were in furious close-quarter combat. The last departing fighters overhead were unable to distinguish friend from foe. Many Germans fell while trying to reach their weapons containers; in the 4th Company every officer became a casualty. The men fought on and held their own, but that was all.

To have the attack thus develop in dribbles proved advantageous to Campbell and his defenders. He reacted swiftly to Channell's melee by sending two platoons from Hill D to block any German movement westward toward the strip and another group to reinforce Channell directly. Campbell ordered the two tanks to drive east into battle; they promptly got stuck. British tanks in Crete made one hard-luck story after another. As the one weapon the Germans could not have and could not cope with on the ground, they simply failed. To review the defense deployment: Campbell had posted three low hills, named A, D, and B, inshore of the airstrip; on Hill A, farthest east, stood Captain Channell and his company, supported by four machine guns and six field pieces; next westward on Hill D was Campbell himself and the remainder of his 2/1 Battalion. On Hill B still farther west was Major Sandover with his 2/11 Battalion, and between these main Australian formations was the 4th Greek Army Regiment. Nearby, concealed in a wadi, were the two Matilda tanks.[13]

Both sides were locked in combat before the bulk of Wiedemann's 3d Battalion dropped into the west end. It arrived in half-strength about one hour late at Platanes village and at once took off westward for Perivolia, a village before Retimo proper. Flanking fire from Sandover's western strongpoints impeded him, but Wiedemann made Perivolia and dispatched an advance guard beyond. By this time increasing fire from the gendarmerie in Retimo persuaded him to pull in his advance guard and go over to the defensive in Perivolia for the night.

13. Long, pp. 256–78; 11th FK Kreta. See also the chart of Retimo, p. 256 above.

In the Center, Colonel Sturm got down close to his drop target. He was alone and covered by Australians. His group landed south of the coastal road under Sandover's guns on Hill B and was for the most part wiped out. Sturm lay low through the night. At the east end Kroh, upon collecting all his men, decided to do the same.

Sandover ordered a general advance of his battalion toward the coastal road. In places the push fell short of the road, yet few attackers remained. The battalion returned to its posts on Hill B with prisoners of war and paper booty. From the captured orders Sandover extracted the good news that no more drops were destined for Retimo. He also found the signal code for supply and ammunition drops. During the following days these came in handy. Curiously, the same intelligence became available in the critical west, but was not exploited.

Campbell could release his report for the day to Creforce with satisfaction—the airstrip and Retimo safe; the attackers stopped at Hill A. The German lodgment there would have to be broken, and for this he requested reinforcement. On the other side, Sturm had no means of rendering report, and his silence deepened the gloom over Athens during the anxious night of the 20th.

No one spoke of it at the Grande Bretagne, but Heraklion's drops had swelled toward climax as the last chance. So eager for good news were the staffs that anything making a favorable sound grew into a full-blown success. They again went astray with unsubstantiated first reports. Before all jumpers were even out of the planes over Heraklion, the corps command was assuring the 5th Mountain Division, which had the big stake in the place, that all drops had gone well—*glatt* (smooth as silk). Then deathly silence supervened. Everything now hung on Heraklion and Group East. The command could console itself; after all, Paratroop Regiment 1 was almost the equal of Sturmregiment, and the leader, Colonel Bräuer, wasn't he among the boldest and most successful? Time was short. No closed columns of numberless Ju's had winged south just above the water, as before, but dispersed flights, hardly a one over twelve planes. The goings-on at the fields had to be guessed at; no line of communication could get through. Heraklion, the last hope, seemed doomed too.

The takeoffs had spread themselves over three anguished hours: units lost cohesion. About 600 men stayed behind for lack of transport. Some of the first planes carried heavy support gear for later troops. Meanwhile preassault fires by the 8th Air Corps fell on schedule and, of course, to small effect. Most of the troops jumped without fighter support. The day ended on a marked downbeat; things were failing instead of building up.[14]

Heraklion's defenders had plenty of notice; their comparatively strong antiair defenses greeted each attack with intense fire. Fifteen Ju's were knocked down and produced a ghastly harvest of horror stories among ground watchers: a Ju afire while its men jumped—each chute lit off and "vanished in a puff of smoke, its passengers hurtling to the ground"; a jumper streamed from a departing plane, his chute caught; a transport faltered while unloading its cargo, "all troops hit the earth before their chutes opened." Many were hit while floating down because the Ju's unloaded high, but more were killed on the ground while trying to reach weapons containers. The casualties totaled well over 200 before ground action began. But begin it did.

Bräuer envisioned quick seizure of the airfield and city by converging battle groups: the 2d Battalion under Captain Burkhardt was to land a strong group east and west of the field, then pinch it off by attack toward each other. The 3d Battalion under Major Schulz was to land west and southwest of the town, take it, and punch through to Burkhardt at the airfield. A reinforced battalion from the 2d Paratroop Regiment was to drop still farther west to fend off interference from that direction; meanwhile the 1st Battalion and Bräuer would drop on the radio station at Gurnes, five miles east of the airfield, to secure the east flank. Field and port thus in hand, the colonel would be ready to receive General Ringel.

The planes reached their drop zones overextended. An attack was nonetheless mounted, principally from the east. Captain Dunz's group made a scattered drop extending from the Australians at the "Charlies" on the south to Buttercup Field on the sea. Within twenty minutes the group was destroyed almost to a man. "Only three men of the 6th Company and two from the machine-gun company succeeded in getting through," not by fighting through to the east as planned, but by swimming along the coast. In that region Captain Burkhardt had jumped into East Wadi with the 5th and 8th Companies. Their commanders gathered what men they could and at once started up the rise toward the aerodrome, guarded by Black Watch. A few men made it to the top and stayed there, but as corpses. At dark Burkhardt was

14. 11th FK Kreta; LF4 Kreta; Generals Student and Trettner to Ansel, Germany, 1960. See also the chart of Heraklion, p. 257 above.

able to reassemble a disheartened remnant of 60 men in the wadi. The attack on the airfield had produced 420 casualties and total failure.

The 3d Battalion, besieging Heraklion town, did a little better in casualties, but not in carrying its objective. The battalion landed late and badly dispersed, managed to clear the drop zone of Greek defenders, and began the assault on the town's lofty walls. Some accounts report German entry and fighting in the streets; others that no entry succeeded and that Major Schulz withdrew his men from the wall to a defensive position in the drop zone. There he was the next morning, plotting to resume the assault.

All through these actions the defenders easily kept the upper hand. Brigadier Chappel in Nea Alikarnassos saw paratroops land all around and took note of the ones most dangerous between him and the airfield. At 1715 he sent a Bren carrier platoon from reserve (Leicesters) to counterattack toward Buttercup Field, then ordered York and Lancs to do the same. These detachments busied themselves with Dunz's group until after dark. By 2130 they had cleared the area. The sinking sun lighted the parachutes of the latest comers floating down in the far east. They belonged to Chappel's opposite, Bräuer, and half of the 1st Battalion.

Though he must have chafed at his own belated takeoff, Bräuer had lost none of his sanguine hopes for quick and easy success. He jumped east of Gurnes at 1840, found his companions of the 1st Battalion, and decided to push west at once. Parts of three companies were on hand; Gurnes radio station was occupied and defenses set up. Radio word may have come from Burkhardt: "Aerodrome under attack." And in turn, word from Bräuer may have inspired the 11th Corps to believe in the aerodrome's capture. Near dark he set out accompanied by a security detachment under Leutnant Blücher. The march turned out much longer than expected. The advance guard reached the approaches to the aerodrome at 2340, and to Bräuer's amazement came under heavy fire (from Black Watch). True to his warrior name, Blücher kept on with a handful of men and at length succeeded in gaining the field's east rim. Bräuer settled for establishment of his headquarters a mile to the east on the coastal road in order to make plans for dawn assault. In Athens the 11th Corps summarized the latest news with "Situation Heraklion unclear."[15]

15. LF4 Kreta; 11th FK Kreta. Hopes for final success faded, except with General Student. He had special confidence in Bräuer.

Prison Valley and Maleme: Afternoon and Evening, 20 May 1941

Shortly after noon Captain von der Heydte in Prison Valley went forward to help his 1st Company; there was a report of trouble down valley toward Canea. Fire from ahead had halted the advance, pinning the 1st Company down in a shallow ditch along the edge of a meadow; beyond were trees that screened the foe (it must have been 19 New Zealand Battalion on the valley's north slope). "We were certainly in a spot," remarked Heydte. No contact with the 3d Battalion on the left, visibility 50 yards; if the enemy attacked from his cover, he could drive a wedge between Heydte and the rest of the regiment. It "would be only a question of time," he felt, "before the British realized the precariousness of our position and attacked . . . such an assault would inevitably have resulted in the destruction of the 1st Company, probably the whole battalion, and possibly the regiment." He recalled how "the minutes crept by slower and slower," while we waited for the end. Suddenly the tension snapped under the dreaded cry of "Panzer!" A small two-man armored thing paddled around a bend in the road, "the first sight of the enemy"; the mere sight of the monster "removed half of the terror." There he was, coming on against a concentrated German fire. He "swerved violently, pulled up with a jerk . . . and remained motionless." Accompanying infantry dispersed. Reinforcement arrived from Heydte's 2d Company. The crisis collapsed.[16]

The panzer was a Bren carrier, one of two called to counterattack along with C Company, 18 Battalion, by Brigadier Inglis of 4 Brigade. The moment was right, the force superior and on the spot—an ideal opportunity. The sole "aggressive action shown by the defense," bogged down in stalemate and darkness. Inglis had ordered the action on his own as a local affair after Division sat on his broader proposal for clearing the whole valley. He was not alone in his proposal, but Division still gave no order. The chance to clear up the valley had been wide open for a time. The Germans retained the initiative, but failed to realize it.

During Heydte's crisis down valley, Heidrich threw his last punch against Kippenberger toward Pink Hill, just below Galatas village. Major Derpa came out of reserve with the 2d Battalion and the 6th Company to make the attack. Like his predecessors, he pushed up

16. Heydte, pp. 79–82; Davin, pp. 160–73; Kippenberger, pp. 56–57. All apply likewise to the passages that follow.

either side of the Galatas-prison road with a thin line of skirmishers. They made some headway against heavy fire from Petrol Company manning the Hill. Colonel Kippenberger called it "a half-hearted attack [that] Petrol Company beat off emphatically," yet Derpa gained enough ground on his left to endanger the defender's west flank. When night fell, the badly mauled Petrol men drew back to reorganize; they had lost three commanders and most of their petty officers. Derpa followed up to occupy Pink Hill. Thus for a while Heidrich possessed an entree into the 10 Brigade position.

When the fighting died down Kippenberger again urged Division to counterattack and received assurance "that something would be done." Shortly thereafter he forwarded reports of a German landing ground under preparation near the prison. This seems to have jolted Division like nothing else to act. Kippenberger's prime concern right along had been the gap left by the 6th Greek Army Regiment, and he was therefore cheered by the arrival of Major John Russell and his Divisional Cavalry, 190 strong. They had trudged a roundabout way through Monodhendhri foothills from their head-of-the-valley outpost. Still fit and ready, the cavalry quickly filled the tender gap. Thus a solid line existed before Petrol Company had to pull out. It appears that Kippenberger at the time was not aware of Derpa's follow-up, for the good reason that soon after reaching the hill he pulled back. It might have been the appearance of two companies from 19 Battalion that scared the new owners off Pink Hill; it might also have been a clanking of tanks down from Galatas. Division had finally ordered counterattack. A hastily contrived foray of three tanks and various uncoordinated infantry units milled around the night through and withdrew to their original posts. The skirmishing killed about twenty Germans, but failed to clear the valley. Heidrich in the bottom was taking stock.

It could not have been a heartening experience, as Heidrich's report to the 11th Corps attests. He had word in about the tanks and about fresh British troop activity. Can he hold against the counterattack sure to come from Galatas in the morning? Only one good line battalion is left, Heydte's; the men are fagged, rations and ammunition are short, casualties are mounting, the adversary is looking down his throat. Should he even try to stand? Or does it not make better sense to break out of this damnable trap toward Maleme and join Meindl? With him he has no communication link, but good contact with Athens. He therefore suggests that he cut his way through to Maleme. Student, who is deep in his own quandary about the whole operation, turns the bid down. He wants Heidrich to hang on, a thorn in the British flank, to tie down forces that could become available to Maleme's defense. And Heidrich stays, but goes over to the defensive. "On the whole the situation was such," notes the 11th Corps's report, "that without possession of the commanding heights of Galatas, further attack against Canea was unthinkable."[17]

In no time the moves are under way: the 1st Battalion will haul back from its forward contacts to secure the south flank; remnants from the 2d and 3d Battalions will hold the north flank against Galatas; for rearguard, Engineer Battalion beyond the reservoir is to close toward the prison and provide a two-company reserve at regimental headquarters.

Elements of a machine-gun company and the engineers had been set down on the Alikianou plain west of the reservoir. German records testify to accurate fire upon the invaders out of hedge, tree, and hillside on every hand as they attempted to retrieve weapons containers and then to force the short bridge into Alikianou village. "Cretan civilians, including women and children, took part." The drops come under the guns of the 8th Greek Army Regiment, Kippenberger's circle on the map; the circle proves itself highly explosive. Greek Army formations give proud account of themselves. Tired bundles of humanity slump in their holes. Of the two sides the Germans are worse off. They have lost the initiative.

At Maleme a more fluid situation obtained, for there was no counterpart to Heidrich who could decide and order for all. It was more of a free-for-all fight dependent on individual action; it really proved a boon to the Sturmregiment and its badly mauled parties, scattered over the landscape. They had to keep fighting. They called out to one another in the night, attempted unit roll calls to get themselves together. A hard day, but Sturmregiment still pressed on.

Having given his orders at noontime, General Meindl rested and hoped for the best. Göttsche carried on at the command post. Gericke of the 4th Battalion was directed by Meindl to continue attack across the Tavronitis against the airfield and Hill 107; Meindl ordered Stentzler of the 2d Battalion to work up the Tavronitis Valley, turn east, and assault Hill 107 in the rear. So Andrew and 22 Battalion

17. 11th FK Kreta; Heydte, p. 94; Student to Ansel, Germany, 1960.

were to be ground up. Frontal pressure on them increased perceptibly after noon.

Andrew is watching and waiting, waiting for thunder on the right from 23 Battalion; but it does not come, and Andrew seems loath to ask for it directly. Presumably the help signal WHITE–GREEN–WHITE has been fired. The record on this is scarce and says nothing about a repeat being fired. A feeling of reluctance to come out with a request for help is implicit in a message to Brigade at 1450; Andrew reported his left giving way and other troubles, "but still thinks the situation to be in hand." Then he repeated the earlier request that Leckie contact his Headquarters Company, "because he [Andrew] needs reinforcements." *This was the message's cloaked meaning, which Hargest never got.* He had already assured Leckie of no need for counterattack from him, and nothing Andrew said had changed this view. Meanwhile the German pressure grew: against D Company on the Tavronitis bank, against C Company around the airfield, and against A Company, around Andrew himself. By 1500 mortar fire forced him uphill toward his B Company. Yet he refused to scream, and Hargest at distant Brigade remained uninformed, unperturbed. Andrew hung on an hour longer before getting down to cases.[18]

At 1600 he asked Hargest outright for counterattack by Leckie, and was put off with the depressing excuse that 23 Battalion had business of its own. His next move, more or less in desperation, was to order counterattack by Johnson and the two tanks. No extra force, Bren carriers, for instance, was added, nor command instructions for the changed situation; the order simply released Johnson and the two tanks. He had been waiting. His view was limited and the tankmen's more so. They knew about Germans in the RAF camp, but nothing about their strength in the riverbed. What could Johnson tell the tankmen about the present fix different from what had been discussed with them only the evening before (Henderson, p. 52)? He tried to get in touch by ringing the bell on the lead tank's hatch for some last words as the two lumbered out of their dugout and passed in front of the

18. Headquarters Company covered a key position on 22 Battalion's line of communication. If Germans got in there, the battalion might be cut off. Moreover, this line was the obvious route of advance for 23 Battalion reinforcement for counterattack. If then 23 helped Headquarters Company, it helped all of 22 Battalion. Andrew made his first request for a check on Headquarters Company as early as 0955. It was on his mind. If he made his WHITE–GREEN–WHITE signal soon thereafter, it fell into competition with the air drops on 23 Battalion. The truth seems to be that Andrew was willing to let Leckie insure his line of communication, but reluctant to have him join directly in the fight to hold the field at this time.

14 Platoon works. The hatch stayed closed, and the awkward brutes rolled on toward the Tavronitis. Lieutenant Donald and his depleted 14 Platoon, joined by eight volunteers from an antiaircraft battery, tagged along between the two monsters. What was this brave little band to do against the German horde?

Thirty yards separated the tanks; soon the rear one turned back; at this late hour its crew had discovered that the gun turret was stuck, and anyhow the shells would not fit the gun chambers. The other tank clattered on around the turn, ignored the Germans in the RAF camp, and went down over the brink above the bridge into the riverbed, teeming with paratroopers.

Lieutenant Sinclair of 15 Platoon, holding desperately to the airfield's western edge, despite his wounds, could see them crawling in the reeds and grasses, then watched them halt at the frightening cry of *Panzer!* The tank swung under the bridge toward the sea and was among them. "They seemed uncertain what to do," Sinclair noted, and Göttsche echoed; "the relentless attacks on the rim of the airfield were interrupted," by the appearance of a tank. Then the pause broke in a rending fusillade from every barrel on hand: "rifles, Pak, flak, machine guns, and hand grenades." No one saw the tank return the fire. Two hundred yards north of the bridge it stopped, bogged or disabled. The accompanying infantry tried to shelter in its lee as those that could withdrew. Only nine out of twenty valiant men made it back, wounded. Sinclair, who was soon overrun, said later, "From where I was, I thought this business with the tank was futile. Of course, I could see more of the opposition lying in wait." The one weapon the Germans could in no way match failed in this last-gasp effort to save the airfield. Two well-handled tanks and infantry could have broken up the German bridgehead in the RAF camp.[19]

Tanks strike terror into any hearts, especially here where there is no counter. There is a German name for it—*Panzerschreck*, tank fright. Yet its converse at times has even greater, and certainly more productive, emotional effects: tank killed! It works up high exultation. The rout of the great Matilda in the Tavronitis cheered Gericke's troops to ever greater feats. Now nothing could stop them. They overran Sinclair, 15 Platoon, and a section of 13 on the seaward side. That gave them solid possession of the western half of the airfield.

19. Davin, p. 110; Henderson, pp. 48–55; Sturmregt B (Göttsche's report) is the only German source that makes mention. He reports the turnaround of the second tank and agrees with Henderson and other Creforce advices on the tanks' actions.

In a little while Johnson's weary 14 Platoon on the inland edge drove off the two Ju's that tried to make a test landing. Fragments of Sturmregiment's 1st Battalion felt the spirit too; they rallied round their regimental medical officer, Dr. Neumann, at the RAF camp and vowed to expand their hold up Hill 107 to the summit. As returning German combat planes (the afternoon waves were over) could distinguish friend from foe on the hill, the air support grew decisive.

From the south side of the hill came more reports of progress: Stentzler's 5th Company pressed against it from the southwest, the 7th Company from the south. By evening there were claims of control over all the southern approaches and 104 prisoners of war. (No British record corroborates the last claim.) Stentzler called in the 6th Company from the far west to stand by near Göttsche's command post as regimental reserve to tide over the coming extremely critical night.

If such was the feeling at Sturmregiment, a kindred spirit of crisis even more compelling ruled 22 Battalion's command post. After 1700 a runner from Johnson confirmed to Andrew the failure of the tank effort and added a request for help. The reply was, "Hold on at all cost." The two Ju's attempt at landing then attested the relentless German drive to exhaust every opportunity. The added pressure could not have helped Andrew's further study of the situation. Planes dove at and strafed his position mercilessly; they confirmed his nakedness here on the hilltop. At 1800 he told Hargest he had to withdraw and got in return a cheerful rejoinder, "If you must, you must." In both minds it was to be only a limited withdrawal.

But once under way, the spirit of retreat heaps up and gathers headway from every report; to reverse it becomes nearly impossible. So Andrew found, at his first halt on B Company's ridge. A report has D Company wiped out; he already knows C Company has lost heavily; A and B are all he has left. And after five more strafings it becomes obvious that the new location is too exposed, not only to air attack, but to the fresh menace (Stentzler) reported on the south. By the time one reinforcing company from 23 Battalion at long last arrives, after 2130, Andrew has made up his mind to withdraw farther into 21 and 23 Battalion territory. He sends Major Leggat to report to Brigade, "We are officially off Maleme." Runners sent to notify the front companies failed to get through; they withdrew on their own in the night, still full of fight. Maybe the difference came in the altitude. German air overhead had occupied the "higher ground," which commanded the terrestrial high ground occupied by Andrew. Sitting on his bald plateau, he became the Luftwaffe's prime target. His companies in the lowlands were far better off. As noted, after the eastern drops the 8th Air Corps was free to concentrate on the critical west with great power. No one could have stayed on Hill 107's flat top; Andrew was right; the hill site was untenable. He and others underestimated the new advantages of low ground and its cover. There during dark Creforce stood its best chances.[20]

Besides one company from 23 Battalion, Hargest sent another from 28 (Maori) at dusk toward 22. It pushed beyond Pirgos on the road and stopped 200 yards short of Johnson's 14 Platoon on the southeast corner of the airfield. Germans could be heard all around. It was dark. The company commander decided against independent attack in favor of first finding 22 Battalion as ordered. At about 0300 on 21 May the three battalion commanders (21, 22, 23) conferred at 23 Headquarters and made their own decision about what next: they would hold where they were; 22 Battalion would reorganize.

Andrew had put in two weary hours on B Company ridge to convince himself that no one remained behind. He was alone with an impasse no one had wanted to face. The two hours must have been hard ones, but he held fast to his decision, unshaken in the belief that withdrawal was his only course. Had the possibility of withdrawal been faced, one final act would now remain: to blow up the runways of the airfield. What consternation on the far bank of the Tavronitis at such a day's end! All hope of an airhead would have exploded. What else would have been left to fight for? Operation *Merkur* would have been finished.

20. Davin, pp. 111–38; Henderson, pp. 54, 70–75. Colonel Andrew was of course not alone in his attachment to the old saw, "Hold the high ground." Improved vision for the commander used to be an advantage. Aircraft have taken that over. Major J. Leggat got through to Brigade to find Brigadier Hargest turned in—he came out in pajamas in total surprise at Leggat's news. In a report to Creforce at sundown he had told of 23 Battalion's feats at bagging paratroops and about the great numbers knocked down around his headquarters, as if this were the main thing. He remarked on help sent to 22 Battalion and concluded that in general things were "quite satisfactory." Creforce had failed to exploit the forenoon after the first drops, and the afternoon, when the 8th Air Corps was busy with the eastern drops. The lack of air cover over Maleme alone, during the lull, showed this advantage up.

Over there Leutnant Göttsche is still on deck doing a thousand and one things—so many that it is 0430 of 21 May before he can break away to his wounded general with the final news of the day and night. Unaware of 22 Battalion's withdrawal, he reports that Hill 107 is still in doubt. Major Stentzler as field commander has issued orders to carry out the general's wishes for 21 May: the 4th and 2d Battalions are to pinch off Hill 107 and the hill southeast (B Company ridge), then to push eastward and establish a security line for the airfield from Pirgos south. In the Tavronitis Valley, the 16th Company would drive farther south; in the far west the 6th Company, when released as head-quarters reserve, is to make contact with the Mürbe party (Kastelli Kisamou). No word in hand yet from it or from the 3d Battalion east of the airfield (destroyed by 23 and 21 Battalions). Air support for these tasks from the 8th Corps has been arranged. Supply and ammunition are dwindling, a fact of which the 11th Air Corps in Athens is aware. That constitutes the full day since takeoff from Megara, ages ago! Meindl has resolved to stay until he is assured his men have all of the airfield. Late in the day a mistaken impression prevails that it is in hand and is so reported to Athens, and then corrected. No mention occurs of Heidrich and Prison Valley. Sturm-regiment is wrapped in its own hard task, still unfinished.

The trouble with Leutnant Mürbe was failure. His party landed in two pieces close under the guns of Major Bedding and the 1st Greek Army Regiment at Kastelli Kisamou. The defenders swiftly destroyed one part and, led by Bedding, dealt with the second. By noon the place was clear: fifty-one Germans killed, twenty wounded, and a number taken prisoner. Some of the dead were later found mutilated, and at the time Bedding had to make special arrangements to keep the prisoners safe from his allies, who had lost fifty-seven killed and sixty-two wounded. The action demonstrated what well-led Greek Army formations could do.

Crisis in Athens: 20–21 May 1941

By evening 20 May 1941 the Grande Bretagne frets in crisis. Not a single item in the assault plan from Kastelli Kisamou to Heraklion has succeeded, not one goal reached. The thing is on the brink of disaster. In the muddled residue it becomes all the more urgent for the chief architect of this colossal misfire, Kurt Student, to get over for a close look to take charge and rescue his dream. Almost by main force his staff members dissuade him. General Löhr will hear nothing of his going in any case.[21]

Student is in the fix of a landing-force commander whose boats have made two trips to the beach with mounting casualties. In them he has committed the elite bulk of his assault troops, who now cry out for munitions, supply, medical stores, and reinforcement. The attacks are stalled; only at one is there a slight prospect of wresting a *beachhead* from a foe much stronger and tougher than expected. But the commander at that point, Maleme, lies wounded. His nearest neighbor force is bottled up in a valley, its leader—Süssmann—killed. From one of the other beaches nothing; from the last, only confused contradictions. These grim realities ring through the louder because they are so far away from the fictitious command ship, the Grande Bretagne. One can't see or smell anything 180 miles away, and imagination runs riot. What to do?

Air Fleet 4's General Alexander Löhr, commanding in chief, wants to know too, and from Student. He puts it up to him. Some of the anxiety shows a pious mix of I-told-you-so and solicitude. It was Student who rejected the need for a center of effort in the west, who insisted on multiple attacks widely spread, who thought he needed no preparatory air strikes. Shall *Merkur* be abandoned before more troops are lost—the 5th Mountain Division, for instance? Or if it is to go on, just how? To these questions Löhr wanted answers. Student tells how he shut himself in his room to wrestle out the answers alone, consoling himself with the thought: "If we only get through this night . . . if we only get through this night, tomorrow we can do something." No hint of sounding taps for *Merkur* entered his mind. It was only what to do first tomorrow that made his quandary.

Victory and defeat teeter on a knife-edge this night. Many bystanders are convinced that a counterattack will throw the paratroops off Maleme. It does not come. But equally unsure prospects at Heraklion and Retimo compete: the solution grows still harder. No, it must be Maleme and prayers for the morrow. Fate has dictated that a landing head be forged there to support the ground conquest of the island.

Richthofen again takes credit for convincing Student of the profits from close air support. His Chronology notes that on his advice, "the Command decides on decisive priority in support to Group West's

21. Staff members—Trettner (Operations), Langguth (Intelligence)—to Ansel, and Student to Ansel, in Germany, 1960.

paratroops, since this group could achieve the most by concentrated attack to open a hope for winning an airfield. (The capture of an airfield is the fundamental requisite for the success of our undertaking.)" All commands now sanctimoniously admit the fundamental need, but fail to name it an air or landing head. This was done later by soldiers.[22]

The same source also brings up to date the war at sea. In the afternoon of 20 May the lost British sea forces were rediscovered. They stood in from the west and south. Bombers reserved for this contingency took the air late in the afternoon: one flight of heavy bombers passed a fleet unit at six miles without contact and went on to unload its heavy load of bombs harmlessly in Suda Bay. A flight of dive bombers also missed contact. Both returned at dark, glad to get down without casualty. These reports of Royal Navy task forces at sea raised command tension over *Merkur*'s amphibians, who, at this point, were pulling into the island of Melos on the north rim of the Cretan Sea.

The inflated fear of a German sea landing capability still gnawed at British confidence from Maleme to Suda. It contributed to Hargest's continued overextension of 5 Brigade and Puttick's hesitance to counterattack in Prison Valley. Late in the evening General Freyberg's own thought about sea attack drew confirmation from a captured *Merkur* operation order; reinforcement by sea was specifically included. Excluded however, was the meager capability of the landing craft and the low priority accorded the sea project by Student. He had intended to seize Maleme and Canea in the forenoon of this day. While Freyberg in the evening was unaware of Maleme's plight and 22 Battalion's, he now knew precisely what strength had been and could be committed against him. His report of the day to Middle East gave a somber account of severe fighting. The Germans have failed to achieve their goals, he said, but there were more to come. He hoped the Navy would crush invasion by sea.

His opponent repondered his own predicament. Little fresh intelligence was available—only a few radio intercepts, which revised the British order of battle upward. Just as he now continued to underrate the British, at the same time he erred badly in their deployment, but on the side of logic, by persisting in a belief that the three identified battalions must be close around Maleme Field and their commander on the heights in 21 Battalion territory. Therefore the free land east of Pirgos should be filled with paratroops from Greece for

22. 8th FK Chrono. Richthofen's parenthetical insert is handwritten.

attack on the east edge of the airfield, while Sturmregiment, after re-inforcement, attacked from the west. That the 3d Battalion had al-ready disappeared in that territory escaped his notice. The obvious first priority was delivery of munitions to Meindl; perhaps a few Ju's could get down on the beach west of the Tavronitis. The great boon of good communication with Göttsche proved itself again and again in arranging details of the developing new plan. Late advices had been more hopeful: there was progress against the west half of the airfield after the tank foray collapsed. Another test landing must be attempted at dawn, and the general had just the man for it. If he succeeded, a battalion of mountain troops must follow immediately.[23]

Thus the *Schwerpunkt* swung heavily and irrevocably to the west. Some top commanders might have congratulated themselves, but to *Merkur*'s progenitor, the shift was almost treason to his Airborne Doctrine, so painstakingly nurtured and brought to maturity in *Merkur*. The doctrine of Vertical Psychological Envelopment had proved a myth.

Approval of the new plan followed swiftly from General Löhr in orders for 21 May. He all but took the battle out of paratroop hands and put it in the hands of a fellow countryman, General Julius Ringel, who was to command both Groups West and Center in the field:

(*a*) *Eleventh Air Corps*
  (i)   Reinforce Group West by drops sufficient for assuring capture of Maleme.
  (ii) Following occupation and securing of airfield, begin transport landing of 5th Mountain Division.
  (iii) After reinforcing, begin attack on Canea and take up contact with *Group Center* in order to effect seizure of Suda Bay.
  (iv) Air Fleet 4 has ordered General Ringel to be new commander of *Group West* and *Center*. He is to be landed at Maleme on 21 May with the first mountain troops.
(*b*) *Eighth Air Corps*
  (i)   Protect drops Maleme-Canea through reduction of enemy re-sistance and continue support to the fighting on Crete, Group West, and Center (Group Canea).
  (ii) Support attack on Suda Bay.
  (iii) Make dawn reconnaissance around Crete; keep in readiness strong forces for attack on enemy sea forces.
(*c*) *Admiral Southeast*
  Use every means to effect landing of 1st Motor Sailer Echelon on 21

23. 11th FK Kreta: Student to Ansel in Germany, 1960. These sources apply also to the paragraph that follows. General Student read from his own manuscript on the operation and interpreted points raised as he read.

May 1941 in the evening before dark, at Maleme, in order to bring in heavy weapons, munitions, as well as another battalion of mountain troops.

Even Axis naval power is invoked, an exceptional concession from the Luftwaffe. Help from Italy's land and sea power is requested. General Löhr's combat report notes that efforts to produce an Italian fleet sortie to pin down British sea forces away from Crete failed in Rome. Göring himself added his voice to this desperate resort, and in addition he urged Mussolini to land Italian troops from the sea on Crete. So high burned the crisis.[24]

24. Weichold (chief of German naval liaison in Rome) to Ansel in Germany, 1960. His Army colleague, General von Rintelen, wrote (Rintelen, p. 142): "Thereupon [at crisis time] I was instructed by OKW to convey to Mussolini Göring's urgent request to have [Italian] troops from Rhodes land in the eastern end of the island [Crete] and go to the aid of the heavily engaged German forces. The Duce at once declared himself prepared to do it. . . ." The troops landed on 28 May. The request direct to Mussolini could hardly have been made without full Führer accession. But Hitler himself stayed out of *Merkur*. It was Göring's responsibility, as witness his request direct to the Duce.

16. Maleme in the Balance

Minute by minute, hour on hour, the night wore away at German headquarters in Athens. No fresh alarms, only confirmations of things already known. Would counterattack stay out? Dawn brought hope that it would. While it was still dark, General Student sent for a certain Captain Kleye, a skillful and daring pilot now attached to corps headquarters. He was there under a cloud; a carefree misstep had landed him in the shade and there he sat, waiting avidly for a chance to reestablish himself. The moment had arrived.

His general expounded the tight situation at Maleme—munitions must be got over, the field tested by landing, and direct contact established with General Meindl. A plane, already loaded, awaited him: go ahead, take off, return, and report. Kleye made it. By 0700 the young man was safely down on Maleme Field's west end. Munitions were dragged from his Ju-52 under scattered small-arms fire, joined soon by artillery bursts. He scampered across the Tavronitis, found Meindl, and spent better than an hour with him; then he regained his plane and took off under renewed fire. A pleased Student received him with forgiveness for all his sins.

Kleye reported Sturmregiment holding well, Hill 107 taken, no sign of counterattack; landing possible though dangerous. His plane suffered hits but survived. Not so with a second Ju that landed farther east on the beach; but two others made the beach west of the Tavronitis to unload more munitions, while a third flew on to look for a sign of life at Retimo. These early morning probes of 21 May were rounded out with a flight by the Corps's chief of staff, Colonel Schlemm, to Maleme. Taken together they fortified Student's resolve to land mountain troops this day, though the continued fall of machine-gun, mortar, and artillery fire counseled delay. A large-scale landing like a mountain battalion, now awaiting takeoff at Topolia, would be battered to pieces. Better to wait for clarification.

What about this artillery? It was almost a new subject, not hitherto bothered with very much. "Once we command the air, we can throw in what we please," had been the accepted view in the vain talk that suggested air power could neutralize whatever deserved it, artillery included. In fact, Richthofen had promised to keep these guns silent during any landing. Yet the boast meant planes policing wide areas and neglected discovery and destruction of guns. The guns kept quiet until no plane was overhead, then came to life in wild rapid fire. German staff guesses on the whereabouts, caliber, and type of guns varied as widely as the shooting: that the fire came from big pieces at Alikianou (over 20,000 yards away), that it came from naval artillery emplaced far back in the hills. The guessers strove for mystery to cover their bafflement, when actually the nine small field pieces of 5 Brigade's artillery support were concealed within 6000 yards of their target and the wildness of their shots was caused by lack of observation, lack of registry, and poor sights, even no sights at all. Proper artillery on call during this crucial period could have become decisive; there were many lacks in Creforce, but this was one that could have been filled. Like tanks, it was something the Germans would have been hard put to counter.[1]

To combat flyers of the 8th Air Corps, Student seemed perplexed and hesitant, when in truth he was still probing and weighing. In their eyes his putting off and further putting off at half-hour intervals added up to a plain waste of costly time. At still another postponement Richthofen broke out: "With this putting off, the predicament of our people at Maleme grows steadily worse! *Ja*! Instead of attacking they let themselves be pushed back. Nor does Air Fleet 4 do any order-

1. If eighteen guns, instead of nine, properly shot-in, had been on hand to interdict Maleme Field, landings of planes on 21 May would have been impossible. Long, p. 216, notes "Australian regiments in reserve [in Egypt] . . . held sixty 25-pounders. . . . The presence on Crete of sixty 25-pounders would have transformed the situation . . . no 25-pounders were sent to Crete . . . but Italian and French field guns (75 mm) did arrive."

ing! . . . blood flows and hours pass uselessly by." Student, as his combat report shows, judged that three New Zealand Battalions, supported by artillery and tanks, had reorganized their defenses around Pirgos and Maleme village as the north anchor of a line reaching inland into the hills; the land eastward between Pirgos and Platanias he persisted in believing empty, and he based his plan for 21 May largely on this mistaken assumption. He aimed to break the Pirgos-Maleme anchor by attacks from the east with newly dropped troops and from the west with Sturmregiment. No cure for the artillery nuisance, further than air patrol overhead, occurred to him. Just when the situation might be ripe for transport planes to land the mountain troops was left to be developed.

Hand-to-mouth, piecemeal, and interminable waiting characterized this forenoon of 21 May, particularly for the eager young men at the hop-off fields. There were other uncertainties. Tank attack was still a worry. An antitank unit was got ready under Captain Schmitt. He left soon after Kleye, with an antitank detachment of one and a half companies, jumped west of the Tavronitis, and by 1030 had his troops pressing forward toward the Sturmregiment command post. He sent one motorized detachment toward Kastelli Kisamou to find Mürbe; the bulk of his force became available to Stentzler and Gericke in the battle for Maleme. Gericke was on the point of reporting to Meindl that his men had reached the east boundary of the airfield. This was the word the general had longed for: fulfillment of Sturmregiment's first task.

What else might become available from the mainland would have to await a muster and inventory at the airfields in Greece. Colonel Ramcke initiated just such a roundup at Topolia. Originally ordered to land with mountain troops at Heraklion, he chafed at waiting for takeoff. Left-behind paratroops, many of them his former pupils at the Paratroop School, rallied round him begging for orders. Ramcke reported the presence of his anxious pupils—there were over 500—to Colonel Schlemm, 11th Corps chief of staff, who directed they be formed into a reserve battalion. Scarcely had Ramcke begun on this when Schlemm called back with combat orders for the windfall reserve: Ramcke is to depart with it by 1300, jump west of Maleme by 1500, and fight the airfield free of all opposition. At last, action for a Lost Battalion.

But to deplane the mountain troops, rerig for jumping, emplane the Lost Battalion, is impossible before 1530 or later. The orders stand. What could have spurred Corps to the sudden shift of pace?[2] Possibly Colonel Schlemm himself was behind the shift. He had flown to Maleme after Kleye, landed on the sand to seaward of the runway, had a look around, and returned to confirm Kleye's opinion: airfield landings would be "hard but feasible." His news inspired extra confidence. Soon thereafter a marked change occurred: things began to happen. First off, Meindl had to be relieved. Schlemm volunteered. Then irrepressible five-foot-five fighter Ramcke, without knowing it, entered the "field" with his Lost Battalion. Here was a leader ready with his own extra troops. He got the job.[3]

Corps ordered up another mountain battalion at Tanagra Field for landing at Maleme at 1600. So arrangements shaped up for fresh assault on the field defenses from the west, but also from the east. Air Fleet 4 had the 11th Corps under crisis pressure. Löhr had ordered Ringel, a rank outsider, to take over Groups West and Center, and specified that he take command in Crete this day. It meant that the 11th Corps's control, Student's control, was in danger; Ringel would take the very post designed for Student, and with it the glory (if he succeeded). The sole chance rested in Ramcke, if only he could get over first. He finally did—Ringel suffered "technical" delays too.

Still, a personal anxiety that may have been the most galling to General Student was that Airborne Doctrine had yet to prove itself, prove the magic of snatching victory from the sky. Faith in his doctrine never left him: take the enemy in the rear ("in Rücken des Feindes") was still his watchword. The catch came in knowing where the rear was. Despite no news from any unit dropped east of the airfield (almost one complete battalion and other detachments) Student argued himself into belief that Pirgos-to-Platanias was clear for another drop. He ordered Leutnant Nägele and two companies to be dropped east of Pirgos at 1500 for attack westward. Though Löhr's *Schwerpunkt* in the west was now supposed to rule, Student could not forgo this last gamble.

For an all-out effort at Maleme, 1500 became another zero hour. The fagged Sturmregiment, reinforced by Captain Schmitt and his antitank detachment and by Ramcke (if he made it), was to launch

2. Schmitt, 18 June 1941; Ramcke GB, 30 July 1941; Ramcke VSJ, pp. 207–22; Ramcke to Ansel, Germany, 1960.
3. Student, Ringel, Langguth separately to Ansel in Germany, 1960. The circumstances surrounding the Schlemm flight are unclear. While witnesses mention it, no record appears in any combat report. Schlemm may have made the flight on his own to get things moving. This evaluation and what follows are my own.

renewed assault from the west. Richthofen was to provide preparatory bombing and strafing from 1400 on. Climax would come at 1600 with the transport landing of Colonel Utz and a battalion of the 100th Mountain Regiment. Ramcke would command in the west. The Navy received final mention: Admiral Southeast was to carry on with Maleme Flotilla and land on beaches west of the Tavronitis, regardless ("ohne Rücksicht") of British fleet movements. That this might mean landing the troops on the bottom of the sea seemed irrelevant. Sea transport had taken a spurt—provision was begun to have another mountain battalion follow up in Italian torpedo boats. The whole program was highly speculative.

On Crete, Sturmregiment struggled at the bitter end of its resources in men, munitions, food, and drink. At daylight Major Stentzler's 7th Company had occupied Hill 107 peaceably and B Company ridge to the southeast. Gericke had reached the east boundary of the airfield and dug in there, dead tired. A few stray shots from 23 New Zealand Battalion beyond Pirgos and an occasional artillery shell were all that bothered. That the coveted airfield and Hill 107 were both in hand made the big and significant news. Gericke reported his part of it at once to his chief. Sturmregiment has achieved its objective. It was 1100 on 21 May. Leutnant Göttsche logged another noonday pause, and this one was well utilized. Stalwart Meindl was carried to the beach west of the Tavronitis, where at 1300 Leutnant von Könitz set his Ju down and carried the general off to prolonged hospitalization. For him also, Airborne Doctrine had proved itself.

On the dot at 1400 combat aircraft began their latest tattoo against inoffensive little Maleme village and Pirgos. The villages intermix.[4] The planes battered the tiny settlements to pieces without achieving a single useful hit. German records take gleeful account of the first successful radio vectoring of planes from Cretan ground onto the targets. Troops entered Maleme village at 1700 and found nothing. Contact came with the defenders beyond Pirgos, first with 23 Battalion, entrenched on hillsides to the southeast, and then with the New Zealand

---

4. Sturmregt B; 11th FK Kreta; Davin, p. 188; Ross, p. 70. German and British accounts are confused by varied use of the names Maleme and Pirgos. Originally the name Maleme belonged to the hamlet and seat of the area's government half a mile due south of the east end of the airfield on a crooked spur road up toward Hill 107. Houses spilled onto the coastal road and carried the name Maleme along to the church half a mile east of the airfield. There the settlement merges into Pirgos on the coastal road. Apparently, German records refer to the newer Maleme, while British accounts stretch reference to Pirgos to include both settlements on the coastal road. The differences disturb the reconstruction of the attacks on 21 May afternoon.

Engineer Detachment and 28 Maori Battalion. 23 Battalion weathered repeated air blastings and a follow-up infantry advance. The advance stopped after heavy German casualties had been inflicted. Farther east Leutnant Nägele's party were in their hardheaded act of jumping on the foe's back. In substance it turned out to be a rerun of the 20 May attempt at the same play. The Maoris wiped out the 5th Company; Nägele with the 6th Company landed closer to Pirgos. He succeeded in gathering together eighty some men and lay low until dusk, then felt his way through toward Pirgos; to seaward of it he built an all-around defensive strongpoint and holed up. The all-out German attack of 1500 achieved no significant gains. It failed to eliminate the artillery, but did keep the defenders under pressure and thus implemented the 1600 climax of transport landings, with the mountain troops.

Here they came thundering in—low columns of threes and in overwhelming power. What a lift and release to the weary men watching from the ground! The planes land with such confidence, dash, and skill. Guiding the lead plane is the squadron commodore, Colonel Ulrich Buchholz. He knows what he is doing: in low from the north, bump over the seaward dune, and then squat the duck to earth in a short south-north run. Out scramble the mountaineers as the Ju slows and turns right to make room for the following chain of three. While taxiing free, Buchholz is hit in the leg, his plane takes fire; eager paratroopers pull him clear. Hours later he is returned to Greece in a luckier Ju. His time on Crete is short, but charged with high adventure. The determined pathfinding lead he made started a decisive upturn in the fortunes of Operation *Merkur*.

Nineteen years later this flight was still sharp in General Buchholz's memory. He told of the hardships at Tanagra, 30 miles above Athens—trouble with dust, fuel, eating, sleeping, with mere existence. A warning order about the flight reached him in the forenoon of 21 May. Planes, sixty-three of them, and the troops were made ready at once; the mixed mountain battalion was emplaned and the men given a chance to try out their seats. They disembarked and sprawled in the shade of each plane to await the word.

Word came by telephone about 1500, and within ten minutes the first trio of Ju's, led by Buchholz, was airborne. The others followed after normal dust delays. He looked back on passing west of Athens and found the formation in good order, column of threes. They were at 1500 feet, course due south. In 1960, by quick strokes on paper, the old flyer illustrated the formation and told how his first thought was to follow the flight plan of the day before—that is, approach Crete from the west. But now the problem was different. He decided, "To hell with that nonsense; go direct; approach under the lee of Cape Spatha, get the planes down quickly and the troops out." Two columns of threes were to land abreast on a southerly course, side wind or no. And so they did, bumping and bouncing to earth. Few casualties to troops occurred; eighteen wrecked planes stayed behind, some damaged in landing, others by gunfire.

The excited mountaineers gathered happily under Tavronitis's east bank below the familiar bridge entry. Even merrier were the admiring paratroopers. They waved, rushed to shake hands as they could; none believed this could happen. But it did, and from here on the German troop numbers swelled. If a single event deserves setting apart for its pivotal significance, this is it: the commencement of reinforcement of German man power on Crete through transport-plane landings on Maleme Field.[5]

Postknowledge tells us this; but at the time, need it have been so? As things stood, or trended, they were by no means irreversible and were not thought to be so by many Germans. In particular, not by General Ringel, who came to the scene twenty-four hours later. He believed the mere start of a landing head could have been cleaned out before noon of the 21st, and even much later. Yet for some British at Creforce the writing of doom was on the wall, notably for Captain Morse, the Navy representative. Admiral Cunningham wrote:

> The battle ashore in Crete had gone badly. After twenty-four hours of heavy fighting the enemy had complete control of Maleme airfield and were able to build up their strength by troop carrying aircraft. Our forces were being inexorably pressed back towards Suda bay. Captain Morse, the Naval Officer in Charge, was already beginning to consider plans for evacuation.

The Creforce doctrine of counterattack was fading into irrelevance without an earnest trial. In London, Churchill's assurances to the

---

5. Lt. General Ulrich Buchholz to Ansel in Germany, 1960. In later landings on the beach alongside the airfield some troop and plane casualties occurred opposite the east end of the field. Of course this area was closer to the Creforce defenders. To the mountain troop commanders the paratroops seemed pretty well used up. AOGA, p. 4, notes that "the only thing that saved the planes landing at Maleme from being destroyed completely by direct fire was the dust cloud in which the planes landed."

Commons of the previous day left his people firm in the belief that Crete would be defended "to the death."[6]

Withdrawal of 22 Battalion ended in a conference of battalion commanders about 0300 on 21 May at 23 Battalion headquarters; Lt. Colonel Leckie as host presided. Andrew was worn down by the day, and his men too, but the other two, Allen and Leckie, and their commands were relatively fresh. No record of the meeting is available, only a note from 21 Battalion's war diary that a decision was reached "to hold our positions next day while 22 Battalion reorganized." Hargest, still rooted to Platanias, let this decision (made for him) stand, reported the situation to Division, and devoted the day to arrangements for a projected counterattack by divisional reserves. We can better understand why Andrew received no help when he so sorely needed it; the spirit for counterattack simply was not there. Instead, a subtle suction to hold, then withdraw seems to have prevailed. Another irreplaceable moment went by the board. The day of reorganizing and holding wasted away, relieved only by the preparatory bombing and the German's afternoon drive east from Pirgos, and then Nägele's drop on Engineer Detachment and the Maori battalion. The paratroop ground offensive was fended off with long-range small-arms fire. These actions subsided after 1730; for the attackers they had at least helped screen the successful landing of the mountain troops. Think what counterattack might have done to the Ju's committed to landing! Of course, that is cutting too fine; yet with four battalions on hand (21, 23, 28, and Engineer Detachment), this landing of transport planes should have been prevented.[7]

Colonel Utz of the 100th Mountain Regiment found no one reporting to him at the airfield and no one to report to; he had some difficulty finding the Sturmregiment command post on the far side of the Tavronitis. For a short time he commanded Group West, now substantially strengthened. His landing made all the difference. Utz sent one mountain company east to beef up Gericke on the coastal road; two others he sent south to counter an alarming report of Brit-

6. Ringel Ms; Cunningham, p. 374; *New York Times*, 21 May 1941. German intelligence gained an insight into Creforce reactions through recorded intercepts of the advice of the naval officer in charge at Suda to his commander in chief in Alexandria. Captain Morse's planning for evacuation soon reached the necessity of establishment of a communications center with proper codes and publications on the south coast of Crete at Sfakia. He dispatched the needed materials on 23 May. Spencer, pp. 224–26. The feared landing from the sea had come from the air. The capacity and versatility of German air transport went unrecognized.

7. Davin, pp. 185–90; Cody, p. 99.

ish advances from that quarter, and the 6th Company went west along the shore to safeguard landing beaches for the already overdue Maleme Flotilla. Hardly had these moves got under way when a still newer commander broke in, a very positive one. Colonel Ramcke jumped down west of the command post about 1800. By 1820 he had assumed Meindl's place and duties and begun issuing orders. Unit commanders Stentzler, Gericke, and Utz he directed to report for orders at 2000. Someone had hold of the tiller at last, but Student's man, not Löhr's.

Marching toward the sound of the cannon is what has plumped diminutive, scrappy Bernhard Ramcke into the center of the Maleme crisis. He was supposed to stay behind at the Paratroop School in Germany, but like the troopers left behind at Topolia, he wangled a way into this great adventure. On some pretext he caught a plane bound for Greece and at once made himself indispensable: first as airborne mentor to the 5th Mountain Division, then as leader of the paratroops left behind, and now as Meindl's relief at crucial Maleme. It was a great break of good fortune, but one encouraged by his initiative. At Topolia he swept together three companies under Leutnants Vosshage, Kiebitz, and Klein. They were equipped for jumping. He was not—no chute, no pads or bandages, no helmet, no jump boots, but worst of all, no knowledge of Maleme and not even a map. One was found. He emplaned after the last of his mavericks, and off they went. Less than half of the planes got through the dust cloud. It was late, but they kept on. Ramcke studied his map at the open jump door and hoped for the best.

Soon after landing, which went well for him but badly for some of his followers, he saw Göttsche hurrying up. "Praise God the Colonel is here!" He got out and at once plunged into what had to be done: take command. Everything is confused. Mountain troops have landed, antitank troops and Schmitt two hours ago. Some have gone forward, others are still assembling. Sturmregiment units are badly mixed. Major Stentzler is forward with his battalion. So ran Göttsche's report. Arrived at the command post, Ramcke reviewed again the whole hodgepodge. He was staggered and strove to get his bearings, going forward for a look.

Dead were all around. At the airfield a house was full of wounded from both sides. Several Ju's were flaming on the runway. But only desultory gun shots came, no machine-gun chatter. Kiebitz and company he sent to Gericke on the east rim, with orders to push on.

Klein went to Stentzler back of Hill 107. That used up Ramcke's reserve, for after he jumped, about forty followers dropped into the sea. Schmitt's antitank outfit and headquarters men finally fished twenty-five of them out. Ramcke made Schmitt his reserve at the command post and prepared plans for the top commanders who had been ordered in.[8]

In his personal story and battle report Ramcke felt his greatest peril to be a British counterattack from the east on either side of the coastal road. Therefore the land east of Pirgos and the battery still active in that vicinity had to be cleared, even though the commanding heights to the south could pour down fire; they must be outflanked farther south, a maneuver which might also be useful for establishing contact with Heidrich in Prison Valley. The orders issued to Utz, Stentzler, Gericke, and Schmitt reflect this train of thought: Sturmregiment's 2d and 4th Battalions under Stentzler and Gericke were to secure the present forward lines, reorganize, and prepare for attack east on the morning of 22 May; Colonel Utz was to secure the south and west. GENERAL PLAN: "Through outflanking movements to the south by mountain troops enable Sturm Battalions 2 and 4 to advance eastward." Ramcke showed a concern for security, but security achieved by rooting out the opposition.

As the evening advanced the precious airfield began to take on a more orderly look; Major Snowatski, a Luftwaffe drome man, had taken charge. He got British Bren carriers going to tow wrecks and trash clear, so that from now on, keeping lanes open for landing was no longer a problem. Random shell and mortar fire offered no great impediment. Over this achievement General Student in Athens exulted: "Reserves succeeded in occupying airfield and town of Maleme. In the evening the First Mountain Battalion as the initial air-landed force could land." This had ever been emphasized as the first report he wanted from his men in the field. Now he had it, twenty-four hours late, and he did not call it a beachhead, an airhead, or as the mountainmen said, a landing head, but he had what he wanted and was happy.[9]

In the upper reaches of *Merkur* command the period of prolonged tension began to ease. It had tautened after the noon decisions; worried waiting ensued. In the middle came a frightening cry for help

8. Schmitt; Ramcke GB; Ramcke VSJ; as elaborated to me by General Ramcke in Germany, 1960.
9. 8th FK Chrono, 21 May 1941.

from Group West: "Strong British forces advancing from south, arrived within ten kilometers of airfield . . . air support urgently requested." The 8th Air Corps responded at once, but sighted nothing; favorable news from Maleme made it easy for the 11th Air Corps to discount the alarm. Its true origin was never established: all stations, including Group West (Göttsche), disowned it. Later the same evening, air attack on own troops in the Kastelli Kisamou region occurred. Nerves were taut. Air Fleet 4 continued to worry; the 11th Corps shrugged it off. The difference in view quickened a brewing disagreement over *Schwerpunkt* building and who was to command it, but Buchholz's success followed by word from Utz and finally Ramcke's hand on the helm inspired a decided upswing. Soon Maleme Flotilla would land a battalion, and in the morning still more would follow over the airfield.

Out of the woods! The German command had expected a vigorous tank-supported counterattack and believed this was thwarted by minutes. Victory fever caught on. Heidrich reported an advance and Bräuer had some troops inside Heraklion town; hoped to do something. That was Ringel's original task. His departure for Maleme had been delayed by so-called technical troubles; it would be too late, for this day anyhow. On second thought, should he go there at all? Ramcke had hold of things; the 11th Corps Command could itself shift over in the morning, which would let Ringel go to Heraklion as first planned. Why, indeed, was that plan ever abandoned? These inner voices rise higher. By 2000 Student was firmly back to the old scheme. He reoriented Ringel, whose diarist Zimmerman recorded the message:

2000: The task of General Ringel falls out, former task stays. Commander 5th Mountain Division redesignated to lead Group East. . . .
Intention 11th Corps for 22 May: *Group West*—Secure Maleme Airfield on all sides; drive toward Canea with all forces. *Group East*—In case tomorrow's attack against airfield [Heraklion] succeeds, air transport landing for 5th Mountain Division. . . .
Midday decision canceled. In general, hold fast and continue execution of the original plan.

Ringel took no exception, but it is clear from his final entry for the day that he was far less sanguine about the situation than the 11th Corps: "The second day's combat has left the decision on a knife-edge; a British counterattack in concentrated force would require a life-and-death effort on the part of every German." He meant of course at Maleme, about which Student's battle report exulted: *"On the evening of 21 May, 11th Corps regarded the crisis of attack on Crete as surmounted."* Before long his conviction would reel under heavy blows from widely separated points.

What General Löhr at Air Fleet 4 thought of the re-shift is not directly recorded, but his expressed "intention" for 22 May insisted on Maleme as the center of effort and Ringel to command it. He personally instructed his ex-pupil of war-college days on his mission, stressing firm possession of the airfield and security provisions for receiving reinforcements. He pressed Admiral Southeast to concentrate Italian torpedo boats for the transfer of yet another mountain battalion to Maleme by sea. Student's resistance to the Löhr design held on. The 11th Air Corps never really gave in to the concept of a center of effort (*Schwerpunkt*); it played along during moments of peril, but once the danger had passed it stalled and shifted, which aggravated differences with Air Fleet 4. Unlike the 11th Corps, *Merkur*'s commander in chief saw more troubles on the way. In his view, Airborne having failed, had to be bailed out, if not superseded, by mountain troop formations. Yet, whether Student's plan or Löhr's, one thing shines out: the Germans all have a cause, one beyond themselves.

Air Fleet 4's combat summary (LF4 Kreta, 21 May 1941) holds added interest because of the lessons it points out:

1. . . . success achieved in bringing airfield Maleme to a certain degree under possession.—An evening report shows the approach of new enemy forces from Palaiokhora to Maleme [the alarm in the south] so that on 22 May strong attacks . . . from the south on the airfield are to be reckoned with. . . . The 8th Corps has found nothing.—Remaining combat troops were not successful in their attacks and had to go over to the defensive to try to hold positions.

2. Lack of heavy antitank weapons and sufficient artillery makes itself felt strongly. . . . In each zone the enemy attacked with tanks, and his well-concealed artillery cannot be discovered from the air.

3. Support of the 11th Corps by the 8th Corps is difficult, since the enemy makes recognition signals that have fallen into his hands. Differentiation between friend and foe is sometimes hard.

4. The British fleet has broken through anew to waters north of Crete and has rendered the sea transport of heavy weapons impossible. . . . It must be assumed that the bulk of the Alexandria fleet, reinforced with parts of the Gibraltar fleet, has been at sea. Lacking sea forces, the Luftwaffe has alone had to take up the battle of eliminating the British fleet.

5. The enemy air force has been eliminated; complete air command over Crete still obtains.

17. Control of the Sea

Early on 21 May little *Lupo*, an Italian destroyer, relieved her older sister ship *Sirio* as guide and protector of Maleme Flotilla, puffing south from the island of Melos for landing beaches west of Maleme. *Lupo*'s noon position report to *Merkur* headquarters brought cheers. Carried forward, the plot of her advance showed that the flotilla might just barely make the landing waters before dark—which meant before the 8th Corps air cover had to end. General Löhr's report noted, "Thereby the hope of having heavy antitank weapons . . . on Crete for 22 May seemed to be fulfilling itself." Ringel of the 5th Mountain Division, the 3d Battalion of whose Mountain Regiment 100 had sailed in the flotilla, also watched the signs of progress with high hopes and low prayers. But later, von Richthofen, the best-informed, through plane contacts, reported a slower advance. At dusk the flotilla would still have 36 miles to go. The watchers and plotters swapped data and worried together, pressing for the happy answer. One man suffered most. Heinrich Bartels, the Channel amphibian, had gone in by air to lay out the landing beaches and prepare the reception, 2 miles west of the Tavronitis delta.

Now he knew time was up. The beaches were ready, judiciously sounded and selected, carefully marked for recognition from seaward but not at night in face of the Royal Navy. Beach and shore parties reinforced by mountain engineers stood ready. Since early afternoon they and Bartels had stared seaward from vantage points beyond Sturmregiment's command post. Now and again Bartels would check in there for fresh news. Where could Österlin and his ragtag mountaineer navy be? He exchanged guesses with newly arrived Commander West, Colonel Ramcke, himself an old sailor. It grew darker and darker, and no answer.[1]

Österlin had tarried only briefly at Melos and hurried on. The run down from Piraeus had demonstrated that time would be short. As the sun of 20 May was setting, he lay to in the entrance to Melos Bay to let his caïques stream in around him and take his word that course south would be resumed at once. Within twenty minutes the flotilla, minus three stragglers, stood out along the rugged west coast of Melos for Crete. A head sea made the sailing order stretch out more than ever; yet sea legs were growing. The established routine of watches and station keeping whiled the night away in satisfactory advance. At the first light of this X-plus-1 Day, *Sirio* left the van for a fast loop around the brood, checking and encouraging a "close-up." Soon *Lupo* steamed up from astern and took over. The course was to follow her, a bit west of south; compared with yesterday's sight of grand Ju formations, only a few low-flying planes appeared to point the way.[2]

At broad daylight the peak outlines of mountains crept up from the horizon ahead; they merged into continuous masses like another mainland. Landing warfare's ultimate water hazard of offshore mines was almost due. The mine menace never stops a landing, but it cannot be totally ignored. A few minutes before 0800 *Lupo* ordered the lead motor sailers to ready their minesweeping gear. The planned waiting zone (*Wartestelle*), 25 miles offshore, lay close ahead. Of a sudden *Lupo* reversed course at high speed. She came charging down from the van, throwing spray, blinking signals. Distant explosions could be heard. She got the message out: "Orders are all ships make best speed to Melos." The flotilla coasted to a stop; the leaders steamed through the formation on a northerly course, passing the word; the others followed uncertainly. Only Österlin and the lead boat knew why. *Lupo* had added, "British naval forces west of Crete," and headed for them. Admiral Southeast had ordered the turnaround. Control of the sea was in doubt.

  1. Ramcke VSJ; LF4 Kreta; the period was discussed with General Ramcke in 1960 and with Captain Bartels in 1953.
  2. Flotilla action reports made between 25 and 29 May 1941 by troop commanders in the caïques form the base of this account. Vidua adds helpful lights.

In Athens, Naval appraisals of the profuse air sightings of ships early on 21 May portended trouble. Day and dark advantage and handicap in the air-vs.-sea conflict were well comprehended on both sides: day was good for Luftwaffe, dark for the Royal Navy—provided it could find the flotilla or the chosen landing spot.

Admiral Cunningham was resolved to sink any seaborne invasion, day or dark. His protective practice settled into a pattern of light force patrols off probable landing areas west and east during dark, followed by withdrawal during day. A Main Body of battleships, cruisers, and destroyers cruised west of Crete to support the light forces and to destroy any sea interference out of Italy. Failing in their efforts to get Italian heavy forces out, the Germans filled the ether with fake radio signals designed to suggest an Italian fleet sortie. Meanwhile intelligence reports and RAF caïque sightings of 20 May fixed the sailing of Maleme Flotilla.

That evening the fleet forces closed in on Crete. A cruiser-destroyer force West under Rear Admiral Glennie patrolled off Canea-Maleme without event, and at dawn 21 May retired on the Main Body under a rain of bombs. A like East Patrol under Admiral King swept the coastal waters off Heraklion, while three destroyers shelled Scarpanto airfield. Six Italian motor torpedo boats were driven off as all the British ships withdrew south through Caso Strait. These early exchanges during the approach of Maleme Flotilla fanned the air-vs.-sea war into full flame as 21 May advanced. The East Patrol was bombed continuously for four hours; just before noon a whole stick of bombs struck down destroyer *Juno*. She was gone in two minutes. First blood! But perhaps in the wrong place. Crisis would be in the west where the German cause needed a clear sea off Maleme. The Main Body together with the West Patrol had been under fire for over two hours in the afternoon as the ships moved off southwest out of air range. Toward evening when Admiral Glennie broke off with ships of West Patrol he was again bombarded. But in the gathering gloom he moved back in for his second night stint. To the German command the welter of reports appeared to show a clear sea north of Crete.[3]

3. Cunningham, pp. 368–79; Dispatch Report Commander in Chief Mediterranean for 4 Aug. 1941 in supplement to *London Gazette*, 24 May 1948, Rumb 38296; LF4 Kreta; 8th FK Chrono. All action reports were of course full of inaccuracies and errors, but more so in the German air story. The flyers' sightings and bomb hits rose to fantastic exaggerations in childish glee, which Admiral Heye, chief of staff to Admiral Southeast, re-recounted in 1960. At the time he had to try to make sense out of the muddled messages; he found it next to impossible.

When the first reports of 21 May were in, the German Naval Command faced a choice like that faced by the 11th Air Corps two nights earlier when intelligence of ships at sea roused that frightful image of Ju disaster at the hands of British antiaircraft gunners on the ships in Kithira Strait. Then General Student decided to go on. Now what should Maleme Flotilla choose? By 0730 Admiral Southeast chose "Go back," and straightaway notified *Lupo*. The flotilla had started from Melos against his judgment anyhow, and the current scene looked unmanageable; it grew more prodigal and confused by the minute: destroyers became cruisers, cruisers battleships—all in great profusion—and for good measure a nonexistent aircraft carrier entered the fray. No two sightings agreed in disposition. Bombs cascaded down, sank, and set fires. Ships took on heavy lists at once or lay immobile. That tyrant of the sea, the Royal Navy, was on the way down—sunk by airpower. But not in the eyes of Captain Heye, chief of staff to Admiral Southeast. Before an hour was out, after turning Maleme Flotilla around, he was besieged by Air Fleet 4 and the 8th Air Corps to reverse to south again. He said later, "The chart plot of these days offered a wild picture (*wildes Bild*) that defied the imagination." Eventually one fact became plain: no British ship was any longer north of Crete. At this instant Maleme Flotilla, at Air Fleet 4 insistence, was turned south again. Six precious daylight hours had been lost, said the air zealots, and they could not be made up. The British ships had not been driven from the sea: they could return. There was no way of knowing that Maleme Flotilla should have kept on, just as Student's Ju's had.

While the 11th Air Corps took little stock in the growing uproar, elsewhere the gravity of the situation on Crete seems only just to have dawned on high leaders. The moment had arrived when the initial reports of whacking success everywhere all at once collapsed and the top Luftwaffe leadership began to squirm. It wanted to invoke magic of its own to insure the truth of the early boasts. Louder and louder came yelps for reinforcement to Sturmregiment in the west by sea, howsoever possible or impossible. In some quarters early Air pretenses were succeeded by near panic—cries to Rome for fleet action, for landing of troops. Admiral Southeast received fresh orders to land a second mountain battalion from Italian destroyers on the open Maleme coast at first light 22 May. The leap from ship to shore by the troops remained unsolved, but leap they must. They embarked.

And Heraklion Flotilla, straggling into Melos, was also to steer for Maleme. In a final summary to his naval superiors in Berlin, Admiral Southeast hoped that the sixteen boats of Maleme Flotilla (some had fallen out) would make their beaches by 2300 this day, 21 May. He sensed trouble if British ships on a logical mission to bombard Maleme runways should tangle with the flotilla landing and catch it red-handed. That would make for a hot time off Maleme tonight. It was the first occasion in which the invincible German arms seemed bound for disaster, and of Luftwaffe making. It would hardly wring a tear from the other services.

Putt-putting along on a southerly course again, Maleme Flotilla leaders noted the fading daylight hours and the failing headway against the seas and wondered. Stukas streaming south overhead must mean something. Could things have gone wrong on Crete? No one could explain the first turnabout nor the second, executed unsurely in a blind follow-the-leader fashion. The ragged column stretched longer and longer astern of the battalion commander's flagship, S-105. Colonel Ehal figured, a staff member recorded, that there could be no landing until early the next morning, 22 May, even if Österlin, ahead there, held his present speed. On *Rosa* (V-4) Leutnant Österlin had her and the sister ship alongside stream their minesweeps. Besides their *Merkur* numbers, these ships carried their proud regular names, like *Adriatico, Patria Eterna, Labor*; yet none of them could match that of Ehal's flagship, towering there near the van—the *Papapopiou I*. She and one other were roomier, speedier, and steadier than any. Since early afternoon her crew had Crete in good sight. Later the headlands marking the entrance to the Gulf of Kisamos stood out. Buchholz's low-flying Ju's passed with many a hand wave. Good; the flight must mean the fight was still going well. Better that, than puking here at sea. Troop leaders rechecked landing arrangements: inflation of life rafts, heavy mountaineer shoes off, life jackets on, Very signal pistols in hand. The outfitting had been well thought out and got aboard, despite the haste. They steamed into their third and certainly most dangerous night at sea. Lookouts complained of poor visibility.

Yet Leutnant Hörmann aboard S-8, bringing up the rear, can still discern the stern lights of the vessels ahead. His ship is quiet, snug, in good order except for the decrepit motor, whose troubles account for the rearmost position. Ahead everything is safe, and to make sure astern, he casts an occasional look over his shoulder. At about 2235 this look stops short on a dark hulk coming up fast. A man-of-war! And as Hörmann realizes the horror of it, sidelights and searchlights flash on and guns blaze. Two salvos fly over him toward the flotilla. A vessel bursts into flames. The warship, a cruiser, passes S-8 so close that only her machine guns will bear; these rake the caïque as the huge ship steams on.

It is no place for his cockleshell, Hörmann decides, and turns north, noting that vessels farther south have opened searchlights and gunfire on the hapless bulk of the flotilla. These new British ships seem to circle inshore to cut off the advance. Another ship has burst into flames, and the first makes distress signals by Very light—her munitions are exploding. Ahead of S-8, a second big ship looms up, rakes her with machine guns, and steams on. The bullets rip S-8 fore and aft; wounded cry for help; the mainmast, shot in two, has jammed the helm. She circles slowly. Hörmann and his Greek crew yank at the mast in frenzy: it comes clear. Just when it seems they are free, the whole play repeats a third time; a third big ship passes. It is too much; Hörmann gives the word, "Prepare to abandon ship." Two men anticipate the final word, cast off a life raft, and jump in. They are smothered at once by machine-gun bullets, at which the rest of S-8's men go prone on deck and stay there. Now Hörmann tries course east, and there he finds surcease. Rising seas add concealment. To the south, five torching hulks light a large semicircle; some burn out, and new torches to the northwest light up—all told, seven. By 0230 on 22 May the searchlights are out; firing has ceased. S-8 resumes course north in relative peace and quiet.

From its remote rear station this vessel offered a plausible account of the action in substantial agreement with the British record. The force of three cruisers and four destroyers (under Rear Admiral Glennie in cruiser *Dido*, with *Orion*, *Ajax*, and destroyers *Janus*, *Kimberley*, *Hasty*, *Hereward*) began a sweep off the Gulf of Canea after dark; at 2200, eighteen miles offshore, radar contact was made on the flotilla. S-8, as the outermost, may have been the giveaway contact. The destroyers in the lead turned to circle inshore and began to pick off the targets, concentrating on the fat ones. The cruisers turned shoreward to join in. A regular destroyer melee ensued; *Lupo* did her part, while the flotilla remnants scattered. The job finished, Glennie headed out, swept east, then north, and finally west out of the Cretan Sea through Kithira Channel. He had broken the back of reinforce-

ment by sea. Had he but known, he could have seriously impaired reinforcement by air too, through bombardment of Maleme's runways.[4]

Glennie's passing target, S-8, carrying 125 soldiers, 3 sailors, and
4 Greek crewmen, stood on to the north. Leutnant Hörmann singled
out the crewmen for individual praise, with an extra "well done" for
the twenty-year-old helmsman, Dimitrin. The soldier master of the
ship had not done badly himself.

The tail and the head of the flotilla had the best of it. When the
shooting began, Leutnant Österlin's *Rosa* (V-4) and two other motor
minesweepers (T-2 and T-3) still held the van. The fourth sweeper,
venerable *Patria Eterna*, had fallen far astern under tow. Her tower—
she was a bigger vessel—was the first thing to be hit hard and immediately burst into flames. *Patria* cast off and started a slow turn northwest, followed by three other ships. They became the torches Hörmann saw later. The three leaders had meanwhile come into searchlight beams and point-blank gunfire; shells splashed all around, but
wide. At this point Österlin and T-3 had to turn off sharply to clear
a ship charging up from astern to interpose. It was *Lupo*; shining her
light on a cruiser's superstructure and banging away. She let go a
spread of torpedoes, for which she claimed one sure hit. For its part
the British command claimed *Lupo*'s extinction by gunfire. Both
claims made good copy in the dispatches. *Lupo*'s devil-may-care
charge into the breach gave cover to the escape of the lead boats; they
went east first, then gradually north toward Melos.[5]

One distinguished ship deserves individual notice, for she came
closest to making Crete, at one point within 350 yards. Her story inter-
twines with that of the flagship, *Papapopiou I* (S-105), which was
instantly recognized as the big prize and concentrated upon. On Colonel Ehal's order, S-105 reversed course to get out of the fire, Leutnant Lindner of the staff recalled. In the glow of searchlights he saw
the ship surrounded by fountains of water, a neighboring caïque cut
in two by ramming; he heard cries for help from below and a shout
to lower lifeboats. The men seemed fearful of jumping into the sea.
He jumped, and four or five followed. They gained the two lifeboats,

4. This action was one of seagoing radar's early successes. At Matapan Admiral
Cunningham had no radar on his flagship, but depended on advices from radar on
another ship. Admiral Glennie must have had radar on *Dido* to coach his ships in
for the kill.

5. After action reports and sketches by Leutnants Hörmann (S-8), Staubwasser
(T-2), Lang (T-3), Commander of 12th Company, Regiment 100 (V-4), Schmidt
(S-105), Siegrist (S-15).

picked up more survivors, and lay low from the searchlight beams. *Papapopiou I* faded into the distance, lighted once in a high flash, and was gone. Lindner organized his new command into five men on three oars and three bailers. So they pulled and bailed through the night. At full daylight on 22 May's morning they sighted a mast in the north; it grew steadily taller. Shortly after midday they pulled happily alongside of Leutnant Horbach's S-14, and clambered on board.

She was simply another motor-troubled straggler just now closing up on the flotilla. Where was everybody? Horbach had had some hints: thunder of guns, a caïque going north full tilt. He decided his orders required holding fast to course south then, and now, even after Lindner's report that the flotilla had been shot to pieces. They could be the last survivors. He could not be shaken. Once again the motor quit and sails were hoisted. Progress toward Cape Spatha continued. With less than 5 miles to go at 1700 the breeze petered out. Horbach had prepared for this one too. He ordered two eighteen-man detachments under Lindner ashore by boat and ponton; they set out at 1800, paddling for "Diktineon" vaguely identified by a break in the cliffs south of Cape Spatha. Lindner was to reconnoiter for a landing place and provide for its security. When he landed, Horbach planned that the whole command would push on to Maleme. Ironically, shortly after the landing party had shoved off, a puff drove S-14 within 350 yards of the shore, then failed; she drifted helplessly out in the offshore current. In any event S-14's doughty captain could content himself with the thought that his landing by sea had half-succeeded. He would hold on.[6]

Surely this landing party had had a fill of alarms and adventures; yet not enough. At dark searchlights from seaward commenced to stab the sky over the paddlers. Out of the gloom ahead rose a sinister shape. Of all things! By conning tower and low-cut deck it looked like a surfaced submarine. Lindner says so in his handwritten report. Soldiers have a faculty for sighting nonexistent submarines; just put them on watch in submarine waters. But who can say? Here was some monster of the deep—to the men frozen at their paddles the thing was a submarine. It slunk off. They saw it go. (In fact, British submarines were on patrol.) After a bit they paddled on, reached shore past midnight, and sheltered under the cliffs. Restless searchlights kept sweeping. About 0300 on 23 May a final fearful horror assailed them; their

6. Lindner report, 5th MD War Diary; Horbach BS-14 for 26 May 1941; Horbach AF.

mother ship was shot to death before their eyes. Three fast-moving destroyers did it, then went on to lob a few shells into Maleme Field. Early morning efforts by Lindner and company to rescue survivors brought in only nine men in two rubber boats. Time passed slowly; a stranded glider crew joined up, then a lone motorboat chugged along the shore. Resourceful Lindner halted her, let her proceed, but with two of his men aboard to see that she returned, and she did. The whole party embarked, said Lindner casually. "We rode over to Maleme."

The true end of *Merkur*'s amphibious pretensions came in the small hours of this day, 23 May 1941, when S-14 blew up. Horbach had ordered all hands overboard after one salvo ripped through the sails; he, his Lieutenant, and their seventy-four men thrashed shoreward. The current proved too strong; it carried them out to sea. He settled on wise crack and song for keeping his men together, and they came through. At 0615 a column of Ju's passed. The seventh plane dropped a life raft, the others followed suit; soon everybody had good flotation. Air-sea rescue planes got busy, so that by 1600 Horbach and the last contingent were on their way back to Greece. He ended his story with a conclusion that "it was irresponsible to use a vessel capable of only two knots for a landing against Crete"; yet he had to soften the charge by laying the decisive blame on wind and motor. If either had held through, his whole outfit would have made it, of this he was certain. Lindner, who did make it, reoutfitted his troops at Maleme and reported for duty on 24 May.

Of course, ifs and buts applied to misfortunes throughout the flotilla. Too many odds against the venture had been accepted; some were unnecessary, some aggravated a circumstance already bad. At the crux was the arrival of the flotilla during dark, the favored period of sea power, and at fault was the time lost during the futile turn-around. The approach route was wrong; it failed to maximize the German air capabilities and minimize the British favors from the sea. A route south under the lee of the Peloponnesian coast, thence across the straits via Kithira and Antikithira islands, had only two short exposures to open water; speed of advance would have been higher, air cover close at hand and more precise; any waiting for a clear route ahead could have been done in the lee of land and planes overhead. In these narrow waters air power gained positive orientation and short runs to the target. British sea power would have been close under the bombs. All this the Germans realized too late.

Reinforcement by sea died; in Athens all thought of it collapsed with the arrival of first disaster tidings: Flotilla destroyed, 1800 men lost! Corrections gradually mitigated the numbers, but having from the start taken small interest in the scheme, Airborne command was only too willing to believe the worst about the attempted sea landing. With *Merkur*'s commander in chief it was different; five months later General Löhr still felt the shock and despair of the moment when he wrote: "The British fleet make the extremely urgent transport of heavy weapons by sea impossible." And at the time he promptly declared a double air war on the Royal Navy. He told the 8th Air Corps

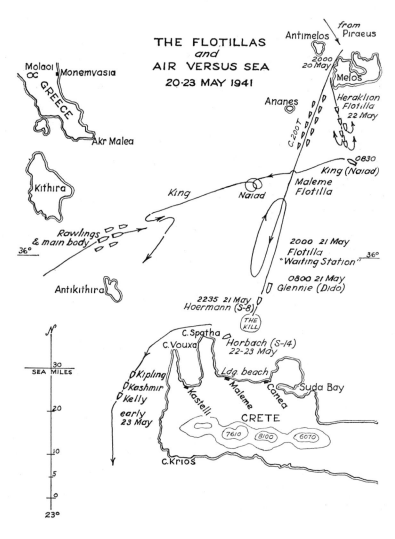

to get busy. The German Navy canceled all amphibious efforts, including the makeshift landing of troops by Italian destroyers. Heraklion Flotilla was recalled, but not in time to avoid all damage. The 8th Corps flyers got sufficiently trigger-happy against men-of-war to include Italian destroyers.

Eight Maleme Flotilla vessels survived to limp toward Melos where Heraklion Flotilla was standing out, early on 22 May. One caïque had already tangled with Rear Admiral King's force of four cruisers and three destroyers. The British destroyers sighted the rest of them streaming along astern. Italian destroyer *Sagittario* now became the hero. She interposed and, like *Lupo*, took up gunfire and added a smoke screen. Under this cover all but two ships regained port at Melos. *Sagittario* and her five sister ships, loaded with troops, then headed for Piraeus. They made it after being pounced upon by their own dive bombers. Many earnest curses, a few hits, and some casualties resulted, but no sinkings.

In recapitulation, eventually, the alarming figures of 20 ships and 1800 men lost reversed themselves to 10 ships lost and 1800 men saved. (British sources, including Churchill, claimed a kill of 4000 Germans.) The final casualty list came to 304 dead or missing. To Lindner's success story a few individual invaders can be added, to make a grand total of 49 Mountain amphibians that reached Crete. If threat of invasion by sea influenced 5 Brigade's deployment and delayed counterattack, its more direct effect was to spur the Luftwaffe to sink Britain's ships at sea.

Sea-Air Battle: 22–23 May 1941

British ships ripped the guts out of *Merkur*'s invasion by sea— a miniature of what might have befallen *Sea Lion* had he ventured cross-channel in September 1940. The English Channel produced stalemate in the air, but Crete produced a trial of deep strategic and historic significance between air and sea power.

At no time did combat action afford German recorders, broadcasters, or indeed, the German people more of a lift than when the Luftwaffe registered a success against the Royal Navy. Reports of such action, real or imagined, got prompt mention and with gusto: the Englanders are sinking; times have changed, for now there is our Luftwaffe to reckon with. Control of the sea from the air grew into something of a sacrosanct cause to Göring and his flyers. They proclaimed its truth over and over; still, their very vehemence betrayed a lurking uncertainty. On the outside, individuals high up seemed unconvinced. The Führer, for example, in a pinch showed deep-rooted doubts. He was afraid of water and of becoming seasick on it, never enjoyed swimming much, and nursed an abiding respect for Britain's use of the alien, sinister sea, his propaganda notwithstanding. Affairs around Crete on 21 May 1941 opened further engaging opportunities to get even. Yet this situation, like others, involved more than denial of the sea to the adversary. That made less than half of it. The decisive half demanded use of the sea for own strategic purposes, which is the ultimate meaning of sea power. Air and submarine enthusiasts often forget the second half. In the case of Crete, both sides needed the sea for transporting reinforcements. Denial alone would not suffice, as 21 May demonstrated.

On that day the British Main Body accompanied by West Patrol cruised in readiness off the west entrance to the Cretan Sea; the ships weathered a forenoon attack and a prolonged afternoon siege. And we can recall how Admiral King's force in East Patrol stood up to attack from mid-forenoon on; destroyer *Juno* sank. Before nightfall Admiral Glennie with his three cruisers and four destroyers took a heavy blasting from Colonel Dinort's Stukas. The Colonel claimed four hits and one cruiser afire, but none stopped. It looked bad for the flotilla, and so it turned out. We know how Glennie went on to rout Maleme Flotilla in the night and thereby double the pressure for an air victory on the day to follow. The lines of battle were thus drawn for 22 May 1941, the day of air against sea.

Another famous name of World War I graced Dinort's command: Squadron Immelmann 2, which was credited this day with the most kills. Fifty of his single-engined dive bombers (Ju-87 Stukas) flew from Argos, below Corinth, thirty-six from Molaoi at the head of the southernmost Peloponnesian bay, from where it not only covered west Crete and its waters but reached 60 miles south of the island toward Africa. Melos and the flotillas battleground off Maleme lay within easy range.

Thursday, 22 May, broke cloudless, light airs, visibility 50 to 60 miles. Reconnaissance flights raised two contacts in quick succession: first on Admiral King's cruisers getting after Heraklion Flotilla south of Melos, and second on the Main Body southwest of Kithira Island in the west entrance to the Cretan Sea. Pursuant to 8th Corps orders, Dinort took on the rescue of Heraklion Flotilla; other tasks on Crete fell out.[7]

Usually the reporting plane maintained contact, while at the fields every flyable Stuka took the air, "even in the smallest formations," some but three planes strong, and sped toward the target. The watchword was "Continuous attack"; "Sink the British!" Pick your target, get over it, peel off, dive, and let go; assemble, return, reload, and get back at them. First the Stukas struck cruisers *Gloucester* and *Fiji*, which, with destroyers *Greyhound* and *Griffin*, were retiring westward to join the Main Body; then they found Admiral King's Heraklion patrol south of Melos. Comdr. Hitschhold gives an eyewitness account of maneuvering ships, hits, explosions, and fires. He counted nine ships (there could only have been seven). He saw Heraklion Flotilla behind *Sagittario*'s smoke screen. Her attackers broke off, turned south, then west; one was lagging. She (flagship *Naiad*) went into a tight circle, giving off only weak antiaircraft fire. Over thirty planes screamed down on her—without a single hit. Hitschhold ascribed the misses to the tight circle. *Naiad* had a steering-gear casualty and felt many near misses; they put out two turrets, flooded several compartments, and reduced her speed to 16 knots. In the only direct hit, *Carlisle* lost her captain. She fought on. The battered ships plowed westward under continued attack. Just after noon a welcome Main Body came into view ahead. Pressure on it from overhead had not been quite so severe. Phase I of air-vs.-sea was over. Actually, King had been driven out.

Colonel Dinort totted up: several cruisers hit, one set afire; one destroyer probably sunk—all for the loss of only two Stukas, though a quarter of them bore wounds. What he left out was the enormous bomb expenditure for one direct hit; he also left out the total absence of air-launched torpedoes, which could have holed hulls and sunk ships. But more important than his "kill ratio" was the claim of a clear-cut strategic victory—that the British ships had been driven out of the Cretan Sea. "The transport movement to Crete could carry on unhindered by hostile fleet forces," he concluded. It was true; the in-

7. In 1940 the Ju–87's were driven out of the Battle of Britain by Spitfires. Here in Crete unopposed, these planes were recouping their name. They could dive out of the sun at 70° along a ship's longitudinal axis, let go a 500- or 1000-pound bomb or four 100-pounders in a blast of machine-gun fire. The thin communications permitted no vectoring; planes simply took off in V's of three and flew toward the reported target. Both Dinort and Group Commander Hitschhold flew and wrote up results. This account bases on their reports, Ms 640 of 1947.

cessant drum fire had made inroads; the flotillas could have sailed the Cretan Sea, but they did not. Instead each side grew wary of making free with the sea. Neither command realized what it had done; and this was entirely normal and natural.

Phase II aimed to drive the even stronger naval force, in fact, the Battle Fleet, from the sea. It began with the junction of Rawlings (battleships) and King. The Main Body had worked through the prelude during the forenoon. Augmented by Glennie's West Patrol, which took a good blasting on the way out, the Main Body presented a juicy collection of targets: battleships *Warspite* (flag) and *Valiant*; cruisers *Dido*, *Ajax*, *Orion*, *Gloucester*, and *Fiji*; and twelve destroyers. Air struck hard after King called for help. At 1125 Rawlings rang up flank speed and headed for Kithira Channel. Cruisers *Gloucester* and *Fiji* led the van. The Stuka chief tells how his divers fell on the formation in massive waves. One stick took out the starboard half of *Warspite*'s antiaircraft weaponry. Dinort watched the meeting forces slow and re-form on an easterly course; it shifted to south and, under increased assault, to southwest. To him it meant the united fleet was leaving the arena, because it could not stay—or, in the British view, because there was nothing to stay for. Air, which had failed to prevent junction, now took up pursuit.

The flyers noted a slackening of antiaircraft fire. Were the ships shot out? they wondered, and tried to step up their assault, but on the fringes. Destroyer *Greyhound*, off by herself, became the first victim. Two Stuka bombs caught her while slowed in quest of a caïque near Antikithira Island. Down she went in fifteen minutes. On orders, destroyers *Kandahar* and *Kingston* and the cruisers *Fiji* and *Gloucester* undertook rescue of survivors. This futility resulted in another casualty, for the air gave no respite. *Gloucester*, veteran of countless adventures, took five 1000-pounders, recorded eyewitness Hitschhold as he circled above. She listed deeply, and in thirty-five minutes rolled over and down. This time no ship stayed to save. The Cunningham rule, "Never detach a ship for any particular task . . . take the whole fleet to it if something must be done," had been disregarded. An hour later, two bombs struck battleship *Valiant* without serious damage. But the breach of the rule was not yet done. *Fiji* had not rejoined. A single fighter found her and dropped his load close alongside. It blew in her hull plates to cause a list. A half-hour later another lone plane finished her off with hits in her boiler room. Her two accompanying destroyers, *Kandahar* and *Kingston*, cleared out, dropping rafts. After dark they returned and pulled aboard over 500 survivors. Phase II ended at dark with both contenders near exhaustion.

Through their weariness the airmen cheered, and the cheers reached to headquarters of the 8th Air Corps at Eleusis near Athens, swelling higher and higher. Commented the Corps's Chronology, "Since 0500 sighting reports of British cruisers and destroyers tumble over each other; they are around Crete, Melos, Kithira." Another "wild picture" churns up on the chart, yet it never daunts the keyed-up staffmen. In von Richthofen's own words:

The British take hit after hit; ships sink and burn. Others turn aside to help and are caught by bombs too . . . the ships are exhausting their AA ammunition. . . . All run at top speed on zigzag courses and wild reverse turns. They are struck down, burn, and sink; some limp along with a list, others with a trail of oil, to get out of this hell.

Flight units that have flown the whole day, bombed, reloaded with time for naught else, at evening begin to let out triumphant shouts of joy. Tired and lame, the *Englander* hauls off for Alexandria. The word *Seeluftschlacht* (sea-air battle) crops up. Results cannot yet be assessed, but I have the secure feeling of a grand and decisive success: six cruisers and three destroyers are definitely sunk, others so damaged they will sink in the night.

We have finally demonstrated that a fleet within range of the Luftwaffe cannot maintain the sea if weather permits flying.

The lopsided story grew with the telling the higher it went. The 8th Air Corps headquarters shook in exultation. Air Fleet 4 was more reserved, requested reinforcement in combat planes. Luftwaffe Chief of the General Staff Jeschonnek lost no time in transmitting the good news to Göring in Berlin, where good news was badly needed. It was of course passed to the Führer at the Berghof. He had kept his counsel through the whole crisis and said nothing of record now: no congratulatory messages, no special commendations.[8]

At Alexandria "as the afternoon gave way to evening," wrote Admiral Cunningham, "our hearts were heavy. . . ." All elation over sinking Maleme Flotilla had burned out as the harrowing events of 22 May pushed toward withdrawal. At one point he told all ships: "Stick it out, Navy must not let Army down. No enemy forces must reach

8. On 22 May, General von Richthofen pressed for resumption of reinforcement to Crete by sea; neither *Merkur*'s commander in chief nor the Navy would budge. 8th FK Chrono continues: "General von Richthofen urges that now the remaining sailers [caïques] go ahead, since these forces are urgently needed on Crete. The British ships, beaten and shot out, are withdrawing . . . cannot come again today or tomorrow. But the shock of the 1st Echelon's [Maleme Flotilla's] destruction made such inroads that retreat is shamefully sounded on the whole thing."

Crete by sea." Then came one casualty after another. At 2130 another sledgehammer blow—the Main Body reported the loss of *Gloucester* and *Fiji* and added that the battleship had "plenty" of AA shells. Instead of "plenty," the first-delivered copy of the message read "empty" of short-ranged shells. That was enough. "The Commander in Chief accordingly decided to withdraw all forces to Alexandria." Two battleships and two cruisers damaged, one destroyer sunk, and now two cruisers to boot—all in one daylight period—and the rest short of ammunition and fuel, short of rest, but short mostly of a lift from accomplishment, a lift of victory. It was not to be had in this sitting-duck environment.

As if to drive home a hopeless feeling of chased-from-the-field, two fresh, new destroyers, just arrived from home via Malta, were sunk early on 23 May. They were trying to close the Main Body south of Crete after a dark patrol off Maleme. It was they at about 0300 of 23 May—destroyers *Kelly*, *Kashmir*, and *Kipling*, on their way in to Maleme—who encountered Horbach's becalmed Ship 14. They banged away at her and went on to shell Maleme airfield, ineffectively. On the way out they bombarded S-14 again and logged the sinking of two caïques crammed with troops. The ships then lit out for Alexandria around the west end of Crete at high speed. Dinort's Stukas espied them at dawn and immediately took them under fire near the limit of flight range to the south of Crete. The first attacks failed to hit; but about 0700 a fleet of twenty-four Stukas, stretching their reach to the utmost, smothered the ships in bombs. Flag *Kelly* and *Kashmir* received mortal wounds; the latter went like *Juno*, in two minutes. *Kelly* listed heavily in a hard turn; she turned over with way still on and then slid under. *Kipling*, coming up astern after a steering casualty, refused to leave. Under three anguished hours of bombing, she survived and rescued 279 men, including the commander of the 5th Destroyer Flotilla, Captain (Lord Louis) Mountbatten. Then she ran all out for Alexandria until her fuel was gone, 50 miles short of the goal. Fleet tug *Protector* hauled her in. Further air-vs.-sea trials would follow, but none would prove so full and portentous as this one of 21–23 May 1941, now ended. To the Luftwaffe, 22 May 1941, the day in the middle, was the joyful day of *Seeluftschlacht* success; to the Royal Navy the sorrowful day of sunk ships and shipmates.[9]

9. Cunningham, pp. 368–76; *London Gazette*, suppl., 21 May 1948. Two other destroyers had in the same night investigated lights in Canea Bay reported by the naval officer in charge at Suda; the lights were onshore. The NOIC's five MTB's in

While Britain's navy had broken the back of invasion by sea, Germany's air force had broken British ability to keep the sea. Yet neither turned its success to profit on Crete. Neither comprehended its success in depth. The Germans failed to reinforce by sea, though the chances were now good; the British failed to adjust the Cretan land defenses, though the threat from the sea had diminished. Neither had precisely established the other's limitations and worked on them, though the information was available. In the air-vs.-sea struggle a stalemate of sorts had supervened. Its reverse effect on Adolf Hitler was strangest of all and may have been decisive: he now feared Britain on the sea all the more.

Maybe Hitler needed respite; maybe he wanted to avoid *Merkur's* stir and troubles while preparing for *Barbarossa*. At any rate, he spent these exciting days in the security of his beloved mountains in the Berghof—with his beloved. If a conference there with Admiral Raeder on 22 May, the day of Air against Sea, offered any clues to Führer interest or concern about Crete, they were all negative. Crete was taken for granted and only received mention once by Raeder as a needed base for eliminating the British from Alexandria and Suez. Hitler offered no comment, simply agreed, according to Raeder's record. No mention occurred of Maleme Flotilla's bitter fate of the past night—they were mountain boys from the Berghof neighborhood who had been lost—or even of its sailing or of the Navy problems connected with *Merkur*. Not a word.

For sea affairs the admiral himself was much more concerned with the sailing of the mighty *Bismarck*; this was the biggest German naval event of the war. But Raeder let it out casually that the big ship and her consort, cruiser *Prinz Eugen*, had departed from Norwegian waters near Bergen on the day before, to round north of Iceland into the Atlantic. With no more ado, the admiral's record went on to other matters, including West Africa and reinforcement of the Canary Islands; this should be speeded, he said. It gave Hitler an opening to go island-hopping again: he wanted the Azores. It was an old, professionally discredited cause that he kept harping on. In high disdain Raeder recorded, "This subject was brought up by the Führer." He could not be dissuaded by the Navy's objections: *"Führer still in favor*

Suda were sunk by air attack. Four destroyers patrolled off Heraklion also on this night. Destroyers *Decoy* and *Hero* embarked the king of Greece and company at Ayias Roumelis Bay on the south coast of Crete. They joined the Main Body and proceeded with it to Alexandria.

in order to carry out long-range bombing against America. The occasion," he said, "might arise in autumn." That meant, when he would be free, after Russia.

It is possible that this renewed wish for a far-reaching swipe at America across the Atlantic was to balance an equally wide swipe in the Pacific against Pearl Harbor. He had been urging Matsuoka and Oshima to attack Singapore during the summer. Why not Pearl Harbor in the fall? To keep the United States occupied was his mission for Japan. When Pearl Harbor came, Hitler, without staff consultation, on 11 December 1941 declared war on the United States, as though prearranged. He could talk about air-raiding America overseas, but got not a word out about Crete's sea problems or her overseas use in the Mediterranean. That water was not his game. The Raeder record omitted mention of Hitler's effort to recall the *Bismarck*. He wanted no tangles with the United States at this critical pre-Russia time. Raeder won out that *Bismarck* should continue. For Germany it was a misfortune.

Midst the mounting sorrows of 23 May Admiral Cunningham took time out to evaluate the experience of the last days and to relay to the Admiralty a straightforward summary. Perhaps it was this message that jolted London and Churchill into a barrage of demands and directions. They turned the heavy sailor hearts in Alexandria to righteous wrath. If OKL in Berlin had panicked a day or so earlier over failure to take Maleme, now it was London's turn; the truth was that the realities of Crete and the East Basin were only now getting home. Cunningham's message (Churchill, p. 292) said:

The operations of the last four days have been nothing short of a trial of strength between the Mediterranean Fleet and the German Airforce. . . . I am afraid that in the coastal area we have to admit defeat and have to accept the fact that losses are too great to justify us in trying to prevent seaborne attack on Crete. This is a melancholy conclusion, but it must be faced. As I have always feared, enemy command of the air, unchallenged by our own Airforce and in these restricted waters, with Mediterranean weather, is too great odds for us to take on except by seizing opportunities of surprise and using utmost circumspection. . . . It is perhaps fortunate *Formidable* [his one carrier] was immobilized, as I doubt she would now be afloat.

Admiralty responded:

If it were *only* a duel between the Mediterranean Fleet and the German Airforce it would probably be necessary to accept the restrictions . . . you suggest. There is however the battle for Crete. If the Fleet can prevent seaborne reinforcement . . . until Army has time to deal . . . with airborne troops, the Army may then be able to deal with seaborne attacks. It is vitally important to prevent a seaborne expedition reaching the island during the next day or two, even if this results in further losses to the fleet.

The two messages speak for themselves. How were ships to prevent a seaborne effort if they could not keep the sea? That was the gist of the admiral's message—that there was no use in sending ships out merely to get sunk. Further losses could only reduce British access to the East Basin. No duel held more significance for Britain than this one that demonstrated the need to husband her waning power at sea. The battle for Crete brought out one manifestation of the main problem: *control of and over the sea*, where needed.

This duel of May 1941 was one of many signals about declining Rule Britannia. Her sea power was out of date. She had neglected a seagoing air component. As Admiral Cunningham realized, the trial began in January near the straits of Sicily when his fleet first encountered German dive bombers. Now the test had been completed. Richthofen and Cunningham were in substantial agreement. And the next question had to be: Without power to control the sea, what was Britain?

Not everyone found the German air prospect so rosy. At *Merkur's* top the tests of air vs. sea had demonstrated to General Löhr that the 8th Corps was too weak. He wrote in his action report:

The course of the fighting demonstrated that the strength of the 8th Air Corps was insufficient for the execution of all combat tasks, since aside from the conquest of Crete, a fundamental battle of Air against Navy in a limited area had broken out. Through the Chief of Staff Luftwaffe . . . immediate transfer of reinforcement from the 10th Air Corps was ordered.

The continued prosecution of this "fundamental battle" became possible only through the arrival of two air groups from the 10th Air Corps in Italy and Sicily. Air thus maintained its edge, and with it the initiative. The opposing navy, on the other hand, could not be reinforced.

A detailed account of the word war between London and CincMed that grew out of London's panic has small use. It teaches again what the policymakers at home should never do, but the lesson will rarely be taken to heart. In the exchanges that developed, Churchill's hand is plainly discernible. It seems as though the reality, that Crete might be lost, of a sudden came home. So much brag and boast about holding the island would have to be eaten. Cunningham was told, for example, that the situation was being allowed "to drag on"; drastic action should be taken; the fleet would have to operate north of Crete by day "though considerable losses might be expected." Another fix was upon troop and material reinforcement to Creforce at this late hour. The urge achieved its peak in London orders direct to a troop ship at sea (*Glenroy*), which CincMed had recalled for good reason, to turn around and rehead for Crete. The cardinal lesson is the same as it has always been, in Cunningham's words, "stop unjustifiable interference by those ignorant of the situation." On the risking of his ships he found London's stand "singularly unhelpful. It failed most lamentably to appreciate the realities of the situation." It is an old problem that modern communications have intensified. Its amelioration will ever depend on the spirit and understanding of the men involved.

Because it had to, air-vs.-sea war held on, but far offshore. At two points back on terra firma soldiers struggled for survival in almost total isolation, oblivious of what went on in the air or at sea. It is time to catch up on Retimo and Heraklion, where grim ground fighting was making a mark.[10]

10. The Germans' official records followed British press reactions closely; often British speculation anticipated German plans. At this time German press notices refuted wide U.S. and British speculations about Crete as a trial run of Invasion England. The two propositions were more different than alike.

18. Isolation of the East

We left Colonels Sturm of the 2d Paratroop Regiment and Bräuer of the 1st Regiment, late on X-Day, each in his own lurch: Sturm bogged down west of Retimo's airstrip, Bräuer trying to set up a headquarters in the eastern approaches of Heraklion aerodrome. Neither had got far with his mission. A kindly nightfall hid them and their scattered formations as they strove to orient themselves and pump up decisive action for the dawn.

The new day, 21 May, proved grimmer still. Sturm's predicament soon grew hopeless. Pinned down under the guns of 2/11 Australian Battalion (Major Sandover) on Hill B, Sturm could not make a move; he could not communicate; he could command nothing but the handful of men huddled around him. He surrendered to a Sandover mopping-up party. *Merkur* orders on his person afforded the defenders a fresh gauge of things. The picture looked good: no more invaders were destined for this sector; only remnants of eight companies dropped east and west remained, while the center drop of one company and headquarters was almost eliminated. On the east, fragments of five companies (Kroh), about 150 men, might threaten the airstrip from Hill A, a part of which they had occupied. In the west two companies (Wiedemann) had been stopped in their drive to take Retimo proper from their strongpoint on its outskirts at Perivolia village. Lt. Colonel Campbell, commanding the defenders from Hill D facing the airstrip in right center, had ordered mopping up in the center and a dawn attack by Captain Channell to clear Hill A.[1]

Beyond the low vineyard-covered spur that formed Hill A the coastal road bent inland at the hamlet of Stavromenos. On the seaward side of this turn stood an olive-oil factory, made prominent by its tall chimney and thick masonry walls. On 20 May the complex of vineyard hill, factory, and hamlet had, except for one strongpoint on the hill, become German territory. Major Kroh planned to launch a dawn attack to take the airstrip. His opponents were ahead of him. Before Kroh's men could get going, Captain Channell at 0430 on 21 May drove in from the hill's south extension in company strength. The two drives collided head on and stopped. Shortly after 0500 Captain Moriarty, sent to support Channell, came on him wounded and his men stalled. Moriarty reorganized at once for renewed attack. On hearing his report Campbell brought over additional troops from Hill D, but left Moriarty in command. He arranged four attack groups and pushed them off downhill toward the olive-oil factory. Kroh and his men gave ground, retreated to the shelter of the factory compound. There they stayed on the defensive, supplied through a drop zone on the coast, four miles northeast. A Greek Army detachment dispatched to this flank by Campbell held the Germans in check. Kroh was bottled up. During the morning, Luftwaffe supporting planes had killed sixteen of his men. He wanted no more such help.

On the opposite flank Captain Wiedemann's two companies had likewise suffered casualties from their own planes through ground signals made by Sandover from his captured code; this kept the Germans from trying to go east. On the west Wiedemann was blocked by hardy Cretan gendarmes astride the coastal road just outside the town. Another Greek Army formation sent by Campbell restrained the German south of Perivolia; he was no better off than Kroh. Retimo attack force, leaderless, bottled up, knew not what to do.

Nor did General Student in Athens. The dead silence of the Retimo force worried him. Observers from the air had no answer: the strip, they knew, was hostile, and they had an idea some of their own might be locked up at each end; yet details were confusing and ground sig-

1. Documentation for Retimo and Heraklion is scarce on both sides for lack of records. The defense story must lean heavily on participant recollection. The attack is treated briefly by the high commands in war diaries and action reports. This writing attempts to reconcile the British and German accounts. Errors and inaccuracies abound on both sides. The 5th Mountain Division lived longest on Crete and had opportunity to piece together a reasonable reconstruction.

nals seemed unreliable. Schemes for bringing relief went the staff rounds. If there were only a tank or two to break in from the west or east! No solution could be settled upon, but the tank notion grew.

In contrast, Creforce could take heart at Retimo's outright success. Campbell reported the airfield safe and the attackers contained, and announced his plan for mopping up early on the 22d. The growing horde of prisoners of war might even become a problem. While all of this was welcome news to General Freyberg, and while the fate of his men was a source of anxiety to General Student, the sector's time had passed. Its strategic significance had shrunk when the main lines of attack and defense were established elsewhere. Thirty-five miles farther east, Heraklion was different; it had more to offer, to defenders and attackers alike.

At least the attack had a functioning command there and good radio touch. Colonel Bräuer gave his ambitious plans for 21 May. Maybe his incisive language dispelled some of the gloom around 11th Air Corps headquarters. Attack on the town and aerodrome, he reported, was set for daylight, from east and west. This was not, however, what came about. In the night Major Walther's 1st Battalion passed the Bräuer command post in driblets; the Major urged them on to link up with Blücher at the edge of the field. The confused files struggled forward in the dark. At first light these men were smothered under furious blasts of machine-gun and artillery fire from Black Watch and supporting guns. Blücher and party were overrun at noon; he was killed. Those that could, tumbled back down the hill. In the afternoon these survivors of the 1st Battalion and a few strays from Burkhardt's 2d Battalion collected half a mile southeast of the airfield on AMES Ridge and began to dig in.

The 3d Battalion, under Major Schulz, southwest of the town, had failed to attack at 0700 as supposedly ordered. The word had not reached Schulz but he had intercepted messages about the 8th Air Corps bombing attack on Heraklion and decided to drive on the town under its cover. Two prongs of his effort were to pass through the thick Venetian walls at the northwest and west gates and go through the town and out the east gate in attack on the airfield. Leutnant Becker and his 2d Company would force the northwest gate, bear left toward the water, seize the port there, and push on to await Leutnant Egger at the east gate. Egger and his 10th Company would meanwhile have forced the west gate, looped through the south end of town, and turned toward the east exit. Both companies were to pass through and then attack the airfield. The plan has interest for its pretentious scope. Yet the town phase came near succeeding. Nothing is said about the bombing prelude, but both parties attacked at 0930, got through their gates, and went to work on the local defenders. Becker reached the port's separate ramparts and there he stalled, unable to breach them. Soon Egger hove into sight in retreat before determined Greeks. By mid-afternoon when the combined parties were running short of munitions, a defending major offered to surrender. At this point the arrival of two fresh British platoons broke up the parley. The defense stiffened. At dark Schulz withdrew his men to the battalion strongpoint outside, where they had started. Night sheltered another failure and its exhausted participants.

No action whatever could be launched on 22 May, so battered and weary were Bräuer's troops. He failed to mount a single move. And this marked the end of Heraklion's meaning; it was out, just like Retimo. The defenses had held at these points and the attack took a decisive turn toward the Löhr plan to build up in the west and fight east. Time elapsed before the reality was conceded by General Student and his staff in Athens, for it counted as a defeat of Airborne Doctrine.

In the evening of 21 May when the landing of transport planes on Maleme was assured, Student "regarded the crisis . . . as surmounted," and in this buoyant mood he advised Ringel of the switch back to the original plan: "If the attack against the airfield [Heraklion] succeeds tomorrow [22 May], the 5th Mountain Division is to land by air transport. . . . *Hold fast to the old prepared plan.*" Where this confidence stemmed from is unclear—possibly from reports of Schulz in the town—but most probably, Heraklion had not a thing to do with it. Rather it was the engaging prospect in the general's mind, now that Maleme landings were going full tilt, of getting over to the island and running the show himself. He could relegate Retimo and Heraklion to their intended ancillary roles while he pushed on to victory at Canea-Suda.[2]

This pleasant prospect faded. In the night of 21 May came the shock of the flotilla disaster, followed on 22 May by the full-blown Air-against-Sea trial of strength. And at Heraklion there was a total absence of ground combat; Bräuer reported rest and reorganizing. At the news, the 5th Mountain Division Diary remarked, "Thus it is not

2. 11th FK Kreta; 5th MD War Diary and action reports.

possible for landings to be made on the aerodrome during 22 May," nor later either for that matter. Now both Retimo and Heraklion lapsed into sideshows, despite continued tough fighting and dying. The 11th Air Corps called it "binding the opposing forces and preventing use of the airfields" by the Royal Air Force. Small comfort to 1200 corpses.[3]

3. There was no good reason for Retimo's isolation. If only one of Vasey's battalions at Georgeoupolis had been sent east to support Campbell, as Vasey had first planned, instead of to Suda Sector, Retimo town could quickly have been freed, and along with it also the airstrip. All battalions would then have been available to the defense of Suda Sector. These experienced and by now blooded fighters could have arrived in time for the crucial Battle of Galatas. After the fact, such shifts on paper are easy to see.

19. Maleme to Galatas

Counterattack: 22 May 1941

Late in the evening of 21 May Captain Bartels, peering seaward from his landing beach, has a sudden start: a light offshore, there another, and a third. Beyond Cape Spatha shafts of light pierced the dark, swept around, then steadied; and now come gun flashes. Automatically the captain counts the seconds: one and two and three and four. . . . The report's arrival is a low rumble that holds on. Out on the water flaming beacons appear. Bartels knows their meaning; so do the signalmen around him; so does ex-sailor Ramcke at Sturmregiment. It means he will get no support by sea. Even the paratroopers on a hill up from Prison Valley see and know the dismal truth. German groans must have matched the British cheers all along the shore. Yet the cheers were strongly mixed with fresh apprehensions about landings from the sea. Already the previous night Captain Morse at Suda had sent out an All Ships alarm: "Lights in bay west of Candia." (It probably should have read Canea, rather than Candia—another name for Heraklion.) To him the lights must have meant that a landing from the sea was about to begin. But it did not begin then, nor this night. These lights, all German watchers realized, could only mean landings on the bottom of the sea. In fact, fear of British naval action against the shore induced Ramcke to order his force reserve out to patrol the waterline. Fear of landings or counter action infected everyone.[1]

1. Ramcke GB; Ramcke VSJ; Sturmregt B; Schmitt; Heydte, pp. 108–9. The

By midnight the scare had subsided on the German shore; the patrol under Schmitt was recalled and sent to support the 4th Battalion (Gericke) on the east rim of the airfield. Schmitt took his anti-tank men around a British Bren carrier that suddenly appeared. Then he made other contacts. Activity was on the rise all along; 22 May's combat started with a wholly unintentional frontal collision. If Wednesday 21 May had been the uneasy Day of Crisis, its successor became the explosive Day of Action—action, counter action, and lightning change, afloat and ashore. Much was at stake, much was decided.

The 11th Air Corps wanted Sturmregiment to get an offensive under way against Canea and so ordered. Ramcke must have known about it before leaving the mainland, and for this reason the choice of commander in the west probably settled upon him: he was a man who would get things going. But on arrival he found a shocking state of affairs: no one in command, confusion, absolute shortages, dead-tired troops on the point of giving up. Reconnaissance showed that the defenders could outflank the advance along the coast from the high ground in the south that they already occupied. The only credible solution was to outflank them in turn by pressure still farther south and swift close-up on any forced withdrawals. So Ramcke sent Colonel Utz and his mountain troops south to pressure the British hill positions.

What Ramcke could not know was that the British were mounting the long-awaited counterattack. Although counterattack was the core of Creforce defense policy, which the detailing and reinforcing of 4 Brigade for the counterattack role exemplified, now when the policy was to be implemented, it took the form of a patchwork job under 5 Brigade to restore its territory, rather than an all-out effort to push the Germans into the sea. The decision to hold the area of 23 Battalion, made by the three battalion commanders at three in the morning of 21 May, had apparently set the pace. Brigadier Hargest at Platanias had accepted this decision in reporting it to Division an hour later. It was not until 1000 that he is reported talking to Puttick about counterattack. Who first raised the subject is unrecorded, but it is clear that Hargest wanted to wait for the cover of dark. He asked for a fresh battalion plus 120 soldiers to replace 28 Battalion around the head-

---

German intercept record of British radio traffic shows two messages about landings; the second reported that four ships were landing troops in the bay west of Candia (Candia for Canea). The ships must have been Admiral Glennie's, seeking out Maleme Flotilla.

quarters at Platanias so that 28 Battalion could join the counterattack. Maps taken from German prisoners suggested that the enemy might strike at Platanias from the south; and then of course there was always the menace from the sea. It was growing obsessive.

A Creforce conference in the afternoon of 21 May confirmed the Hargest-Puttick outline of a two-battalion effort in the night: 20 Battalion from division reserve and 28 Battalion from 5 Brigade, supported by three light tanks. For assault preparation fire, the Navy and the RAF would bombard the airfield. In division reserve, 20 Battalion would be relieved before Canea by 2/7 Australian Battalion from Georgeoupolis (an arrangement that fouled up the whole works). As the conference broke up, the arrival of a message, probably from Cairo, stirred new alarm. According to Brigadier Inglis it ran something like this: "Enemy attempting seaborne landings beaches west of Canea tonight. Navy informed." Two hours later Creforce passed the word on to Division in such forcible language about its responsibility to crush seaborne attack that Brigadier Puttick insisted on almost a man-for-man relief of 20 Battalion before it could move to the line of departure for counterattack. The delays became cumulative and, together with fresh invasion scares, blunted the spear of counterattack before it could be launched. Counterattack had fallen into competition with repulse of sea landings. In short: standing by for the landings took precedence over regaining Maleme Field, where the Germans already had a functioning airhead.[2]

In the early evening (21 May) Brigadier Hargest expounded his plan at his Platanias headquarters to the commanders concerned, except for Major Burrows of 20 Battalion, who was trying to get relieved as division reserve. Hargest's proposition was a straight-ahead frontal drive, which he probably thought was about all that would be practicable at night. The three tanks (Farran) were to lead along the coastal road, flanked on the right (north) by 20 Battalion (Burrows), whose task was to punch through and take the airfield, and on the left in the hills to the south by 28 Battalion (Lt. Colonel Dittmer) whose goal was Hill 107. Hop-off was scheduled for midnight from a line 300 yards west of Platanias, depending on 20 Battalion's arrival. Pirgos village, two miles from the start, was the first objective; after taking it, the advance would halt to rest and re-form before pushing on to the final objectives. (Pirgos included Maleme 2, south of the road.) Once the airfield and Hill 107 were in hand, 20 Battalion was

2. Davin, pp. 191–99, 206; Pringle and Glue, pp. 95–117.

to redeploy on a line from Maleme 1—old Maleme village—to Hill 107, so as to command the airfield, while 28 Battalion would return to its post at Platanias. Meanwhile 21 Battalion was to extend the new front line southwestward from Hill 107, and as an afterthought, 23 Battalion would mop up in the rear of the attack. Noteworthy is the return to commanding the airfield from the slopes of Hill 107—a stance which had already failed once. In end effect, 20 Battalion merely replaced 22, and from distant Platanias Hargest would be no more able to command than before. There were other counts against the plan: its lack of strength in depth; the lack of reconnaissance in force to explore and clear the approaches to Pirgos; the lack of orders about command in the field—no one had charge; neither battalion commander could order the tanks or the other. Nevertheless, here toward dawn of 22 May both contenders for Crete hoped to take the offensive in designs destined to collide head on; and if they ground to a halt, the Germans had only to hold and grow stronger, whereas the New Zealanders had to advance while growing weaker. The Germans hold the airfield from the flats, not from the heights of Hill 107, though they occupy the hill. To complete the uncertain picture, there is poor ragtag Maleme Flotilla, an odd caricature of a fleet in being. All commands along the shore see it burn, yet it still exerts power, still causes fatal delay to 5 Brigade's counterattack. Perhaps three hundred drowned mountaineers of the flotilla became the pivotal price paid for Crete.

After midnight Brigadier Hargest still watches the fireworks at sea while he waits, at the little Platanias schoolhouse on the coastal road, for 20 Battalion. He cannot account for the delay; his confidence oozes away with the passage of time and his wonderings. What chance has the attack? Burrows knows nothing about the terrain of the plan. It will be hard. At last Burrows arrives, alone; his C and D Companies pull in, half an hour later. He takes in his orders and huddles with Dittmer, who has been waiting long at the ready. Burrows makes his own dispositions, proposes that they take off without waiting for the rest of his battalion; his A, B, and Headquarters Companies can follow in the wake of C and D. Hargest is unsure. He rings Division to ask if the attack "must go." The answer comes back, "It must." And it does, in its reduced strength. About two hours of indispensable dark remain.

Dittmer and his Maoris advance rapidly through Engineer Detachment into the edge of 23 Battalion country. Burrows advances with his C Company, paralleling the coastal road; his D Company on the far right follows the seashore. These men have never been here before; not only is the country doubly strange in the dark but also the men know nothing of 5 Brigade's wire and other obstacles. It is their commander's first action. Almost at once pockets of paratroops are encountered. The fire fight begins and rages confusedly, hot and heavy. It reaches the three light tanks rattling along the road single file. Lieutenant Farran rides the second tank; he strives to keep up with 28 Battalion on his left. Farther back, Burrows and C Company uncover nest after nest of paratroopers in the scrub growth and holed up in houses. Many are caught with trousers and shoes off. "The Germans were helpless in the dark," said Captain Upham of C Company. Their casualties are heavy; prisoners are sent back to Brigade. They must have belonged to Leutnant Nägele's drop of yesterday. Their resistance stiffens as the advance approaches Pirgos, and darkness is fading. It is broad day 22 May when the tanks halt at a crossroads only a mile and a half out to talk things over. Captain Dawson is there from Brigade to see how the battle goes; to him the tankmen seem "very dubious of the whole show." He is unable to find Burrows and returns to Brigade to report, "The situation seemed unstable and unsatisfactory."

But if these surprised Germans belong to Nägele, back of him toward the airfield is Gericke with the remnants of his 4th Battalion of Sturmregiment, reinforced on his left (north) by Kiebitz's company and on his right by Schmitt's antitank outfit. It is placed exactly right for the attacking spearhead. Ramcke has already made his round to familiarize himself and urge his men forward. Above all else he stresses to hold, and if the foe falters, to follow fast. He goes on to see Stentzler up toward Hill 107.[3]

Any reliance the British placed on the tanks was misplaced here as everywhere else. Soon after the contact with Captain Dawson the tank thrust collapsed before Pirgos. Farran saw his leader hit and set afire. The driver managed to turn off and quench the fire, but the mortally wounded sergeant and gunner could not be freed. By this time the sky overhead throbbed with planes, screaming and strafing at

3. British sources are Davin, pp. 215–30; Farran, pp. 94–98; Cody, pp. 91–93. German sources are 11th FK Kreta; Ramcke GB; Schmitt. Accounts from the two sides are difficult to mesh. Confusion of names Pirgos and Maleme tangles the tales. Maleme 1, the inland old Maleme, belonged to Stentzler up toward Hill 107, while Maleme 2 on the coastal road belonged to Gericke, Schmitt, and company. Pirgos proper lay a quarter of a mile east of Maleme 2. It was now coming into dispute.

anything that moved. Farran, with his two heavy machine guns jammed, took cover in a bamboo thicket and thereby disabled his tank. The third tank was still able. Major Burrows said the infantry would continue; Farran was to follow when he could. Later, when hard pressed, Burrows did send a Bren carrier back for tank support; none responded (Davin, pp. 217, 218).[4]

New Zealand infantry carried on into Pirgos on both sides of the road and there experienced its toughest ditch-to-ditch, house-to-house combat, Major Burrows admired the Maori advance on his left, which helped Upham and his C Company forward. "Two Bofors pits were overrun and the guns destroyed," wrote Upham, and concluded that one more hour of dark to fight in would have brought his company through the airfield. Yet when he had got through Pirgos it was already 0700. Things were pushing toward crisis; Pirgos had cost too much time. Burrows began to sense it. D Company on his far right was unclear; B Company under Captain Rice was closing up behind D, whose Lieutenant Maxwell soon checked in to say that he was the only officer left on his feet. He was told to carry on. His later account tells how close the attack came to recapturing the airfield and how far from it:

We reached the clear part of the drome, all right—there were stacks of aircraft. . . . fired two shots into one . . . made a mess of it. Broad daylight—at this time we had come under most intense mortar and MG fire with the clear ground of the drome in front of us. I pulled the Coy back about 100 yards back into the cover of some bamboos [Davin, p. 218].

Rice saw D Company pull back and so reported to Burrows, who told him to hold his own B and D Company where they were. Fresh fire on the right, which Rice reported at once, with request to withdraw, decided Burrows. He could see it would be impossible to take his first objective, the airfield, and have anything left for the second, the line on the slope of Hill 107. If he could now get back of the Maoris (28 Battalion) to take over the second objective, should they achieve Hill 107, he would have a position from which the airfield could be taken later.

4. Why no more than three tanks were committed to this obvious chance to turn the German tide is hard to answer. They were bound to have casualties. Those left behind in Inglis's force reserve could not repulse a landing from the sea near Canea. Cairo sent its cast-off junk in tanks, and artillery, the other serious German shortage. Creforce deserved the best, if holding the island was sincerely meant. What could be more important than depriving the Germans of their one beach or air head? The niggardly allotment of three tanks to this main counterattack is as incomprehensible as the weak allotment of infantry.

On the opposite side, Schmitt of the Antitank Force stands out; he professes to carry the bulk of the load. Though close to the road, his actions swung wide. By 0500 he sensed that counterattack was under way against Pirgos and Maleme 2. His whole force and part of the Kiebitz command joined in the confused melee that sawed back and forth until after 0800. By 0830 he could record the power of the opposing drive broken, and added his own concern to trail the attackers back through Pirgos. He failed because of British "protective fires." His 1st Company had to be reinforced by the 3d Company; together they regain Pirgos. The time is 0930. Thereupon a troop of mountaineers, fresh out of a plane, screams for help on the airfield's far-eastern edge near the sea. Schmitt sends the last reserve to stiffen the mountain troops. The alarm may have been 20 New Zealand Battalion's A Company, which reached the airfield while covering B Company's withdrawal. Captain Rice of B Company became a casualty. Schmitt seems sure of himself in a belief that the field was made safer by this morning's work.[5]

The outlook from the command post of Colonel Dittmer and his Maoris was even less encouraging than that from 20 Battalion. By hard fighting the Maoris' drive south of the road reached points from which the streets of Pirgos and Maleme 2 could be enfiladed, and this helped 20 Battalion greatly; yet from those vantage points the probes up toward Hill 107 failed, though parties from 23 and 22 Battalions joined the fight. Daylight overhauled and cut short all these brave efforts; Major Dyer, of D Company, 28 Battalion, set them forth (Davin, p. 220):

> We must get forward . . . mortars and bombs cracking round us. . . . We collected in small groups and worked forward. Men were hit . . . the din of fighting incessant. There seems to be a German machine gun behind all the trees.
> Maoris in a scattered mob under the trees going forward crying Ah! Ah! and firing at the hip.

Not much of a forward line was gained for Burrows and the remnants of 20 Battalion to get back of. Yet Dittmer thought the fight could still be pressed. In the afternoon he returned to 23 Battalion for support to renew the assault. His brother battalion commanders demurred. All that could be done, in their opinion, was to hold what ground they

---

5. In the Ramcke reorganization of 21 May, the Schmitt command is listed as an independent command directly under him. While Gericke may have been on the scene to give general direction, his record does not furnish the blow-by-blow account that Schmitt's does.

had and stop the constant infiltration. Earlier in the forenoon Leckie and Andrew advised Brigade that the counterattack could not win through unless more infantry, artillery, and air support came. Now after its failure, they were all the more convinced against another attempt. Thence the rest of the day was devoted to stabilizing a line that ran south from the coastal road at the crossroads east of Pirgos, past 23 and 20 Battalions, then 28 in a gap to 21 Battalion.

Though 21 Battalion has slipped out of notice, it is not because it has been idle; in fact it had gone through a series of brisk actions on the left (south) flank and was now serving as anchor for the stabilized front there on old Vineyard Ridge. Early in the morning Allen had from that spot launched successive company attacks toward the Tavronitis back of Hill 107. In heavy combat his troops took the village at the bottom of Vineyard Ridge and pushed on in relays; by 0930 they had the Tavronitis riverbed in sight. Forward elements who came from D Company of 22 Battalion gained a look at their original defense posts. Then came disquieting news from the main attack along the coastal road. One by one Allen pulled his units back to their starting points and re-formed on the ridge. The good forenoon's work was enlivened in the early afternoon by a German call for surrender under a white flag of truce. "A German in British battle dress appeared bearing a white flag." His reception may be gathered from Colonel Allen's terse comment: "Sent a Hun with a flag of truce about his business. He was demanding surrender!" (Davin, p. 222). Neither Allen nor anyone else realized that he had opened a tender German flank to exploitation. Maybe this should have been the main effort. Instead, it went for naught.

Back at 5 Brigade in Platanias, spirits rose and fell with the small bits of real news or rumors through prisoners of war and wounded men, all fed by wishful personal speculation. The brigadier was an optimist. He could fasten his binoculars on Maleme Field and see planes landing, but also taking off in a constant stream. To him the off traffic seemed to increase in tempo and density; he counted eleven fires on the drome. At 0942 on 22 May he advised Division: "Steady flow of enemy planes landing and taking off. May be trying to take troops off. Investigating," and followed up twenty minutes later with: "From general quietness and because eleven fires have been lit on drome it appears as though enemy might be preparing evacuation. . . . Do any other reports from other sources show further evidence of this?" Division replied, "No other indications as you suggest but it is possible." With Division thus infected, Hargest sticks to his fantasy; it is obviously self-inspired by poring and straining at the airfield through glasses to glean some gem to report. The field is a dreadful jumble of burning and wrecked planes and planes landing and departing. Men are seen running toward the planes at takeoff, as though left behind—which is also reported to Division at 1130. Just before noon the odd performance climaxes with a terse message of success: "Reliable reports state aerodrome occupied by own troops line now held east side of drome." Apparently Division did nothing about the message, which was soon overtaken by events. The initiative passed to the Germans and there it stayed.[6]

Now Nothing More Can Happen!: 22–25 May 1941

General Student was not so sure about 22 May when he wrote in summary, "The heights south of Pirgos remain in possession of the tough, dourly fighting opponent." He knew that Schmitt's drive had secured Pirgos and freed the airfield from heavy rifle fire [23 Battalion] and he was firmly convinced that reinforcement over Maleme would soon make up for the deficiencies in men, weapons, and supply. And as he had held from the first, Air Fleet 4's storm over British attack from the south had proved unfounded. All these positive pieces gave him good reason to fetch a deep breath and build an urge to hop over and take command himself. Already early in the day the 11th Air Corps's chief of staff, Colonel Schlemm, accompanied by staff forward elements, had flown to Maleme to pave the way, just in case.

Schlemm landed on bustling Maleme Field at 0700 and set up shop with Ramcke and Göttsche to explain the reinforcement program. But first, he should send back a cheering bit of news: "The mass of the Light Echelon [Maleme Flotilla] has arrived Maleme after all." No one dared stop him, and off the message went, as big a boggle as Hargest's claim that the aerodrome was British-occupied. No one

6. The Hargest performance accounts for earlier 5 Brigade lapses, specifically for the failure to take in and respond to Andrew's need for support on 20 May. The brigadier now stuck to his own evaluations against field advices and those from his staff. In a message to Division at 1225 he acknowledged that the forward position was confused, saying that "officers on the ground believe enemy preparing for attack and take a serious view. I disagree, but of course they have a closer view." His reaction to reports of Germans in his rear was different; he thought they had worked up from Prison Valley toward Ayia Marina. He requested attack by the 10 Brigade to check. Uneasiness about being cut off may have been 5 Brigade's root trouble.

knows where either got his strange idea. Solid evidence quickly dispelled Schlemm's fanciful cheer and left nothing but a dampened drive for an early takeover of command by General Student. Ramcke reported the situation to Schlemm, who fully sanctioned his moves and assured him of his continued command in the west. Then Ramcke shoved off for one of his rounds at the front on the back seat of a motorcycle. He watched the 5th Mountain Division troops deplane, assemble, and pass up the Tavronitis to their work, all fully equipped, ready for combat; in sharp contrast, thought Ramcke, to the poor beset paratrooper, who must cut loose from the tangle of his parachute and assemble his arsenal under hostile fire.

Yes, business is booming at the airfield. The captured Bren carriers tow the wrecks out of the landing lane. Ju's come and go; many crack up, yet the casualties are within limits. They disgorge heavy weapons, munitions, artillery pieces, and mountaineers: on this day, three battalions of them, one engineer outfit, and a field hospital. A Captain von Richthofen has arrived to vector planes against the at last identified Creforce artillery pieces that still throw an occasional shell into the airfield. Under its dust shroud a booming airhead has come into being, a teeming base never visualized in this expanded role by the 11th Corps command, now packing up in Athens for the move to Crete.

Such a move, Generals Löhr and von Richthofen are convinced, won't do, and they say so. They agree that the commander of the 5th Mountain Division should take command as already ordered; meanwhile the 11th Corps should stay on the mainland to run logistics. The 8th Corps Chronology notes

General von Richthofen presses with all means at his disposal to have . . . General Ringel sent to Maleme to get the ground fight into a firm hand and organized. Prestige matters arise—Army versus Luftwaffe. General Jeschonnek is cut in and even Field Marshal List, commander in chief Southeast. Finally General Ringel flies to Maleme, well protected. . . . The impression now is that things will get cracking with necessary energy, clarity, and decisiveness!

Löhr rejected Student's proposal to move, in order to insure uninterrupted direction of supply and reinforcement. He hammered this home in fresh and specific orders, which required the 5th Mountain Division command and staff to fly at once to Maleme and take over. Student, set in his own views, was hard to handle, yet *Merkur* would never have gone at all without his drive and faith in himself and Airborne.[7]

In Athens at 5th Mountain Division headquarters, Omonia Plaza, General Ringel received word of his re-revised mission to assume overall "command on Crete." Transport for himself and staff is arranged in five Ju's that are to take off at 1700 on 22 May from Phaleron, Athens's seaside airport; five fighters are ready to cover the flight and landing. Having stood by since yesterday's orders to go to Heraklion, the staff is set. General Löhr is on hand to shove his old friend off; he had already explained his wishes to Ringel:

Task (1) Secure airfield Maleme.
    (2) Fight Suda Bay free.
    (3) Relieve paratroops Retimo.
    (4) Make junction with Heraklion.
    (5) Occupy the whole island.

With Löhr's farewell blessing of, "*Servus* Ringel! Goodbye, make it good!" they were off. It was a smooth flight, ending with a belly landing of Ringel's plane on the beach west of the airfield, which at the moment was under fire. The other planes landed nearby. A small reception party led the short way to headquarters on Tavronitis's west bank. Of one thing Ringel can now be sure: Crete is up to him.

He notes the drawn, worn paratroop visages, the broken, inhospitable terrain. Objectives can perhaps best be given in heights to be scaled; it is surely mountain-troop country. By dark the newest commander is ready with orders for the assembled unit commanders. In the presence of Colonel Schlemm he instructs them in a plan that diverges very little from Ramcke's. Three combat groups are constituted:

(a) *Major Schätte*, Mountain Engineer Battalion 95, will protect Maleme Field against the west and south.

(b) *Colonel Ramcke* will assemble all paratroops by battalions into one regiment and with it will secure the airfield through action eastward along the coastal road. Attack only in concert with Utz group.

(c) *Colonel Utz* will operate three mountain battalions in close touch on Ramcke's right in pushing eastward; remaining forces will go south

7. LF4 Kreta; 8th FK Chrono; 5th MD War Diary; consultation with staff members of the 11th Air Corps and with General Ringel, and correspondence with him. Ringel was the first of record to name Maleme Field a bridgehead. In his preliminary combat report "Kreta" of 4 June 1941 (5th MD CR) he for the first time calls Maleme a *Brückenkopf*, a term he later changed to *Landekopf*, "landing head." See note 4, p. 206 above.

around the enemy wing to eliminate his artillery batteries (special task).

Before leaving the mainland Ringel had heard of Heidrich's somewhat improved chances in Prison Valley, thanks to increased drops of heavy weapons and munitions. Direct communication with him from Maleme was yet to be established. Immediately on arrival, one mountain battalion had headed inland for that impressive bulge in the distance, Signal Hill, that seemed to hold the key to Canea.

Here toward the end of *Merkur*'s third day a quick survey shows there were more Germans stalled or on the defensive than on the make. Before Heraklion, Bräuer's 1st Paratroop Regiment was stopped in two pieces; at Retimo, Colonel Sturm of the 2d Regiment was a prisoner. His troops were fighting for their lives in two dwindling stands. In the far west outside Kastelli Kisamou, Mürbe's remnant had been beaten and imprisoned; and in the bottom of Prison Valley, Heidrich and the 3d Regiment were still locked in. The whole spread made a depressing picture.

Yet the images that Creforce headquarters could summon up were even more depressing. After it was clear toward midafternoon of 22 May that counterattack had failed, General Freyberg and Brigadier Puttick conferred. The result was an order for renewed counterattack, this time with the works, 4 Brigade as well as 5. On returning to get things going, Puttick found Hargest's alarm of Germans in his rear (see note 6 above) and news of Heidrich's thrusts in Prison Valley. These reports exerted a decisive influence on the course of the battle. Both originated in the valley.

The lock-up galled Colonel Heidrich; boredom, hunger, and munitions shortage depressed his men. Morale was slipping, thought Captain von der Heydte, still holding a defense line on the valley's south slope. Scavenging a captured strongpoint had produced a few cigarettes, bits of bread and cheese, and a prize diverter, a phonograph. One record lasted through an ordinary routine artillery shelling from over there where guns and men locked them in. Somehow the lock would have to be sprung. Late on 21 May, Heidrich ordered a renewed assault straight up the same Galatas spur road from the valley bottom by Major Derpa's 2d Battalion. When Derpa raised doubts about the repetition, Heidrich blew up, accused him of cowardice. Derpa spoke up for his men but got nowhere. The attack went and he with it late the next day, 22 May. That night he came back on a stretcher and died. The assault failed, but it furthered a smaller parallel drive of far greater potential.[8]

To-and-fro fighting of the day before (21 May) had been grueling enough to delimit a no man's land around two knolls on either side of the spur road, halfway down from Galatas. The knolls were Cemetery Hill on the east and Pink Hill on the west. The odd Hargest rumor about German evacuation at Maleme led Puttick to order aggressive probing for 22 May. This encouraged Kippenberger to mount a two-company attack on his left to regain 6th Greek Army positions below Cemetery Hill. He kicked off the attempt from 19 Battalion's lines about 1400 and later recorded, "After three hours of desultory scrapping in very broken ground both companies withdrew." Thereupon under air and mortar support Derpa made his bid up the spur road. On his right he confronted Russell of Divisional Cavalry; on the left, Rowe with Divisional Petrol Company above Pink Hill. Derpa pressed harder than ever over a 700-yard front. His men reached the no-man's-land knolls from which they could cover an advance into Petrol Company. It gave ground in the center; Kippenberger hurried a reserve group into the breach while he and Captain Carson took a second group over to threaten the German left flank. They were, he wrote,

abreast . . . a beautiful opening for Carson. . . . I was waiting for him to line up his men . . . to charge, when the most infernal uproar broke out . . . over an open space in the trees near Galatas came running, bounding and yelling like Red Indians about a hundred Greeks and villagers, including women and children, led by Michael Forester twenty yards ahead. It was too much for the Germans. They turned and ran. . . . We went back to our original positions.

Forrester reassembled his Hellenes behind Galatas, and "a very busy day ended."[9]

The day (22 May) had begun for Colonel Kippenberger on the happy news of Germans abandoning Maleme Airfield; it ended on a somber note of strain among the men: more of them slightly wounded, and the wounded being brought in by "three or four friends in no hurry to go back." The most fateful change came at Division late in

8. Heydte, pp. 120–22.
9. Kippenberger, pp. 58–59. Captain Forrester had been a member of the British military mission in Greece. He was given charge of the Greek troops left over from the 6th Greek Army Regiment and collected them in Galatas. These men plus the villagers made the stirring charge.

the day; it was directly chargeable to the parallel, less noticeable drive of weak company strength, alongside Derpa.

Heidrich had ordered Heilmann of the 3d Paratroop Battalion to gather his bits and pieces, add to them from the Engineer Battalion, and set out northward across Signal Hill to cut the British main artery, the coastal road. Left in the valley would be only Heydte on the south slope and a few engineers around headquarters at Mandhra near the prison. So Heilmann probed through the rough eastern slope with his new combat command of 141 men and 9 officers; his first objective was Stalos village, half a mile west of 10 Brigade's defense lines. Stranded paratroopers may have taken potshots earlier from this area at the coastal road and thus alarmed 5 Brigade. Heilmann did not enter Stalos until dawn 23 May. He was driven out by patrols of 10 Brigade, but reentered and took most of another day to reach the road. Nevertheless the early random shots, confirmed by his skirmishing, did the work of raising a fright.

Two perils bothered the defenders more than all others: invasion by sea and isolation by land. After 22 May's counterattack had failed and General Freyberg had ordered renewed attack, Puttick heard of the actions in the valley and of machine-gun fire on the main artery. He wanted 5 Brigade to renew the counterattack, but went to 4 Brigade headquarters first. There his concern deepened: 10 Brigade confirmed heavy attacks and increased activity toward the coast. Meanwhile Hargest gave notice that his men were too tired for counterattack. That was enough for Puttick; he saw both brigades in peril of isolation if the counterattack should go. These ideas he discussed with Freyberg by telephone and urged 5 Brigade withdrawal. In essence this course confirmed abandonment of Maleme and freedom for German reinforcement. For Freyberg, however, withdrawal of any kind raised harder immediate questions. Where would one withdraw to for a stand, or indeed, could one stand at all? The details of withdrawal worked out by Creforce chief of staff and Puttick at Division Headquarters evaded direct answers: "5 Brigade will withdraw night 22–23 May to a defensive post along coast between former post held by 28 Battalion [before Platanias] and North and South line through 046572." 10 Brigade was to extend westward to link up with 5. Heidrich's puny drive toward the coast had done all this through fanning the fear of isolation. No one dared think of a far worse isolation on the south shore of Crete.[10]

10. Davin, pp. 238–40; Pringle and Glue, pp. 120–21; Cody, p. 93; 11th FK

In the west, isolation also took a toll of General Ringel. His first night on Crete passed in "unreal quiet," his diarist recorded. In the gray dawn, fresh alarm thundered in from the sea. A fight was in progress out there. For forty-five minutes the general and his staff strained through glasses at the fireworks off Cape Spatha: gun flashes and searchlights, a burning hulk flared high. British destroyers were shooting up an Italian torpedo boat, concluded the wiseacres. It was of course Horbach's S-14 and Lord Louis Mountbatten's destroyers. The rest of the night passed quietly.

23 May 1941: The day broke clear and cool. Ringel sent off an up-to-the-minute report to the 11th Air Corps in Athens—"Nothing new in the west." By 0720 Ju's were landing on the airfield with heavy cargo; mountain artillery and ammunition were important items. The guns were combined into a combat group under Lt. Colonel Wittmann as a most welcome fire support addition. When little or no progress could be seen in reorganization of the fragmented paratroop units, another order was issued to expedite action. A favorable break in unification came at about 0800 in the establishment of direct radio contact with Heidrich, toward whom Utz was pressing south around Signal Hill with his mountain troops. Ramcke was to plug down the coastal road toward Platanias. A fresh force task organization brought the various groups into sensible order.

TASK ORGANIZATION

Group Ringel	Overall command
Group Utz	Three mountain battalions
Group Ramcke	All paratroops, Maleme
Group Heidrich	All paratroops, Prison Valley
Group Wittmann	All artillery
Group Schätte	Mountain engineers and all paratroops west [Kastelli Kisamou]

Ramcke's headquarters drew off and set up in a new command post west of Platanias. Already the paratroops felt the competition of the mountaineers. Ramcke gave Gericke the lead role to advance eastward on either side of the road while Stentzler kept pace in the hills;

Kreta; 5th MD War Diary. Postknowledge demonstrates that Heidrich could have been eliminated. He was vulnerable: his air supply was weak, combat air support was only fair. Troops and command were slipping. Sufficient British forces were available to wipe him out, which, had it been done, would have adversely affected the German situation at Maleme. Heidrich turned out to be exactly what General Student hoped: a thorn in the British flank. All hindsight though this may be, vigorous action could have developed possibilities.

Schmitt with his heavy weapons was to keep abreast in the center, ready to support either wing. Noting withdrawal ahead, Gericke pushed forward to the edge of the Platanias riverbed with Schmitt in line southwest of the village. There he soon made big news by finding two abandoned field pieces. Schrank, commanding the nearest battalion of the south-circling mountain troops, laid claim to the same discovery. Ramcke then halted the advance in the face of artillery fire from ahead. Apparently, not all artillery pieces had been found.

Signal Hill, that massive lump in the way ahead, impressed Ramcke; he gave it a detailed binocular reconnaissance; on the western slope he thought he could make out cleverly camouflaged defense works and recorded, "This position Monodhendhri is without question the main defense west of Canea. A frontal attack can only succeed if the mountain troops first work in over the south peak." A breakthrough here, he thought, could be the first sign of victory. His orders for the next day specified a cautious approach: Stentzler in the hills was to hold back until he knew the mountain troops farther south had outflanked the defenses ahead, and Gericke on the coast would stop altogether until ordered forward by Ramcke himself. This bulging hill mass, he felt sure, would tell the tale.

An early report to Ringel on this day, 23 May, trumpeted the incredible news that the 1st Battalion of the 85th Mountain Regiment sat on Monodhendhri's summit awaiting orders. "We catch our breath," wrote the general, "for if there they sit, all is already won." Colonel Utz undertook personal verification by motorcycle via the Platanias Valley trail at the base of the hill. Almost at once his doubts were confirmed when protective fires for his dash issued from the wrong side of his route. The 1st Battalion sat on a slightly lower peak on the west side of Platanias Valley, not on Signal Hill's summit. It looked down on them, by a few feet. But the mistake spurred the mountaineers to drive harder, now that the unbelievable, the peak undefended, seemed borne out. Two link-ups were the prescribed goals: (1) between Schury's 2d Battalion and Heilmann's paratroops in and around Stalos, and (2) between Utz and Heidrich in Prison Valley.

Without halt, the air war had been running the hard, fast pace that von Richthofen demanded, with closest linkage to ground action. He already had plane-vectoring teams on the ground and dispatched in addition Leutnant Gerlach with communicators and Leutnant Döling of operations to Ringel. Staffs and air operating forces felt the strain. Stuka Group Brücker on Scarpanto had but four operable planes left. Jeschonnek ordered replacements; Scarpanto became an advanced airfield for the main concentration on Rhodes. Late on 23 May the long-looked-for transfer of "a swarm of fighters to Maleme" was attempted in the middle of clutter from over 110 wrecked Ju's and numerous shell holes. The transfer proved "totally impossible," Air Fleet 4's report to the contrary six months later notwithstanding.

RAF actions, uncoordinated with British sea or ground efforts seemed desperate, futile. Had the planes at night coordinated their bombardments of Maleme with ship's gunfire from sea, something might have been achieved. The random bombing did nothing.

At the end of 23 May Ringel collected his thoughts and recorded, "On the whole the operations have run off favorably," and the greatest bugbear, logistics, all by air, had kept abreast of the game. For 24 May he intended to hold at Platanias on the left, to advance in the center and on the far right on either slope of Prison Valley to the level of Galatas, and when reinforcements permitted, to attack toward Canea. Also on his list were: "Seize Kastelli Kisamou" and "Scout out Palaiokhora on the south coast."[11]

These days made names—each new day after the break-in felt as if it could be the last. To the attackers: the unproductive X-Day of 20 May followed by interminable crises over Maleme Flotilla and the expected British counterattack on 21 May; the spectacular sea-air combat and British counterattack of 22 May. It signaled a change. And now, the day of decision, 23 May 1941. The West has been won. Its finality was demonstrated by its successor, 24 May.

Ringel's satisfaction stopped short. The 11th Air Corps objected to his plan for 24 May. Student wanted more action toward Suda to cut off the British retreat on Retimo, so that relief could be brought there to his silent paratroops. He was being egged on by optimistic hints from Ramcke about "plunging on after the broken defenders." Ringel's plan stuck, though in fact, a drive along the coast could have produced a sensation, for 5 Brigade had been in trouble at Platanias before noon of the 23d, and within the next two hours Creforce decided to withdraw to a new Divisional line before Galatas. Close pursuit might have cut up the retreat and redeployment all in one.

11. 5th MD War Diary; Ringel HG, pp. 134–39. Reflecting on these days later, he wrote, "My troops crawled over land that the devil created in anger . . . man by man, overloaded, gasping, bathed in sweat." Motored vehicles could not have done it; it took men. "Sweat saves blood": it was another Division motto.

During the morning (23 May) Kippenberger at 10 Brigade made another round to check his ramparts and his men. Above him on Signal Hill in plain sight, Germans went about their business of preparing assault. There was not a thing he could do to interfere. An uncomfortable conclusion bore in on him—10 Brigade is in no condition to meet the heavy attacks that must come soon. At midday he so reported to Division and very promptly 18 Battalion received orders to relieve Composite Battalion on the hill. The worry grew under a fierce Luftwaffe preparatory blasting. (It was the prelude of the full support that Ringel had urged.) In the British command the thought occurred of more paratroop drops; none came. As Kippenberger now watched dazed men of 20 Battalion, his old command, pass through to the rear from their counterattack ordeal of the day before, he for the first time smelled approaching defeat. He shook it off and returned to his local duty: to hold the main front line. Division issued the orders; the moves would take place this night.

The trial of a last stand before Canea drew closer. The position was as ill suited as ever; but now its defense had grown frighteningly compulsive. Even if it held, could the German tide be reversed? The cause had long before been lost in neglect of the grim business of the ground fight. It went begging.

RAF planes lighted up the night of 23–24 May with flares and bombs on Maleme Field; moreover, fighters landed at Heraklion. Report of them caused a stir at Air Fleet 4. General Löhr saw his command of the air menaced. Fresh orders followed for paratroop attacks by Bräuer's command to seize, or at least deny, the Heraklion aerodrome. This alarm was more than balanced in the strategic scales by the consummation of German unity on the ground in the west: troops from Utz and Heidrich joined forces on the slopes of Signal Hill, and the two commanders met at Mandhra. Combat patrols from 10 and 4 New Zealand Brigades had forced out Heilmann's advance guard on 23 May at Stalos. After the New Zealanders drew back, the Germans reentered the village and went on toward the coastal road. By the time they reached it, 5 Brigade had already passed.

Colonel Utz promoted the meeting with Heidrich on 23 May. In a motorcycle sidecar he wound his way farther up Platanias Valley. The flat, barren plateau of Alikianou, its water reservoir and electric plant, came into view. There he turned down Prison Valley road and soon was halted by posted paratroopers. They could not believe their eyes and ears—a German Colonel—but directed him to a few houses on the slope west of the Prison. It was Mandhra, and there came Heidrich, followed by staff, toward him proffering a cigar—one of his last two. He could hardly get out: "Good, you've come!" The 3d Paratroop Regiment was sprung. His host prepared a feast of burnt chicken. He was just as incredulous about mountain troops as his men.[12]

Ringel refused to crowd his luck. He stuck to his intention for 24 May: to hold on the coast (Ramcke), to push forward in the center, to seal the junction of Utz, Heidrich, and Ramcke, and to swing down Prison Valley on the extreme right (Krakau's 85th Mountain Regiment) towards Galatas. The newest British defense line from the Turkish fort across the valley and up west of Galatas was unknown, and the valley entry to Canea plain received no particular notice. Events soon cleared the scene.

In conformity, Ramcke on the left held Gericke in check astride the coastal road. By 0800 (24 May) mountain troops could be made out on the slopes of Signal Hill; Stentzler's 2d Paratroop Battalion joined them, whereat Ramcke released Gericke with his newly acquired heavy weapons. His van quickly passed through Platanias and then Ayia Marina, half a mile inland. By early afternoon Gericke's troops were shaking the hands and slapping the shoulders of Heilmann's road blockers. This time it was paratrooper meeting paratrooper in the latest junction that certified the continuity of the offense in the field, from the impassable highlands in the south to the sea in the north. There on the coast the Germans stood before the northern anchor of Creforce's latest defense line. The name of the place was Staliana Khania.

Gericke went over to the defensive for the night (24 May). Stentzler was in reserve, and nearby was Ramcke in a new command post, ready for 25 May. Radio traffic with Group Ringel stood at an all-time low (they aren't speaking). Ramcke made no bones about his independence and confidence in his command of a reconstituted Sturmregiment, supported by a combined mountain-airborne artillery group. And it was on this artillery group, commanded by one of his officers, that Ringel had to depend for news of the situation on the left.[13]

Meanwhile Utz's men had combed over Signal Hill and cleared the picture. The hill was indeed unoccupied, and it could now make a useful springboard for pouncing on the more clearly outlined

12. Utz told the story to Fleckher and Dobiasch, pp. 101–2.
13. Sturmregt B; 11th FK Kreta; Sturmregt TB; 5th MD War Diary.

Galatas position. The British works and wires gaped wide open. To probe still closer, Utz sent his 2d Battalion toward Stalos and the 1st toward Galatas during the afternoon. News of this encouraged Ringel to believe that Galatas might be taken before dark. But the tests merely established the defense strength and offense need of air neutralization before assault. That recommendation was adopted for 25 May. The 5th Mountain Division War Diary summary at this point recognized the Galatas line as the last stand before Canea, which the combined forces were to seal off on the south in order to move against the second major objective, Suda Base, with the southern wing. This wing would at the same time cut off the route of British retreat on Retimo. That the defenders would attempt this was constantly stressed.

REPORT OF 24 MAY 1941 BY COLONEL UTZ, MOUNTAIN REGIMENT 100

FROM: Mountain Regiment 100, Electric Works, Ayia, 24 May 1800
TO: 5th Mountain Division

1. Strong enemy position Galatas (6 machine guns on west side, 2 guns) in well-constructed fieldworks identified. Wire obstacles and barriers established. Enemy position runs north from Galatas to the sea and south over road to the vicinity of Pirgos.

Enemy established in Alikianou (British, Greek, and many snipers). Reconn leader was shot in the place.

2. Because of the established strength of the position, attack on Galatas dropped out 24 May; it would in any case, because of shortage of time, have been a hurried effort.

3. Attack on Galatas will be carried out on 25 May by 2d Battalion from northwest and north, by 1st Battalion from west.

I propose attack early afternoon to permit insuring artillery support and coordination with Group Heidrich and Group Ramcke.

4. For support I hold necessary:

(*a*) Strong Stuka preparation on Galatas;

(*b*) Combining of all artillery before start of attack and attachment of two artillery sections to this regiment;

(*c*) Simultaneous attack by Group Ramcke on enemy position north of Galatas and attack by Group Heidrich on enemy line running from Galatas to Pirgos, with the aim of at least eliminating, by tying down, outflanking of the attack on Galatas.

5. Galatas is most probably the backbone of the last switch position before Canea. Readiness of strong forces for immediate exploitation of success at Galatas by means of a penetration into Canea is therefore desirable. . . .[14]

14. Ringel to Ansel, Germany, 1960; 5th MD War Diary; Ringel Ms.

This final written report for the day formed the basis for most of 25 May's action. The message had to go by hand to Ringel on the Tavronitis.

While Utz thought of pushing through to Canea, Ringel had in mind sealing the city off and passing on to Suda. The arrival of the Utz message lifted a load from Ringel. Of the occasion he wrote in 1947, "The overall view on the evening of 24 May provided a complete and clear picture for me." On the basis of Utz's report he prepared an attack order and released it with a sigh of relief, musing meanwhile, "Now, nothing more can happen!" ("Jetzt kann nichts mehr passieren!") It was only a question of time, and not so much time at that.

Ringel checked off the tasks accomplished during his two full days of command with great satisfaction. Word arrived that his command would no longer be independent: General Student was to arrive early on the 25th. If only he could wait until after tomorrow's battle!

The winning of far-western Crete had still to be accomplished. It entailed two tasks: seizure of Kastelli Kisamou and occupation of Palaiokhora on the south coast, opposite Kastelli. A detachment from the 55th Motorcycle Rifle Battalion (last noticed at Platamon and Peneus Gorge) was dispatched south over the stony track on the left bank of the Tavronitis toward Palaiokhora. The mythical Major Buck on motorcycles met fire from both sides as he advanced south. At noon 24 May the troop leader, Major Schäcke, reported stumbling progress against the snipers; by nightfall he had established that, contrary to reports, no British force was anywhere in the area.

Kastelli Kisamou was more easily accessible and real. Long ago on X-Day the men of the 1st Greek Army Regiment, coached by Major Bedding and a small party of 19 New Zealand Battalion, had foiled Leutnant Mürbe's paratroop attack by 73 men. About 50, including Mürbe, had been killed and 15 wounded, and the rest were taken prisoner. Isolated at the end of the line with only BBC broadcasts to inform him, Bedding sat tight awaiting further attack from the east. It came on 24 May at 0830 when Stukas opened a furious blasting. In the uproar some German prisoners broke free, found arms, and caught Bedding and Baigent, his assistant, going out to rally their men. Now on their own, the Greek soldiers fought hard against Major Schätte of the 95th Mountain Engineer Battalion, reinforced with antitank elements. His casualties were heavy and he could not close in until near noon. By 1430, when Bedding had just about convinced his captors that their lot was hopeless, Schätte broke through the defenses. Kastelli Kisamou fell; the German now had a small port. Captain Bartels surveyed it for unloading two tanks to be brought over in a towed lighter from Piraeus. They were wanted to relieve Retimo paratroops.

If Major Bedding found the BBC short of Crete news, it was for good reason. A story at sea overshadowed Crete—the story of the *Bismarck* on the prowl in the Atlantic. She was making gloomy news for Britons and glad news for Germans. Toward evening of 24 May General Student radioed the latest exciting item to his command in Crete: "H.M.S. *Hood* sunk by *Bismarck*." On her decks sea cadets capered in a snake dance of victory. Far at the other end of the line in the Mediterranean, a like exuberance had moved German Air zealots to cheer their victory over the Royal Navy.

Surveillance around Crete from sea had fallen off sharply after 23 May; it was in part due to the replenishment of ships at the Alexandria base. However, two destroyers that made a swift sweep of the north coast on the night of the 23d, to deliver munitions and meager reinforcements to Suda, were followed the next night by a cruiser-destroyer patrol. Admiral Cunningham, who felt he could no longer attempt to blockade Crete's north coast without prohibitive losses, had to deal with London's woefully weak understanding and insistence that he must accept the risks. The risks were not at all the question. Cunningham meant that taking losses without compensatory strategic gains was folly. Nevertheless, on 25 May he sent a strong force to sweep the danger area, and at noon the same day dispatched a task force that included the carrier *Formidable* (8 planes) to attack Scarpanto's air base. Heavy bomb damage to *Formidable*, destroyer *Nubian*, and battleship *Barham* was the result.

London pressure on Cairo to reinforce Creforce on the ground mounted with the increasing gravity of the situation. Because of near bomb misses General Freyberg moved to naval headquarters at Suda. The Naval Officer In Charge (NOIC) was deep in planning evacuation. On the night of 26 May he docked the last installment of troops and supply from Egypt. The time for reinforcement was long past.

Just these outside pressures were the ones hardest to bear. No war has ever been free of these Johnny-come-lately solutions, but their harm can be minimized if the authors at home must deal through one supreme commander on the scene. German possession of a secure Maleme airhead was plain, yet the London chiefs of staff seemed ignorant of this. A message on 24 May to Wavell and Cunningham ran:

> ... If we stick it out the enemy's effort may peter out ... imperative reinforcements in greatest strength possible be sent as soon as possible ... to ensure destruction of enemy already landed before they can be seriously reinforced ... great risks must be accepted.

The message must have been inspired by one from Churchill to Wavell on the day previous:

> Crete must be won ... fighting must be maintained indefinitely. ... Hope you will reinforce Crete every night to the fullest extent. Is it not possible to send more tanks and reconquer any captured Aerodrome? Following for General Freyberg: The whole world is watching your splendid battle, on which great events turn.

The effusive praises, designed to encourage and cheer, succeeded only in doing quite the contrary through their ignorant absurdities.

Loose talk about reinforcement further confused a rapidly deteriorating supply situation. Without supply, nothing could be done; operations would cease. Such thoughts were already intruding on Freyberg before 24 May as the NOIC began advance preparations for evacuation. In Freyberg's later report he recalled:

> At this stage I was quite clear in my own mind that the troops would not be able to last much longer against the continuation of air attacks. ... We were gradually being driven back on our base areas, the loss of which would deprive us of our food and ammunition. ... I really knew at this time that there were two alternatives, defeat in the field and capture, or withdrawal.

There was no way out.

The two top commanders on Crete, Freyberg and Ringel, came to this conclusion on the very same day. While Freyberg's had to be the sorrowful decision for "withdrawal," Ringel's rang out in relief: "Now nothing more can happen!" On this day also the German press for the first time broke its total silence about Crete with fresh cries of another smashing victory.[15]

15. Churchill, pp. 292–303; Long, pp. 241–43; Davin, 274–94. Davin describes the enormous supply problem and the many solutions proffered. They added up to increased frequency of small deliveries direct to Suda for the improvement of the road leading from there over the mountains to the south-coast fishing port of Sfakia. These improvements made only slow and insignificant progress. The message traffic

If Freyberg and Ringel thus shared a common conclusion about the end in sight, so did Freyberg and Student share a worry about the outlying posts of Retimo and Heraklion. What about them? In the thoughts of both men, Retimo stood closest.

---

between London and the scene reflects the deficiencies of the British command structure. No supreme commander was responsible for Crete. Such a commander could have recognized that further German landings by sea were very unlikely (as von Richthofen implied) and that therefore all defense forces in the west could be committed to night counterattack.

20. Retimo and Heraklion

22–26 May 1941

Student's concern for the Retimo paratroops continued to raise differences about just how the ground fight was to develop. He wanted the road cut beyond Suda to lock up the British well enough, but his more urgent cause was to rescue his men in Retimo. They meanwhile had never ceased trying to break out on their own. Hard combat had gone on day in and day out, and with little interference or help by air. The eastern combats thus set themselves apart as soldier fighting tests.

Major Kroh with the residue of the 1st Battalion was still locked in the olive-oil factory compound; in the late afternoon of 22 May, Colonel Campbell's latest attack by two companies was beaten off. Early in the action the Australian company leaders became casualties; many wounded and dead lay in a no man's land outside the factory walls. At midday of the 23d under a truce the wounded were moved to a combined Australian-German dressing station, where the totals now reached 147 Australians, 51 Greek Army, 252 Germans. During the truce Kroh sent an officer to Campbell to demand surrender; his message was that landings at other points on Crete made the local Australian cause hopeless. Campbell at once rejected the demand and for good measure at the end of the truce had artillery shell the German compound.[1]

Like Kroh, Captain Wiedemann sat trapped at the west end within

1. Long, pp. 262–67; Davin, pp. 270–72, 292, 324, 325, 363; 11th FK Kreta; LF4 Kreta; 8th FK Chrono. These sources likewise apply to the rest of this chapter.

the walls and houses of Perivolia. Late on 22 May Captain Honner of 2/11 Australian Battalion drove in close to the edge of Perivolia. Firing from houses and from behind walls and the yard of St. George's Chapel, the Germans halted Honner. The chapel capped Hill C and thus dominated the entire western front; it became the key. Australian shelling in the forenoon of 23 May almost forced the Germans out, but late in the afternoon Wiedemann received strong air support. Fifty planes worked over the Australian positions for two hours. Though pinned down, the attackers held, and when at sundown Wiedemann launched a counterattack, he was driven back with severe losses. He retained the chapel. At dawn the following day (24 May) a surprising attack hit in on him from the west—not from the gendarmes, but from a company of Rangers. They had been sent by bus from Suda. But Perivolia's stony ramparts held them off too. They returned to Suda with their casualties. 24 May ended with no change.[2]

By the 25th the two Australian tanks were again ready for combat. One joined in another infantry attack in the morning against St. George's Chapel. It had made only a little headway when the tank blundered into a creek and stuck. So did the rest of the attack. In the evening the tank was got out and cleared for another attempt on the 26th. But there a shell struck the turret, the tank stopped and the infantry drive petered out. In the east the second tank covered a minor operation against a nonexistent foe.

Kroh in the factory must have decided during the night of 25–26 May to clear out for Heraklion. Campbell noted only weak fire response on the forenoon of 26 May. He sent a platoon under cover of the second tank forward close to the factory wall. The men hopped over into the midst of wounded and unwounded paratroops, all of them ready to give up. It came out that Kroh with two officers and thirty men had decamped at two in the morning. Left behind were forty-two wounded and forty able-bodied men. The total in the prison cage beyond Hill D rose to 501.

That left only Wiedemann at St. George's Chapel, against whom Campbell could now concentrate.

In the Heraklion scene, meanwhile, toward noon of 23 May Major Schulz and his battalion, encamped to the southwest of the town, did nothing but watch two British tanks trundle in from the south. They

2. Campbell had hoped for the Ranger attack on the preceding evening to press Wiedemann from both sides. On arrival in time for this, the Ranger commander saw that his arms were too light for the job; he asked for confirmation of attack from Suda. He was ordered to attack, which he did, and failed.

with some field pieces and the Argyll and Sutherland Battalion had on 18–19 May landed at Timbaki on the south coast. At about the time that the tanks entered, six or seven Hurricanes circled the airfield and came under fire from their own on the ground. Two were knocked down, three flew away, and one hearty landed. When a heavy German air raid came later, six more Hurricanes dove out of the blue to engage. All six landed when the raid ended. These startling air events shook General Löhr in Athens. What did the return of the RAF signify? Was it the first action of air strength held back, as over England, just for this moment? The alarm added pressure to the abortive attempts to operate fighters from Maleme this day. Heraklion, now back in the game, had either to be taken or denied by ground fire. A fresh battalion of paratroops was scraped together to reinforce Schulz. As the bombing was stepped up, he sent a messenger forward through the pall of smoke and dust to tell the Greek Army Defense Commander to surrender or be destroyed. The message was rejected. Early on 24 May Schulz received orders to join Bräuer in the east.

During an interlude in the promised destruction on the 24th, Schulz's reinforcing paratroops descended. This sparked a rare encounter between two reinforcing columns, for the paratroops dropped spang on top of the Argyll and Sutherland Battalion marching in from the south. A wild riot exploded. After taking about twenty casualties, the Highlanders drew back a bit and the paratroops gravitated toward Schulz's compound. On the following day the Scots entered Heraklion. At nightfall Schulz began his trek east, and finally on 26 May the long-separated Bräuer forces were united. Schulz received orders to seize the airfield. These were the effects of the RAF plan to save Crete at the eleventh hour by rushing in with planes from Egypt at just the right moment. They did create a short-lived hubbub.

Brigadier Chappel's defenses had nowhere been breached. He had news of crumbling defenses in the west and considered whether to open a road westward or toward the south.

21. Last Stand

The Battle of Galatas: 25 May 1941

By nightfall of 24 May the lines of battle before Galatas had been clearly drawn. Throughout the day deployment, probes, and testing had established them. On both sides the troops knew where they were and why. This was it.

New Zealand Division had been pressed into a tight little sector of rough ground between the two western road entries to Canea. The familiar road junction just outside the town was the sector origin, and the two roads—coastal and valley—formed the radii boundaries that extended westward about three miles. In the middle on a foothill saddle sat the adjoined villages of Galatas and Karatsos. The northern boundary stopped beyond Kolimvithra on the coast; from there an arc of defense works swung south and then east over a series of heights that described the present mile-and-a-half front line of battle. Only a day before, Brigadier Puttick in his Order No. 6 still defined the line as it was on 20 May; since then the lower half had been lost, so that the remainder, which would now be fought over, lay north of the valley road. Divisional headquarters during the battle were still near the Canea end of that road. Conduct of the battle Puttick entrusted to Inglis of 4 Brigade; his command post lay northeast of Karatsos.

Except for two notable changes, the picture differed little from Kippenberger's former layout: (1) now 18 Battalion under Lt. Colonel Gray had relieved Composite Battalion, which drew back 700

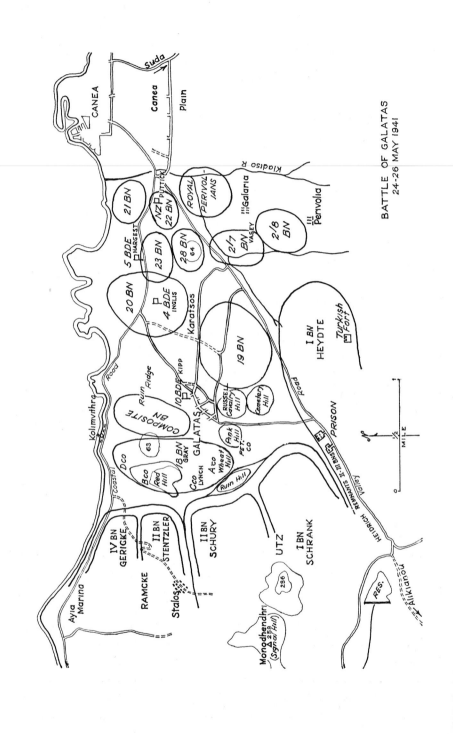

BATTLE OF GALATAS
24-26 MAY 1941

yards in support; and (2) the Germans were closer in front. Indeed, the two opposing mountain battalion commanders, Schury and Schrank, had occupied the height called Ruin Hill at the south edge of Gray's front. Gray had been unable to man it for lack of troops. On the other flank, 19 Battalion stood where it had begun. In between, Russell's force of Divisional Cavalry and Petrol Company occupied two knolls on either side of the spur road from Galatas to the prison. The one on the west—Pink Hill—Petrol Company held; the other—Hill 114—can be called Cavalry Hill. Kippenberger acted as front commander from his command post at the northeast corner of Galatas. In reserve Inglis had 20 Battalion around his headquarters above Karatsos. Also available was 5 Brigade still farther along in and around the sector's origin.

On the Galatas firing line were about 1800 riflemen, supported by nine field guns and two 12-pounders. Three tanks stood by. In reserve Inglis had more than 1600 men, so that the division's grand total reached at least 3400 infantrymen. To these could be added the 1065 men of two Australian battalions south of the valley road on the far left flank. For holding still another line closer before Canea, Creforce was forming a new Suda Brigade of 2000 fresh, fully equipped troops. Yet now if ever was the time to be strong at the Galatas front; the Germans had to be given a sharp rebuff, had to be made to give ground.

There were 4100 of them, supported by about fourteen field pieces, facing the Creforce disposition. Group Ramcke on the north flank had Sturmregiment's 4th Battalion on the coast and its 2d Battalion inland alongside. Next inboard, directly opposite Galatas, were the two mountain battalions of Group Utz. Then came remnants of the 2d and 3d Battalions of Group Heidrich and finally on the right flank, the 1st Paratroop Battalion (Heydte), which had ranged far ahead on the south side of the valley road to the vicinity of Perivolia. There 2/7 and 2/8 Australian Battalions under Brigadier Vasey blocked the way.

From the head of the valley near the reservoir and electric power plant, Colonel Utz moved his command post forward. He expected Colonel Krakau of the 85th Mountain Regiment to join up with a battalion or two for attack against the 8th Greek Army Regiment around Alikianou. This action was to kick off the day at 0700 on 25 May; the main effort against Galatas would then follow at 1220.[1]

1. Davin, pp. 262–63, 283–316; Kippenberger, pp. 62–70; Long, pp. 242–45;

An uneventful night of 24–25 May passed over west Crete. To be sure, RAF bombs fell around Maleme Field, but on the whole harmlessly. The night alarms had become commonplace, but not the daylight ones that followed on 25 May. Hard upon General Student's smooth landing at 0800 an air attack came in, and still another two hours later. Ringel's staff noted the sequence; also that hits were creeping closer to the command post on Tavronitis bank where the two generals were conferring. Stronger fighter cover was requested. Student approved the day's planned actions, which closely followed the Utz proposal. One failure Ringel already had for report: his prelude attack by the newly arrived 85th Mountain Regiment (Krakau) on Alikianou had not gone in at 0700, for lack of Stuka preparation. Ringel wondered if the main effort against Galatas would suffer delay too. This was no way to begin business with Student. 8th Air Corps promised action soon. Fighters roared up and down Prison Valley, small-bombing and strafing, but still no dive-bombing at designated targets. Under the fighter cover, the troops before Galatas moved to their stations. Hop-off was to be 1220.

A merciless Cretan sun blazed down on the craggy slopes of Monodhendhri, into the steaming valley and onto the sweaty deploying attackers in heavy green-gray uniforms. Colonel Kippenberger watched from his ringside seat and wrote, "Numerous parties moved into cover opposite 18 Battalion's front on the north . . . about midday a column . . . 1500 strong moved by three's to obvious assembly positions." The fighter tempo overhead mounted, accompanied by increased machine-gun and mortar fire. Yet no troops moved forward. The Stukas had again failed.

A message from Utz cheerfully and routinely reported—approach to assault under way according to plan, but without Stukas or artillery (which was to descend after the bombs); he asked pointedly, "When Stukas?" After half an hour he warmed up with an "urgent" message, "Request urgent reply. Are Stukas still coming?" Artillery boss Wittmann, itching to cut loose after the bombs, chimed in, "Urgent, where is Stuka attack?" Ringel did not know, nor did the newly attached air assistants from the 8th Corps. He tried to notify the front commanders of rescheduled dive bombing in two waves at 1620 and 1645. This most important message of the day suffered long delay in delivery. Ringel saw his big moment stalled in anticlimax.

5th MD War Diary; 8th FK Chrono; Ringel Ms; Ramcke GB; Ramcke VSJ; consultations with General Student and General Ringel in Germany, 1960.

Not so at the front. The message was delayed because the attack went in without preparation. It was under way.

Mortar and machine guns flayed the defenders as the assault battalions closed; then the attack troops began probing. Their efforts proved productive. But Schrank's 1st Mountain Battalion, making for Pink Hill and entry to Galatas, found itself under flank fire from Pink Hill and Russell on Cavalry Hill 114. Prompt notice to artillery chief Wittmann brought down shells ahead to steady the advance. In the center the Ruin Hill salient poured bullets into Wheat Hill opposite to test its holding power, while farther north Ramcke attempted to circumvent Gray's D Company next to the sea on Red Hill. There on this north flank Ramcke was keener than ever. Had not his chief Student within the hour made him a surprise visit and decorated him on the field of battle? So Ramcke saw his chance and acted as Stukas finally dove in. He released his poised men. So did Utz in the wake of a shattering dive bombing of Galatas.[2]

The main assault plunged forward from the sea to the valley bottom. The best eyewitness is still Kippenberger. He tells how Ramcke's drive hit 18 Battalion: "The crackle of musketry swelled to a roar, heavily punctuated by mortar bursts . . . six in a minute in one company sector alone." Gericke and Schmitt fought toward the coastal chapel of Kolimvithra; Stentzler kept pace inland as the link to Utz in the center. Some posts of 18 New Zealand Battalion on the sea had been overrun, and they surrendered just before Colonel Gray "hove in sight armed with rifle and bayonet," reported New Zealand Corporal Bishop; Gray was "leading perhaps twenty men and yelling no surrender, no surrender! Sergeant Scott took a half dozen men . . . the rest of us following. We had just got to the top of the ridge when we met Gray coming back, Scott and the others having been killed." This incident was probably the one Ramcke described in his battle report when he said two officers and four men fell from fire at short range by New Zealanders who had already given up. By 1600 Gericke had

2. The Stukas caused casualties in Russell's cavalry force and among civilians in Galatas; houses were fired and telephone wires cut. The second wave at 1800 dropped bombs on Schrank's battalion. The growing unreliability of the planes remains unexplained. Some planes may have been diverted to a frantic bombing at sea near Kithira island to dispose of a fantastic air sighting of four submarines. At the time two precious tanks were en route to Crete via Kithira in a towed lighter under the command of Österlin. However, dive-bombing support slacked off perceptibly after 25 May, even though the 8th Air Corps had been reinforced by Stuka Squadrons 1 and 77 from the 10th Corps. It may be that some squadrons had been withdrawn for *Barbarossa*. Heydte, pp. 138–41, writes about General Student's struggle to keep them for *Merkur*.

Kolimvithra and halted. Stentzler reached a point almost abreast to the south and also stopped. Group Ramcke thus chopped the first hole in the Galatas line and half-opened the shortest (coastal) route to Canea. General Student took prideful note, "The Sturmregiment proved by this success that its power of combat had not been broken by the previous fighting." Airborne felt an urge to prove its mettle over and over.

The threat to the north flank looked deadly to Kippenberger, as he showed by throwing in his first and last reserves, two companies from 20 Battalion. A new line north from Galatas held by degrees, either through this counter action or because Group Ramcke halted. Ringel's orders had indeed barred deep penetration; an incipient break-through was, however, at hand, as Utz had suggested the day before. Reserves for this were ready and well positioned. The truth was, no front-line authority was present to order them in. A deep thrust might have become decisive. The capital city, bombed and rebombed, was ripe for picking. Maybe Ramcke realized this. At 2121 he advised Ringel that "Canea is ablaze" and went on, "it offers a suitable target for night attack." He also reported shelling from ship's guns (H.M.S. *York*) in his rear. From seaward there were no shells.[3]

In the center the fight raged on. Major Schury's advance (adjoining Stentzler) slowed perceptibly against fierce resistance by Major Lynch and his C Company. The double assault against Wheat Hill's A Company of 18 Battalion gained ground. Farther along the bend, Schrank labored over the approaches to Pink Hill. He took the no man's land of days gone, Cemetery Hill; its mate Pink Hill, as we shall see, offered heavier going. The front thus fragmented into rocks and channels: on the coast, the start of a channel; in the center a rock solidly occupied by Lynch and his C Company; and finally beyond the turn, another strong bulwark at Pink Hill and Cavalary Hill 114. Full credit for clearing the central rock Ramcke heaped on Stentzler, who had promptly ordered his right-hand company (Leutnant Barmetler of Hill 107 fame) to swing south. Lynch of defending C Company stayed, himself manning a rifle in the front line. Though he later had to give way, it was not because of Barmetler's action, but because his southern flank was threatened when Wheat Hill gave way. A break there decided things. It was a renewed drive by Schury's

3. Two cruisers and three destroyers which swept the Cretan north coast on the night of 25–26 May had the bombardment of Maleme among their tasks. For lack of time this action was omitted. No task to bombard ground targets so obvious to the army was assigned.

7th Company, led by himself, which marked Wheat Hill as a primary German objective. Its fall, about 1800, opened a channel from the west to the center of Galatas.

The gravity of the threat struck Colonel Kippenberger when he went forward to check repeated requests from A Company on Wheat Hill to withdraw. At that point "the position worsened," he said. "Wheat Hill was abandoned. . . . Lynch was forced to fall back. Suddenly the trickle of stragglers turned to a stream. I walked in among them shouting, 'Stand for New Zealand!' and everything else I could think of." The men stood and he got them started at re-forming a new line north from Karatsos "where a white church gleamed in the evening sun." The sharpest trial was only beginning. Russell reported fire in his rear. It could have meant Germans in Galatas and may have been so taken; more likely, the fire came from just outside on Pink Hill, toward which Schrank's 1st Company was moving.[4]

On X-Day and the two succeeding days, Heidrich had driven at that balding ridge, which Galatas Day, 25 May, claimed for its own. A series of humps guarded it on the south. In fact, the last one provided the entrance stoop into the village and control over it; a side terrace held a few houses and ruins. One was pink, already mentioned as Colonel Kippenberger's first command post. The whole position had lapsed into a no man's land, but on 23 May a detachment of gunners under Lieutenant Dill reoccupied this vital height, which now became Schrank's objective. Utz at 1710 posted himself nearby. The stench of foul flesh assailed the advancing 1st Company—dead paratroopers. But the hill must then be unoccupied, and so it seemed on first reaching the crest through wire and works.

But defenders of this key point there were: besides Dill near the south tip, a party from Petrol Company was on the lower western slope and at about this time Russell ordered his reserve from 19 Battalion forward as reinforcement. When 15 Platoon then moved along low on the east slope, it at once encountered Germans. A spirited grenade charge led by Robertson's section drove them back. Russell

4. Actions and reactions of the two sides can be brought into fair coincidence. The accounts by Ringel HG, 5th MD War Diary, and 5th MD CR, Fleckher-Dobiasch, Tietz-Manz, have to be meshed with accounts by Davin, Farran, Pringle and Glue, Ross, Kippenberger, Sinclair. German reports tend to overcolor the action and German bravery, while British accounts aspire to devil-may-care nonchalance. They were firmer in identification of landmarks. Lacunas remain on both sides. For example, the second Stuka bombing at 1800 (German time) is not mentioned in British reports. At this point Colonel Kippenberger saw his second turn for the worse. It was when Russell's belated runner reported pressure and fire in his rear.

then recalled the unit. The other reinforcers of 7 Platoon under Lieutenant Scales fought a harder, longer engagement, possibly the crucial one of the day; it delayed the Germans just enough. On arrival at Pink Hill's north end, Scales split his command in order to work the upper west and east slopes simultaneously. Sergeant Rench took the west group, Scales the east. Rench led off, and with one follower gained the dwelling on the southern end that sheltered Dill and his gunners. From there he crossed to the east slope and rejoined Scales. By this time fire from the south and east was heavy; Russell and his men were suffering from overhead fire. While Scales moved up one terrace, he found the cause: a machine gun in action. A grenade attack silenced it, and from that post Scales fought back the advancing Germans below. Dill and his troop joined in and the cavalrymen too. In a little while a total lull ensued. It must have been the chance Russell grabbed to pull east into 19 Battalion; Scales noted the move and conformed. One by one his men broke off, and Dill's handful— except Dill. He had been hit. Petrol Company on the west slope fell back through Galatas.

The spirited action by about twenty men brought the Schrank attack to a dead halt: the 1st Company stopped, the 2d tried to hurry up in support. "Not a rosy picture," mused Ringel on Tavronitis bank. He wonders if the job can still be managed before dark, when British counterattack must surely come. But hark, the throb of motors, that peculiar thrum of the Stukas. It must be the 8th Air Corps's second wave, already two hours tardy. Ringel quickly flashes the good word to his front commanders. The message is scarcely out when the planes and bombs scream down. British records make no specific mention, but Germans on the ground do. Utz growls to Ringel about bombs among his men. The citation which Lt. Colonel Schrank won tells how after the bombs fell, he personally swung his 1st Company right to deal with the flanking fire from Hill 114 (Russell); and thus freed, the 2d Company stormed Pink Hill. Both hills were overrun, though, contrary to German billing, against zero opposition. The 2d Mountain Company went on into broken and empty Galatas at the south end, whence it could shield the 7th Company's approach from the west toward the village center. Soon Schury's 6th and 8th companies advanced from the northwest. The ruins filled with strangers, while at the northeast exit Kippenberger strove with men and tanks to mount a countercharge. It is his and Britain's very last chance.

After Ramcke halted on the north flank before the patched line there, the situation stabilized some; Kippenberger remarked, "Things looked more hopeful. . . . It was no use trying to patch the line any more," he decided; "obviously we must hit or everything would crumble away."

Lieutenant Farran rattled up with his two tanks and was immediately dispatched to reconnoiter Galatas. Then 23 Battalion's C and D Companies marched up from reserve. The men, about eighty in each company, halted alongside the road. Kippenberger quickly ran a practiced eye over them. "Tired but resolute," he decided with satisfaction and set about instructing their commanders, Captains Manson and Harvey: on return of the tanks they together are to retake Galatas. "Move straight in up the road, one company either side, in single file behind the tanks and take everything." Volunteer parties from other units begin to join: Lt. Colonel Gray and two squads from his headquarters company, the Bren carrier platoon of 20 Battalion, Lieutenant Carson and men of Petrol Company, Captain Forrester of the Hellenic charge. Farran returns and bursts out, "The place is stiff with Jerries." Would someone help lift two wounded from the second tank? Volunteers replace them and are given a short practical training course up and down the street. The course ends with Farran's short blessing, "Of course, you know you seldom come out of these things alive." To which volunteer Ferry later remarked, "That suited me all right—it seemed a pretty hopeless fight with all these planes knocking about, and a couple of my bosom friends had been knocked." New Zealand's blood is up.[5]

Spirits are rising, and most of all the colonel's. "Now get going," he exhorts Farran—who pulled down his hatch and went. Light is failing, bright tracers crease the sky, the din of battle grows louder and louder as the clanking tanks disappear into the village. The men cheer and follow, first at a walk; then without signal they break into a run and shout blood-curdling yells. War whoops and gunfire mix. "By the time we entered the narrow streets . . . the whole line breaks into battle cries . . . every man firing and flushed with confidence you could feel it . . . nothing could stop us," wrote Lieutenant Thomas

5. Volunteer Ferry expressed the feelings of many New Zealanders. The unrelenting pressure overhead bore in on all ranks; its effect has been reiterated by participants again and again. At the same time these men, never before exposed to such tough ground fighting, were becoming blooded to it. Their change can be felt as one works through the records. Now they know. Farran, p. 99; Kippenberger, p. 66; Ross, p. 76; Davin, p. 309.

who led 15 Platoon. The tanks sprayed either side of the street. Farran, leading, reached a turn at an open space, a small plaza. Heavy fire from ahead overwhelmed him and ignited a wild melee that decided the night.

The fusillade came from the 2d Mountain Company troops who only minutes before had entered the village at the opposite end and felt their way forward along unfamiliar streets and alleys. A glow from air-attack fires gives some light. They pass the church and are joined by the 7th Company from the west entry; together they press on, when an arresting hum and clatter calls a halt: tanks ahead for sure. "Panzer!" Up go signal stars for mortar support, and all at once the street is alive with flat helmets. They can just be made out. A tank is leading them into the plaza. The mountain men cut loose with rifle and machine gun, with machine pistol, grenades—indiscriminate. Two main German parties engage: Leutnant Bauer has two machine gunners on a low balcony over a house entrance; under him Sergeant Burghartswieser leads another group. He lives to tell his story and be named the Hero of Galatas, but not Bauer, whose lance corporal must speak for him.

The dread cry "Panzer!" rings out. "Firing out of all barrels, one rolls up within twenty meters. We are blinded as well as deafened. The riflemen shoot what they can; we throw grenade after grenade, . . . finally his track breaks. He keeps shooting," said the sergeant. From the balcony Bauer's corporal adds, "A comrade runs down the staircase and lays a balled charge under the tank's belly . . . down we go into the street! Suddenly we are faced by a whole bunch of Tommies, recognizable by their flat helmets and lowered bayonets. Lightning-fast Leutnant Bauer whips out his machine pistol and empties a magazine into the attackers." There is no time to do more before Lieutenant Thomas and 15 Platoon charge. Bauer becomes a casualty.[6]

Lieutenant Farran tells how a blinding flash lighted the inside of the tank. His gunner sank to the bottom of the turret and he himself felt a pain in his thigh. The driver tried to turn around and was hit in the shoulder, which made him pull to turn all the harder. He ran

6. Ringel HG, p. 163; Tietz–Manz; Fleckher–Dobiasch. The accounts in the last source from the lance corporal and the sergeant have been tampered with. The facts sift out by comparison with other evidence. German photographs taken the next day nail the thing down. Several depict Farran's stalled tank No. 17/660; but the labeling of the photographs goes wide of the mark in location of the scene. The second tank does not appear. Both German accounts have it rushing through the thick of the fight. British accounts imply it never reached the plaza.

head on against a lighting pole. "We sat there crouched in the bottom of the turret, while anti-tank fire carved chunks out of the top." The gunner was bad off. Farran, though hit again, got his crew and himself out and then on his elbows pulled himself under a wall. There "in the infernal din" he lay and prayed for the infantry to come. They came (Thomas's platoon), hesitated momentarily, then plunged ahead. "Firing from the hip we advanced across the square," Thomas reported, "screams and shouts of desperate panic in front of us . . . we had caught them ill prepared and in the act of forming up [Bauer and his men down from the balcony]. From doors, windows and roofs they swarmed . . . falling over one another . . . there was little aimed fire at us now. The earlier exhilaration returned, victory seemed assured." Thomas fell wounded; his men surged on, and parallel, to the left, D Company did the same. Resistance gave way until the last cluster of dwellings at the southwest exit toward Pink Hill had been reached. There the Germans under Utz built a strongpoint and linked it to the Hill's southern summit. The fight was over.

Galatas regained! The first and only real German setback in west Crete, where it could count. "The battle field . . . became quiet," said Kippenberger. His timely counterattack, so resolutely carried through, ranked among the fiercest actions fought by New Zealanders in the war (Davin, p. 316). The Colonel rated 23 Battalion's performance "one of the best and most effective efforts made by any single battalion in the Division throughout the war," to which General Freyberg added Amen. He designated this counterattack the highlight of the Crete campaign.

Galatas regained, but for what? A straggler passed through the plaza with a rumor about abandonment of the hard-won prize. Under his wall, Farran turned to cursing. "All the world seemed quiet after the battle," he wrote, "and I felt deserted, lost in a village occupied neither by Germans nor British."

Inglis reconnoitered the north end of the front with a view to further attack, spearheaded by 28 (Maori) Battalion. He saw that the ground was difficult and he knew the Maoris would be thinly spaced, yet not to attack meant the end. He requested Brigadier Puttick to join his conference for decision. Instead, Puttick sent Lt. Colonel Gentry, his G-1 (Operations), who arrived after the assembled battalion commanders had offered their comment. Colonel Kippenberger gives a graphic account of the gathering in "a tarpaulined hole in the ground," the conferees around a table, a dim lamp lighting the map before them:

It was clear to all of us if this was not feasible Crete was lost. . . . Dittmer [of 28 Battalion] said it was difficult; I said it could not be done and that it would need two fresh battalions. Inglis rightly pressed, remarking that we were done if it did not come off—"Can you do it George?" Dittmer said, "I'll give it a go!" We sat silently looking at the map; then Gentry lowered himself into the hole. . . . Without hesitation Gentry said, "No."

He explained that the remaining fresh troops were needed to hold a new line. Apparently Puttick, with only meager news of the successful counter action in Galatas, had already set his mind on withdrawal to a shorter line, which Gentry was to explain. It was the prelude to pullout. The conferees now knew. They "quickly decided Galatas must be abandoned and everyone brought back to the present Karatsos line before morning." It was done. The sequence of Maleme and Prison Valley repeats itself. Here it vitiated a courageous and inspiring last stand.

Crises about who should have Crete are over. The drops of 20 May brought the break-in, whose efficacy no one could know. It tested a new doctrine of quick conquest, which was immediately cast into doubt by 21 May's crisis over failure of both lodgment by air and reinforcement by sea. 22 May saw the trial of air against sea, and the Creforce land counterattack too little and too late. 23 May confirmed German possession of a landing head at Maleme, with a good prospect of expansion. Finally, Sunday 25 May 1941 sealed the outcome. From here on, the German offensive from decisive west will seek to bind and cut off the defenders, who aim to disengage and withdraw by sea.

The Germans have Crete and one can begin to wonder what they may do with it.

22. Pursuit and Pullout

26 May 1941

On neither side did the top commands grasp the true post-Galatas situation of 26 May 1941. The 8th Air Corps remarked, "The British are still exceedingly tough." Diarist Zimmermann at the 5th Mountain Division entered: "25 May has brought the division a great success." He said nothing about the New Zealand counterattack, nor did his general, as was his wont, cheer about a fresh victory. While Ringel probably never knew of the late-evening fracas that threatened his progress, Utz took the cool view when he reported merely: "Galatas taken, though street fighting still in course." He mentioned no tank encounter. It was Student, doubtless egged on by Ramcke, who raised questions. At midmorning on the 26th he confirmed the presence of tanks to Ringel and suggested clarification about Galatas.

On the spot, at dawn Sergeant Burghartswieser and his depleted platoon tiptoed back into the rubbled village. They found it empty, stepped over plenty of corpses, but encountered no opposition. Not a single gunshot rang out. The platoon then posted a new line toward Karatsos on the land saddle between the two villages, just in case. The men were all alone; they could not believe their good fortune.

On the coast Ramcke "pressed forward slowly" as ordered by the 5th Mountain Division. The basic plan stressed reinforcement of the right (south) wing for a wide outflanking thrust. There was where Ringel wanted to make news. He shifted his command post forward to Padhelari village on the west side of Platanias Valley, which he hoped would place him in back of the middle of the front with easy access to his main effort on the right (south).

In Creforce command, knowledge about the Galatas front was even sketchier. Brigadier Puttick at New Zealand Division either did not take in or did not credit the evening gallantry that regained Galatas and offered fresh opportunities. Instead, late on the 25th he forwarded Freyberg a discouraging summary gleaned in good part from Hargest; it omitted the successful counter action, exaggerated the enemy pressure, and mistakenly represented his troops as badly shaken. The effect on Commander Creforce makes the message important. It read:

> Heavy attacks about 2000 hrs. have obviously broken our line. Enemy is through at Galatas and moving toward Karatsos. Right flank of 18 Bat. was pushed back . . . 20 Bn moved forward and 23 and 28 Bns moved to 4 Bde assistance. Tanks were moved forward toward 18 Bn area to assist in restoring line. Hargest says Inglis is hopeful of establishing a line.
>
> Am endeavoring to form a new line. . . . A second, or support line, will be established I hope. . . .
>
> Reports indicate that men (or many of them) badly shaken by severe air attacks and TM fire. . . . Am afraid will lose our guns through lack of transport. . . . Am exceedingly doubtful on present reports whether I can hold enemy tomorrow [the 26th].

Forgotten was that Galatas had always been the linchpin of coastal and valley defense. Possession of it had discouraged advances down the Prison Valley road up to this very moment.

When he received the bad news shortly after midnight 25–26 May, General Freyberg was drafting a cheerful summary of the day's events for transmittal to Cairo. Puttick's message brought the drafting to a halt. He had written of the day's anxiety, of the air attacks at 1700 and the ground action that followed, which, he said, "is still in progress and I am awaiting news. *If we can give him a really good knock it will have a very far reaching effect.*" He relates how he struck out the last sentence on receipt of the Puttick news and added, "I have heard from Puttick that the line has gone and we are trying to stabilize. I don't know if they will be able to. I am apprehensive. . . ." The message went off at 0200 (Davin, p. 326). He had got his "good knock" but could not know it. At this point thinking about pullout accelerated.

At 0400 on the 26th Freyberg then responded to Puttick in a note delivered by officer messenger. Puttick was to hold his newest line and to counterattack if any part should go. "It is imperative that the enemy should not break through," the general wrote, and Major Saville, the messenger, was to explain the plans settled upon with Brigadier Stewart, the senior Creforce staff officer. The plans intended evacuation by sea from the south coast, but could not be brought into the open until ordered by Cairo. How to bring understanding there would be a problem among the compelling local ones, such as that fundamental affliction, command.

For example, would the New Zealand forces under Puttick, about to flow into Suda sector with the tide of battle, come under Weston's command? At first glance Freyberg decided No; Puttick and Weston would command jointly, while Inglis, still under Puttick, held back the Germans with force reserves. This plan Saville passed on to Puttick while Freyberg explained it to Weston, Beamish of the RAF, and Morse of the Navy at about 0830 on 26 May. From here on, the day turned into a confused and perilous deadlock of no command. At fault could have been the ambiguous joint arrangement between Puttick and Weston. It had to be dropped. Puttick was subordinated to Weston, an arrangement which likewise failed because Weston failed to act. A breakdown of communications and an unannounced shift eastward of Creforce headquarters undoubtedly contributed to the deadlock.

Also near 0830 on 26 May, General Freyberg, with the concurrence of RAF and Navy representatives (Beamish and Morse), sent off his initial message to Middle-East about evacuation:

The limit of endurance has been reached by the troops under my command. . . . No matter what decision is taken by the Commanders in Chief . . . our position here is hopeless. . . . The Difficulties of extricating this force in full are now insuperable. . . . Provided decision is reached at once, a certain proportion . . . might be embarked. . . . reduction of Retimo and Heraklion will only be a matter of time. The troops we have, with the exception of Welch Regiment and the Commando, are past offensive action. If you decide . . . that hours might help we will carry on. I would have to consider how this would be best achieved. Suda Bay may be under fire within twenty-four hours. . . .

In the end Puttick on his own withdrew New Zealand Division from the makeshift position about a mile and a half west of Canea. At its southern end Vasey of 19 Australian Brigade, by arrangement, conformed. So by dawn 27 May five New Zealand and two Australian battalions had withdrawn to a final line called 42d Street. It ran south from the coastal road a mile west of Suda village. Replacement in the old position by Inglis's force never materialized, but Weston did belatedly order reserve forces forward for that job; they included Lt. Colonel Duncan and his 1 Welch Battalion, 1 Rangers, and the Northumberland Hussars. Duncan put his own battalion on the north next to the sea and the other two units to the south. What he did not know was that this southern flank below his last unit was wide open, for the so called Suda Brigade, a composite outfit of marines, 2/2 Australian Field Regiment, and a mixture called the Royal Perivolians all under Lt. Colonel Hely, had left that flank.

On the opposed side Utz's amazed mountain troops on the east rim of Galatas had pushed through Karatsos and into 19 New Zealand Battalion territory to establish contact during 26 May. On the north there was some skirmishing as Ramcke's group pulled abreast. In the right center Heidrich's men pressed forward too. They had the easiest alley south of all British opposition.

But rather than pushing forward frontally, General Ringel's primary interest ran to the southernmost efforts. He squeezed Colonel Jais with two battalions of his 141st Mountain Regiment in between Heidrich and Krakau (85th Mountain Regiment), who had finally passed Alikianou on the far south. The sharpening object was to reach the Suda shore cross-country before the British could disengage and withdraw along the coastal road. To insure this, Ringel now committed his highly mobile reconnaissance battalion from reserve to a still wider-swinging thrust southeast, under Prince Castell-Castell. He was to end up at the entrance of Suda Bay.

Ringel turned over to the Luftwaffe the serious work in the north. He gave them open season in that sector until 1600, at which time he expected to launch a general assault. The flyers stretched their extra air freedom too far, for German troops far south in Krakau's task force came under heavy air attack. Group Ringel screamed for the scalp of the offending flight commander. Krakau, who had shown little enterprise anyhow, slowed his advance still more. The mistaken attacks forced the postponement of the general assault to the following day. The delay proved costly. If attack had gone as scheduled at 1600 on 26 May, it would have caught the defenders fumbling between stand and pullback.

At 1600 Heidrich launched an attack below the valley road anyhow, with Heydte's hungry 1st Parachute Battalion—at last, release from hunger and boredom. The troops progressed rapidly without opposition and by nightfall occupied the villages of Pirgos and Peri-volia (19 Australian Brigade had already pulled back to 42d Street). "Absolute calm prevailed," said von der Heydte as he looked out on the plain of Canea before him. He bedded down, grumbling over orders for the morrow (27 May): Ramcke and Utz were to take Canea while he was to press on to the land neck of Akrotiri Peninsula and clean it out. "The others would reap the glory" whilst he did the dirty work of mopping up a large unknown quantity.[1]

Where Is the British "Main"?

General Ringel's orders for 27 May gave a dual purpose: (1) cut off Canea at Suda Bay and (2) punch eastward with strong forces to the Stilos–Neon-Khorion line which spanned the main and secondary routes toward Retimo. Ringel said nothing about pursuit of the British "main," possibly because he expected to lock it up in Canea. Strategy demanded for this day news of the British main body, *das Gros.* Where was it? Under the jubilant, congratulatory hot air of stupendous success promised for Tuesday, 27 May, only a week after X-Day, who could care? An easy obvious answer grew firmer: it would be locked up in Canea. To make sure, in the early hours of the morning, Colonel Jais of Mountain Regiment 141 drove east on Heydte's right. Just before Suda village his 1st Battalion under Major Forster ran afoul of the Creforce 42d Street position. Things began to happen.

Hargest and Vasey, under Puttick, had played the withdrawal from the Canea line by ear and feel. Now lacking precise orders, they whacked out between them what would be done; a like rapport governed among their subordinates. Indeed, on several occasions these Dominion formations had had to make decisions when directive or inspiration from above failed them. In this instance the brigadiers arranged for 2/8 Australian Battalion to defend the junction at the head of Suda Bay between 42d Street and the Canea-Suda road. Thence due south the battalions would man the 42d Street ramparts in order from the north: 2/7 Australian, 21, 28, 19, and 22 New Zealand, and in a rear-guard station backing the center, 23 Battalion. Higher

1. Heydte, pp. 143–67. Hunger was no joke to the paratroopers locked in Prison Valley. Repeated messages give evidence of ration shortages. Ringel got priority on rations for Heidrich's "starved" troops. Airborne logistics were just barely getting by.

orders had issued for general withdrawal commencing at dark this 27th of May to Sfakia on the south coast. At 42d Street men washed their bodies and drank gallons of plentiful new water. Down the line they agreed with their next neighbors on a single doctrine: when the Germans came close, the line would open fire and charge. They packed themselves into their tight 2000-yard front with fixed bayonets.

For Jais and Heydte the fine bright morning broke auspiciously. Both made good cross-country progress, generally northeastward toward their goals. Jais's Major Forster of the 1st Battalion pointed for the head of the bay; Heydte, at the midpoint of Akrotiri's land neck. By 1000 his 3d Company on the left reached the radio tower Genz was to have put out a week ago. The men scrambled up to be first in the flag-raising coups of the day. Firing could be heard from the west, where Utz and Ramcke were just taking off against isolated Duncan. Ramcke had his "first" flag raising too, but only as a display on a very stubbornly defended rock. Forster and the 1st Mountain Battalion meanwhile hurried east. His radio link to Jais in the rear began to fail, and he had no contact with Heydte. Both battalions passed and plundered British works and dumps as they went. All at once 42d Street in front of Forster burst into flame.

Probably Forster had his northeast-advancing companies echeloned north and south, for they bumped the street simultaneously and evoked the same response. First a few skirmish shots, then 2/7 Australians in the north and 28 Maoris in the center charged full tilt;

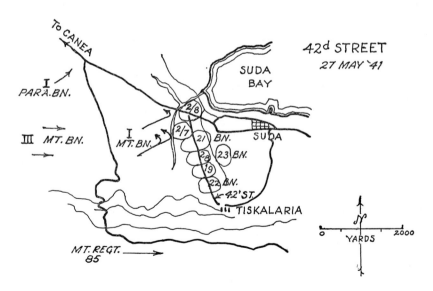

they were quickly joined by the others. They repeated Galatas, yet in greater force and ferocity, for it was daylight and each man could see his work. The mountaineers tried to rally, but when the Australians and Maoris got deep among them, it was too much. "They commenced to panic," said Captain Baker, and in no time, "their disorder became marked . . . they disappeared very quickly from the scene of battle." The action turned into a rout. Jais's 3d Battalion coming up met the fragments of the 1st Battalion and immediately went over to the defensive half a mile short of the Street, to which its defenders returned and held fast. They were in great spirits; here was something to fight for. Their sole worry was the sight of a steady procession of troops (Krakau's Mountain Regiment 85) streaming east through the highlands in the south. Could they cut off withdrawal southward?

None of the 42d Street noise disturbed Heydte's battalion approaching Canea. He and his staff "arrived at the fine Canea/Suda road much earlier than expected" and before his advance guard. The sound of battle still echoed from the west, and soon from that quarter a lone British truck appeared, loaded with troops. A quick crackle of German rifle fire captured truck and troops, who reminded Heydte that Canea must still be British. For him to try to mop up Akrotiri to the north as ordered would be folly. He decided to take Canea in rear. "It proved a march, rather than a combat advance," a flag-waving march of recognition signals and a horizontally held swastika flag to repel aircraft, who had been busy blasting the town. Stepping over debris, around ruins and rotting bodies, the companies entered without a shot. A plaza came into view; nearby, a hospital poured out wounded Germans shouting in wonder and joy. There Heydte set up headquarters, talked to the wounded, and considered what next. They were the only humans around. Where was everybody? Surely he was the first into Crete's capital.

While Heydte wondered if he should take Suda as well and began issuing orders for this, his Leutnant Abratis marched into headquarters with two Cretans. The younger of them introduced his elegant companion as the mayor of Canea, who wished to contact the senior officer present.

The mayor found it hard to believe that the rough character before him, with clothes in tatters, a week's beard, and a knotted handkerchief for headgear, was the troop commander. It could not be. Yet on being courteously received and ushered out into the shade of the hospital to a chair, he became persuaded and explained his wish to surrender the city and to request "clemency" and help for his people. Solemnly the youthful commander vouched for all and sealed the deal with a tin-cup toast, "to peace among men." The binding beverage had just been discovered in a nearby cellar. The mayor raised his cup, but hesitantly. As the party emerged again into the sunlit plaza the "German flag could be seen hoisted on the tall minaret of the mosque" at the harbor. Heydte then knew his 2d Company had reached its objective. The thunder of battle to the west died out.[2]

Even before noon 27 May Lt. Colonel Duncan, commanding 1 Welch and by accident the force reserve as well, found his situation in the Canea line untenable. Although the Germans delayed their main assault until after the "flying artillery" had by 1000 blasted a way, earlier probes and skirmishes got into Duncan's middle. The decision fell on Ramcke's right, where Stentzler adjoined Schury's mountain battalion. There another sergeant did his stuff. His name was Barnabas and he belonged to the Sturmregiment. At dawn he worked his scout troop forward right through the defense lines, taking out strongpoints in his way as he went for the central height that dominated the whole field. Barnabas's seizure of the rock enabled Stentzler and Schury, paced by Wittmann's mountain artillery, to advance at the cost of only two dead and four wounded. In a similar tactic Gericke, supported by flanking fire from a post at the sea coast, pulled abreast. About noon Duncan moved to get out: first to man a line on the east bank of the Kladiso River. When the first two companies under Major Gibson reached the far bank, there was nothing for it but to keep going. With other troops, some from the Rangers and the Hussars, they picked a precarious way along and eventually got through to Suda. Their commander, Lt. Colonel Duncan, with the remaining two companies of his own and other remnants, did not make it. One dauntless fire team of a dozen or so, led by a British Barnabas, stayed in action at his seacoast post until early on the 28th. The rest of the line was no more after 1500 on the 27th.

When Ringel heard of Ramcke's speedy progress, he urged him to press on and take Canea; air reports had Suda full of fleeing British; some might still be caught. Meanwhile, Utz should bend toward

2. The Heydte account is documented by photographs with shadows of mid-afternoon. Other German records say that the surrender of Canea was consummated by Colonel Utz at 1700 and also at 1800 on 27 May 1941. These could have been the more formal ceremonies. Records about hoisting colors also give several answers. General Student's combat report solved the rivalry by having all contestants credited with entry and hoisting at the same moment.

Suda too. Ramcke executed the verbal orders with Gericke's battalion on the coast, supported by the versatile Schmitt's heavy weaponry, and the prideful thought became "Thus paratroops, shoulder to shoulder with mountain troops pushed into Canea." The motorized Schmitt group in the van at *1615* hoisted "the *Swastika Flag* on the *red church steeple* in the center of the town, Canea." An advance motorized group under Leutnant Kurtz sped on toward the British consulate on the east rim. There, near the seashore, the group encountered the old settlers, von der Heydte's people. They were already sea bathing and bedding down in a seashore villa. As Heydte's adjutant put it: "The battle for Canea is over, sir. The fight for comfortable billets has now begun."

Still, in the town's backyard toward Suda, fighting and dying were far from over. By late afternoon Colonel Jais had assembled the remnants of his mauled 1st Battalion and pushed the 3d Battalion forward to cut the coastal road short of 42d Street. But that did little good; patrols sent farther forward all bogged down. Jais convinced himself he faced a greatly superior concentration that "launched counterattack after counterattack." He settled for a "firm defensive position" from which he could "beat off these despairing . . . thrusts throughout the night" (5th MD War Diary; Davin, p. 379). These sallies by the British brigades at 42d Street made time for the bulk of Creforce to gain a night's head start into the hills—toward Sfakia. "The severe counterthrusts" Jais took were a series of feints designed to deceive him.

An incredible worm of humanity crept south over the hump toward hoped-for rescue by ship. If one got locked in its coils, there was no escape. How could anyone command? It was chaos—just what Freyberg had hoped to forfend. Weston, named to command the cover for withdrawal, found himself caught in it; he never got out. Later, Freyberg fared little better. At dockside late on 26 May he instructed the last reinforcement from Egypt—parts of two commando battalions brought into Suda by minelayer *Abdiel* and destroyers *Nizam* and *Hero* (Davin, p. 565). Then he regained his headquarters to read the last messages. Instead of orders from Cairo confirming evacuation at Sfakia, he found Wavell's suggestion to retire on Retimo.

Patiently, General Freyberg drafted his reply, the last message from the Suda command post, and dispatched it in the first minutes of 27 May. Retimo not only lacked the resources to support Creforce, he said, but the defenders were cut off on all sides; the ebbing combat powers could not continue without air cover. The sole hope left was withdrawal to Sfakia, while fighting a rearguard action; for this he needed more commandos to help cover. Retimo force should be moved forthwith, presumably by sea. During the same hour Churchill, alarmed by Wavell's warning of failure, cabled, "Victory in Crete essential at this turning point of the war. Keep hurling in all you can." Nothing could have better demonstrated the unreal grasp of strategy on the part of the political leadership than this incongruous piece. Under any circumstances, it would have been out of place. Wavell replied with the gravity of the situation as revealed by the latest developments and ended with justifiable testiness, "There is no possibility of hurling in reinforcements." Shortly after midday on the 27th, Wavell, who knew Churchill was sacking him, ordered the evacuation of Crete. London added its approval in the evening.

The London professionals were even more culpable. Churchill was guilty of only draping the current unrealistic thought in language inappropriate to the realities of the battlefield. A belief flourished that German Airborne was wearing itself out; the breaking point must come soon. If Creforce could but hold to that point! Throughout they had been fighting Invasion England, on Crete. England doctrines, evolved against the gripping peril of Invasion cross-channel, were invoked to save remote Crete, in totally disparate circumstances. The professionals had entered the wrong alley as eagerly as Churchill, though he waxed more vocal.

Frantic last-minute efforts were made at reinforcement. The latest commando units for Layforce landed at Suda on the night of 26–27 May. General Freyberg personally directed them to rearguard duties. The fast transport *Glenroy* and escorts tried to bring 800 troops in to Timbaki on the south coast but failed. She returned to Alexandria. Navy talk there was already centered on the bad subject of another evacuation. The mood was black; not even the Atlantic news of the *Bismarck*, sunk this day, could relieve it.[3]

If London insisted that time must soon tell, a strong German voice sounded off to the same tune. This was General von Richthofen, tireless driver, and more often than not, in the right direction. Through

---

3. Cunningham, pp. 376–77. 8th FK Chrono remarks on the air difficulty of silencing the guns of H.M.S. *York*, beached in Suda Bay. She was expending herself firing against ground forces before Canea during the night of 26–27 May. Both Ringel and Ramcke remark on this. Harassment at night of the German lines on shore by fire from sea might have offset some of the day-long German air harassment. As the crisis in Crete worked up, Wavell, at Churchill's behest, was in Syria.

his tight liaison with Ringel, he had first-hand information. One of his liaison officers returned on 26 May to report; his news was bad: paratroops at a low level of fitness, no discipline, at loose ends. He urged the "absolute and immediate need" on Crete of "reinforcement by sea shipment of heavy weaponry if the operation was to get ahead at all." Richthofen packed the young man off to Athens to tell his story to Jeschonnek at Air Fleet 4. Late on the 27th a high conference resulted: Generals Jeschonnek, Löhr, and von Richthofen and Admiral Schuster, whom Richthofen described as "depressed by the loss of Maleme Flotilla, some steamers, and today the mighty *Bismarck*." The airmen showed him no mercy: heavy weapons—first off, tanks—must be got to Crete before "the Englander claws himself erect again; our people require help; no time to lose; air cover is guaranteed." After long heaving and hauling it was agreed that the two tanks currently en route in a towed lighter via Kithira would at once be expedited. The project had been under way for two days; the goal was to land the tanks at Kastelli Kisamou. The story makes a mark of its own.

The leader of ill-fated Maleme Flotilla, Leutnant Österlin, hardly had time to set foot on the mainland, after the flotilla ordeal, before the Navy braced him with another most urgent and risky job: to somehow or other get a couple of tanks over to Crete; it might mean saving the whole operation. He set to work on 24 May, found a suitable wooden lighter in Piraeus, lowered the medium tanks into it, one astern of the other, and secured them for sea. At dusk 25 May, lighter in tow of a small harbor tug, he crept out the net gate of Piraeus and set a southerly course past the many Peloponnesian capes. All went well until alarms of the Royal Navy on the prowl induced Admiral Schuster to order the tow into the tiny harbor of German-occupied Kithira island, off the mainland's south tip. The conference of the 27th in Athens probably got Österlin sprung from his haven by fresh radio orders on 28 May: he was to proceed to the south shore of the Gulf of Kisamos, where Captain Bartels waited at a selected and marked beach. Under way again, Österlin steamed for the horns of the dragon head. "Smoke cloud ahead to starboard"; the covering planes circle it, then head off. Shortly, home base explains that the planes have sunk a boat loaded with British soldiers. The tow plows on and enters the gulf; after a time Österlin spies Bartel's marker on the south shore. He puts the lighter ahead now and with full power rams it up on the beach, nearly high and dry. An eager party of mountain engineers jumps to assist; the men throw off the tank-securing gear, stuff demolition charges in the prow and blow it clear. The tank motors roar above the cheers as the precious monsters roll ashore. There is work at hand. General Ringel orders the tanks east with all speed. They are to bring down Retimo and round up the British "main." But first, thought a local authority, let them round up some British soldiers loose in the Kisamos area. The delay almost proved fatal.[4]

The tanks were too popular: just what was needed to beef up the newly organized Advance Detachment under artilleryman Lt. Colonel Wittmann. Elements assembled near the Prison Valley reservoir during 27 May—a motorcycle battalion, the Reconnaissance Battalion, an antitank party, a motorized artillery troop, and some engineers in a truck. They made an all-purpose task group that was to "strike out from Platanos [southwest of Canea] at 0300 on 28 May in pursuit of the British 'main' via the coastal highway to Retimo"; after relieving the trapped paratroops there, Wittmann was to press on to Heraklion. Swift follow-up seemed all the more in order to Ringel on 27 May as he realized that Canea's defenses had crumbled; but in determining what direction the pursuit should take, he lost himself. He vouched that not the faintest hint of the British going south entered his mind. Instead he followed the general conviction that they must have fallen back on Retimo (as Wavell suggested to Freyberg). An extra urge east was General Student's concern for his paratroops there. No one raised a diverging thought. By noon of 27 May it was clear that the British had pulled out of Canea; early air reconnaissance confirmed it, but at this point Air lost contact. In accord with Ringel's request, the flyers concentrated their scouting toward Retimo. They found nothing. The British had disappeared. Still, no one worried; perhaps they had gone east, in a hurry.[5]

Meanwhile, because of radio failure General Ringel remained ig-

4. Vidua tells the story, which as a navy crew member under Österlin he apparently witnessed. Österlin's success on this second try again raises the question whether this route might not have been better for Maleme Flotilla than the one via Melos. Exposure to British sea power would have been shorter, the two channel islands provided convenient waypoints, and caïques would have been in sight on land, and air cover close at hand could have been more efficient.

5. Ringel mentioned Student's concern for his marooned paratroops and added that he, Ringel, at the time had no idea (*keine Ahnung*) that Creforce had turned south across the island (Ringel to Ansel in Germany, 1960). Failure of the air reconnaissance is obscure, notwithstanding the Creforce practice of avoiding exposure during daylight on the trek. German flyers attacked the British concentrations at Stilos and another way-point beyond. Reconnaissance farther along belonged to another outfit. Later the movements of columns were identified, but the ground force still did not grasp the significance of these reports. Coordination between ground pursuit and air reconnaissance was poor.

norant of the holdup at 42d Street; he nevertheless forced rapid advance along the south shore of Suda Bay, personally telling Utz to push. Schrank's battalion therefore lunged ahead and soon encountered Jais and the tangle at the Street. There the advance halted.

By 1500 (27 May) back at Canea, Germans streamed in on all sides. Colonel Utz took time out to seal the earlier surrender deal of Heydte with the same mayor in a more formal and official ceremony. Report of the event rattled out through radio to Athens and beyond. The news roused jubilant responses on high. The most prized message came from Field Marshal List, commander in chief Southeast: "Bravo Ringel," he fairly shouted. "Appreciation and best wishes to the mountain troops—List." A holiday spirit took over.

The 5th Mountain's orders for 28 May faced most of the fresh troops east. Wittmann's Advance Group would spearhead the movement: "First objective, Retimo and the relief of the paratroops." Krakau was to follow with the Mountain Regiment 85 in close support; then Jais. Bringing up the rear would come the 5th Mountain Division command and staff itself. Utz was to "mop up a strip either side of the road Armenoi–Askifos–Sfakia, including the port of Loutro, and then provide for the security of the south coast." It was a much bigger job than realized. Mention of the only south-leading road of the region occurs here for the first time, and so naïvely that the command's innocence of knowledge about British withdrawal over this route cannot be doubted. The soldiery had already started to make free with British summer clothing. "To avoid mistaken identity," the order continued, "troops are forbidden to use New Zealand hats. All men wearing such headgear shall be taken under fire." Apparently, shorts and khaki blouses were not banned. At 0400 of 28 May, Advance Group Wittmann took off. It would first have to pass through the final defenses before Suda.[6]

The 42d Street defenders remained without orders throughout 27 May, and as the day drew on, the threat of cutoff by Krakau's mountain troops in the south plagued Vasey and Hargest. They decided to get out that night: 19 Brigade would head for Neon Khorion, 5 Brigade for Stilos. This was done.

A self-appointed and self-directed rear guard, composed of a commando battalion and two depleted Dominion brigades, supported

6. 5th MD CR; Ringel HG, pp. 170–77; Ramcke VSJ. Ramcke was made responsible for the security of Canea and the west to Maleme; Heidrich for the security of Akrotiri; Mountain Engineer Battalion for security west of Maleme. Österlin and his tanks received no mention.

by three tanks, Bren carriers, and a troop of artillery, made up the fighting British main body that Ringel, Krakau, and Wittmann so earnestly sought. Later, 4 Brigade and a battalion of marines joined these actions. After clearing Stilos, this stubborn rear guard blocked German advance before Babali Khani and Kaina, three miles from Vrises, the turning-off point for the south.

Beyond it on the trail up over the mountains a dreadful drama unfolded. No words can paint the scenes better than General Freyberg's own:

There were units sticking together . . . but in the main it was a disorganized rabble making its way doggedly and painfully to the south. There were thousands of unarmed troops . . . including Cypriots and Palestinians . . . without leadership, without any sort of discipline. . . . Somehow or other the word Sfakia got out and many of these people had taken a flying start in any available transport they could steal. . . . Never shall I forget the disorganization and almost complete lack of control of the masses on the move . . . that endless stream of trudging men.

The stream had first to gain the Askifos bowl at the high halfway milestone on the trek south. But for the men it meant much more; it meant they were over—the rest would be downhill. Accordingly, 4 New Zealand Brigade was assigned to guard the bowl's north entrance. The rearguard meanwhile held Krakau and Wittmann at bay. General Wittmann tells the story.

His men needed water. "What a priceless beverage water is!" he remarked on reaching Stilos. There was a cool spring that provided bountifully. They drank up and rushed on. They passed several abandoned tanks and an hour later ran head on into a well-prepared position. It was Babali Khani, where "the heads got bloodied." The defenders struck back "desperately," wrote Wittmann, "probably to gain time for evacuation. . . . At midafternoon, support from Krakau on one flank and Jais on the other begins to tell. Yet the position held. . . . Toward midnight our probes met no foe. The road is again clear." The rearguard had pulled out for Vrises and beyond. The last action on the near side of the hump thus ended.[7]

---

7. Davin, pp. 395–402; Wittmann.

23. All Over

Wittmann's Advance Detachment had now by 28 May passed the objective line originally prescribed—Stilos–Neon Khorion—yet no British had been uncovered. For the moment search and pursuit receded as General Student's anxiety for his troops at Retimo surged still higher. They must be sprung. Wittmann passed the crossroads at Vrises, noted the signs of previous heavy traffic on the south fork, but kept on eastward, leaving a security detachment to await the arrival of Mountain Regiment 100, which was to explore the south. By dawn of 29 May the Advance Detachment arrived at Georgeoupolis Bay and so reported to General Ringel in his newest command post at Stilos. He was anxious about the Österlin tanks.

Germans were tank-conscious. Had tanks not won the astounding victories in France and Africa? Indeed, the Führer counted himself a tank expert, a support which gave them extra meaning. Ringel insisted upon an exact accounting of his approaching tanks. The latest report had them fueling at Maleme; shortly after midday on the 29th they were welcomed at Stilos and at once ordered to join Wittmann on the approaches of Retimo. Away they went.

During the forenoon General Student's arrival at the 5th Mountain Division Command Post spurred an exchange of news and views. Air reconnaissance, said 5th Mountain Division War Diary, had sighted truck traffic on the road south to Askifos. It could be that a high British staff was setting up there, for Creforce radio had cut out during the night. The 8th Air Corps had news of Heraklion: the town was in German hands; the aerodrome was to be occupied later this day. Italian forces sortied from Rhodes to land by ship in the east at Sitia on 28 May. Interrogation of British prisoners indicated that their main body had retreated on Loutro (near Sfakia); ships were approaching there and at Heraklion on the 28th. Air reconnaissance confirmed two groups of paratroops holding out at Retimo. General Student set out to join Wittmann for their relief.

In truth, that front had only one isolated group still fighting— Wiedemann and his company, holed up in Perivolia and St. George's Chapel at the sector's west end. By 27 May Campbell's defenders (2/1 and 2/11 Australian Battalions) had buried 550 paratroopers, made over 500 prisoners, were themselves still fit, well-armed, and equipped (including two unruly tanks), had a dwindling supply of munitions and a shorter supply of rations. The battle for the airstrip had been won, and Campbell was free to concentrate against Wiedemann. Misfortune dogged such plans for the 27th. Both tanks, manned by infantrymen who had practiced at night, soon became casualties, and for good, during a dawn attack on Perivolia by two companies from Sandover's 2/11 Battalion. Campbell saw that further daylight assault would be futile and ordered Sandover to try again in the dark before the next dawn, on 28 May.

Like Major Bedding at Kastelli Kisamou, for news Campbell depended on the BBC, whose reports grew gloomier and gloomier. During the night (27–28 May) Navy Lieutenant Haig again beached his landing lighter from Suda. He brought badly needed rations but also the startling word that after ration delivery he was to tramp cross-island to Sfakia. This was disturbing, especially since Creforce radio had gone off the air. (Campbell had radio but no ciphers.) It must have made a bad night of soul searching for Colonel Campbell. Nevertheless, he let Sandover's two-company attack, scheduled for 0220 on 28 May go through.

Again bad luck. Premature fire by Greek Army units gave the attack away. Captain Jackson's company in the lead got through the outer German defenses, but was turned off toward the sea by heavy fire when close to Perivolia; a following company of Captain Wood encountered heavy mortar and grenade fire in closing the houses; all officers became casualties but one. The company had to withdraw. Jackson made a loop around Perivolia along the shore westward and then inland and finally reached home base about noon on the 29th. Inexorably, the picture darkened: evening brought Greek reports of a new German force advancing from the east, possibly from Heraklion, already reported in German hands; Retimo Sector's own Greek Army formations withdrew to the hills. By midnight local agents in the west warned of an approaching German column (Wittmann and Student), spearheaded by 300 motorcyclists. Campbell had the beaches patrolled with signal equipment to respond to signals from sea. Perhaps ships would come to take his men off. None came.[1]

The midnight intelligence of motorcycles was behindhand, for Wittmann had in the early afternoon of the 29th clashed decisively with the Cretan defenders at the west end; they had surrendered, and the Wiedemann group was sprung. Student wanted to go on to free more paratroops, but Wittmann's probes indicated the need of greater power. He proposed a pause while the rest of his men closed up, and attack on the morning of 30 May after a regular artillery preparation. In approving the plan, Ringel added news of the two Kastelli Kisamou tanks; they were speeding forward to add still more power. "They roll up," related General Wittmann, "just in the nick of time at dawn." Artillery had already blasted the defenders on the hillsides. The British replied with mortar and machine-gun fire. Corporal Young from 2/11 Battalion posted the coastal road with three men. They waited until the tanks were in close range and then cut loose with a Bren gun. The tanks turned off the road for the hills to the south; motorcyclists followed. The position was about to be taken in flank from the south. His mind made up, Campbell ordered his quartermaster to break the readied white flag. Said General Wittmann, "A fine colonel, well turned out, reported the capitulation of an Australian regiment with artillery." By 0830 of 30 May 1941 action at Retimo Sector ceased.

Surely this sector had well earned General Freyberg's high praise, and all the more was this true of its commander, Lt. Colonel Ian R. Campbell. The end was a fact, and his next thought must have been for his men. He decided to capitulate in good order, but left a choice for those who might want to take to the hills. Some chose to.

---

1. Long, pp. 267–75; Davin, pp. 339, 390, 411–13, 438–39; Wittmann; 5th MD War Diary. All of General Freyberg's efforts to instruct Campbell on evacuation failed: via Lieutenant Haig (who left Suda before the general's message to Campbell arrived), by air drops from Egypt, and by his own radio in clear. On 23 May Freyberg had sent in clear: "You have done magnificently," and then dispatched the Rangers from Suda to make their vain effort to reinforce Campbell.

Of these, eventually about 15 officers and 50 men reached Egypt. Over 900 became prisoners of war; 96 had been killed, and double that number wounded. Loyally, in the best tradition of the warrior Campbell led his men into honest surrender. More power to him and his integrity!

Detachment Wittmann plunged on eastward—over hill, down dale. Although a headquarter's summary of 29 May had announced "town Heraklion and airfield in own hands," Wittmann and his men still worried and wondered about the British "main." The 5th Mountain Division Command, bringing up the rear, wondered too. Back at Alikambos on the road to Sfakia Colonel Utz was finding strange signs, but here on the approaches to Heraklion not a thing out of the way happened; only gasps of ohs and ahs at the natural wonders. Finally the last height was scaled and the last turn negotiated to open that marvelous sight of city and port spread out below on the coast. Wittmann's men raced down to establish contact with Bräuer's paratroops in handclasps and shoulder thumps. A brief rest at the aerodrome and Advance Detachment took the road again to the final objective—Ierapetra, on the south coast in the east. It was reached without incident and contact established with the Italian force landed at Sitia on 28 May. *Merkur* had reached the prescribed final objective.

To go back to Heraklion of a day before: evacuation by sea did take place on the night of 28 May and is noteworthy chiefly for what happened to the ships and their passengers during the run to Alexandria. The last days of sector defense had passed in relative quiet. Brigadier Chappel was told to get ready for evacuation by sea on the night of the 28th. The Greek Army commands were not informed. Thus, defense at Heraklion came to an end. Retimo held the longest. These isolated sectors put on superior performances. They had no higher headquarters at hand to look to for succor. They were on their own. It was so with Bedding at Kastelli Kisamou, with Campbell at Retimo, and Chappel at Heraklion. Each carried out his assigned task of holding until overwhelmed or ordered out. The clarity of their independent positions helped. It is a common experience: often, the farther you are from headquarters, the better you do.

Cruisers *Orion* and *Dido*, screened by six destroyers, arrived off Heraklion late on 28 May for the first big troop lift out of Crete. It was to be the easiest in embarkation and the toughest at sea. En route incessant air attack had damaged cruiser *Ajax* enough to force her return to Alexandria. Flagship *Orion* (Rear Admiral Rawlings) and

Dido, later a firm shipmate of mine, lay off the port while the destroyers brought out the troops. All went very well: some 4200 men were embarked and the ships sailed as scheduled at 0220 on 29 May for Caso Strait at the east end of Crete.

Within half an hour they were overhauled by bad luck. A steering-gear casualty swung destroyer *Imperial* into a wild turn that threatened to cut down two of the other ships. It was a machinery failure caused by previous bomb damage, and it proved irreparable. Rawlings faced a hard choice, but he decided quickly: *Hotspur,* standing by *Imperial,* was to take her load and then torpedo her. The sorry job was got over quickly with two torpedoes. *Hotspur* now crowded on steam to catch the others. The precious hour thus lost would add to the daylight time the formation would be under Stukas from Rhodes and Scarpanto. Still worse, the carefully planned air cover from Egypt at maximum range would get fouled up. In result, from their dawn arrival in Caso Strait until midafternoon the rescue ships fought off the heaviest air concentration since 22 May's big battle for control of the Cretan Sea.

Ships and soldiers suffered severe casualties—the latter, more in proportion than in Greece and Crete combined. When they disembarked at Alexandria almost 22 percent were missing. A second destroyer was missing; three of the remaining ships were badly damaged. German planes had been hit too, but very few; about a quarter of them bore antiaircraft holes. This was the final massive air-sea action of the Crete campaign. Its immediate forerunner of 26 May and this last one deserve another look and an assessment of the air-vs.-sea contest.

Air-vs.-Sea Finale: 26 May to 1 June 1941

On 21–22 May the Germans wanted to land troops and heavy weapons by sea under air cover, while the British, unable to compete in the air, wanted to foil the landings by ship's gunfire. This they did at night when they caught Maleme Flotilla on the last reach of the crossing and shot it to pieces. It became clear, however, during the succeeding daylight that British sea power without close air cover was helpless. Their own sea air-power available locally was what was needed, and Admiral Cunningham effected it when, as already noted, he sent the carrier *Formidable* to sea with a task force of battleships and destroyers on 25 May. The move was not billed as such an effort, but it led in the direction of another test of air vs. sea.

On *Formidable*, Fleet Air had patched together a dubious twelve fighters and half a dozen torpedo bombers to blast Scarpanto's Stuka base. Pridham-Wippell commanded from battleship *Queen Elizabeth*. From a hundred miles off to the southwest the planes went in at dawn of 26 May, achieved surprise, and destroyed, they said, planes on the field. German records log the attack as of no consequence, since Colonel Dinort's Stukas habitually overnighted on Rhodes just to avoid surprise visits. Scarpanto had become a forward base for daylight actions only. After furious 22 May, Dinort shifted his eighty some planes from the Peloponnese to the area of Rhodes and Scarpanto to bring a counter closer to the Royal Navy's movements through Caso Strait, east of Crete.

Shortly after *Formidable*'s Scarpanto strike early on the 26th, German evaluators noted signs of something different. A reconnaissance plane reported himself under fighter bullets and then went off the air. By noon German planes penetrated *Formidable*'s flimsy screen and counted fifteen ships guarding a carrier (the actual total was eleven). Here was the target the 8th Air Corps had yearned for. As on the 22d, all available planes were thrown into the charge: long-ranged heavy dive bombers (Ju-88's), high-level bombers (He-111's), and Dinort's own workhorses, the single-engined Stukas (Ju-87's). But *Formidable*'s cover held tight in the north; no one got through. Then a break. About twenty Stukas out of Libya flew in from the south and scored. *Formidable* took two hits that put her out of action indefinitely, and destroyer *Nubian* one. It blew her stern off. But Richthofen wanted sinkings. He bewailed the low-grade bombs his flyers had to use (yet said nothing about lack of something—like torpedoes—that could hole hulls). Even so, bomb damage cleared the sea on the following day. Long-range Ju-88's found the task force 66 miles off Alexandria and severely damaged battleship *Barham*. It was enough. Admiral Cunningham called the force into port. It could not keep the sea.

Rawling's evacuation run to Heraklion, already noticed, offered additional proof. He sailed on 28 May with cruisers *Orion*, *Ajax*, *Dido*, and six destroyers. Snoopers duly reported his sortie to the 8th Air Corps and raised concern for the Italian landing by sea about this time on the eastern end of Crete. In the end Rawlings, innocent of any knowledge about the Italians, got through to Heraklion with near misses by Dinort planes on *Ajax* and destroyer *Imperial*. *Ajax* returned to base, and *Imperial* continued, only to have her near-miss damage catch up with her; she was the ship that had to be torpedoed after leaving Heraklion. Air action began against the whole evacuation group as it steamed south through Caso Strait, right under Colonel Dinort's bombs.

This time Dinort's planes could zero in easily from their island landmarks. Three of them struck destroyer *Hereward* almost at once; she was barely able to move. Rawlings had to decide fast again, and it had to be to leave her. She limped toward the tip of Crete's tail. There her Captain, Lt. Commander Munn, put her on the beach. Most of the crew and passengers were rescued as prisoners of war by Italian Scarpanto-based motor torpedo boats. Meanwhile the fury of the fighting over the other ships built up swiftly to a climax. But these ship handlers knew all the dodges—when to start a radical turn, then turn again at 28 knots. The count on attacks and numbers of planes ran into hundreds; they returned again and again. Destroyer *Decoy* (an old China hand) and flagship *Orion* were slowed to 25 and then 21 knots. Captain Back of *Orion* succumbed to wounds. Admiral Rawlings was hit but managed to hold on. Both cruisers were struck on the forward turrets. Flagship *Orion* took fire and went out of control; eventually emergency steering gear took charge. But her speed grew erratic from salt water in the fuel. Soldiers crowded into the mess deck for cover; a bomb struck there squarely in the center and mangled the lot—260 killed, 280 wounded. That any ship survived was remarkable. Near their range limit of about 150 miles the Stukas thinned out. At last they were gone. By 1900 Rawlings brought his battered ships into Alexandria. Ten tons of fuel remain in *Orion* and "very few rounds of ammunition," wrote Admiral Cunningham. "Guns awry, one or two broken off and pointing forlornly skyward. Upper decks crowded with troops, marks of their ordeal only too plainly visible." Score in ships: two destroyers sunk, two cruisers and one destroyer badly damaged, against about ten planes shot down.

The 8th Air Corps continued to believe that this crucial engagement turned on the Italian landing—that the British ships were intent on another Maleme Flotilla slaughter. Dinort must have thought he had expanded on the air-sea battle of 22 and 23 May by corroborating air superiority. What he did prove was that sea power required its own seagoing air cover; and that because the British lacked it, German air power could control the East Basin. What this could mean strategically at this point of the war failed to get through even to the able von Richthofen.

The experience was nowhere fully understood. Both sides entertained obsolete theories about undisputed command over the sea or air, like the mistaken German drive for command of the air over England, to permit Invasion. The true requirement is local sea (or air) control within a mobile bubble of security provided by fleet fighters and combatant ships. Such security enables landing forces to assault hostile shores and convoys to traverse oceans. *Formidable*'s bubble failed for lack of fighters. Integrity of the bubble takes precedence over all else. Total command of sea or air through prior destruction of the opposed arms, often touted as a prerequisite for success, has no absolute validity. At sea the air components of carrier task forces provide the best answer, a solution that Britain deprived herself of when toward the end of World War I she turned her budding Royal Naval Air Service over to the shore-based and shore-minded RAF. Seagoing Air was neglected. From this error she continues to suffer.[2]

Sfakia: 28 May to 1 June 1941

In marked contrast to Luftwaffe air-sea supremacy at the east end of Crete, the RAF based on Egypt successfully disputed control off Sfakia in the west. From the narrow half-moon beach there, embarkation and overseas withdrawal proceeded in relative safety. The movements began in force on the night of 28 May when four destroyers brought in small arms and some food and lifted out over 1100 men, 230 of them wounded. Only one attack enlivened the return voyage with the downing of one Stuka. Not many Stukas were on hand because of withdrawals for overhauls and RAF opposition.

Air intelligence about the evacuation was incomplete and slow to reach German ground forces. Communications were poor; yet one would have expected a tighter air follow-up of the reported sightings. Colonel Utz had orders to clean up the trail south from Vrises to Loutro; his signals to the Air Command had to go through the 5th Mountain Division in the east, 60 miles away in thought and deed. The colonel was not happy about his assignment in a vast mountainous waste against an unknown hostile force armed with tanks. Near noon

2. Macintyre BM and Macintyre PNR develop the importance of the Fleet Air Arm. See also on this subject Hittle.

of 29 May a personal message from von Richthofen to Ringel set things straight about the British. He scribbled a delighted "Oho!" across the top.

Oho!
Appears enemy resistance collapsed after yesterday's bomb attack. Aerodrome [Heraklion] occupied. . . . Suda all clear. Enemy withdrawing to Sfakia. Enemy movements at points 8 and 10 on route to Sfakia. Impression about withdrawal same as before.

That evening Schrank's battalion engaged a strong concentration at the northeast entry to Askifos. Now at last they were hot on the trail.[3] During the night Schrank pushed his battalion through the Askifos bowl, then early on the 30th started downhill toward Imbros, a station on the local bus line. British tanks and Bren carriers soon came into play again, leapfrogging each other in sharp delaying fire fights. About 0900 the mountaineers came hard against another position.

It was the last of the last stands on Crete. It was held mainly by Australians of 2/7 and 2/8 Battalions under Brigadier Vasey, who had first halted the Germans high up on Vevi Gap in Greece. He now had Royal Marines on his right (east) and 21 New Zealand Battalion backing up his own battalions in the center.

In accord with Utz's orders, Schrank pinned down the center, while fresh companies began wide flanking movements west and east. His 1st Company flanked eastward; and then came the great discovery. The men gained the top of a commanding foothill, Point 892, from where they overlooked everything: to the south the sea, and to the southwest the whole British evacuation layout. Just under the hill toward the sea, troops were wiring-in a flank protection on the shore; southwestward toward the village of Komitadhes on the escarpment were hundreds of men apparently in bivouac, and in the distance beyond, there gleamed some white houses above a narrow beach— Sfakia.

A regimental observation post was quickly established on Point 892, and more slowly, a light mountain gun was dragged up and emplaced. "The obvious strength of the enemy," Utz wrote in his official report, "caused me to postpone the original encircling plan against the last stand . . . until strong Stuka attacks and artillery prepared the

3. 8th FK Chrono; 5th MD War Diary; Utz. Ringel was happy. Late on 29 May he vented his usual victory cry of "Hurra die Gams!" (Hooray for the mountain goats!). He quoted commendations, paid tribute to fallen comrades and to the paratroops.

way." He dispatched an officer messenger on a seven-hour motor trip to request air and artillery support. Early on 1 June only four Stukas, escorted by four fighter-bombers, showed up. But the lone gun on Point 892 did the trick. It opened on the British cover spots; "men left their cover to mill aimlessly about in search of shelter. . . . White flags appeared in places." The German wing companies closed in. At about 1000 the company on the east entered the defense line before Komitadhes, and at 1330 the western company broke into Sfakia. The end had come.

Before noon on that day of misfortune for British arms, 1 June

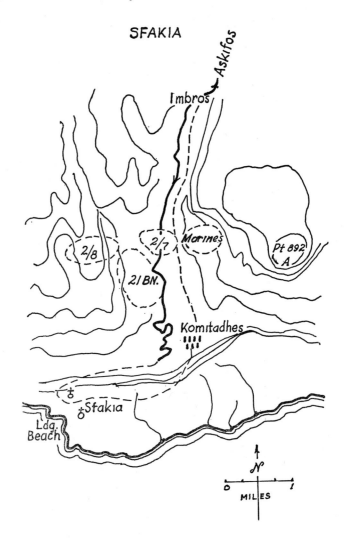

1941, Lt. Colonel Walker, commander of 2/7 Australian Infantry Battalion, clambered up from the beach to Komitadhes to carry out the melancholy duty of proffering surrender to an Austrian officer of Mountain Regiment 100. It had become Walker's duty by accident, for he and his veteran battalion were supposed to be speeding for Alexandria in the final troop lift of the night before. After leaving their last real stand, the delay of crushing through the human obstructions on the way down to the beach had made arrival there too late for the last boats. Then, said Major Marshall, Walker's second, as at the head of their column they watched the departing boats, "came the greatest disappointment of all: the sound of anchor chains through the hawse . . . all our efforts and skill wasted."

In the morning Walker met Commando Lt. Colonel Colvin, a newcomer on Crete, to whom General Weston, before departing by seaplane the night before, had given written orders to capitulate. (Weston had succeeded Freyberg when he departed on 30 May.) Thus Walker and Colvin were the two senior officers remaining, and it soon developed between them that Walker was the senior. Colvin thereupon handed over Weston's document. It read:

The position must be considered in the light of the following facts—
1. There are no more rations available and men have had no food for three days.
2. The wireless set can only last a few hours and the risk of waiting for further instructions from H.Q.M.E. cannot be accepted.
3. The decision to give priority in withdrawal to fighting troops has reduced the numbers below the minimum necessary for resistance.
4. No more evacuation is possible.
5. You will collect as many senior officers as possible and make known to them the contents of this order.
You are ordered to make contact with the enemy and arrange capitulation [Davin, p. 447].

Walker was trapped! He should not have been, nor Colvin. No matter what the future needed, nor in what rhetoric of extenuation the act is rationalized, the captains had abandoned ship and left their crews to shift for themselves: the sorry last of many command failures. Again, no one was in charge.

Of course not everyone could go, nor should everyone have stayed. Nevertheless, at the very least, a duly selected and officially appointed officer of flag rank should have been charged with the duty of capitulation in good order and in the unbowed spirit that the mettle and courage of the troops demanded. If ever they needed high authority to speak for them, it was here in a surrender not of their making.

The record describes instances of self-sacrifice; there must have been many more unrecorded. Take Major Burston of Australia, who became a prisoner of war (Long, p. 305). He tried to bring order out of chaos that last night:

Organization had completely broken down . . . troops were reaching the beach by the alternative route or just across country in small batches. . . . The situation became hopeless.

He declined to embark so long as others of his regiment were still left. A like feeling is expressed by Colonel Kippenberger of New Zealand (Kippenberger, p. 76):

We had a tramp of some miles to the beach, the last lined with men who had lost their units and were hoping for a place with us. Some begged and implored, most simply watched stonily, so that we felt bitterly ashamed.

It was doubly tragic that the bulk of 2/7 Australian Battalion, the marines, and Layforce Commandos, the very stalwarts whose rearguard fighting during these last days had made any evacuation at all practicable, should have been left behind.

By three in the afternoon of 1 June Utz was asking for prisoner of war arrangements at Canea for around 3000; by the next day the number rose to 190 officers and 6650 men, of whom 900 were Cypriot or Palestinian laborers. (Utz's written report gave final totals of 256 officers, 9103 men.) At this exciting news General Ringel signaled, "Division congratulates on the magnificent success!" It made the biggest single bag.

Surely the ones who missed the boat are the most unsung heroes of history. No drill has been devised for surrender. At Sfakia Lt. Colonel Theo G. Walker, as at Retimo Lt. Colonel Ian R. Campbell, both commanders of crack Australian battalions, rate special mention. Their fighting records stand on their own. Out of warrior tradition, extra credit is due them for assuming and discharging the warrior's most repugnant duty with honor. To lead men in victory is easy; to lead them in surrender is hard.

The troop lift Walker missed was the final one of four that began in the night of 28 May. On the next night came the big lift of about 6000 by Admiral King in four cruisers (two lay off for antiair protection), a light troop carrier, and six destroyers. Three air attacks were weathered on the return run under RAF cover out of Egypt; only one German plane got through to damage cruiser *Perth*. Meanwhile the casualties suffered by Admiral Rawlings out of Heraklion counseled caution. So for the night of the 30th only four destroyers started, and they were dogged by misfortune. Two had to give up and return because of material failure; this left *Napier* and *Nizam* under Captain Arliss to go on and do what they could. They reached Sfakia after midnight and by 0330 achieved the remarkable loading of all 1500 troops, intended for the four ships. One near-miss alongside *Napier* was the only event of the return voyage. Admiral King undertook the final lift of 31 May–1 June with cruiser *Phoebe*, minelayer *Abdiel*, and three destroyers. They brought out a whopping load of 4000. With practice the numbers were rising; yet this was the last load.

Seaplanes had meanwhile taken out the top commanders and staffs. To help the final ship lift into Alexandria, Admiral Cunningham dispatched antiaircraft cruisers *Calcutta* and *Coventry* to cover the last reach into home port. They got barely a hundred miles out when two planes attacked out of the morning sun. The first just missed *Coventry*; the second got *Calcutta* squarely. She went under in minutes. *Coventry* picked up 235 survivors and returned to port. This loss, said the admiral, came as a final blow.

The fleet had shrunk. Left operable were two battleships (one of them damaged), one cruiser, one antiair cruiser, a fast minelayer, and nine destroyers. No crucial sea battle had inflicted these losses, and no enemy fleet had been sunk. "The battle was fought between ships and aircraft," Cunningham put it, and the aircraft had won. Tall talk about immediate fleet reinforcement issued from London. But reinforcement with what? London had nothing that could enable the fleet to keep the sea. In the fighting ring Britain was on the ropes, and nothing but the bell could save her. She had neglected to add enough seagoing air to her sea power.

The Mediterranean story began in November 1940 with a useful Cretan extension of British naval strategy. It found its end seven months later as a sequel to a British political maneuver in Greece. In between, the moves had been halting and unsure. An old problem of timing took hold; it often slides easily into debate over what to act with, policy or strategy, or if with both, in what proportion and when. The danger comes when political bluff dabbles in unsound strategy, as it did in Greece. It made the whole thing a bluff. When the bluff was called, the Battle of Crete began, not by strategic choice, but out of dire necessity. The political leaders had failed to properly differentiate between policy and strategy and allow each its due. They are not at all interchangeable. They complement each other.

For Britain the contest thus came to a dismal end—this exciting and significant trial of strength over an island far from home in the war's first really combined action of all arms; it tested land and sea power and for the first time, air's power over the sea. As fought, the island battle could have gone either way at several crucial pivots. The pace was fast and furious; throughout, the British seemed to lack a clear-cut goal of victory, something to fight for.

Hindsight commentary has attempted to rationalize Crete's loss into good riddance, almost a boon: the island would in any case have been untenable; or if saved, how could it have been supported? Churchill jested about thousands of Germans on Crete, captive on the island, as good as prisoners of war who fed, maintained, and guarded themselves. But hindsight may not brush off a lost chance at victory so lightly. Here in May 1941 fate presented an opportunity for Britain alone to deal Hitler his first outright defeat. Better than anyone of the time, Churchill understood the prestige at stake as he strove too late to exploit the chance. He knew that Britain needed a clear victory of her own.

The Germans won the island in Maleme Sector when they capped their seizure of the airfield with the occupation of Galatas heights. The crucial pivots that marked the progression were these.

> On 20 May: Lodgment in the RAF camp and possession of half of the airfield.
>
> On 21–22 May: Landing of mountain troop reinforcements on the airfield. Repulse of the belated main British counterattack.
>
> On 25–26 May: Consolidation by the Battle of Galatas of a German offensive front from the sea through Galatas to Prison Valley.

It took the cumulative effect of these achievements to decide the issue. Had the progress been reversed at any of the mentioned points, the story would be different. In each critical instance the vital élan of the initiative was at stake; each time the Germans kept it and pressed relentlessly on until reversal was no longer conceivable.

Crete proved sterile to German arms; the plunging eagle died. Not so among the Western Allies: *Merkur* demonstrated airborne possibilities that were applied later in the war and are yet under test and development. The eagle himself, the jumper, seems to have been superseded today. He now lands with a whole fire team that comes out with guns blazing. Perhaps his loneliness has been conquered.

Command became critical: if the Germans at times suffered from someone too much in charge, the British time and again suffered from no one in charge.

STATISTICS OF ACTION IN CRETE, MAY 1941

Casualties

	GERMAN	BRITISH	GREEK
Killed	3,986	4,051 (=1,751 Army, 2,000 Navy, 300 during evacuation)	One source gives Army and Civilians killed as 1,500, prisoners of war, 5,000
Wounded[a]	2,594	1,738	
Prisoners of war	17	12,254	
Lost (= killed plus prisoners)	4,003	16,305	

[a]Usually the number of wounded is far larger than the number killed.

Evacuation

From Sfakia 12,600; from Heraklion 4,600, of whom 600 became casualties en route as prisoners of war or killed. Total rescued, 16,600—about equal to total losses, 16,305.

German Aircraft Performance

Air transport set a record: 503 Ju–52's flew over 1,500,000 miles; 151 were lost; 23,500 troops were transported, plus 5,358 weapons canisters, 539 guns and mortars, 731 motorcycles, 1,100 tons of supply, 3,173 (German and British) wounded evacuated; 33 combat aircraft were lost.

Casualties of the Royal Navy

	SUNK	HEAVILY DAMAGED
Battleships	0	2
Carriers	0	1
Cruisers	3	2
Destroyers	6	2
Merchant shipping	Tonnage lost, over 285,000 T	

24. Phenomenons Hitler

Crete Lost in Delusions: June 1941

The Germans had won well enough, but just what, and why, soon fell into doubt. General Ringel at his comfortable Knossos headquarters wondered even on Whitsunday 1 June 1941 as he totted up the booty and set the sum against the uncheerful figures of casualties. Of the cost in lives he wrote afterwards, "This sacrifice would not have been too great if the Crete campaign had meant a beginning and not an end"—a beginning, maybe, of German dominion over the East Basin. In mid-July he and General Student attended at the Führer's headquarters for a ceremony of *Ritterkreuz* awards won on Crete. In the ensuing talk Ringel extolled the virtues of the island: in coming days of peace, he ventured amiably, Crete would provide a fine trip goal for sunbathers. Hitler thought otherwise and replied ("darkly"): "For that, Crimea has been reserved." Except as a bar to the Aegean, he had no use for Crete in his private plans, nor any use for the Mediterranean. His planners in L Section of OKW, however, did, and so did the planners at Luftwaffe—and strongest of all, those at Navy. This cleavage is what Ringel sorrowed over: on the highest level his island lost out.

Not alone that: Airborne lost out too. Führer confidence in paratroops had slumped badly. At this very time of awards he remarked to Student, "Crete has proved that the day of the paratrooper is gone. The parachute arm is a weapon of pure surprise. The surprise factor has in the meantime worn itself out." Already on 1 June, when Crete was barely finished, he had assured Mussolini that such an operation would not be repeated. The heavy casualties upset him. He would have no more big airborne operations.

Offhand remarks like these were by no means final; yet their frequent reiteration gave off signals that established the trends of Hitler's thought. It was negative about Crete and positive about the Crimea. On 18 June Hitler signed a treaty of friendship with the Turks because Crete alone was not enough for *Barbarossa*'s security. At the anniversary of the Crete Campaign a year later, he said, "I do not intend to make Crete a German strongpoint. If I did, I should have to keep a German fleet in the Mediterranean and . . . create perpetual conflict with Turkey." And again, in the "interest of pure economics and as we have no interest in the Mediterranean, this should make for amicable relations with the Turks." He was using the Turks to hide his own reluctance to have anything to do with the water. The Crimea had a land connection to the mainland; Crete was 'way off there at sea.[1]

Whitsunday 1941 on Crete passed more easily at 5th Mountain headquarters as messengers from Colonel Utz at Sfakia unfolded the story of the lost British main. An endless column of prisoners of war labored a way back over the hump toward the north shore. Life was already returning to the grim scenes of battle; the people of Canea streamed down from the hills and began poking around the rubble of their city. In and around it the paratroops swapped tall stories and made merry. It would be a short holiday; orders for return to the mainland and new tasks were already in hand. Creforce supply stocks did well by these men, and by Ringel's mountaineers too. Ringel's occupation order could even prescribe khaki shorts as troop uniform. Otherwise security was provided by dividing the island into the same old sector commands: West, Center, and East, plus one in the far east for the Italians. Nothing was said about air defense except to restrain opening fire; not a word about Axis planes flying from the captured fields or their protection by ground forces. This was Luftwaffe business that could wait.

Relief of the 8th Air Corps (bound for Poland and *Barbarossa*) by the 10th Air Corps from Sicily and Italy was only one change of many in this close-off of one campaign and the poising of another. Führer Directive No. 31, which was to establish command lines for

1. Hitler SC, pp. 56, 378, 388; Documents GFP, 12:946; Gundelach, p. 125.

certain tasks in the Southeastern Theater, suffered delays at Göring's hands. Meshing of Air commands with those of other services was always troublesome because Göring insisted on Air's independence, and in the southeast it was now to predominate. Thus Crete was promised a "special position under an Air general as commandant." So appointed was General Waldemar Andrae, who took over from Student on 2 July 1941. Ringel remained to rule benevolently over Center Sector. Contrary to his hopes, Crete was not used for much of anything. The 10th Air Corps seemed to lack punch. When Ringel departed at the year's end, his Cretan subjects bestowed on him honorary citizenship of Heraklion and gave his name to one of its fine plazas.

Führer directive No. 31 cannot, any more than others, be taken at face value. The degree to which Hitler's private schemes agreed with the strategy implied by the directives, written by L Section OKW, always required careful study. The written word often had to build a modicum of sound strategy around his private intent; he would then use the apparent logic of the inside professionals to screen the true intent from the professionals on the outside. Such logic often bothered him until he had argued himself around it to get his own way.

During this period of Crete's rise and fall, one area of intrigue that briefly interested the Führer was the incitement of anti-British conspiracies among the Arab states. His nimble imagination rambled around the Fertile Crescent as though he were a new Lawrence of Arabia, liberating Arabs from British slavery. An opportunity of promise came early in May when Rashid Ali of Iraq tangled with the British at Habbaniya airfield. On 11 May Admiral Darlan's visit to the Berghof gave Hitler an opening to ask the French for aid from Syria to Rashid Ali. Though not well informed on Syria and French General Dentz's stocks, Darlan seemed willing to help. He had already made clear his government's wish to cooperate with Hitler as the conqueror of Europe. Here was a way to make good.

The Darlan visit led to ten days of renewed negotiation of German-French military agreements between the head of L Section, General Warlimont, and General Huntziger of France in Paris. They hammered out an agreement on cooperative military matters that was soon called the Paris Protocol. On 29 May Warlimont presented it to the Führer. OKW showed small interest. Hitler listened attentively, but that was about all. Besides being preoccupied with *Barbarossa*, he still mistrusted the French. Darlan did not move him as Marshal

Pétain had done at Montoire. Yet here after Crete, if East Basin strategy was called for, the Darlan visit and the Paris Protocol provided another political opportunity to pursue a South Plan in union with France. The moment passed, never to return.

The shorter-range cooperative measures among the Arabs with the French fizzled out too. German planes landed in Syria en route to Iraq. In response, British and Free French forces pressured General Dentz. He himself required reinforcement from France. An ambitious plan was developed to bring men and stuff by rail from France to Salonika, whence all would go by sea to Levant ports. Even wilder, one scheme proposed that the battleship *Strasbourg* and cruisers should dash out of Toulon for the East Basin under air cover by Luftwaffe from Crete. German fighters did get into Aleppo; sharp fighting ensued on the ground and off the coast. Nothing came of the Toulon fantasy. German timing and much else found itself badly out of step. Revolt in Iraq collapsed in early June, and General Dentz gave up on 10 July. In the end, Britain's Palestinian flank emerged stronger. Some difficulties of supply for a German 1000-mile march through Turkey and Palestine to get at the back door of the Suez Canal were brought out. Still, in this era of invincibility, Hitler and most Germans could accept such ventures by land as normal. Over the collapse of the scheme he was not in the least dismayed: at any rate, a start had been made with the Arabs; it could be pursued later, that is, "after *Barbarossa*." This phrase covered a multitude of monstrous German delusions.[2]

One of them Partner Mussolini could not share: that Russia would collapse all of a sudden when earnestly attacked. On 6 June 1941 he growled to Ciano, "I would not be at all sorry if Germany in her conflict with Russia lost many feathers, and this is possible." The Axis leaders had met at the Brenner on 2 June. Just why, except to give Hitler a chance to brag, Mussolini was unable to see. He complained of Führer verbosity, of the bell-ringing call to conference, of tears over Hess and the *Bismarck*, of failure to go to the bottom of any problem or make any decision. The two had conversed privately for almost two hours before Ribbentrop and Ciano were drawn in. Hitler's rambling recital surely had a purpose: possibly his own solid decision

2. Skl War Diary, May and June 1941; OKW Ops SitConf, pp. 248–88; Lossberg, pp. 101–2, and in conversation to Ansel; Documents GFP, vol. 12, Doc. 491. Warlimont IH, pp. 139–40. Cunningham, pp. 397–98; FD No. 30, which set up guidelines for liberating support to Iraq and others. Luftwaffe General Felmy was in charge.

to invade Russia needed sounding out with Mussolini (between them the subject was not new), but without a firm date for commencement. That could come later, after the event, as usual. He spoke of the imminence of England's collapse, speculated on a change in the British government—maybe Lloyd George would be the new prime minister—reviewed the Iraq-Syria scene and gave the Mediterranean a superficial brush through. Excessive losses on Crete he deplored, renounced any repetition, touched on Gibraltar, whose defenses had hardened since first considered. On the following day Ciano by letter urged Serrano Suñer to bring Spain in now. Hitler summed up: "The fight has been hard, but the hardest is behind us." He was in a talkative mood of high expectation, and now Mussolini was on vague notice about Russia.

A few days after these exchanges, Hitler received Admiral Raeder at the Berghof for a prolonged conference—historically, one of great importance. Two urgent matters lay on the admiral's heart; both concerned the war at sea, and one had the power to change the whole course of the war. The first was to account for the *Bismarck* action and draw from it lessons for the Battle of the Atlantic; the second was to elaborate the situation after Crete for the Battle of the Mediterranean. The Navy's own sorrowful story of the *Bismarck* deeply overshadowed the exciting opportunities now presented in the Middle Sea.

Hitler at once got down to cases on the *Bismarck* by putting two questions. "Why," he asked, "did the fleet commander [Admiral Lütjens] after the engagement with the *Hood* not return to port?" He meant, why had not Lütjens, having sunk the great battle cruiser *Hood* and damaged Britain's last word in battleships the *Prince of Wales*, called it a day, reversed course, and returned to his Norwegian refuge? Raeder replied that another "break through the northern straits would have been more dangerous than retirement into the broad reaches of the Atlantic." Hitler then asked, "Why did not *Bismarck* after sinking *Hood*, in reliance on her fighting strength, renew attack on *Prince of Wales* . . . in an all out fight?" Admiral Raeder was hard pressed; evidence had to be circumstantial. The fleet commander, he said, had to keep his primary mission in view, which was to sink merchant shipping. Further combat with *Prince of Wales* could have resulted in own damage and jeopardized his ability to carry out his main mission. He spoke truly when he continued that "retrospect" can always contrive better answers. Hitler had hit on the obvious questions. His position was good: not only had he argued against the *Bismarck* sortie at the last conference on 22 May but he had urged her recall. The Navy's wish to continue had prevailed (Puttkamer, pp. 47, 48).

What Hitler and other questioners failed to realize was that radar in Denmark Strait between Iceland and Greenland had deprived *Bismarck* of stealth. Once contact beyond gun range could be held by cruisers *Norfolk* and *Suffolk*, *Bismarck* could have been trailed anywhere, including a turn back through Denmark Strait into an ambush of superior British sea power. Admiral Raeder made the radar case clear in a twelve-page study. Along with it he submitted a reevaluation of German surface-ship operations in the Battle of the Atlantic. The aim had never been to sink British combatant ships for achieving parity of sea power; it was to cut the British lifeline of supply. Now radar blocked breakthrough into the Atlantic; it could concentrate Britain's sea power upon the kill of any German ship sortie. Inferior German sea power was again locked up. It numbed Raeder's zest for the Atlantic big-ship strategy—a mistaken doctrine, theorized upon in the dim past and painstakingly brought to fruition after German arrival on the French Biscayan coast. It had been unsound from the start. Any ship commitment of this magnitude that depends wholly on the exorbitant chance of achieving and holding surprise in this well-traveled sea expanse is unsound. The Germans proved it. They lost their fine capital ships one by one in unsound commitments.[3]

Strategically and politically the current German naval operations by submarine and surface ship in the Atlantic were unsound. If World War I had taught the Germans anything, it should have been that the United States must not be brought into another war. Hitler seemed to understand this better than his sailors; their strategy westward was just as hopeless as his eastward. Both were perverse delusions. Sounder might have been a drive by sea and air to seal off the "narrow seas" of the English Channel, the kind of thing that was all but done in the East Basin of the Mediterranean.

Raeder tried to close out the *Bismarck* on the brave note of resumed big-ship action in the Atlantic—the old impracticable blue-water dream of German sailors. Hitler at once demurred, and this reaction may have made the sum of his uncomfortable feelings about

3. FC, 6 June 1941, supported by conversations with German officers of Skl who had to prepare and account for the *Bismarck* operation. Raeder, p. 271, wrote: "The consequences of the loss of the *Bismarck* were decisive for the war at sea. . . . Hitler's attitude changed . . . he became more critical . . . prohibited sending surface ships into the Atlantic, as a first step." At OKW, talk made a scapegoat of the Navy, especially with Jodl—which meant, with Hitler.

the misfortune at sea: he countered with a claim of a rapidly deteriorating situation in England. She was in bad shape, "a collapse might occur all at once." By the middle of July he would be able to judge *Barbarossa*'s results and "their effect on the situation as a whole." (Could he have thought that, at Russia's collapse, Britain would have to choose between her own collapse and coming around? And that she could well choose the latter?) Until then, mid-July, the Führer continued, it would be imprudent to take big risks in naval surface warfare. Then, too, surface craft could in any case play an important role if Britain was truly on the brink; there might be need of a cross-channel blitz. Speculations of this character were current on both sides of the Channel—recall *Haifisch II* planning and alarms to Washington from Ambassador Winant in London. If there was substance to these, the logical German strategy would have been to redouble the pressure and to force decision. But fantasy is stronger than logic, doubly so in Germans. East Plan champed at the bit, demanding its day, and so did Hitler's dream of colonial Russia. With or without England, it came first. She had become a contributing side issue of limited war. The few weeks till mid-July would make this plain.

In direct contest with that prognosis was the final conference topic. It was a closely reasoned case by the Naval Operations Office, Skl, for action in Crete and the East Basin, now that forward bases and control over the sea had been won. The caption of the brief ran:

> *Examination of the Strategic Situation in the Eastern Mediterranean After the Balkan Campaign and Occupation of Crete and the Further Conduct of War Operations.*

We can guess that the fertile mind of Admiral Fricke in Operations guided a young officer assistant, Lt. Commander Heinz Assmann, in reducing thoughts about Crete to paper. The ideas were discussed and firmed in an Skl conference on 3 June for their submission to the Führer by Admiral Raeder. Assmann had produced and edited other noteworthy papers on German naval thought. In retrospect, this was a crucial one and the most significant he produced. Trailing in last, after the prolonged and heavy-hearted *Bismarck* accounting, the Assmann production had small chance. What a big difference a resounding *Bismarck* success—like one of Rommel's feats—could have made! Raeder recorded that he presented only "a sharply reduced summary of the Assmann study." The admiral requested pressure on the Italian Navy for naval action against British supply lines and improved security of German lines to North Africa. This old, old plea was almost as threadbare as questioning the validity of *Barbarossa*.

Perforce, this newest Skl estimate put up with the Russian mania to urge concurrent pursuit of the striking opportunities in the East Basin. Though the Luftwaffe felt the same, its views failed on consistent presentation. Army had been brainwashed into accepting *Barbarossa*'s preventive virtues. At the present conference Raeder laid no special stress on the changed East Basin; Hitler could easily agree with all that was said: the chances were favorable for action; talks with the Italian and French navies might become productive. Hitler's promise to support such ideas in a letter to the Duce came out easily. (Meanwhile, *Barbarossa* would be in course, making history.)

The effect of Assmann's paper on OKW was inconsequential. The paper is nevertheless worthy of record. First he outlined the new power position of the Axis secured by possession of the Adriatic coast through Greece to Crete, the Aegean and its islands. All outside threats to southeast Europe had been eliminated and *"control of the easterly Mediterranean* is no longer completely in the hands of the foe but is exercised by the Axis." Vital supply lines, petroleum for Italy, France, and Spain are assured, and grain for Germany.

Possession of Crete and the Dodecanese not only cuts off the Aegean, but enables the Luftwaffe on Crete or naval forces (from Italy or France) to police from Suda Bay the western entrance to the East Basin at the 165-mile gap between Cape Lithinon on the south coast of Crete and Ras el Tin in Libya. A British approach (out of Alexandria) toward the Central Basin and Rommel supply convoys would thus be flanked by Axis forces. Dominion over the Adriatic and the Aegean insured that the Balkans and Turkey would not go over to the enemy. Finally, Italy's staying powers were strengthened in policy, economy, and military freedom for outside employment. The new positions "are decisive for the further prosecution of the war."

Launching sites for the decisive battle against the British power position have been gained: "the most vulnerable points of British world power now lie within effective range of German weapons." The enemy was aware of the deadly danger; he had combined his own reinforcement with the hope of timely arrival of promised American aid via the Red Sea.

Britain's "fleet alone can protect the sea communications needed to control and preserve a political influence over the countries of the Middle and Far East." Therefore the aim of German/Italian war waging remains as always to destroy this controlling element, drive it out of the Eastern Mediterranean, and eliminate its bases and operational facilities in the whole Mediterranean.

Skl believed achievement of this goal must now be, the goal of a determined effort of German strategy, not only to hold the positions (until after Russia) but to exploit them with utmost speed in an energetic and systematic "*offensive* against the British stand in the Eastern Mediterranean."

The magnitude of *Barbarossa* places it in the foreground of the Armed Forces Command; this "must in no case, after the great strategic successes in the southeast, lead to the abandonment, reduction, or postponement of operations in the Eastern Mediterranean. On the contrary, everything must be done to keep the initiative firmly in hand, carry on, and even step up the fight with energetic power-packed blows."

Skl envisioned the following imperatives:

1. Make the strongest commitment of German and Italian air forces against the British fleet, if possible under German leadership, with heaviest-caliber bombs and torpedoes aimed at destruction of the capital ships and carriers (up to now *no* battleship or aircraft carrier had been sunk by the Luftwaffe). Production should be tested on suitable bombs and torpedoes. . . .

2. Call for transfer of Italian submarines from the Atlantic to the Mediterranean for attack on British sea communications. . . .

3. Push comprehensive mining by air from Crete and Rhodes against the Suez Canal, Port Said, Alexandria, and the Egyptian coast and Palestinian ports.

4. Call on Italy to give up her defensive war and to operate cruisers, destroyers, and small craft to exploit possibilities of Crete and Peloponnesus in continuous harassment and damage to opposing supply and transport. It is urgently desirible to get conduct of further operations into German hands.

5. Influence France to shore up her Syrian position to rule out British action there. Test air possibilities from Syria against Suez, the Red Sea, and the supply line to Cyprus.

6. Seize Malta to further restrict British operational possibilities toward the East and to diminish the threat to North African supply. (A final cleanout of the Mediterranean by the capture of Gibraltar is not a requirement at this time.)

7. Bring pressure on Italy to close the Strait of Sicily effectively (with German help) in order to disrupt the link between Gibraltar and Malta/Alexandria and to rule out further reinforcement and supply to the Eastern Mediterranean from Gibraltar.

8. Capture Tobruk through reinforcement in Libya and air concentration from Crete, plus Italian submarine activity in order to remove the flank threat at sea to Rommel, free him, and improve control over the sea area between Crete and Africa. Marsa Matruh could be very useful for operating against that key position. "The end goal of the North African campaign remains Alexandria/Suez."

What Assmann left out, because Skl was wedded to the war at sea in the Atlantic, was an equal call for commitment of all possible naval power in submarines and small craft to the now crucial Middle Sea. He launched a final shaft at *Barbarossa*: Skl is still convinced, he said, that control over the Eastern Mediterranean through wiping out every vestige of British power or influence would be of such "decisive significance to the whole war that vigorous attack on problems and exploitation of all opportunities, despite other strong demands (*Barbarossa*), must be brought about without reservation" in order to reap the Mediterranean harvest before American aid should ruin it. The case so stated was about as strong as any official writing could make it. No one dared to condemn *Barbarossa* outright; instead, he had been worked around, maneuvered around, and ignored, but eventually had been accepted as a fact of life. He had grown into an overpowering possessive monster who demanded his day in *unalterable Führer resolve*.[4]

There rested the case for Crete, the East Basin, and all that went with it. An unforeseen materialization of all the former prerequisites, so earnestly sought on behalf of the forgotten South Plan, had come about. A fair chance to alter the war drastically, if not to end it, could be discerned. If these proposals had been carried only as far as the Strait of Sicily, could British-American forces have risked a landing in Algeria in November 1942? Today's knowledge blots out 1941's practical problems of difficult relationships within the Axis and of demanding *Barbarossa*. Skl alone seems to have achieved sufficient detachment to apprehend a basically altered situation, its values and its urgency; yet Skl, at the same time, failed to reevaluate what contribution the submarines in the Atlantic could make in the Mediterranean. It probably would have been as hard for the Navy to cut back on its very own main effort in the Atlantic as for Hitler and the Army to give way on *Barbarossa*. Nevertheless the fresh challenge was there: Britain under serious pressure in the East Basin on land and at sea. Ground, air, and sea initiative were up for taking. This was the message of the hour.

No German in his right mind would have openly proposed a call-

4. The estimate was written up by Heinz Assmann, approved by Skl and the Navy's commander in chief. It appears as Annex 4 to FC of 6 June 1941 in a translation. In German records, the original of the paper is numbered Annex 5 of the same date. The brief is my translation and interpretation.

off of *Barbarossa*; such a radical shift General Halder declared "absolutely unthinkable," and so did many others. Most of the military had become converts. Failure to reevaluate was one hitch; the decisive one remained, however—Hitler himself. He could not have changed.

On the opposite side, Stalin, under building tensions, ruled as head of government as well as of party; Molotov acted as deputy. Both of them did their utmost to placate Hitler—by speeding material deliveries, by closing anti-German embassies in Moscow, by withdrawing troops from so-called offensive frontier deployments, by prohibiting fire against German aircraft incursions, and by salving the German ambassador with declarations of friendship. Day on day Hitler's case for preventive war was falling flat; yet he persisted. Without pause or ripple he forced his personal design against Russia toward fruition and thereby "committed," in the words of Admiral Weichold, *"the greatest strategic blunder of the war."*[5]

Warlimont of OKW wrote (Warlimont IH, pp. 144, 145): "An unforeseen strategic situation arose which offered a prospect of altering the whole course of the war. . . . It was an occasion for a fresh examination of the further plan of war." At the time this aspect was never fully perceived. Assmann's study had no effect. L Section OKW would have had little trouble in regarding the Navy paper as merely a matter of timing, that is, the recommended steps could come "after *Barbarossa*" better than in the crowded now. A delay of six or seven weeks until Russia should be out would make little difference in the end. Meanwhile let Göring's 10th Air Corps whittle away at the Eastern Mediterranean from bases on Crete. Undoubtedly Hitler felt the same way. He cherished the thought that Britain might still come around. How badly her sea power had been crippled, and how attractive this made the hour, never got over to him. On the Channel the principal excuse had been lack of air supremacy. Here such supremacy was a fact and had all but assured total control of the sea. Hitler still feared the sea and Britain on it.[6]

5. Werth, pp. 117–27. According to Werth (an experienced journalist who arrived in Moscow early in July 1941) Stalin aimed to put off the war, which he thought inevitable, to 1942 when Russia would be better prepared, even well enough possibly to take the initiative. This Hitler wanted to keep ahead of.

6. Weichold, pp. 155–161, as elaborated to the author in talks in Germany, 1960; Skl War Diary, June 1941; IMT Doc. 066 C, in which Admiral Raeder discusses his efforts to dissuade Hitler from attack on Russia. Raeder found he had to go along. Consultation with General der Flieger Paul Deichmann, chief of staff to Field Marshal Kesselring, commander in chief South from late 1941 on, is another source, as is discussion with General Halder, in Germany 1960, who agreed that

On 4 June the 10th Air Corps took over from the 8th Air Corps and went to work with over three hundred combat planes, including about a hundred in North Africa with Rommel. Führer Directive No. 31 emerged on 9 June. It rearranged the southeastern commands and gave status to Crete as the main base for the air effort. Field Marshal List commanded the theater, and under him an Air general commanding southern Greece (General Felmy) was to combine staffs with Admiral Southeast to make what amounted to a joint command over the East Basin. Felmy's deputy was to command "Fortress Crete" as "special commandant." Tasks included operating sea communication to and from Crete, directing supply, and supervising military governments. The primary task was the air war against Britain, according to orders of the commander in chief Air. While L Section, in producing the directive, had to be content with turning over planning and targeting to Göring, the wording shows a sharp awareness of Crete's potentialities. The pertinent paragraphs ran:

6. The *Island of Crete* will occupy a special position in the southeastern area. It will be the operational base from which to carry on the air war in the Eastern Mediterranean, in coordination with the situation in North Africa. . . . At present organizing, strengthening, protecting, and supplying this base are the most important tasks in the southeastern area. . . .

Fortress Crete is to be put under an Air Force general as *special commandant.*

7. The air war in the Eastern Mediterranean is to be carried out according to the orders of the commander in chief Air. He is to make appropriate arrangements with the Italian Air Force directly.

This was as far as the case for Crete ever got.[7]

---

an opportunity had been missed, but emphasized that a switch away from *Barbarossa* would have been "absolutely unthinkable." General Warlimont expressed himself in like terms in his KFA, p. 216. His later writing was stronger on the side of "something should have been done." Admiral Raeder approached Admiral Riccardi, head of the Italian Navy, with a proposal to shift the offensive to the Mediterranean. Riccardi replied that the offensive belonged in the Atlantic, where it was, while the Italian light forces protected the heavy ships against the British naval offensive. Admiral Raeder did not himself intend to make a total shift to the Mediterranean with the forces engaged in the siege of England, which he regarded as his primary, Führer-approved task. Assmann's choice of words reveals the German attitude toward the partners: they were to be called on to do this or to do that, as the Germans saw things. Their limitations were well known and their sensitive awareness, from Mussolini on down, of shortcomings. There at the top was where unified planning and execution had to begin: between Hitler and Mussolini.

7. Although the Luftwaffe was to break open the gates into Russia and thence be heavily committed, several officers in its higher echelon wanted no part of *Barbarossa* and sought to replace him by air war in the East Basin. In some such hope

It was not far; Crete remained a paper dragon. Air power available was inadequate, and on top of that came Göring's capricious remote control. He knew that Hitler's interest ran low, despite the free hand offered the Luftwaffe, in much the same fashion as on the Channel in August 1940. The same dubious result followed. Main target here should have been the British fleet in Alexandria and at sea, but Göring wavered, incapable of staying on target. Nothing much was done about bringing the Italian flyers into the game, and after the first few flurries the 10th Air Corps bogged down in maintenance and supply troubles on Fortress Crete. Shipping was short and grew shorter; so did stocks of fuel and munitions. Although an ideal air arena presented the best chance of the war to the Luftwaffe, no sustained air offensive developed. Once again, hard-won strategic initiative dribbled down the drain as British power revived in well-executed jabs at North-Africa-bound convoys. Rommel was short of supply. Cairo breathed easier while Crete died on the vine. Instead of symbolizing control over the East Basin, the island stood for the death of the plunging eagle, symbol of German airborne. In terms of high casualties, Crete memorialized the mightiest and last German airborne effort of the war.

It is true the number of German airborne divisions increased after Crete; yet the proportion of jumpers in each sank lower and lower. They were no longer strictly parachute formations, but special ones for special tasks. Except for the Battle of the Bulge (winter of 1944–45), in which a weak, poorly executed airborne effort failed, the so-called German paratroops fought as infantry. They defended Monte Cassino, and Heidrich of Prison Valley was with them. No, where Crete really made the heaviest impact was on the Western Allies. It speeded their development of airborne as a new arm immeasurably. And in all the world, paratrooper became a fearsome name to scare children with. He was the strongest and fiercest fighter.[8]

Göring, who never favored the East Plan, had arranged for Student to see Hitler in April about airborne seizure of Crete. Student, who knew nothing of *Barbarossa*, thought to go on from Crete to Cyprus and the Suez. Air Force Chief of Staff Jeschonnek, who knew about *Barbarossa*, accompanied Student and sympathized with his ideas. Ideas similar to Student's Göring had heard a week earlier from Löhr of Air Fleet 4. His chief of staff, Korten, who later succeeded his friend Jeschonnek, was a strong advocate of the South Plan in place of the East Plan. Whether Korten influenced Löhr or the other way around makes no difference. The idea was alive and had been spread around. The discussion probably helped to obtain Hitler's approval of at least a show of air war continued in the East Basin, as Führer Directive No. 31 prescribed.

8. In November 1942 Student taxed Göring by letter on the nonemployment of

Now, back in 1941, the last truly offensive opportunity of winning the Battle of the Mediterranean is gone. The story grows anticlimactic. Indeed, it has tended so ever since Mussolini leaped into Greece in October 1940. He wanted to show Hitler he could go it alone; instead, he demonstrated, to Hitler's deep disgust, that unified war waging by the Axis could result only in *Schweinerei*. Therewith Hitler dropped his toying with the Jodl-Raeder South Plan, to find fulfillment in his very own East Plan. Molotov's sour rejoinders in the Berlin conference of mid-November reinforced Hitler in his earlier resolve. The compulsive private Front he had piled up against Russia could not give way to a changed situation in the East Basin or even to reports of England tottering on the brink at home. The time was right for pause and counsel. But in spirit he was already plundering Russia—and soon most of his people joined in greedily.

Events bore out the case for Crete as the war's great what-might-have-been that got lost in the deepest of Hitlerian delusions: he might not have to invade England after all.

Crusade in the East and Hopes for Its Sequel

Even at this moment of commitment the German people knew little about these goings-on. By press and radio they were still fighting in Crete or flying against beleaguered Tobruk or toward the Suez Canal and smothering Britain's fleet at Alexandria in a "hail of bombs." Reports on Crete only began to appear after 24 May (when Ringel heaved his sigh of relief) and thereupon Crete news fired up: Britain is tumbling; her days in the Mediterranean are numbered; the conquest of Crete has done all this and more. Göring commended his Crete warriors in a special order of the day: "With boundless pride and happiness I report to the Führer, his order has been executed. Before the whole world you have proved the Führer's words: there are no impregnable islands." People soon shortened the cry to, *There are no more islands*. Plane crews splashed the slogan on fuselages, complete with signature—Adolf Hitler. What magic will he work next? Will it be England at last or continuation in the Mittelmeer? To them in their paradise of dreams it was all one. News advices seemed to

his arm since Crete. He extolled the Airborne cause, for which, he thought, "the greatest possibilities of surprising successes" still existed. The new techniques and weaponry developed since Crete had great promise. Göring did nothing about it.

favor action in the south where Rommel was driving into Egypt. Not a solitary word issued on mounting tension with Russia.

Outside Germany, however, public opinion discussed and rediscussed an approaching storm in the east. Crete's fall was deplored; Britain's Lower House raised questions of neglect in her defense materials and wondered if the rest of the Mediterranean came next or Russia. It could even be a switch back to England. Across the Channel Goebbels printed a piece entitled, "Kreta als Beispiel" (Crete as an Example), which OKW promptly suppressed, to make it appear that Goebbels had talked out of turn about actual plans, namely, Invasion England. Increased warnings and orders on one subject indicated the Führer's growing edginess. The subject was evasion of untoward incidents with the United States at this wrong time; he wanted to steer shy of them at all costs. In mid-Atlantic U-203 skirmished with the U.S.S. *Texas* and her destroyer escort; earlier (21 May) another submarine sank the American freighter *Robin Moore*. Orders issued to forfend all such actions and they were repeated and reemphasized. For, as Hitler reminded Admiral Raeder, by mid-July *Barbarossa*'s prospect should be manifest, and Britain's reaction too. Now at this tender time England must merely be held down; there must be no new uproar, let alone a declaration of war by the United States. The extraordinary precautions seem to show that the Führer expected *Barbarossa* to have a decisive impact on British policy.[9]

While Crete was being relegated to the sidelines in German staffs, *Barbarossa*'s sequels were taken in hand under a working draft of Führer Directive No. 32. Post-Russia designs had brewed in OKH for months and in OKW where L Section attempted to keep abreast of the Führer brainstorms. If his Atlantic island fancies were wild enough to embarrass sailor conversation, his post-Russia continentalism should have made the soldiers ashamed. Yet they seemed to tolerate it as they gradually did *Barbarossa*. Moreover, they did some dreaming of their own. One thing was sure: *Barbarossa* was going to go and most soldiers who knew came to believe in him. Speculation about strategical aftermath began as early as February 1941 when Jodl gave orders to study the invasion of India via Russia and Afghanistan. Likewise, Hitler's infamous extermination speech of 30 March had included hints

9. FC and Skl War Diary, June 1941; *Völkischer Beobachter*, May and June 1941; OKW Ops SitConf; Lossberg, p. 117. Goebbel's example was naturally that Crete was a curtain raiser for Invasion England. British newspapers wondered about this too.

of a shift in armament, after Russia, to the Luftwaffe and the Navy. Army would be able to get along with fifty some divisions in Russia; a few more might be needed for Gibraltar and Northwest Africa. Then in April, when Rommel had shown the way, another inspiration struck: in the fall there would be an African offensive. OKH began making up tables of troop allocations for the coming tasks in such places as Spain (Gibraltar), Morocco (to close off the Strait), Libya and Egypt (to drive on Suez from the west), Turkey (for passage to drive on Suez from the east), and Afghanistan (maybe simply to equal Alexander).

It is evident that OKH had kept abreast of Führer thinking with ideas of its own; and now as B-Day drew near, it would be natural to seek clarification. During a series of review briefings, begun with the field commands on 4 June, General Halder stressed the need of rapid execution and added, "After *Barbarossa*: Malta, Egypt, possibly from southeast Russia; through Spain to Northwest Africa," and ended, "Basis of the Army for tasks after *Barbarossa* have long been in the works." On this same day of 4 June at a regular L Section conference, post-Russia plans were queried, probably by the Army member on OKH instructions. General Warlimont, the section chief, gave his own reaction as a rough starting outline for his assistants in three short but all-inclusive projects:

1. Clean out the Mediterranean by seizure of Gibraltar, Malta, Cyprus, and the Suez Canal.
2. Build up a European–West African ground position against a British-American coalition, and help France to regain territories held by de Gaulle.
3. Invade England for the kill.

These made a very general but sound progression out of the many plans that had been discussed since *Sea Lion*'s demise in the fall of 1940. The East Basin's current advantages were, however, ignored while emphasis rested on a western combination with France. Nothing was said about an offensive against the British fleet to gain control of the Mediterranean Sea. Spurred by these ideas—some from OKH and some in Assmann's Skl study (which Army would naturally want to stay ahead of)—L Section got busy on a draft of Führer Directive No. 32. Its date was 11 June 1941, a day before the Führer and OKW moved down from the Mountain to pump up things for B-Day. General Jodl held the draft for more than a week, then released it to the top service commands with a signed memo of transmittal on 19 June.

By that time *Barbarossa* pressure was high and the chips were down. That Jodl was the releaser adds significance.[10]

One of his galling chores was to steer drafts of directives through to Führer approval. Some of the papers Jodl simply sat on, well knowing they would never make the course. But with *Barbarossa* and his preliminaries there was no trouble; indeed the Führer took the lead. These plans were food and drink to him. Thus Jodl's release of Directive No. 32 in draft form certified his Führer's full approval. The language itself smells of Hitler. If any paper revealed his thinking, this one did so for his long-range continental strategy. Above all the draft confirmed his and professional faith in *Barbarossa*'s swift victory. He more than half-expected the first shattering blows to bring Britain around on his side. Might she not even join his crusade? A place for her he still held in his postwar world. Among many delusions, this one ran deepest and fondest: to be accepted by her. After the campaign had begun, he often burst out with something of the sort while monologuing to aides: he must not give up on England; eventually she would see the light. Here was one more chance.

In itself the draft is noteworthy because it culminated Hitlerian-German strategical thought in the same way as the ugly orders of 30 March 1941 pointed up the prospective Nazi sociopolitical frame for continental Europe. At this time, 6 June 1941, these orders were implemented by an addition to a basic martial law decree of 13 May. It is idle to speak about one of these manifestations—strategy and policy—without the other. They were authentic Hitler. Inside him the sociopolitical plan had long been firm; its strategical companion left room for the fond hope that the sudden catastrophic downfall of Russia would eliminate need for the last actions against Britain, especially the final one: Invasion England.

The draft's power words carry the ring of triumph as they picture a gratifying closing scene: "After smashing the Russian armed forces to bits, Germany and Italy will be military masters of the European continent. . . . Serious danger to the European land spaces will no longer obtain." Emphasis on armament can shift to the Navy and the Luftwaffe. Deeper German-French collaboration will tie down British forces, eliminate any threat from North Africa, restrict the movement of the British fleet in the western Mediterranean, and protect the

10. Hubatsch, pp. 120–39; FD, 1939–41, pp 183–96; Warlimont KFA, pp. 400–426; Warlimont, IH, pp. 148–49; OKW Ops SitConf, 4 June 1941; H. Greiner, pp. 391–92; Klee; Halder, 2:335, 441–43; Lossberg, pp. 107, 127; discussion with Warlimont in Germany, 1960.

southwestern flank of Europe against Anglo-Saxon incursion. Spain will soon be challenged to decide whether or not she will join in driving the British from Gibraltar. The possibility of bringing pressure on Turkey and Iran will improve the prospect of making them useful in the fight against Britain.

From the triumphant ending of the East Campaign the following strategic tasks can arise for the armed forces during the late fall of 1941 and the winter 1941–42:

(1) Organize, secure, exploit the economy of the east spaces; fifty to sixty divisions should suffice.

(2) Continue *the fight against the British position in the Mediterranean and the Middle East* with concentric attack out of Libya through Egypt and out of Bulgaria through Turkey, and possibly from Transcaucasia through Iran.

    (*a*) In North Africa it is important to reduce Tobruk as a base of continued attack on the Suez Canal [from the west] in November 1941.

    (*b*) Plan to attack Suez from the East by an operation from bases in Bulgaria, through Turkey [and Palestine].

    (*c*) Commit a motorized expedition corps from Transcaucasia as soon as the Russian collapse permits against Iraq in combination with Operation *b*.

    (*d*) Exploit Arab Freedom uprisings.

(3) *Close the west entrance to the Mediterranean* by eliminating Gibraltar. . . . Operation *Felix* with French participation.

(4) Besides these possible operations . . . the siege of England must be taken up again in full force by the Navy and Luftwaffe. . . . Preparations for a landing in England will have the double objective of tying down British forces in the homeland and finishing her off by a landing at a sign of her collapse.

The time of commencing these strokes in the Mediterranean and Near East could not yet be fixed, said the draft, though strongest operational effect would result from simultaneous launches against Gibraltar, Egypt, and Palestine. Such a combination would depend mainly on the Luftwaffe's ability to support all three at once. In customary personal admonition by Hitler (which for Warlimont clinched the surmise of his direct involvement) the draft closed with a request to service chiefs that they meet their preparations along the lines given and advise the Führer in time of their results so that "my definitive directions may still be released during the East Campaign." It would not take long.

Jodl's first version, released on the eve of battle, 19 June, soon felt the influence of *Barbarossa*'s amazing initial victories. On 30 June Warlimont accordingly released a revision. (Its main points are included above.) Rommel's first priority was shifted to Tobruk, followed by attack toward Suez, while a concentric advance against Suez from the east was to develop from a main force based in Bulgaria, for advance through Turkey and Palestine. Land power's terrific effects through mobile forces seemed already to have been demonstrated by *Barbarossa*'s armored columns; they ate up whole landscapes. Against this early proof, fresh troubles had arisen over Rommel's supply by sea. So why not stay on the land? The march on Suez through Turkey and Palestine was promptly upgraded.

Nothing was salvaged from Assmann's Navy plea for control of the sea through a combined air-sea effort. The new strategic springboards in the East Basin went begging as Army influence prevailed. Nor did the finished draft heed Warlimont's thought for a definite return to the west and a cleanout of the Mediterranean from there. The new version omitted Malta entirely, and Cyprus too, probably in the glib old thought that possession of Gibraltar and Suez would render Malta and Cyprus harmless. Yet if Tobruk stood enough in the way to be taken out first, so did Malta, and even more. For his own reasons, Hitler feared Malta. Hitler could only do with a soldier's finish on land.

In June 1941 Hitler again stood on the sea and again was charged with victory. Yet for this second and last time he felt less at home, more uncomfortable, than that first time, on the Channel. If anything, the interim had made him more wary of the sea. Even in the glow of prospective victory over Russia, he had to hedge for the final action against England—"a sign of her collapse"—before he set sail, not to slug it out, but to take over in a police action. To be sure, it might never come to a crossing; his private sequel might do away away with the need for both the long march through the Holy Land and the Channel crossing.

From 5 June on, when Hitler at the Berghof approved the definitive *Barbarossa* timetable, hop-off tension tightened. Transport by rail and road had been rumbling eastward since 23 May at highest density. On 9 June the adjutant offices of OKW distributed "invitations" to a final Führer briefing and luncheon for 14 June with the same high commanders as had attended on 30 March, plus a few more from Navy and Air. On 12 June he and his entourage descended from the Mountain to watch for outside reactions against B-Day preparations. For example, Navy minelayers had to depart for the Gulf of Finland to lay a barrier; back of them in the Baltic, five small submarines took up stations in readiness. OKW and the foreign office fell to weaving a web of fake reports about border violations by Russian forces. Of course there had to be a direct, intolerable offensive spark to ignite the explosion.

On Saturday 14 June the invited officers made their arrivals in staggered order at the various entrances of the Chancellery, timed to fit the progress of the presentations and to screen the meeting from the curious. Two and a half months had passed since the confrontation of 30 March when Hitler held aloof and told them their duty curtly and forcibly. They had now had time to digest these orders, received since in written form, and to get used to them. Hitler had won, felt relaxed, confident. He greeted the arriving individuals genially in the Bundesrat Chamber as each entered to speak his particular piece in the portrayal of the operations. This went along very well toward a break at 1400 for a pleasant, mellowing lunch.

After that came Hitler's own turn. General Halder recorded it as a "comprehensive speech of policy, giving reasons for . . . attack on Russia and the development of his estimate that the fall of Russia would induce Britain to give up the fight." Germany and all Europe would benefit if "I sweep Russia away and thereby kill Bolshevism." Hitler's whole demeanor beamed friendship and confidence in his field commanders; no direct reference to the orders of 30 March occurred. His audience seemed to feel better. Its members could hardly applaud as he finished with a flourish about *"the world will thank us,"* but they could beam back and they did. There is record of a unifying confidence pervading the room. He had moved them. Much later one officer remarked that if he had reservations about the campaign before, he lost them at this meeting. The general reaction was favorable. Thus Invasion Russia got set in body and soul through the "will power of one man alone to lead German soldiery into the heaviest fighting of its long history."[11]

11. Philippi and Heim, p. 52; Heusinger, pp. 120–23 (Heusinger was operations officer, OKH); Halder, 2:455; H. Greiner, pp. 390–91; Warlimont IH, pp. 161–65; Raeder, 2:251, plus discussion and correspondence with four officers present. On this same day of 14 June 1941 Stalin had Tass release a dispatch which countered one of Hitler's arguments to his officers and drove hard in a last attempt to clear away rumors of war. It named the stories about British–Russian collaboration after Cripps's arrival in Moscow from London as "clumsy propaganda," and then made four points about Russo-German relations: (1) No German claims have been made on Russia. (2) Germany is fully observing the conditions of the Nonaggression

The Führer trumpet having sounded, presentations resumed with a new aplomb; they covered the sea tasks of Navy in the Baltic, the three-pronged drive of Army into the Russian middle, and the support from the Air. The pieces fitted together in a dress rehearsal of far deeper impact than hundreds of written plans. At the tail end came a checkout of Zero Hour for B-Day, a mere day and a week off. Decision settled on 0300 Sunday 22 June 1941.

A definitive warning order to carry on would flash out on 17 June, still under proviso of call-off up to 1300 on the 21st by the code word *Altona*. Since January two notable instances had caught an exalted Führer as he contemplated *Barbarossa*'s mighty works. At each he exclaimed, "The world will hold its breath." The moment was almost upon him, and he vouchsafed to his inner circle, "We shall witness on the Russian side in less than three months a collapse such as world history has never seen." On the evening of the 20th his *Word to the Troops* goes out, in "an extraordinary politically canted exposition," and hard upon it comes the irrevocable, full-blooded code word *Dortmund*, "Go!" The die is cast. History's most ambitious land offensive gets under way.

Seventy-five years before 22 June 1941, Tolstoi wrote about another launch into Russia:

Millions of men perpetrated so great a mass crime—fraud, swindling, robbery, forgery, issue of counterfeit money, plunder, incendiarism, and murder—that the annals of all the criminal courts of the world could not muster such a sum of wickedness in whole centuries, though the men who committed those crimes did not at the time look on them as crimes.

Hitler was one day ahead of Napoleon and aimed to stay ahead.

The unworried German public got the exciting news by radio at 0700 on 22 June when Propaganda Minister Joseph Goebbels solemnly intoned a declaration of war against Russia. It was the Führer call-up to his *Volk*. He used eleven printed pages to review the unknown case against the old friend and new foe. He wound up with a remarkable half-apology to Self for having passed up his prime opportunity in the East Basin:

The victory of the Axis Powers in the Balkans . . . thwarted the [opponents'] plan to involve Germany this summer in month-long battles in

Pact. "Rumors of her intention to tear up the Pact and to . . . attack the USSR are without foundation." Transfer of German troops to the north and east "one must suppose" have no bearing on Soviet–German relations. (3) The USSR intends to abide by the Pact, and is not preparing for war. (4) Summer rallies of Red Army reserves are training exercises that take place every summer. Werth, p. 125.

southeastern Europe, [while they combined in order] finally, together with Britain, supported by supply from America, to crush the German Reich and Italy. *I therefore decided today to lay the fate and future of the German Reich and our people in the hands of our soldiers.* May God help us specially in this fight!

To Mussolini, Hitler confided a feeling of immense spiritual release. He had what he had to have.[12]

What luck! A year ago to the day, 22 June, he had accepted the surrender of France at Compiègne in that refurbished railroad coach of 1918.

12. Hitler's letter of 21 June to Mussolini pursued the established line: England has lost the war; her present situation is bad; she places hope in Russia and America. He is about to take out Russia, and America matters little since she is already at her maximum capacity of assistance. "Whatever may come now, Duce, our situation cannot become worse . . . it can only improve. . . . In conclusion, since I struggled through to this decision, I again feel spiritually free." Mussolini replied on 23 June in full approval: Egypt in the fall after Tobruk; play both France and Spain; the United States is already doing all it can.—Documents GFP, vol. 12, Doc. 660; Roussy de Sales, pp. 977–87; H. Greiner, pp. 390–92; Lossberg, p. 113; Halder, 2:457–59; Puttkamer, p. 44; OKW, L Section, Situations Evaluation, 21–22 June 1941.

25. Aftermath I

In Russia: Summer and Fall of 1941

The 3d Battalion of Regiment 228, 101st Light Infantry Division, was a crack outfit of south Germans who wondered why on 14 June 1941 they had ended up at an out-of-the-way frontier point under the Carpathian Mountains in Polish Galicia. The thought never entered any of their Swabian and Bavarian heads that the battalion would have the honor of guarding the extreme right wing of a mighty drive into Russia. True, over there to the south, across the placidly winding river San, lurked a few Russian soldiers among deserted houses; they were accepted as friends, though distant furtive friends, who seldom appeared except at the railroad bridge 200 yards downstream from the schoolhouse billet of the 3d Battalion. Rail traffic crossed over every once in a while with Russian deliveries to Germany. Downhill from the schoolhouse lay the remains of a demolished road bridge that bore witness to the continued total separation of the German and Russian halves of an old fortress town. As a key position in World War I it had earned fame through its unpronounceable name—Przemysl. Before the 1939 occupation by Germans and Russians, 50,000 Poles had lived in this thriving center, now a ghost of its old self. Why should the 3d Battalion be stuck with it?

Rumors circulated about a through passage of German troops toward the Middle East, which Russia had acceded to; this made sense because Britain was surely due for attack there. Perhaps, on the other hand, Russia had demurred and it was more a case of stiffening the frontier line to show her. But war "against friendly Russia"! And to be set off by friend Germany! No one could think such a dirty thought. On 18 June important news arrived for the battalion commander, Lt. Colonel Hans Kissel; but for him alone.

For the first time he learns of Operation *Barbarossa*; he is to prepare, but in highest secrecy, to make a demonstration against the opposite side of the river to tie down the Red force. On Saturday 21 June comes word of B-Day on the morrow and zero hour of 0330 (which is the original hour instead of the new one of 0300). By 2300 the battalion is deployed northwest of Przemysl; it has hauled out farther on the flank in readiness "for attack." At midnight the Führer's "Call-up to the Soldiers of the East Front" is read to the troops gathered at each assault station. It is the first they have heard of "the Red Army opposite preparing to strike Germany in the back in its fight for life and freedom. This move must be got ahead of. In this campaign, the brutal and cunning foe must be treated with the greatest harshness." What silly rubbish!

No soldiers or sailors are that stupid. "Every soldier," wrote Kissel, "probably experienced a peculiarly disagreeable feeling at opening fire in the middle of peace on an unsuspecting ally. . . . The battalion commander too felt depressed this night." Yet he has to admit a paucity of knowledge about political actions in course, and repeatedly in the past his own misgivings about Führer actions have seemed to prove false—later. Then too, maybe he alone has had doubts, for the overwhelming majority of the German people are faithfully committed. Enough. This is no time to burden oneself with these problems. The soldier's duty is to carry out orders. At 0300 a long freight train passes over the bridge bound for Germany with Russian deliveries, maybe the last on the whole 500-mile front. It puffs on; gradually the clank of the wheels fades out.[1]

1. Major General Kissel and I met on a number of occasions in Germany during 1953 when he was engaged on his book (Kissel). The story and quotations above are taken from his book, which gives a vivid and instructive account of actions on the firing line of the Russian campaign. Presumably at this eleventh hour, battalion commanders also first learned of the *Kommissarbefehl* and its queer companion piece. Both were generally ignored. Field Marshal von Manstein, pp. 176–77, writes of hearing about these odd orders shortly before B-Day. He commanded the 56th Armored Corps in *Barbarossa*'s northern wing. He considered the orders "unsoldierly" and notified his superiors they would not be carried out in his command. He and his troop commanders were in close agreement on this and he thought this attitude obtained generally throughout the Army. He found it so when he took over the 11th Army in the south during September 1941.

Of a sudden, there, beyond the disappearing train, the heavens flame red—ah, Division Artillery opening up! One can count seconds until the boom of the guns arrives and the whoosh of shells overhead. The first hit strikes in across the river, then another and another. The bursts flash dusky red. There are so many, count is lost. What about the Russians? Not a sign or a sound. Own preparation fire holds on; after a good hour the rifle company on the right creeps past the houses to the river bank. Mortars and machine guns rake the far side; still no reaction. A lieutenant and nine men form a scout group to paddle over in an inflatable boat. They disappear on the other side. Rifle fire crackles, then dies out. Toward 0600 the scouts reappear on the far bank, and a quick count and recount shows three extras; good. The group and three prisoners cross back. Now maybe some news. One of the extras is an artillery lieutenant. When asked why he has not fired back, he answers, "We have received no order to." Smiling, he then throws himself flat in the grass, asks for a cigarette. What a strange business.

What does it mean? Does it characterize a Russian what-the-hell tolerance for anything? Or is it a small but significant sample of the cheerful fatalism that carries these people along? Perhaps both. Soon another stronger, spiritual force would make itself felt: unfailing allegiance to Mother Russia, who has been violated. Stalin will bring her forward. First must come trial and trouble. In the north Leeb drives for Leningrad, in the middle Bock toward Smolensk, and in the south Rundstedt (past Przemysl) through the Ukraine toward Kiev.

Bock in the middle carried the killing punch in his two armored groups—Hoth (Group 3) on the left, Guderian (Group 2) on the right. In one pincer combination after another these two, trailed by regular infantry divisions, executed massive encirclements on the way to Minsk and then on toward Smolensk, which Guderian took on 16 July. Behind him on his north flank were still masses of trapped Red formations. The advance had carried 400 miles, and German forces stood on the autobahn to Moscow, 200 miles off. The overall bag in aircraft, tanks, guns and prisoner of war ran to unbelievable figures like 2582 planes, 2500 tanks 1500 guns and over 700,000 men. These reports surpassed even those of Hindenburg and Ludendorff in World War I. German high commands were elated.

Leeb's territory in the north broadened as he advanced; his forces became separated, the terrain grew heavy with rains, and resistance stiffened. Yet by mid-July he was through the Baltic states and poking into Russia proper, about 130 miles from his objective, Leningrad. While the bag had not been as spectacular as Group Center's, it had been big. It was obvious there could be no swift crashing advance on the target. By 11 July the first German supply ships put in at Riga.

Rundstedt's southern prong encountered the dourest defense. At first his tank blitz in the center achieved no decisive breakthrough as the defenders overcame their initial shock and threw in everything at hand with prodigal abandon—yet only to hold, not to advance. For

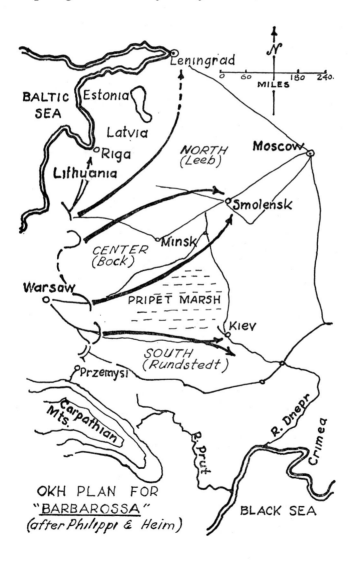

OKH PLAN FOR
"BARBAROSSA"
(after Philippi & Heim)

five days a border battle raged. Beginning 27 June the Red formations gave ground slowly while confining the German thrust to a narrow spear with tender flanks. Farther south, Lemberg (east of
Przemysl) fell on 30 June, a success which broadened the front as it
approached the Stalin Line. The breach made in the line by 9 July
in the area of Zhitomir and Berdichev secured a favorable springboard
for operating east and southeast. Fresh Red forces in stubborn defense
actions denied rapid German progress. But after 13 July Russian
strength weakened, so that on the 14th, German tank and motorized
forces were within range of Kiev, the large industrial target in the
south; the strategic line of the Dnieper Valley hove into sight; the
Pripet Marshes west of Kiev were sealed off. "Therewith the tactical
crisis of the break-in, Phase I, had been surmounted."[2]

All along the front the German war machine gained more ground
in three weeks than its World War I predecessor had gained in three
years. By 4 July Hitler's cup was running over. "The Russian has
lost the war," he told his personal staff. His favorite weapon, surprise,
had scored beyond belief, not only on the ground but in the air and
even on the sea. Red planes were caught under covers around their
fields by the hundreds, and in flight without fighter support. Luftwaffe's
air action, close support to ground forces, and long-range intelligence
had been very effective. The air belonged to the Germans again and,
negatively, so did the Baltic Sea. General Halder so early as 3 July
ventured that the campaign was won in these fourteen days. Similar
thoughts circulated in other commands, but abroad too, especially in
London. Not so in Moscow.[3]

Alexander Werth tells of his arrival in Russia from London on this
very day, 3 July 1941; of the long plane voyage via the Shetlands,
which ended in the estuary of the Dvina south of Archangel; of how
the Russian Army hosts made the arriving British comfortable at an
all-night supper, how they spoke of Churchill's broadcast call to Russia on 24 June, and how today Stalin had spoken to his countrymen.

2. Philippi and Heim, pp. 54 ff.; Heusinger, p. 127. Kiev could probably have
been taken at the end. The 2d Army Corps (Motorized) with the 2d Panzer Division stood poised for the job on 12 July. But Hitler had forbidden the move to
Rundstedt direct. It became another costly Hitlerian "tankhalt" order. Russian defense power thickened around Kiev and a line to the northwest. Kiev became a sort
of Verdun-like salient that refused to give up. During September it was cut off in
the rear at heavy cost.

3. Halder, 3:3–84; Philippi and Heim, pp. 54–74; Warlimont IH, pp. 187–212;
Werth, pp. 131–188; Liddell Hart RA, pp. 101–111.

It would be a long hard war, but Russia, they knew, would win in the end.

Stalin's appeal was long overdue—war all around for nearly two weeks and no word out of him. Now he began in a heart-warming salutation: "Comrades, Citizens, Brothers and Sisters, Fighters of our Army and Navy! I am speaking to you!" He told them the bitter truth; the Nazi Invasion continues despite heroic defense efforts. Nazi troops have occupied Lithuania, part of Latvia, western Byelorussia and western Ukraine. "A serious threat hangs over our country." But Hitler's army is no more invincible than Napoleon's or than Wilhelm II's. The truth is, this war began in conditions favorable to the Germans and unfavorable to the Red Army. He explained the main difference— German treachery. "This war has been inflicted upon us and our country has entered on a life-and-death struggle against its most wicked and perfidious enemy, German Fascism. . . . Our people should be fearless in their struggle and should selflessly fight our patriotic *war of liberation* against the Fascist enslavers. . . ." His words kindled a fire of fierce nationalism that filled a void Russians were hardly aware of—one that encompassed God, hearth, home, and country in Mother Russia. At last they had a bond to unite them. Through Stalin the German attackers had given it to them. He concluded, "All the strength of the people must be put to smashing the enemy. Onward to victory!" They had a leader of great strength to look to.

General Fedyuninsky, commanding the 15th Infantry Corps on the north flank of the Kiev front north of Przemysl, wrote later, "It is hard to describe the enormous enthusiasm and patriotic uplift with which this appeal was met. We suddenly seemed to feel much stronger." The 15th Corps struggled and suffered like all the others against a totally unexpected assault.

The overwhelming might of the German Army came as a complete surprise. Ammunition had not been distributed. . . . We deployed to our defense positions under constant shelling and bombing. Our officers did not lose control. We reached the defense positions where the frontier guards had been waging an unequal struggle. Even the wives were in the firing line.

By 8 July the 15th Corps had withdrawn to Korosten on the fortified line inside the old frontier. Stories of neighboring forces up and down the front were worse still: inability to make high headquarters believe, continued insistence on their part on keeping the peace; then impossible orders to counterattack. Leaflets dropped from German planes said that Moscow had surrendered. The men got angry. Morale ebbed low, but it held. Would the real test come just east of Smolensk in the center, on the road to Moscow?

Smolensk to Moscow? Why, that was the route of Napoleon 129 years before. And just as the German leaders preparing to invade England had engrossed themselves in Julius Caesar's landings there, so they now went after Napoleon in Russia. He had taken Smolensk. What did he then do wrong? He frequently repeated, "Peace lies in Moscow." Was that the error? Among the questioners was Adolf Hitler, who developed an aversion for the Napoleonic route and a stronger dislike for Napoleon's objective, Moscow. This twist, which involved the aim of Phase II and the whole campaign, came out by bits as *Barbarossa*'s Phase I progressed and as Phase II tried to get under way. Far back in the early planning of late 1940, Hitler and his professionals had differed at this very point; it was then left for actual operations to clear up.

From *Barbarossa*'s first days onward, the Führer weather at OKW in the new woodland headquarters near Rastenburg, East Prussia, recalled all the instability experienced during the West Campaign. The high and low pressures and the changing wind effects were passed on to OKH in nervous concern (*Sorge, Besorgnis*) followed by meddling, jealous care to stay ahead of OKH evaluators—diffused and unnecessary ordering. Braided into this pattern was the former unsureness about targets. It already showed when Hitler visited OKH to felicitate General Halder on his fifty-seventh anniversary, on 30 June.

Hitler did not come right out with it, but maneuvered around, first with the north flank—Leeb. Swift freeing of the north coast on the Baltic and Gulf of Finland was important so that ore traffic by sea from Sweden might accelerate. Thereupon he leapt over to Rundstedt in the south: the Ukraine was needed for foods and industrial power. This he mixed with another reference to Leeb in the north; he should get going quickly for Leningrad. Did he have sufficient power? After Smolensk was taken by mid-July, it would require until August for infantry to take Moscow. Armored forces would not do for that job. During that time the table could be cleared by turning the armored forces to the north; then they could assemble east of Moscow. This talk revealed several significant trends: Hitler, in the interests of his old scheme, was working up the importance of the flank drives north and south. And most telling, he continued to disparage the importance of Moscow.

About this time he again spoke about Britain's collapse. But on 9 July he extended her time limit to Raeder. The Navy chief had appeared for the customary conference. Two days earlier President Roosevelt, contrary to his professions, had marines land in Iceland. Raeder asked, "Is this to be considered an entry into the war or an act of provocation which should be ignored?" Hitler explained in detail that he was most anxious to *"postpone the United States's entry* into the war for one or two months" (that is, past mid-July). No air power, he explained, could be diverted from the East Campaign [toward America], and on the other hand "victory in the East will have a tremendous effect on the whole situation and probably also on the attitude of the U.S.A." Therefore, for the time being, he did not wish existing instructions changed, but rather, wanted "to be sure that incidents will be avoided." Raeder warned again about Northwest Africa; "France must receive all necessary help." But Hitler responded with continued mistrust of France. The admiral persisted. Meanwhile, Britain's collapse and war with America had to be postponed a coupled of months.

The day before, Hitler had heard OKH on the situation and its plans, which simply continued the current actions. In response he hinted at sending the tank prongs of Group Center (Bock) "not against Moscow" but one group (Hoth) to join Group North (Leeb toward Leningrad) and the other (Guderian) south or southeast to work with Group South (Rundstedt). For no apparent reason he cut loose with a barbaric resolve "to raze Moscow and Leningrad to the ground," so that no humans could remain there to be fed in the winter. Luftwaffe would batter the cities into such "a national catastrophe that Bolshevism is not only done away with, but is deprived as well of Moscow as a center and Leningrad as its cradle." The outburst might have been tough tall talk to rouse and bolster Self for expected decisions.[4]

If England's turnabout was a bit delayed, Russia's seemed well enough forward at this mid-July period for implementing the post-campaign intentions. Directive No. 32 had been a working draft; it now took on authority. On 14 July Hitler signed and released a paper

4. Halder, 3:53. At this conference Hitler spoke for the first time of record about winter quarters. Troop winter barracks were not to be built near settlements, so that these could always be bombed by planes if disturbances arose.

that "laid down . . . guiding principles covering personnel and equipment pursuant to the objectives of our war aims announced in Directive No. 32." After Russia, "when our forces will control Europe," the size of the Army can be considerably reduced. Navy can be limited to "the needs for war against Great Britain and against the United States if she should enter the war. *Military preparations will be concentrated* above all on the Air Force, which will be greatly expanded." It seems Göring has huddled with his Führer and assured him he not only could finish off this war but could take care of any tasks left over. To anyone familiar with Göring's practices, this is the impression that emerges from the specific directions for each service. Navy got three lines limiting her to the submarine program; "any expansion [i.e., to surface ships such as aircraft carriers] over and above this is to be stopped. . . . The overall armament program is in the main to concentrate on carrying out the expanded Air Force program, which I have approved. It is of decisive importance to the whole war to complete it by the spring of 1942. All facilities and means available. . . . will be employed to accomplish this." It was patent Göring-Hitler language.

The two plotters must really have talked themselves into a happy, self-congratulatory mood, which they did by habit, often at Göring's reassuring instance. Here their exuberance led to fatal consequences: The Army, now carrying the brunt, could soon subside to a lower strength and "effective immediately all additions to Army armament and equipment will be adapted to the future reduced strength"; moreover, "the powder and explosives program," to the extent of Army reductions, will take its cue from Air Force needs in bombs and antiaircraft ammunition. "Only too soon it became manifest that these orders were as wide [of the mark] in the strategic lay of things as they were prejudicial to the further runoff of the East Campaign" (Warlimont). Shortages developed very soon. Yet so sure and confident were Hitler and his crony of the outcome.

Still another incident bears witness. In the afternoon of 16 July a seance took place in OKW about post-*Barbarossa* plans for Russia itself. For five hours Hitler and his top Nazis indulged in a fantasy rape of Russia. There was Rosenberg, the expert who was to administer the new lands, Lammers, Keitel, Göring, and Bormann, who recorded (Jacobsen, p. 255). To set the pace Hitler explained that German conquest did not mean pie in the sky for all Europe, a view which he had often righteously voiced by himself, but which now, when seconded in a French newspaper, became a deadly affront. German plans would be carried through without announcement to anybody; "the important thing is that we ourselves know what we want." He then elaborated.

We can do whatever our power permits. . . . For tactical reasons we shall stress we were forced to occupy a region to bring order and security in the interests of the inhabitants; we must show care for peace and quiet and subsistence without revealing the ultimate order of things. Nonetheless, we will pursue all necessary measures such as shooting, resettling, et cetera. The Crimea must be cleared of foreigners and be settled by Germans. . . . In Russia the iron rule shall be that only a German may carry arms. Forever the soldier must preserve the security of the regime. Out of the newly won east territories we must make a Garden of Eden.

The various lands were then inventoried, estimated, and parceled out. The master again reverted to the virtues of the Crimea for Germans alone; it must be protected by a buffer belt in Russia. After Leningrad is razed to the ground, the Finns can have it. Nazi bosses of the regions were selected. "The gigantic space," said Hitler, "has naturally to be pacified as quickly as possible. This can be best done by shooting dead anybody who even looks at anything sideways." Churches were in no case to be reactivated. On this high note the gangsters closed their binge; they were drunk with the prospect of power. "Practice," said Hitler, "makes perfect; the fighting will quickly end—witness the outstanding cooperation between the Army and the Luftwaffe at the front." As a finishing touch, they decide that the new Baltic lands shall be called Eastland (*Ostland*).[5]

Depraved fancies of this sort were what Hitler and a good many Nazis lived by, and had for long. Moreover, the fancies were coming true. With his cronies Hitler had already leapt over the strategic imperatives to feed on the spoils. A striking, childish example was his mounting Crimea craze. Nazi Germany had to have its very own Riviera; the Crimea would do admirably. He held forth about it at the meeting on the 16th and had enough left over to apprise General Ringel, up from Crete for special awards, of the Crimea's attractions. It would do better than Crete because it was out of the Mediterranean and accessible by new highways. Hitler even trumped up a weak strategic excuse for its speedy occupation: it would remove

5. Jacobsen, pp. 255–60. Hitler's mess talk of the time reflects the same lines of thought in Hitler SC, pp. 4, 5, 11, 13, 20, 28, 29.

the last Russian air threat against the Rumanian oil preserves. He was always at pains to satisfy strategic logic, often with comic results. But here as a prime target, the Crimea, of all places, began to compete with Moscow.

Of course there were very personal reasons for holding back on Moscow. Napoleon had fought for it to force the tsar to conform with the French Continental System and to discourage his flirting with England. Hitler, while claiming a like objective, was truly more interested in rubbing out Russia and her Bolshevism to make room for his Nazi empire. This demanded taking her economy as well as her capital city. Since most of her economic resources based in the Ukraine, that region had to come first, with the Crimea for good measure. If Rundstedt in the south took Kiev and the Ukraine while en route to the Crimea, Moscow could burn at any time later. Still more did he want to avoid a life-and-death Borodino before Moscow. Slugging matches were not his dish; he feared them.

OKH, however, knew that Russia's armed might had to come first and figured that it could be run down operationally en route to and before the capital, the nerve center of Russia. Signs of this fundamental difference in strategy became marked over the designation of Phase II's objective. The aim had to be stated as well as supported by forces and actions. At first glance Führer Directive No. 33, "The Continuation of the War in the East," of 19 July seemed to do this. Moscow remained a general objective. Yet on examination the detailed orders turned the requisite armored forces off toward the wings. And the whole South wing—toward Crimea—received extra emphasis. Three days later the truth came out in a supplement to No. 33. The South took over: east of the Dnieper a panzer army, formed from Center and South, was to strike east, take Kharkov, and roll on toward the Caucasus. "The bulk of the infantry is first of all to occupy the Ukraine and the central Russian lands up to the Don River." The northern thrust toward Leningrad was reinforced with the rest of the Center's armor, whose drive on Moscow was thus emasculated. The picture grew more and more jumbled. Commanders were admonished to use Draconian methods to scare the people into submission. It is a characteristic Hitlerian reach for the lash to toughen his own spirit. He tightened the screws on OKH slowly by adding objectives ever wilder. His *Wunschbild* had always included the Caucasus and he had to have it. A conflict of rising acerbity ensued between Führer and OKH over the prime objectives. These were the Days of Decision.[6]

Nervous tampering with field commands over tactical situations, over orders and directives, followed by shifting supplements, plus perceptibly stiffening Russian resistance, agitated these hot humid times of late July and August. On 30 July General Halder, who carried the fight for OKH, received hopeful word from General Jodl at OKW to stand by for a new directive that would clear the air. At midnight thereafter Colonel Heusinger, head of OKH Operations, broke in on his chief with Directive No. 34 in hand. It looked good. "It subscribes to the ideas we have striven for," Halder exulted and added, "This solution frees every thoughtful soldier from the frightful nightmares of the last days in which one could discern the complete disintegration of the East Operation through the obdurate stand of the Führer. Once again a beam of light!" Apparently Russian counter action and Jodl's intervention had induced Hitler to delay his southern fancy and, in effect, the northern one too. In the center, Bock was to go over to the defensive to refresh his armored groups. Acceptance, however, of target Moscow stayed out, a decision which Hitler soon made plain by playing that campaign down during early August visits of subversion to front commands. He electioneered for his *Wunschbild*.

Again the double-dealing of the West Campaign all over, only worse, for this time there could be no end. It could be fatal, and the staffs knew it. Halder's beam of light fluttered out. An estimate by him, a study by the L Section's young Turks at OKW, a study by Operations at OKH—all heaved with might and main to move the Mountain. In an extraordinary move the last study went forward to the Führer on 18 August over the signature of the Army commander in chief, and as follow-up, OKH sent its producer, Heusinger, to General Jodl at OKW on 20 August in the hope of winning his support as intermediary.

General Heusinger wrote his recollection of the exchanges on this day in the form of a colloquy. It lends an authentic feel of close participation in the impasse and reveals Hitler's private reasons for its insolubility. He was repeating the mistake of 1940 in France.

HEUSINGER (after stating his mission): This [study] is the only means left to us. . . . May I review the problem as we see it? The Führer wishes to hold back Army Group Center and divert from it mobile forces to Army

6. Halder, 3:78–197; Philippi and Heim, pp. 67–76; Warlimont IH, pp. 196–207; Hubatsch, pp. 136–50; Heusinger, 127–31.

Group South. He has stressed that from the beginning Moscow was of no importance, but instead, above all, that he wanted the wings to drive ahead. . . . Further, he assigns great importance to the Donets region, whose capture will deal Russian industry a deadly blow and at the same time provide a substantial lift to our armament situation.

JODL: Just a moment. Very early the Führer told me of his intention after arrival on the Dnieper line . . . while holding in the Center, to drive ahead with the wings, in case by this time Russia had not collapsed. He had surely eagerly hoped for that. So, he says now he is merely returning to his old plan. . . . For the rest, he instinctively shies away from taking the same route as Napoleon. Moscow means something sinister to him. He fears a life-and-death fight there with Bolshevism.

HEUSINGER: And for that very reason we want to choose that course. We must beat the living fighting forces of the foe. That is just the point. Then all the rest will come along of itself. We must not rush around after economic targets so long as the Red Army has not been destroyed. . . . On the way to Moscow the Russians will scrape up everything they can throw at us. There's where great success beckons, not in the Donets region.

JODL: That's what you say. Now let me tell you what the Führer will answer: At the moment a much better prospect to beat the live Russian forces is offered. They will make a stand with their strongest group east of Kiev, after these forces have not been destroyed west of the Dnieper. Aside from that, our Group Center cannot push farther east at all so long as the menace to its south flank has not been eliminated. Finally, of what further use are the foe's armies to him if we take the Donets area, his essential armament base, and threaten its link to the oil wells in the Caucasus? We can take Moscow later. Then it will be easier.

HEUSINGER: To pick up at the last point, Russian winter will break into the North and Center Sectors first. . . . This demands a reverse arrangement: first center, then south. . . . Moscow has similar industrial significance. . . . We should not give in to the hope of achieving decisive successes through reducing armament potential. The main argument is, finally, the importance of Moscow as the primary center of communication. All north and south linkages go through Moscow. By taking it we tear the opposing front into two pieces between the sea of Azov and Ladoga. . . . The damage to Russian lines of communication will be catastrophic!

JODL: I'll do what I can. But you must grant that the Führer arguments are well taken and cannot be summarily run down. Don't grow any gray hairs over his holding fast to his view. One must not try to force him against his inner conviction. His instinct has for the most part been right. That one surely cannot deny.

HEUSINGER: Unfortunately, not always! I recall Dunkirk, and we are afraid that this time, also, a decisive moment will be missed.[7]

---

7. Heusinger, pp. 132–35. Jodl said that Hitler's stand against Moscow was something that he had worked into a basic, unalterable conviction. As recounted earlier, at the conference on 5 December 1940 he said, "Moscow can wait." He reiterated the thought time and again as 1941 advanced. Just as firmly, OKH's plan had always

To Heusinger's Dunkirk and its prologue could have been added the succeeding quandary of June and July 1940, when inner conviction told Hitler that the British, once chased from the Continent, would talk. He had no plan for the case they might not. Now his conviction of Russian collapse having proved false, he has indeed a plan, based not on strategy, but again on an impossible private policy aimed, as an excuse, at economic booty. But more, it was dictated by inner fear. Dictators must always be right. This one mistrusted his own powers to handle a Borodino before Moscow, as he mistrusted his powers to handle overseas operations. No one knew this better than Jodl, who had never been so candidly recorded.

How do you persuade a dictator that he is unequal to a task? Certainly not by a proposal that runs counter to a convention based on fear. A double-barreled response promptly blasted back almost immediately from the enraged Führer. Two sensitive counts probably contributed: (1) Whose campaign was this anyhow? His! It was his fulfillment. He alone had dreamt it up and would put it over, not OKH! (2) He had been found out—he is afraid of Moscow. To cover both, he reached instinctively for spite. With one barrel he fired a directive of rejection, written by Jodl; with the other he let go an abrasive critique of the Army leadership, written by himself. After scanning Jodl's directive, General Halder remarked, "It is decisive for the outcome of this campaign."

The proposal of the Army for the continuation of the operation . . . does not at all agree with my intentions. I order as follows:

(1) The most important objective to be reached, still before winter, is not Moscow, but the Crimea, the industrial and coal region of the Donets, to force the shutdown of Russian oil supply from the Caucasus; in the north, the isolation of Leningrad and establishment of contact with the Finns. . . .

(4) Seizure of the Crimean Peninsula is of the very greatest importance for the security of our oil supply out of Rumania. . . .

(5) Only close isolation of Leningrad, joining up with the Finns, and destruction of the Russian 5th Army [south] will achieve the prerequisites and free forces to attack the Timoshenko Army Group [before Moscow] with a prospect of success, in the sense of supplement to Directive No. 34 of 12 August.

ADOLF HITLER

---

headed for Moscow as the prime target. Now the two plans came to the decisive clash, as they had in France. It was old stuff. One reason the issue was never resolved earlier was that everyone believed in Russia's and therefore Moscow's early collapse. Why worry about Moscow? The mistake of 1940 was repeated.

By cautiously holding back, the Führer was giving the Russians time to consolidate.

Hitler's sharp personal criticism added bitterness to the disappointment caused by the directive. He undertook to educate the Army leadership in the employment of mobile forces; they should be operated the way Reichsmarschall Göring handled his planes. No comparison could have been less welcome and more insulting. It was an outrage that sounded to General Halder like a vote of no confidence. He proposed that his commander in chief request his own and his chief of staff's relief. Brauchitsch, who was not at all well in heart and spirit, demurred. How keenly Halder felt the gravity of the moment is disclosed by his final despairing effort. He arranged for Guderian, who had the armored group that would be diverted south, to present his opposed views to the Führer. Tank man Guderian, the first to crash onto the Channel in May 1940, stood well with Hitler; yet here he failed his own and the Army views. Hitler talked him out of them. OKH had to issue orders to conform. This decided the campaign's fate, and Germany's.

But within a week the Führer privately received von Brauchitsch, who on his return to own headquarters presented all as sweetness and light once more: the Führer had "really not meant it that way." He has given assurance that as soon as at all possible, through success in the south, forces needed in the center before Moscow will be placed at disposal.

Time is nevertheless a-wasting. It is now 30 August 1941, the seventieth day of the campaign. The drive of the offensive is petering out.[8]

As operations in the south thenceforth permit, forces begin to concentrate toward the Battle of Moscow. Hitler in fact presses to get them to move faster than they can. Preliminaries come on 2 October with the fanfare of a Führer special order of the day. Giant strides are made immediately; the prospect is good. Then come rain and mud.

Kiev had ended with September, giving up hundreds of thousands in prisoners and commensurate treasures and material. The drive on Moscow accelerated. Vyazma fell to encirclement on 7 October, Bryansk on the 9th. Every man jack, horse, and machine strained forward in Operation *Typhoon* for Moscow, only 108 miles off, a mere two-day march for the mobile units. Hitler ordered rejection of all

8. Halder, 3:206–7.

proffers of capitulation. The city was to be razed, obliterated, with the Russians in it.

Toward mid-October the truth set in. Rain and more rain made a quagmire of the approaches. No man, beast, track, or wheel could move in the knee-deep sludge. Shoes and clothing went to pieces; follow-up supply began to fail. "Phenomenon of mud" the Germans called it. It bound them. Three weeks in the south made the difference. Typhoons are unreliable.

On 10 October an Associated Press dispatch had quoted a German High Command release: "The military decision has fallen, the most essential condition," as set forth by the Führer in a special order of the day of 2 October, "has been achieved." This seemed so, for on 14 October the Soviet government had moved to Kuibyshev, 550 miles southeast, as a temporary capital. People streamed out of Moscow. American press notices wondered about Ambassador Steinhardt and his staff. In Washington two Russian officers, sent there to expedite Lease-Lend aid, confided their concern to their American opposites in terms that came close to asking prayers for Mother Russia and her capital. In Berlin, a general just arrived from the east said, "Everybody here makes like peace."

October ran out in deepening cold and local actions. Rear forces closed up some by mid-November. Dour Field Marshal Fedor von Bock, commanding in the center, held that waiting for the rest "only brings the danger of winter snows closer; one could get stuck in them." Relentless, he strove to launch the "final" thrust at Moscow. "The last battalion will do it!" as it should have done it on the Marne. This is Bock's watchword as he goes forward to lead the charge from an advanced post (Halder, 3:287–303). By 29 November Moscow is almost within striking range of Panzer Groups 3 and 4, northwest of the city. The 2d Panzer Division is in the lead beyond Istra, pushing into the outskirts through fire from flanks and front. It is too much. On 30 November the tanks grind to a halt, exhausted, 18 miles short of the goal. This is the closest approach. A last despairing effort on 1 December by the adjoining 4th Army goes deep into the defenses on either side of Naro Fominsk, but is forced to haul back in the night of the same day to avoid encirclement. It is the unspectacular end of the Battle for Moscow, and the end of the German offensive. Though Hitler wanted to fight on, his Führer Directive No. 39 made failure official in orders to go over to the defensive.[9]

9. Philippi and Heim, pp. 97, 98; Werth, pp. 253–56; Halder, 3:318.

Barbarossa nears the 180th day, old and feeble, his crusading spirit flagged. At the start he had the finest ground war machine ever fielded, led by tried and proven leaders. Now his machine lies in bits and pieces, men in tatters, leaders falling out. Those remaining know well they will never again be so strong. The toll has been heavy, almost 776,000 men (Halder, 3:345). Half a year of steady fighting through ever-lengthening lines and constantly reappearing Russians, who fight hard in weather and sludge that have locked whole armies. Whatever solace such reflections may grant, it is not enough. Why are the Germans in the Russian mud in the first place? The mud may have denied Moscow, but would her capture have been enough? Enough to bring Russia under in the Nazi plan?

To make sense at all, war must ultimately aim to pacify in the new balance it means to create. German strategic capability was ample to lay waste a great part of Russia's people, lands, cities, and resources; yet that this, Moscow included, could have led to pacification is highly problematic. Russia was big, her people hardy, numerous, and ingenious and unexpectedly loyal. No other people endured heavier hardships or contributed more pain, blood, and treasure to Germany's defeat. How could any strategy bring this vast country under and impose its alien policy, let alone the monstrous Nazi fantasy of partition and enslavement? Its denial of the bedrock principle of all policy—survival—could only encourage eternal war. It offered the Russians no prospect but extinction. It was ignorant; it was mad. Yet it was at the core of Hitler's private policy, alongside his cherished dream of marriage with Britain. Even now, irrevocably committed in Russia, he chatters about a deal with England "at the expense of France," which he despises. These twin hopeless delusions, the enormity of their ignorance, their incongruity, left no room for peace—only more war.

Things had turned out other than imagined, radically so—even as they had after the fall of France in 1940. The two seasons had much in common. General Jodl had reacted early as before; by 28 August he had produced a Hitler-Jodl estimate of the situation entitled "Strategic Situation of Late Summer 1941." The possibility of retarded progress figured foremost. Though it received Führer sanction, this did not bar his entertainment of ideas far different. The estimate was of the official variety, seasoned with private hopes Hitler had fed into Jodl. While in the paragraphing, phraseology, and thought division Jodl attempted to follow his own style, the discursive jumpiness of the whole sounded like a speech or monologue of Hitler's. The points raised disclose the Führer in a fresh dilemma. He strains to solve his old twin troubles and their interplay. Of course, Russia again came out ahead.[10]

In assuming early hegemony over the Continent, Directive No. 32 [after Russia] expressed the fundamental Nazi aspiration, Britain aside. Yet to cement professional support we have heard Hitler preach the *Barbarossa* crusade as a preventive thrust against the infidel Bolshevik menace on the one hand and as a detour toward England on the other. This double-take he got over. Yet now in late August, with the campaign but two months old, we hear no more about preventive crusade or even the name *Barbarossa*; we do hear of England as a final goal, and a sinister note about the campaign's prolongation in total commitment. Problems bulk huge and baffling. How shall they be surmounted? These first signs of uncertainty are what lend Jodl's estimate significance. In notable fidelity, Hitler strives to stick to the strategic precept (as he had in 30 June 1940) of continued war with England. But total commitment against Russia is now the main point more than ever, in a feeling of uneasiness instead of bold thoughts about certain conquest. These have begun to sink under a load of horrifying doubt.

Recapitulated, Jodl's findings for "the further conduct of the war" (recall this identical phrase) read:

(1) The breakdown of Russia is the next and decisive war aim, which through the commitment of all dispensable forces from all other fronts must be forced. Insofar as this is not completely realized in 1941, the continuation of the East Campaign in 1942 stands as first priority.

(2) Only after the elimination of Russia as a power factor is the battle of the Atlantic and Mediterranean, if possible with the help of French and Spanish positions, to be taken up in full measure. Even if Russia is in the main overthrown this year, the Army and Luftwaffe will hardly be available for the Mediterranean and Atlantic and in Spain before the spring of 1942.

(3) In the time until next spring it is important not to let military and political relations with France and Spain deteriorate, but to deepen them; hold France on short tether and induce her to reinforce West Africa

10. Halder, 3:226; Warlimont IH, pp. 205–7; Warlimont KFA, pp. 420–436; IMT, Doc. 1776. Hitler's reconciliation with the Army commander in chief came on 30 August 1941, two days after Jodl's estimate appeared. Thereupon the Führer began his own drive to get the soldier's drive on Moscow going. A new directive of 6 September 1941 (FD No. 35) came in support. Finally he had given in, but too late.

against British-American attack there. Since France is absolutely necessary for the overthrow of England, agreement with her must be tried.

(4) On this expanded basis a stepped-up submarine commitment with full air support can come about for greater success in the siege of England.

(5) Operations in the Eastern Mediterranean are possible only if Transcaucasia is reached. . . .

(6) Invasion England can be taken in view in earnest only when, despite Russia's downfall, measures to bring Spain or France into the war . . . fail and therewith the Battle of the Atlantic or Mediterranean does not show enough success that the subjection of England can be counted upon in this way.

Discussion preceding this summary started with the categorical resolve that "the aim remains to overthrow England and force her to make peace." To be at peace with her was surely a long-standing objective, but the involved hedging used for wiggling out of Invasion as the final horror reveals Hitler's abiding fear of direct overseas assault. From the beginning it had been an alien uncomfortable thought, and so it remained. First came Russia and then thoughts about after Russia, which had to mean showdown with England. There they trailed off into uncertainty. The present paper made the last attempt to claim Russia as "a detour on the way to England." Significantly, the Middle Sea rose to rank on a par with the Atlantic. Jodl had updated and watered down the ambitious Führer Directive No. 32. It had lasted less than two months. Even the spirit had changed.

Jodl wrote, further, "Future armament plans will depend on whether England is to be attacked at home on the island or on the periphery [in the Mediterranean]. . . . Just as important as the Battle of the Atlantic is the Battle of the Mediterranean." That Hitler concurred implies a wish to preserve German initiative in the south. A Rommel offensive in October or November had always been on his agenda in talk to the Italians. Now he wanted all the more to keep the Mediterranean option open; retardation of *Barbarossa* had forced it.[11]

If this cheerless study of late August thus revealed concern and uncertainty, what must the feeling in high places be now, after three months of flailing at Moscow in vain, the last drive stalled in freezing mud and Russians everywhere taking the offensive?

As usual, men of the time and place manage to live with mounting crisis. They lower their sights, they get used to it; its finality eludes them. Bock's diminishing progress shows plain in the record, in which

11. Halder, 3:226–229; Warlimont IH, pp. 206–7.

allowances for the possible, instead of the wished-for, creep in. Winning winter quarters in the outskirts becomes a rationalized substitute for winning the whole city of Moscow. By 29 November General Halder writes, "At best the north wing [of Bock] can be shoved up against Moscow while Guderian clears out the bend of the Oka River northwest of Tula for winter quarters." (Such quarters are about 55 miles from Moscow.) So early as ten days before, Hitler had offhandedly admitted to Halder that he expected the two opposed camps to realize that *neither could annihilate the other*; the result would be a negotiated peace. Not only is Moscow being discounted as a big prize; the Nazi philosophy is drooping.

A paraphrase of this rank heresy by Hitler was handed along by General Halder to his general staff deputies in the various Army commands on 23 November, with his own interpretation. The Army, he told them, would never again equal its state of June 1941: "We must keep in mind that neither of the two chief contenders may succeed in destructively striking the other or decisively subduing him. The war may move from the military level to that of morale for holding through and economic resource." Still, Britain could no longer use Russia as a "continental dagger." Militarily, Russia no longer presents any danger to the build-up of Europe. Her total destruction cannot be achieved "*this year*"—indeed, it is doubtful if total destruction can ever be reached in this "land of unending space and inexhaustible human power." So the attack must be continued until a "favorable break-off situation for continuing next year has been achieved." The preventive crusade is over; moreover, German leadership is in the market for negotiating peace.

Much as these admissions may have softened the impact of failure before Moscow, a more immediate and direct diversion was provided by Führer uproar over operations in the south. According to plan, Rundstedt's 1st Panzer Army (Kleist) drove on Rostov at the head of the northeastern arm of the Sea of Azov. He took it on 21 November—an important gain; for Rostov meant a stronghold in the Donets basin and entree to the Caucasus. But heavy, well-ordered Red counter action cut short the rejoicing at Führer headquarters and hove the place into great tumult, reported Keitel to OKH on 22 November.

"Kleist is in crisis" went the word, "and no one doing a thing about it!" By 28 November the tension burst decisively: he gave up the city and hauled back 9 miles. What could spring him? Stukas? Guderian tanks? Although the withdrawal succeeded, the Russians still pressed hard; pullback farther to the Mius River came into consideration. That touched off the fireworks. Hitler forbade further retreat, summoned the ailing commander in chief of the Army, and belabored him with insults and nonsensical orders. Beaten down, Brauchitsch gave in to an order forbidding Rundstedt to pull back to the Mius all at once. Rundstedt replied to OKH that he could not comply and requested that the order be lifted or he be relieved. Word for word the message went on to Hitler. That might stay things, thought OKH, for on high Rundstedt stood well, and besides, at issue was a pure field command decision.

Late in the night, having heard nothing, OKH inquired of Jodl

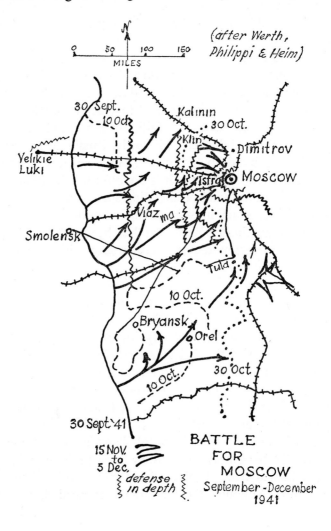

and got an unbelievable answer: "Not at all, the Führer has not changed the order. Rundstedt is relieved; Reichenau of the 6th Army is to replace him." Impossible! Reichenau is the laggard who failed to close his 6th Army in support. An old favorite of Hitler's, he took over and the next day was forced to request permission to pull back; he got it. Whereat General Halder wrote, "We are now where we could have been yesterday evening. Men and time have been sacrificed and von Rundstedt has been lost." Madness!

Even worse: the instability of the Supreme Command had been demonstrated and the growing fatigue of the field commanders. Rundstedt started a series of departures: Field Marshals von Bock of the Army Group Center (because he was ill); von Brauchitsch, commander in chief of the Army (because of a heart ailment); von Leeb, commander of Army Group North, who left in January over Führer disagreement. On Christmas Day Guderian, the bad boy of the front, was fired. He had differences with Hitler and his own Army superior.

At this crucial juncture top command in the field has been wiped out. It is incomprehensible, unbelievable. Still more alarming is Hitler's announcement on 19 December of his intention to take over direct command in chief of the Army himself—not as an extra cabinet office in government, not as chairman of an important committee to give it a lift, but in the guise of a ruling sovereign as commander in chief of the professional German Army. Perhaps he is Frederick the Great. The incredible story tells itself. After World War I a lance corporal, dissatisfied with German policy, talked and tricked his way to the political top through emphasis on German grievances and personal image building. Once at the top, he always knew better and gave proof through drastic housecleaning and German annexations. Professional officers who counseled against these forays he proved mistaken. He knew better in policy and pursued the same method in strategy. He took that over. Now he commands in chief old Germany's greatest pride, her Army. In near chaos the top commands staggered along, beset by merciless winter and Russian hordes. The greater danger lay, however, in the omniscience of Germany's maladjusted Führer. Each day at headquarters becomes a heavy burden—"Noch ein schwerer Tag!"[12]

12. Heusinger, pp. 144–56; Warlimont IH, pp. 219–237; Hitler SC, pp. 24–131; Halder, 3:354–71, especially note 2 on p. 354. After their first exposure to Hitlerian manners at the war helm during the Polish campaign, von Brauchitsch and Halder agreed that if either had to step down because of Hitler, both would go. Now when it was von Brauchitsch's turn he urged Halder to stay on for the sake

On the north flank, operations were being shattered by icy blasts off the Baltic. Leeb's men struggled to isolate Leningrad and to link up with the Finnish Army of Karelia. They hemmed Leningrad in, but the second objective stalled in zero weather and failing supply. Only by personal appearance before Hitler could Leeb get authorization to shorten his line to one running from Lake Ilmen to Schlüsselburg along the Volkhov River. By Christmas the line was established. From there south along a thousand-mile front, Soviet forces had taken over the initiative.

Never had Germans worked in spaces of this magnitude nor over terrain so diverse and difficult and peopled by such multitudes of hardy men and women. The scale was expansive—in its own way, grand. The Germans had always been cooped up in their own cockpit of explosive power. They had to dream of breaking out into wide open spaces or onto broad blue seas. The land dream stirred up for Hitler a politicostrategic formula of land warfare that proved fatal. His policy of annihilation often overrode normal strategic considerations, for old-fashioned peace was not what he was after. By December these confusions, added to others more personal, had the remaining strategic power laboring from day to day in tactical extremis. The outlook was bleak. About the time of Brauchitsch's departure, near 19 December, the OKH chief of operations, Heusinger, commented (Heusinger, p. 152): "We stand at a crucial point of the war . . . failure before Moscow, merciless onset of winter, our bad supply situation, miscarriage of the Tikhvin operation [the final operation in the north]—all this has buried hope of a decisive stroke in the east. In Africa Rommel has been thrown back again. In the west the

---

of the fatherland and its army. Halder agreed he should at least try. And try he did, during the nine more months he bore the burden of making the crazy chain of command work. The new commander in chief had no conception of what the radical shift meant to the functioning of the complex machine. He had no use for these complexities; directing from the top was easy. He simply directed by telephone to battalion commanders at the front. At the time of this shift he remarked, "This bit of operational direction anyone can do. The real task of the commander in chief of the Army is to bring up the Army National-Socialistically. I know no general in the Army who can fulfill this task in my way. Therefore I decided to take over command of the Army myself." Warlimont IH, p. 227. General Halder wrote, "Most frightening is that the top leadership does not comprehend the condition of our troops and works on a petty shoe-mending and patching basis when only great decisions can help." Staff reorganizations were undertaken to fit the new command lines. Hitler showed small interest. L Section (OKW Ops) became the Wehrmachtführungsstab (Wfst.). H. Greiner, pp. 16–17; Warlimont IH, pp. 229–31. In effect, two army operational and planning staffs and directors—Jodl and Halder—each with his own staff, functioned. The thing grew steadily more unmanageable and self-defeating.

United States with their vast war potential have formally entered the war."

Everywhere German soldiers fight for survival; from here forward the strategy of their leaders takes on a defensive cast. They are trapped in Russia. It is the black aftermath of neglected opportunities in the west, specifically those in the Mediterranean after Crete. There was the final fatal turning.

The temptation is strong. Suppose the professionals had been left to do their job in Russia. Kiev could have been taken early, Moscow by September. What then? To judge from the basic elements of Jodl's estimate of 28 August, it would even by this time have been clear that Russian collapse was in any case a vain hope, as was surely negotiation. The fight would have gone on into the winter of 1941 anyhow. Russia was in every way too big, unmanageable. Neither in 1812 nor in 1941 was she susceptible to conquest or domination in the narrow classical pattern of western Europe's wars. On 11 December 1941 Hitler compounded his troubles by declaring war on the United States, to which global expansion there could be only one end: disastrous defeat. Field Marshall Kesselring closed his appraisal (Kesselring, pp. 133–37) with the question, "Did this war have to take the apocalyptic end that it did?" Because of Hitler alone, the answer must be affirmative.[13]

13. After the Russians' collapse Hitler had thought to pacify them and keep them in order with fifty army divisions. But Russia's land proved too expansive, her people too hardy and strong in spirit for such simplistic plans.—Today similar doubtful assumptions are applied to the nuclear stalemate between Russia and the U.S.A. Both are too vast in land and resources for conquest or pacification by intruders. While the world might get along without Russia, it badly needs the U.S.A. The threat of nuclear war grows more and more unreal and preposterous—almost childish. From the very beginning it has been a purely political weapon on the highest level, though surrounded by the most barbarous implications. Suppose Japan had stood fast. Would the United States have continued a policy of her gradual reduction by atomic bombs? Hardly. The policy would have become untenable. Nuclear weapons have made the top game pure political bluffery. The bottom has dropped out of massive war waging.—Let us devote ourselves to professional police action by conventional forces, geared to handle each imaginable contingency that concerns U.S. interests directly. Let us work toward international law and order. In this law, civilians are not eligible targets.

26. Aftermath II

In the Mediterranean: Late 1941, Early 1942

In mid-September Field Marshal Kesselring at his Air Fleet 2 command post near Smolensk had received a casual telephone query from General Jeschonnek at Luftwaffe headquarters: Did the Field Marshal have any liking for Italy and Africa? Something more would soon have to be done down there, if the fall of the North African position was to be avoided. Kesselring, engaged at the time in preliminaries for the Battle of Moscow, made a noncommittal reply and forgot about it. In the first days of November he was taken aback by orders to shift his Air Fleet 2 command to Italy as commander in chief South. The Mediterranean's case had grown urgent.

How good to feel the sun, to search out the sharp blue line of the southern horizon! Clear they are and inviting, but also challenging; for under the blue skies these waters have swallowed many supply ships bound for Africa. Ashore a resurgent British army threatens Rommel's existence. He waits for sufficient strength to resume the offensive and capitalize on the favorable German strategic stance in the East Basin. Yet besides short supply, 10th Air Corps support is failing. The RAF has the upper hand too often. Air Fortress Crete has simply lacked the stuff to neutralize Alexandria and its fleet, reduce Tobruk, and close not only Suez but the Strait of Sicily as well. British ships still get through Bomb Alley between Crete and Africa when they must to help Tobruk and even Malta. Nowhere has the

10th Air Corps been able to force a decision, and Crete is a logistic drain. People begin to wonder about "the blunder of Crete" that cost so much.

A reorganized, reequipped British army had taken the field in the Western Desert in the Tobruk-Sollum sector. In pace, the RAF achieved a general edge over Axis air power, particularly at Malta. Moreover, during September, Malta submarines gutted three vital supply convoys, the last composed of three Italian liners jam-packed with troops. Only seven of thirteen ships got through—and only one of the liners. Thanks to the British shift to the German over-and-under-sea attack system (instead of on it), British success boosted Axis losses from 20 percent in July to 40 percent in September. The acceleration looked bad.[1]

These were the losses that caused Jeschonnek to call Kesselring. The whole Axis stand in North Africa was again in peril, and Hitler behaved as he had before—loath to act overseas. As a convenient resort, he turned again to the Luftwaffe and, against Navy advice, ordered submarines to be deployed south. Navy objection had two main thrusts: (1) the main Battle of the Atlantic could be won only by more submarines, and (2) the clear southern waters robbed the submarine of its chief advantage—stealth. Hitler's compelling counters were that Britain would attack Rommel to relieve German pressure on Russia, and loss of North Africa would kill the Axis cause (an old Navy argument). Here he was, trying to implement the sailors' own South Plan in naval terms much stronger than they had ever proposed. They had recommended small-craft deployment south, and this was in course. By 17 September the Navy chief seemed to have shifted ground, for he reported two submarines en route south and four others to follow. A miniature German Mediterranean fleet, which acquitted itself well, was taking shape—something the sailors had never dreamed of.[2]

1. Macintyre BM, pp. 98–124; Cunningham, pp. 408–38 and app. 2. Chiefs of German Army and Navy representatives in Rome warned of increasing losses, as did Admiral Raeder on 22 August and 17 September.
2. Warlimont KFA, pp. 447–58; FC 1941, 2:23–53. Deployment of both submarines and small craft had been urged by Navy Command South in a special trip to Berlin by the command's chief of staff. In OKW, Navy was losing face. Marginal notes by Jodl on Navy papers show as much, and Navy representatives noted the feeling. Hitler had in the past held the sea and its followers off at arm's length and was circumspect in his talk. The *Bismarck* disaster swept this awe away. Now he knew better than his sailors. He grew critical and captious toward the Navy and Admiral Raeder. This feeling led finally to Raeder's departure in a January 1943 explosion very much like that with Brauchitsch.

Another paper submitted by Raeder analyzed President Roosevelt's speech of 11 September 1941. In the admiral's eyes it constituted a declaration of war and should be met by liberalization of the open-fire rules against American ships. Again Hitler took refuge in Russia. Her imminent collapse would change everything. The situation demanded peace with America, for the time being. Raeder recorded the Führer words: "The end of September will bring the great decision in Russia; therefore the Führer requests that care be taken to avoid any incidents in the war on merchant shipping before about the middle of October." At first it had been mid-July; then mid-August; and now October. How incurably wishful! Yet no more mistaken than Raeder's wish to make war on the United States. For Germany, war with either Russia or the United States was strategically and politically unsound; there was simply no chance of winning.

A revived Battle of the Mediterranean bumbled through October into November. Göring got the orders for air protection to convoys watered down to air escort for only specially designated convoys. By October another influence came into play. Under the impression that Moscow and the East were as good as won, Hitler let Keitel release a warning order in late October "for transfer of important air units to the central Mediterranean." Moscow troubles delayed Führer Directive No. 38 until 2 December. It provided the charter for the new command South of Field Marshal Kesselring—which, as such, lasted the war out. He arrived in the new theater a few days before the directive and began establishing his staff and himself within the Italian chain of command. Ship casualties had risen to prohibitive figures, and supply to North Africa had shrunk to a tiny trickle.

On shore in North Africa the fighting season reopened. Rommel had planned a main fall effort against Tobruk, while holding at Sollum on Egypt's border. Fortress Tobruk was as sharp a thorn in the Axis flank as Malta, and as a prize even more valuable; for, once taken, it would make an excellent front-line coastal base, opposite and linked to Crete, for operating farther eastward. For the moment, everything depended on Tobruk.

Pending reinforcement during September and early October, the landward Axis ring around Tobruk was tightened and entry points were selected for later penetration. But through losses at sea, fill-up and reinforcement fell so far behind that attack had to be postponed until the last half of November. Early in the month, when still somewhat short, Rommel felt attack was urgently necessary to insure the initiative. OKW favored postponement; Rommel, however, knew that on the ground the British could only grow stronger while he grew weaker. His forebodings proved correct. A new British 8th Army beat him to the punch by launching a major offensive on 18 November. His attack on Tobruk had to be dropped.

Severe fighting and heavy losses during November and early December convinced Rommel he lacked the men and staff to beat back General Auchinleck's forces. (Wavell had been moved on by Churchill.) Rommel decided to lift the siege of Tobruk and retire. By 12 December the Axis was back in its Ain-el-Gazala positions 30 miles west of Tobruk, the key.

Here was to begin a race westward, thought the German leadership; by the Axis, to gain the comparative safety of its starting point, Agedabia, 250 miles across the hump of Cirenaica; by the British to get there first and cut the Axis off. Rommel reported his choice to OKW in far away Rastenburg, East Prussia: "After four weeks of unremitting combat with severe losses, troop effectiveness declining and all the more for total lack of supply . . . withdrawal night of 16–17 December unavoidable to escape encirclement and destruction by superior enemy." Crisis in the east and now, crisis in the south.

Commando Supremo in Rome quailed in fear of political repercussions. A high delegation, including Field Marshal Kesselring, bearded Rommel in his cave command post southeast of Gazala. He refused to budge from his already issued order for swift withdrawal. It crashed into high gear, and by Christmas he had the bulk of his men back at their starting points around Agedabia. That a stronger British force had not joined in closer pursuit mystified the Germans, but Britain's 8th Army had suffered severely too. Slowly Rommel's forces disengaged and retired farther toward the lowest bend of the Gulf of Sirte, to man the familiar old El Brega line.

Great good news arrived that two German tank companies and some supply had reached Tripoli and Bengasi; yet there was a sour note: two other companies and a battery of artillery had been lost to Malta's counter action. So the fresh supplies would soon be used up. Bits of supply salvaged from the battered hull of a steamer stranded in the gulf saw the force through. A crack at Tobruk had been lost, and Malta still threatened. Something more had to be done about her to win this Battle of the Mediterranean.[3]

These days are packed with widely distributed heroics and drama

3. Rommel, pp. 78–96; Warlimont KFA, pp. 427–436; Kesselring, pp. 138–60.

on land and sea. Out of Malta, Force K, a newly constituted British attack group of cruisers *Aurora* and *Penelope* and destroyers, now ruled the sea. On the night of 8–9 November they fell on a convoy of seven steamers, escorted by cruisers *Trieste* and *Trento* and ten destroyers. Force K opened fire in total surprise with its rapid-firing six-inch guns and slaughtered the steamers. Two Italian destroyers sank; one limped out badly damaged; the other ships escaped. Two weeks later, five Italian cruisers, aided by seven destroyers, hovered around one section of four southbound freighters and a second section that was to break off on a diverging route. On the first day torpedo planes from Malta damaged a cruiser; in the following night a submarine struck cruiser *Trieste*. It was enough; the ships were recalled. The recall failed to reach the second section of two German merchantmen bound for Bengasi with fuel and munitions. Force K overhauled them and blew them up. Even under the heaviest escort, casualties continued. A battleship and four cruisers and a convoy of five ships lost all but one. For Axis shipping, November was a black month.

Then came a British turn at losses. As a routine practice Admiral Cunningham backed up Force K with additional ships at sea on call. He put to sea himself on 24 November with three battleships and destroyers to patrol Bomb Alley between Crete and Africa. In the afternoon of the next day he was having tea in his sea cabin when he felt the cabin door give "three distinct rattles." AA fire, he thought as he made for the bridge. There, an awful sight astern: battleship *Barham* churning on her beam ends to port; in a minute, a deep rumble and "a terrific explosion . . . a great cloud of yellowish-black smoke eddying high in the sky. When it cleared . . . nothing remained but a bubbling oily patch on the calm sea, dotted with wreckage and heads of swimmers." Lt. Commander von Tiesenhausen in U-133 had pierced the destroyer screen and scored three torpedo hits on *Barham* from a spot so close no gun could get on him, as he broached and slithered down the side of battleship *Valiant*, next astern.

Only a little while before, on 13 November, another of the newly arrived German submarines had sunk carrier *Ark Royal* in the West Basin. She had just finished flying off fighters toward Malta. In the Tobruk run, still another submarine torpedoed the troop carrier *Glenroy*, and off Alexandria in mid-December U-557 sank cruiser *Galatea*. Submarines were creeping nearer that base and with greater effect than air had scored during the Crete campaign.

Climax came through actions by Italy's 10th Light Flotilla when it struck right inside Alex on 18 December 1941.[4] The flotilla's men constituted a brotherhood of skill, daring, and hardihood that equaled today's astronaut teams. While these probe high to explore space, the flotilla probed low to get under ships and explode them. Membership was open to any navy volunteer who could qualify and endure the prolonged, rigorous training. They worked in two-man crews, each astride a mini 20-foot electric submarine, affectionately known as a pig, but officially as an SLC (for *siluro a lunga corsa*). The adversary called their game limpet attacks, for, each minisub carried a heavy explosive charge for attachment low to an unsuspecting hull. Lieutenant Luigi Durand de la Penne commanded a 10th Flotilla task group of three pigs, supported by two more in reserve. His group was charged with the momentous task of blowing up the three most important ships moored in Alexandria.

The group embarked in the specially fitted submarine *Scirè*, which had the pigs secured in caissons on deck. Two days later at Leros island in the Dodecanese the great adventure began. *Scirè* doffed her camouflage cover and put to sea. In the early dark of 18 December 1941 she arrived close off Alex. It was a fine, cool, clear evening.[5]

But it was not clear and cool in the submarine, sitting on the sandy bottom to hold her position. It was hot and humid as the attack crews struggled into their tight black rubber suits and checked their respirators and luminous wrist watches. Commander Prince Iunio Valerio Borghese, commanding *Scirè*, meanwhile assigned targets; two battleships and many other ships, including tankers, were known to be in port. De la Penne and his backer-up, Chief Diver Bianchi, got the first battleship, H.M.S. *Valiant*. Lieutenant Marceglia, naval engineer, and Diver Corporal Schergat got the second battleship, H.M.S. *Queen Elizabeth*. Lieutenant Martellotta, naval constructor, and Chief Diver Marino were to take any aircraft carrier, and if none was present, a tanker, with the thought that her load might ignite and set the waters of Alexandria ablaze. *Scirè* surfaced, the hatch opened, and as each hydronaut mounted the ladder, Prince Borghese gave him a friendly boot in the stern for luck. It was not the first time this ritual had been gone through by these men. They were ready, confident.

4. Cunningham, p. 424; Macintyre BM, pp. 112-24. *Barham* took with her Captain Cooke, 55 officers, and 1806 men.
5. De la Penne; Cunningham, pp. 433–37; Macintyre BM, pp. 120–24; Maugeri, pp. 68–74.

On deck, one caisson gave trouble and a reserve member collapsed from oxygen poisoning. These difficulties were mastered: the
assisting reserves returned inside *Scirè* and the hatch snapped shut with
finality. The conning tower sank lower, the pig men mounted their
craft; *Scirè* departed. The group was on its own, under way at about
2 knots, two heads in tandem showing from each pig; they formed a
line abreast on a southwesterly course to seaward of the long Alexandria breakwater. De la Penne in the center tells of arrival "off Ras
el Tin Lighthouse" two hours later (about 2300) and "ahead of
schedule. We lay to and broke out our emergency rations and had
something to eat. . . . Cold, fresh air had given us a terrific appetite,
and we felt it necessary to eat in order to be in top shape when we
neared the targets." Earlier he remarked that the "worst obstacle to
success was not the foe but the extreme cold. There was no alternative
but to accept the hardship imposed by the cold. . . . The best results
could only be had by using bare hands."

The lighthouse structure stood out clear. Of a sudden the light
went on, which could mean that entering ships needed it for making
port. Between the long south-trending breakwater and the short southern one jutting out from the mainland was the boomed entrance with
a gate. Toward it De la Penne, now sure of his bearings, decided to
close, prepared for sneaking in. The group slowed and submerged to
periscope depth, that is, with only the forward rider showing his head
above water. Then shortly after midnight, signal lights flashed at the
gate. Ships were surely coming in. From this point on, the pigs proceeded independently. "I thereupon decided," said De la Penne "to
attempt to run in with the entering ships . . . rather than attempt to go
under or through the net," and that is what succeeded.

Dark shapes approached from seaward—three British destroyers.
The pigs submerged completely and moved toward the gate. Their
commander recounted: "A destroyer passed at what seemed like a few
inches over my head . . . her bow surge forced me down, where I
touched bottom; happy to have missed the screws, I put on full
speed . . . , entered with the second destroyer, and then came up to
the surface." He was in. And so were the others. Lieutenant Marceglia slipped in when the gate signal lights came on just before the
first destroyer. It narrowly missed Lieutenant Martellotta on Pig 3
as he was negotiating the gate entrance. Proceeding independently,
these two—Nos. 2 and 3—turned shoreward along the inner side of
the south breakwater and then to a northeasterly course between the

shore docks and an inner breakwater. Looking ahead or northeast from there, they could see the two heavies: *Valiant* outboard to the left and *Queen Elizabeth*, as flagship, close to the dock on the right. No. 2 went after the Queen; No. 3 passed between the targets to look for a carrier or tanker beyond.

No. 1 had passed under the stern of the third destroyer (as her crew prepared to anchor) and then along the outboard side of the inner breakwater, where two cruisers were moored, and thence on a generally northeasterly course under the stern of the French battleship *Lorraine*. Now at last De la Penne could make out his target, *Valiant*,

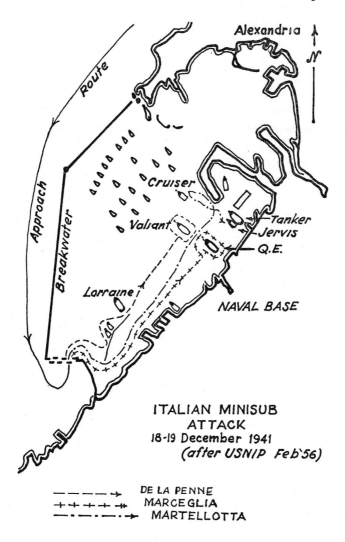

ITALIAN MINISUB
ATTACK
18-19 December 1941
(after USNIP Feb'56)

DE LA PENNE
MARCEGLIA
MARTELLOTTA

dead ahead—"enormous 31,000-ton battleship." He soon made contact on the ship's antitorpedo net, dismounted, and with Bianchi pushed the pig through between two net floats. "Intense cold" bit into their fingers, he remarked, and added, "I was now within 100 feet . . . no obstructions. It was 0200 December 19, 1941. My present position was the result of six years study and strenuous training." Now to go to work!

The great ship's stack towered up amidships; that would be about the right spot for the big blast. De la Penne pushed No. 1 down to 20 feet and inched forward, but not slowly enough, for the pig banged the hull and went down out of control, down to 50 feet into the deep muddy bottom. Stiff fingers had refused to work the controls properly. Trailing a line made fast to the pig, De la Penne swam to the surface for a check, and found himself about 45 feet forward of the stack; it would still do. He clawed back on the line to the pig. It had not moved, but Bianchi had; where could he be? Nowhere to be found. What about pig's motor? It refused to turn. In the thick mud everything had to be done by feel; ah, here was the trouble—a wire wrapped tight around the propeller. That decided things, the torpedo would have to be dragged under the hull by main strength. Guided by the beat of a pump in the ship, De la Penne struggled and sweated with his charge. Inch by inch it moved. Sea water seeped into his mask; he swallowed it to avoid drowning and flailed on, growing thirstier and thirstier. The depth diminished, the pump beat closer, his head bumped the hull. "At last I had arrived. I was nearly exhausted." Attaching the warhead and setting the fuses went quickly, and then to the surface. As he swam away, a voice on deck hailed him to stop. He kept on until a blast of machine-gun fire induced him to try to make the ship's mooring buoy for shelter. He made it. But, but! there on the buoy for everlasting joy sat Bianchi. He had passed out down below, floated to the surface, revived, and found the lee of the buoy. Voices from *Valiant*'s bow were now shouting. The culprits lay low, but soon a boat took them off. Under escort they boarded their prey. About two hours had done the trick.

De la Penne identified himself and with Bianchi thereupon went into a stubborn silence. Guards escorted them ashore for futile interrogation in Italian, then back to *Valiant*. Her captain had reported his catch to the flag on *Queen Elizabeth* and at once received orders to "confine his prisoners in one of the forward compartments well below the waterline." This was done. Bianchi dropped asleep; his companion "reflected on my future at this point." Time was waning; only ten minutes remained. At his request he was taken to Captain Morgan and warned him to sound Abandon Ship, for *Valiant* was about to blow up. More questions brought no answers, but orders for return to the dungeon. As he went below, the ship sounded the alarm. Then came a terrific thump. "The blast shook the vessel with extreme violence, lights went off," wrote De la Penne, "the hold filled with smoke. . . . I was unhurt. The ship rapidly heeled over to port. . . . Groping my way through the open hatch I went toward the stern where a number of officers were watching the *Queen Elizabeth* a hundred yards away." Admiral Cunningham was far aft, watching too; only yesterday he had "warned the fleet . . . these attacks might be expected."

Already blown was tanker *Sagona* nearby, and destroyer *Jervis* alongside damaged, but no oil had caught fire. Then came *Valiant*, and "four minutes after that," according to the commander in chief, "when I was right aft by the ensign staff, I felt a dull thud and was tossed five feet in the air by the whip of the ship and was lucky not to come down sprawling. . . . I knew the ship was badly damaged. The *Valiant* already down by the bows; the *Queen Elizabeth* took a heavy list to starboard." In a few days Admiral Cunningham informed the First Sea Lord in London, "We are having shock after shock . . . damage to the battleships at this time is a disaster. . . ." It was indeed a disaster, but also an achievement for Lieutenant de la Penne and his companions, one of the war's great exploits.[6]

Italy supreme on the sea! Her fleet could presumably stand off Alexandria and pound to bits what the British had left: three light cruisers and one antiaircraft cruiser plus destroyers, against four Italian battleships, six cruisers, and many destroyers—that is, on paper. Nothing of the sort happened. For quite a time the Italians had no true word on the success—not until 1944, wrote Admiral

6. Lieutenant de la Penne and Bianchi were again put below to encourage talk; with still no change, they were taken to Ras el Tin and officially made prisoners of war, as were the other crews. Marceglia and Schergat (bound for the *Queen Elizabeth*) got ashore, evaded detection by posing as French sailors, and made their way to a bar in Alexandria. When they paid with a British pound note instead of an Egyptian, they drew attention. On the following day near Rosetta (off which Italian submarine *Saffiro* was waiting) police took them in. Martellotta and Marino reluctantly gave up on a cruiser opportunity and finally found tanker *Sagona*. They made it ashore at the coal pier, but in trying to leave the port compound they were arrested. In 1946 Admiral Sir Charles Morgan "wished to do Commander de la Penne the honor of pinning on his chest the gold medal Valor Militare, which had been awarded him by the Italian government."

Maugeri, head of their Naval Information Service. Days passed. A tender balance ruled the sea. "Each side," wrote Captain Macintyre, "was able to use the Central Mediterranean for own purposes but was unable to prevent the enemy from using it, neither could control it." Britain's prestige took another dip.

But how much stronger on the sea the Axis would have been had these late 1941 efforts of submarines, surface, and air been brought to bear in the summer after Crete. Control and use of the sea could have been established, Tobruk taken, and Malta eliminated. The later demonstration proved it. But now, chained to the East, all German Mediterranean action took on the defensive cast of purchasing time until after Russia.

Malta raised a dilemma; signs of it were already evident in December 1941. Führer Directive No. 38 of 2 December talked around the island without taking direct aim. Kesselring was actually only to "lay a foundation for protecting and expanding our position in the Mediterranean . . . in order to influence future developments." This meant after Russia. His tasks were to:

(1) Gain air and sea supremacy for the establishment of safe shipping lanes to North Africa. "It is important to hold Malta down."
(2) Cooperate with forces deployed in North Africa.
(3) Interdict British west-east ship traffic, including supply to Tobruk and Malta.

Although Kesselring came under the Duce's command via the Commando Supremo, his own authority stayed sharply limited to German air forces and cooperation with Italian Air. No command over Rommel or German naval forces appeared. As is often the case, Kesselring had to establish his authority by wielding it. To the "brotherly cooperation" promised, Mussolini reacted with small enthusiasm.

The contrast between grim combat tasks in the east and the Italian unawareness of a war, gay city life, and laissez-faire shocked Kesselring. Where was the crisis so carefully set forth by Hitler, Göring, and Jeschonnek? He was to improve radically "the unfavorable state of North African supply by fighting down British sea and air forces based on Malta." Why not then take the island and be done with it? It was his very first reaction and it never left him. The word was lack of forces at present; the alternative therefore had to be neutralization from the air. Hitler had again covered his aversion for storming an objective at sea by bombing it into harmlessness—as he had thought to do with England. He reckoned without Kesselring, who like Rommel, would open unexpected vistas and choices.

The shipping crisis eased. From November's high of twelve, ships lost dropped to eight. Still British forces had exhibited remarkable accuracy at sighting and relentlessly pursuing their prey. In fact in the eyes of the Johnny-come-lately Germans, British performance was so unerringly perfect that something had to be wrong. Suspicion grew that ship movements and connected plans were being divulged. It is normal for the Mediterranean to seethe with intrigue and mysterious transmission channels; remarkable here was the steady pace of results. It could mean for the British to have air reconnaissance verify information already in hand and then proceed to the kill. (The same mysterious performance had struck Admiral Iachino after Matapan.) In mid-December Kesselring confided his concern to General Count Cavallero, chief of Commando Supremo: "News of the convoys is being disclosed." This alone could explain the regularity of so many bad breaks even in face of drastic corrective measures.

With Air Fleet 2's growing experience, losses during January fell to two. General Rommel felt stronger and stronger as men and material came through. This time the foe was not going to get in the first punch. Without aye, yes or no to anyone, not to his Italian allies or even his own high command, he took off on a fresh thrust eastward on 21 January, caught the widely scattered British units cold, just as he did his own superiors. He charged on, so that by 30 January the old stand at Gazala was again in hand, with the general itching to get at Tobruk, the next prize. The hesitant Italian formations joined at the new front. News advices "Rommelled" far and wide once again. A day earlier he had become *Generaloberst*. Egypt called.

By mid-February Kesselring felt enough at home in his new surroundings to break off for a report to the Führer at Rastenburg in East Prussia. The session proved warming and "full of emotion." Again Kesselring urged "the seizure of Malta to create healthy condition in the Mediterranean," as he had pressed it on Göring, the Italians, and Rommel, who was to command the operation. The latter two at times supported him, and on this occasion Hitler joined them. At the end of the talk, holding his visitor's arm tight, he said, with moving emphasis, "Just take it easy Field Marshal Kesselring, I'll do it all right!" It proved to be the time of decision and he was trying so hard to measure up.

We note how independent operating by highly capable leaders tore strategy along at such a pace that the higher leadership, engrossed in its own immediate problems, was not only unprepared for the new vistas but was incapable of grasping their true import. Moreover, these two, Kesselring and Rommel acted independently with only loosely integrated moves by planes and tanks. No general plan with specific objectives and priorities governed. There should have been one.[7]

On Sicily and in neighboring Italy, Air Fleet 2 of the Luftwaffe worked up to the full power of some 560 planes and pilots, plus accompanying ground facilities, fuel, and munitions. All through March 1942 as power grew, so did the pressure grow on the target, 55 miles south of Sicily. On 2 April full-scale sorties began to smother Malta and everything on it. Knock out all defenses for a late-May invasion became the thought, though no such objective had been officially fixed. Joint German-Italian staff work, training and firm allocation of German units, with Führer sanction, pumped the hope all the higher. Just as one of Rommel's moves sparked another by newly opened strategic possibilities, Air Fleet 2's complete silencing of Malta thrust forward, as the next logical act, invasion.

Commander in chief South, his Italian colleagues, the Duce, and even Rommel (provided he lost no time for Tobruk) agreed that invasion should come next. The old dreams took on reality as the furious pace of bombing progressed. It could point only one way, or it made no sense. Already in mid-March, von Rintelen and Kesselring had emphatically replied affirmative to OKW's query whether the Italians were truly in earnest about it. Of course the German landing-craft program required speeding up. General Cavallero, chief of Commando Supremo, thought training Italian paratroops under German General Ramcke and readying an airborne division might require extra time, but he was for invasion. Thus the answer to OKW established a positive attitude between the partners.

German planning gave the project the striking name *Hercules,*

7. Kesselring was unaware of Raeder's strong support in the Führer conferences of March, April, and June for the early occupation of Malta, but its priority failed to get through. Many sources establish the developing outcome. Raeder, 2:278–79; OKM Malta; Warlimont KFA, pp. 462–97; Warlimont IH, pp. 238–55; and Warlimont IM, with the critique by Weichold; Suchenwirt; Rommel, pp. 111–74; Kesselring, pp. 138–84. Opportunity occurred to discuss the situation with Kesselring in 1953. Basically, while the Italian professionals wanted Malta reduced and even seized by combined forces, their first concern was always for the security of Tripoli and Libya, rather than marching on Alexandria. At times Mussolini shared this view.

growing stronger and stronger. Hopeful progress reports arrived from commander in chief South with precise regularity. In a report of 12 April, he warned that the widely separated objectives, Malta and Tobruk, or vice versa, had to be taken in sequence for lack of air power to do both at once. By this time he had convinced the Italians the operation could go as a coup de main (*Handstreich*), which meant earlier readiness, say during May. Mussolini felt so elated over the first ten days of full-scale bombing that he ordered readiness by the end of May. By then, only three Italian paratroop battalions could complete their training; Kesselring asked his home office to fill out with German troops. The project moved.

Then on 29–30 April came the belated Axis communion on the Obersalzberg to decide definitively which should come first, Malta or Tobruk. Both ends of the Axis were hemmed with their usual private reservations; still, a happy air seemed to prevail. A bad winter lay behind, fresh opportunities beckoned ahead. Mussolini came out for Malta; he was reluctant about going farther east without her. Hitler wanted Tobruk and a drive east to set the pace for the future. He won. Of course after Tobruk anything could happen. Some further talk back and forth, and then agreement, in reasonable-sounding terms, but other than the Italian expectation: "At the end of May the Panzer Army should attack and, as feasible, take Tobruk, but then halt on the Egyptian border so that in mid-June, or at the latest by full moon in July, *Hercules*—seizure of Malta—can be carried out." In truth no choice any longer existed. It had to be Tobruk because Rommel could not wait past 1 June to get in the first punch. Polishing off Malta before then was by now manifestly impracticable. Had decision been made in January to take Malta after the air neutralization, *Hercules* could have come first. The choice should have been faced earlier, as Kesselring wanted.

The outcome suited Hitler so well that it whetted his generosity. He at once made more than one parachute division available for Malta, assault engineers, tanks out of Russian booty, and the strongest possible concentration of German landing craft. Kesselring's air fleet would of course be on hand in time; meanwhile it would carry out other duties. If Hitler was soft-soaping his partner, the men of his own naval headquarters also took him at his word and acclaimed the decision with cheers: now something might really get under way in the Middle Sea; with Führer support the thing would go; without it, nothing could. The sailors were happy.

By 31 May 1942 a full-blown *Studie* (advisedly so named instead of "order" or "plan" to spare partner feelings) for Invasion Malta, complete with an action timetable, enjoyed general approval of the leaders on the scene. In this noteworthy paper Kesselring outlined the forces and steps of deployment by air, sea, and land units, set preparatory air barrages, designated landing spots, arranged the complex meshing of the actions, and provided for their logistics and troop reinforcement. The planning evinced an awareness of *Merkur*'s errors on Crete, especially in the concluding restatement of the initial objective: "The establishment of a bridgehead (see Annex 7) agrees with my explicit purpose." Thus in thought and spirit *Hercules* felt ready enough to set practical preparations in course toward the awaited signal, *Execute*!

Hitler welshed. The signal never came. Of course, the final word would not have been his to give in any case, but it would have required his accession. And this he never felt able to give. On returning to Rastenburg after the Axis meeting, he began to squirm with doubts and let them drop to OKW underlings. Doubt as to whether the commitments at the meeting were spoken in good faith arises. Göring had nosed in, and the sequence of that hour of truth before England on the Channel in September 1940 repeated itself. During that travail Göring had likewise huddled with his Führer, consoled him, and counseled him to default on Invasion. Neither of them had wanted *Sea Lion*, nor do they now want *Hercules*. What is the need of taking Malta if she can, like England, be kept neutralized by bombs? Why add unnecessary risk? Even if taken, the island would have to be held and supported overseas, something that the Italians have already proved they cannot do. Members of the planning staff (WF St) became alarmed at Hitler's growing skepticism. It was arranged that General Student should come to reassure the Führer through a report on the progress of his training and operational readiness planning in Italy and Sicily.[8]

Hercules would be Student's third great exhibit of airborne power; he yearned to retrieve the confidence lost just over a year before on Crete. Again present in support on 21 May 1942 was Jeschonnek (despite Göring's opposite views). Admiral Krancke, the senior naval adviser at Führer headquarters, Jodl, and Warlimont also attended.

8. Warlimont KFA, pp. 502–7. Warlimont was present at the Student-Führer conference of 21 May 1942. In a written report General Koller, the last chief of staff of the Luftwaffe, recorded that Göring took credit for counseling and deciding Hitler against *Hercules*. Suchenwirth, p. 95 and n. 41; Kesselring, pp. 148, 169.

At the Axis meeting of 30 April the problem had been twisted into a choice of timing; now it became the stark decision of whether *Hercules*, which the British feared as a coming catastrophe, should go at all. Student, showing no doubt whatever, sailed into his masterpiece with utter faith in the plan. Nothing but praise came out for the growing Italian paratroop units and confidence in the facile meshing of various difficult maneuvers. As he breezes on, the Führer grows more and more fidgety, until he finally bursts out: "I am not of a mind to let the attack on Malta be executed." Before the flabbergasted Student can utter a word, an effusion of well-rehearsed predecision reasons descends: Italians cannot be trusted to keep the plans secret; the successive steps, one depending on the other, demand a punctuality and exactitude they are incapable of. Moreover they lack the necessary aggressive spirit of attack. British sea power will interrupt supply, the Italian Fleet will haul off, and "you will be sitting on the island alone with your paratroopers." What then? Krancke and Jeschonnek took up for the Airborne chief. It was no use; the wrought-up Führer would not listen. To him Malta was a piece of Britain; he wanted no part of her, no part of being pitted against the sea, which he dreaded. When the argument of possible British revival on Malta arose, the cat slipped out of his bag: Tobruk when taken would receive Rommel's supply via Crete, by which direct route Malta would be evaded. That was it! (Later Göring and Hitler rejoiced when Tobruk's fall freed them of Malta altogether.) As for the Italians, fooling them bothered Hitler not at all. Theoretical planning could continue, assembled German troops and material would remain ready in pretense of the coming operation. Student's return to Italy he at once forbade, just to clinch his own perfidy (and to remind us of last year's Schmundt-transmitted prohibition of dissent about Malta). *Hercules* was as dead as *Sea Lion*.

And so he stayed, in the face of fresh naval efforts to keep him alive. The eager young men of old L Section OKW drove to have Admiral Raeder again present the gravity of *Hercules*'s abandonment. Lt. Commander Junge summarized the case in these well-reasoned words:

Just because the Italians have these weaknesses, we must take part with them to give them a lift in morale. The halfhearted handling of *Hercules* kills it just as surely as *Sea Lion* . . . whose neglect the Führer himself now points out as an error. . . . His reinforcement of the plan before the Duce [on 30 April] could hardly have been so seriously meant as taken.

It is a fact that with the firm will of the Führer, everything goes; without it nothing does.

Disapproval of *Hercules* fails to recognize two factors, (1) the decisive importance of Malta to the African traffic and the very existence of our position there and (2) the limited span that the present favorable situation in the Mediterranean can last, never more to return. If *Hercules* drops out and we leave the Italians to their own devices, the conditions of the summer and fall of 1941 will recur. . . . We do not yet have Tobruk. . . . If the foe succeeds in putting Malta on its feet again, Libya and the whole south coast . . . will fall into his hands. The consequences will be terrible. . . .

That *Hercules* is a risk is clear, but to omit now to carry *Hercules* out is a still greater risk. . . . We know how to take risks . . . , but I fear the strategic challenge that should cause us to take the risk is not fully recognized.

These sound arguments failed to stir a Navy crash drive to convince the Führer, but they did instigate a fresh study in support of *Hercules*. Its findings Admiral Raeder only routinely brought to Hitler's attention at the conference of 15 June 1942. The need of Malta's reduction, Hitler readily acknowledged, but doubted it could be done "during the East Campaign . . . especially not with Italian troops." Whereupon he came out with an irrational excuse for leaving things as they were: "Malta, as she is," he held, "attracts British ships that become targets for inflicting more ship losses." Since the Schmundt uproar of a year ago nothing in him had changed. Then he seemed to fear the record of his own timidity; yet that did not send it away. He will have no *Hercules*, no part of him, and soon, as it turned out, no Mediterranean.

Hitler's latter-day feelings about Crete were likewise uninspiring. The island, he persisted, was to be a defensive bastion against Allied entry to the Continent via the Balkans. This fear about the south entry plagued him as had the fear on the north through Norway. Crete's abandonment was several times recommended. He insisted steadfastly not only on holding the island but as well on reinforcing it—with force no longer available.

What remains of the Hitler Mediterranean story, at times comic, but finally tragic, deserves recounting only for terminal emphasis. Rommel dashed on, in skirmishes and hot engagements with "mobile land craft"—and also in tough ground war slugging. By 21 June he had Tobruk and the baton of a field marshal. Göring and

Hitler rejoiced, as noted, over their deliverance from Malta. On Rommel surged, beyond the agreed limits. At Sidi Barrani, his command post 40 miles inside Egypt, consultation with Cavallero and Kesselring on 26 June 1942 settled on Cairo, bypassing Alex for the moment, rather than Malta, as the agreed next target. Rommel vowed to have the prize within ten days. Booty out of Tobruk, he held, would make it possible. Kesselring objected on the solid ground of serious air shortages. He was outtalked, so that Cavallero could report agreement on Cairo to his Duce. Hitler's distant yet heavy backing decided. A special Führer message played on Italian vainglory in these inspiring words: "The Goddess of luck in battle comes nigh but once. . . ." It was enough to persuade Mussolini that his time had come. He packed up, crossed to Africa and stood by at Derna for the call—the call to lead the triumphal parade into Cairo, of course. Kesselring received dispatch orders to cease "objection . . . and to support the drive with all available force." This political meddling created, as always, the gravest uncertainties at the front. For a time Rommel charged on, yet resistance stiffened visibly on the ground and especially in the air. The British halted him; by July they had the action pretty well stalemated before El Alamein, 142 miles short of the goal. A disenchanted Duce re-returned to Rome, which news the British gleefully recorded as a positive sign of crisis finished. It was indeed.

No Axis reinforcement nor Rommel magic could relieve the deadlock. Poor health impaired Rommel's own powers, and also later, those of his first-class relief, General Stumme. At the close of August the long overdue and final Axis offensive got under way. Two days of bitter fighting inconclusively on the ground, and decisively in favor of Britain in the air, forced the Axis back into the starting positions before El Alamein. During September Kesselring worked up another all-out effort at reduction of Malta. But by this time it was a different ball game. His main effort of mid-October had to be broken off because of excessive German air losses. On 23 October the British launched the opening actions of their big offensive at El Alamein. In concert, on 8 November British and American forces landed in Algeria. From that beachhead and Egypt the Allies reestablished firm control of the Middle Sea, from which they laid siege to Italy. It meant the beginning of the end for Germany—the so often mentioned practical turn of the tide.

Control of the Mediterranean became decisive. It could still be so today. How long would western Europe remain free if the Russians should gain hegemony over the Great Middle Sea?

In 1941 the Germans could have insured control over it from Crete. And even in 1942, had they taken Malta, the Allies could hardly have risked the November landings in Algeria. The war's balance would have remained in doubt. Malta's specific significance lay in her role as a sea-going part of Britain that Hitler could not bring himself to attack. He corroborated in full the depth of his infirmity whenever he had to deal with the sea. Not even the Mediterranean's engaging natural and strategically favorable circumstances could convert him. Thus, our long voyage, rather than closing on exciting new discovery, ends on this now firmly established fact of Hitler's failure at sea.

We have watched the foibles and fantasies of one Self act as powerful drags and motors of history: not as the reality of logic, but through compulsive fears and irrational hope about personal fulfillment. The meaningful memory that history may keep for the troubled story of Hitler and the Middle Sea could be the forfeiture of his last advantageous offensive opportunity in the war: conquest of the East Basin after Crete. The whole Middle Sea would have followed.

How eagerly Hitler always admitted his sea failing! As though the admission absolved him and accounted for his low-keyed interest in operating overseas. It lay outside of his toasted infallible competence. Many actions and witnesses bear out the peculiarity. To his naval adjutant he used to quip: The sea, that is "only for adventurers." Throughout the tensions of Invasion England, any signs of improving chances seemed to worry him—they might eventually demand invasion. At the peak of the period he exclaimed to his army chiefs, "On land I am a lion, but with the water I don't know where to begin." There were other versions. He explained to senior officers at a *Sea Lion* meeting that the operation could not go because the Navy and the Air Force were unable to guarantee success, "and besides," he added, "I am water-shy (*ausserdem bin ich wasserscheu*)." At heart may have been a fear no dictator can tolerate—the fear of losing control. He must command and feel secure in doing so. For Hitler such feeling failed to reach the Channel, much less the remote Mediterranean. We have noticed how easily he drummed up reasons for finding the whole southern area smelly, repugnantly Levantine. The time, place, and fighting factors were right for fixing the war on a German course. He spurned the chance, though well aware of it. It lapsed by default with his pursuit of heart's desire in Russia. Germany and Adolf Hitler there passed the point of no return.

So, Germany's war can be said to have foundered on the negative fact of her Führer's sea shyness. Had he wanted the Middle Sea as badly as he wanted Russia, he could have had it. And he made a feeble try, but it proved no go. Signals inside hemmed him, made him uneasy, unsure. The commanding influence of such signals could have been discerned at the time, their effect forecast and countered with greater power and accuracy. Much and many could have been saved from harm and horror.

What happened then, or failed to, because of Hitler, can today be computed out by machines on the data available at his time. He provided data constantly, as "unpredictable man" still does and by this very fact becomes predictable. A man's innate aims, actions, and reactions can be sorted out and arranged in plus and minus patterns. These repeat, and as they do, they check and refine and correct themselves. They can show, within useful limits, what this or that man is most likely to cause to happen or not happen. Conceivably, computer analysis can likewise be applied to the restraints and urges of a group of men—for example, a controlling group in government: witness the repetitious moves by the Russian controllers. They return to basic motives and always surprise the West by doing so. Russians can hardly do otherwise.

However, for the individual the spirit within remains the final arbiter. Let man therefore beware? Not at all. Let him rejoice in his freedom and go forth to defeat the delusions of today. Think how stupid and unforgivable if a command in the field or at sea or in the air should fail to keep its operating abreast or ahead of the material, technical, tactical, and strategical lessons of everyday combat! Or if a command should fail to switch targets as combat closed old ones and opened new ones! Soon after arrival in North Africa, Rommel tore the hesitant time-buying strategy and policy of his superiors wide open, and along to fresh vistas; yet higher up no change in either resulted. And Churchill, when operations opened the possibility of Tripoli's capture, instead of holding fast, switched to an impossible political goal in Greece, which in Grenfell's words "turned passage of the Mediterranean from a British asset to a liability." But the prize blunder belonged to Hitler for his irrational political drive into the east when the combat-won Mediterranean prospects were at their peak. His wishful eastern goal was not only mistaken, it was unworthy of the fighters who died for it.

Wishful preconceptions—what a bane they have been to man! Then comes history bent on making everything rational. . . .

If nothing else, policy must keep faith with our men: it must pick honorable goals capable of opening tangible targets worth dying for. Even in this day of "kill ratios" and limited goals there is no limited way of dying. Our fighters need their Suribachis and Hamburger Hills.

And the great Middle Sea? It must be kept free. A vigilant and helpful posture toward the key of the East Basin, the island of Crete, can do much toward ensuring freedom for the whole sea.

1. A try-out for German paratroop attack: at top, the Corinth Canal after 25 April 1941, with the bridge blown up; bottom, German paratroops and matériel dropping from Ju-52's. See page 183. [National Archives; General Trettner.]

2. Spacious Suda Bay. Suda village on the south bank and its pier are visible across the water on the right.

3. Canea from the vicinity of the Creforce Battle Command Post. Canea's tiny port can be made out, and in the left background the exit from Prison Valley. Above it is Monodhendhri. At the right the background shore curves toward Platanias and beyond, to vital Maleme Airfield.

4. Heraklion's lofty walls had to be scaled by the Germans.

5. Hill 107 from Maleme Airfield, May 1941. Note the wrecked Ju-52's. [Courtesy, OCMH.]

6. View north from top of Hill 107. Tavronitis bridge crosses on the left. The flat cultivated summit of 107 shows in the middle ground, in 1960. [Courtesy, Commander Magopoulos, RHN.]

7. A German paratrooper dives through the open door of his transport plane. [Courtesy, General Buchholz.]

8. A German 22–mm gun in action. Terrain was rough and fields of fire were sharply restricted. [Courtesy, General Trettner.]

9. A lone paratrooper finds company. On the far right and left are abandoned chutes.

10. "If we could only get through to headquarters!" [Courtesy, General Trettner.]

11. The first one down: General Ulrich Buchholz's plane afire on Maleme Field. [Courtesy, General Buchholz.]

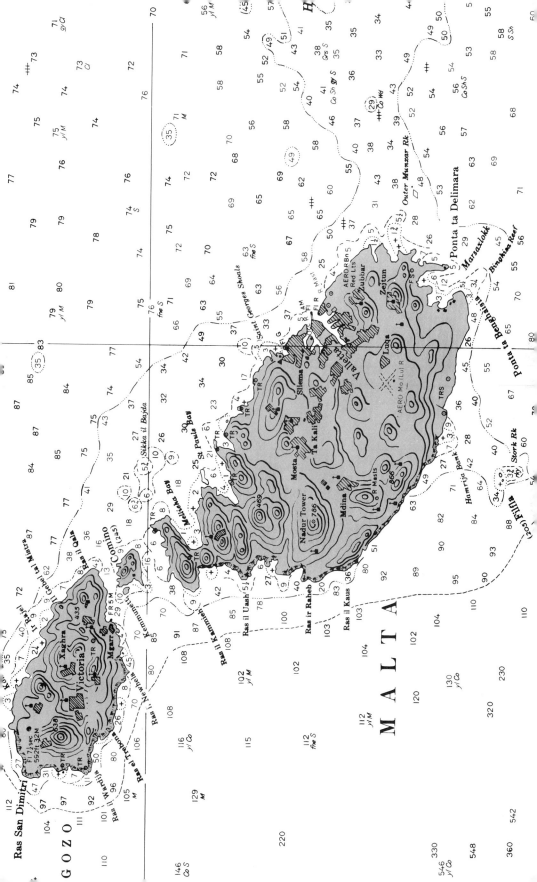

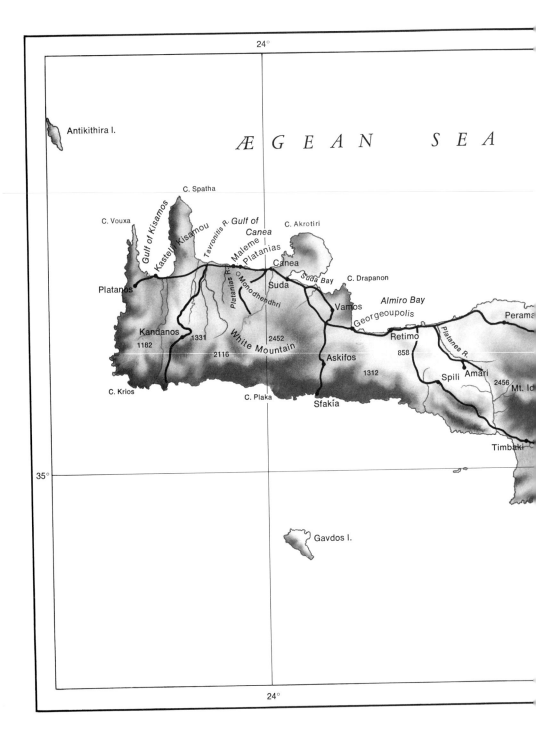

AE G E A N   S E A

Antikithira I.

C. Spatha

C. Vouxa

Gulf of Kisamos

Kasteli Kisamou

Tavronilis R.

Gulf of Canea

Maleme

Platanias

Canea

C. Akrotiri

Suda Bay

C. Drapanon

Platanos

Platanias R.

Monodhendhri

Suda

Vamos

Almiro Bay

Georgeoupolis

Perama

Kandanos

1331

White Mountain

2452

Retimo

Platanes R.

1182

2116

Askifos

858

1312

Spili

Amari

2456

Mt. Id

C. Krios

C. Plaka

Sfakia

Timbaki

35°

24°

24°

Gavdos I.

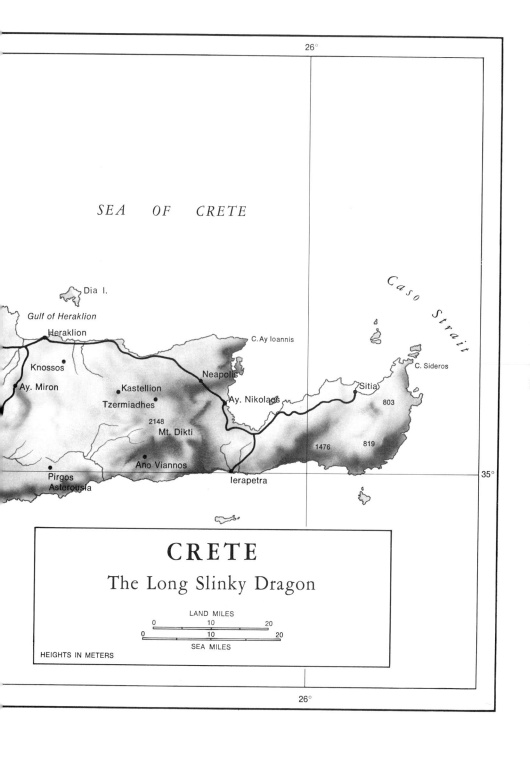

SEA OF CRETE

Dia I.

Gulf of Heraklion

Heraklion

C. Ay Ioannis

Knossos

Neapolis

Ay. Miron

Kastellion

Ay. Nikolaos

Sitia

803

Tzermiadhes

2148
Mt. Dikti

1476   819

Ano Viannos

Pirgos
Asterousla

Ierapetra

Caso Strait

C. Sideros

35°

CRETE
The Long Slinky Dragon

LAND MILES

0   10   20

0   10   20

SEA MILES

HEIGHTS IN METERS

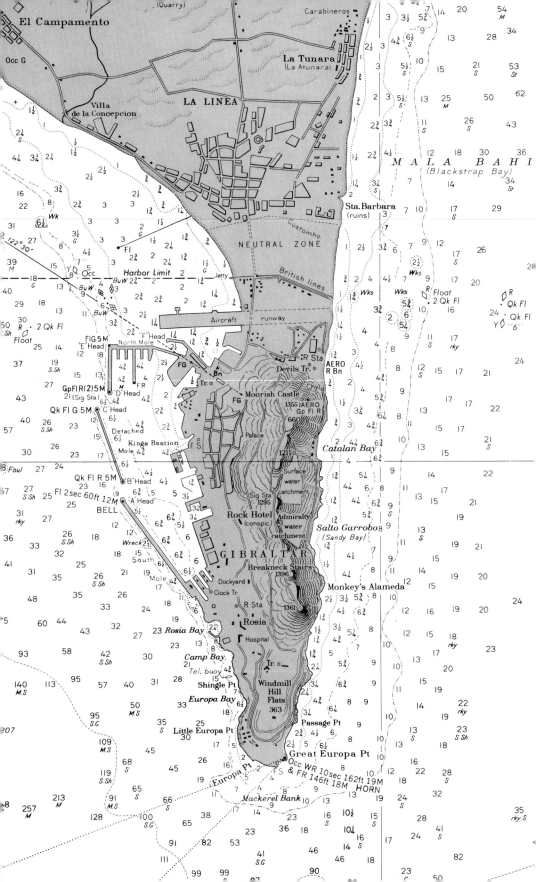

12. A German glider landed in Crete, as did many others; they did not pay off very well. [Courtesy, General Buchholz.]

13. Maleme Field as General Ringel first saw it from his plane on 22 May 1941. [Courtesy, General Ringel.]

14. The 19 Lindner Amphibians arrive off Maleme Field on 23 May 1941. They were the only infantry troops who made it from Greece by sea, but not in this craft. [Courtesy, General Ringel.]

15. General Julius Ringel during the Battle of Galatas, 24–25 May 1941. [Courtesy, General Ringel.]

16. Mountain troops deploy for the Battle of Galatas, 24 May 1941. [Courtesy, General Ringel.]

17. German mountain troops moving to Crete, 21-22 May 1941, in the ill-fated caïques of the Maleme Flotilla. See pages 327 ff. [S. Horbach.]

18. A German fighter-bomber circles over crucial Pink Hill in the Battle of Galatas, 24–25 May 1941. The house looks like the pink house (from which the hill took its name) once used as his forward command post by defending New Zealand Colonel Kippenberger. [Student, *Kreta–Sieg der Kühnsten*, Graz, 1942.]

19. Generals Ringel and Student confer on Crete. [Student, *Kreta*.]

20. General Student decorates one of Colonel Ramcke's men in the field, 26 May 1941. Ramcke is at the right.

21. Field Marshal Kesselring (left) and General Rommel in North Africa, December 1941. [Courtesy, General Beppo Schmidt.]

References

Admiral SO
Records of Admiral Südost. U.S. Dept. of the Navy, Office of Naval History, Washington, D.C.

Air Ministry RFGA
Air Ministry. *The Rise and Fall of the German Air Force, 1933–1945*. London, 1948.

AOGA
Airborne Operations: A German Appraisal. Ms P–051. U.S. Dept. of the Army, Office Chief Military History, Washington, D.C.

Bashmore
Boyd T. Bashmore. "Sword of Silk," *U.S. Infantry Quarterly*, Oct. 1956.

Burdon
Randal M. Burdon. *24 Battalion*. Official History of New Zealand in the Second World War. Wellington, N.Z., 1955.

Churchill
Winston S. Churchill. *The Second World War: The Grand Alliance*. Vol. 2. Boston, 1950.

Ciano D
Galeazzo Ciano. *The Ciano Diaries, 1939–1943*. Edited by Hugh Gibson. New York, 1946.

Ciano DP
Galeazzo Ciano. *The Ciano Diplomatic Papers*. Edited by Malcolm Muggeridge; translated by Stuart Hood. London, 1948.

Clark
Alan Clark. *The Fall of Crete*. New York, 1962.

Cody
   Joseph F. Cody. *21 Battalion.* Official History of New Zealand in the Second World War. Wellington, N.Z., 1953.

Cunningham
   Andrew Browne Cunningham. *A Sailor's Odyssey.* New York, 1951.

Davin
   Daniel M. Davin. *Crete.* Official History of New Zealand in the Second World War. Wellington, N.Z., 1953.

De Guingand
   Sir Francis W. de Guingand. *Operation Victory.* New York, 1947.

De la Penne
   Durand Luigi Durand de la Penne. "The Italian Attack on the Alexandria Naval Base, as Told to Captain Virgilio Spigai, Italian Navy," *U.S. Naval Institute Proceedings* 82, no. 2 (Feb. 1956): 125–35.

Documents GFP
   R. J. Sontag et al., eds. *Documents on German Foreign Policy, 1918– 1945, From the Archives of the German Foreign Ministry,* ser. D. U.S. Dept. of State Publication 3277. Washington, D.C.

8th FK Chrono
   Deichmann (Lt. Colonel), ed. VIII Fliegerkorps Chronologie. Munich, 1954.

11th FK Kreta
   Gefechtsbericht XI Fliegerkorps, Einsatz Kreta. National Archives, World War II Records Division, Washington, D.C.

Farran
   Roy Farran. *Winged Dagger.* London, 1948.

FC
   Führer Conferences on Matters Dealing With the German Navy, 1939– 45. U.S. Dept. of the Navy, Washington, D.C., 1947.

FD
   Führer Directives. U.S. Dept. of the Navy, Washington, D.C.

Fergusson
   Bernard Fergusson. *Wavell: Portrait of a Soldier.* London, 1961.

5th MD CR
   Fifth Mountain Division. Preliminary Combat Report "Kreta," 4 June 1941 (Ringel). National Archives, World War II Records Division, Washington, D.C.

5th MD War Diary
   War Diary of the Fifth Mountain Division. National Archives, World War II Records Division, Washington, D.C.

Fleckher-Dobiasch
Sepp Dobiasch and (Major) Fleckher. *Gebirgsjäger auf Kreta*. Berlin, 1942.

GCB
The German Campaign in the Balkans. U.S. Dept. of the Army, Pamphlet No. 20–260. Washington, D.C., 1953.

H. Greiner
Helmuth Greiner. *Die oberste Wehrmachtführung*. Wiesbaden, 1951.

J. Greiner
Josef Greiner. *Das Ende des Hitler-Mythos*. Zurich, 1947.

Grenfell
Russell Grenfell. *Main Fleet to Singapore*. London, 1951.

Gundelach
Karl Gundelach. "Der Kampf um Kreta 1941." In *Entscheidungsschlachten des zweiten Waltkrieges*. Edited by Hans-Adolf Jacobsen and Jürgen Rohwer, pp. 95–134. Main, 1960.

Halder
Franz Halder. *Kriegestagebuch*. Edited by Hans-Adolf Jacobsen. Stuttgart, 1963.

Hampshire
A. Cecil Hampshire. "Triumph at Taranto." *U.S. Naval Institute Proceedings* 85, no. 3 (March 1959):71–79; together with Comment (W. Ansel), *ibid*. 86, no. 2 (Feb. 1960): 101–2.

Henderson
Jim Henderson. *22 Battalion*. Official History of New Zealand in the Second World War. Wellington, N.Z., 1958.

Heusinger
Adolf Heusinger. *Befehl in Widerstreit*. Tübingen, 1950.

Heydte
Friedrich A. von der Heydte. *Daedalus Returned*. London, 1958.

Heyking
Rüdiger von Heyking. Ms B–639. U.S. Dept. of the Army, Office Chief Military History, Washington, D.C., 1947.

Hitler MK
Adolf Hitler. *Mein Kampf*. Munich, 1939.

Hitler SB
Adolf Hitler. *Hitler's Secret Book*. Translated by Salvator Attanasio. New York, 1961.

Hitler SC
Adolf Hitler. *Hitler's Secret Conversations, 1941–1944*. Translated by Norman Cameron and R. H. Stevens. New York, 1953.

Hittle
J. D. Hittle. "Montgomery and Conflicting Philosophies of Sea Power." *U.S. Naval Institute Proceedings* 81, no. 5 (May 1955):521–27.

Horbach AF
H. Horbach. "Die Argonautenfahrt Reichenhaller Gebirgsjäger: Teilstück aus dem Kampf um Kreta 1941." *Die Gebirgstruppe*, 1945, Heft 2, pp. 35–41.

Horbach BS-14
H. Horbach. Bericht über die Fahrt des Bootes S-14 nach Kreta, 26 May 1941. National Archives, World War II Records Division, Washington, D.C.

Hubatsch
Walther Hubatsch, ed. *Hitlers Weisungen für die Kriegführung, 1939–1945.* Frankfurt am Main, 1962.

Iachino GM
Angelo Iachino. *Gaudo e Matapan.* Rome, 1947.

Iachino SM
Angelo Iachino. *La Sorpresa di Matapan.* Rome, 1957.

IMT
Trial of the Major War Criminals Before the International Military Tribunal, Nuremberg, vol. 29. Nuremberg, 1948.

Jacobsen
Hans-Adolf Jacobsen. *1939/1945: Der zweite Weltkrieg in Chronik und Dokumenten.* Darmstadt, 1959.

Kesselring
Albert Kesselring. *Soldat bis zum letzten Tag.* Bonn, 1953. English version: *A Soldier's Record.* Translated by Lynton Hudson New York, 1954.

Kippenberger
Sir Howard K. Kippenberger. *Infantry Brigadier.* London, 1949.

Kirkpatrick
Sir Ivone Kirkpatrick. "The Inside Story of Rudolf Hess." *Atlantic Monthly* 205, no. 2 (Feb. 1960):42–48.

Kissel
Hans Kissel. *Gefechte in Russland, 1941–1944.* Frankfurt am Main, 1956.

Klee
Karl Klee. "Der Entwurf zur Führerweisung No. 32." *Wehrwissenschaftliche Rundschau* 3 (1956):27–141.

LF4 Kreta
Luftflotte 4. Bericht "Kreta." National Archives, World War II Records Division, Washington, D.C.

Liddell Hart RA
Basil H. Liddell Hart. *The Red Army*. New York, 1956.

Liddell Hart RP
Basil H. Liddell Hart, ed. *The Rommel Papers*. Translated by Paul Findlay. New York, 1953.

Long
Gavin M. Long. *Greece, Crete, and Syria*. Canberra, 1953.

Lossberg
Bernhard von Lossberg. *Im Wehrmachtsführungsstab*. 2d ed. Hamburg, 1950.

Macintyre BM
Donald Macintyre. *The Battle for the Mediterranean*. London, 1964.

Macintyre PNR
Donald Macintyre. "Point of No Return." *U.S. Naval Institute Proceedings* 90, no. 2 (Feb. 1964):36–43.

Manstein
Erich von Manstein. *Verlorene Siege*. Bonn, 1955.

Maugeri
Franco Maugeri. *From the Ashes of Disgrace*. Edited by Victor Rosen. New York, 1948.

Merkur B
Befehl für den Einsatz XI Fliegerkorps im Fall Merkur. National Archives, World War II Records Division, Washington, D.C.

Ms 640
Reports, Dinort and Hitschhold. Ms 640, 1947. U.S. Dept. of the Army, Office Chief Military History, Washington, D.C.

Ms B-250
U.S. Army, European Command. Ms B-250. 1946.

NSR
R. J. Sontag and J. S. Beddie, eds. *Nazi-Soviet Relations, 1939–1941*. U.S. Dept. of State Publication 3023. Washington, D.C., 1948.

NZ Docs
New Zealand. War History Branch, Dept. of Internal Affairs. *Documents Relating to New Zealand's Participation in the Second World War, 1939–1945*. Wellington, N.Z., 1949–1963.

OKM Malta
Oberkommando Marine. File 31032, 1941–1942, "Malta." U.S. Dept. of the Navy, Office of Naval History, Washington, D.C.

OKW Ops SitConf
Record of Situation Conferences of the Defense Branch, OKW, 8 Aug. 1940 to 25 June 1941. German edition. Ms C-065 L. U.S. Dept. of the Army, Office Chief Military History, Washington, D.C.

OKW Ops War Diary
Draft Entries, War Diary of Defense Branch, OKW, for Aug. 1940 to March 1941. Ms 065j. German edition. U.S. Dept. of the Army, Office Chief Military History, Washington, D.C.

"Operation Felix"
Ms 065h. U.S. Division of the Army, Office Chief Military History, Washington, D.C.

Pack
S. W. Pack. *The Battle of Matapan.* New York, 1961.

Papagos
Alexander Papagos. *The Battle of Greece, 1940–41.* Translated by P. Eliascos. Athens, 1949.

Philippi and Heim
Alfred Philippi and Ferdinand Heim. *Der Feldzug gegen Sowjetrussland, 1941 bis 1945.* Stuttgart, 1962.

Pringle and Glue
Dave J. C. Pringle and W. A. Glue. *20 Battalion and Armoured Regiment.* Official History of New Zealand in the Second World War. Wellington, N.Z., 1957.

Puttick
Sir Edward Puttick. *25 Battalion.* Official History of New Zealand in the Second World War. Wellington, N.Z., 1960.

Puttkamer
Karl Jesko von Puttkamer. *Die unheimliche See.* Munich, 1952.

Raeder
Erich Raeder. *Mein Leben.* 2 vols. Tübingen, 1957. English version: *My Life.* Translated by Henry W. Drexel. Annapolis, 1960.

Ramcke GB
Ergänzung Gefechtsbericht Sturmregiment. National Archives, World War II Records Division, Washington, D.C.

Ramcke VSJ
Hermann Bernhard Ramcke. *Vom Schiffsjunge zum Fallschirmjäger General.* Berlin, 1943.

Ringel HG
Julius Ringel. *Hurra die Gams!* Göttingen, 1955.

Ringel Ms
Julius Ringel. Ms D-190. U.S. Dept. of the Army, Office Chief Military History, Washington, D.C., 1947.

Rintelen
E. von Rintelen. *Mussolini als Bundesgenosse.* Tübingen, 1951.

Rommel
Erwin Rommel. *Krieg ohne Hass.* Heidenheim, 1950.

Ross
A. Ross. *23 Battalion*. Official History of New Zealand in the Second World War. Wellington, N.Z., 1959.

Roussy de Sales
Adolf Hitler. *My New Order*. Edited by Raoul de Roussy de Sales. New York, 1941.

Schmidt
Paul Schmidt. *Hitler's Interpreter*. Edited by R. H. C. Steed. New York, 1951.

Schmitt
Gefechtsbericht des Fallschirm Jäger-Abteilung. U.S. Dept. of the Army, Office Chief Military History, Washington, D.C.

Seibt
Konrad Seibt. Einsatz Kreta, Mai 1941. Ms B-641. U.S. Dept. of the Army, Office Chief Military History, Washington, D.C.

Seth
Ronald Seth. *Two Fleets Surprised*. London, 1960.

Sinclair
Donald W. Sinclair. *19 Battalion and Armoured Regiment*. Official History of New Zealand in the Second World War. Wellington, N.Z., 1954.

Skl Haifisch
Seekriegsleitung, File "Haifisch." U.S. Dept. of the Navy, Office of Naval History, Washington, D.C.

Skl Harpune
Seekriegsleitung, File "Harpune." U.S. Dept. of the Navy, Office of Naval History, Washington, D.C.

Skl Malta
Seekriegsleitung, File "Malta." U.S. Dept. of the Navy, Office of Naval History, Washington, D.C.

Skl Merkur
Seekriegsleitung, File "Merkur." U.S. Dept. of the Navy, Office of Naval History, Washington, D.C.

Skl Seelöwe
Seekriegsleitung, File "Seelöwe." U.S. Dept. of the Navy, Office of Naval History, Washington, D.C.

Skl War Diary
Seekriegsleitung, "Kriegstagebuch," Part A. U.S. Dept. of the Navy, Office of Naval History, Washington, D.C.

Spencer
John Hall Spencer. *Battle for Crete*. London, 1962.

Sturmregt B
Gefechtsbericht des Stabskompanie/Sturmregiment für den Einsatz Kreta, 20–28 Mai 1941. National Archives, World War II Records Division, Washington, D.C.

Sturmregt TB
Tagebuch 23 April–20 Mai 1941, Sturmregiment. National Archives, World War II Records Division, Washington, D.C.

Suchenwirth
Richard Suchenwirth. "Historical Turning Points in the German Air Force War Effort." *USAF Historical Studies*, no. 189, pp. 89–97.

Tietz-Manz
Tietz and Manz. *Gebirgsjäger in Griechenland und auf Kreta.* Berlin, 1942.

Utz
W. Utz. Mountain Regiment 100, Short Combat Report, 29 May–2 June 1941, to Commander 5th Mountain Division. Included in Annexes to 5th Mountain Division War Diary. National Archives, World War II Records Division, Washington, D.C.

Vidua
Josef Vidua. "Gebirgsjäger im Seegefecht vor Kreta." *Leinen Los*, nos. 5 and 6. Gräfling/München, 1961.

Warlimont EM
Walter Warlimont. "Die Entscheidung im Mittelmeer 1942." In *Entscheidungsschlachten des zweiten Weltkrieges,* edited by Hans-Adolf Jacobsen and Jürgen Rohwer, pp. 253–68. Main, 1960.

Warlimont IH
Walter Warlimont. *Im Hauptquartier der deutschen Wehrmacht, 1939–1945.* Frankfurt am Main, 1962. English version: *Inside Hitler's Headquarters, 1939–1945.* Translated by R. H. Barry. London, 1964. All references are to the German edition.

Warlimont IM
Walter Warlimont. "Die Insel Malta in der Mittelmeerstrategie des zweiten Weltkrieges." *Wehrwissenschaftliche Rundschau* 8 (Aug. 1958): 421–36.

Warlimont KFA
Walter Warlimont. Die Kampfführung der Achsenmächte im Mittelmeerraum. Ms P-216. U.S. Dept. of the Army, Office Chief Military History, Washington, D.C.

Weichold DF
Eberhard Weichold. "Die deutsche Führung und das Mittelmeer unter dem Blickwinkel der Seestrategie." *Wehrwissenschaftliche Rundschau* 9 (March 1959): 164–76.

Weichold WM

Eberhard Weichold. The War in the Mediterranean. Unpublished manuscript.

Werth

Alexander Werth. *Russia at War, 1941–1945*. New York, 1954.

Wittmann

A. Wittmann. "Von Kreta, der Insel der Rätsel." *Die Gebirgstruppe*, 1954, Heft 2, pp. 5–20.

ACKNOWLEDGMENTS

My grateful esteem goes out to editors John W. Dowling and Carol Thompson—they understood and were anxious to help; to manuscript producers Nancy Gannon Gearing and Lois Grimm Sowell—they read, reread, and typed until it made sense; to kindly critics Dan M. Davin and Walter Warlimont—they offered first-hand knowledge and critique of authenticity, each from his side of the struggle.

My earlier research in Europe and England paved the way to new exchanges with many participants in the Mediterranean story. Every one of them responded to my inquiries graciously and frankly. Often, personal knowledge and material available nowhere else filled out the picture. Such generous and vital cooperation bolstered confidence in the project and made its work a pleasure. To the same end Dr. Ford K. Brown coached and encouraged me at home.

There the offices of the Chief of Military History and the Director of Naval History, the Library of Congress, and the Library of the U.S. Naval Academy contributed importantly in making records and books available. Thomas Parnell Ridley deserves credit for his fine map-making. The U.S. Oceanographic Office and the U.S. Naval Academy chartroom helped by furnishing and letting me adapt the charts for the illustrations of Malta and Gibraltar.

Walter Ansel

Annapolis, July 1971

Index

Index